KOSMOS

AN EVOLUTIONARY-WHOLISTIC ACCOUNT OF CREATION

BY
DENNIS MILNER

Visit us online at www.authorsonline.co.uk

KOSMOS: AN EVOLUTIONARY–WHOLISTIC ACCOUNT OF CREATION

is a sequel to:

THE LOOM OF CREATION: A STUDY OF THE PURPOSE AND THE FORCES THAT WEAVE THE PATTERN OF EXISTENCE

by Dennis Milner and Edward Smart

published by Neville Spearman, London, 1975

and

EXPLORATIONS OF CONSCIOUSNESS

Edited by Dennis Milner

published by Neville Spearman, 1978

DEDICATION

TO THE NEXT GENERATION

WHO HAVE TO FIND THE
WAY FORWARD

KOSMOS

The title 'Kosmos' was chosen, partly to avoid the connotation that modern science has given to the more usual term 'cosmos' but primarily because of its intrinsic meaning. According to a study by VLASTOS of the early Greek philosophers' concepts of the nature of the Universe, Kosmos describes, not a thing, but an intelligible dynamic activity. This activity is an ordering with aesthetic and moral aspects to it; it seeks beauty (from which 'cosmetic' derives) and harmony within an organic whole. The word was used by early Greek philosophers to describe the rational activity by which the Universe comes into existence and operates, as opposed to the earlier mythological viewpoint that everything happens according to the whims of gods. This view of the Kosmos as a dynamic, organic, self-organising, self-developing activity is the theme of this book. 'Kosmos' is larger than, and encompasses, the scientist's 'cosmos' that is concerned with the structure and workings of the Universe, i.e. its galaxies, stars, planets and life on Earth. Kosmos deals with what existed before the Universe and how and why the Universe arose as part of a larger system of creation.

The term 'Kosmos' could be equated with 'God' but we have avoided the use of the term 'God', because of the various connotations it already has. In particular 'God' usually refers to an entity separate from creation and directing it from outside, whereas the viewpoint put forward in this book is that there is nothing but God, God is everything and everywhere and evolving through the experiences of creation:

God sleeps in the mineral,
Dreams in the vegetable,
Stirs in the animal,
Awakens in Man

ACKNOWLEDGEMENTS

This book grew out of an extra-curricula research, carried on into post-retirement activity, that was an extension and integration of three strands of our activities in the Department of Metallurgy and Materials at the University of Birmingham, England. These were: first, from our metallurgical and materials researches, a realisation of the central role of the creativity of the human mind and attempts to understand this, which led to seeking deeper understanding of human nature: second, researches into the complex inner structures of materials developed an interest in morphology, i.e. how forms come about in Nature: third, the development of a lecture course on the evolution of humanity's use of materials, starting with the evolution of substances in stars to give rise to the substances in the Earth's crust, and how early hominids and successive civilisations have exploited these, which led to the development of an evolutionary-wholistic way of thinking.

Many people have, directly or indirectly, played a role in these activities, particularly a succession of Heads of the School of Metallurgy and Materials who have tolerated this research and people who have provided the finance for it. The late Professor Eric Rollason took an interest in, and supported, its early stages. Subsequently the late Professor Donald Wilson, followed by Professors Raymond Smallman, Michael Loretto, John Knott and Rex Harris, although not themselves committed to this investigation, upheld the principle embodied in the University's mission statement of supporting academic freedom, which has allowed us to search for understanding wherever this has led us.

Andrew Wilson, Richard Wilson and the Board of the charity for which they have been successive Chairmen have provided the financial support. Without this we could not have achieved anything.

Among the many other people who have helped in one way or another, we particularly thank Michael Watson for his contribution to the electrophotography researches reported in Part IV of the book, Dr. James Binns for useful discussions from an humanities standpoint, Edward Cottam for much photographic help, Christine Hardy for producing clear diagrams and illustrations from our hazy ideas, Paul Osborne and Jeff Sutton for much patient help and guidance in dealing with the mysteries of the working of computers, Mark Ashworth for designing the book cover and providing the photograph on which it is based, and David Milner for organising the layout of the book.

Illustrations

OVERVIEW

One of the great scientific advances of the nineteenth century was the realisation that all living things on Earth have come about by evolution over a long period of time. A major advance of the twentieth century was the realisation that the Universe as a whole - its Galaxies, Stars and Planets, have likewise come about by a lengthy, cosmic evolution. Thus, it is now possible to view the Universe, and everything in it as a vast evolving system. In this book it is proposed that evolution works by simple basic principles and that it is possible to comprehend everything, including the purpose of our lives, in these terms. In this 'Kosmic Metaphysics' the Universe is traced back to a state of dormant energy that becomes active and thereby gets a sense of self (in the same way that a baby first gets a sense of self from its activity). In seeking to enhance its sense of self, the energy increases in activity and, as a result, becomes a state of turmoil, that differentiates into a large number of separate centres of activity (Kosmic Bénard cells), each of which experiences a sense of self out of its activity. These comprise the basic framework of energy/activity out of which the Universe develops. In order to increase their sense of self these centres become more active and their interactions create a further level of turmoil, out of which further centres of activity – galaxies arise. The galaxies interact with the basic Bénard cell activity and the stress that this creates in their zone of interaction causes them to break down in this region, to give rise to hydrogen atoms. The hydrogen atoms caught up in the on-going turmoil give rise to stars that transform them into larger atoms of substances from which planets form. It is postulated that there was not one Big Bang but an on-going sequence of 'little bangs' that create the physical universe.

It is proposed in this book, that our Universe is the latest in a sequence of Universes brought about in this way, i.e. it is part of an 'Omniverse'. There thus exists a hierarchy of Omniverse entities created in previous Universes. These 'older generations', out of their greater experience, seek to encourage the development of the later generations, and it is the activities of these that mystics and religious leaders refer to as a Spiritual World. The totality is here called 'Kosmos' but it could equally be called God, which is everything and everywhere.

Life starts on Earth in watery regions where prebiotic droplets form, that evolve into single, then multicellular organisms and finally hominids. To gain the special experience offered by Earth existence entities from the Omniverse Hierarchy incarnate into hominid bodies, to give rise to modern day humanity. As a result of arising in this way Humanity is cut off from the Omniverse Hierarchy and, like the prodigal son, has to find its own way forward. In order to do this Humanity seeks to understand the workings of the Universe and the Earth situation in which it finds itself. In doing this it is developing the ability to contribute a new, objective understanding of how and why the Omniverse has developed and works, whereby Kosmos/God develops a new level of consciousness of itself.

Each stage of development opens up new activities with potentials for further developments and the pursuit of these gives rise to the activities and entities that make up the Universe as we know it. This is the 'purpose' of our lives, as part of this system, to realise our potentials and, in so doing, to open up new potentials for further developments.

When we look around us we see the workings of the Kosmos on Earth in the forms, behaviour and functions of substances and organisms. In this book it is proposed that forms arise out the stresses that substances and organisms create in the underlying basic energy activity, as they strive to express their natures. Experimental results drawn from electrical discharge photography, crystallisation, liquid flows and capillary dynamolysis are presented to show how stress fields create the shapes that we see in the natural world.

Humanity, however, does not exist in isolation, it has to learn to work with the Omniverse Hierarchy to produce a harmonious integration of the new with the old and vice versa and there is evidence of a drawing together of the Omniverse Hierarchy and Humanity's activities on Earth. But this requires an expansion of Humanity's consciousness and the development of a new evolutionary-wholistic understanding. These are seen as major tasks for the next and future, generations and this book is offered as a contribution to this end. As well as providing a deeper (and simpler) understanding of everyday life and of the observations of science on the workings of the Universe and on religious beliefs, this evolutionary-wholistic approach throws light on so-called fringe phenomena, e.g. alternative healing practices, psychic phenomena, UFOs and the growing body of so-called channelled communications in which people claim to get messages from a spiritual world.

CONTENTS

PART II: APPENDICES AMPLIFYING THE BASIC PRINCIPLES OF KOSMIC METAPHYSICS

CHAPTER 6: Appendix to the Introduction

CHAPTER 7: Appendix to Chapter 1: The Kosmos Stirs and Thereby Begins to Experience a Sense of Self

CHAPTER 8: Appendix to Chapter 2: The Evolution of the Superstructure Entities Leads to the Beginning of the Universe

CHAPTER 9: Appendix to Chapter 3: The Arising of Substances, Stars and Planets out of an on-going Turmoil

CHAPTER 10: Appendix to Chapter 4: The Arising and Evolution of Life on Earth

PART III: HOW KOSMIC-METAPHYSICS CAME ABOUT

CHAPTER 15: The Beginning

CHAPTER 16: Experiences of Expanded Consciousness (ECEs)

CHAPTER 17: ECEs on the Human Situation

CHAPTER 18: ECEs on the Forces of Nature and the Natures of Substances

CHAPTER 19: ECEs and the Experimental Investigations

CHAPTER 20: Homoeopathy

CHAPTER 21: An Evaluation of This Phase of Our Work

INTRODUCTION

The Imminence of a New Era of Understanding

The objective of this book is to assert that we are poised to make a major leap forward in our understanding of the nature, purpose and workings of the Universe and of our role in it and that this will lead to an awareness of as yet untapped forces and potentials for further development. This is because the human characteristic that sets us apart from the rest of Nature – our rational consciousness – has now evolved to the point at which we can objectively evaluate the phenomena of the Universe and of life on Earth and come to comprehend what lies behind it all.

When we look at the sky on a clear night we see large numbers of stars. Scientists have found that these are organised in a collective pattern, or galaxy – the Milky Way, which comprises many millions of stars, of which our Sun is one. With advanced high-powered telescopes scientists have found that the Milky Way is only one among many millions of galaxies, each of which comprises many millions of stars.

We exist on planet Earth that, along with a number of other planets rotates around the Sun and together form the Solar System. By examining the genealogy of the Solar System scientists deduce that this came into existence in the Milky Way galaxy about four to five billion years ago. Prior to this there was no Solar System and no Earth. By examining the genealogy of the galaxies, from which stars and the Solar System derived, scientists deduce that these evolved from an earlier primeval state and that the Universe first came into existence as an explosion of energy and primal substance and started on its path of development about 15 billion years ago.

When we look around us we see that our Earth planet comprises many different substances that have evolved in stars, out of the original primal state. In seeking to understand the nature and behaviour of these substances scientists have found that they comprise assemblages of vast numbers of minute atoms and that each atom consists of a nucleus with a surround of electrons. Scientists have hypothesised that atoms come together to make substances as a result of invisible interatomic forces and that substances come together to make cosmic bodies as a result of the invisible force of gravity.

We see that living on Earth are multitudinous plants of many different types and vast numbers of animals of different species. By examining the genealogy of the rocks of the Earth's crust and the distribution of fossilised remains of organisms therein, scientists have established that the abundant and multifarious life that we see around us has evolved over a long period of time from primitive beginnings. As we go back in time life on Earth becomes increasingly more primeval, until we reach a state when life existed only in the seas and the land was bare. Further back there was no life of any sort on Earth.

Science has thereby generated a great deal of knowledge about how the Universe works, how the Earth planet came into existence and how life arose on Earth. These investigations show what the Universe comprises and how it works but not why the Universe is the way that it is. They do not show why the Universe consists of galaxies of stars, why atoms exist and why these comprise a nucleus with an electron surround, where the invisible interatomic forces and gravity come from, why life has arisen on Earth culminating in human beings, why the Universe is evolving, what the driving force is behind it and why in fact the Universe exists at all. Yet if we are to have a real understanding of the Universe and our life in it we need to understand not only how it works, but also how and why it all came into existence and its underlying meaning or purpose.

The astrophysicist science writer John GRIBBIN claims that scientists' descriptions of the evolution of the Universe are becoming so similar to those for describing the evolution of life on Earth, that scientists are coming to see the Universe as a living evolving entity and that the development of this living evolving Universe viewpoint is the next stage in the advance of scientific understanding. In order to understand a person's activities we need to understand his/her inner nature, how this has developed to become what it is and how this causes them to behave as they do. And so it is with the Universe. This book claims that the development of the understanding of the Universe as a living thing will lead to an evolutionary-wholistic understanding that relates its behaviour and workings to its underlying nature and purpose. At the same time this will throw light on phenomena that science cannot, as yet, deal with, such as psychic experiences, the phenomena of parapsychology, UFOs, mysticism and complementary healing therapies. We think that this will be a major aspect of the contribution to be made by the next generation and this book suggests a framework to help them with this task, in which we endeavour to show that striving for the goal of an evolutionary-wholistic understanding is realistically feasible.

The 'Inner Nature' of the Universe and a Kosmic Metaphysics

The essential feature of the Universe and everything in it is that it is evolving. The question is, 'What has brought this evolution about?' At one time the evolution of the Universe was believed to take place by a sequence of random events. But by examining in detail the processes involved, scientists have found that the Universe is very finely balanced, so that it could not have occurred as a result of chance. These scientists have therefore concluded that the Universe is, in some way, 'purposive'. In this book we take the view that the purpose of the Universe is simply to do what it is doing, i.e. its purpose, or rather its nature, is to evolve.

We propose that the Universe and everything in it is a self-evolving totality and we are concerned with the underlying principles and processes by which this takes place. To this totality we give the name 'Kosmos'; the principles by which it evolves are described as a 'Metaphysics'; so that what is presented in this book is called 'Kosmic Metaphysics'.

The Two Basic Principles of Kosmic Metaphysics

The Universe is infinitely complex in its range of activities and phenomena but according to Kosmic Metaphysics, underlying all these complex manifestations there are two simple, readily understood, principles at work. The first principle is concerned with the driving force that causes things to happen. The second principle relates to how this driving force works to bring about the multifarious activities of the Universe. Since we are part of this evolutionary development these two principles determine the way in which we live our lives, so that it is in this form that we present them.

What drives us is our sense of I. That is, in everything that we do, feel, or think, we experience that we exist, that we are someone. This may be simply a matter of carrying out the routine, mundane tasks of life, or expressing our innate creative potentials in various ways. We may be involved in happy or unhappy, or even tragic, events, but in all cases we get a sense of self - I do this, I feel that, I think so and so - which drives us to behave in the way that we do. According to Kosmic Metaphysics the sense of I is something that first arose in a very primitive, unconscious way (far removed from what we know now as a sense of I) and it has evolved, and exists, in everything. It is the maintenance and pursuance of sense of self that drives all evolution, from sub-atomic particles that seek to maintain their patterns of energy activity, the smallest organism in its determination to survive against environmental pressures that threaten to destroy it, ourselves in our seeking for self esteem and ego growth, to the so-called God or gods in their roles in the evolutionary process.

The second principle is that an evolving thing, in doing what it does, progressively opens up new potentials to pursue. Thus, when we come into the world as small babies we express our innate energy by becoming active - sucking, kicking, grasping, etc. In doing these things we become aware of our potential to perform different activities. Then, as we grow up we develop an increasingly wider range of activities, which bring us into contact with more and more things in the world around us, as a result of which we develop interests and goals in life. Each activity opens up new potentials in ourselves, so that one goal is replaced by another, in terms of developing skills, educational achievements, careers, forming relationships, marriage, family life, etc. When we came into life as babies we did not know, and nor did anyone else, how our life would work out; there was no preconceived plan. Human activity in general works in the same way. For example, in the sequence of developments of motive power - wind power - water power - steam engine - internal combustion engine - gas turbine - rocket propulsion: as each of these developments has been worked out it has opened up a new potential for a further phase of development. According to Kosmic Metaphysics this is the way in which evolution works; there is no preconceived purpose and no final or fixed goal or aim, because by pursuing one perceived goal, further, as yet unknown potentials and goals are opened up.

In order to understand Kosmic evolution it is therefore necessary to recognise the arising of a potential, its development and the new potential that arises out of it, and the phases of evolution that this gives rise to. We start with the Kosmos in a primeval state of dormant or 'unawakened' energy, long before anything that we know as the Universe exists. To use a simplistic description, the Kosmos is in a state akin to a deep sleep. This Kosmic energy stirs into activity in a simple way and this gives it a very dim sense of self. In seeking to increase its sense of self it increases in activity more and more until it reaches a state of turmoil that then differentiates into many separate energy-activities, i.e. entities. Each of these centres of activity gets a sense of self as a result of the interaction of its own activity with that of the other entities around it. Their pursuance of sense of self causes them to exert stresses on each other which results in their zones of interaction breaking down, to give rise to further centres of energy activity or entities, that again seek sense of self out of their activities and this is how the Universe arises. Thus, as with an evolving human organisation (which is part of, and therefore operates on the same principles as, the totality) simple basic activities give rise to more evolved and diverse ones, which develop out of what has been achieved previously. In this way, from its initial awakening into activity the Kosmos has evolved in complexity and diversity of activities and entities, to give rise to the Universe. This book is concerned with the story of how and why this evolution has happened.

Differences Between Kosmic Metaphysics and Science

With the development of high-powered telescopes, scientists discovered, in the 1920s, that galaxies appear to be moving away from each other. This led them to conclude that as we go back further and further in time the galaxies were all closer and closer together and the Universe was smaller and smaller, until we reach a state where all the energy and substance of which it consists existed in a very hot intense condition, compressed into a 'pinhead' size, from which it exploded out in a 'Big Bang'. The Big Bang is thus regarded as the source of everything, from which the Universe as we know it now, and life on Earth have evolved. As the energy and substance of the Big Bang exploded outwards it cooled down and simple atoms (hydrogen and helium) formed. These became concentrated into galaxy formations, which then broke down into stars, in which the hydrogen and helium were 'compressed' into larger atoms. Then, in a further stage of cosmic evolution, more stars were formed, among them the Sun, with its surrounding planets that developed out of substances formed by earlier stars. Science then sees life on Earth - living cells, plants, animals and Man as arising out of the activities of the substances of the Earth's surface.

The scientific view is that all of the developments since the Big Bang arise from two forces, firstly gravity, whereby substances exert forces on each other to come together on a large scale in the formation of galaxies, stars, the Earth, etc. and secondly, interatomic forces that substances exert on each other when they are brought into close proximity and that cause them to relate to each other in the way that they do. These forces thereby bring about the ways in which substances behave, to make up the world as we know it. It is thought that the origin of the forces lies in the nature of the substances and that since these consist of assemblies of atomic constituents that formed in the Big Bang then, if the nature of these constituents could be determined, this would give a basic understanding of the ultimate nature of the Universe. The Kosmic Metaphysics' viewpoint is, however, that substances - atoms and their sub-atomic constituents, are not the ultimate driving force behind the Universe that makes it what it is, but are a manifestation of what the driving force produces.

According to Kosmic Metaphysics the initially dormant energy became active, from which it got a sense of self. In seeking to enhance this sense of self it increased in activity and thereby developed into a state of turmoil. The turmoil became stabilised as a collection of centres of activity, each with its own sense of self. These exist everywhere and comprise the invisible 'space' of the Universe and everything takes place inside them. In pursuing a greater sense of self these 'space entities' increased in activity until their interaction (friction) caused break up at their peripheries. The peripheral fragments gave rise to the visible Universe and the substances of which it consists. These then perturbed, and created stresses in, the basic pattern of activity of the space energy entities and it is these stress fields, which science calls gravity, that force substances together, into galaxy, star, planet, etc. formations. If 'space' did not possess the properties that it does and was 'nothingness', there would be no gravitational force between substances and nothing would ever happen. Once substances are brought together by gravity they interact by interatomic forces that arise from localised stress fields in the space-energy created by the different constituents of atoms. According to Kosmic Metaphysics substances do nothing themselves, what substances do is brought about by the stress fields which they cause in the space-energy, which then determines what they do.

From the examination of the fossil evidence, scientists conclude that life on Earth first arose in the form of minute cells, from which all other organisms subsequently evolved. Science explains the arising of the cells and their subsequent evolution in terms of substances combining together to form genes, which somehow give rise to the activities of the cells and to all the different forms and functions of the living organisms that evolve from them and furthermore, somehow bring about awareness and consciousness. The Kosmic Metaphysic's view is that where the stress field acting on substances results in a stable on-going activity, the space-energy caught up in this situation develops a sense of self and it differentiates out as a self-actualising entity that carries out this activity for itself. Thus, behind all the living organisms of the world there exist self-actualising activities that have developed out of force fields in the space-energy. In seeking to enhance their sense of self these entities then carry their activities further and the organisms thereby evolve. This process gives rise to more evolved and different organisms, culminating in human beings. We are not just our genes; we are active, feeling, thinking people working with substance bodies that have developed through stages of evolution reflected in their genetic make-up. In the same way that the components of a computer give a pattern to a flow of electrical energy that is passed through them, genes channel, and give a pattern to, the flow of the will, feeling and thinking energies that we express through our bodies.

Thus the scientific view is that substances are primary and all else derives from them due to the gravitational and interatomic forces that they exert on each other, through 'space'. In contrast the Kosmic Metaphysics' view is that the space-energy existed before substances and is therefore primary. Substances arose out of the space-energy and it is the way that the space-energy interacts with substances that makes everything happen. The emphasis is therefore, not on substances but on the space-energy and it is the evolution of the space-energy, through its experiences that lies behind the evolution of everything.

Science views the Universe as a vast mechanism, operating according to fixed, mechanical laws of behaviour. But because science also sees the Universe as evolving, the questions arise, how do living organisms arise out of a mechanical non-living background and how can something that is purely mechanical and following fixed laws of behaviour evolve? In Kosmic Metaphysics these problems do not exist because the whole Universe is regarded as a living thing, in the sense that it is self-sustaining - it is not dependent on anything or anyone to maintain it and make it behave in the way that it does. There is thus no problem in accounting, either for the arising of life on Earth, since there is nothing that is non-living; or for the fact that life evolves, since in seeking increasing sense of self everything evolves. (The special feature of organisms on Earth is not that they are living but that they procreate).

It is a fundamental feature of science that it describes the activities of the Universe as happening in space and time. But these are not the basic characteristics of the Universe; they are creations of the human mind to provide a framework for describing our experiences in relation to the world around us. Using them to explain the nature of the Universe leads to peculiar anomalies. For example, in the Big Bang theory of the Universe, in which all the substance and energy of the Universe explodes out from a pin-head state, if the Universe is all that there is, there is in consequence nothing for it to expand into, so scientists have had to propose that space itself is expanding. But the concepts of all the energy and substance of the Universe existing in a 'pinhead' and of space expanding do not fit in with our everyday common-sense experience of the nature of the Universe. Either there is something wrong with our common-sense experience of things or there is another way of understanding the Universe that is more in accord with our common sense. Kosmic Metaphysics offers such an alternative.

Man has invented the concept of time to compare the rate at which one activity takes place in relation to another. Thus it is necessary to have a basis against which to measure other activities. This basis was first of all the duration of light from the Sun as a measure of the passage of the day and the cycle of seasons and years. Since the length of a day varies throughout the year, mechanical devices, clocks, were invented to give a more constant measure of time. Today, to provide optimum accuracy of measurement, the basic event against which all others are measured is the vibration of a particular type of atom. When scientists describe the very early events of the formation of the Universe in the Big Bang, they do so in terms of fractions of a second. This is to say, in effect, that while an atom is making a certain number of vibrations the Universe is doing such and such, but since in this theory atoms and their activities have not yet come into existence to compare events against, this does not make sense.

According to Kosmic Metaphysics these anomalies come about as a result of trying to describe the behaviour of the Universe in terms of space and time. The concepts of space and time were created by humanity to provide a basis for describing its activities in relation to its environment. But humanity has then gone on to analyse the larger and different problems of the nature and evolution of the Universe in terms of space and time. And to do this ideas such as the expansion of space and time, curvature of space, extra dimensions beyond the four provided by space and time, have had to be postulated. In this way the space-time descriptions of the Universe have become ever more convoluted. According to Kosmic Metaphysics the basic characteristic of the Universe is not space-time, it is the fact that it is evolving, so that any fundamental explanation has to be in terms of states of evolution and how these arise one from another. And since we are evolving ourselves and living the principles by which this occurs we should be able to understand the Universe in these terms, without having to understand the convolutions of the space-time descriptions. However, truly to understand the workings of the Universe, it is not enough to know how it is evolving but also why it is evolving and the driving force behind it all which, according to Kosmic Metaphysics, is the seeking by everything to enhance its sense of self.

There is, however, no question of Kosmic Metaphysics being at variance with the observations of science, indeed these have been used in formulating Kosmic Metaphysics. But, with Kosmic Metaphysics, we seek a deeper, evolutionary-wholistic interpretation of these observations, to give a more basic understanding of the workings of the Universe and everything in it. The problem is to put the contribution of science into perspective; what does it explain and what does it not explain?

A Personal 'Jotting' by the Author on Scientific Explanations

Although I am a scientist this book is not written from the point of view of a scientist, but from that of a human being who happens to have pursued a career in science (one operating in technology at the level of scientific common-sense and not involved in high-powered, frontier-breaking science). My first studies and qualifications were in physics and although I learned enough to get a degree, in two respects I never really understood the subject. First, I found the concepts of modern physics abstract and difficult (but I was very impressed by the clarity and logic of the thinking involved). Second, I was confused by the attitude of physicists who believed that physics was the ultimate way of understanding everything. My difficulty began early on, when I was introduced to Newton's Laws of Motion. Newton's first law of motion states that:

> *'Every body continues in a state of rest or uniform motion in a straight line, except in so far as it is compelled by some force or forces to change that state'.*

Scientists use the term 'body' to describe any agglomeration of substance (typically a billiard ball). At my first exposure to this way of thinking I did not know this; the only meaning that the term 'body' had for me was the every-day one of a 'human body'. So, there was this body/lecturer expounding this law, who had left his state of rest, in bed, and was marching up and down in front of the blackboard, without any obvious force that compelled him to get up from his rest state, and to change direction. This made no sense to me until the lecturer went on to show how this law described the motion of billiard balls. Out of all the wonderful and interesting things going on in the world, why pick on something comparatively dull, such as the motion of billiard balls? Surely if a law of motion is important and universal the first thing it should explain is our everyday experience of the motion of the human being? I thought at any rate that the lecturer must know what he was doing and I did my best to understand him. (It wasn't until I gave lectures myself that I realised that lecturers do not necessarily understand fully the topic of their lectures).

The point about this digression is to ask, exactly what can scientists explain and not explain? Starting with billiard balls, in searching for ultimate origins they have gone on to explain the behaviour of smaller and smaller 'bodies', i.e. atoms and then sub-atomic particles, with the assumption that when they arrive at the ultimate particle, in the next experiment, they will arrive at an understanding of the foundations of the Universe. But will they then be able to explain simple everyday happenings, like why the human being gets up from a state of rest every morning and his/her motion throughout the day?

My basic education was many decades ago, before recent developments in modern biology with its genetic explanations for the behaviour of organisms. Doubtless now-a-days biologists would isolate a gene that governs marching up and down in front of blackboards, but would this constitute an adequate explanation? According to Kosmic Metaphysics this is not the whole story.

The Difference Between Kosmic Metaphysics and the Mystic's Viewpoint

Another way that describes the nature of the Universe is that of the mystics. Mystics claim that, in states of enhanced consciousness or enlightenment, they perceive the activities of spiritual beings, God and/or gods, who bring the Universe into existence and make it work in the way that it does and this viewpoint is the basis of the world's religions. Kosmic Metaphysics certainly sees everything as the activities of 'beings', in the sense that the Kosmos and the activities into which it differentiates maintain themselves in existence, and in this respect they are 'living entities', but it does not see events taking place at the behest of any external God or gods pursuing predetermined goals. Instead, it sees the Kosmos as evolving out of itself, starting from an unconscious and inactive state. If it is desired to consider this in terms of God, then the Kosmic Metaphysics' viewpoint can be expressed as God (the Kosmos), which is everything and everywhere, evolving:

> *God sleeps in the mineral,*
> *Dreams in the vegetable,*
> *Stirs in the animal,*
> *Awakens in Man.*

That is, everything is part of a totality, for which we have chosen the term Kosmos but which could equally be expressed as God, which, in its multifarious parts, is evolving in activity, awareness and consciousness.

In these evolutionary processes, once substances have arisen, themselves self-sustaining activities, then further evolution takes place by substances creating stress fields in parts of the space-energy that give these a sense of self so that they become self actualising, to give rise to living organisms. As these organisms become more evolved then, in humanity, they develop mental abilities by which they begin to come to a conscious understanding of how things happen. At first humanity applied its mental activity to understand and control the surrounding world, on which its existence depends. But, as humanity has evolved further it has become aware that it is part of a larger pattern and it has used its mental abilities to seek understanding of this and to wonder about what lies behind it all. And it is by experiencing a state of consciousness that gives them some awareness of the forces and beings that have evolved out of the space-energy, that lie behind the manifestations of the Universe, that mystics conceive of the existence of a Spiritual World that they regard as the expression of God. But according to Kosmic Metaphysics, the mystics' spiritual world did not pre-exist and bring about creation but itself arose out of the Kosmic evolutionary process.

As we have stated, Kosmic Metaphysics starts with the Kosmos in a state of dormant energy. This dormant energy then becomes active, and this activity evolves and becomes a state of turmoil that differentiates into numerous activities and entities. Thus everything develops as a pattern of evolving activities. There is nothing mystical, or mysterious, involved, simply a coherent and comprehensible evolutionary sequence of events that arise one out of another according to their own 'internal logic'.

What the mystics have to say has given rise to the religious viewpoints and their beliefs about the workings and purpose of creation. As with the findings of science, there is no question of Kosmic Metaphysics being at variance with religious beliefs. With Kosmic Metaphysics we seek a deeper understanding of how creation works that gives a basic explanation for these beliefs. The Kosmos works in its own ways regardless of our scientific theories or religious beliefs. If we lived in a different culture or time our theories and beliefs would be different. Our theories and beliefs are ephemeral, but the workings of the Kosmos are not, and if we properly understood these we would see that our theories and beliefs are different ways of looking at the situation.

The Contributions of the Mystical and Scientific Ways of Understanding

As we have stated, the way of the mystics to seeking understanding of existence is to enter into higher states of consciousness, in which they establish contact with whatever beings and their activities that have brought it into existence and to find from these the purpose behind it all (the Platonic Way). It led to accounts of creation in terms of the workings of God/gods, which gave rise to the religious viewpoints by which people understood and ordered their lives. This way led to an authoritarian type of existence in which people sought to perform the will of their gods, in much the same way that young children develop under an authoritarian system at school, in which they seek to perform the will of their teachers. But under this system as people, and children, develop the abilities to understand and do things, they seek to understand things for themselves out of their own thinking, and to decide for themselves how to lead their lives. In Western civilisation this way has led to modern science that seeks to understand things by observing what they do and then thinking out their underlying behaviour, (the Aristotelian way). If we want to understand something that is vast and beyond our ability to comprehend it in its entirety we break it down into parts of a size that we can examine and understand. The past three hundred years, dominated by the development of modern science, have been characterised by this 'reductionist' approach of breaking existence down into its multifarious facets and examining these in detail. In this way science has sought to develop an understanding based on the facts of existence, instead of an understanding based on beliefs derived from mystical experiences. But in so doing we have lost the overall pattern provided by the mystical approach to seeking understanding.

In this book we propose that we are now entering an era that will be characterised by reintegrating the parts to recreate a whole, by integrating the way in which science shows the individual parts to behave with the mystical approach to seeking the cause and purpose of it all. This will require advances in both scientific and mystical understanding and readjustments of both viewpoints. It is, in fact the way that Kosmic Metaphysics has come about. One possible outcome of this integration is that the many divisions in humanity, that are based on different religious, scientific, economic and political viewpoints and which lead to antagonism and wars, will become healed as they are seen to be different aspects of a unified whole.

The Purpose of Life in General Terms

It is a commonly held view that it is not possible for us to know the purpose of our lives - that this is something known only to God who created us and is beyond our comprehension. However, given that the basic nature of the Kosmos is to evolve then this is the purpose of our lives, that is, as part of the Kosmos, simply, to evolve. We enter the world by being born into a situation - parents, nation, environment, etc. that provides a set of conditions that we have to 'work out' as we grow up. And, as we become adult we enter, by conscious decision or unconscious impulse, into other situations that we have to work out. And, by working out these situations we evolve and develop qualities as human beings, and what we develop is what we become and what we have to contribute to the Kosmos from which we have arisen. From the point of view of Kosmic Metaphysics the simplest exposition of the purpose of life is that of the prodigal son, who is given talents to go out into the world to develop and return to his Father with what he has accomplished.

We can assess what we achieve in life by imagining that when we get towards the end of it we look back and evaluate what we have done in evolutionary terms. There are two aspects to this; first, the personal qualities that we have evolved and second, how we have used these qualities to contribute to the evolution of others and the world around us.

The Structure and Nature of this Book

While the basic principles of Kosmic Metaphysics are simple, their ramifications to the various aspects of existence are vast. So we present the book in four parts. In Part I we set out the Kosmic Metaphysics' view of the evolution of the Universe and life on Earth, in as uncomplicated a form as we can, seeking to preserve the simplicity of the overall picture, without getting lost in detail. In Part II we have put in a series of Appendices in which we try to elaborate the general story of Part I. In Part III we explain how Kosmic Metaphysics arose. In Part IV we try to apply the viewpoint of Kosmic Metaphysics' to some experimental researches that we have carried out. Each part is separate and self-contained. As we have stated, the key features of Kosmic Metaphysics are presented in Part I and, according to their background and orientation, readers may not find Parts II, III, or IV, or sections of these, to be of interest to them.

As we have stated, we are all living the basic principles of Kosmic Metaphysics all the time. We do not have to be experts in philosophy, science, or anything else, to understand the simple underlying principles of evolution at work in ourselves and everywhere around us, on which Kosmic Metaphysics is based. Although we have used the term 'Kosmic Metaphysics' as the best description we can think of, for what is put forward in this book, we want to avoid any implication of 'Kosmic Metaphysics' as a 'higher physics' that is even more difficult to understand than conventional physics, or as signifying a vast, mind-stretching, philosophical, conceptual structure about how the Kosmos works. So, from this point on we reduce the term 'Kosmic Metaphysics' to the less imposing K-M.

Before we proceed to our exposition of K-M, we wish to reiterate the objective and nature of this book. As we have stated, our claim is that humanity is poised to make a step forward by developing an evolutionary-wholistic understanding of the nature of life, the Universe and of its own existence. We have tried to make a tentative step in this direction by putting forward a Kosmic Metaphysics based on the idea that the Kosmos is self-evolving and that there are two principles by which this takes place. These are, first, that the basic driving force in evolution is seeking for greater sense of self and second, that this continually opens up new potentials for development that give rise to new phases of evolution. How these principles bring about all the complex manifestations of the Universe is, however, very difficult to work out. While we have tried to make a step in this direction, there is much that we have not considered, while in many cases we have been dealing with matters for which we have no competence or expertise. Thus no claim is made for the adequacy or validity of our story: it is all very tentative and hypothetical, some of it extremely so, and designed only to promote the seeking for an evolutionary-wholistic understanding which readers will have to work out for themselves according to their own perspectives. To stress the *hypothetical* nature of the Kosmic Metaphysics that we expound, we designate it *h*K-M. Where positive statements are made this is only to make clear what our hypothetical speculations are and not to assert their validity. It will require a great deal of effort and thought by many people now and in future generations to work out a valid evolutionary-wholistic understanding of things.

PART I

THE BASIC PRINCIPLES OF KOSMIC METAPHYSICS

(CHAPTERS 1 TO 5)

In Part I we sketch out the evolutionary-wholistic viewpoint of hK-M in as brief a form as possible, so as not to obscure the total picture with too much detail.

Chapter 1

The Kosmos Stirs and Thereby Begins to Experience a Sense of Self

Going Back as Far as We Can in the Evolution of the Kosmos - To A State of Dormant Energy

As we go back to earlier and earlier stages of evolution, life on Earth becomes increasingly more primitive, until we arrive at a state where life has not even begun to exist. When we go back further still there is no Earth and no Solar System. And if we go back yet further there are no stars, galaxies, or anything that comprises the Universe. Thus, by going back further and further in evolution fewer and fewer features of the Universe exist, until we reach a state of a uniform, undifferentiated, Kosmos.

In this uniform, undifferentiated state the Kosmos is the same everywhere. There is no space, because space requires that one thing is here and another is there but there are no different things - it is all one. Equally there is no time, because time measures the rate at which one activity takes place relative to another, and there are no different activities. There is no consciousness, because consciousness requires the perception of something and there is nothing to be perceived and no perceiver. Thus, in the uniform condition of the Kosmos, when there are no parts to be distinguished from one another, to our 'space-time' consciousness it is as though nothing exists. Looking back on this situation from the vantage point of our present level of evolution, perhaps the best way to describe it is as a state of dormant energy.

According to the metaphysics described in this book there is a pattern to the evolution of the Kosmos, whereby each phase of development arises out of stresses that develop in the previous one, due to seeking greater fulfilment. Thus, when the Kosmos transcends the limit of its potential to evolve in its 'dormant energy' state, it experiences a stress to be more than that, so that it 'breaks out'. Or, to put it in more simplistic terms, 'the Kosmos stirs'.

[It is difficult for us to relate to this remote primeval state, perhaps the best that we can do is to think of the situation when we are in a deep sleep, and some slight inner disturbance arises, but without interrupting our deep sleep].

The Kosmos Stirs Into Activity and Thereby Experiences Itself

When a part of the Kosmos stirs this creates a disruption and thereby a stress in its otherwise uniform, quiescent state. This stress then forces the active part back into the quiescent state, in line with the rest of the Kosmos. But then the activity breaks out again. And again this creates a disturbance and stress which forces it back into the quiescent state, fig. 1.1.

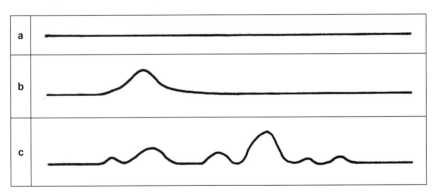

Fig. 1.1. (a) In this diagram the initial uniform state of the Kosmos is symbolised by a straight line. (b) There is then an eruption of activity and this creates a stress between the active and the inactive parts, in a way analogous to that which an 'eruption' would create a stress in a rubber sheet. (c) At first the activity is experienced as a disturbance; the stress, however, gives a sense of self that seeks to increase by becoming more active here, there, and everywhere.

This cycle of events is repeated again and again. But as this happens something new occurs in the Kosmos - in that the stress of interaction between the active and the inactive parts gives rise to a sense of self. Thus, where the activity occurs this gives a sense of self due to its interaction with the resistance of the quiescent part, and where the quiescent state is dominant an experience of self arises from the interaction of this with the pressure of the activity trying to break out.

[This is comparable, but at a very much less-evolved level, to the situation where we are enjoying a comfortable relaxed state and an urge spontaneously arises in us 'to be active'. We then experience a conflict between our desire to continue in a relaxed state and the urge 'to be up and doing'. But this analogy does not really capture the situation because the Kosmos, unlike ourselves, has no I, or centre, to register the experience. It is more like a disturbance that comes and goes at different places in an unformed, featureless, 'water-like' state of existence].

The Kosmos' experience of itself is something that had never happened before. Because it was a uniform thing with no part interacting with another part, it had never before experienced that it existed. By comparison with the much more evolved state that exists now the experience of self at this early stage is at a very low level - just a sort of unconscious diffuse disturbance.

[Again, perhaps the only way that we can relate to the Kosmos's experience of self is to think of the very low, almost non-existent, experience of self that we get from a slight inner disturbance while in a deep sleep].

Although this is a very dim level of experience, to the Kosmos at that time it is a totally new potential to be able to experience itself and this gives rise to an impulse to pursue this experience. As a result, the spontaneous activity that at first produces an uncomfortable, or negative experience of stress becomes a positive striving to be active and to experience a sense of self, which leads to a new phase of development.

[It is a basic principle of *hK-M* , that stress, or stimulus, drives evolution. Thus, for example, we experience the pressures of life as, on the one hand, stressful and, on the other hand, as stimuli to our further development].

The Kosmos' experience of self is by virtue of the stress, or stimulus produced as each upsurge of activity acts against the state of quiescence and vice versa. Through repetition, the ability to be active and to accommodate to the stress increases, so that there is no longer the same degree of experience of self. As a result, the striving to experience a sense of self increases the level of activity and produces a greater stress, thereby maintaining and enhancing the experience of self. Thus the activity increases with each upsurge.

This is how a sense of self first arises in the Kosmos and, as explained in the Introduction, it is the pursuance of sense of self that drives all further evolution.

The Activity Becomes Turmoil Which Breaks Down Into 'Superstructure Entities'

Eventually, in striving to increase its sense of self, the activity of the Kosmos reaches a state of turmoil, fig. 1.2a. In this turmoil the part of the Kosmos that wants to be active and the part that wants to be quiescent struggle against each other, which intensifies the turmoil. Where these two parts interact there arises a diffuse, ever-changing experience of self, here, there and everywhere. But as the sense of self becomes stronger, in some parts it becomes momentarily centred and stable, fig. 1.2b but then it is overcome by, and dispersed into, the surrounding turmoil.

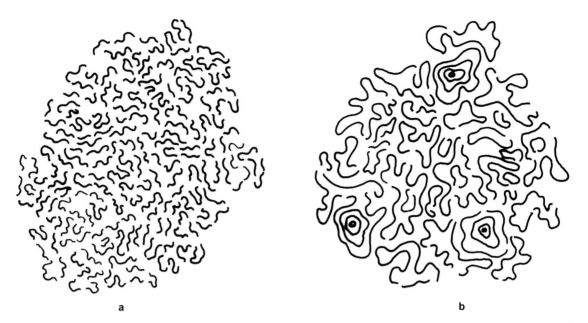

a   b

Fig. 1.2. (a) As the activity of the Kosmos's striving for a sense of self increases there arises an increasing turmoil of interaction between the active and inactive parts. (b) As this activity increases further, regions arise that temporarily experience being a centre of activity.

As the desire to experience a sense of self increases, the turmoil becomes greater and more and more centres arise that experience a transient sense of self. Eventually centres arise with the ability to maintain a permanent existence and thereby a permanent sense of self, so that the Kosmos becomes a collective of multitudinous stable centres of activity, fig. 1.3.

Fig. 1.3. As the experience, of striving for a sense of self increases, more and more transient centres of activity arise and their life spans become longer, until the Kosmos becomes a stable collective of self-actualising activities, or 'superstructure entities'. Each superstructure entity is a centre of activity that flows out to its confines [the surrounding superstructure entities] and back again.

Each centre is concerned with the sense of self that it acquires from expressing its activity so that its activity flows out from it. But because it is only one among many centres, its activity collides with that of the others around it doing the same thing, which deflects its activity back to itself. So it develops a continuous circulation but it is not aware of its pattern of activity, only of being a centre of activity.

[At a much more evolutionary advanced state of development an analogous sense of self arises in an embryo when it kicks out and experiences its will and ability to do this, due to the resistance of the surrounding womb].

Each centre is active on its own account, so that it is an 'entity', or I, in its own right, (but only as an unconscious 'mechanical' activity), and the Kosmos as a whole no longer exists. We call these centres, with the patterns of activity that they produce, 'superstructure entities', since these then form the basic structure of the Kosmos.

This transition from a state of quiescence can be reproduced in a laboratory experiment. If we take a stationary, featureless layer of liquid and make it increase in energy, first it takes up a random turbulent motion and then, as the energy increases further, centres of turbulence arise. These become stable, so that the liquid breaks down into a collection of separate circulations, known as Bénard cells, figure 1.4.

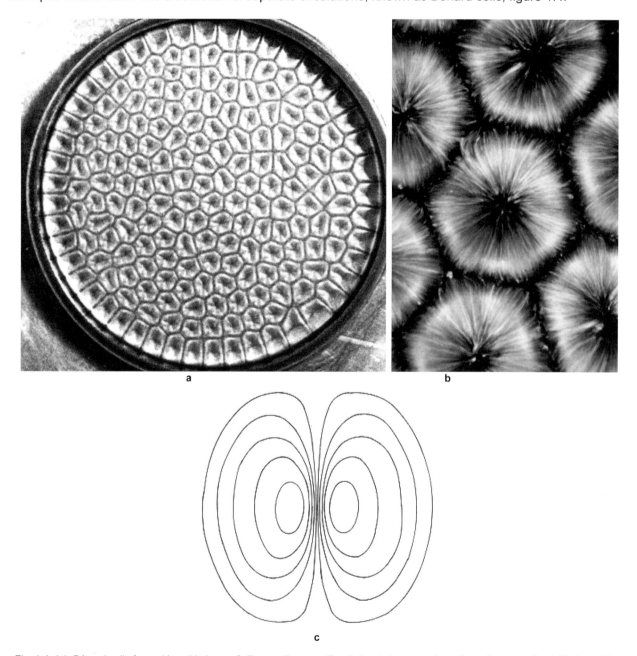

a   b

c

Fig. 1.4. (a) Bénard cells formed in a thin layer of silicone oil on a uniformly heated copper plate; the cells are made visible by adding fine aluminium powder to the oil. (b) A group of the Bénard cells in (a) at higher magnification, showing their flow pattern. (c) Diagram of Bénard cell motion.
Figs (a) and (b) Courtesy of Professor M.G. Velarde http:fluidos.pluri.ucm.es

This is what the Kosmos now comprises - a large number of superstructure entities, like Bénard cells on a vast Kosmic scale. Each entity is unconscious and exists simply as a self-actualising mechanical activity, independently pursuing its sense of self.

The idea of an initial state of 'nothingness' from which all else has arisen is not new. For example, Egyptian creation myths recognise such a state of existence, when there was no sky, no earth, no air, nor even gods, 'the infinity, the nothingness, the nowhere and the dark', which was described as the 'Primeval Waters', (PLUMLEY). Early Greek thinkers also refer to an indefinite, unformed, infinite 'apeiron' state from which came into being all the heavens and the worlds as a result of a 'whirl'; a state which existed before gods, (KIRK et al). The findings of modern science also lead to the conclusion that the first event is that 'the cosmos stirs', but scientists express this in a somewhat more sophisticated way:

> *'A microscopic quantum blob of ten-dimensional space suffers a spasm which inflates three dimensions to form a Universe, and traps the remaining seven in a permanent microcosmos from which they are manifested only indirectly, as the forces of Nature'*
>
> [DAVIES (1)].

Chapter 2

The Evolution of the Superstructure Entities Leads to the Beginning of the Universe

The Superstructure Entities Increase in Activity

Each superstructure entity gets a sense of self from its experience of being self-actualising, i.e. by expressing its ability to be active from its centre, with the other superstructure entities around it causing its activity to return to it, so that it reactivates what it gets back, to give rise to a continuous circulation. Its experience is at an unconscious, mechanical or 'will', trance-like level but with a stable, centred, sense of I, compared with the diffuse, unstable and changing sense of self that initially arose in the Kosmos.

This sense of self that derives from being an active self-actualising entity is a new experience that provides an impulse for a new phase of evolution, in which each superstructure centre strives for increasing experience of itself by increasing in activity.

[It is akin, again at a much more primitive level of evolution, to the sense of self that a baby gets by repeatedly pushing with its feet against the side of its pram, or against someone's hands. It knows nothing about being a body with arms and legs, or about prams, its only experience is of being active from inside itself against something outside it].

The Interaction of the Superstructure Entities Creates Turbulence at their Boundaries

At first the increased interaction with its 'environment' of the other super-structure entities, that are also increasing in activity and therefore pushing back on it, gives each entity an enhanced sense of self. But as they increase in activity this creates friction between them at their peripheries. When the distortion created by the friction exceeds the stability of flow imparted by their centred activity, they break down at their peripheries.

Before this breakdown the Kosmos consists of vast numbers of self-actualising superstructure entities in a formation akin to a three-dimensional pattern of mutually interacting 'cosmic bubbles'. When they break down at their peripheries this creates small turbulences along the boundaries of interaction between the bubbles, fig. 2.1, and these constitute the beginnings of the Universe.

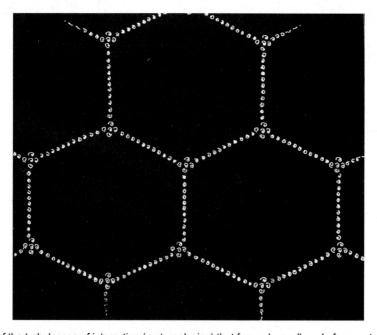

Fig. 2.1. The distribution of the turbulences of interaction (proto-galaxies) that form when a 'layer' of superstructure entities break down at their peripheries. (In actuality the proto-galaxies are even smaller in relation to the superstructure entities than this diagram portrays)

The Turbulence Gives Rise to the Beginning of Galaxies

The turbulence comprises a mixture of the different activities of the adjacent superstructure entities from which they were separated off. Under the pressure created by the activities of the surrounding superstructure entities these different activities are forced to interact and, as a result they adjust to each other (the more active increasing the lesser and vice versa) and they combine. At the same time the pressure of the activity of the superstructure entities compresses them. The activity of each region of turbulence then increases until a centre, or centres arise in it, (as in fig. 1.2). In these centres the sense of self, which was there when they were part of the large organisation of a superstructure entity, is reawakened, and they develop their own, enhanced, sense of self, so that each region of turbulence becomes one, or a group of, self-actualising activities. These thereby become small versions of the superstructure entities that 'gave birth' to them and they comprise the beginnings of 'galaxies'.

At this early stage of their formation these galaxies are nothing like they are now. No substances have yet arisen and what is described here is purely a self-actualising activity, which we designate a 'galaxy entity'. (As will be seen later, as evolution progresses these galaxy entities break down into the first substance of the Universe - hydrogen, which creates further turbulence leading to the formation of stars which 'process' the hydrogen. This is what we see today, by modern telescopes, as the galaxies of the Universe).

[A way of visualising these early developments is to think of the confluence of two massive rivers that are flowing steadily at slightly different speeds. In the comparatively narrow region of their interaction turbulences are formed. The pressure of the massive steady flows causes the turbulences to increase in activity that results in them forming whirlpools. If we then imagine that these whirlpools become self-actualising, then they are equivalent to the turbulences that form 'galaxies' at the peripheries of interaction between the superstructure entities].

When scientists plot the distribution of galaxies they find that they do not exist uniformly throughout the Universe. They find, instead, that the galaxies occur in skeins and clusters as though along the boundaries of a three- dimensional bubble pattern, as in the diagram in fig. 2.2, in which several 'layers' of fig. 2.1 have been superimposed.

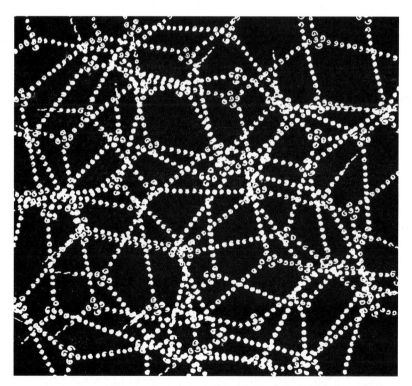

Fig. 2.2. The skein and cluster-like distribution of proto-galaxies that arises with the over-laying of several 'layers' portrayed in fig. 2.1

The Big Bang theory of the Universe posits that all the energy and substances of which the Universe consists, initially existed in a highly compressed 'pin-head' state before expanding out and condensing to form the galaxies that are the basic features of the Universe. One of the problems of this theory is to explain how the energy and substance became concentrated into localised galaxy formations that exist in skeins and clusters throughout the Universe. After all, if everything is expanding outwards from a point source, why does it not do so uniformly in all directions? A number of theories have been proposed to resolve this problem. From the *h*K-M viewpoint this is not a problem, because the substance and energy of the Universe arose in the first place as a multiplicity of 'little bang', galaxy formations distributed along the peripheries of interaction of the superstructure entities.

The vast array of superstructure entities make up what we know as the space of our Universe. They continue with their self-actualising activities and, in so doing, exert a pressure on the much smaller galaxy entities and thereby bring about further developments. In this way all further evolution can be viewed as the 'creation' of the superstructure entities, brought about by the pressure of their mutually interacting activity, which exists everywhere. But this creation is not by design, or out of any awareness on the part of the superstructure entities; it is purely inadvertent, as they continue their unconscious mechanical self-actualising activities. In fact, rather than seeking to create something, their activities act to eliminate anything that disturbs their equilibrium, but, inadvertently, this pressure provides a stimulus to further development on what it acts.

. . . .

Continual reference will be made in what follows to the superstructure entities and their activities. To simplify the otherwise cumbersome phraseology we adopt the following notation:

Superstructure entities: s-entities

Superstructure entity activity: s-activity

Superstructure entity pressure: s-pressure

Chapter 3

The Arising of Substances, Stars and Planets out of an On-going Turmoil

The Formation of Hydrogen – the First Substance of the Universe

As described in Chapter 1 the Kosmos starts as a state of dormant energy that becomes active and the activity increases to create a state of turbulence that differentiates into self-actualising s-entities. As described in Chapter 2 the s-entities seek enhanced sense of self by increasing in activity and the build up of their interaction creates turbulence at their peripheries, that differentiates into self-actualising galaxy entities.

The galaxy entities seek enhanced sense of self by increasing in activity and in so doing conflict with the much larger s-entities, to bring about mutual breakdown of their zone of interaction, thereby creating a further state of turbulence. This turbulence comprises two different levels of energy activity, a ponderous part that derives from the breakdown of the large s-entities and a more active part that derives from the much smaller galaxy entities. The s-pressure forces the two energy states to interact and the stresses that their different levels of activity exert on each other results in them breaking each other down, to give rise to hydrogen atoms. In the hydrogen atoms the ponderous s-entity-derived part forms the atomic nucleus and the more active galaxy-entity-derived part forms the outer electron energy of the atom, fig. 3.1.

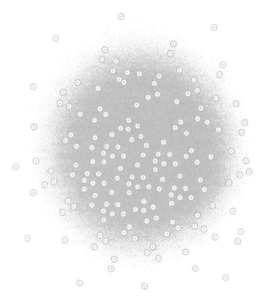

Fig. 3.1 A cloud of hydrogen atoms, each comprising a nucleus of ponderous s-entity energy activity and an electron surround of more active galaxy entity material, forms out of the mixed s-entity – galaxy entity turbulence. This creates a non-coherent 'grey' area in the s-entity activity.

The Formation of Stars and Heavier Atoms out of the Hydrogen

The clouds of hydrogen that develop in this way cause localised turbulence in the activity of the s-entities. The coherent undisturbed part of the s-entities' activities exerts a pressure on this turbulence that compresses and intensifies it, causing it to differentiate into self-actualising star entities, (in the same way, but on a much smaller scale, to that in which the initial turbulence of the Kosmos broke down into s-entities, figs. 1.2 & 1.3). The star entities develop a Bénard-cell-type flow pattern of activity and the combination of this and the s-pressure concentrates the hydrogen atoms to their centres where they collide to form larger atoms, fig. 3.2(a). The increasing concentration of atoms at the centre of the star entity creates congestion and stress in its self-actualising activity, so that its thrusting against the s-pressure is reduced. When the stress becomes greater than it can accommodate to, the star entity contracts under the s-pressure. This increases the intensity of its activity, which causes an ejection of stress-causing material, fig. 3.2(b), until it settles down to a new balance of its activity acting against the s-pressure. This new, increased level of its activity results in increased collision of atoms at its centre, so that these form larger atoms, fig. 3.2 (c).

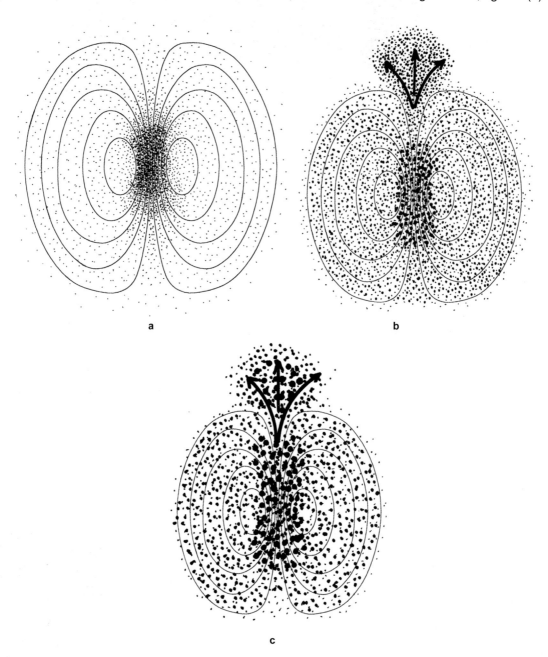

Fig. 3.2(a). The cloud of hydrogen causes turbulence in the s-entity, out of which self-actualising star entities arise, in which the B-cell flow pattern of the star entities brings about collision of the hydrogen atoms to form larger atoms of helium. The concentration of atoms at the star entity's centre causes congestion and reduction of its activity so that it collapses under the s-pressure, with the stress of reaction causing it to eject some of its congestion-causing material, fig. 3.2(b). The increased intensity of the star entity's activity results in an increased intensity of collision and the formation of larger atoms at its centre. This sequence of events is repeated a few times with a small star entity, fig. 3.2(c) and many times with a large star entity

The sequence of build up of congestion and contraction happens a number of times, with each contraction resulting in the formation of larger and larger atoms and rejection of excess stress-causing material into the surrounding s-entity. This ceases when an impasse state is reached at which the atoms at the centre of the star entity have increased to a size at which its activity is no longer great enough to collide them together to form larger atoms and the star then becomes inactive, with further contraction under the s-pressure concentrating these into a 'dead' planet.

When hydrogen forms into larger atoms in stars light is given off and the visible Universe begins to come into existence, fig. 3.3.

Fig. 3.3. When stars begin to form larger atoms from hydrogen, light is given off.   This is what we see when we look out to the heavens but, according to hK-M, the creation of stars and the substances that they work with, have come about as the result of the activities of s-entities that fill the whole of 'space' and are invisible to us. Within each s-entity there are billions of galaxy entities, which are again invisible to us. Each galaxy in turn contains billions of stars, which contain billions of atoms, the interactions of which gives out light, and this is all that we see.

Photo Jeff Sutton

The Formation of the Solar System

As further star entities arise out of the turbulence, fig. 3.4, these encompass not only hydrogen atoms but also larger atoms formed by previous stars.

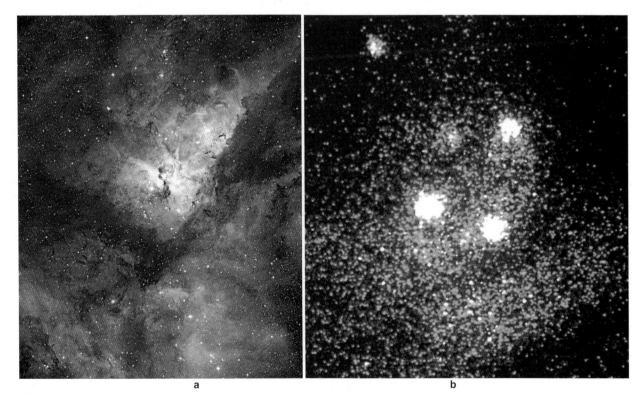

a   b

Fig. 3.4(a). Photograph of a typical region of cosmic turbulence containing cosmic dust, made visible by the impinging light of near-by stars, in which, by X-ray photography, scientists observe new stars to be forming, fig. 3.4(b).
3.4a The Corina Nebula: Anglo-Australian Observatory/David Malin Images 3.4b Photo by courtesy of NASA

The Sun entity is formed in this way. The combination of the s-pressure and its Bénard-cell flow pattern cause the Sun entity to concentrate hydrogen and larger atoms, formed in previous stars, to its centre, fig. 3.5(a). The collision between the larger atoms causes these to form particles of substance. The build up of this concentration of substances at its centre creates a stress that resists the Sun entity's centrally-driven activity so that it contracts under the s-pressure. This intensifies its activity, and gives rise to a burst of energy that causes excess stress-causing material to be rejected from it as a cloud of gas and cosmic dust, fig. 3.5(b). The rejected material creates disruption and turbulence in the surrounding s-entity from which one or more self-actualising Bénard-cell-type entities arise. These concentrate the material that they encompass to their centres, to form asteroids or planets, fig.3.5(c).

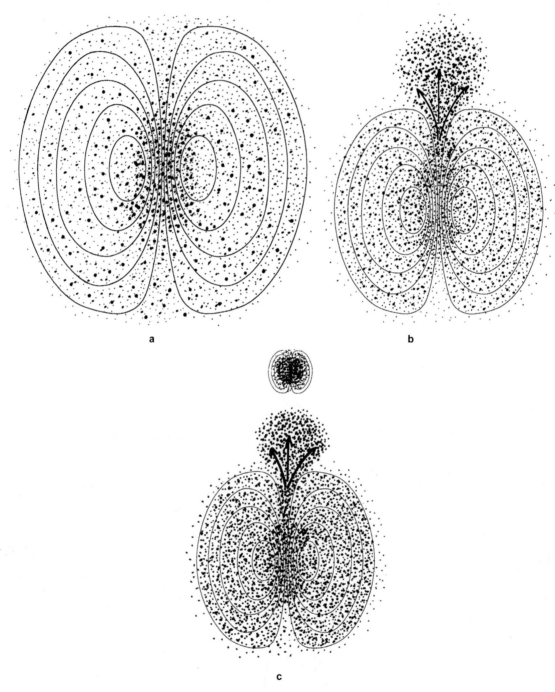

a   b

c

Fig. 3.5. The Sun entity is differentiated out of the s-entity background as a cloud of hydrogen and cosmic dust that impedes the s-entity's pattern of activity. The Sun entity at this stage is large, existing out to the periphery of what is now the Solar System, (a). As the Sun entity concentrates substances to its centre, this causes congestion in, and a reduction of, its self-actualising activity, so that it collapses under the s-pressure with rejection of excess stress-causing material, (b). The ejected material causes turbulence in the surrounding s-entity and the formation of a planetary entity that concentrates the substance to its centre to form a planet, (c). This happens a number of times as the Sun collapses to a size at which the increased intensity of its activity causes hydrogen atoms to combine together into helium atoms, thereby reducing the congestion and slowing its collapse.

This rejection process happens a number of times, as the Sun entity contracts under the s-pressure, to give rise to the formation around it of a succession of asteroids and/or planets, of which the Earth is one. This ceases when the Sun entity does not contract any further under the s-pressure, which occurs when its activity has intensified to a level that causes hydrogen atoms to combine together into helium atoms, which reduces the resistance to its centrally-driven flow and boosts its energy to give rise to the Sun as we know it now. The Sun then enters its present period of stability in which the resistance to its centrally-driven flow as more hydrogen atoms concentrate there, is counteracted by them being compacted to form helium atoms. Eventually, when there is no more hydrogen to 'burn' the Sun entity will contract under the s-pressure and compact whatever cosmic dust and atoms that are at its centre, to form a dead (inactive) planet.

[This explanation for the formation of planets differs from the commonly held scientific view that rings of gas and cosmic dust formed around the Sun, (akin to those observed around Saturn), the material of which slowly agglomerated into planets. However, recent examinations of meteorites have shown that they possess features that can only be explained by more violent processes taking place in the formation of the asteroids and planets of the Solar System. At the same time ejection processes are observed as playing a significant role in cosmic phenomena].

The Universe at this stage of its evolution consists of a vast number of large and small self-actualising entities that pursue their sense of self by increasing in activity in an unconscious 'mechanical' way, each seeking increased sense of self without any awareness of, or concern for, the others. This results in an on-going turbulence of interaction, out of which further entities arise. The developments that take place in the turbulence are brought about by the (unconsciously creative) pressure of the s-entities' activities acting on it.

*   *   *

We use the description 'Bénard-cell-type flow many times in this book so, to shorten this cumbersome phraseology, we reduce it to B-cell flow.

Summary of the Evolution of the Universe According to hK-M

The Kosmos starts in a state of dormant energy.

The energy becomes active and turbulent.

The turbulence differentiates into self-actualising s-entities. This is the invisible background state of the Universe that exists everywhere.

The s-entities interact to create turbulence at their peripheries.

The turbulence differentiates into self-actualising galaxy entities. This is the beginning of galaxies but they are not yet visible.

The galaxy entities interact with the s-entities to create mixed s-entity – galaxy entity turbulence.

The mixed turbulence differentiates into hydrogen atoms.

The clouds of hydrogen create turbulence in the s-entities.

This turbulence differentiates into star entities that force the hydrogen atoms together to create larger atoms that are expelled as cosmic dust into the surrounding s-entity. At this stage the visible Universe arises, as the formation of larger atoms out of the hydrogen creates reverberations (light) that marks out the underlying pattern of galaxy activity, fig.3.6.

As more stars form these encompass hydrogen together with cosmic dust formed from the larger atoms created by earlier stars. Our Sun is a star of this type.

The Sun is initially large, (the size of the Solar System). The mixture of hydrogen and cosmic dust creates stress in its centrally-driven activity and it contracts under the s-pressure, which increases its activity and results in some of its material being ejected into the surrounding s-entity.

This happens a number of times and the ejected material creates turbulence in the s-entity that differentiates into self-actualising entities that compress it into the asteroids and planets of the Solar System.

Fig. 3.6. This is a photograph of the Antila spiral galaxy that is similar to the Milky Way in which the Solar System exists. The dark background comprises invisible s-entity energy. The pattern of turbulence was formed by the interaction of s-ents to create an (invisible) galaxy entity. The interaction of the galaxy entity and the s-entity has then created further turbulence that has given rise to stars in the galaxy. The stars force hydrogen atoms together to create larger atoms and it is this activity that gives out light and thereby makes visible the stars and the turbulent pattern of the galaxy.

Anglo-Australian Observatory/David Malin Images

Chapter 4

The Arising and Evolution of Life on Earth

The Formation of the Earth with its Atmosphere and Watery Surface

As a result of the s-pressurised B-cell activity of the Earth Entity, the gases, cosmic dust and agglomerates that make up the substances of the Earth come together to form Planet Earth. But there is a division of substances, in that light ones, that circulate more readily, get circulated out to form a gaseous atmosphere comprising various carbonaceous and other gases and water vapour. As the Earth and its atmosphere cool down, water vapour in the atmosphere condenses to form rivers, lakes and seas on its surface. As the water vapour condenses to (hot) water it carries with it, in solution, some of the other gaseous materials in the atmosphere. Then in its hot state it dissolves some of the solid mineral substances of the Earth's surface.

The Arising of Life in the Form of Prokaryotic Cells

As the watery 'soup' of the lakes and oceans cools, its constituents come closer together and the dissolved carbonaceous and mineral substances create a stress in the uniformity of the watery state, which results in them separating out. In this process small droplets rich in carbonaceous constituents separate from the rest of the water that contains predominantly mineral substances. The stress at the droplet boundary causes carbonaceous substances to concentrate there and they form a membrane around it. The s-pressure then acts on the imbalance between the substances within the droplet to those outside it, to cause some substances to flow from outside into it and other substances to flow out from inside it. Some of the substances in the membrane-enclosed droplet combine together, which releases energy. The released energy and its associated increase in activity gives the Earth Entity (the E-energy) in the droplet a sense of self in which it experiences itself as a 'droplet entity' taking substances in from, and rejecting others to, its environment. It takes over this activity and makes it self-actualising. As, in seeking increased sense of self, the droplet entity takes in and combines more and more substances, this stresses the membrane until it can no longer contain them and the droplet divides into two. This gives rise to microscopic procreating single-celled organisms (prokaryotic cells) in which the E-energy caught up in the cell situation ingests substances, brings them together and excretes substances that create excess stress in it. (Scientists have reproduced in the laboratory the formation of membrane-enclosed droplets in these conditions, that grow and divide to give rise to forms resembling early microfossils, fig. 4.1).

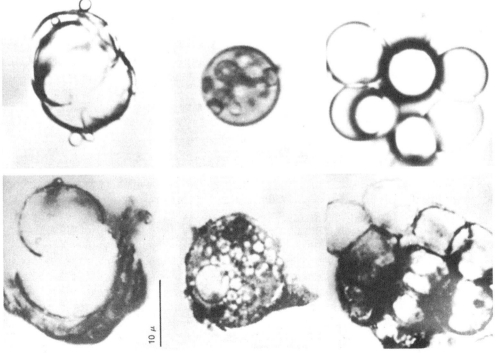

Fig. 4.1

Top: various stages in the development of minute membrane-enclosed droplets which divide into two, that scientists have observed to form when they re-create the conditions that existed in the early stages of the watery environment of the Earth planet.

Bottom: photomicrographs of microfossils showing the very early forms of life.

From Molecular Evolution and the Origin of Life by FOX and DOSE

[This is the basic principle underlying the evolution of life on Earth. The s-pressure causes activities in which the part of the E-energy involved experiences a sense of self. This part takes over this activity and makes it self-actualising, to give rise to entities that carry out this activity for themselves. At the stage of evolution that we are now considering, this is simply a matter of microscopic entities in the watery environment manipulating substances to maintain their existence and sense of self. But we see the same principle in operation at a more advanced level when, for example, at school we are 'pressurised by a higher force' into going through the activities involved in, say, arithmetic and we then take over these activities and make them our own. Thereby we become self-actualising entities that carry out arithmetical calculations for ourselves. In this way we similarly develop many other abilities as we go through life].

As with water finding a way through mixed terrain, in which it organises substances as it develops its flow pattern, the prokaryotic cell entity does a similar thing, thereby developing a structure to the cell and its membrane that arises from the pattern of this activity. Thus the prokaryotic cell entity's pattern of activity is determined by the substances involved (the genetic aspect) but its existence and its basic striving energy derive from its nature, as a differentiated-out part of the E-energy seeking an enhanced sense of self.

As the E-energy gathers increasing experience of operating as a prokaryotic cell, it becomes able to maintain this self-actualising activity with combinations of substances other than those that gave rise to the first type of prokaryotic cell, so that different species of prokaryotic cells arise.

The Arising of Eukaryotic Cells

As different species of prokaryotic cells come into existence, some of them interact with each other, by substances rejected by one species being used by other species to support their activities. As a result different species form symbiotic relationships. In this way a pattern of activity forms in the E-energy that encompasses and integrates the activities of different species of prokaryotic cells. The E-energy involved in this localised pattern of integrating activity thereby experiences a sense of self and it takes it over and makes it self-actualising. Then, in seeking increasing sense of self, it expands its activities until these become more than it can control and the resulting stress causes it to disintegrate. This awakens its prokaryotic cell experience that the way to avoid this is to divide into two parts and thereby procreating eukaryotic cells come into existence. These combine and integrate the activities of several prokaryotic cells, with the encompassing eukaryotic entity monitoring and harmonising the flow of substances between its prokaryotic components and the environment. Although a eukaryotic cell is a combination of several prokaryotic cells it is still a small, single-celled organism, (akin to a primitive amoeba).

As was the case with prokaryotic cells, as the E-energy builds up experience of maintaining its sense of self with the symbiotic interaction that gives rise to the first type of eukaryotic cell, it becomes able to do so with different symbiotic interactions between prokaryotic cells, so that different species of eukaryotic cells develop.

The Arising of Multicellular Organisms

In seeking increased sense of self, eukaryotic cells multiply and form colonies, to give rise to interactions between the members of the colony. This results in a further, larger pattern of activity in the E-energy. This region then experiences a sense of self, so it takes over this activity and makes it self-actualising. This gives rise to a multicellular organism that comprises a multiplicity of eukaryotic cells encompassed and controlled by a multi-cellular entity. At this stage this multicellular organism is only a small blob of jelly-like living activity (like Trichoplax) in the watery environment, in which the multicellular entity monitors and controls the flow of substances between its 'body' of eukaryotic cells and the environment.

As the E-energy gathers increasing experience, in seeking enhanced sense of self it becomes able to maintain a self-actualising multicellular existence in which it integrates the activities of larger and larger numbers of eukaryotic cells; thereby larger and larger multicellular entities arise. At the same time, in response to stresses imposed on them by different environments, these develop patterns of activity in which they can maintain their sense of self in these different conditions. Thereby more and more new species, of increasing variety of forms and ways of functioning arise in different regions of the watery environment. The more that this happens, the more experience the E-energy brings to bear on the situations that it encounters, so that the forms of life in water become increasingly evolved. Thus, from primitive soft-bodied creatures (like rudimentary worms and jelly fish) there develop more complex forms, such as trilobites, shelled organisms and multitudinous types of fishes, which become increasingly varied and larger as the E-energy gathers more experience. Then the build up of experience in the E-energy reaches a point that enables it to maintain a multicellular existence in the conditions at the water-land borderline, giving rise to amphibians, fig. 4.2.

a   b   c   d   e

Fig.4.2   This picture (from HENBEST) summarises from left to right, the origin and early development of life on Earth. (a) Violent volcanic activity created an atmosphere of carbon dioxide, water vapour and ammonia. (b) Lightning and other violent activity created simple organic molecules from these substances that then became dissolved in the water that was condensing onto the Earth's surface, to form a watery 'soup'. (c) As this cooled, prebiotic carbonaceous droplets separated out in the mineral-containing waters of the oceans, the activity of which built up a body of substances within them. (d) This activity became self-actualising to give rise to microscopic living, prokaryotic single-celled organisms. From these there developed more complex eukaryotic, and then multicellular, organisms to give rise to early plants and animals. As these sought enhanced sense of self there developed multitudinous varieties of creatures in the sea, out of which some evolved the ability to exist on land. As these organisms developed and proliferated they combined carbon with hydrogen from water, thereby freeing oxygen so that the atmosphere became the mixture of oxygen and nitrogen that it is now, (e).

Artist Jon Wells, courtesy Marshall Cavendish Picture Library

As the amphibian experience of surviving out of water builds up in the E-energy, multicellular organisms arise that are able to maintain a sense of self in a totally land-based environment. Then, by surviving in a range of different environments on land the E-energy builds up ever-greater experience, on which multicellular organisms draw, to adapt to an ever-wider range of environmental conditions. Thereby the evolution of new species of organisms on land becomes increasingly rapid and varied and a great multiplicity of creatures arises that develop abilities to exploit different environments. In particular some 50 million years ago, monkeys arose that evolved from earlier primates that were small tree-living creatures that had developed a grasping hand and stereoscopic vision to enable them to live in this environment. To this monkeys added a degree of bipedalism, with an increase in brain size and the ability to coordinate these functions.

The Arising of Hominids

The exposure of monkeys in some regions to environmental conditions that required them to develop their bipedal movement then resulted in the arising, about 5-7 million years ago, of a basically bipedal creature, Australopithecus. Thus, out of the build up in the E-energy of vast experience of adapting to, and coping with, many different environments there arose a bipedal creature with co-ordination of movement and dexterity of manipulation, capable of functioning in a range of environments on Earth, namely a hominid. Since then further responses to environmental stresses have been met, not by changes in biological form, but by the increasing skill with which hominids function; performing increasingly complex tasks with the only biological change being an increase in brain capacity to co-ordinate this.

During multicellular evolution many animals develop the ability to use the materials of their environment to maintain their activities and their sense of self. (Birds build nests; beavers build dams, etc.). A few animals also develop the ability to use materials from their environment as primitive tools to help with their activities, (e.g. chimpanzees use sticks as levers, and twigs to dig out termites; sea otters and thrushes use stones as anvils on which to break open soft-bodied shelled creatures).

The arising of hominids, with their greater freedom in the use of their hands, led to them developing the ability to make stone tools. Because of their durability and because they have been found in large numbers these portray a well-defined pattern of development. The first event could have been the use of a stone that had adventitiously been broken and developed a rough edge as a result of some natural occurrence, for getting access to food, e.g. tearing through the tough skin of a dead animal or digging for roots, etc. This registered in the E-energy that, by its continual integrating activity, brought it into juxtaposition with the experience that the stone had developed its rough edge by being broken. Then, as hominids were faced with the situation for which they had found a broken stone useful this triggered off this connection and activated them to deliberately break a stone to obtain one with a rough edge. (This is how our minds as conscious, individualised parts of the E-energy would put things together and the way that the E-energy is all the time working unconsciously). This gave rise to homo habilis who developed a routine of breaking stones to make rudimentary tools about 2.5 million years ago, fig.4.3.

Fig. 4.3 Crude stone 'tools' made by the first tool-making hominid, homo habilis, about two and a half million years ago.
From LEAKEY Robert Harding World Imagery

Looking back with hindsight we can see that this offered great potential for further developments and that it would have been very easy to make better tools, but at the time the only thing that homo habilis knew was the use of a broken-edged stone for rudimentary hacking at something. Some broken stones must have performed better than others and over a period of a million years this experience built up in, and was activated from, the E-energy to culminate in a deliberate breaking of stones to give a more efficient 'tear drop axe shape', fig. 4.4, which then became the established pattern of tool making for a further million years.

Fig.4.4.   The more efficient 'teardrop' hand axe shape that developed a million years later.
From LEAKEY Robert Harding World Imagery

Attempts to make the required tear-drop shape gave rise to other shapes and as a result of trying to use these for various tasks the experience slowly built up in, and was activated from, the E-energy that a variety of shapes could be made to suit specific purposes. This led to the making of 'tool kits' that covered a range of requirements, fig. 4.5.

At the same time, the stress to make tools for specific applications activated in the E-energy the experience that other materials, that possessed different properties to stone, could be more suited to some requirements and so there developed tool making using also bone, horn and antler and this was the situation with Neanderthal man 100,000 years ago.

This shows the long period required in the evolution of hominids for the build up of experience in the E-energy to give rise to new developments, which with hindsight, seem simple and obvious.

In carrying out their activities different Neanderthal hominids developed specialised skills that gave them an ego sense of self, as possessing abilities different from the other members of their group. Thereby each individual began to experience a personal sense of self that was different from those of the other members of the group, due to his/her specific way of functioning.

Fig. 4.5 A variety of stone tools that hominids developed a further million year's later (75,000 years ago) to make up a 'tool kit'.
From F.Clark Howell: Old World Archaeology, Scientific American, 1952

The Arising of the Hominid Feeling Soul

As with the arising of prokaryotic, eukaryotic and multicellular entities, the parts of the E-energy that experience a sense of self from each of these different activities make this self-actualising. Thereby each group member acquires, and out of its further experiences draws on and develops, its own individualised 'ego', activity. This is then superimposed on its bodily functioning hierarchy of multicellular-eukaryotic-prokaryotic activities.

At first the ego is concerned with satisfying the needs of the individual's multicellular body (which in turn satisfies those of the eukaryotic-prokaryotic activities that it encompasses). But as it evolves it becomes concerned with developing and satisfying its increasingly stronger ego sense of self, as well as the needs of its body. That is, it seeks self-fulfilment, using the multicellular body to achieve this. It then develops feelings or emotions of satisfaction or frustration, according to the degree to which it achieves this. In this way it becomes the body of 'soul-feelings', which then uses the hierarchy of its bodily activities as the means to exert its will to satisfy its desires.

[We can perceive the effect of soul feelings by two examples from our own experience. First, food: our multicellular body experiences stresses when its eukaryotic cells require substances to maintain their activities. However, the effect of our feeling soul is not only to experience this basic need for food but also a gourmet-type feeling of satisfaction from the experience of consuming it (which sometimes leads to consuming more than our multicellular body needs and thereby imposing stresses on it). Second, sex: the multicellular entity of an animal experiences biological bodily sexual needs/stresses that it seeks to satisfy. But we seek also feelings of soul satisfaction from sexual relationships].

The drive for soul satisfaction causes the hominid ego to seek feelings of enhanced sense of self. Thus there arises primitive jewellery and other articles of adornment to enhance its sense of self (archaeologists have found such items in the graves of Neanderthal hominids dating from about 100,000 years ago).

The Arising of the Hominid Thinking Spirit

As the soul seeks the best way to satisfy its desires it draws on the E-energy's integrating activity of its experiences, so as to achieve its ends. In this way it develops a rudimentary thinking, which gives rise to a thinking I, Ego or 'spirit' which then superimposes its activities on those of the feelings of the soul-body and wills its thoughts into actions through the multicellular body complex. There thereby arises a hominid that is a rudimentary thinking, feeling, willing hierarchy of activities.

Its thinking ability enables the Ego to realise new potentials in the things of the world around it and in its own creative abilities. Animals have developed many highly creative activities with the materials of their environment, such as the building of bird nests. But this has arisen by things happening inadvertently in the first place. This registers in the E-energy and then, when the animal is faced with the relevant situation, this activates this memory and the animal re-enacts, and thereby reinforces, this pattern of activity. (The bird nest situation evolves from the bird initially depositing its eggs on a naturally occurring clump of material and then taking over this experience and making it self actualising, so that it builds such a clump and then re-enacts and reinforces this process, making the clump/nest conform more and more to the stresses of its needs). Thus, whereas everything that animals (and early hominids) do, first happened inadvertently, thinking hominids, faced with a stress/need situation, can think how best to apply their experiences to find a solution. This conscious thinking faculty arose with homo sapiens Neanderthalensis (sapiens = wise), for whom archaeologists have discovered evidence of considerable advances in skills and conceptual (thought out, purpose built) design of tools and the invention of the bow and arrow, the needle and sewing.

[The development of dwellings by hominids follows the same evolutionary principle as the sequence of developments that led to the bird's nest but with a conscious realisation of the situation. Primitive hominid seeks out sheltered regions provided by Nature, e.g. in woods and caves. Then he modifies these to improve the shelter that they provide. Then he builds shelters from branches or stones from scratch. This gives him an awareness of his ability to do this and an associated enhanced sense of self. Over long periods of development, this leads to greatly improved dwellings that provide better for his needs. This, in turn makes him further aware of his creative potentials and the resulting enhanced sense of self causes him to enlarge and embellish his dwelling. Then, as a result of the acclamation that he gets from doing this, which further enhances his sense of self, the creation of the necessities for his dwelling takes second place to striving for artistic expression and acclamation. In this, like the development of the highly ornate nest of the weaver bird, or the peacock's tail, the end result can become more concerned with creating an impression so as to get an enhanced sense of self, by superfluous achievement which can become excessive and, in some cases, more than the entity can sustain and hence be self destructive].

The members of a hominid group develop this rudimentary thinking ability, according to the pressures on them to perform and improve their role within the group and their own desire to enhance their sense of self. As members of the group become older they develop more experience and wisdom and the other members of the group turn to those that develop these qualities to the greatest extent so that these members of the group take on the role of leaders. Fulfilling this function gives the leader an enhanced sense of self and, in seeking to maintain and increase this, the leader further develops his/her Ego activity.

When the leader's body dies the members of the group experience the need for the leadership that they have lost and this stimulus keeps the leader's Ego spirit in a state of continuing activity. The members of the group then experience this wisdom and leadership as coming from the 'spirit' of the dead leader.

The awareness of the members of the group thereby begins to encompass the idea of a life after death of the leaders, (and of ancestors who influenced their lives - giving rise to ancestor worship). As a result, they start to bury their dead and to provide them with articles that they imagine will maintain them active on their behalf in their afterlife, and to practise 'magical' ways of communicating with the dead. According to the archaeological evidence these activities first occurred with Neanderthal Man about 100,000 years ago. (Animals, by comparison, probably live in their immediate experience; it is unlikely that an animal is aware that it was once born into the world and will one day die out of it).

Some members of the group (shamans) become more capable than others of communicating with the Ego activity of the discarnate leader and the more that they accomplish this, the more they 'merge with' and are taken over by the leader's spirit. The spirit of the leader, having no sensory contact with the world seeks to perceive that of the shaman with whom it is in contact. In order to do this it seeks to interpret the sensory/brain activity of the shaman's soul-body and to construct from it an image of its experiences, (in much the same way that we form an image from the pattern of electrical activity on a television screen). That is, instead of experiencing the world around it directly, as it did while associated with a body, it experiences it indirectly through the sensory and brain activity of the soul-body of the shaman, so that it then has to interpret this activity by forming 'concepts' for what it thinks is going on and work out of these.

This development of a conceptual understanding of things is what characterises modern man but to see how modern man (homo sapiens sapiens) arose and carried this development further, we have to introduce a new and larger dimension to our considerations of the evolution of life on Earth, which we do in the next Chapter.

The Central Role of the Earth Entity (Memory) Energy

The key to the arising and evolution of life on Earth is thus the E-energy. Everything in the Kosmos comprises energy that was originally in a dormant state that, as a result of the way in which it has evolved, has become its present activity. Thus the experiences of the E-energy constitute its nature and abilities. (Just as our experiences and abilities constitute our nature). At each stage of the evolution of life - prokaryotic cells, eukaryotic cells, multicellular entities, soul-feeling and spirit-thinking entities - there has been a flow of the E-energy into and out of the entities involved. The E-energy thereby comprises a memory energy of everything in which it has been involved in the formation of the Earth and of life on Earth. We therefore re-designate the E-energy the Earth Memory Energy (EM-energy). When it enters into a prokaryotic cell, eukaryotic cell, multicellular entity or hominid, the situations/stresses that it experiences activate the relevant part of the EM-energy to maintain these self-actualising activities, in the way that the relevant part of our memory experience is activated and determines our behaviour by the circumstances that we encounter.

Each member of a species draws on, and contributes to, the build up of the experiences of the species. Thus, while the EM-energy contains the totality of all Earth and life experiences, there develops within it integrated species patterns of experiences that become activated by the individual members, in the same way that our memories are not just a jumble of everything that we have experienced but, when they are activated, arise as patterns of events and associated responses. It is the activation of such 'species memory patterns' that gives rise to 'instinctive' patterns of behaviour. It is because all members of a species activate the same memory pattern that they have common patterns of behaviour. Later on in evolution the species memory pattern becomes individualised in each hominid. And this is the situation which we inherit so that, in addition to communal patterns of behaviour that derive from the collective unconscious, we each have our own specific memory pattern, which consists of our past experience in a dormant state, the relevant aspects of which become activated in response to the situations that we encounter. Our behaviour is a localised, individualised part of the overall behaviour of the EM-energy.

[The evolution of life takes place by basic hK-M principles that operate universally, so that the developments that brought about the increasing organisation of life on Earth can be seen as analogous to what happens later in the evolution of human organisations. Thus, prokaryotic entities are akin to workmen who derive their sense of self from working with the substances of the Earth. The eukaryotic entity is akin to a foreman who gets his/her sense of self from integrating the activities of a group of different workmen and ensuring that they have the supplies of materials that they need, so as to maintain their patterns of activity. The multicellular entity is akin to a Works Manager who derives his/her sense of self from integrating the activities of a group of foremen who in turn integrate those of groups of workmen. It is the sense of self that is got by playing a larger role in the activities of life. The hominid activity is akin to that of management that derives its sense of self from developing the further potentials that it perceives in the organisation and it does this out of intuitive feelings or rational thinking. With both the biological evolution of life and that of the human organisation, these levels of development come about as the experience and abilities to utilise the potentials of the substances of the Earth become more advanced, leading to the arising of a higher level of organisation to control and integrate these activities.]

Summary of the Evolution of Life on Earth

Scientists estimate that substances came together to form the Earth planet about 4,500 million years ago. At first the Earth was hot and liquid but it then began to cool and the oceans condensed onto its surface. Small regions of pre-life activity, called 'carbonaceous droplets' probably came into existence in the oceans, in vast quantities, early on. But these were very small and it took a long time for the EM-energy to build up sufficient experience of circulating through this state for it to become self actualising, which then gave rise to prokaryotic cells. From fossil evidence scientists estimate that these arose some 3,500 million years ago. There then followed a long period of evolution, lasting some 2,000 million years, in which the EM-energy acquired increasing experience of a sense of self through its activity in ever-increasing numbers and species of prokaryotic cells. As a result of this increasing experience prokaryotic cells became more evolved and complex. They exist now, in the watery environment, as bacteria and blue-green algae that are more evolved than the simple prokaryotic cells that first formed.

Different species of prokaryotic cells formed symbiotic relationships, to give rise to eukaryotic cells. From the fossil record scientists estimate that these arose after 2,000 years of prokaryotic development, i.e. about 1,500 million years ago and the minute prokaryotic and eukaryotic cells in the watery environment were the only forms of life for 3,500 million years of the Earth's existence.

About 800 million years ago groups of eukaryotic cells acted in concert, to create small jelly-like multicellular organisms in the watery environment.

According to the fossil evidence many different species then evolved in the lakes and seas until, about 400 million years ago, organisms arose, in the form of insect-like creatures, primitive plants, fungi and then amphibious animals, with patterns of activity that enabled them to survive on land. Thereafter more and more types of land-living organisms arose that were capable of existing in an ever-wider range of environments.

Some 50 million years ago, monkeys arose that evolved from earlier primates which were small tree-living creatures that had developed a prehensile, grasping hand and stereoscopic vision. To this monkeys added a degree of bipedalism, with an increase in brain size and the ability to co-ordinate these functions. The exposure of some of these to environmental conditions that stressed their bipedal movement then resulted in the arising of the first basically bipedal creature, Australopithecus, that had a brain size of about 500 cc, compared with 400cc for that of an ape. According to the fossil evidence this happened about 5-7 million years ago.

About 2.5 million years ago there arose a hominid, with a brain size of about 800cc, that made crude chopper tools from stones, (homo habilis). For the following million years this continued to be the only type of tool made.

About 1.5 million years ago a more-evolved hominid arose - homo erectus - that made a more-advanced shape of tool (a pear-shaped hand axe) and a few other shapes. Homo erectus also carried out organised hunting, used fire, and built campsites. This hominid had a brain size of about 1100cc.

Again there was a long period, of over a million years, when no further significant advances occurred. Then, some 100,000 years ago Neanderthal Man arose who was a skilled maker of a variety of tools in stone, wood, bone, antler and ivory and who made clothes from animal skins sewn together with sinews. This was a period of rapid advance compared with that of earlier hominids. Neanderthal Man had a brain size of about 1400 cc, slightly larger than that of modern man.

Chapter 5

The Omniverse and a New Dimension to Hominids

In this Chapter we add a further dimension to the previous account of the arising and evolution of our Universe, by setting it within a larger framework, in which our Universe comes about as the latest in many Universe-creating pulses of s-activity. The totality of the so-far created Universes, we call the Omniverse. Each Universe starts with peripheral break up of the s-entities, to give rise to self-actualising energy entities (substances), as has been described for our Universe. As the earlier generations of energy entities interact with those formed in subsequent Universes they develop qualities of sensation-feeling and awareness-thinking and thereby they become progressively more evolved Beings. As a result an Omniverse Hierarchy builds up, into which the activities of each new generation are assimilated. The interaction of the Omniverse Hierarchy with the rudimentary thinking Neanderthal hominids gives rise to a major new hominid development, i.e. modern man, or homo sapiens, who carries thinking to a higher level of development.

The Formation of the Omniverse and an Omniverse Hierarchy

After the Kosmos has broken down into a collective of s-entities, these seek enhanced sense of self by increasing in activity until the energy of their impulse to be active is expended, when they revert back to an inactive state. But then they lose their sense of self and so they become active again, until once more their impulse to be active is expended and they revert to the inactive state. This happens again and again, so that the s-entities enter into a cyclic existence of increasing and then decreasing activity.

In each cycle, when the stresses that the s-entities exert on each other become excessive they break down at their peripheries. This separated-off energy-activity becomes a Universe and we have described how this gives rise to our Universe but this is only the latest in a sequence of Universes. When a new Universe and its new generation of differentiated-out entities arise, the s-pressure causes the already-existing entities to interact with these and their interaction brings about an integration of the new activities with the existing ones and vice versa.

This is repeated with each new Universe-creating pulse and as a result there develops a hierarchy of entities in the Omniverse. Those at the 'top' were created in the early Universes, so that they have experienced the greatest number of Universe-creating cycles and integrating and harmonising with new levels of activity but they have become increasingly remote from the 'working face' where new developments take place. Those at the 'bottom' are concerned with developing their sense of self, as self-actualising mechanical-energy activities. In between are intermediate levels of entities that, from their experiences in successive Universes, develop from mechanical, working-face activity to become increasingly able to contribute to the activities of the Omniverse as a whole.

[This organisation is akin to that of a family business created by successive generations. The oldest generation started the business in a simple way. Subsequent generations then make their successively more-advanced contributions to it. Each new generation is concerned with developing its sense of self that it derives from its 'working-face activity'. But it does not possess the awareness and sense of direction of the older generations. On the other hand, the older generations do not possess the impulses for a new level of activity at the working face. The activities of each new generation require integrating and harmonising with those already established by previous generations, as a result of which the whole organisation evolves, from top to bottom].

The Stages of Development of the Omniverse Hierarchy

As successive generations of Universes come into existence the entities created in previous Universes evolve. When entities first arise and become self-actualising they are purely energy, or will, activity. When a further generation of entities is created the members of the previous, first generation try to maintain their pattern of activity but this is changed by their interaction with the new generation. This gives the members of the first generation a new sense of self, not simply of being active, but of adjusting their activity to the stress, or 'sensations' which they experience, due to the impinging activity of the new generation. This is the beginning of the evolution of beings whose will activity is controlled by their ego desires arising from their sensation-based, soul-feelings.

[This is akin, but at a very primitive level, to the change in experience that a baby gets from pressing its feet against its environment, for example, the side of a pram (equivalent to the s-entities' sense of self got by being active against the uniform s-pressure), to experiencing interacting with a variety of simple toys, e.g. rattles, little bells, rubber figures, etc. that respond differently to it and thereby give it a range of sensations which elicit variations in its activity].

When a further Universe and its associated new, third generation of entities arises the first generation finds that the second generation no longer responds to it in the way that it did before (because this is adjusting to the activity of the third generation). And as a result of not having direct 'sensory' contact with the new activities taking place, the first generation is forced into trying to interpret, from the behaviour of the second generation, what is going on at the working face. It then adjusts its activity according to its evaluation of what is happening. Thereby it begins to develop a rudimentary, conceptual, spirit-thinking, level of activity. And this gives it a new and greater sense of self, of an awakening of a potential to become aware of what is going on in its existence, to give rise to beings whose will activity is driven by a combination of the ego desires of their soul-feelings and their Ego generated spirit thinking.

[This is akin, again at a very primitive level, to the way in which, as a child develops it becomes increasingly aware of its place in the larger pattern of activities in the world around it, and starts to act out of its Ego-generated thinking, as well as its ego desires arising from its feelings].

Then, when further Universes and their associated new generations of entities arise, the first generation develops its awareness, so as to encompass these new activities, and it adjusts its own activities to those of successive generations. In so doing the first generation develops increasing understanding of the situation in which it finds itself and it makes this self actualising, giving rise to beings who seek to increase their understanding of, and to exert their influence on, new developments. The first generation thereby experiences a new sense of self, as beings who have the power, understanding and responsibility to be contributing Creators to future developments.

[This is akin to the way that, when we become parents, we change from a purely ego/Ego-centred existence to recognising a responsibility to integrate our drive to fulfil our own potentials, with helping the development of our children].

As the beings of the first generation continue to relate their activities to those of the increasing numbers of generations beneath them they begin to get a new experience, of concern for the well-being of the new generations. They then become beings whose purpose in existence is to foster the development of the potentials of succeeding generations. And, they thereby become beings whose nature is loving concern for the development of the successive generations of creation.

[At a Kosmic level they are akin to (idealised) grandparents who recognise that later generations have to work out for themselves their impulses in the situations in which they find themselves, while at the same time providing support in terms of wisdom, understanding and loving concern].

With each cycle, the s-entities, in seeking increased sense of self, increase in activity, so that the parts that become separated off in their stress of interaction are more energetic. This results in each new Universe comprising more break up and a more extensive range of more-active entities. This means that with each new Universe a stronger and more varied level of will activity is added at the working face of the Omniverse, which in turn engenders more evolved soul-ego feelings and spirit-Ego thinking in the higher levels.

Three Streams in the Omniverse Hierarchy

The Omniverse Hierarchy does not, however, operate as a harmonious totality. As the first generation develops its ability to feel and think and to exert its will to influence the developments of subsequent generations, three streams arise. There is a central stream that gets its sense of self from promoting harmonious developments. There are also two side streams. One of these gets an enhanced sense of Ego-self out of its ability to think out ideas for further developments, without ensuring that its ideas will produce harmonious development. We call this the 'Idealist' stream, which gives rise to insubstantial illusory ideas. The other stream develops an enhanced sense of Ego-self by exerting its will to make new developments at the substance working face, without ensuring that these promote harmonious progress. We call this the 'Materialist' stream.

The reason for the existence of the different 'poles' of beings arises from their origins in the mutual breakdown of the s-entities and 'galaxy' entities. In the current cycle this gives rise to the two poles of entities that make up substance - the more active electrons and the more substantial protons. The energy-activity entities that were created in this way in the early cycles of breakdown then evolved, in subsequent cycles, to become feeling, thinking beings but the polarisation of their natures, between greater activity (Idealist) and greater substance involvement (Materialist), still exists. Only where their interaction brings about a balance of the two aspects, does a central stream arise.

[We can appreciate this feature by considering our own situation. We develop our abilities by working in the physical, substance world, as part of an ever-evolving creation. The ideal role of humanity is to develop ever-greater ego-feelings and Ego-thinking and to apply these to furthering harmonious evolution. But it is possible to diverge from this in two ways. As we develop feelings and ideas we can become gripped by the sense of ego/Ego self that these give us, so that we pursue the development of ever greater feelings and ideas, without properly evaluating them and ensuring that they promote harmonious evolution. We can then acquire an enhanced sense of self by seeking to impose our beliefs and ideas on others, instead of working out our own down-to-earth existence. This gives rise to a self satisfying, high-flown but illusory world of feelings (beliefs) and ideas (philosophies, etc.), which are not based on practical experience and implementation at the working face. Alternatively we may direct our feelings and ideas to performing practical activities in the world of substance and obtain an enhanced sense of ego/Ego self out of our abilities to do this, without concern as to whether what we are doing gives rise to harmonious evolution. We can then get gripped by the ego/Ego sense of power that results from our material achievements or, on a larger scale, from setting up and controlling organisations of people to achieve these things for us. The activities of these three streams, the intellectual-ideas-driven, the substance-results-driven and the balanced-harmony-seeking, can be perceived in all human activities, e.g. industry, politics, education, the medical field, the arts, etc.].

The Interaction of the Omniverse Hierarchy With the Earth Situation Gives Rise to Homo Sapiens Sapiens

As explained in the last Chapter, the evolution of life on Earth gives rise to the independent (from the Omniverse Hierarchy) development of entities of will, feeling and thinking, which culminates in Neanderthal Man who comprises a hierarchy of levels of activity that are like a miniature version of those of the Omniverse Hierarchy. However, there is a major difference. With the development of the Omniverse Hierarchy each new generation is 'born' into, supported by, and integrated with, the 'family' of the preceding generations. But because Neanderthal Man arises out of a biological evolution that occurs separated from, and independent of, the activities of the Omniverse Hierarchy, he is not controlled by them and he lives his own life in his own way. And because his spirit/Ego is encapsulated in a body-soul complex that develops independently and cuts him off from the 'family background' of the Omniverse Hierarchy and its 'tradition', he has to work things out for himself. By doing this he develops a stronger sense of self, i.e. a stronger will, soul-feeling ego and spirit-thinking Ego, than he would have done as a new generation within the Hierarchy family.

[It is as though, in the family business created by successive generations, each of which is brought up within the system to further its development in the established way, a new generation of 'outsiders' enters. These have no knowledge of how the established situation works and no awareness of the organisation and the entities that created it and they have to find their own ways forward in the circumstances in which they find themselves].

The concern of the Omniverse Hierarchy is to integrate with the new developments taking place at the working face. They realise that, while most of the activities of the current Universe follow the established pattern of development, i.e. the substance-energy behaviour of galaxies, stars, etc. there is a small region (the Earth planet) where unusual and uncontrolled activities are taking place. They see that in these regions beings are arising that manipulate substances and in so doing develop qualities independently of them.

The Hierarchy therefore strives to experience and understand what is going on and, in so doing, some of its members inadvertently get caught up in this new development. They find that this gives them a greater sense of self and so they then seek positively to experience the Earth situation for themselves. This gives rise to the era described in ancient mythologies in which the gods interacted with the hominids on Earth. This is described, for example, in Jewish mythology:

> 'when men began to multiply on the face of the Earth and daughters were born unto them, the Sons of God saw that they were fair and they took to wife such of them as they chose'.
>
> Genesis 6

As a result of this interaction there develops a new race of hominids - homo sapiens sapiens. Thereby two types of thinking hominids come to exist, one that develops by biological evolution, homo sapiens Neanderthalensis, while the other, homo sapiens sapiens (modern humanity), is due to pre-existing 'spiritual beings' from the Omniverse Hierarchy incarnating into biologically-evolved bodies on Earth.

Unlike Neanderthal man, the spiritual beings from the Omniverse Hierarchy have no experience of working with a biologically-evolved body system, so that it is difficult for them to incarnate and to grasp what is going on in the Earth situation. We have to imagine an entity that exists in the Omniverse Hierarchy where it moves according to 'sensations' that arise from its interactions with beings of its own, lower and higher levels of development: i.e. it 'flits around' in the way that our feelings and thoughts do. It has no knowledge of the biological evolution that has taken place on Earth but, through interaction with Neanderthal Man, it has become aware of stronger qualities of sense of self that seem desirable to it, that it could develop by experiencing and understanding what Neanderthal Man experiences. Accordingly it seeks to enter into the Earth situation, by entering into a body as this is being born, and it formulates its experiences by making images of what happens to it, in the same way that we create images of our experiences that we express in drawing/paintings, sculpture or descriptions in words. Its first experiences are of the process of entering into the world by emerging from something (the body of a woman which, at this stage it does not properly comprehend) that then provides sustenance for it. It formulates this experience by making a sculpture that shows its experience of the part of the woman's body through which it undergoes the birth process and the part (the breasts) that then provide sustenance, fig. 5.1.

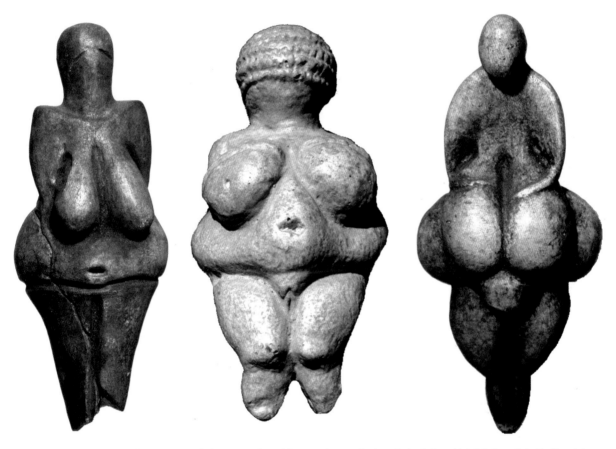

Fig. 5.1 Examples of the Omniverse entity's expression of its experience of a female body by which it is born into Earth existence.
Ancient Art and Architecture Collection

At this stage there is only a limited awareness of any other aspects of the woman: the head, legs, feet, arms and hands are portrayed in rudimentary fashion, if at all.

As members of the Omniverse Hierarchy began to incarnate into hominid bodies then, in order to understand what hominids were experiencing, they had to learn to interpret the sensory and brain activity of the hominid. That is, they had to form images from the sensory impulses transmitted to the hominid brain, as the first stage of their awareness of the Earth situation. This, as we have stated in Chapter 4, is akin to the way in which we form an image from the pattern of electrically-induced activity taking place on a television screen.

[Forming an image is the first stage of conscious awareness of a baby as it incarnates into the Earth situation when, out of the confusion of light, colour, forms and activities taking place around it, it isolates and forms an image of separate things, e.g. its Mother's breast, feeding bottle, etc. It is also the first stage of awareness of a scientist when he/she looks down a microscope at an unfamiliar field of vision and isolates, and forms images of, features that he/she perceives].

As the Omniverse entity incarnates further into the hominid body it becomes aware of the nature of hominid existence and it formulates its understanding of this in paintings of hominids hunting animals on cave walls, fig. 5.2a and of its experience of its hominid body in hunting them, fig. 5.2b.

a

b

Fig. 5.2. (a) The incarnating spirit's formulation of its awareness of the hominid existence into which it has entered by painting hunting scenes on cave walls, as 'stick images', akin to those painted by children. (b) Its expression of its self awareness of the body and activity that it has incarnated into, of thrusting against the ground and reaching up and out with its spear (or bow and arrow).
5.2a Prehistoric painting from a cave in Valencia, Spain. 5.2b Reproduced from 'The Social History of Art' by Arnold Hausen, by courtesy of the publishers Routledge and Kegan Paul

These 'stick-people' images are comparable to those that a young child paints as it portrays its developing awareness of the people and their activities going on around it. In painting (and modelling in clay) animals of significance in their lives and their own experiences, the homo sapiens that did this got an enhanced sense of self, which caused them to pursue further these 'artistic' activities. It is the same with contemporary artists (like Lowry), who get an enhanced sense of self from portraying the activities and people in the world around them.

When members of the Omniverse Hierarchy incarnate into hominid bodies, the brain of the body serves as a link between its awareness of its Hierarchy state and its experiences in its incarnate state. As a result it changes to become more dome shaped, associated with greater internal reflection, compared with that of Neanderthal man, who was more directed to seeking and processing information from his environment fig. 5.3.

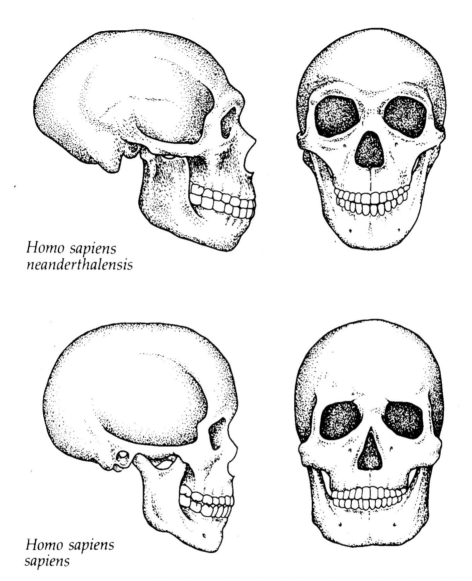

Homo sapiens neanderthalensis

Homo sapiens sapiens

Fig. 5.3. The forward directed skull shape of Homo Sapiens Neanderthalensis and the more dome-shaped skull of Homo Sapiens sapiens.
From Roger Lewin: Human Evolution, Blackwell, 1984

The Neolithic Era

Before incarnating into hominid bodies, the members of the Omniverse Hierarchy who did this were part of an extensive organisation, from the higher levels of which they experienced impulses for what they should do and to whom they looked for guidance. When they first incarnated they continued to do this. They believed that there was a world of 'higher beings' (gods) that had superior wisdom and who could help them to cope with life on Earth and they created shrines and practices for contacting these gods. The help and guidance that they got from the gods they received as visions, in their dreams, or in 'mystical practices', in which they sought to retain their contact with the Omniverse Hierarchy. In this way homo sapiens began to consciously work out of 'ideas' that came to them from the gods, as opposed to progress taking place by the unconscious combination of inadvertent developments and the integrating activity of the EM-energy, that had determined previous biological evolution. This conceptually-led development had begun in a small way with Neanderthal Man, whose practice of burying his dead showed that he had a belief in a discarnate existence and a post-mortem world and that he had begun to tap into the wisdom of the gods was evidenced by the development of the bow and arrow and the sewing needle, which could not have arisen inadvertently out of natural events but required a conceptually-generated idea.

With the incarnation of members of the Omniverse Hierarchy into hominid bodies and their conscious pursuit of guidance from the higher levels of the Omniverse Hierarchy, Homo sapiens evolved much more rapidly than hominids and Neanderthal man ever had, giving rise to what is known as the Neolithic Era, in which there were many wide-ranging developments in a period of some 10,000 years, compared with the previous slow progress in making tools from stone that had taken several million years. Homo sapiens greatly advanced the skill of making of stone tools, fig. 5.4, and also, made of stone, complex hollow vessels, querns, mortars, pounders and pestles for crushing grain, together with rudimentary sculptures.

Fig. 5.4. An example of the much more advanced skill of Neolithic Man in making a stone tool, compared with that of hominids illustrated in figs. 4.2, 4.3 and 4.4, in the previous chapter.
Ancient Art and Architecture Collection

They also made a greater variety of bone implements. Then they made vessels out of the more plastic material of clay, for which they developed the technique of firing to make them robust. They developed greater skills at woodworking; they developed weaving of rushes to make baskets and weaving to make cloth; and they began to use naturally occurring metals (gold, silver and copper) and to extract copper from its ores by heating with charcoal. This resulted in more thought-out, conceptually-based developments, fig. 5.5.

Fig. 5.5 The evolution of conceptual thinking expressed in clay pot making. (a) a more durable version of a gourd that was the established type of pot. (b) a realisation of the potential of clay to be formed into a more useful shape. (c) the realisation that pots can be made to suit a range of different purposes, with the addition of self-expression in ornamental designs. (d) a truly 'thought out' pot, made to suit a specific purpose.
Figs. 5.5 a-c. from The Dawn of Civilisation, Ed. Stuart Pigott, Thames and Hudson 1961, Photographer Josephine Powell, Courtesy of the Publishers. d. Athens Archaeological Museum.

In doing this Neolithic peoples began to experience themselves as thinkers, fig. 5.6.

a   b

Fig. 5.6. Two examples of Neolithic Man's awareness of becoming a thinker about the existence in which he finds himself and in (b) not feeling very happy about it.
a. Greek Neolithic era (Athens National Archaeological Museum) b the Cernovada Thinker, BERCIU, Romanian Neolithic period, (Ancient Art and Architecture Collection)

We recapitulate the experience of becoming conscious of ourselves as thinking beings at about 12 or 13 years of age, fig. 5.7.

Fig. 5.7. 'Thinking' drawn by a thirteen year old boy.
From Creative and Mental Growth by Harriet, B. and Lowenfeld M. 6th Edition 1975 p.309, reprinted by permission of Pearson Education Inc. Upper Saddle River N.J. U.S.A.

The Neolithic way of life brought about a change from that of a hunter-gatherer existence to a settled agriculturally-based one, together with the domestication of animals and the creation of more advanced social organisations in settlements of several hundred to several thousand inhabitants, fig. 5.8. The people lived in single and two-storey buildings, made from stone and/or clay and within the settlement there were workshops for stone and bone working, making beads and jewellery, butchers shops and shrines for worshipping the gods.

Fig. 5.8. Reconstruction by archeologists of the Neolithic settlement Khirokitia, Cyprus (about 5,500 BC). It comprised several hundred huts made of stone and mud bricks with wood-framed doors and stairs to an upper storey. There is evidence for the domestication of sheep and goats (and possibly pigs), the cultivation of corn and olive trees, spinning and weaving of wool, basketry, stone carving and the making of simple jewellery. The Neolithic era established the essential features of modern civilisation – a far cry from homo habilis – in a comparatively short period of time compared with earlier hominid development.
From Dawn of Civilisation, Ed. Stuart Piggott, Thames and Hudson, 1961 Artist Gaynor Chapman, Courtesy of the Publishers.

In this way the basis of many craft skills practiced today and the structure of society as we know it now was laid down in the Neolithic era. At the same time Neolithic Peoples developed the thinking-based evolution of homo sapiens, with advances arising out of a combination of personal thinking and wisdom received from the gods, compared with previous biological evolution that had occurred by stresses activating experience registered in the EM-energy, as described in Chapter 4. This took place in three regions: in the Fertile Crescent in the Near East about 10,000 years ago, in an area of China about 7,000 years ago and in Mesoamerica about 5,000 years ago, from which more-advanced cultures developed. In this book we deal only with the sequence of evolutionary developments that took place in the Near East and how these led to modern Western Civilisation but RENFREW points out that all cultures follow a somewhat similar pattern of development. This we would ascribe to the universality of the EM-energy, which encompasses all experience and on which everything draws to give a communality of development, as we have described for biological evolution on Earth.

Once members of the Omniverse Hierarchy established themselves on Earth, because of their prior evolution the homo sapiens beings developed more rapidly than the Neanderthals and thereby became dominant and the Neanderthals died out. (Fossil evidence shows that Neanderthals existed from about 100,000 to 35,000 years ago and that homo sapiens arose about 40,000 years ago).

The Uniqueness of the Earth Situation and Its Consequences

According to *h*K-M, biological evolution and the incarnation of Omniverse Hierarchy entities into hominid bodies, leading to the development of thinking entities on the Earth planet, is a unique event in the Kosmos, which results in an unprecedented development, with far-reaching consequences. Because of this, some aspects of our existence that we consider to be 'normal' are, in fact, quite abnormal when viewed in relation to the larger picture of the development of the Omniverse. In order to appreciate this situation it is necessary to contrast the nature of existence in the Omniverse Hierarchy with that on Earth.

The Nature of Existence in the Omniverse Hierarchy

As new generations of the Omniverse Hierarchy come into existence, to give rise to a new level of working face activity, each of the established levels experiences developments from the activity of the level below, to which it has to adjust, and it also experiences changes in the impulses from the levels above, as these adjust to its own changes. In this way the activities at the working face, and the effects that these have on the levels above pass up to the top, with each intermediate level making its own contribution to the interchange, while conversely response-impulses to these changes pass down from the top in the same way. Thus the Omniverse Hierarchy is a communal organisation, in which all entities are continuously interacting with each other.

Existence within the Omniverse Hierarchy is therefore different from that which we experience on Earth. Here we exist as soul-feeling and spirit-thinking entities encased in physical bodies that separate us from each other and from the world around us. If we want to express our soul-feelings or spirit-thinking we do so through our bodies, e.g. feelings through music, dance, physical interactions, etc. thinking by communication in speech, writing, etc. But we have control over whether we do this or not. Thus we can have feelings or thoughts which we keep to ourselves, or we can express them differently in ways that we think may be more acceptable, or which will achieve what we want without other people realising our true aims, or we can do nothing much with our lives and 'opt out'. Being encased in bodies gives us a degree of individuality and control over our activities that results in us having a freedom of choice and a degree of free will that the members of the Omniverse Hierarchy do not possess. The entities of the Omniverse Hierarchy are not confined in, and separated off, by bodies; they exist as individualised centres of activity in a continuum. They do not express their natures; they are their natures, (akin to the way that plants and animals do not express their natures but are their natures). They are continuously acting individualised patterns of activity, within an energy totality that is filled with 'vibrations' created by the activities of the entities of the various levels of the Hierarchy. Each entity is aware of, contributes and responds to, these according to the state to which it has evolved.

At the top of the Hierarchy are the entities that came into existence in the first phase of break up of the s-entities. These have developed the highest level of ability to think and the most understanding, to influence the further development of the Omniverse. In them, individualised parts of the erstwhile unconscious energy of the Kosmos become self-conscious 'Creators'.

As the top levels of the Hierarchy 'think', the activity of their thinking energy Being changes and this causes a change in their interaction with the beings of the lower levels of the Hierarchy who experience this as an energy or impulse acting on them, to which they respond according to their level of development. In this way impulses to influence further developments 'radiate' away from the top levels of the Omniverse Hierarchy.

[According to hK-M there is no external Creator (God) planning and directing what happens. The basis of what we call creation is due to the collective activity of the entities differentiated out in successive Universes contributing their creative-manipulation to what is going on. There is no such thing as true *ab initio* creation. Thus, for example when we 'create', we take something that already exists and realise new potentials in it, i.e. we creatively manipulate. Reverting to the analogy of the family business, those at the top, out of the experience and understanding that they have gained in working with successive generations have thoughts about how the new level of activity at the working face should develop. They then try to influence the activities of those lower down in the hierarchy along these lines. The working-face entities get their sense of self by expressing their innate energy/natures guided by stimuli from the higher levels, in a collective evolution].

Two Basic Types of Homo Sapiens Experience: Inner-Spiritual and Outer-Material

When members of the Omniverse Hierarchy first incarnate on Earth they retain an awareness of, and contact with, the 'world of the gods', which is described in ancient mythologies and they continue to be controlled by the guidance from the gods (the higher levels of the Omniverse Hierarchy), in their Earth existence, fig. 5.9.

Fig. 5.9. The Egyptian Pharaoh Horemhep (the smaller figure) carrying out his functions under the guidance and support of the god Amun who, in turn, receives a 'shaft of wisdom from above'.
Luxor Museum

However, their achievements on Earth under the auspices of the 'gods' give them an enhanced sense of self which they make self actualising, (in the way that, as pointed out earlier, when we master what we are taught at school we acquire an enhanced sense of self and we take over and develop these abilities further ourselves). This enhanced sense of Ego-self derived from doing things under the auspices of the gods and then progressing further out of our own resources (and thereby getting a yet greater sense of Ego-self) is portrayed, for example, in the description of metallurgical activities carried out by Sennacherib, King of Assyria, 705 to 681 B.C.

*'I, Sennacherib, first among the princes, wise in all craftsmanship wrought great pillars of bronze, colossal lions, open at the knees, which no king before my time had fashioned, **through the clever understanding which the noble God Nin-igi- kug had given me and in my own wisdom**. I pondered deeply the matter of carrying out the task ..... over great posts and crossbars of wood, twelve fierce lion colossi, together with twelve mighty bull colossi .... clothed with exuberant strength and with abundance of splendour heaped upon them, - at the command of the god I built a form of clay and poured bronze into it .... '*

(LUCKENBILL Courtesy of the University of Chicago Press)

There then occurs a division of orientations in outlook. Some cultures become more and more immersed in the sense of self that they get from manipulating the substance energies of the Earth situation. This gives rise to material developments on Earth and the arising of a mechanistic, substance/energy-based outlook and an understanding of the workings of the Universe in these terms, e.g. Western cultures. Other cultures are less concerned with generating material developments and they seek more to retain contact with the 'spiritual world' of the Omniverse Hierarchy, e.g. Eastern cultures. This leads to meditation practices that seek to eliminate material sense impressions and to concentrate on soul and thinking, spiritual activities. This gives rise to a mystically-derived viewpoint of the workings of the Universe in terms of the activities of a pantheon of greater and lesser 'gods', or spiritual beings.

The Spiritual and Material Viewpoints

The Eastern, mystical approach depends on raising one's level of consciousness to perceive the workings of the Hierarchy and it seeks to describe the events of the world in terms of the activities of spiritual beings, God or gods. Because it is concerned with perceiving the workings of the Hierarchy it does not reach back to a basic understanding of how or why this came about in the first place; it is not concerned with seeking basic principles to explain these activities and any description of the basis of creation is usually in vague abstract terms or stated to be the work of an unknowable God. When it comes to dealing with day-to-day existence in the material world it seems to see incarnation into Earth conditions as a mistake and that the thing to do is to free ourselves from the wheel of continual rebirths and return to a 'Nirvana-like' spiritual existence.

The mystical way of life retains an awareness of the existence of the Omniverse Hierarchy and it can lead to a living at-one-ness with it. People who achieve this can develop the powers and abilities possessed by the Hierarchy. For example; omnipresence, that is, the ability to be in contact with what is going on anywhere; communication at a mental level independent of the physical body, that is, telepathy; they can become channels for the energies of the higher levels of the Omniverse Hierarchy, as in healing; they can co-ordinate with these powers to produce 'magical' psycho-physical manifestations. (We give examples of these phenomena in an Appendix to this Chapter). Awareness of the existence of the Omniverse Hierarchy, our origins in it and our descent into the material world from the Omniverse Hierarchy, can provide a counterbalance to the purely materialist viewpoint.

The Western-oriented view is concerned more with developing the potentials of material existence and the enhanced sense of self that Humanity gets from doing this. Because we exist in the conditions at the working face as complete hierarchies in ourselves, we can formulate, and evaluate the validity of, our thoughts out of our direct experience. (As opposed to the thinking levels of the Omniverse Hierarchy that have to rely on information passing back and fore through intermediate levels of entities to and from the working face). We then act according to how we think things happen and, because our ideas are not an accurate reflection of the workings of existence, we sometimes do things that would not otherwise occur that open up different new potentials for development. In this way we can become conscious, thinking creators operating at the working face. This way of life tends to develop human creativity and an associated sense of self with its potential Ego problems, and because what we do is not harmonised by the Omniverse Hierarchy, we can create disharmony by our activities on Earth.

The outstanding feature of the materialist approach is however, that we find that, according to what we do, various things happen, sometimes things work out and sometimes they go wrong and this can cause us to think about why this should be and to seek to formulate laws by which the Universe works. And this leads on to seeking the cause, origin and purpose of the Universe. This is something that the members of the Omniverse Hierarchy do not do, because they are concerned only with playing their roles in this; nothing in their existence has caused them to conceive that it could possibly be any other way than it is and therefore they do not ask, Why is it this way? Thus, by becoming more and more immersed in our Ego-thinking activities and thereby getting more and more cut off from the Omniverse Hierarchy, in Western society we develop a detached, objective, external, view of things. And this leads to a more basic understanding of the Omniverse but one that is 'hypothetical' and not a living integration with its activities. But it has the potential to contribute a new dimension to the understanding of the Universe/Omniverse, by formulating the laws by which it works and explaining why it is the way that it is.

The Human Situation

The first point to make about the human situation is that we do not belong here. We, that is our spirits, are part of the stream of evolution that has developed from members of the Omniverse Hierarchy incarnating into the Earth situation. We came here to gain experience and to evolve in various ways and then to 'return home' to rejoin the Omniverse Hierarchy. But we have become so immersed in coping with the problems of life on Earth and the enhanced sense of ego/Ego self that Earth existence gives us that we have become cut off from our origins. This is why we find ourselves in the peculiar situation that we inhabit bodies that are not ourselves. Although we often regard ourself as our body, in fact we have very little understanding of it and very little awareness of the multitudinous activities that are going on in it. It is a 'vehicle' that we have taken over to gain experience of life on Earth; it arose out of biological evolution, in ways that we can only hypothesise about and we simply make use of it.

In our Earth incarnation we (our spirits) experience sensations/feelings, think about what is happening and carry out actions which register in our memory, that is, our individualised part of the EM-energy. When we become discarnate we find ourselves embroiled in any stresses, confusion and problems that have arisen from our Earth experiences, and the only way that we can deal with these is to reincarnate into Earth conditions to try to sort them out. When we do this we gain more experience and understanding and thereby we build up our individualised part of the EM-energy further. We are not free to return to the Omniverse Hierarchy and its state of harmony until we have sorted out our ties and commitments to the Earth situation. But in this sorting out process we gain in understanding and wisdom.

We incarnate into bodies and situations that developed by biological evolution on Earth, with their associated predator-prey relationships, insecurity, and competition for survival, and we inherit this pattern of behaviour. At the same time, by becoming embroiled in pursuing ego/Ego development for our self satisfaction we become more and more cut off from our Omniverse Hierarchy origins. As a result we experience loneliness and this activates our inherited, programmed-in feelings of insecurity, fearfulness, defensiveness and aggression. However, this drives us to try to understand the situation that we are in, fig. 5.10, and to try to remedy it and thereby we develop our inner resources.

Fig. 5.10. Modern Man as a thinker: sculpture by Auguste Rodin sited above what are known as the Gates of Hell that portray a chaotic conglomeration of human activities and emotions, mostly tormented ones. The thinker seeing life in this way seems to portray, in a more sophisticated way, the sentiment expressed by the Neolithic thinker in fig. 5.6(b)
'Philadelphia Museum of Art, The Rodin Museum:Bequest of Jules E. Masbaum, 1929'

[This aspect of leaving the security of our existence in the Omniverse Hierarchy to gain Earth experience is akin, on a more intense scale, to the comparable feelings that we get when we leave the security of our family environment to go out into the world on our own in teenage].

But we are not totally alone; although on our side we have lost conscious contact with the Omniverse Hierarchy it still exists, with its desire to influence developments. However, as described earlier, there are three streams in the Hierarchy, the Idealistic, the Materialistic and the Central Balanced stream. Mystical and expanded-consciousness experiences, the sleep state and even, at a subconscious level, ordinary feeling and thinking, can lead to contact with the inspirations and energy from these different types of beings, who seek to influence the activities of Man on Earth. But it is our responsibility to work things out for ourselves at the working face. Our attitude determines which types of beings and energies we open ourselves up to. The Idealistic beings are behind the illusory ideologies and cults that can control a person's life. The Materialistic stream controls people when they become gripped by a mania for power and material status. The central stream does not seek to control people, as the other two streams do, because it does not seek Ego/ego power. Instead it gets its sense of self by responding to those people who seek to follow a path of balanced evolutionary development. Such people are then not under 'outside' control but follow freely a path of their own choosing.

[People controlled by the non-central streams can tap into their immense powers, as demonstrated by the Idealistic cult leaders and the dictators and tycoons of life, who then take over and control the lives of large numbers of people. It is the existence of the two side streams and the conflicts that they cause that is the source of disharmony and 'evil'. But if they did not exist and we all followed a balanced harmonious existence we would have nothing to sort out and we would all be cabbages. Resolving the problems that they create, so as to regain a harmonious state gives rise to evolutionary progress].

In its integration of its spiritual and material activities Humanity has to find a balance between these two streams and, because it was having problems in doing this a member of the highest level of the central stream of the Omniverse Hierarchy incarnated in a human body as the Christ, to teach and show the balanced way forward and to promote awareness of Man's 'spiritual origins'. When Humanity, with its strongly developed will, feeling-ego and thinking-Ego re-develops its relationship with the Omniverse Hierarchy, carrying these qualities with it, it will be the prodigal son returning to the Father with the fruits of his labours.

The Purpose of Life in More Specific Terms

In the Introduction it was stated that, according to *h*K-M, the purpose of life is simply 'to evolve'. This simplicity may have been lost sight of in the complex material that has been presented in these Chapters and so we reiterate it at this point, while amplifying it slightly.

While the purpose/nature of the whole of creation is continually to evolve by developing its potentials, we consist of three parts - will activity, feeling and thinking and it is by developing these further that we evolve. If we do not do anything much with our lives we do not evolve our will. But it is not good simply to be increasingly active, without concern for the significance of what we do. We need also to evolve our feelings so that we are sensitive to the effect of our actions on the mineral, plant, animal and human kingdoms of Nature around us. But it is not enough simply to be sensitive; this can slide into ineffectual sentimentality. We have to evolve our ability to think about and to evaluate our feelings that arise from our will activities, so as to make this activity both sensitive and wise, in a way that contributes to evolution.

In short, the purpose of our lives is to evolve in will, feeling and thinking in a way that contributes to harmonious evolution.

Summary of Part I

According to *h*K-M there is no supernatural God external to and directing creation. Everything is part of a self-evolving Kosmos (God) that 'pulls itself up by its own bootstraps'. And as it does this it establishes patterns of behaviour that can be rationally comprehended. There is nothing mystical or mysterious about it.

The Kosmos(God) starts in a state of inert dormant energy. Parts of this become active and the interaction between the active and the inactive parts gives it a very rudimentary and, by our standards unconscious, sense of self. The pursuance of increased sense of self causes all further evolution of the Kosmos.

In seeking an increased sense of self the Kosmos becomes increasingly active, reaching a state of turbulence that breaks down into a large number of separate self-actualising centres of activity that we call superstructure entities (s-entities), because they create the superstructure of the Universe.

In their drive for increasing sense of self, the s-entities increase in activity and thereby increasingly interact until they break each other up at their peripheries. This break up gives rise to a network of on-going turbulence that develops into further centres of activity, or entities, namely the galaxies, stars, substances and planets of the Universe.

The Earth planet starts as a conglomeration of substances in a hot state of turmoil. As these cool and condense a solid surface forms onto which water condenses out of the atmosphere to create seas, lakes and rivers. The water contains carbonaceous substances from the atmosphere and minerals dissolved from rocks. As the water cools and contracts, carbonaceous rich droplets separate out from the mineralised surrounding water. The s-pressure induces a flow of substances into and out of the droplets that give the part of the Earth energy involved in the droplet condition a sense of self, so that it takes over these functions to give rise to self-actualising prokaryotic cells. These developments are brought about by the s-pressure so that, inadvertently and unconsciously, the s-entities are responsible for the creation of life on Earth.

As the Earth Energy cycles through the experience of life in prokaryotic cells, this builds up and becomes the Earth Memory energy of these events (and all subsequent events in which it is involved.)

In pursuing increased sense of self by increasing in activity, prokaryotic cells multiply and spread into different environments and their seeking to maintain their sense of self/existence in these different conditions gives rise to new species of prokaryotic cells.

As a result of the s-pressure, interactions occur between different species of prokaryotic cells that form a pattern of activity in this part of the Earth Energy that gives it a sense of self and it becomes self-actualising, resulting in a symbiotically integrated pattern of behaviour of these prokaryotic cells, to give rise to eukaryotic cells.

In pursuing increased sense of self eukaryotic cells multiply: as a result of the s-pressure they form interacting groups, which gives this part of the Earth Energy a sense of self and it becomes self actualising, to give rise to an integrated behaviour of groups of eucaryotic cells, i.e. multicellular entities.

In pursuing their sense of self, multicellular entities multiply and encounter different environments. Their drive to be active and maintain a sense of self in these different conditions gives rise to new species that are in harmony with these environments. The more that different environments are encountered the greater the variety of experience that builds up in the Earth Memory energy and, as a result, the more evolved are the new forms of organisms that arise.

Eventually an entity arises (a hominid) which is so evolved that it has the ability to cope with further environmental pressures, without change in its biological form and functioning, by modifying its pattern of behaviour. The stresses of its existence lead it to develop the ability to use the materials of its environment, as 'tools', with only an increase in brain size to deal with the necessary co-ordination involved.

As a result of developing different skills, different members of a hominid group take on different roles. Thereby, the part of the Earth Memory energy associated with the activity of each group member becomes individualised and self actualising to become the hominid's soul which senses, feels, and seeks to supply, its needs.

In drawing on the ever-increasing build up of experiences in the Earth Memory energy the hominid soul selects and integrates from the totality of these, to suit its specific requirements. As this pattern of activity associated with each soul develops it becomes self-actualising to become the hominid's thinking spirit.

Our Universe is only the latest in a series of Universes that make up an Omniverse and the sequence of entities created in each Universe make up an Omniverse Hierarchy. The already-existing members of the Omniverse Hierarchy seek to integrate, and to integrate with, the activities of each new Universe that comes into existence.

As members of the Omniverse Hierarchy integrate with the activities that have arisen by biological evolution on Earth they experience a situation that gives them an enhanced sense of self and they become more and more identified with hominid bodies, to the extent of 'incarnating' in them. This gives rise to a more-advanced hominid, i.e. homo sapiens sapiens or modern man.

This is what we each are, a 'spirit' from the 'Spiritual World' of the Omniverse Hierarchy, that has incarnated into the living situation that has evolved on Earth, a prodigal son that develops experience of the Earth situation and returns, eventually, to the Omniverse Hierarchy with the fruits of this experience.

By leaving the Omniverse Hierarchy and entering into hominid bodies members of the Omniverse Hierarchy get an 'outsider', more detached 'objective' view of the Kosmos, which they see as a 'object' outside themselves, and thereby they develop a more conscious understanding of its workings. At the same time, they use this conscious understanding to develop their own potentials and those of the world around them. Thereby, in the part caught up in Man, on Earth, the initially unconscious Kosmos (God) becomes consciously creative.

PART II

APPENDICES AMPLIFYING THE BASIC PRINCIPLES OF KOSMIC-METAPHYSICS

(CHAPTERS 6 to 14)

As stated in the Introduction, the objective of this book is to make the claim that Humanity is poised to make a leap forward in understanding the nature of the Universe and its role in it, by coming to a all-encompassing understanding of how and why it is what it is. In order to substantiate this claim such an understanding has been presented in Part I as a Kosmic Metaphysics, which has been kept to as brief an outline as possible, so that the overall picture does not get lost in detail. To expound this metaphysics properly would require a degree of elaboration that is beyond our ability. What follows now is a series of Appendix Chapters that comprise a collection of jottings that amplify here and there the hK-M viewpoint. To some of the Chapters in Part I we have little further to add but others we expand on more. In particular Chapter 5, 'The Omniverse and a New Dimension to Hominids' requires a great deal of elaboration, so that there are four Appendix chapters devoted to this. However, we repeat again what we stated in the Introduction, that no claim is made for the validity of any aspect of this. We are simply trying to demonstrate the feasibility of developing an evolutionary-wholistic understanding.

The account of hK-M given in Part I has been deliberately kept as free as possible from references, as it is not intended to be something that is substantiated, only to suggest a way of thinking about things. In the Appendices where references are quoted these are printed in capitals and relevant details are given in the reference index at the end. We have not provided a comprehensive list of references – this would be beyond our capabilities but for the areas that we touch on we have tried to refer to works which themselves give references, sufficient to provide a basis for anyone who may wish to, to follow up the aspect being dealt with.

Chapter 6

Appendix to the Introduction

The Universe as 'Purposive' - The Anthropic Principle

When scientists showed that life on Earth and the Universe at large are evolving, this raised the problem of what causes evolution to happen. At first it was thought that evolutionary change took place as the result of chance events. But increasing understanding of what evolution entails has made this unlikely. Thus, by making a detailed analysis of the Big Bang and subsequent developments scientists have found that the odds against the Universe evolving in the way that it has by chance are too great for this to be possible. For example, if there had been a slightly higher ratio of energy to mass in the Big Bang, the Universe would have expanded without gravity being able to pull substances together to form stars and planets, and without the existence of the Earth planet, life on Earth could not have arisen. If, on the other hand, the ratio of energy to mass had been slightly less, then gravity would have caused the Universe to collapse back on itself long since and there would have been insufficient time for the evolutionary processes that have given rise to life on Earth to take place.

The possibility of many other factors, e.g. the processes involved in the formation of carbon in stars, which is the basic substance on which the chemistry of all living organisms is built, coming about by chance, has also been shown to be highly unlikely - the reactions involved are too 'finely tuned'. This has led to what is known as the Anthropic Principle, the view that the Universe has evolved purposefully to become what it is. The problem then is, 'What is this purpose?' Wheeler, one of the physicists who proposed the Anthropic Principle argues that if the Universe has evolved purposefully, then what it has become must be its 'purpose'. And, since in our locality on Earth, it has achieved Humanity as its highest level of evolution, and thereby an intelligence by which it is becoming conscious of itself, then this must be its purpose, fig. 6.1.

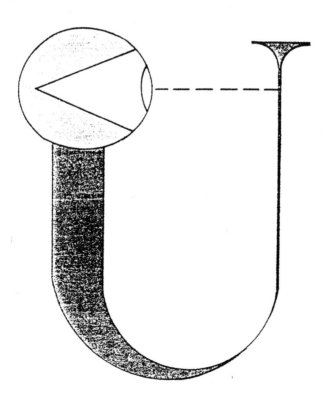

Fig.6.1. The viewpoint of the theoretical physicist, Wheeler, that from the initial manifestation of the Big Bang, giving rise to the energy and substance out of which the Universe is created, there evolve entities that look back on what has happened and thereby the Universe becomes conscious of itself.

The hK-M viewpoint is that initially there was a state of unconscious dormant energy that became active and turbulent and out of the turbulence there arose centres of activity that experienced a sense of self and became self-actualising. The pursuance of their sense of self by these entities led to further turbulence and the generation of further self-actualising entities. The first beings that arose were beings of (will) activity; as further entities arose the first ones experienced the activities of these through the sensations/feelings that they invoked in them and, as later beings arose, the first ones developed understanding and thinking about what was happening. In this way the Kosmos differentiates into entities by which it becomes conscious of itself, in accordance with Wheeler's view, although the hK-M explanation for this is a much more simplistic one than the complex quantum physics that led Wheeler to it.

The Universe As a Living Entity

GRIBBIN, in a survey of the developments of modern cosmology, has pointed out that scientists are increasingly describing the evolution of the Universe in similar terms to those used by biologists to describe the evolution of life on Earth. Thus cosmologists talk of the birth and death of the Universe and its life cycle and equally of the birth and death and life cycles of galaxies and stars. Their analysis of the behaviour of galaxies also shows that, like living organisms, these have an element of self-regulation of their patterns of activity; their behaviour is not explicable simply in terms of the dynamics of the force acting on them. Also there is a developing view of the Earth and its atmosphere as a living ecosystem. Gribbin takes the view that, while these terms are currently used metaphorically, they are leading inexorably to viewing the Universe as a living thing and that this is the next, impending major advance in scientific understanding. However, if the Universe is a living thing the problem then is to understand its basic nature and how this leads to it becoming what it now is. This is the problem that this book tries to address.

The Universe As a Self-Organising System

The idea that the Universe is self-organising is emerging from recent developments in science. A number of scientists have become dissatisfied with the inability of the reductionist approach to account for patterns and organisations in Nature in terms of the components of which these consist. These scientists take the view that, instead of the reductionist view that the whole can be understood in terms of the properties of the parts, the whole possesses properties that the parts do not have. For example, a living cell possesses properties that the atoms of which it consists do not have, and plants and animals possess properties that the cells of which they consist do not have. These scientists have therefore turned to the study of 'wholes', i.e. the study of patterns, organisms and organisations in Nature. From these studies, they have come to the conclusion that patterns and organisms arise out of the relationships between their components, that spontaneously gives rise to self-organising systems.

This wholistic view is in accord with that of hK-M but from the hK-M viewpoint the concept of a 'self-organising system' is an abstract one that requires further development to show how it leads to things being the way that they are. To be self-organising infers a self that is carrying out this activity, and for something to do this it needs to be self-actualising and pursuing a sense of self, as with the hK-M explanation for these things. The idea that the 'relationships' between the components of a system give rise to the overall system requires that the 'relationship' possesses properties that enable it to do this. As explained in Part 1 of this book, hK-M takes the view that behind everything there exists the s-pressure which forces things together and thereby brings about relationships. These relationships are formed in the space-energy, i.e. the s-entity energy or some evolved derivative from it, which on Earth is the Earth Entity energy. Through the experience of being involved in forming these relationships parts of the Earth energy experience a sense of self which they take over and pursue, to become self actualising.

The 'systems scientists' see two aspects to self-organisation first, how does the pattern or organisation arise and second, how does it maintain and regulate itself? According to hK-M the pattern of the activity arises from the dynamic stress patterns created by the movement of substances in the space-energy, while the maintenance and regulation of it arises from the self-actualising entity that this gives rise to, with its drive to maintain and enhance its sense of self.

In order to account for the behaviour of self-organising systems, some scientists have proposed that they possess the qualities of cognition, by which they 'know' and appropriately respond, to interactions with their environment, together with the abilities of learning, memory and decision making. That is, on this view, even the less-evolved organisms that do not have brains must possess 'minds'. According to hK-M everything starts from energy that, as it evolves, possesses the qualities of its experiences. The EM-energy, through its experiences of life cycles of organisms, possesses all of the experiences of these, and the relevant part of this experience is activated when it is 'incarnated' in an organism, by the stresses of the situation in which it finds itself. (In the same way, we are our experiences, with our relevant past experience activated by the circumstances that we encounter, to give rise to the way that we behave). Thus it is not the individual organism that recognises a situation and works out its response to it, and learns from it. It is a 'channel' for the expression of the collective experience of the EM-energy.

When the EM-energy is not 'incarnated' in an organism, the s-pressure is acting on it and thereby causing it to form relationships between its stored experiences. Incompatible things when forced together create stress, while things that fit together reduce stress. Thus there exists an interacting world of memories of experiences, which can come up with new possibilities for development. We experience this when we sleep on a problem and, without giving it conscious thought, a new idea comes to us. This results from the inter-relating activity of our memory, i.e. our individualised bit of EM-energy; an activity of which we are not conscious.

However, hK-M goes beyond explaining the self-organising systems that scientists study, in that it explains why these scientists exist and why they are doing what they do. A scientist is a thinking person and thinking homo sapiens exist because members of the Omniverse Hierarchy incarnated into body systems that evolved biologically on Earth. Because they do not have the direct contact with their environment that, through their sensory systems, plants and animals do, homo sapiens have to 'overshadow' and interpret the brain activity of the hominid body systems that they have incarnated into. That is, they have to form concepts by thinking about what is happening. Having developed the ability to live and maintain a sense of self in Earth existence by interpreting the hominid brain activity, homo sapiens has then sought enhanced sense of self by 'thinking things out', to try to understand the nature of existence. This is what scientists pursuing these investigations into the basic nature of the phenomena of the world are doing - because they thereby derive their enhanced sense of self.

This is not to say, of course, that only scientists seeking to understand the basic principles of the Universe make a contribution to understanding existence. Valuable as this work is, such scientists often arrive at abstract, mathematical concepts that do not help us in our daily lives. In seeking to understand the feelings and behaviour of ourselves and other people and the organisms of Nature around us, we each make our own contribution to the understanding of the whole. In the end it is what we each contribute to the evolutionary development of ourselves and of the people and things around us that matters.

While hK-M offers a deeper interpretation of the meaning of 'self-organising systems' it does not conflict with the basic concept of systems' scientists that everything consists of networks of self-organising systems at different levels of development. And the few cursory comments made here in no way do justice to the work involved in developing this viewpoint and its contribution to understanding. For this the reader is referred to 'The Self-Organising Universe' by JANTSCH and 'The Web of Life' by CAPRA.

Chapter 7

Appendix to Chapter 1: The Kosmos Stirs and Thereby Begins to Experience a Sense of Self

The Superstructure Entities

Although we have come across references to the idea of the Kosmos starting from an unformed, homogeneous state, (see end of Chapter 1 and the next section on cyclic creation), the only account that we have seen that could relate to it forming into a collection of cosmic 'Bénard cells' is a description by the mystic STEINER of the first stage of creation as:

> *'picture to yourself a mulberry or a blackberry composed as it is of ever so many tiny berries',*
>
> Occult Science p. 121

This is part of Steiner's highly complex cosmology of creation by a Hierarchy of Beings who first create these 'berries' which have the property of warmth (activity?) and then bestow on them life and a sense of I, (we consider Steiner's cosmology at some length later in this book). Although, according to Steiner, this refers to the first stage of creation, he attributed it to the activity of a Hierarchy of Spiritual Beings who must therefore have come into existence prior to this, thus it does not get back to ultimate origins. So, although the observation may describe Steiner's mystical experience of the first stage of creation, presumably obtained from his exploration of the 'Akashic Record' (the memory experience of the space energy), we have doubts about his interpretation of it; (as we explain in Chapter 11, we have doubts about the validity of a number of aspects of Steiner's cosmology).

There is, of course, the basic problem of where the energy of the Kosmos came from in the first place. Steiner stated that, in his mystical observations, the world was 'boarded up' at this point and he could not get further back and, equally, accounts by other mystics seem to refer to events taking place in the evolution of the Kosmos from an initial unformed state, without any explanation for where the energy/activity to do this came from. In our own investigations, described in Part III of this book, when we tried to get back beyond an initial uniform energy state of the Kosmos, we were led to an 'Absolute', a term that portrayed the origin and totality of everything, that was initially in an unconscious state.

Cyclic Creation

ELIADE, in a study of the difference between the mythological views of archaic societies and modern historical views, points out that the mythological views were based on cycles of renewal of creation, instead of the contemporary linear-development, cause and effect view. The mythological, cycles of renewal, view was based on creation on Earth being a re-enactment of celestial activities of the gods, with a multiplicity of cycles within cycles, (of which the human life cycle is one), with the largest cycle being a cosmic one in which the entire Universe fades out and is then regenerated. This viewpoint was particularly expounded in the ancient Indian culture but, Eliade claims, is discernible in other archaic societies. Cyclic creation is a central theme of mystically derived cosmologies such as Theosophy and that proposed by Steiner.

LAWTON surveyed creation myths and cosmologies from around the world (the Middle East, India, China, Japan, Greece, Polynesia, Africa, North America India) and found that a common theme is that of repeated cycles of emergence from nothing (according to hK-M, unmanifest dormant energy), followed by a return to nothing, with this cycle taking place over a very long period. In Hindu cosmology this is referred to as a day and night of Brahma, each lasting for 4.3 billion years.

The idea of a cyclic Creation that alternately expands out from a Big Bang and contracts down in a Big Crunch has been, and still is, considered a possibility by scientists but it has been difficult to formulate an appropriate mathematic model [CHOWN (2)]. Those theories that have been proposed tend to involve obscure and difficult to comprehend mathematical abstractions. According to hK-M, the cyclic activity in the Kosmos arises because the collective of the s-entities, that comprises the totality, increase in activity so as to get an enhanced sense of self, until the stresses that they exert on each other brings about a cessation of their activities that thereby die down. But they then lose their sense of self and this gives rise to an impulse to become active again and the cycle of events is repeated. In each of these cycles the build up of stresses of interaction between the s-entities causes them to break down at their peripheries, which gives rise to a Universe. On this basis each Universe comes about as a result of the basic energy of creation seeking to experience and express an enhanced sense of self, that propels a Universe into existence that then dies down as the force to express itself becomes exhausted, so that each successive Universe is a more evolved expression of its nature.

On the basis that the same principles of evolution operate at all levels and that the Kosmos, in its striving for a sense of self, manifests a sequence of Universes, i.e. an Omniverse, that differentiate into a multiplicity of parts that undergo different experiences and thereby contribute to the evolution of the whole, perhaps the Kosmos itself has differentiated out of something larger (the Absolute) that evolves in this way. If this is so then our Kosmos/Omniverse is only one of many to come into existence to work itself out, which would be in accord with theories of modern science that our Universe is only one of a multiplicity of Universes that exist in other space-time dimensions, (REES). (The activities of each Universe create its own particular space-time framework).

Chapter 8

Appendix to Chapter 2: The Evolution of the Superstructure Entities Leads to the Beginning of the Universe

Kosmic Metaphysics and the Big Bang Theory

It is impossible to write a book purporting to give an account of the origin and evolution of the Universe without taking into account the Big Bang theory. This has been developed by many competent scientists from the findings of astronomy and extensive theoretical analyses.

Redshift

The first, key observation that led to the Big Bang theory was that the wavelength of light from distant stars is elongated, which causes the colour to move towards the red end of the spectrum, the so-called redshift, as though while they are emitting light these stars are moving away from us, which led to the conclusion that the Universe is expanding. By taking this observation and extrapolating it backwards scientists have concluded that the Universe came into existence in a 'Big Bang', in which all the energy and substance of which it consists arose in a pinhead, or 'point source'. But this then posed the problem that if the Universe is all there is, then what is there for it to expand into? This problem was solved by proposing that the Universe is not expanding into some pre-existing space but that space and time are themselves expanding. However, as pointed out in the Introduction, the concepts of space and time are inventions of the human mind by which we describe our existence in relation to the world around us. The use of these concepts to describe the processes of creation is like trying to use a map of our location that we use to find our way around, to explain the processes by which the features of the location came into existence and how it developed. The nature of the Universe is that it is evolving and any basic understanding of it needs to be in terms of states of evolution and how these arise one from another, and not in terms of space and time.

There is, in fact, evidence to show that redshift observations are not a valid basis for the hypothesis of an expanding Universe. A phenomenon astronomers have observed is that of quasars which are intense sources of light. These show a very large redshift so that, in accord with the expanding Universe viewpoint, they were at first considered to be the oldest and most distant objects in the Universe. However, ARP and others have found that quasars are emitted from the centres of highly active galaxies. Thus quasars were not formed in the early stages of the Universe but are part of its later development. This undermines the redshift basis, on which the concept of the Universe expanding from a point source in a Big Bang was developed

To explain the high redshift of quasars ARP proposes that they consist of concentrations of matter more recently created in, and ejected from, the active centre of a galaxy and that the mass of particles of matter increases with age, so that the energy-activity of more recently created particles is weaker, which results in a redshift in the light which they emit, compared with the older particles that now emit light of higher frequencies.

Arp's concept of the mass of particles increasing with age is in line with the basic hK-M concept that everything, even a particle, is evolving. Thus the activity of a particle entity, in seeking increased sense of self, increases, which results in an increase in the frequency of the reverberations that it gives off in its interactions. Thereby the reverberations from more recently created particles have a lower frequency and are seemingly red-shifted.

Since Arp's observations made the redshift basis for an expanding Universe no longer valid, he had to formulate another theory for the origin of the substances of the Universe. From the observation that, in quasars, substance comes into existence from the centres of galaxies, Arp concludes that the Universe episodically unfolds from many points within itself and was not created once and for all in an initial Big Bang. This is in accord with hK-M, which does not see the substances of the Universe as arising from a single initial Big Bang but from a large number of sources that progressively develop throughout the Universe, i.e. from the mutual breakdown of s-entities and galaxy entities as they interact.

Another feature of the observations on redshifts, which has been difficult to explain, is that these do not occur as a continuous sequence but there is a periodicity to them. According to hK-M this is because in seeking increased sense of self the activities of entities increases, thereby building up a stress against the s-pressure until this overpowers them, when they break down or transform. This build up and reduction of stress results in a periodicity to phenomena, which we deal with shortly, under the heading 'punctuated equilibrium'.

According to an article in the New Scientist (22nd May 2004), there is a developing reaction against the dominance of the Big Bang theory of the Universe, by a number of scientists who claim that in order to make the theory fit with observations a growing number of 'fudge factors' have had to be postulated, e.g. inflation, dark matter, dark energy, for which there is no observable evidence. But because believers in the Big Bang theory control cosmological research there is no opportunity to develop alternative viewpoints. Any observations that do not fit in with the Big Bang theory, such as those on red-shift, are rejected.

According to the Big Bang theory the Universe came into existence from a 'pinhead' source in which all the energy and substance of which it consists, and space and time, existed in a highly compressed state, from which they subsequently expanded out, with no explanation for where they came from in the first place. According to hK-M the Universe started off as energy in a dormant state that derived from a larger system of which it is part. This dormant energy became active to give rise to turbulence in which the parts of the energy involved experienced a sense of self and became self-actualising entities. In seeking increased sense of self these entities became increasingly active, which created more turbulence to give rise to more entities, in an on-going pattern of increasing activity and breakdown of the initial dormant energy, to give rise to the features of the Universe in ways that have been described. The problem is, which of these viewpoints makes most sense?

The Distribution of Galaxies

On the Big Bang theory of the energy/substance of the Universe expanding from a point source, one would expect it to be uniformly distributed, whereas it exists in localised concentrations, in the form of galaxies that are distributed in a skein-like pattern throughout the Universe. To deal with this problem it is assumed that somehow there exist non-uniformities in the expansion that result in localised concentrations of substances which act as centres of gravitational attraction that cause more substance to build up around them, in opposition to the thinning out of the expansion. As explained previously, this problem does not exist with hK-M, in which galaxies are formed from turbulences that develop along the boundaries of interaction of the s-entities, to give rise to the skein-like distribution portrayed in fig. 2.2.

The Creation of Hydrogen and Helium as Galaxies Break Down

According to the Big Bang theory all the energy/substance of the Universe came into existence in a highly-intense compressed, interacting condition, in which the groupings of energy-activities that make up atoms would have been unstable and therefore could not then exist, so scientists propose that the first substances comprised minute, highly-energetic sub-atomic particles. These then came together to form the first atoms - hydrogen and helium - as the Universe expanded and cooled and the conditions of their existence became less intense.

In order to determine what sub-atomic particles existed in the Big Bang, scientists have broken atoms down by colliding them at high energy and examining the resulting sub-atomic particles, on the basis that these were the constituents out of which atoms formed. From the hK-M viewpoint the internal structures of atoms arose, not by a coming together of particles that existed in the initial Big Bang, but were formed as the atoms were created, from a state of turbulence that comprises a mixture of two interacting levels of energy activity, a slow ponderous activity that derives from the s-entity and an intensified level of activity that derives from the galaxy entity. The two levels of activity form a turbulent mixture that contracts under the s-pressure, which intensifies its activity. This increases the rate of flow of the more active galaxy-entity derived part in relation to the more ponderous s-entity derived part, so that the more active part flows over the less active part. At their zone of interaction the more active part is held back by the less active, in the same way that the water of an incoming sea is held back where it is in contact with the underlying sand of the shore, while the water above flows on, to form a series of collapsing waves. The 'waves' of the more active energy fragment and 'wrap up' parts of the less active energy, fig. 8.1(a) that, compressed and separated off in this way, become individualised and experience a sense of self.

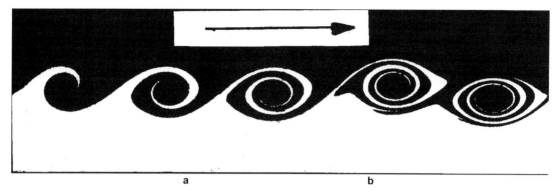

Fig. 8.1 The way in which more active energy, top, flowing from left to right over less active energy, bottom, forms waves that encapsulate the less active energy: (a) as a single event of less active, surrounded by more active, energy; (b) as a multilayer mixture of the less and more active energies. (Diagram based on a photograph of interacting liquid flows given in VAN DYKE).

These then form what scientists know as protons, the nuclei of hydrogen atoms, while the more active galaxy-derived material, forms a cloud of electron energy around the proton nuclei. By its greater activity this holds the slower, ponderous activity of the nucleus in place to create hydrogen atoms.

The proton is a self-actualising entity but the electron energy is not, because it does not determine its own central activity. The ponderous proton nucleus acts on it to do this. Driven from the centre in this way the electron energy pushes back the surrounding s-entity until its level of activity attenuates to that of the s-entity. Because of its highly active nature, the electron energy expands a long way to reach this degree of attenuation. As a result the electron region constitutes by far the larger part of the hydrogen atom, so that scientists find it to be one hundred thousand times larger than the proton. A balance is then set up, in which the proton experiences a sense of self from generating its activity, which interacts with the electron surround, while the electron energy responds to the driving force of the proton at its centre and, at its outer perimeter, interacts with the space-energy around it.

When the turbulence breaks down into hydrogen (and helium) atoms it changes from being increasingly compressed by the s-pressure, to a large number of self-actualising entities that form an expanding cloud of gas. When, in this expansion two hydrogen atoms collide, their electron surrounds come together to form a communal electron energy cloud, the activity of which is driven by both proton nuclei and thereby they combine together, to form a hydrogen molecule.

When hydrogen atoms that are more energetic collide, as happens in the intense activity in stars, (and as can be caused to occur in laboratory experiments), the more 'rigid' small self-actualising nuclei carry on in the direction of their motion, thereby separating from their electron energy surrounds. This leaves the electron energy parts devoid of a driving force at their centres, so that they contract under the s-pressure until the increase in intensity of their activity creates a stress in them that gives them a sense of self and they become centred and self actualising. Because of its highly-active nature the electron energy contracts and increases in activity a great deal before it becomes stressed and gets a sense of self, so that it is then very small, (about one thousandth of the size of the proton). The electron energy thus experiences existence in two states, one in which its activity is determined by that of the proton constituent of an atom and the other in which it is an independent, highly condensed self-actualising 'electron particle'.

[In their experimental investigations scientists found that electrons can exhibit an extended wave-like behaviour or condensed particle behaviour. They developed equations to describe this by combining the equation governing wave behaviour with that governing particle behaviour. They then attribute the contraction from wave to particle to the 'collapse of the wave function', which hK-M attributes to the electron energy contracting from a spread out pattern of activity, determined by the proton constituents of an atom, to an isolated self-actualising particle, as described above.]

As the s-pressure forces the s-entity and galaxy-entity derived energies into closer interaction, the more-active galaxy entity derived energy not only fragments and encapsulates parts of the s-entity derived energy to form hydrogen atoms but it also penetrates the s-entity energy to form a (spherical) 'swiss roll' configuration, fig. 8.1(b). The high level of interaction between the layers of energy causes the galaxy-entity energy to fragment and wrap up the s-entity layers, [as in fig. 8.1(a)], to form coiled up strings of 'miniature' protons, fig. 8.2.

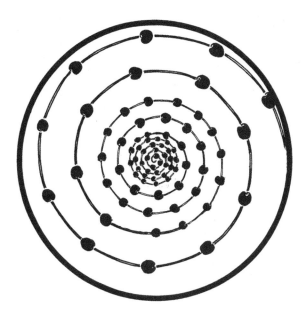

Fig.8.2 The structure of the neutron as a coil of miniature protons.

In their close interaction the greater activity of the galaxy entity derived energy and the lower activity of the s-entity derived energy 'neutralise' each other and this composite particle/activity gives rise to what scientists know as a neutron. Because of the different interpenetrating activities that make up a neutron it is unstable. However, the s-pressurised B-cell motion of the star is all the time acting on the melee of particles/activities within it and in some places this creates a zone of interaction between electrons and protons where the greater activity and lesser activity tend to cancel each other out, to give rise to a 'neutral' region and a composite 'neutron' gravitates to this region where it stabilises. In fact what happens is that the interaction of two 'electron' and 'proton' regions from two hydrogen atoms creates a double neutral region that accommodates two 'neutrons' and this, together with two further hydrogen atoms stabilises as a helium atom. We deal further with the structure of neutrons in Chapter 27.

A basic premise of hK-M is that everything comprises patterns of activity in the basic, initially dormant, energy and further developments take place by activities differentiating out of those already existing and by activities combining together. We need to think of everything, not in terms of inanimate 'things' held together by abstract forces but as living dynamic activities that interact by the effects that they have on the underlying energy from which they have arisen. A way to think of the dynamic activities taking place in the formation of atomic structures is to visualise a vast slow moving river. This is comparable to the s-entity activity that is slow, ponderous, powerful and fills the space in which everything exists. Out of developments taking place within it there arises a region of the river where there are multitudinous self-actualising minute whirlpools of two types. One (electron) type is very minute but highly active and exerts a positive, outwards force on the s-entity activity, the other (proton) type, although still minute, is much larger, slower and ponderous and exerts a negative, suctional force on the s-entity. The movement in the river brings these entities into close proximity so that they interact and the highly active (electron) whirlpool then gets wrapped around and encompasses the ponderous (proton) one, in the way that a highly active whirlpool entrains an object and takes it to its centre, to create the equivalent of a hydrogen atom.

Galaxy Breakdown and the Punctuated Equilibrium Principle

The fossil evidence pertaining to the evolution of life on Earth shows that organisms developed smoothly along established lines for long periods and then there was a sudden change, when many organisms died out and new species arose. Biologists have given the name 'punctuated equilibrium' to this type of development. According to hK-M, punctuated equilibrium is fundamental to the evolutionary process. It arises because entities evolve, and develop their sense of self, by increasing their pattern of activity against the s-pressure. This creates a stress of interaction and ultimately this stress becomes more than they can withstand and they break down or transform. In the case of galaxies, the galaxy entity's increase in its activity builds up a stress in the surrounding s-entity and in the peripheral regions of itself, until the zone of interaction breaks down to form hydrogen and helium atoms. These clouds of gas then cause turbulence in the s-entity, giving rise to the formation of stars that process the hydrogen into larger atoms. After the peripheral breakdown, the galaxy entity continues to seek increasing sense of self by increasing in activity, until again the build up of stress between its activity and the adjacent part of the s-entity causes peripheral break down, forming further hydrogen and helium atoms and leading to further star formation. Thereby galaxies undergo a succession of outer 'shells' of break down that give rise to the formation of hydrogen, helium and stars, the residual effects of which can sometimes be observed by astronomers, as in fig. 8.3.

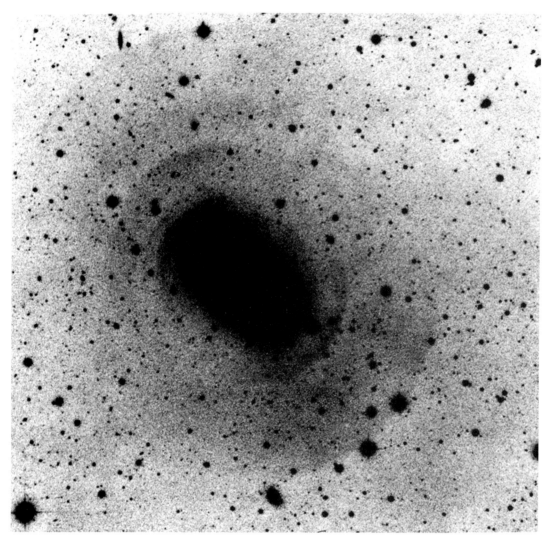

Fig 8.3 The shell pattern observed around galaxy NGC 3923. The general pattern of stars registered all over this photograph exist in the Milky Way, through which all astronomical observations from Earth have to be made.
Anglo-Australian Observatory/David Malin Images

According to *h*K-M galaxies came into existence as something larger than they appear now and they have been progressively breaking down. Thus when we look at a galaxy, (as in fig. 3.6), we see it smaller than it was originally, in the process of breaking down, giving rise to stars that are working through their life cycles. There exist also old stars, from the earlier periods of breakdown of the galaxies that have worked through their life cycles and are now 'dead' (and invisible). These exist as a sort of halo around what we see as a galaxy and they could be the source of the invisible matter that scientists have calculated must exist to a considerable extent in the Universe.

Although it is common practice to refer to galaxies as though these can be perceived (through telescopes), in fact galaxies are invisible and cannot be seen. What is actually observed is a large number of stars that are made visible by the energy given off in their activity of creating heavier atoms out of lighter ones. The stars are distributed in a pattern and it is this pattern that is called a galaxy but the basis of the pattern cannot itself be seen. According to *h*K-M galaxies arise as self-actualising entities that develop out of the turbulence of interaction of the s-entities, so that the pattern of their activity follows that of the turbulence from which they were formed and the stars that subsequently develop as a galaxy breaks down then mark out this pattern. What is observed now is the current state of galaxy breakdown, as it results in star activity and substance formation, that started from something bigger.

Galaxy entities are much more active than the surrounding s-entity. So a way to imagine their interaction with the s-entity and their mutual breakdown is to visualise vigorously stirring something fluid, e.g. water into a much thicker tar-like substance (with which there is no mutual solubility). Then imagine the rapidly moving water slowly eroding the tar in a way in which fragments of the tar break off, each within a globule of water, analogous to the atomic nucleus within an electron surround, which then become luminous and light up the background stirring pattern of activity, to look like the galaxy portrayed in fig.3.6.

Other Features

According to the Big Bang theory the initial explosion of energy/substance produced reverberations (radiation) that permeate the Universe. A major factor supporting the Big Bang theory is that scientists have measured very accurately this 'background radiation' to the Universe and found that it is exactly what is predicted from mathematical calculations based on the Big Bang model. *h*K-M proposes that the Universe began with a multiplicity of little bangs which gave rise to galaxies. It could be that a collective of little bangs would produce the same result as a single Big Bang.

If all the energy/substance of the Universe came into existence with the Big Bang, this leaves the problem of where did it come from prior to its concentrated 'pinhead' state? According to *h*K-M this is not the situation that has to be considered; the energy of the Universe already existed but in a dormant state prior to it becoming active and the Universe thereby arising.

One of the unresolved problems of the expanding Big Bang model of the Universe is whether it expands forever or reaches a limit and then collapses back onto itself, to rebound and expand out again as another Universe. With a succession of Universe creating pulses of s-activity, giving rise to an Omniverse, *h*K-M comes down on the side of a cyclic activity.

For an authoritative account of the Big Bang theory, its development and ramifications, see GRIFFIN, for an account of possible alternative explanations see ARP. There is much here for the next generation to sort out, to arrive at a satisfactory explanation for the arising and nature of the Universe.

Chapter 9

Appendix to Chapter 3: The Arising of Substances. Stars and Planets out of an on-going Turmoil

In this Appendix we go into further detail on the creation of substances, stars and planets, to supplement the outline given in Chapter 3 in Part 1. Once again, the ideas presented are highly speculative compared with the precise sophisticated theories and mathematical analyses of modern science and we reiterate that we make no claim for their validity. Their purpose is give continuity to our effort to demonstrate the feasibility of developing a deeper, evolutionary-wholistic understanding along hK-M lines.

Scientists investigate the substances of the world and conclude that these comprise atoms, that are made of nuclei consisting of protons and neutrons, with an electron surround. Scientific analyses show that invisible forces, namely gravity and interatomic forces, determine the behaviour of these. But science offers no explanation for why substances should consist of atoms and why atoms should consist of nuclear components and electrons, or for the existence of gravity and interatomic forces. hK-M attempts to explain why and how these features arise.

In the previous chapter we dealt with the formation of hydrogen and helium out of the interaction of s-entities and galaxy entities. We now consider how the presence of hydrogen and helium gives rise to stars, heavier atoms, cosmic phenomena and planets.

The Formation of Stars and Heavier Atoms

When the hydrogen and helium atoms form an expanding cloud of gas this destroys the pattern of s-entity activity in this region, (that is generated by the centre from which it is remote), and makes it turbulent, so that it becomes separated from the coherent centred activity. This region then contracts under the s-pressure and its activity increases until it develops self-actualising centres in it, (as in fig. 1.2), to give rise to star entities. These inherit from the s-entity, from which they differentiated out, a B-cell pattern of self-actualising activity.

The s-entities, in maintaining their activities and sense of self create a universal s-pressure that acts on anything that obstructs their activities, in effect seeking to press the obstruction out of existence. This compresses the star entity, which intensifies its activity. The s-pressurised B-cell flow pattern of the star then causes it to concentrate the hydrogen and helium atoms that it encompasses towards its centre, where they create a resistance that reduces its centrally generated activity. It then contracts under the s-pressure, which increases the intensity of its activity. This causes some of the galaxy derived electron energy/particles to penetrate into s-entity derived protons to form neutrons and these combine with hydrogen atoms to form helium atoms, as described in the previous chapter.

The compacting of hydrogen atoms into helium atoms reduces the resistance to the star's self-actualising activity, so that it ceases to contract under the s-pressure. It then enters into a stable period of existence, in which the increasing resistance to its flow caused by its B-cell motion concentrating hydrogen atoms to its central region is counteracted by them being converted to a more compact form as helium atoms. The release of stress that occurs in these rearrangements creates considerable disruption, heat and turbulence in the Sun's pattern of activity, as shown in fig. 9.1, which is a photograph of its surface, showing a granular structure that is thought to be due to the turbulence taking the form of Bénard cells, (LANG).

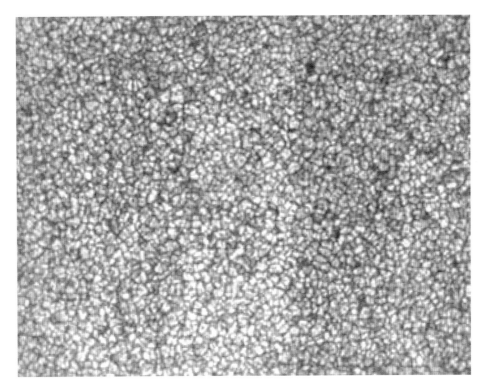

Fig. 9.1.   The Sun, photographed by astronomers, showing a 'granulated' surface, in which the 'granules' are the tops of Bénard convection cells.
Richard Muller and Thierry Roudies, Observatoire du Pic-du-Midi et de Toulouse

When most of the hydrogen has been converted to helium the resistance to the star's centrally driven B-cell activity is reduced so that it expands, casting out its outer, helium rich, region.

Fig. 9.2 The way in which a star expands and expels substances that it has been creating, at the end of its period of activity. (The Helix Nebula).
Anglo-Australian Observatory/David Malin Images

The central zone continues to convert atoms entering it into neutrons so that this region becomes a mêlée of neutrons and residual hydrogen and helium atoms. The s-pressurised B-cell motion of the star is now more concentrated and intense, so that it compresses together larger groupings of these constituents, to form larger, heavier atoms of substances. Again when this process is complete the resistance to the star's centrally driven pattern of activity is reduced, so that it expands casting off its outer region containing the heavier atoms. This cycle of events is repeated again and again, so that the star undergoes a succession of contractions, each time leaving behind an outpouring of heavier atoms, fig 9.2.

In this way stars create larger atoms and undergo successive shells of breakdown by the punctuated equilibrium principle of sequential build up of stress and transformation, as described for galaxy breakdown.

The end-point of this sequence of developments depends on the initial size of the star entity. If it is 'small' it only goes through the first phase of forming helium from hydrogen. If it is a medium-sized star it goes through several phases of forming increasingly larger atoms. Then, when its centrally-driven activity is no longer great enough to convert the atoms there into neutrons and larger atoms, it becomes clogged up by the atoms accumulating there, which then become compacted by the star's s-pressurised B-cell activity, to give rise to a 'dead' star, that is, a star entity that no longer generates the movement that causes collision and interaction of the substances that it encompasses.

If the star is larger, then as it contracts, its activity increases to a point at which the intensity of collision of the atoms that it now encompasses becomes so great that they are all converted into neutrons. These are then forced together into a highly compacted state to create what is known as a neutron star.

If the star is larger still then, on contraction, its activity intensifies to a level at which collisions between the neutrons reach a point at which these break down. When this happens the impediment to the star entity's flow pattern is greatly diminished and it expands out explosively, in the phenomenon known as a 'black hole'.

As a star contracts it leaves behind a cloud of the atoms that it has been creating, in the form of cosmic dust that permeates the region where more hydrogen, helium and stars are forming. As with the old stars, these new stars cause hydrogen atoms to be compacted to form helium atoms. This is the situation with the Sun, which is a smallish star, in which helium is forming from hydrogen, and which also contains a smattering of cosmic dust of heavy atoms formed by previous stars.

The hK-M viewpoint on the formation of stars is different from the current scientific one, which starts from a diffuse, expanding distribution of hydrogen and helium arising from the Big Bang. In this, somehow, inhomogeneities arise that, within the overall expansion, give rise to localised concentrations that, by gravitational attraction, accumulate further hydrogen and helium until this builds up to create a galaxy of stars, in which a combination of gravity and interatomic forces bring about transformation of the hydrogen and helium to heavier atoms. As ARP has pointed out, it is difficult to envisage a concentration of substance as taking place out of a formless diffuse cloud in this way; as the cloud condenses collisions between particles would cause it to heat up and it would then expand and disperse. It requires some sort of force or activity to bring it together which, according to hK-M, is a self-actualising star entity, which concentrates the hydrogen and helium to its centre to give rise to a star.

Astronomers observe stars to be continuously forming and the problem then arises as to where the hydrogen and helium come from, for this to happen. According to the Big Bang theory all the hydrogen and helium came into existence in the beginning and localised concentrations arose that gave rise to galaxies and stars, and it is assumed that sufficient hydrogen and helium remain to account for the fact that galaxy/star formation is still going on. According to hK-M, hydrogen is forming all the time by the interaction of galaxy entities and s-entities, as they progressively break down. Self-actualising centres then arise out of the turmoil created by the clouds of hydrogen and helium to give rise to stars, so that further hydrogen, helium and new stars are continually being formed.

Planet Formation

The Sun starts as a large diffuse cloud of hydrogen, helium and cosmic dust that disrupts the s-entity activity and this part of it thereby gets separated off and develops into the self-actualising Sun/star entity. This contracts under the s-pressure, which builds up the intensity of its activity until this converts hydrogen to helium. However, the Sun entity contracts a long way before this point is reached and this does not occur smoothly but by the punctuated equilibrium principle, with the build up of stress and its release by transformation. In this sequence of events the s-pressurised B-cell activity of the Sun entity causes an increasing concentration of hydrogen and dust in its centre that creates a resistance to its self-actualising motion. When this stresses it to the limit of what, at its state of evolution, it can withstand, i.e. when it becomes more than it can 'digest', the s-pressure causes it to contract and its activity then intensifies until it opposes and equals the s-pressure. As its activity increases, this acts on the substances clogging up its centrally driven motion and it spews out, or ejects, the excess of these into the surrounding s-entity. This creates turbulence in this region of the s-entity, out of which a self-actualising centre arises that concentrates the ejected material to form an asteroid or planet.

After the rejection of the excess material clogging up its centre the Sun settles down at a level of activity that again equals and opposes the s-pressure. But again, in seeking increased sense of self its activity increases which builds up a further concentration of hydrogen and dust that reduces its centrally-driven activity, so that it comes under increasing stress until once more the s-pressure causes it to contract. Again the intensification of its activity results in it ejecting excess clogging-up material from its centre, which leads to further asteroid or planet formation in the surrounding s-entity. In this way the Sun entity contracts in jumps and each time that it does so it ejects excess material from its centre that creates turbulence and asteroid or planet formation in the surrounding s-entity. (The way that planetary or asteroid entities concentrate substances to their centres is similar to star entity activity but the smaller turbulences that form asteroid or planetary entities are much weaker, so that they only cause substances to aggregate and not to break down and transform, as they do in stars). The Earth is formed in this way, from material ejected by the Sun that created turbulence in the surrounding s-entity that developed into the self-actualising Earth planetary entity.

The s-pressurised B-cell activity of the Earth Entity causes the agglomerates of substances to concentrate towards its centre, which create a resistance to its activity and the pattern of what happened with the Sun is repeated, whereby it undergoes a jump contraction and excess substances are rejected. These then undergo, on a smaller scale, the same process that gave rise to the Earth in orbit around the Sun, to give rise to the Moon in orbit around the Earth.

This hK-M viewpoint of the formation of the Solar System differs from the current scientific one. This starts with a diffuse, spread-out distribution of hydrogen and cosmic dust in which, somehow, an inhomogeneity develops which, by gravitational attraction, concentrates the hydrogen and cosmic dust into a more-dense cloud that forms the beginning of the Sun. As this cloud contracts (under its own gravity) rings of cosmic dust are left behind in which inhomogeneities arise which, by gravitational attraction, draw further substances towards them to form planets in a long slow gentle process. However, as pointed out in Chapter 3, there is now evidence from the structures of meteorites that shows that these have been subjected to high temperatures, so that the formation of the Solar System took place by more violent processes (MUIR). Additionally it has become clear that the formation of planets in other Solar Systems that have recently been discovered cannot have taken place by the slow condensation from dust rings, so that a rethinking is required (ADLER). ARP states that, in addition to it being difficult to envisage a reason for the concentration of substance out of a formless diffuse cloud, it is against the observed evidence that shows an ejection mechanism. Thus, T Taurus stars, which are stars in the process of formation, show jets of ejected material seemingly forming into planets. (Quasars are seen to be formed in the same way, in this case by material ejected from the core of intense Seyfert galaxies).

The Earth Planet

As the Earth Planetary entity pursues its self-actualising B-cell activity this carries substances towards its centre. However, when they come into proximity the stress fields that they create in the Earth Entity activity interact. There then occurs a division of the substances. Heavier atoms in which their interacting stress fields prevent the Earth Entity's B-cell activity forcing them closer together then form the solid Earth, light atoms, mainly hydrogen and helium, that continue to respond to the Earth Entity's B-cell activity continue to circulate and they form the Earth's atmosphere; atoms that cohere together but move en masse under the B-cell motion form liquid, water, on the surface of the Earth.

Where the B-cell activity impinges on solid substances it permeates slowly through, and exerts a force on, them, in the way that a stream of water coming up against a barrier will penetrate it according to its permeability. In the interior of the Earth where temperatures are high and solid substances are viscous and plastic, this B-cell activity engenders a slow movement in them. The B-cell activity creates more dynamic circulation patterns in the watery environment and even more so in the gaseous atmosphere.

When the Sun starts to convert hydrogen to helium this creates an outwards pressure that drives the hydrogen and helium atmosphere away from the Earth. As the Earth continues to contract, lighter gaseous substances that are caught up with the heavier ones concentrate into pockets that are circulated out as volcanic activity, to form another atmosphere around the Earth that, scientists deduce, comprised largely carbonaceous gases, nitrogen, ammonia and water vapour.

As in the formation of the Sun, the Earth Entity contracts in jumps as it becomes stressed to the limit of what it can withstand, giving rise to discontinuities in the pattern of its activities and thereby in the effects of these on the background s-entity space energy. This, in turn, affects the distribution of the light elements that are present in 'space' that thereby mark out these regions of its B-cell flow pattern. Scientists know two such 'marker zones' as Van Allen belts around the Earth, fig. 9.3, (named after their discoverer).

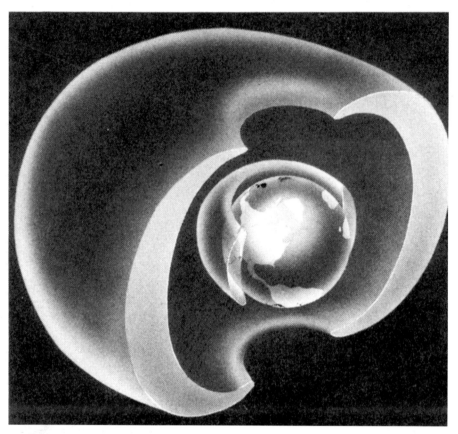

Fig. 9.3 The B-cell-like form of the Van Allen belts around the Earth that exist at an altitude of 2,000 to 16,000 kilometres. *From: The Solar System by Roman Smoluchowski, courtesy of the publishers W.H. Freeman*

The Earth's Magnetic Field

The Earth possesses a magnetic field that regularly reverses: the cause of this field and its behaviour are something of a mystery to science. As explained above, according to hK-M, the Earth Entity is an s-pressurised, self-actualising B-cell activity, that has been differentiated out of the s-entity space energy by the presence of substances, which it concentrates to its centre to form the Earth planet. The Earth Entity's pattern of activity acts on the patterns of activity that comprise the substances that it embodies, producing responses according to their natures. Thus, for example, with the naturally occurring mineral magnetite (lodestone), the pattern of its activity is in harmony with that of the Earth Entity so that it tends to align with it, (which resulted in the Earth's stress field being called a magnetic field). A number of other substances, such as iron respond in the same way, which has given rise to the magnetic compass needle and other devices. However, the Earth's magnetic field and its effect on magnetic materials, is only one aspect of the nature and behaviour of the Earth Entity's pattern of activity that acts on everything that it encompasses.

By comparison with the activity of the s-entity space energy out of which it has differentiated, the Earth Entity is more active, so that at its boundary of interaction there is a retarding stress. As, in seeking increasing sense of self, the Earth Entity increases in activity this builds up this stress in the more static surrounding space energy activity until this overpowers the activity of the Earth Entity that then loses control and becomes driven by the stress that has built up in the s-entity, which, as it releases, acts on and reverses the motion of the Earth Entity and thereby reverses its magnetic field.

Thus, the presence of substances in the s-entity space energy activity gives rise to stress fields that become self-actualising entities and their self-actualising activities create further stress fields in the space energy. The interplay of these stress fields with substances gives rise to the structure and activities of the

Universe, for example, to the formation and activities of the Solar System in the way that has been described. The activity of the Sun entity creates a stress field in the s-entity activity, which like that of the Earth, undergoes reversals that act on the Earth planet. These stresses, and particularly their reversals are the cause of, sometimes catastrophic, changes that take place in the structure of the Earth planet.

The substances of all planets are brought together by B-cell planetary entities but the relationship of these to the substances of their planets is not necessarily the same as that of the Earth Entity to the magnetic substances of the Earth planet. Thus using the means by which they detect the Earth's magnetic field scientists find that other planets have weaker or stronger magnetic fields or, as with Venus and Mars, none at all, (LANG).

The Universe is full of interacting stress fields and activities that exert effects on each other. Thus, the Sun, in its activities gives off a continuous stream of high-energy particles as a very dilute 'gas' (known as the solar wind) that interact with the Earth Entity, fig. 9.4. This is equally true for the other planets of the Solar System and in this way the Sun and its planets interact with each other. The hK-M viewpoint is that the Sun and its planets interact via the dynamic stress fields that their activities create in the space energy and by reverberations given off as a result of changes in these but that we only observe this when we monitor the behaviour of the gas/plasma particles that exist in space, as in fig. 9.4

Fig. 9.4. The interaction of the solar wind with the Earth and its magnetic field.
Courtesy NASA

The Basic Nature of Substance

As we have described, substances comprise intense concentrations of the energy activities of 'protons', 'neutrons' and 'electrons' that are held in place by the forces of interaction between them.   As the number of the components of atoms increases it is more of a problem for them to exist in an unstressed relationship, so that some large atoms are unstable and break down spontaneously into smaller atoms, in the phenomenon of radioactive decay. When this happens energy involved in the formation of the disintegrating material is released. By isolating and concentrating the material that breaks down in this way scientists can produce intense concentrations of energy generated from the radioactive breakdown of substances, as in the atomic bomb, fig. 9.5, which can be regarded as a near instantaneous reversion of the series of condensing processes that the energy has gone through over eons of time in creating substance.

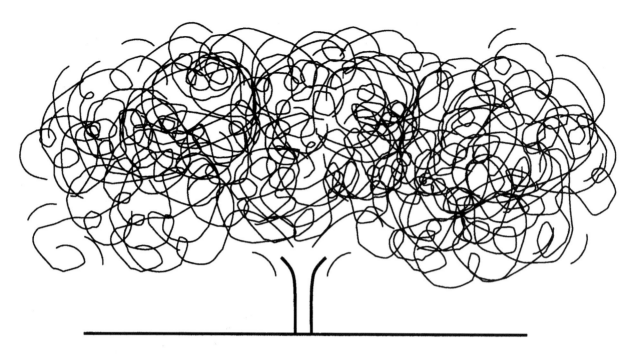

Fig 9.5 The way in which the energy of substance, that has been created by the concentration of the energy/activity in turbulent cosmic processes, is released and re-expands in the activity of the atom bomb.

Where scientists can control this reversion of substance to free energy it gives atomic power.

The findings of science about the nature and behaviour of substances are expressed in terms of mathematical equations that govern the relationships between the parameters involved in a situation and allow calculations to be made of what happens when these are varied. The correlation between predictions made by the equations and measured substance behaviour shows the equations to be valid. However, it is not always clear what is actually happening and why this should be so. This is particularly the case with fundamental phenomena concerned with the basic nature of substances, described by the equations of quantum mechanics. These equations have been verified by experiments but there is considerable debate about what the basic nature of substances must be, to give rise to their observed behaviour. In fact a famous Nobel-prize winning quantum physicist (Richard FEYNMAN), has stated:

'I think I can safely say that nobody understands quantum mechanics'.

*h*K-M, with its deeper, evolutionary-wholistic viewpoint, offers an explanation for what is taking place to give rise to the behaviour expressed by the mathematical equations and of why this should be so. It is only a qualitative explanation but it could complement the quantitative theoretical equations to create a total picture.

We experience solids and liquids as though they are a continuous 'mass' of substance: however, the investigations of science which showed that substances comprise an assembly of minute atoms held together by interatomic forces acting through space, posed the problem of what exactly is a 'mass of substance'?

The finding that the atoms that make up substances consist of a nucleus of proton and neutron 'particles' with a surround of electron 'particles' led scientists to break down the nuclear particles to find out what substance ultimately consists of. This resulted in the detection of many types of much smaller particles. At the same time scientists found that these are not stable and can form and disappear, transforming into or out of, energy as they do so, according to Einstein's famous equation $E = mc^2$, where E is energy, m is mass and c is the velocity of light. Since c^2 is a vast quantity this means that a small amount of mass is equivalent to a very large amount of condensed energy. This led to the conclusion that what we call the 'mass' of a particle of substance is in fact a highly ordered concentration of energy.

But this poses the problem of what is meant by, 'a highly-ordered concentration of energy'. If space is nothingness, i.e. a vacuum, then how can particles, as localised concentrations of energy emerge out of, and disappear into, it. Scientists therefore now think of space as a continuum of energy (in accord with *h*K-M) from which localised concentrations of energy (particles) can emerge and return, (McTAGGART). But it is not possible for a concentration of energy to be stable - it would disperse into its surroundings. Something must organise it and keep it in place. So, either there is some unknown force that acts on it to do this, or else the energy does it for itself. This problem is resolved by *h*K-M that regards the 'particles' as self-sustaining, self-actualising stable patterns of energy-activity that have been generated out of the basic space energy, by the interaction of s-entities and galaxy entities in processes that have been described.

Things comprise agglomerations of the patterns of activity that make up the 'particles' of substances of which they consist, held together by the forces that they exert on each other, that derive from the distortions/stresses that they create in the s-entities' pattern of activity. The pressure of this activity acts on everything everywhere, so that when something moves through the s-entity it requires a force to bring this about. The resistance of the s-entity pressure to this movement is determined by the nature and amount of the particles (patterns of activity) of which the thing consists, i.e. by its mass, (this is what its mass comprises) and by the increasing rate at which the movement is taking place. Thus scientists have found that the force required to bring the movement about is proportional to the mass and acceleration of the thing moving through the pressure of the s-entity activity, (F=ma). [This applies only to mineral kingdom 'bodies of substances' that are moved by external forces and not to the bodies of organisms that have developed the ability to self-actualisingly move around].

The more evolved the energy-activity, the more active it is and the less evolved it is the more effort that is required to get it to respond and move (as with human beings), i.e. the more 'inertia', or 'mass' it has. Thus the mass of a proton in the nucleus of an atom, which derives from the break up of the ponderous s-entity energy is one thousand times greater than that of an electron, which derives from the break up of the more-active galaxy entity energy.

[The more-evolved energy-activities of life processes, namely soul-feeling and spirit-thinking are massless by comparison.]

For particles, and the agglomeration of particles that make up substance, to exist and not to be crushed out of existence by the s-entity activity their own activity must oppose that of the s-entity and, as explained above, a measure of this is the 'mass' of the particle, or agglomeration of particles in substance. If, in some event, part of the mass of the particle/substance is lost, then this reverts to the basic s-entity energy state from which it derived, according to Einstein's equation $E = mc^2$, which relates the transformation of energy from its basic s-entity (E) state, to a self-actualising 'particle' (m) state and vice versa, with c being a measure of the resistance of the s-pressure-driven space energy to the change.

Since the self-actualising activities that comprise substances are 'mechanical', i.e. simply striving to maintain the patterns of activity that give them their sense of self, they can be described by mechanical laws of behaviour. Thus the laws and mathematical equations formulated by scientists that describe the behaviour of substances are not in dispute with hK-M. It is understanding the basic nature of the Universe that gives rise to these laws, with which hK-M is concerned.

The Force Fields of Substances

The activity of the s-entities exerts a pressure on all the entities which they encompass that make up the Universe which, by their self-actualising activities, react back, thereby creating a stress in the s-entities' pattern of activity. This results in the 'gravitational stress field' around the Earth and all other cosmic bodies, so that throughout the Universe an overall balance of action and reaction is set up.

When the proton nucleus and electron surround are together as a hydrogen atom that is part of the Earth, they make their, minute, contribution to the gravitational stress field. When they are separated they create different levels of stress from that of the overall gravitational field around them, because of their different levels of evolution/activity. The electron activity being greater creates a stress in one (more-active) direction, while the ponderous proton creates a stress in the opposite (less-active) direction. In these regions therefore the pervading s-entities' gravitational stress field is modified, which gives rise to what scientists know as positive and negative charge stress fields. If a separated-off proton and electron come within the influence of their opposite stress fields this brings them together and the electron switches to its 'nucleus driven' state, to reform a hydrogen atom.

The scientific viewpoint is that the component parts of atoms are held together by fields of force that they exert on each other. These fields of force are described mathematically but there is a problem in understanding how they operate across the intervening space. At one time it was thought that space was filled with an aether which was the medium through which the forces acted but experiments designed to detect the aether did not do so and the idea of its existence was therefore abandoned: as long as the mathematics of 'fields of force' described correctly what happened it was regarded as unnecessary to know anything further. But this is only a partial understanding of the situation. According to hK-M there is no such thing as empty space, equally 'space' is not filled with an inert aether; everywhere there is Kosmic energy in some state of development and it is the stress fields that the activities of electrons and protons create in the s-entity space energy activity that gives rise to the forces that cause them to combine together to form atoms.

[When scientists sought evidence for the existence of an aether through which the Earth was moving, two physicists (Michelson and Morley) devised a famous experiment to test this. This was based on the assumption that if the Earth is moving relative to an aether then light sent in the direction of movement and reflected back would take longer to cover a set distance than light sent out perpendicular to the direction of flow. (As is the case with a boat travelling at a fixed speed in the direction of flow of a river and back again and across the river and back). However, they could not detect any difference and this was taken to disprove the existence of an aether. From the point of view of hK-M any stress on the aether (s-entity activity) caused by the movement of the Earth parallel and perpendicular to its direction of movement would act equally on the 'ruler' (equipment) used to measure the difference which would therefore not detect it. But that there is such a stress is shown clearly in fig. 9.4].

When activities develop in the space energy that force atoms together until their stress fields interact, then atoms of the same type relate to each other to form a liquid or solid collective of the atoms of the substance. If they are of different types then, if their interaction results in a reduced stress, they form a collective compound of the different atoms, but if it results in an increased stress they oppose forming a relationship. In all cases the final configuration is one in which their stresses of interaction oppose and equal the activity forcing them together.

Types of Atoms and the Periodic Table

Scientists list the different types of atoms in terms of increasing heaviness, which relates to the way that stars form successively heavier atoms. However, scientists find that heaviness is not all, and that there is an underlying pattern in the properties of atoms, which is expressed as the Periodic Table of the elements. While listing the atoms in terms of increasing heaviness this then arranges them in a rhythmical pattern according to their qualities and characteristics of behaviour.

This pattern of atom characteristics arises from the way in which the atom constituents fit together as these increase in number in increasingly larger atoms. The patterns of activity that comprise protons and neutrons cohere closely together to form a nucleus around which the patterns of activity that comprise electrons pack together in increasingly larger onion-like layers. The nature and behaviour of an atom, i.e. the way that it interacts with other atoms, is determined by the 'face' that it presents, i.e. the outer layers of electrons. If the nucleus is completely surrounded and sealed off by electron energy activity, it forms what scientists call a 'closed shell' around the nucleus that balances out and is balanced out by, the positive charge of the nucleus and the atom is 'inert'.   This occurs when the number of electrons around the nucleus is 2, 10, 18, 36, 54, or 86 (the inert gases). But if the number of electrons increases above that for a closed shell the atoms exhibit qualities associated first with an excess of electrons above the closed shell and then, as the number of protons/electrons approaches that of the next closed shell, the qualities associated with an incomplete closed shell. This accounts for the rhythmical similarity as layers of electrons build up around the nucleus. Thus for example, increasingly larger atoms with just one electron in excess of a closed shell possess similar properties. Atoms of opposite lack of inner balance (i.e. with more or less than the harmonious arrangement of constituents), attract each other and form shared relationships which gives them both a degree of completeness, (a sort of forerunner of biological attraction between opposite sexes caused by the stresses of their inner make-up). This is the basis of chemical interactions and the way in which atoms fit together to make up the substance natures of everything that we see in the world around us (DICKERSON and GEIS).

Quantisation and 'Wave Packets'

If an atom increases in energy, as it does when colliding with other atoms of higher energy, then its behaviour follows the punctuated equilibrium principle.   That is, it increases in energy/activity in its established state until this creates a stress that exceeds what, at its level of evolution it is able to withstand, and it then undergoes a convulsion in which it jumps discontinuously to a higher level of energy/activity. This can happen a number of times in which it exists in a sequence of discrete levels of increasing energy/activity.

Conversely if it loses energy, by collision with atoms of lower energy, then it drops down through its sequence of energy/activity levels, with the convulsion of each reduction of energy reverberating through the s-entity space energy that presses on it. These reverberations travel through the space energy at the speed of light, that is the rate of response of the s-pressurised space-energy to this activity, which scientists know as light, X-rays and other radiations. However, instead of the reverberation spreading out uniformly in all directions, the omnipresent s-pressure 'clamps down' on it and confines it. As a result the change in the space-energy radiates away from the event in a form that scientists know as a quantum of reverberation, or 'wave packet'. It is the resistance to disturbance and the 'clamping down' by the omnipresent s-pressure that brings about the individualisation and quantisation of these activities.

Once created the 'wave packet' of energy reverberation travels through the space-energy ad infinitum, until it encounters an obstacle, e.g. as light from far-away stars, after travelling vast distances, encounters the Earth. Scientists have recorded the characteristics of the wave packets of vibrations associated with known and controlled atomic changes taking place on Earth and when they find that the wave packets from stars have the same properties they deduce that the same substances and atomic changes exist there.

Scientists regard these wave packets of energy reverberation as particles (photons) but according to hK-M they are not true particles; a particle is a self-actualising will activity entity that, once it is created continues to exist in its own right. The energy quanta of vibrations, when absorbed by entities on which they impinge contribute their energy to the activity of the pattern of activity of the absorbing entity and thereby lose their identity and separate existence.

If the wave packet impinges on a substance that is 'in tune' with it, i.e. the constituents of the substance are 'on the same wavelength', the energy of the reverberation activates these and it is absorbed. If, however, the reverberation frequency of the wave packet is too high or too low to interact with the substance, then it passes through, or bounces back from, it. If the wave-packet is of a frequency that would interact with the substance but it does not impinge directly on it and passes close to it, it is distorted by the substance's space-energy stress field, in the phenomenon known as diffraction.

[Such wave packets are all the time being given off by, and impinging on, all the activities that comprise the entities of the Universe. In this way entities experience, and can be influenced in their development by, what is going on elsewhere as for example in the way that the plant kingdom is influenced by the wave packets of radiation from the Sun. Then, as entities experience an enhanced sense of self from this activity they actively seek it out and thereby develop systems and organs that give them an awareness of it and a subconscious understanding of it. Then, in homo sapiens, there develops mental, thinking, abilities that give a conscious understanding of what is going on. The energy of the Absolute, out of which the Omniverse collective of Universes and their entities have been created, is full of multitudinous activities reverberating through it. But we are not aware of the majority of these because we do not have senses or instruments that respond to them, so that we have only a limited awareness of the activities of the Absolute].

Electrical Conductivity

As we have stated previously, when separated from the balanced state in which they exist together in substances, electrons and protons by virtue of the difference in their activities (greater and lesser respectively) create stress fields in the space energy around them. If they are stationary then once the situation around them has adjusted to these stress fields everything settles down. However, if they are moving, the stress field is maintained and on-going. With substances in which the atoms have one, or a few electrons outside a closed shell, as in metals, then these electrons are not tied to any particular nucleus and are free to move through the material. In such a substance, extra electrons can be continually put in at one end of it and taken out at the other end, to give rise to a continual current of electrons through the material and an associated (magnetic) stress field in the space energy.

Magnetism

The pattern of activity of the electron energy of each atom of a substance creates a minute localised electric current and stress field. In most substances these currents and stress fields are randomly orientated and tend to cancel each other out. But there are a few materials (iron, nickel, cobalt and their compounds and alloys) in which they can be caused to line up with each other so that the material as a whole then exhibits a (magnetic) stress field in the space energy, fig. 9.6.

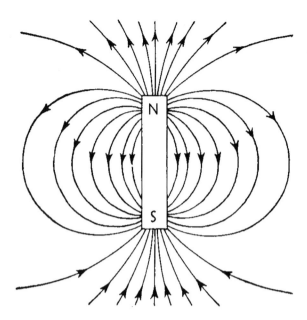

Fig. 9.6 The B-cell magnetic field around a bar magnet, produced by the line up and mutual reinforcement of the B-cell fields of the atoms of which it consists that, in a pivoted compass needle responds to, and aligns with, the B-cell activity of the Earth Entity.

Such materials respond to the B-cell activity of the Earth Entity so that a small piece of the material, if free to move, lines up with it, as in a magnetic compass needle.

In the same way that a current of electrons creates a (magnetic) stress field, a moving magnetic stress field acting on free electrons, e.g. in a metal, causes these to move, thereby creating an electric current. The first of these principles is the basis of the electricity generator, in which an electric current is produced by rotating magnets whose stress fields act to move electrons in a coil of wire, while the second principle is the basis of the electric motor, in which a current through a coil of wire creates a stress field that acts on magnets that are attached to the drive shaft of the motor causing it to rotate.

The Activity Fields of Substances

When atoms come together as a collective, their activity creates a stress field in the background s-entity activity that encompasses the substance. Some psychics claim to perceive these activity stress fields as auras around substances. REICHENBACH published in 1844, the results of an extensive series of tests that he carried out with people who he selected because they were sensitive to the physical and emotional conditions around them. After conditioning their eyes by being in total darkness for an hour or so, these people could see luminous activity associated with crystals, plants, animals, chemical reactions, sound, friction, electrically-charged bodies, human breathing and 'flames' around magnets. Reichenbach gave the term 'odic force' to what was observed and stated that, from the tests he carried out, it was different from electric and magnetic phenomena and that it permeated all things. From the hK-M viewpoint we would equate Reichenbach's odic force with the stress field that a substance, regardless of its electrical or magnetic properties, creates by its presence in distorting the surrounding space-energy activity.

In the 1970s KARAGULLA carried out a similar investigation to that of Reichenbach, with a number of people who claimed to be able to perceive energy fields associated with substances, plants and people. Among her findings she cites the case of a person who saw a bluish haze around the north-seeking pole of magnets and a reddish haze around the south-seeking pole and who also perceived an interaction between these 'energy fields' and her aura. This person reported seeing energy fields associated with crystals that were like a B-cell activity, in that there was a flow from the centre of the crystal to its periphery and back again. The pattern and intensity of flow varied with the type of crystal being examined. In some cases there was an interaction between the energy field of the crystal and that of the environment and there was an interaction with the energy field of the human body. This could be the basis of the 'mythology' of the healing properties of crystals.

Some people who claimed to perceive these energy fields (e.g. STEINER, PAYNE, GARRETT), have stated how difficult it was for them at school, when the teacher was demonstrating phenomena, e.g. associated with musical instruments and the manifestations of electricity and magnetism and giving the scientific explanation for them, which they could see by their 'etheric' vision, was not true. This, we regard as an important area where the direct observations of mystics and people with 'etheric vision' of activities taking place in 'space', that scientists can only hypothesise about, could make a contribution to advancing understanding. As we have pointed out, this is a 'grey area' between science and hK-M, in that hK-M sees etheric (space energy) activity as a central factor by which evolution occurs, whereas science has ruled out the existence of an 'ether' and devolved into mathematical abstractions about fields of force in 'space'.

Reichenbach's odic force permeating everything equates with the space-energy of hK-M. Ancient cultures have claimed the existence of such an energy, e.g. prana - Hindus; Ch'i - Chinese; nous and pneuma - Greeks; mana - Polynesians; and many others, while modern attempts to define and explore such an energy are Reich - orgone and 'energy of the vacuum state', see WHITE and KRIPPNER. DAVIDSON gives an account of a number of inventions designed to harness the space-energy activity. But from the hK-M viewpoint we are already doing this, in that all motion derives from patterns of activity in the space-energy. We harness the stress fields that electrons and protons create in the space energy to produce motion as, for example, in electric motors. All substances, by their presence and the activities of the atoms of which they consist, create stresses in the s-pressurised space-energy. When substances are brought together in a way that forces them to interact so that energy is released, then this can be harnessed to provide heat and/or to drive mechanisms, as in the burning of fossil fuels or the generation of atomic energy. From the point of view of hK-M, all substance energy/activity and the energy that powers life, feeling and thinking, derive from, and are evolved manifestations of, the space-energy. It is not inconceivable that human beings could find further ways to tap into this energy, perhaps by something like the methods described in DAVIDSON's book that would give a source of cheap, non-polluting energy. There is a lot in this area to be worked out by the next generation.

Space-Time Considerations

As we stated at the beginning of this book, according to hK-M the Kosmos starts in a state of uniform dormant energy in which, because it is the same everywhere there is no space because space requires one thing to be here and another thing to be there and there are no different things. Equally there is no time because time is the measure of the rate at which activities take place relative to each other and there are no activities.

Each level of entities is differentiated out of the space-energy by the pattern of activity that creates it. Once differentiated out, the entities at each level become self-actualising and pursue further, out of themselves, the pattern of activity and the sense of self given them 'at their birth'. Thereby each level of entities creates its own structure of activities or 'space-time' framework within which it operates.

The Kosmos first differentiates into a collective of self-actualising centres of activity, i.e. s-entities. These then interact and break up at their peripheries to create galaxy entities and the galaxy entities and s-entities interact to create the first substances – hydrogen and helium. The clouds of hydrogen and helium then differentiate further centres of activity out of the s-entities to create stars that 'compress' the hydrogen and helium into heavier atoms. These permeate further stars that form, to give rise to solar systems with planets circulating around the star centre, like the one in which we exist. Scientists do not recognise the s-entity energy states of the Kosmos that occurred before the arising of atoms of substances, although the mystic Rudolf Steiner (of whom more later) described a first state of pure energy activity, STEINER (2) P.116, in which, if one could move through and experience the Universe at this time one would experience different states and patterns of warmth/activity, which we think could relate to the world of the s-entities. It is only with the arising of substances and stars that it becomes possible to describe events in terms of what we call space and time, in that it is then possible to describe different constellations of stars and their relationship to each other and the rate at which events are taking place within them.

As life evolves on Earth each level of entities creates its own structure of activities or 'space-time' framework within which it operates, e.g. atoms interact with each other in chemical activity, biological entities interact with each other in their life processes, human beings interact in their soul-feeling and spirit-thinking activities. Because all levels of activities are reflected in substance activity that, in Western culture is regarded as the basis of everything, we have adopted the habit of relating everything to the space-time framework of events in the substance kingdom. That is, to the daily rotation of the Earth in relation to the Sun and to measure and record the passage of time in this event by the movement of pendulums and springs in clocks or the rate of vibration of atoms, which we describe in terms of seconds, minutes, hours, etc. But this is not a satisfactory way of describing higher levels of activity. Thus, it would be more realistic to relate biological events to the phases of the life cycle of the organism involved, such as childhood, maturity, etc. and, in the comparison of different organisms, to differences in their life cycles. Equally soul-feelings, e.g. pleasure and annoyance, joy and depression, take place in their own 'space-time' framework and cannot be described as happening in seconds, minutes, etc. Again, spirit-thinking creates its own framework of ideas, understanding and flashes of insight that cannot be expressed in terms of seconds, minutes and so on. Each level sets up its own 'space-time' framework of activities and, in humanity, all four levels of activities exist and interact as a hierarchy that comprises – substance activities – biological life processes - soul feeling - spirit thinking.

Each level maintains its existence and sense of self by its interaction with the level/s below. Thus our biological activity is dependent on manipulating substances, e.g. food by which it maintains its existence and sense of self, and incompatible substances, e.g. toxic materials, such as thalidomide, etc. cause a disruption in its biological activity. While feelings, such as happiness and joy, loneliness and depression, take place in their own space-time, they arise out of and find their expression in, biological activities. Thus our feelings derive from the interaction of the biological activities of our body, e.g. touch, sight, hearing, with the phenomena of Nature and the people around us and if we want to express our feelings we do this by a biological activity such as talking, embracing, etc. Biological activity is, in turn, dependent on manipulating substances in the substance space-time framework and it is possible to ingest substances that make us feel happier or depressed.

Thinking, that produces enlightenment, takes place in its own space-time but it derives from our seeking to understand our sensory soul experiences and if we desire to communicate our thinking this requires making soul contact with other people. We do this by biological activities, e.g. talking or writing, which are in turn dependent on manipulating our substance body and, as with soul feelings, we can ingest substances, such as hallucinogenic drugs that affect our thinking.

While higher levels express themselves via substances, substance activities move out of the purely physical world and into a higher frame of reference when they take place under the control of a higher level, as in a biological entity. That is, the needs of the biological organism determines where and to what extent they take place, but the biological activity can only work according to the principles of the reactions of the mineral kingdom. To consider an example, imagine a man running. The rate at which he does this is determined by his limb movement that, through a chain of biological activities is dependent, among other things, on him inhaling oxygen from the air and expelling carbon dioxide. This produces a localised imbalance or 'stress' in the air that, because of the unifying action of the omnipresent s-pressure, causes movement to take place in it to correct the imbalance. This movement is determined by the laws of the mineral kingdom, (diffusion, convection): the 'higher level' biological activity of the runner determines where, and the extent to which it occurs. This, in turn, is determined by a combination of the yet higher levels of seeking emotional-soul and mental-spirit expression and satisfaction.

But it is not necessary for soul feelings and mental thoughts to be communicated via substance interactions; they can be communicated between people in their own space-time framework. Thus we can experience soul contact, attraction or antipathy, from our interaction with another person without any physical contact. Mental thoughts and awareness can be communicated between people without them even being in each other's presence, in the phenomenon of telepathy.

There is also evidence of a 'telepathic' type of communication at the substance level of existence. Thus scientific theories have led to the view that there is a connectedness between twin particles (particles that are created together), in which the behaviour of one of the pair that is exposed to a stimulus determines the behaviour of the other, without any physical interaction between them and this has been confirmed by experiments. This reflects the total interconnectedness of the all-pervading underlying basic space-energy, in which time and space do not exist.

The 'Energetics' of the Universe

According to the Big Bang theory of the Universe, in the beginning all energy and substance were together in a highly confined, very hot, condition in which everything was in equilibrium. This expanded out and cooled at a rate that was too fast for the necessary amount of substance-energy interaction to take place to maintain equilibrium. Thus the Universe consists of substances and energy 'frozen', or trapped, in a non-uniform state so that if any part is activated in some way, i.e. becomes free to move, it tends to even itself out. (If all the substance and energy of the Big Bang had expanded uniformly in equilibrium there would be no localised concentrations and therefore no galaxies, stars, planets, etc. that is, nothing that we know as the Universe). Scientists have formulated the energy aspect of this as the theory of thermodynamics that governs the energy changes in all physical movements, which take place towards a more uniform distribution of energy. But in its non-uniform condition, everything in the Universe is also in a state of stress and when anything is able to move it does so towards a less-stressed condition. Thus, as well as the existence of universal laws of energy behaviour that govern activity and movement, there could be universal laws of stress behaviour, which govern the configuration of activities that arise as movement takes place towards a less-stressed state. (We touch on this again in Chapter 26).

Although *h*K-M sees the Universe as arising from a collective of little bangs, instead of a single Big Bang, the principle of it existing in a state of non-uniformity of energy and stress is the same. The *h*K-M viewpoint is that in the beginning there was energy, in a 'dormant' state. This became non-homogeneously active, so that stresses arise between the different parts. These stresses determine the patterns of activity that ensue. Thus, according to *h*K-M, stress is the basic factor in determining patterns of behaviour and energy changes result from the movements/activities brought about by stress. If we perform an action we redistribute energy in so doing, but it is not the energy that initiates the action, it is the stress or impulse that is the source of it. And so it is with the Universe as a whole. In the physical world stresses bring about activities. In the biological world stresses to maintain existence and life styles bring about activities and their associated energy changes. In ourselves there are, additionally, emotional stresses, desires and other soul impulses and thoughts and ideas that bring about activities and the associated energy changes.

Chapter 10

Appendix to Chapter 4: The Arising and Evolution of Life on Earth

From the fossil evidence, scientists have concluded that the first living organisms appeared on Earth, in the form of minute prokaryotic cells in the oceans, soon after it formed some 4,500 million years ago. Since then there has evolved an increasing variety of prokaryotic cells and, from these, larger, more complex organisms. In this ongoing biological evolution some 99% of the organisms that have arisen have become extinct, but such is the proliferation of new evolutionary developments that millions of species of organisms currently exist, (an estimated 30 million species of animals alone, MARGULIS and SAGAN [1]). Much effort has been put into classifying organisms into major groupings (phyla) identifying different species within these phyla and establishing from the fossil record when they came into existence and how currently existing species fit into this scheme. Although a framework of understanding has been established, because of the complexity of the situation biologists are still not clear on some aspects of it. Currently there is a great deal of activity on many fronts, in which scientists seek to identify the different types of organisms that exist, their patterns of behaviour, how they have evolved to become what they are and the nature and workings of the cells and the substances of which they consist. Not having studied and worked in the biological field we have found it difficult to grasp the current state of biological understanding but there would be a large gap in our evolutionary-wholistic account if we did not include biological evolution, so we have done the best that we can to give some account of it from the hK-M point of view.

Living organisms build their body structures out of the substances of the world. With the development of an understanding of chemical reactions and the energetics that drive these and the identification of the molecular structure of DNA which is a central feature of the chemistry of cells, there has been a tendency to concentrate on these aspects of the nature of organisms. While this has resulted in considerable progress, the story is far from complete and new advances are being made all the time. But however much scientists develop accounts of the way that things are, they do not explain why they are the way they are. In putting forward a simplistic, hypothetical account based on the two principles of, first, everything seeking a sense of self and, second, this creating stresses out of which new developments arise, we seek to illustrate how an evolutionary-wholistic hK-M based explanation for the key features of life on Earth may be possible.

The Arising of the First Prokaryotic Cells (Bacteria)

The water on Earth is surrounded on one side by solid - rock, and on the other side by the atmosphere. When it first condenses onto the Earth's surface the water is hot and it takes into solution some of the substances of the rock that it contacts, as various salts. At the same time, as it condenses it brings with it some of the substances of the atmosphere, particularly carbonaceous gases.

As the water cools, it contracts and the substances that it had dissolved at high temperatures create increasing stresses in it. This results in salts crystallising out of the water, while excess gaseous constituents bubble out. In this separation process there arises an intermediate situation in which carbonaceous-rich droplets differentiate out of the salt-containing bulk of the water. The stress set up by the change of conditions across the droplet boundary then causes carbonaceous substances to concentrate there, to form a barrier or membrane. The out-of-balance difference in conditions within the membrane-enclosed droplet to those outside it cause transfer of some substances into the droplet and vice versa.

The pressure of substances inside the droplets causes some of these to combine, where this reduces the stress, which frees energy. This gives the EM-energy undergoing the droplet condition an experience of possessing greater energy and increased activity that gives it a sense of self, i.e. of being a centre of activity, that derives from the flow of substances into, and out of, the droplet. And the more that this happens, the stronger its experience of this sense of self becomes, until it seeks to take over and maintain this pattern of activity for itself, taking in and combining those substances that reduce its internal stress and free energy, and thereby enhance its sense of self and rejecting outwards substances that increase its stress.

In seeking to enhance the sense of self that it gets from the experience of reducing stress and freeing energy, the EM-energy associated with the droplet brings more and more substances together to combine, building up a chain of (DNA) reaction products while, at the same time, inadvertently, creating a structure of substances in the droplet. Thus, as more and more substances enter the droplet from outside and combine together, the encompassing droplet membrane becomes increasingly stressed until it breaks down and divides into two droplets.

[As pointed out in Chapter 4, scientists have reproduced the formation of pre-biotic, membrane-enclosed carbonaceous-rich droplets that grow and divide, in laboratory experiments, (FOX)].

The EM-energy associated with the droplet thereby experiences dividing into two parts when its activity builds up substances to the point where it becomes too stressed to carry this build up further. The two droplets that are formed then go through the same processes of development as the 'parent droplet', until they too divide into two, and so on. In this way small, microscopic, self-procreating organisms - prokaryotic cells (bacteria) come into existence in the watery environment.

[When the EM-energy is pursuing a self-actualising activity within a prokaryotic cell we designate it a prokaryotic entity, and similarly a eukaryotic entity and multicellular entity when it is performing these functions].

In the tempestuous conditions that prevail in this early period of the Earth's existence there is a variety of droplets with different chemical compositions. When the EM-energy experiences that dividing into two is the way to overcome the build up of stress in one type of droplet, it does the same in other types of droplets. Thus, there arises what biologists call a 'radiation' of different types of prokaryotic cells out of the developments taking place in the prebiotic state.

The pattern of stress involved in the prokaryotic entity taking in and rejecting substances gives rise to the formation of a network of flow paths, which gives the cell an inner structure. Likewise, the stress of maintaining itself as an entity separate from, but interacting with, its environment by controlling the flow of substances into and out of the cell causes the prokaryotic entity to develop the structure of its separating membrane. Thereby the cell develops a form and function that represents the activity of the prokaryotic entity. This is the beginning of the principle by which biological organisms develop structures that enable them to carry out the functions (ingestion, digestion, excretion, etc.) that enable the parts of the EM-energy incarnated in them to maintain their existence and sense of self.

The s-entities thereby 'create' life by, inadvertently, pressurising into existence in the EM-energy, interactions between substances that differentiate out of the EM-energy entities with a sense of self that enables them to maintain these activities, in opposition to the s-pressure. Furthermore, in maintaining their existence/sense of self these entities, inadvertently, procreate thereby giving rise to yet more self-actualising entities. They do not do this by intent and they are not concerned with the well-being of their 'progeny', they are not even aware that they have produced any, they are concerned solely with preserving their own activity/sense of self.

The Evolution of Prokaryotic Cells

As the prokaryotic entity divides it loses its sense of self, although it is 'reborn' as two cells. As experience of the stress leading to division builds up in the EM-energy, in its striving to hold onto its sense of self, in some types of cells, instead of a division taking place there occurs a controlled break-out which, as it grows, forms a 'bud'. The part of the EM-energy in the bud then develops its own pattern of activity and sense of self, while the main part retains its integrity. This sets up a stress between these two parts, as a result of which the bud separates off and goes its own way. The prokaryotic entity thereby retains its sense of self and it carries on its activity, to produce another bud that separates off and so on, and the buds grow into independent self-actualising cells and they too bud and reproduce. Thereby two forms of procreation take place, cell division and cell budding and there is great proliferation of the dividing and budding organisms.

It is a basic feature of hK-M that as entities seek a sense of self from their interaction with substance, a spectrum of variations arises. Thus some prokaryotic entities get their sense of self more from the energy of their activity while others are concerned more with the experience of their interaction with their substance bodies. (This is akin to the difference between the sense of self that ballet dancers get from their expression of their high level of activity and lithe bodies compared with weight lifters with their low activity but development of their strong heavy bodies). Where the prokaryotic entity gets its sense of self from increased interaction with substance it builds up its 'body' and thereby its chain of DNA until this becomes stressful and greater than it can control. This causes it to reject the excess DNA that it has built up, (by the same principle as described for the Sun spewing out excess material to give rise to planets). Other prokaryotic cells, which have a high activity but low substance nature, absorb the rejected material and combine it, or part of it, with their own DNA, to reduce the stress of their over activity, in the process known as conjugation. In this way the DNA of different prokaryotic cells (bacteria) becomes mixed, leading to new strains of bacteria more adapted to their environment. This is the beginning of an interaction between different 'sexes' of the same organism, although at this stage it is not linked to reproduction, which continues to take place separately by cell division and cell budding.

[Later in evolution, where a prokaryotic cell rejects excess DNA that it has built up, this can be taken up by a multicellular entity that, because it has a more developed and fixed pattern of activity, cannot accommodate it in the way that a prokaryotic cell can. Then it interferes with the multicellular entity's pattern of activity as a 'virus' in its system.]

The prokaryotic entity maintains its activity, and gets its sense of self, by manipulating substances. Where the reverberations of sunlight penetrate into the watery environment and make its constituents more mobile, this makes it easier for the prokaryotic entity to manipulate substances so as to maintain its activity. Many types of prokaryotic cells thereby arise in which the prokaryotic entities make use of this (photosynthetic) activity to maintain their existence/sense of self. But some prokaryotic entities continue to maintain their activity by combining substances without help from sunlight. These (chemotropic) cells exist mainly in regions around hot vents coming up into the bottom of oceans and in some hot springs.

The substances of the prokaryotic cell body derive largely from the carbonaceous and other gases, which dissolve in the water. As prokaryotic cells proliferate, more and more of these substances are taken up to form them. Thereby they denude the atmosphere of its original constituents and they replace them with those that they expel. From analysis of the gases given out in volcanic activity and the composition of deposits laid down during different eras of the Earth's development, scientists have deduced that the early atmosphere was rich in carbonaceous and sulphurous gases, ammonia and nitrogen, but contained very little oxygen. As the prokaryotic entities combine these constituents with hydrogen from the water, they give out oxygen, resulting in the composition of the Earth's atmosphere as we know it now. At the same time the stresses caused by the changes in the atmosphere bring about new types of cells that maintain their self-actualising activity with the new balance of substances in the environment.

As the prokaryotic entity takes in substances for its sustenance and denudes the surrounding area of these, this creates an out-of-equilibrium stress that moves it towards a region that still contains the substance that it requires for sustenance. The prokaryotic entity thereby experiences satisfaction of its need for sustenance and it takes over this activity and makes it self-actualising. That is, it develops stress-induced self-actualising movement towards substances that maintain its activity, which in turn leads to the development of the ability to 'sense' where higher concentrations of nutrient are. Similarly cells develop the ability to sense the intensity of light so as to move to regions that aid them in carrying out their photosynthetic activity. (The cells that carry out this sensory activity are the forerunners of those that later develop into sense organs in multicellular organisms).

In some areas the substances that prokaryotic cells reject cause them to stick to a base on which they are procreating. Thus, today some ancient rocks (stromatolites) exist which have been built up from layer upon layer of deposits of prokaryotic cells over a period of some 3,500 million years.

Some prokaryotic cells, as they procreate, form agglomerations. However, where cells in the centre of such agglomerations are cut off from their surrounding source of nutrient they die, thus only chain-like formations and mats of prokaryotic cells develop, (as with the algae mats that are seen floating on water now-a-days), in which all cells have sufficient contact with nutrient to survive. In some cases e.g. myxobacteria, when nutrient becomes scarce the overall stress which they experience causes large numbers of individual prokaryotic cells to behave collectively, (like a school of fish or a mass of human beings subjected to a common urge) so that they move together as a whole, inadvertently trapping and absorbing other types of prokaryotic cells i.e 'prey'). Because of their different positions in the collective, cells have different experiences, so that they differentiate into plant-like behaviour, in which outer members of the colony 'reach out' for nutrients, thereby forming a stalk with branches, on which cells that are deprived of nutrient 'hibernate' and form spores that disperse and give rise to new prokaryotic cells when nutrient becomes available, in a seasonal pattern of activity, (STARR and TAGGART). Although this is akin to multicellular behaviour, it is not truly multicellular, in the sense that the cells are not interacting with, and dependent on, each other, as part of an integrated unity that procreates to form another multicellular entity.

The fossil evidence shows that for the first 2,000 million years of the 4,500 million years of the Earth's existence prokaryotic cells in its watery regions were the sole forms of life. As a result of this long period of its prokaryotic cell entity existence the EM-energy acquires vast experience of operating with many substances and of many interactions in which genes are transferred. It thereby becomes very flexible in its abilities, so that innumerable different strains of prokaryotic cells (bacteria) develop that are capable of surviving in many different environments and of coping with environmental changes. When a prokaryotic entity encounters a situation it activates the relevant part of the EM-energy's collective experience to deal with it. Thus, for example, now when a bacterium solves the problem of developing resistance to an antibiotic that threatens to destroy its existence/sense of self in one part of the world, similar bacteria everywhere else draw on this EM-energy experience and likewise develop resistance to the antibiotic. And once bacteria have developed the principle of becoming resistant to one antibiotic they draw on this experience to develop resistance to other antibiotics.

Prokaryotic cells lay down the basic chemistry that sustains all life forms and they are the basis of all living activity. Thus, all living organisms develop out of, and are dependent on, the activities of bacteria. MARGULIS and SAGAN(1) state that our bodies comprise one hundred quadrillion (100,000,000,000,000,000) bacterial cells, together with ten quadrillion eukaryotic cells which have developed from bacterial cells.

The Arising of Eukaryotic Cells

In the 'sea of interaction' taking place in the prokaryotic world there are instances where prokaryotic cells form symbiotic relationships, by one type of cell making use of the excreted products of other types of cells. Where this happens the EM-energy in the region of interaction between the cells experiences a pattern of activity imposed on it, which invokes in it a sense of self, as a centre of activity. The stronger the build up of the sense of self that the EM-energy experiences, the more it seeks to maintain the activities that give rise to it. The only way that it knows to do this is from its experience as a prokaryotic cell, so it seeks to become 'a larger prokaryotic cell', that is, a 'super-cell' that encompasses the interaction of the group of prokaryotic cells. However, the autonomous prokaryotic cells are pursuing their own, independent, patterns of activity. As a result of the stress that it experiences in its striving to control these it uses one type of prokaryotic cell as a control centre, a nucleus, by which it monitors and controls the flow of substances through its super-cell, in relation to the activities of the other prokaryotic cells that it encompasses. When it is able to do this, in pursuing its sense of self it builds up its super-cell more and more, until it becomes larger than it can control which creates a state of stress in it. This then triggers its prokaryotic memory experience that the way to cope with this is to divide. And at this stage stable procreating eukaryotic cells come into existence.

Once this new level of sense of self becomes established in the EM-energy for one symbiotic relationship, it develops it in other relationships and it thereby becomes able to maintain a eukaryotic existence with other symbiotic interactions and hence a 'radiation' of a variety of eukaryotic cells occurs.

As a prokaryotic cell takes in and expels substances from its environment, this disturbs and creates non-uniformity in their distribution in the mineral kingdom. The s-pressure acts to unify this situation, resulting in diffusion of substances to restore equilibrium. In the eukaryotic cell the motion of substance is driven by the interacting prokaryotic components of which it consists, which the self-actualising eukaryotic entity takes over. This manifests as a more intense activity and motion that can be seen in eukaryotic cells, compared with the more passive 'drifting' movement in prokaryotic cells, MARGULIS and SAGAN (1).

Whereas the sense of self of a prokaryotic entity is analogous to that which a workman gets from manipulating the materials of the world, the sense of self of a eukaryotic entity is analogous to, but at a much less evolved level than, that of a 'foreman' who controls the activities of a group of workmen. It is the sense of self got from playing a larger role in the activities of life.

In some types of eukaryotic cell, as with prokaryotic cells, the eukaryotic entity experiences that as it divides it loses its sense of self and this activates its prokaryotic experience that the way to overcome this is by separating off a bud, so that it retains its integrity. In this way some eukaryotic cells develop procreation by budding. However, whether the eukaryotic entity procreates by division or budding, it has no awareness that it is procreating and it has no concern for its progeny, it seeks only to maintain the activity that gives it a sense of self.

In its seeking for sustenance from its environment the larger eukaryotic cell encounters prokaryotic cells and, in pressing on with its pattern of activity, it wraps itself around, and encompasses the smaller prokaryotic entity. The prokaryotic cell then disintegrates and the encompassing eukaryotic cell absorbs the disintegration products. As this experience builds up in the EM-energy, the eukaryotic entity makes the capture and ingestion of prokaryotic cells a self-actualising activity. At the same time, the stresses of disintegrating and absorbing the prokaryotic cell cause the eukaryotic entity to develop a rudimentary gut system. Thus an evolved eukaryotic cell, such as the paramecium comprises, in limited form, many of the functions that later become highly developed in more-evolved multicellular organisms.

As they evolve, eukaryotic entities recapitulate the experiences of the EM-energy of conjugation developed by prokaryotic cells, in which 'male' cells eject excess, stress-causing substances (DNA) which is then absorbed by 'female' cells, thereby reducing the stress in these. Repeated experience of this 'male–female' interaction builds up the association in the EM-energy that it is stress reducing. Some eukaryotic entities experience seasonal stresses due to lack of nutrient and/or prokaryotic cells on which they feed, particularly where photosynthetic activity is involved. This stress causes the 'male' and 'female' versions to come into closer interaction, which results in them mating and fusing. (The principle by which eukaryotic cells reduce their stresses by fusing together is same, but at a much less evolved level, as when, in a male-female relationship, we experience emotional stress and seek solace by coming together, and also the way in which positively and negatively charged particles mechanically come together to neutralise their stress fields). The fused cells then enter into a hibernation state, as dormant spores, until nutrient becomes available again, when they divide and continue their separate existences, as with the single-celled algae Chlamydomonas. This gives rise to seasonal biorhythms of growth, and fusion with spore formation and hibernation in these cells (MARGULIS and SAGAN[2]), that the eukaryotic entities take over and make their own.

Since they encompass several prokaryotic cells, eukaryotic cells are larger organisms, but they are still very small, only just visible to the naked eye; a common example is unicellular amoebae. As with prokaryotic cells, as they procreate some eukaryotic cells form colonies and again, as with prokaryotic cells, in some cases when food becomes scarce the overall stress causes the members of the colony to act in concert, to form a 'slug' that moves around seeking food (slime moulds). With the scarcity of nutrient then, as with the myxobacteria prokaryotic cell-type of behaviour, it forms a stalk with a 'fruiting body' that forms spores which, when nutrient becomes available, develop into amoeba-like cells and the cycle is repeated. As with prokaryotic cells, although this is multicellular-like behaviour, the slug is not a truly multicellular entity in that cells do not differentiate to become part of an overall integrated pattern of self-actualising activity that procreates to produce a replica of itself.

The fossil evidence shows that the eukaryotic era existed for a period of 1,500 million years after the 2000 million year prokaryotic era, so that minute single cells, prokaryotic (bacteria) and eukaryotic were the only forms of life on Earth for the first 3,500 million years, out of the 4,500 million years of its existence.

[As we have stated, once the first prokaryotic cells appeared there was a 'radiation' of different types and similarly, once the first eukaryotic cell arose there was a radiation of different species of these. These are examples of the 'punctuated equilibrium' principle, in which developments take place for a long time along established lines in the only way then known until, out of this situation, there arises the potential for a new type of development. Once this new potential is experienced it is exploited in all its possibilities, to give rise to a radiation of many forms of the new development. An example of this principle, that we are currently in the middle of, is the evolution of the computer era. This arose from an initially small aspect of the era of mechanical-electrical developments that gave rise to our modern industrialised society. As mechanical-electrical mechanisms grew larger and more complicated, increasingly larger control systems were required, which created a stress/need for a smaller, more compact way of doing this. Out of research into ways of trying to improve the situation, (in this case specifically the problem of the increasing size and complexity of telephone exchanges), a new development emerged, the transistor, which offered a simplified non-mechanical way of miniaturising control systems, (BRAUN and McDONALD). There followed a period of intense activity of pursuing the potentials of this new development, giving rise to ever-greater miniaturisation, leading to the development of the modern computer that then 'radiated' out into all areas of human activity. This is thus an example of punctuated equilibrium, in which the evolution of engineering activity, that had been steadily taking place along established mechanical-electrical lines, underwent a jump to a new electronic level].

The Arising of Multicellular Organisms

As with prokaryotic cells, when eukaryotic cells proliferate and form colonies, chain and mat formations develop where all cells are in contact with nutrient. But also, in some cases the cells form a cluster, in which the deprivation of a supply of nutrient to the cells in the centre of the cluster creates a pattern of stress in the EM-energy encompassing the colony. Because they are multi-component, eukaryotic cells possess greater flexibility than prokaryotic cells so that, instead of cells cut off from nutrient dying, as with prokaryotic cells, the other cells respond to the stress in a way that brings about a flow of nutrient to the cut-off cells. The encompassing EM-energy involved in this integrating activity experiences a sense of self and it becomes self-actualising, and it takes over control of the integration and functioning of the colony of cells. In pursuing its sense of self it then builds up the colony until this becomes more than it can control and this activates the EM-energy's experience that the way to cope with this situation is for it to divide into two or to bud. In this way small procreating multicellular organisms arise, in which a 'multicellular entity' controls the activities of a number of eukaryotic entities, which, in turn, control the activities of prokaryotic entities. This gave rise to small multicellular amoeba-like organisms (like Trichoplax) in the watery regions of the Earth about 700 million years ago.

Once the experience of multi-cellularity is established in the EM-energy it is triggered in many situations, to give rise to a radiation of a number of different types (phyla) of multicellular entities that procreate by division or budding.

As multicellular organisms use up the nutrients in their environment, proliferate into different environments and/or the environment changes and/or they grow larger, they experience stresses, which they impose on the group of eukaryotic cells that they encompass. The multicellular entities and their bodies of cells that comprise the adult organisms are too established in their patterns of activities to be able to change, but the buds that have not yet developed the pattern of activity of the parent organisms experience the stress. As a result, the buds develop differently to the parent organism, in a way that leads to the arising of new species of multicellular entities that are adapted to the new environment.

As with the prokaryotic and eukaryotic levels of evolution, there develop different balances between the activity of the multicellular entity and the substance with which it interacts, to give rise to male and female versions of the species. These interact by conjugation in which the 'male' ejects material that is absorbed by the female, in the way developed by prokaryotic and eukaryotic organisms. This leads to a new method of procreation, in addition to dividing and budding, in which the female organism, in relieving the stress of excess activity, ejects material as egg cells, while the male ejects sperm cells. When these 'sex' cells separate from the parent organisms, because of their different imbalances between activity and substance, they create opposite stresses in the EM-energy, that cause them to come together and fuse, to complement each other. They then form a fertilised egg that grows and divides to build up a fully formed organism. Thereby, instead of asexual dividing or budding that produces copies of the single parent, sexual procreation takes place as a result of the interaction between male and female parents, each of which makes its contribution to its progeny. But, again this is not by design or with any concern for the progeny, it occurs entirely inadvertently, with the parent entities concerned solely with maintaining their sense of self.

Out of the many lines of evolution of multicellular organisms that develop sexual procreation, three give rise to larger organisms, namely animals, plants and fungi, that by their extensive proliferation and evolution transform the face of the Earth, (some members of each kingdom also continue to procreate asexually).

In sexual procreation animals develop from embryos that form from a male-fertilised female egg that divides and grows to form a ball of cells that, with further growth becomes hollow - a blastula - that, with continued cell division, the formation of communicating cell junctions, the realignment of cells and their movement over each other, and the death of some of them according to an overall scheme, takes on the shape of the embryo which then grows into the adult animal. These activities require considerable mobility of the substances involved so that animals first arose in the watery environment of the oceans about 600 million years ago, and many species of animals are still ocean dwellers but ways of procreating in a non-aqueous environment then developed, to give rise to animal life on land.

Plants evolved from multicellular colonies that remained attached to a base on which they were dividing, that spread out of marginal areas of water onto land and developed ways of absorbing nutrients in non-aqueous conditions, so as to maintain their existence and sense of self. They develop from embryos formed from a male-sperm-fertilised female egg but the development of the embryo is simpler than with animals, in that each cell is fixed in place in relation to its neighbours, there is no movement or realignment relative to each other. Cells simply divide and differentiate to take up the form and functioning of the plant. In their growth plants absorb energy from the Sun and they provide nutrition for animals that cannot do this for themselves.

The other type of multicellular organism that arose and has evolved to become a major part of life on Earth is fungi. Some fungi live by breaking down and recycling dead organisms, some live parasitically off live organisms and some live symbiotically in association with plants. They create a supply of nutrients on which plants and in turn animals depend for their existence. They comprise networks of fine threads or tubes (hyphae) that interpenetrate the organism that they are living off and they procreate asexually by dividing or budding. Also hyphae of the same, or different fungi fuse and 'mate' sexually to give rise to fruiting bodies, such as mushrooms: they do not create embryos as animals and plants do.

We consider briefly each of these three kingdoms of Nature, starting with the animal kingdom.

The Evolution of the Animal Kingdom

The first animals to arise were very small jelly-like creatures, like Trichoplax, which resembles a large amoeba. Because it is not confined within a limiting membrane, as the EM-energy incarnated in multicellular entities seeks increasing sense of self, it becomes able to deal with increasing procreation of the eukaryotic cells taking place within it, leading to larger animals. The forms and functions of the animals that develop are determined by two factors. First the stresses that arise from seeking to maintain a sense of self in relation to their environment, that comprise primarily stresses for survival, i.e. seeking nutrition, capture of prey and/or escape from predators. These in turn create stresses for movement that give rise to locomotive systems, stresses for awareness that give rise to sensory systems, also digestive systems, etc. which form the animal's body structures and patterns of behaviour. Second, procreation stresses that progeny create by their striving for a sense of self that react on and modify the parental biological organisation and behaviour.

Nutritional – Survival Stresses

As we have already stated, nutritional-survival stresses come about as organisms multiply and/or grow larger and use up the nutrients in their environment. Also stresses arise due to changes in the Earth situation. Fossil evidence shows that there have been many catastrophes as a result of which large numbers of species have been wiped out, as with the catastrophe that obliterated the dinosaurs, as well as a number of ice ages that changed the climate in which organisms had to survive. The causes of these catastrophes are thought to be large impacting meteorites and the break up of the Earth's crust from a single world continent, Pangaea, into the different continents of which it now consists, MARGULIS and SAGAN (1). Whatever the cause there is no doubt that there have been major events that have had a dramatic effect on life on Earth, wiping out many of the types of organisms that then existed, with stresses arising from the changed environment giving rise to new species.

The first era of animal development took place along 'established lines', that is, from the first small Trichoplax-like organisms there developed a variety of larger soft-bodied creatures of worm-like and jelly-fish-like shapes that resulted from, and were adapted to, the stresses which they experienced in maintaining a sense of self in their environment. This era took place about 700 million to 600 million years ago.

In some cases, in its cycling of substances, the materials that the multicellular entity rejected were not absorbed by the water of its environment so that they built up a layer around it. This reinforced the organism's sense of self as something separate from its environment (as with prebiotic droplets that developed separating membranes) and it took over this activity and made it self-actualising. In some cases the rejected substances derived from dissolved rock and the rejection of this gave rise to a 'rock-like' shell around the organism. In other cases the rejected substances were carbonaceous materials and these caused a chitin (finger nail-like) type of substance to form around the organism. The rejected material followed the stress pattern of interaction of the organism with its environment and gave the organism its characteristic shape. At the same time it gave firmness and support to an otherwise jelly-like body, which enhanced the sense of self of the multicellular entity. The rejection of 'rock' around the organism gave rise to a radiation of shelled creatures and the rejection of chitin to trilobites and similar creatures, about 600 million years ago.

The stresses involved in organisms seeking for nutrient to maintain their sense of self gave rise to more efficient locomotion and body shapes, paddles, fins, etc. which promoted this. The operation of these body features created internal stresses that resulted in substances being deposited out along the internal stress lines and thereby organisms developed a cartilaginous or skeletal internal structure that strengthened their functioning.

[We consider substance formations developing along stress lines/patterns for the simpler case of crystallisation from solution, in our experimental work described in Part IV of this book].

This gave rise to an era of vertebrate fishes with their skeletons and jaws that came into existence about 500 million years ago. With the development of jaws predator-prey activity evolved, so that instead of living off prokaryotic and eukaryotic cells, jawed fish also consume smaller multicellular organisms.

The stresses that arose from the need for the distribution of nutrient to the different types of cells that make up the multicellular entity gave rise to a digestive system and specialisation of cells to do this and similarly to an excretion system. The more-advanced locomotion system led to specialisation of cells for this function and, similarly, the evolution of the predator-prey activity was associated with specialisation of cells. As each system became established, the part of the multicellular entity involved got its own specialised sense of self. In this way, as with an expanding human organisation, semi-autonomous sub-systems arose within the overall system, giving rise to discrete organs and systems within the multicellular entity. As these developments took place the multicellular entity experienced stresses in maintaining the co-ordination of these different systems. This resulted in the development of a central region to which the activities of the other regions were monitored and controlled, giving rise to a brain with a nervous system that follows the stress pattern involved in the monitoring and controlling processes.

Procreation Stresses

During these eras of evolution, at first the male and female organisms, in relieving the stresses that built up inside them randomly jettisoned sperm and eggs. Where these met and fused, as a result of a combination of chance and the opposite, mutually attractive, stresses that they created in the space-energy, they gave rise to progeny that developed a sense of self. But in this random process many of the eggs and sperm did not meet and therefore did not get the opportunity to develop a sense of self. As the experience of the sperm and eggs built up in the EM-energy, that the way to achieve a sense of self was for them to come together and fuse they exerted a stress on the multicellular parent entities to bring this about. Thus, the female became impelled to eject her eggs in coordination with the male ejecting its sperm, as many fish and frogs now do, which increased the possibility of fertilisation of the eggs by the sperm and the survival of the progeny. However, many of the fertilised eggs were consumed by predators and, in its stress to avoid this and maintain its sense of self, the egg exerted stresses that registered in the EM-energy which caused it, in its incarnated state in the mother to provide protection for the eggs' development. Thus, mouth-brooding fishes carry their eggs in their mouths until they hatch. Nile crocodiles guard their eggs against predators until they hatch and they then carry the baby crocodiles around in their mouths to protect them. The females of star fishes, sea urchins, sponges and the edible oyster retain their eggs inside their bodies and draw in sperm from the surrounding water to fertilise them and the embryos then grow protected by the mother. At the same time the stress to ensure fertilisation of the eggs resulted in more positive methods by the male to transfer sperm to them. For example, octopuses, sharks and rays eject their sperm in enclosed packets (spermatophores) that they thrust into the female's genital tract, (CATTON and GRAY).

As they proliferated, organisms spread out into the environment around them and they sought to maintain their sense of self in any new circumstances that they encountered. The fossil evidence shows that about 500 million years ago creeping and crawling creatures emerged from the watery environment onto land (McLEOD and BRADDY). About 100 million years later photosynthesising plant-like organisms adapted to existence on land. This provided nutrition for larger animals then to move onto land. As animals moved from an aqueous environment to a land-based existence stresses to obtain nutrient in the new situation gave rise to a variety of body forms, that could reach into vegetation, dig down into the earth, capture and/or escape from prey. At the same time, sexual activity and procreation developed to adapt to the new environment. At first organisms continued their established patterns of behaviour, i.e. they returned to the watery environment to procreate, as the amphibians such as frogs, toads, newts, etc. now do. As they continued to expand onto land a stress developed to procreate on land but the fusion of sperm and egg and the development of the embryo in the egg required movement of substances in a fluid environment and hence protection of the egg from drying out. The stress that the egg then exerted on the Mother, activated the experience of the EM-energy (from its shelled creature existence) that a shell provides such protection. This resulted in the animal producing a shell around the fertilised egg, which gave rise to the age of reptiles. At first, once the egg was fertilised the female ejected it and left it to fend for itself, as with turtles, (but the fertilised egg exerted a stress on the female to lay its eggs at a time and place which was activated from the EM-energy as suitable for the development of its existence and sense of self). Then the stress that the fertilised egg exerted on the female caused her to retain it and to gestate it within the protection of her body, as with crocodiles and birds, so that she gave birth to live young. (The power of the sense of self of the embryo in the egg can be seen from the behaviour of the cuckoo which, as soon as it emerges from the egg as a weak scrawny, sightless hatchling, sets about ejecting the rightful eggs and hatchlings from the nest, so that it is the sole occupant to be brought up by its 'foster' parents, STARR and TAGGART).

While the embryo was gestating within the body of its Mother it drew on her for sustenance to develop its body and sense of self. After it was born it continued to exert a stress for sustenance, which gave rise to mammary glands to feed it, as with the egg laying platypus, the marsupials and the placental mammals. The mother then experienced an enhanced creative sense of self by carrying out this process of protecting and caring for her progeny.

Where fertilisation of the egg takes place within the female body it creates an embryo that, in seeking a sense of self, imposes stresses on the parents that affect their development and behaviour. We can get some feeling for the effects of stresses created by progeny by looking at how they work now, in more advanced form, in our own lives. We experience stresses that cause us to form a sexual relationship with someone of the opposite sex. In many cases this sexual activity is not concerned with desire for progeny but if it results in fertilisation of the egg within the female, then progeny inadvertently arise. The embryo then grows inside the female until it exerts a stress that causes her to eject it. The Mother then experiences stress from the demands made on her by the infant for care and attention, the provision of which gives her an enhanced sense of self, from the fulfilment of her creative potential, and evokes in her feelings of love and concern. As our children grow up they exert stresses on us that cause us to modify our life styles to satisfy their demands and we experience an enhanced sense of self from being concerned with their well-being. Then, instead of simply responding to stresses/pressure from our children, we make this self-actualising and positively seek to promote their well-being, and thereby we feel ourselves to be actively participating in advancing creation by contributing to the development of the next generation.

The more experience that the EM-energy acquires, the more it has to draw on when it cycles through the multicellular state and encounters different environments and stresses. After the extinction of the dinosaurs and many other forms of life about 66 million years ago, there remained small shrew-like mammals that moved around rapidly from branch to branch in trees. In pursuing a sense of self without the presence of large predators they got bigger, while the stresses of this form of existence gave rise to grasping hands and feet to hold more firmly onto tree branches, together with stereoscopic vision to judge distances accurately, giving rise to monkeys and then apes. Changing environmental conditions then gave rise to bipedal movement and a more versatile use of their hands, that were no longer required for holding onto branches. Scientists used to think that this came about as the result of deforestation of some areas of their habitat, so that they had to move around upright in savannah. But the fossil evidence now points to hominids arising in watery forest margins, living on a succulent diet of marsh and riverside vegetation and leading a partially aquatic existence that supported an upright posture and freed hands for the development of manipulation of objects, leading to the use of stones for tools to break open shell fish, as some sea otters do. This is in accord with physiological evidence that, unlike other primates we are not covered in hair and we possess a layer of fat which promotes buoyancy, so that new-born babies can swim and float, together with other physical and biochemical features that support this hypothesis (DOUGLAS). Whatever the cause of this development, bipedalism gave rise to the first hominids

The Evolution of Plants

It is thought that the first land-based plants evolved from photosynthesising algae that existed in wet, sunlit shallows around the peripheries of oceans, lakes, rivers, etc. During periods when these shallows dried up the algae retained sufficient moisture for the male sperm to swim to and fertilise the female egg. This gave rise to small plants on land that were only a few centimetres in height, without stems and only small branch-like outgrowths to support photosynthesis, akin to modern mosses and liverworts. These 'amphibious' plants were comparable to the development of amphibians in the animal kingdom in that, although existing on land; they were tied to water to reproduce.

The cycling of the Sun's and Earth's force fields acted on the multicellular entities associated with the algae. This resulted in them extending down into the earth and developing roots to increase their contact with the supply of water and nutrients, and up into the atmosphere, with the development of foliage which increased their exposure to sunlight and their photosynthesising of substances, together with the development of stems that transported fluid and substances from roots to leaves and vice versa. In seeking an enhanced sense of self, plant entities pursued this activity, resulting in root, stem and leaf systems that follow the stress patterns generated by them doing this.

In moving from water to land, plants, as with animals, encountered two types of stresses, first a stress to survive and maintain a sense of self, that required obtaining nutrient and secondly a stress to adapt to the stresses created by progeny seeking a sense of self. Because it is fixed in place, the plant's nutrition system is simpler than that of animals, so that this aspect of the plant kingdom's evolution was limited to developments on the root-stem-foliage theme. The response of plants to the stresses of progeny followed a similar pattern to that of the animal kingdom, i.e. increasing protection of the embryo by the mother but the plant had to resolve this problem in situ. This led to three major phases in the development of plants that are characterised by the way in which they procreate, (THOMAS).

The first rudimentary 'non-amphibian' plants, fully adapted to a land-based existence, arose about 400 million years ago; they were like bundles of green stems that photosynthesised substances, with a rudimentary root-like contact with the ground. From this small beginning, in seeking nutrient to pursue an enhanced sense of self, plant entities generated larger and larger structures, with larger and larger root formations for getting greater amounts of water and nutrients, larger and larger leaf systems for photosynthesising more substances and larger and stronger stems to transport materials up and down to support these activities. This led to an era of forests of great fern-like trees that developed about 350 million years ago. At the same time, in the same way that animals rejected substances, to give rise to shell or chitenous material that outlined their patterns of activity and increased their sense of self, plant entities similarly rejected cellulosic substances and, with the development of trees, lignin. Thereby the plant entity developed a rigid outer layer to its root-leaf-stem structure.

As with the animal kingdom, as plants became more evolved they developed internal stresses due to imbalances in their energy-substance activities which caused them to develop male or female characteristics. And, again as with animals, the female rejected eggs and the male rejected sperm. Where they fell on moist and fertile ground these grew into small plantlets, which then produced eggs and sperm (on separate plantlets or sometimes on the same plantlet) with the sperm swimming through a film of moisture to fertilise the egg, from which a spore-producing plant grew and the cycle was repeated. This is the way in which the tree ferns and other plants that arose in the first phase of the development of land plants procreated. Although these have largely been replaced by the plants of the subsequent two phases of development, they continue to exist in a few places.

As plants developed roots to take in water from deeper in the earth they became able to survive in drier terrain but in the absence of a moist surface for the male sperm to travel to the female egg, their spores did not survive for long. As with the animal kingdom, in their seeking to survive the spore entities exerted a stress on the parent plant entities to maintain their sense of self. Then, instead of expelling the spores, the parent plant entities retained them so that they started their development within the moist tissues of the parent plants. The female plant entity invested the egg with a surround of starch-like substance that provided an initial source of nutrition and a protective coating, (comparable with the yolk and shell provided for the animal kingdom egg), while the male sperm was encapsulated and kept moist, in pollen grains. The egg remained on the plant and the pollen was freed, and where it was transported by the wind to come into contact with an egg it fertilised it to form a seed that contained an embryo for a new plant. The seed then separated from the parent plant and, where it came into contact with moist and fertile soil it grew into a new plant and the cycle of developments was repeated. This is characteristic of conifers where the female cone harbours the egg and the male cone the pollen that contains the sperm.

Because of its protective coating and food store the seed has a much greater chance of survival and of developing its sense of self than does the spore, so that seed-bearing plants became prolific and largely replaced the seedless spore-producing plants. Thereby large forests of conifers arose during this second phase of plant evolution. The plants that arose later, during the third phase of development, have replaced many of these but they still exist in appreciable numbers.

Although seeds have a better opportunity to survive and to maintain the embryo plant's sense of self, they require the precarious wind transport of sperm to egg to produce the fertile seed. The stress for survival to develop a sense of self, exerted by egg and sperm on the parent plant led to a further phase of plant evolution. In this it activated from the inadvertent experiences registered in the EM-energy the transport of pollen to the female egg by insects and birds, to form seeds within the protective environment of the female. At the same time the plant produced coloured petals, nectar and perfumes that attracted the insects that carry pollen to the egg, which is a more efficient and positive process than wind transport. In a further stage of development, in some plants the transport of seeds into the environment was aided by the growth around the seed of a fleshy edible fruit covering, as with blackberries, cherries, etc. that ensured dispersal when eaten by birds and animals. This has led to co-evolution of some plants and insects to such an extent that the shapes and colours of flowers and insect body shapes have become perfectly adapted to their complementary roles. In some cases this has occurred to the point where the flowers and insects (butterflies, moths and small birds) have become totally dependent on each other, so that if the type of flower, insect or bird were to become extinct the partner would not be able to survive, (STARR and TAGGART). The success of flowering plants has led to them becoming dominant, largely replacing the other types of plants.

The fossil evidence suggests that a primitive form of flower first developed on a magnolia type of tree about 130 million years ago, by some of its leaves developing a bud and flower-like structure with coloured leaves. This is an example of a key feature of *h*K-M, i.e. the punctuated equilibrium principle, that evolution continues in the then established way until this, inadvertently, throws up a new potential for development that opens up a new era of evolution. During the evolution of the period in which plants developed better leaf systems for absorbing sunlight and thereby generating, photo-synthetically, more nutrients for its growth and procreation, the striving for increasing sense of self and the stress to achieve this gave rise to changes in colour and composition of the leaves, that insects found more satisfying. This led to increased procreation that registered in the EM-energy and was activated by the stress of the eggs/sperm that were seeking sense of self. Then, as experience of the success of the flower in giving greater opportunity for the development of a sense of self by the egg built up in the EM-energy, this became activated again and again in more and more circumstances. Thus a great range of flowering plants of all types developed, e.g. trees, shrubs, grasses, crop plants such as wheat, annual and perennial plants, cacti, etc. As a result there arose the wonderful profusion of flowering plants around us, where none existed before. There are now about 250,000 known species of flowering plants and more are being discovered all the time, compared with about 10,000 species of the other types of plants.

The protection and fertilisation of the female egg by male sperm in plants occurred at the same time as these processes took place in the animal kingdom to give rise to mammals, MARGULIS and SAGAN(1). This is because in both cases the stress to survive and maintain a sense of self acted on the experience that had built up in the EM-energy to produce a similar response.

The Evolution of Fungi

Fungi live by breaking down dead organisms, by living parasitically off live ones, or by forming symbiotic relationships with plants. Most fungi are multicellular but a few, like yeast, remain at the unicellular eukaryotic stage of development. A few grow under water or in the sea but they are mostly land organisms. Fungi can be the cause of diseases in animals and plants but mostly they form constructive relationships. Scientists think that probably a symbiotic relationship had formed between the first algae that lived on land and fungi, so that they developed the ability to live on land together. Most plants seem to depend on this symbiosis, with fungi supplying their soil phosphorus and nitrogen; fungi are synergistically intertwined in the roots of more than 95% of plant species, as root growths (mycorrhizae) that result from the dual growth of fungi and plants; more than 5,000 different mycorrhizae have been discovered. Orchid seeds will not germinate unless a mycorrhizae invades them. Some of the oldest plant fossils show evidence of symbiotic fungi, (MARGULIS and SAGAN [3]).

The fungus makes nutrients available to the plant, while the plant supplies the fungus with photosynthetic products. Lichens, for example, are a combination of fungi and green algae or blue-green bacteria. The fungi break down rock and turn it into nutrients on which the algae, (and subsequently other plants), can live, with the algae supplying the photo-synthetically produced substances that the combination needs to live. There are some 25,000 species of lichens and they exist everywhere, even in the most barren environments.

Fungi develop from spores and usually grow as elongated cells that form thin tubes (hyphae) that spread out to locate food, to give rise to undifferentiated masses of fungal threads with no clear borders that can cover a vast area and be very ancient. The hyphae cell walls, that are strong and tough, are made of chitin and there are passages between the cells that allow nutrient to move from the absorptive parts to other non-absorptive parts, such as reproductive structures.

Fungi do not require sex to reproduce but as they spread out, hyphae of the same type or different types meet and fuse and from this 'sexual mating' mushrooms, puffballs, shelf fungi and the like are formed that give off millions of fine spores that are spread everywhere by the wind, and when these settle on anything on which they can germinate, further fungal growths develop. While fungi have developed sexual procreation to produce fruiting bodies, they have not developed the formation of an embryo that is protected by the mother, as animals and plants have.

There are vast numbers of species of fungi; 50,000 have so far been identified out of an estimated one and a half million. They are able to thrive on a great variety of substances and they inhabit seemingly inhospitable domains.

From the point of view of hK-M, fungi develop from eukaryotic cells that, in their striving for a sense of self, evolve the ability to live off, and derive nutrient from, the substances of the earth and thereby to colonise land. They did not themselves develop photosynthesis but by interaction with cells that had evolved this ability they developed a symbiotic relationship that registered in, was activated from, and built up by repeated experience of the EM-energy, to give rise to the situation that exists now. The evolution of the structure of multicellular fungi has been driven by the fungus entity seeking a sense of self that has given rise to the stress to seek nutrient which, in turn, has led to the spreading hyphae form of the fungus, that follows the nutrient-seeking stress pattern. As we have stated previously, we deal with how plant-like stress forms arise in Part IV.

The Pattern of Life on Earth

The popular view of Nature is that it comprises three kingdoms, namely, mineral, plant and animal. But biologists who have greater awareness of the diversity of the organisms that exist on Earth and the ways in which these have evolved, are not satisfied with this simple division into plants and animals and they have sought better ways of classifying them to reflect their evolutionary development, exemplified by MARGULIS and SCHWARTZ. This approach is in accord with the evolutionary-wholistic viewpoint of *h*K-M, in which the basis for understanding anything is the way in which it has evolved from, and is part of, the whole. However, there are some differences between the scheme described by Margulis and Schwartz and the viewpoint of *h*K-M.

Margulis and Schwartz propose first a major division into prokaryotic organisms that existed for the first 2000 million years of life on Earth and eukaryotic cellular life that came later. The eukaryotic cell comprises a symbiotic association of prokaryotic cells and scientists regard its primary distinguishing feature as that it possesses a membrane-enclosed nucleus. According to *hK-M* the symbiotic integration of several prokaryotic cells led to the arising of a new level of controlling eukaryotic entity differentiating out of the EM-energy and it is the controlling eukaryotic entity that is the distinguishing feature of eukaryotic cells, with the cell nucleus through which it regulates the prokaryotic activities, as a secondary feature. There are in fact, many instances of eukaryotic cells that possess more than one, even many, nuclei which makes the criterion for classification as the possession of a cell nucleus difficult but from the viewpoint of *h*K-M all of these single or multi nuclei eukaryotic cells are organisms that are under the control of a eukaryotic entity.

As a result of symbiosis a large variety of interacting combinations of different prokaryotic cells arose, to give rise to a multiplicity of single-celled, and multicellular eukaryotic organisms, which Margulis and Schwartz call the kingdom of Protoctista. These exhibit a variety of sexual and procreative behaviour. In some cases, like prokaryotic bacteria, the 'male' ejects excess DNA into the environment that is absorbed by the 'female' in the process of conjugation. In other cases there is an exchange of DNA by intimate contact between the two 'sexes', which in some instances leads to complete fusion between them. Some protoctists have developed sperm-egg procreation. Out of these, in their classification system, Margulis and Schwartz define three lines of development of larger organisms, i.e. animals, plants and fungi, depending on the way in which these procreate. Animals develop from embryos that arise from sperm-egg unions; fungi grow from spores that are asexually or sexually produced without sperm-egg embryo formation; plants develop both from spores and sperm-egg sexually produced embryos.

This aspect of Margulis and Schwartz's choice of a basis for classification is not entirely in accord with *h*K-M, in which the key features are the number of levels and the corresponding hierarchy of controlling entities in an organism. Thus Margulis and Schwartz's kingdom of Protoctista includes single eukaryotic cells that, according to *h*K-M are under the control of a eukaryotic entity, and multicellular eukaryotes that are under the control of a multicellular entity and therefore represent a more advanced phase of evolution. Again, according to *h*K-M, the sexual and reproductive behaviour, on which Margulis and Schwartz's classification depends, is not primary but a secondary manifestation of the way in which an organism develops its response to the sexual stresses that arise in it, i.e. whether it simply discards its eggs or sperm, or acts to bring them together to give rise to progeny and the degree to which it supports the development of these.

Another feature of Margulis and Schwartz's classification is that it does not see any significant difference between homo sapiens and earlier hominids, with them all being part of the pattern of biological animal evolution on Earth. In fact Margulis and Schwartz (and most other biologists) emphasise that there is no foundation for the old view of humanity being a 'special creation'. *h*K-M, however, sees homo sapiens as possessing a spirit that derives from an entity in the Omniverse Hierarchy that inhabits a biologically-developed body and which therefore is a 'special creation' that cannot be classified as part of the animal kingdom.

Some Specific Aspects of Biological Evolution

In this section we consider three aspects of biological evolution, namely Symbiogenesis, the EM-energy and the Genetic Viewpoint

Symbiogenesis

The idea that eukaryotic cells arose out of symbiotic activity between prokaryotic cells is one that has been proposed by a number of scientists, particularly by MARGULIS. This has been supported by the finding that the different components of a eukaryotic cell possess different DNA from the nucleus but similar to those of free living prokaryotic cells, from which they are therefore presumed to have derived. Margulis has given the name 'symbiogenesis' to the coming together of prokaryotic cells to make eukaryotic cells and eukaryotic cells coming together to make multicellular entities. But there is a difference between this viewpoint and that of *h*K-M. The scientific view is that in the formation of a eukaryotic cell, a group of prokaryotic cells develop symbiotic relationships in which they fuse and act in concert, with one cell absorbing the others and, through the activity of its nucleus, controlling the others. According to *h*K-M, it is the pattern of activity which the symbiotically-interacting prokaryotic cells create in the space-energy that gives this a sense of self to cause it to differentiate out and take over this role and become self actualising, using the activity of one type of prokaryotic cell as the basis to monitor that of the other cells against. According to *h*K-M, this is a general principle that also accounts for the arising of the integrated activity of a multicellular organism, by the differentiation out of the space-energy of a multicellular entity. It is difficult to imagine extending the Margulis symbiogenesis viewpoint to account for the large number of cells in a multicellular entity acting together in an integrated way as a result of one cell, or group of cells, taking over control of the others. According to *h*K-M, the general principle that, as entities evolve they create a higher level of activity in the space-energy which then differentiates out and becomes self actualising, operates at all levels. It explains the formation not only of eukaryotic and multicellular organisms, with their controlling centres, but also the formation of the feeling-soul and thinking-mind, into which an entity (spirit) incarnates from the Omniverse Hierarchy, as explained in Chapter 4.

MARGULIS finds that with her symbiogenesis theory she cannot explain how the first prokaryotic cells arose, whereas with *h*K-M the same principle that gave rise to prokaryotic cells, eukaryotic cells, multicellular entities, the hominid feeling soul and spirit thinking activity, also accounts for the coming into existence of prokaryotic cells in the first place. Thus, as explained earlier, environmental forces induced chemical reactions between substances in pre-biotic droplets that gave the EM-energy involved a sense of self, so that it took over this activity and made it self actualising to give rise to prokaryotic entities which control the activities of prokaryotic cells.

The Earth-Memory Energy

According to *h*K-M the key factor in the evolution of life on Earth is the EM-energy, i.e. the part of the space-energy that has experienced, and is associated with, the formation of the Earth planet. As life arose on Earth this energy experienced existence as self-actualising prokaryotic, eukaryotic and multicellular entities. It has thereby undergone a continual build up of experiences as it has striven to maintain a self-actualising existence in an ever-greater variety of increasingly complex organisms in different environments on Earth. In this respect it could be called the 'collective unconscious' of Earth experience. And it is the relevant part of this memory experience that is triggered off by the situations that it encounters when it is 'incarnated' in an organism, that gives rise to the organism's pattern of behaviour. For example, the hominid embryo develops from the fertilised egg cell by triggering and recapitulating all the developments 'registered' in the EM-energy that this has passed through to become a hominid body, from an early tadpole-fish-like state, etc.

A simple example of the progressive build up of an EM-energy pattern of behaviour comes from Beavers, that carry out a complex system of creating dams and the building of lodges, etc. According to *h*K-M, this occurred in the first place by beavers living in pools formed by water that carried branches to places where they built up barriers by meeting with rocks. Each time that these barriers broke, the stress that the beavers experienced on losing their pools activated the memory in the EM-energy of the existence of the pool being created by the barrier of branches until the association between the barrier breaking and the loss of the pool became strong enough that it stimulated the beaver entities to actively guide branches to restore the barrier. Since the beavers chewed up branches and trees for sustenance then, because these were readily to hand they automatically used them for repairing dams. Then, when no pool existed in a stream or river, the stress/need for the beavers to live in a pool activated in the EM-energy the impulse that they could create a dam from scratch by specifically chewing off and transporting branches to do this. In this way, little by little the beavers, in their striving to survive and maintain a sense of self, built up a highly-developed pattern of species behaviour in the EM-energy, the totality of which is then triggered off by the stress needs of individual beavers, which in no way work this out for themselves.

As well as the build up of species patterns of behaviour from what were initially inadvertent events, symbiotic relationships between flowers and insects developed in the same way. The build up of patterns of experiences in the EM-energy, also accounts for the development of the complex social organisation of bees, ants, termites etc. The activities of the individual entities are brought together into a unity by the integrating and controlling activity of the collective memory pattern in the EM-energy and this then determines their roles and behaviour. Groups of bees do not work out the organisation of the hive for themselves and individual bees are not aware of the total pattern of the activity of the hive and of their role in it. This is the same as the way that human organisations build up by developing and integrating the different skills of the members of which it consists. The total pattern of behaviour exists as a mental construct built up from memory/awareness of the abilities and potentials of the members of the group, so as to fulfil the desire for increased sense of self in the prevailing conditions.

The EM-energy and its memory bank of experiences exist, and can be tapped into, everywhere. Thus, for example, tits in one place learned to peck at milk bottle tops to get at the cream below and this behaviour subsequently spread over a wide area, apparently faster than tits with the ability to do this spread into these areas, [SHELDRAKE(1) gives an account of this and similar phenomena]. And, as stated previously, the resistance to antibiotics developed by bacteria in one place becomes universal. This is because, as explained in the previous chapter, the EM-energy exists everywhere and what it experiences permeates throughout it and can be tapped into and activated anywhere.

The Genetic Viewpoint

When a prokaryotic cell divides it produces two daughter cells that are copies of the parent and the same is true with the more complex division of eukaryotic cells. In a multicellular organism that commences with a fertilised egg cell this grows and divides many times, to develop first into an embryo and then an adult version of the organism. The progeny, on the one hand inherit characteristics from the parents and on the other hand changes occur so that the situation is not identical, allowing evolution to take place. The problem is, how do progeny inherit parental characteristics, with flexibility for evolution?

With the development of microscopical methods of observing cell behaviour it was seen that cells contain thread like structures (now known as chromosomes) and that before cells divide the chromosomes are duplicated and the cell develops two 'poles' and separates into two parts, to give rise to two daughter cells. According to hK-M these activities have evolved so that, as cells seek increased sense of self by taking in and processing substances beyond what they can accommodate, instead of disintegrating they develop the ability to divide into two parts each of which possesses a sense of self with an ability to carry out the activities of its parent cell.

Experiments by Mendel on peas, in the 1860s, showed that in interbreeding pea plants that produced yellow or green peas, the resulting peas were either yellow or green and not some shade in between. This showed that there are discrete inheritable characteristics. Furthermore, only where both parents produced green peas did the interbreeding result in green peas; where either (or both) of the parents produced yellow peas interbreeding led to yellow peas, so that the inheritance of yellow peas was dominant, and that of green peas recessive. Subsequent investigations have shown that this principle applies to all living organisms. This led to the idea that the cell possesses an innate structure of inheritable characteristics that are somehow connected to the thread-like chromosomes. Many years of investigation have shown that the chromosomes comprise a chain of chemical compounds called 'genes' that 'code for' the characteristics of the organism. The key chromosomes/genes are found in the cell nucleus but there are others associated with the other organelles of the cell. The number of genes in each cell of an organism is very large (29,000 in each of our cells) and the problem is to understand how these give rise to the various characteristics of an organism. Investigations have shown that despite the large number of genes there is a core group that is common to all organisms and that within the common core group there are genes that control the development of specific features, e.g. appendages/limbs, eyes, heart, blood cells, etc. and that all organisms are built from this basic 'tool kit', with the differences between organisms coming about, not as a result of them possessing different genes, but due to differences in the way that the tool kit genes are used. This is determined by other control genes that determine when and where the different genes are 'switched on', (CARROLL). The tool kit genes are very ancient, being found in organisms that have an ancient lineage, as well as organisms that appeared more recently on the evolutionary scene.

A basic theme of hK-M is that once substances are formed, by the interaction of s-entities and galaxy entities, these interfere with the activity of the encompassing s-entity space energy. This decouples this part of it, while the interactions of this part with the substances that caused its decoupling gives it a sense of self. In this way the Sun entity formed with the substances that it encompassed and, within the Sun the Earth planet and, on the Earth, living organisms – prokaryotic cells, eukaryotic cells and multicellular organisms. In each case the interaction of the part that is cut off with the substances that it encompasses gives it a sense of self and the resultant combination of 'entity' activity and substance gives rise to the observed behaviour. Take away the activity of the organising entity, as with living organisms at death, then the substances revert to non-living physical/chemical behaviour. According to this view cells have associated with them a cell entity or 'etheric energy body' that controls their behaviour, while multicellular organisms also have a multicellular entity. Homo sapiens comprises a hierarchy of organising activities, namely prokaryotic, eukaryotic and multicellular 'etheric' energy body activities that confer 'life' and the ability to express will activity, together with soul/feeling and spirit/thinking levels of activities.

From the hK-M point of view the characteristics of the first organisms were brought about by them experiencing stresses to maintain their sense of self by ingesting and excreting substances, by sensing where sustenance could be found, by striving to move around, etc. These stresses gave rise to body shapes and structures that enabled them to carry out these activities and this registered in the EM-energy. In its incarnated state in organisms, as these experienced the same situations as earlier organisms they activated the relevant experience in the EM-energy so that this repeated its previous pattern of behaviour with substances, to give rise to the same body form and structure. Where for some reason the situation changed, so that the stresses were altered, then this registered in the etheric energy body, which changed the way that it manipulated the substance body. This is how evolution occurs as organisms strive to express themselves in more advanced ways or to meet changes in the conditions in which they exist. The change in stress and its effect on the activity of the etheric energy body can derive from any level, chemical substance (as with the effect of thalidomide), or physical, or emotional, or mental activity.

[The EM-energy works in the same way in generating activities as the way that our minds work, since we are small parts of the whole. Thus the way that humanity has developed complex dwellings is akin to the way that organisms have developed more evolved body forms. The first, primitive dwellings required ways in and out of them, access to light and air, warmth/heating, storage facilities for accoutrements, etc. As humanity has evolved, these structures have evolved by making improvements on their component parts and in their assembly, akin to the way that 'tool kit genes' and their assembly have been upgraded in the evolution of organisms. It is not the dwellings that have evolved but the minds of human beings have evolved in response to the stresses of their existence, to come up with new developments for organising the forms of the substances that make up the dwellings, in the same way that the EM-energy has evolved in its response to the stresses experienced by organisms, to give rise to more evolved body forms].

The unravelling of the structures and workings of cells and particularly those of the genes that code for various characteristics have led to explanations for cell behaviour in these terms but there are problems with this type of explanation. Thus, when scientists observe a cell dividing under a microscope and see that its DNA is replicated to provide two lots, one for each of the cells that it divides into, it is assumed that when a molecule reaches the level of complexity of DNA it somehow acquires the ability to replicate. If this is so, then the problem is, how does this happen? There is nothing known about the basic chemical nature of a molecule that enables it to reproduce itself in this on-going living way. A molecule comprises an assembly of atoms that, in turn are made up of a nucleus with a surround of electrons. In molecules atoms form relationships through the interatomic forces/stress fields that they exert on each other. There is no evidence that the make up of the atoms, i.e. their nuclei and electrons develop any abilities in a living organism that would cause replication. Atoms are the same after they have been part of a living system as they were before. Since it is the force/stress fields acting in 'space' that cause atoms to behave as they do, if the molecules/atoms replicate, and they have not changed their intrinsic nature then it must be the activities of the parts of the force/stress fields in space that are associated with the physical substances that make up the body of the organisms, that are responsible for this phenomenon and, according to hK-M the workings of these derive from the E-M energy repeating its previous experiences.

The current scientific view is that substances somehow out of themselves get together and cooperate to form living organisms. But this view causes a problem because the substances that make up the body are continually changing, it is the body's organisation that is the permanent feature and, according to hK-M, this is provided by the self-actualising energy field of the EM-energy incarnated into the body. Some aquatic animals such as polyps, starfish and flatworms can regenerate bodies from severed sections while 'higher' animals such as lizards and salamanders can regrow a lost limb, which suggests the pre-existence of the organising pattern. Human beings have lost this ability, although children can regrow a lost fingertip, (BECKER and SELDEN).

It is often stated in biological textbooks that DNA is the memory of the organism, since its replication is associated with reproducing the pattern of the parents in the procreation process. But there is nothing known in the properties of the substances of the DNA molecule that would give it a memory, according to hK-M memory is the property of the EM-energy which, when 'incarnated' as a cellular entity repeats the pattern of its experiences to re-create what it has done before, unless conditions have changed in a way that modifies what it is striving to do.

A partial analogy for the cell's EM-energy - substance interaction is the flow of a stream of water through a mixed terrain of earth, pebbles, rocks, etc. The pattern of flow of the stream is determined by the response to it of the different parts of the terrain, while it, in turn, acts on and determines the distribution and relationships of these, to develop a structure and arrangement of them. This is comparable to the way in which the flow of the cell's EM-energy takes on a pattern as a result of its interaction with substances, while at the same time organising these. If, with the stream we were to rearrange the distribution of the pebbles, etc. this would alter its pattern of flow. In particular, we could rearrange the pebbles so as to eliminate blockages to its flow or to make it flow differently, analogous to the way in which scientists, in genetic engineering, rearrange the distribution of genes to alter the pattern of activity in the cells of an organism. The behaviour of the cell entity (its etheric, will activity body) is purely mechanical, so that if parts of the DNA (genes) are removed and replaced by other genes then the cell entity will continue to try to do what it was doing before but its behaviour is then modified by any difference in the stresses created by the gene substitution.

When medical scientists state that a malfunction of the human body is due to a particular gene this is only part of the story. All the structure and functioning of our bodies is brought about by the interaction of the various levels of energy flow (prokaryotic, eukaryotic, multicellular, will activity, soul-feeling, spirit-thinking), interacting with its substances, particularly with its genes. In this way the functioning, or malfunctioning of our body has substance/genetic, will activity, soul-feeling, spirit-thinking energy aspects to it, in a balance that varies according to the situation and circumstances.

The view that the nature and behaviour of the body are determined by the types of atoms and their arrangement in the DNA molecule is akin to saying that the nature and behaviour of a car is determined by the atoms and their arrangement of which it is constructed. This takes no account of the hierarchy of activities that make metals and alloys with specific properties out of the atoms, the processes by which these are shaped into components that perform specific roles in the car, the assembly of these into an integrated functioning whole and the role of the driver in determining the car's behaviour. According to *h*K-M the human being comprises a hierarchy of a vast number of procreating prokaryotic and eukaryotic cells under the controlling influences of a hierarchy of prokaryotic, eukaryotic, multicellular, soul-feeling, spirit-thinking entities/activities. Substances of themselves do not combine together to produce a car, or a human body.

When scientists manipulate the gene structure to produce changes in the organism they are changing the pattern of activity of the lowest level of a hierarchy of activities each of which is dependent on the activity of the level below it. Thus changes at the bottom level reverberate all the way up. In the car analogy any change at the basic atomic structure level can affect the properties of the components and the workings of the car and, in turn, the way that the car behaves when the driver operates it. Equally of course, the behaviour of the car is determined by the experience and maturity of the driver, in the same way that the experience and maturity of our soul and spirit affect the way in which they operate our body.

*h*K-M and the Darwinian Theory of Evolution

Before the discovery and interpretation of the fossil evidence on which the ideas of evolution are based, the general viewpoint was that life on Earth came about by divine creation. However, as the studies of geological formations and of fossils developed, these showed that the present structure of the Earth and the organisms living on it have not always been as they are now and the idea that we live in an evolving world began to develop, culminating with Darwin's theory of evolution. The background to Darwin's theory arose from a five-year voyage around the world on HMS Beagle, during which he visited many countries and saw many fossils and different species of animals and plants. A key observation was that in the Galapagos islands he saw thirteen species of finches that existed on different diets; some lived on buds and fruit, some on insects and others on seeds, with each species possessing a shape of beak suited to its diet. He deduced that these different species had all evolved from one initial species of finch and he was then faced with the problem of explaining how these evolutionary changes took place. Darwin proposed that, (1) small random chance variations are continually taking place in living organisms and, (2) there is a continual struggle for existence, in which the changes that give an organism a better chance of survival are selected in competition with those that are less efficient. Thus, in the case of the finches, the idea was that their beaks were subject to small random changes and those that made the birds more efficient in their life styles built up until the beak of each species was adapted to its diet, while the initial species and birds whose beaks changed to be less efficient died out. With the development of the genetic basis of the characteristics of organisms it was then assumed that Darwin's random changes occur by mutations in the genes, and how these take place scientists are still seeking to determine. The integration of Darwin's theory with the modern genetic viewpoint became established as what is known as neo-Darwinism.

The viewpoint of *h*K-M is in accord with Darwin's theory in seeking a self-evolving type of explanation for the phenomena of Nature, without any divine intervention or preconceived plan. However, there are problems with Darwin's theory and, at a detailed level, differences from *h*K-M.

One problem with Darwin's theory is that the fossil evidence shows that evolution does not occur continuously by a series of small changes. There are long periods of comparative stability, with only small changes and adaptations of organisms to their environment, as proposed by Darwin, but these are interspersed by brief periods of rapid change and the arising of markedly different species, not explicable by Darwin's theory, in what is known as punctuated equilibrium. In some cases such major changes seem to be associated with catastrophes that wiped out many species and resulted in new ones and that this took place rapidly, without leaving a sequence of observable developments in the fossil record to show how it occurred. According to hK-M, when species are wiped out in catastrophes the EM-energy species-patterns of behaviour are then activated in different and changed ways by the entities in the remaining organisms that are striving for a sense of self in the new circumstances. It is akin to when we encounter new circumstances and mull over our memory stock of past experiences to see how we can use and modify them to cope with the changed situation, only this is something that we do by conscious decision, whereas the EM-energy activity works automatically and unconsciously. Another cause of a major change is that which we have referred to as giving rise to the computer era where, out of a sequence of steady developments along established lines, a new feature inadvertently arises that is then applied to, and changes, many different situations. The important point is that, in both cases, evolutionary developments result not from the manifest physical processes themselves but from the 'behind the scenes' forces of the EM-energy activities.

Another feature that it is difficult to account for by Darwin's theory of evolution taking place by a sequence of small changes, that could involve 'behind the scenes' activity is that of metamorphosis. It is possible to imagine the variety of finches observed by Darwin arising as a result of a series of small developments from a common 'source' finch but it is difficult to see how this could result in a butterfly arising from a caterpillar. It is as though the evolution of the buttterfly's life cycle occurs by one pattern of development followed in the development of the caterpillar from the egg that is then curtailed, almost killing it off, so that its expression of its sense of self is suppressed until circumstances change and the pressure to express itself 'bursts out' in the new form of the butterfly. As a result of multitudinous occurrences this pattern of behaviour becomes built into the EM-energy which is then activated by the relevant stress experiences of caterpillars. Similar metamorphoses take place in the development of the mammalian embryo that recapitulates the phases of evolution, from a fish-like state when it possesses gill slits, through a stage when it has a tail, to become a miniature version of an adult human being. All of these changes involve a 'behind the scenes' EM-energy activity.

When the situation stabilises then further evolution occurs by small changes, as Darwin envisaged but according to hK-M it does not take place by random chance events. The basic feature that determines what happens is that entities pursue a sense of self and where this gives rise to a state of stress, the stress acts on the store of experience of the EM-energy to cause modifications that harmonise them with their environment. Thus, in the case of Darwin's finches a possible scenario is that, as a result of one of the catastrophic terrestrial changes that occurred, a flock of finches found themselves on the Galapagos Islands in circumstances different to those that they were used to. To continue to maintain a sense of self, i.e. to survive, they had to feed on the available materials. Some made use of insects, some fruits, some seeds, etc. and the stress to acquire these brought about the various beak forms, in the same way that the forms of many organisms have developed from the stresses that they experienced in maintaining their sense of self, as with the form of the human skeleton.

It is, in fact, as TAYLOR points out, extremely difficult to account for many evolutionary developments taking place randomly by chance. A simple example is the arising of limb joints that require bones precisely shaped to accommodate the stresses to which they are subjected, supporting cartilage, tendons, ligaments and lubricating synovial fluid, all organised to make an integrated functioning whole. Another example is the ostrich, which is born with calluses on its rump, breast and pubis just where it will press on the ground when it sits. In some cases, such as the complex structure of the eye, it required many coordinated changes, which again it is difficult to imagine coming about by chance mutations. The hK-M viewpoint is that these developments arose as the result of stress, to move in the case of limb joints, the stress experienced in sitting in the case of the ostrich the stress to become aware in the case of the eye. These stressful situations are experienced by the E-M energy incarnated in the organism and they activate its integrating activity to seek solutions from its store of experiences to resolve the problems, which are then triggered and developed by the organisms until the stress is resolved.

D'ARCY THOMPSON has pointed out the role of stress in creating the form of organisms where mechanical adaptation clearly takes place to give rise to the organism's fitness for its function. He quotes, for example: the way in which the wing of a bird or the flipper of a penguin are shaped to give the flow of air and water required for the creature's movement through its environment: the structures of the bones in a vulture's wing that are arranged along the lines of stress that it experiences: the way in which the shape and structure of the human femur are perfectly adapted to carry the stresses to which it is submitted. He points out how the skeletal structures of different quadrupeds vary according to the stresses exerted by their body's mass and its distribution. To illustrate the role of stress in the formation of an organism Thompson refers to experiments carried out in the 1860s where most of the tibia in young puppies was removed, leaving the whole weight of the body to rest upon the fibula that was normally about one fifth of the diameter of the tibia. Under the increased stress the fibula grew to be as thick or even thicker than the tibia. He states that among plants, the strength of the stalk of a pear increases as the pear grows without any obvious increase in bulk and experiments on loading shoots of a sunflower showed these to increase in strength with the magnitude and duration of the load. These features are difficult to explain in terms of random genetic variations with survival of those that most fit the circumstances. They could be conceived to show design for fitness of purpose but this would invoke the existence of a designer with a preconceived purpose. According to hK-M there is no designer and no preconceived purpose, everything works itself out to realise its potentials as it evolves, as part of an interacting collective, with further as yet unknown potentials arising out of the developments that take place as it does this.

TAYLOR quotes many other cases that are difficult or impossible to explain as happening by chance. An outstanding example is the behaviour of the planarian worm microstomen that intermittently feeds on small hydra. The hydra possesses stinging cells (nematocysts) that contain a coiled poisoned hair which can be ejected with explosive force. The microstomen worm varies its normal diet by eating these hydra but it does not digest the nematocysts, instead it somehow passes them through its body and positions them onto its skin with the stinging points outwards. Then when enemies approach it discharges the nematocysts. When fully armed it ceases to feed on the hydra and returns to its normal diet but after discharging the nematocysts it feeds on hydra again to rearm itself. As Taylor points out, it is extremely difficult to envisage such a complex integrated pattern of behaviour as arising from a series of chance events. It is equally difficult to see how microstomen could work out such a complex routine for themselves, as they are creatures with no brain or nervous system. As Taylor says, it implies a memory and an instinctive pattern of behaviour. The hK-M view is that, as a result of the stress to maintain its sense of self that the microstomen entity exerts on the EM-energy, this builds up this pattern of behaviour from its numerous experiences. This 'memory pattern' is then triggered off, as the 'instinctive' behaviour of the individual microstomen.

There are many examples of complex patterns of sexual behaviour that are very difficult to imagine as building up by a sequence of small chance events. Thus male butterflies secrete a 'plug' after they have transferred their sperm to the female, to prevent other males from fertilising her and guinea pigs, hamsters and chimpanzees behave in a similar way. The damsel fly goes even further than this, since the male cleans out the female's genital tract to empty her of sperm from previous matings before passing his own sperm into her (CATTON and GRAY). Again the hK-M explanation for this would be of stress-induced events occurring that are integrated and coordinated by the EM-energy and then triggered off by the circumstances of the organism.

There are a number of other features of evolution which Taylor points out are difficult to explain by Darwin's theory. For example, parallel evolution in which similar developments took place in different lines of evolution. Thus mammalian characteristics appeared simultaneously in more than a dozen different groups, while marsupials arose on different, unconnected landmasses, namely S. America and Australia. According to hK-M this parallel evolution arose because similar situations in different places triggered off the same patterns of behaviour in the EM-energy, which exists everywhere.

Another feature of evolution is what biologists call 'pre-adaptation', which is where developments arose that at the time had no significance but later became important. Two examples of this were the arising of the feather, which occurred before organisms needed it for flight and the amniotic egg, itself a very complicated structure difficult to account for by chance, which developed before the arising of reptiles that would need it to be able to live on land. Many 'neutral' developments have also arisen which have no obvious advantage or disadvantage to the survival of the organism concerned. These occurred because in the 'milling around' of experiences taking place in the EM-energy all sorts of relationships are formed which may be triggered off by the situations encountered by organisms and are thereby tried out. This accounts for the 'experimental' nature of evolution, in which many different types of organisms have arisen that did not fit in with the on-going circumstances and therefore died out.

[We show in Part IV that feather-like and plant-like stress patterns can form in non-living systems and organise substances into these shapes, without being connected to the evolution of organisms].

Another feature of evolution pointed out by Taylor is that of 'overshoot', where organisms follow a path of development long after it offers them any evolutionary advantage and which, in fact may bring about their demise. An outstanding example was that of the Irish elk which developed antlers that evolved to become twelve feet across and weighed a quarter of a ton that must have adversely affected its activity and contributed to its demise. The male peacock has developed a large and colourful patterned tail with which to impress the peahen but this is now so large that it has resulted in the loss of the power of flight. Similarly the male lyre bird has developed a long dangling tail for display which is a handicap in walking around and flight. The dinosaurs, in seeking enhanced sense of self became larger and larger which was then a disadvantage to them in their long-term survival. This is because once a pattern of development is formed in the EM-energy that gives the organism a sense of self, it is triggered again and again, so that the process is reinforced and continues mechanically on and on until some external circumstance causes it to cease. The integrating activity of the EM-energy that brings about these patterns of behaviour is purely mechanical and devoid of judgement, what is feasible is determined by how well it works in the Earth situation.

Another feature of evolution that is difficult to explain by Darwin's theory of random changes is that of mimicry. Thus some species express their aggression, on being attacked by predators by their fearsome eyes. The success of this registers in the EM-energy and is then activated and mimicked by other species such as butterflies that thereby develop fearsome eye patterns on their wings. The *h*K-M explanation for this is that because the EM-energy exists universally and is tapped into by all species, a pattern or part of a pattern, developed by one species can be activated in appropriate stress situations by another species. It is akin to the way in which we take a development from one situation and use it as an 'idea' for another situation. According to *h*K-M we are individualised parts of the EM-energy or, to put it the other way round, the behaviour of the EM-energy is the same as the behaviour of our minds, writ large.

A basic feature of Darwin's theory is that it envisages life being a struggle for existence, in which less efficient organisms are replaced by new ones. On this basis we would expect all earlier organisms to have died out and been superseded, whereas many older species continue to survive much as they were. Examples of this are the coelacanth that was thought to have become extinct some 150 million years ago and specimens of which have in recent years been found to be living unchanged, sharks which are the same now as their fossils of 150 million years ago, bees that were trapped in amber some 30 million years ago that are virtually identical to bees living now and prokaryotic cells (bacteria), which seem to have survived with little change for three and a half billion years. According to *h*K-M when a part of the EM-energy experiences a sense of self by 'incarnating' into an organism it seeks to maintain this sense of self and continues to do so unless some external force destroys it. Thus, where environmental conditions allow it to continue to maintain its sense of self by its established pattern of behaviour it carries on doing so.

Furthermore, instead of evolution occurring by competition between organisms there are many examples in Nature of different species living non-competitively with each other as, for example, with the different species of fish that live alongside each other feeding on coral. This is an example of different animals that, instead of being competitive, respect each other's, territories. In some cases, far from being competitive, different species form symbiotic relationships, as when small 'cleaner fish' remove parasites from the bodies, and even the mouths, of larger voracious fish, which could easily eat them. In fact, instead of evolution arising as a result of competition, many developments occur by symbiotic cooperation, as with prokaryotic cells symbiotically cooperating in the formation of eukaryotic cells and eukaryotic cells forming multicellular organisms. The most hardy and widespread of organisms, namely lichens, are a cooperative combination of algae and fungi. Some plants and insects or birds form symbiotic relationships and then evolve together. We are an example of this, in that homo sapiens has evolved by the selective breading of plants and domesticating animals, thereby affecting the development of these in a process of co-evolution.

Evolution is a matter of co-evolution. According to *h*K-M 'creation' started with the space energy differentiating into superstructure entities. Then within these there differentiated out successively galaxy entities, star entities and planetary entities, as with the Earth and the other planets that form within the Solar System. Within the Earth planetary entity there has differentiated out a sequence of living entities – prokaryotic cells (bacteria), eukaryotic protoctists, animals, plants and hominids. If any level evolves to a point that exceeds the flexibility of the other levels to accommodate to it, this creates stresses and strains in the other levels that react back on it to bring it into line with the overall situation. As each level becomes self-actualising it reacts on the other levels. (This is in accord with Lovelock's Gaia concept of the Earth possessing a unity that integrates, and maintains equilibrium between, all the activities that it encompasses, as described by MARGULIS).

New developments do not replace the established ones but build on them; in fact they depend on them for their existence. If all of the first 'primitive' organisms to come into existence, i.e. the prokaryotic bacteria, were eliminated, all other, 'more advanced' organisms, that are totally dependent on these, would die out. Biological evolution is an on-going experimentation of what can be achieved by the stresses of organisms seeking to maintain their sense self in changing circumstances, activating impulses for further developments from the experiences of the collective unconscious of the EM-energy.

TAYLOR points out that as a result of their studies, a number of biologists have concluded that there must be an element of purpose or design in evolution. After extensive analyses of these studies he concludes that evolution takes place from 'an inner necessity' and that there is some, as yet unknown, factor involved. From the *h*K-M viewpoint the 'inner necessity' is the seeking by organisms to pursue their sense of self and the unknown factor in current evolutionary thinking is the EM-energy and the part that this plays in the evolution of organisms.

As LOYE has pointed out, the generally accepted view of Darwin's theory of evolution taking place by random variations with the survival of the fittest is not the whole story. This is the view that Darwin put forward in The Origin of Species to explain the evolution of lower organisms. In his later Descent of Man Darwin proposed that higher organisms, particularly humanity, evolve a sense of morality (although in many cases exhibiting great depravity). Thus, instead of acting purely out of self-interest, they can act to support the needs of other organisms, in the extreme case sacrificing their lives in doing this, with the drive to behave in this way coming from within them according to their moral standards.

Darwin proposed that the moral drive developed through three major stages, biological, social and psychological. It began in the biological stage where the male and female of a species formed a relationship that determined their behaviour towards each other. With the generation of progeny, the Mother developed concern for their well being, with the Father involved in this to a greater or lesser extent, according to his commitment to the family. In some cases this care and concern extended beyond the family with the adoption of orphans from other families.

The social level arose where animals lived in groups when moral concern extended to other members of the group and to the group as a whole. For example some animals groom each other: in dangerous situations some animals post sentinels to warn one another when danger threatens: some animals mutually defend each other and hunt in concert. When attacked some groups of animals surround their young to protect them. The behaviour of the individual is then determined by its interaction with the group and with the group's attitude towards them. If animals are kept as pets the moral level may be raised by the animals developing love for, and seeking love from, their owners.

The psychological level arose with the development of moral sensitivity. This requires the ability, probably only possessed by humanity, to compare past and future actions and motives and to perceive where these have led to adverse consequences and to feel remorse for this. This leads to the expression of blame or praise, with dread of the former and love of the latter then playing a major part in determining behaviour. Education, religion and spirituality, i.e. the belief in powers beyond physical existence, then become contributing factors in developing moral sensitivity and its manifestations of sympathy, love and mutual aid. Moral sensitivity evolves from concern for one's family to concern for one's community to concern for one's race to concern for humanity in general, to concern for all living things, culminating with the golden rule, 'Do unto others as you would have them do unto you'.

All of this is largely in accord with the hK-M viewpoint except that hK-M emphasises that everything arises 'inadvertently', out of stress, in the first place with the inadvertent activity giving rise to an enhanced sense of self that is then taken over and made self actualising by the entities concerned. Thus, as described previously, parental concern arose from progeny exerting a stress on the Mother by seeking a continuation of succour and support from her and in responding to this the Mother experienced an enhanced sense of self, as a result of carrying out a more advanced role in the processes of creation of which she is part. Where the stress of their existence drives animals or human beings into group activity, this gives the individuals an enhanced sense of self, as being part of a community. And where individuals move beyond community behaviour and act out of their own resources according to impulses received from the spiritual world, they get an enhanced sense of self as playing a higher role in the creative process.

The theoretical physicist Paul DAVIES (2) has reviewed the problems involved in accounting for the creative power and self-organising ability of Nature. He states that the 'reductionist' view, that attempts to explain the behaviour of organisms in terms of the atoms/molecules of which they consist does not work. This is because as molecules of substances come together and behave cooperatively new patterns and principles of behaviour arise which are not explicable in terms of the atomic forces of the molecules. In the same way it is not possible to explain how living organisms arise in terms of the forces between substances. Similarly it is a major problem to explain the morphology and behaviour of a living organism in terms of the forces of interaction of its DNA molecules and how small random events in these give rise to major changes and evolution of organisms. Equally it is not possible to explain behavioural skills, such as the migration of birds, and mental events, thoughts, feelings hopes, fears and consciousness in terms of the forces of interaction between the molecules of which organisms consist. In order to explain these phenomena scientists are seeking to formulate principles of collective and organisational behaviour. Davies concludes that the fact that the Universe has organised itself and developed self-awareness is evidence for 'something going on behind it all'.

According to hK-M the evolution of living organisms does not occur as the result of a preconceived plan by a grand designer (God), nor does it occur, as proposed by the neo Darwinian theory of evolution, as a result of random changes in the genetic code, of which advantageous ones are naturally selected. It takes place as the result of entities that have become differentiated out of the EM-energy by the presence of substances using the potentials of these to combine together and free energy and, in so doing, to form structures in which the part of the EM-energy bringing this about gets a sense of self and becomes 'incarnated'. If the natures of substances were different, the evolution of organisms would be different, so that, in this respect substances determine the pattern of evolution. But it is the activity and striving for sense of self of the parts of the EM-energy that have become embroiled with substances, that seek to maintain their existence, to express themselves and to become aware of their situation and of themselves, that create stresses that give rise to the forms and functions of organisms. It's like the building of houses; the nature of the materials available determines the potential structures of houses but without the drive and energy of the builders, who seek fulfilment and expression of their sense of self by creating structures in which to live, there would not be any houses. The basic nature of substances and the ways in which they interact have been formulated by scientists as the principles of physics and chemistry and in making use of substances organisms are restricted to using them according to these principles. Thus, as D'ARCY THOMPSON has shown in his extensive survey, the patterns of the growth and form of organisms can be simulated and described in terms of the principles of physics and chemistry but not the driving force that causes them to exist and to make use of these principles.

Chapter 11

Appendix 1 to Chapter 5: The Omniverse and a New Dimension to Hominids

The Evolution of Humanity and the Human Being

In Chapters 1 to 4 in Part I and their associated Appendices' Chapters 6 – 10, we have been dealing with well-established understanding of the structure of the Universe and the biological evolution of life on Earth, which we have sought to relate to the evolutionary-wholistic viewpoint of hK-M. In Chapter 5 we put forward the concept that our Universe is the latest in the development of an Omniverse sequence of Universes and that there exists an Omniverse Hierarchy of Beings created in previous Universes. Furthermore, we put forward the idea that we, i.e. Homo sapiens, are beings from the Omniverse Hierarchy who have incarnated into hominid bodies that have developed by biological evolution on Earth. These are different and contentious issues that need a great deal of examination; hence this Appendix is very long, (whole books could be written on these subjects). It is divided into four Chapters; in this Chapter we continue surveying the evolution of life on Earth, dealing with the post-biological developments that have taken place since members of the Omniverse Hierarchy started to incarnate into hominid bodies. In Chapter 12 we consider how some, often rejected, psychic and mystical experiences become understandable in terms of, and contribute to, this viewpoint. In Chapter 13 we look at the constitution of the human being in the light of this viewpoint and some of its implications, particularly for heath and healing. In Chapter 14 we consider phenomena that could be manifestations of the existence of the Omniverse Hierarchy.

The Incarnation of Members of the Omniverse Hierarchy Into the Earth Situation

According to hK-M the Omniverse Hierarchy builds up from the beings that arise in successive Universes. When a new Universe arises, the already-established members of the Omniverse Hierarchy are forced by the s-pressure to interact with the new generation of beings that arise from the new Universe. Each established level thereby adjusts to the new developments and, in so doing, imposes a stimulus on the levels below it to integrate with the overall situation. Thereby all levels experience stimuli to which they respond, from which they get a sense of self as contributing creators in what is happening, which they take over and make self actualising. (In a way akin to the enhanced sense of self that we get in dealing with and helping a new generation when it is born into the world). Normally when a new Universe arises the Omniverse Hierarchy experiences only a new level of energy-activity (substance-will) beings with which they work. However, in their interaction with the Earth situation they find that there has occurred something further - the evolution of a race of hominid physical-soul-beings that are undergoing experiences, and from them developing an enhanced sense of self, that in some ways is greater than what has happened to themselves. Some members of the Omniverse Hierarchy therefore seek to become involved in this.

We have referred in Chapter 5 to the statement in Genesis about the sons of the gods coupling with women on Earth. A more extensive account is given in the apocryphal Book of Enoch, (SPARKS:- reproduced by permission of Oxford University Press):

> 'And it came to pass, when the sons of men had increased, there were born
> to them fair and beautiful daughters. And the angels, the sons of heaven,
> saw them and desired them. And they said to one another, Come, let us
> choose for ourselves wives from the children of men, and let us begat for
> ourselves children.'

But, according to Enoch, God disapproved of this, saying:

> 'Why have you left the high, holy and eternal heaven and lain with the
> women and become unclean with the daughters of men, taken wives for
> yourselves and done as the sons of Earth and begotten giant sons? And you
> were spiritual, holy, living an eternal life, but you became unclean upon the
> women, and begat children through the blood of the flesh, and lusted after
> the blood of men and produced flesh and blood as they do who die and are
> destroyed. And for this reason I gave them wives, namely that they might

sow seed in them and that children might be born by them, that thus deeds might be done on earth. But you formerly were spiritual, living an eternal, immortal life for all the generations of the world. For this reason I did not arrange wives for you because the dwelling of the spiritual ones is in heaven.'

Further relevant comments from the Book of Enoch and more material from other works are given by VON DANIKEN. The problem with Von Daniken's books is that, particularly with his first book, he made spectacular unsubstantiated claims; in later books he paid more attention to giving the sources of the material on which be based his claims. Von Daniken has a passionately held conviction that humanity was created by gods who came to the Earth. He has travelled the world collecting mythological evidence to prove his thesis and he presents archaeological evidence for the remains of past highly evolved civilisations (e.g. in the Middle East, South America, Easter Island in the Pacific Ocean), which he claims were set up by the gods. He quotes from the myths of many cultures, Egyptian, Sumerian, Indian, Aztec, African, Amerindian, Eskimo, and Japanese, to show that they all refer to a time when gods were active on Earth. A common theme of the myths is that gods came to the Earth planet, established humanity, taught them basic skills and then returned to their world (heaven) promising to return. (Some of these myths also refer to an earlier time, at the beginning of creation, before the existence even of gods, when all was unformed, or chaos).

Von Daniken views the gods as extra-terrestrial beings from more advanced civilisations that have developed elsewhere in our Universe and as travelling to Earth in space vehicles akin to, but more advanced than, those being developed by modern man. He views the angels and other beings referred to in the myths as 'flesh and blood' beings and the heaven that they came from as a physical region somewhere in the Universe. According to *h*K-M the gods are beings from the Omniverse Hierarchy, who arose in previous Universes and exist in the space-time conditions relevant to these, but whose continued development of their sense of self depends on them interacting with the new developments that take place at the working face i.e. each new Universe that comes into existence. The way in which they do this depends on their level of evolution within the Hierarchy. Higher levels are thinking entities so that they interact with humanity by seeking to implant thoughts or ideas, which are sometimes perceived as visual imagery. Lower levels of the Omniverse Hierarchy have not developed to this point; they are more 'physical', which leads to them incarnating in hominid bodies.

The Development of the Civilisations of the Near East and Western Europe

As members of the Omniverse Hierarchy incarnated into Earth existence, giving rise to homo sapiens the qualities that they brought with them resulted in a major change in the erstwhile biological evolution on Earth giving rise, in a period of a few thousand years, to the development of a sequence of human civilisations. In this book we deal only with the developments that took place in the Near East and Western Europe.

In Chapter 5 we summarised how, by incarnating into hominid bodies, members of the Omniverse Hierarchy experienced the situation on Earth and how partaking in this existence gave them a new level of self-awareness. At the same time, being cut off in hominid bodies led to the development of a conceptual understanding of what was happening on Earth. The combination of transmitted wisdom from their contact with their origins in the Omniverse Hierarchy (the gods) and their conceptual thinking, led to wide ranging developments resulting in the Neolithic era and the beginnings of advanced civilisations.

The Egyptian and Mesopotamian Civilisations

Out of the developments of the Neolithic era in the Near East, there arose two great civilisations, one in Egypt and the other in Mesopotamia. The Egyptian civilisation existed from about 3000 BC to about 500 AD. During this period it was disrupted by civil wars and invasions but the main features on which it was based remained much the same. At the head were the all-powerful Pharaohs, the divine kings, who were considered to be incarnations of, or in contact with, the world of the gods and who governed their peoples according to the wisdom that they received from the gods, fig. 11.1. Under the Pharaohs there was a hierarchy of priests and a highly organised body of professional classes who were skilled in administration. There was intense preoccupation with life after death, as evidenced by the pyramids, mummification procedures, etc.

(a)   (b)

Fig. 11.1 (a) Egyptian Pharaoh (Amen-hetep) receiving dispensation from the Sun God. Because of his divine connection the Pharaoh was portrayed as larger and god-like compared with ordinary mortals; his wife was regarded as less divine but still much above everyday people. (b) The Pharaoh Chephren dispensing to his people the wisdom of the god Horus who is portrayed as possessing the qualities of a falcon.
a from Fetish to God in Ancient Egypt by E.A. Wallace Budge, by courtesy of the Estates Bursar, Christ's College and University College, Oxford b Egyptian Museum, Cairo

[As we grow through child-hood we experience, and we develop, by living in an 'authoritarian' environment, in which our parents and teachers take on the role of the 'omniscient Pharoahs' in our lives].

The Ancient Egyptians did not believe in life after death, in the way that we might or might not do. To them it was simply a fact of existence; they were aware of their origins from, and return to, the Omniverse Hierarchy (the world of the gods) and they had not become so immersed in life on Earth that the idea that there might not be life after death had arisen. Humanity, was regarded as being of the same type, but of lower order than, the gods and its job was to be active on Earth and how a person behaved determined what happened to him/her after death. There were detailed principles laid down in their Book of the Dead (FAULKNER), copies of which were put into the graves of those affluent enough to possess one, to help a person in his/her journey in the afterlife. This book comprises a number of 'spells' in which the deceased protests his/her innocence of wrong doing during life on Earth, expounds his/her virtues, praises the gods, and seeks protection during the perils and vicissitudes encountered during the journey into post-mortem existence. It was believed that a person had a Ba and/or Ka(soul and/or spirit) that separated from the body at death, fig.11.2(a); this was weighed by the gods and if they were pleased with what the person had achieved he/she was given a small place in a paradisiacal existence with the gods, fig. 11.2(b).

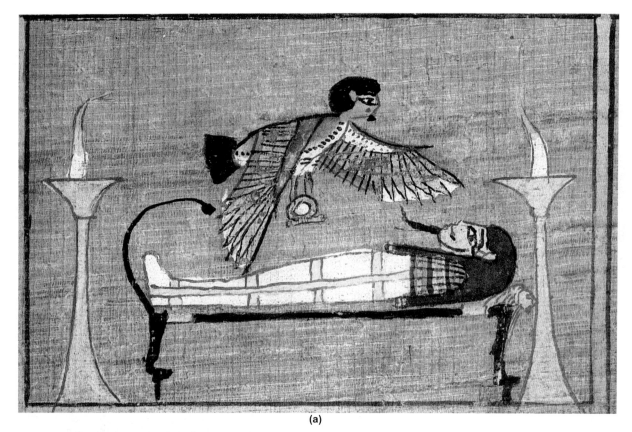

(a)

(b)

Fig.11.2 (a) Egyptian wall painting showing the Ba (soul/spirit) separating from the body at death. (b) The Ba being weighed before a tribunal of gods to determine its post-mortem future.
Copyright: The Trustees of The British Museum

The first civilisation in Mesopotamia was the Sumerian that was highly developed well before 3000 BC. The Semitic Babylonians and Assyrians displaced the Sumerians as the dominant power after 2000 BC but these peoples retained much of the Sumerian culture; the Hebrews also based their way of life on that of the Sumerians. The basis of Sumerian culture was the belief in a democracy of gods whose activities and arguments were enacted out by man on Earth. The basic unit was the city-state owned by, and under the auspices of, a local god and administered by the King and priests of the city temple on behalf of the god. The purpose of the people was to ascertain and carry out the wishes of their god, fig. 11.3 and as the gods were always quarrelling and seeking supremacy over each other so did the cities go to war to achieve domination over each other. The workings of the gods were divined from patterns made by oil cast on water, from the investigation of the livers of sacrificed goats and sheep and from the movements of stars and planets. In this latter activity Babylonian astronomy reached a high level of development.

a

b

Fig. 11.3 (a) The Sumerian priests looked to the gods for guidance and (b) considered themselves to be servants of the gods (the all powerful King of Lagash).

[In child-hood we look to our omniscient parents and teachers for security and help and we feel that our happiness depends on gaining their approval].

Whereas with the Neolithic era we have to rely on the interpretation of archaeological evidence to understand what was taking place, the Egyptian and Mesopotamian societies developed hieroglyphics and writing, by which they left extensive records of their activities and beliefs, so that the situation is much clearer.

The Egyptians and Sumerians both had a complete world picture. They believed that initially there was an unformed state (chaos) out of which the world was created. This was done by a hierarchy of gods working under one supreme God, who created the gods working under him. Thus every aspect of Nature and of humanity was considered to be the work of gods, so that in each feature could be seen the quality that the god had built into it, or the personification of the work of the god. In their mythology God, gods, qualities and things all flowed into, and were more or less synonymous with, one another (FRANK FORT et al.). This comprehensive philosophy was expounded in terms of animal and nature qualities understandable by comparatively simple peoples. The wisdom of the gods was conveyed to those able to receive it – the Pharaohs and priests, in visions that arose in dreaming and mystical experiences in their temples. This knowledge gave to humanity law and order, the fundamentals of language, writing and literature, arithmetic, surveying, accountancy to support growing trade, astronomy, anatomy and medicine. There was also the development of a higher level of arts and crafts than in the Neolithic period, in stone, pottery, metal, wood and the invention of glass, in which again a high level of craftsmanship was achieved. In many of these activities the methods used and the level of craftsmanship, some 4-5000 years ago, were unsurpassed until the Industrial Revolution, fig. 11.4.

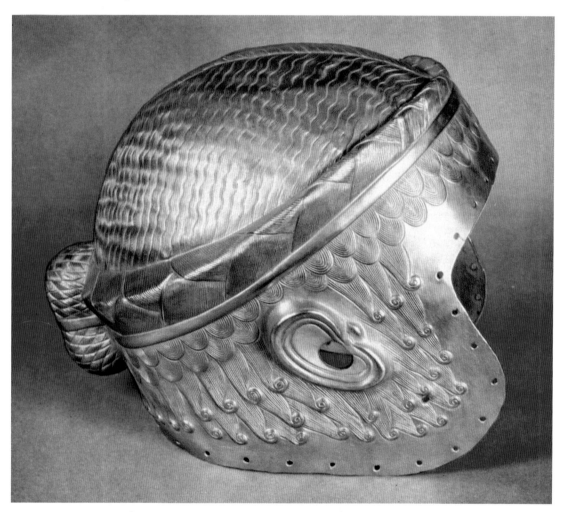

11.4 An example of the high level of craftsmanship achieved 4,500 years ago in the Sumerian culture. Many of the craft skills of the Egyptian and Sumerian cultures of that time were not surpassed until the Industrial Revolution.
From The Dawn of Civilisation Ed. Stuart Piggott, Thames and Hudson, 1961, Photographer Eileen Tweedy. Courtesy of the Publishers

[We recapitulate this phase of developing under guidance when, as young children, through play, school, parental and media influences, we gain some understanding of the forces of Nature and experience some expression of the forces within ourselves, by fairy story and myth. This imparts a feeling for meaning and purpose to our lives. Then, as we go through early school years we experience an authoritarian way of life, under the guidance of which we develop abilities and skills].

The Arising of Self Actualisation

While Neolithic peoples, out of the wisdom that they got from the gods and the development of their own thinking abilities, had begun to create conceptually, thought out things, this was carried much further in Egyptian and Sumerian societies. We have mentioned in Chapter 5 how Sennacherib the King of Assyria made a large bronze basin supported on bronze lions and bulls, (a formidable metallurgical achievement), out of the understanding given to him by the god Nin-igi-kug and out of his own wisdom. Thereby, in the same way that the 'higher guidance' that we are given at school leads to the development of our potentials to do things on our own account, this happened in the evolution of humanity. Thus, as with Sennacherib's casting, experiencing how to achieve things by following the guidance and wisdom of the gods led to humanity's awareness of the capability of achieving things out of one's own inner resources. This is illustrated by fig. 11.5, in which the Pharaoh and his wife, no longer dependent on receiving guidance from the gods, can be considered as representatives of humanity going forward on their own account, as yet only at a simple stage of development, with the masculine, striving aspect stepping forward into the world and the feminine understanding, sustaining aspect supporting him. We recapitulate this stage of development when we begin to act independently of family and guiding authorities and form relationships with the opposite sex and go forward together on our own account in early adulthood.

Fig. 11.5 Humanity begins to step out into the world on its own account, as personified by this statue of a Pharoah and his wife, no longer portrayed as god-like beings but as simple, down to earth folk.
Museum of Fine Arts, Boston, U.S.A.

[When he begins to step out into life on his own account the young man is fulfilling an inner experience of the need to find a path through life for himself. He also experiences a desire for the warmth of a feminine companion to support and strengthen his striving forces. The young woman, on her part, experiences the desire for the security of this relationship].

The situation is not, however, that we carry on developing indefinitely but that when we have worked out our lives, we die and subsequent generations take over that recapitulate and improve on, the achievements of previous ones and then go on to make their own contribution to evolution. And so it is with civilisations; civilisations die out to be replaced by new ones that recapitulate, and improve on, the phases of development made by earlier ones and then go on to make their own contribution to evolution.

The Greek Culture

The next phase of development of Western Civilisation took place in Greece and emerged from the background of the comparatively barbaric peoples of Mycenae and Minoa that are portrayed in the Iliad and Odyssey. The culture of these peoples had the same 'given by revelation' and mythological basis as that of the Egyptians and Sumerians, with belief in the creation of the world by a hierarchy of gods. In their activities the wishes and support of the gods were sought by consulting seers and oracles, (POLLARD) but they also acted out of their own resources. In doing this people gained a greater awareness of their physical nature and physical abilities and they expressed this in a new high level of artistic portrayal of the human body, fig. 11.6.

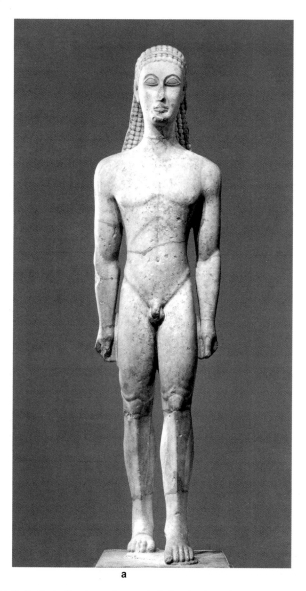
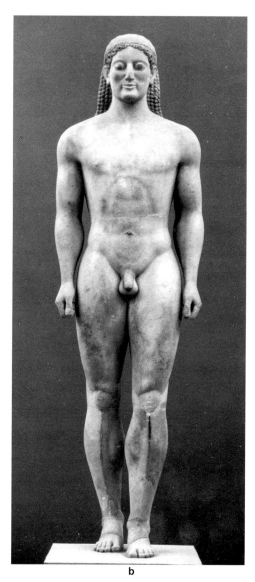

a   b

Fig. 11.6(a). Early Greek youth recapitulating the 'stepping out into the world' stage of development. (b) A later stage of 'stepping out into the world' development showing a more-advanced stage of awareness of the physical body but with little head development (as in teenage).
a Metropolitan Museum of Art. Fletcher Fund, 1932 b Athens National Museum

[As children we exist naturally and unself-consciously in our environment. Then, around the time of puberty we become increasingly aware of ourselves and we become 'self-conscious'. Our first awareness of ourselves is primarily as physical beings, so that we become concerned with our shape and appearance. Boys often perform body-building exercises and become sports devotees. Girls become very conscious of their features and figures. Both sexes feel very strongly that they must wear the right clothes so that they have the 'right appearance'. This is essentially a stage of physical development and relationships between the sexes in particular have a strong physical element to them].

This enhanced physical sense of self caused them to extol physical virtues and they inaugurated the Olympic and similar games and they exalted the physical qualities of the warrior. We recapitulate this phase of development in teenage with its emphasis on physical activity and self-consciousness of our body shape and appearance and we seek physical prowess in sport or adulate those who achieve such prowess.

The Arising of Philosophical Thinking

In this way human beings became aware of the striving forces within them and they felt that the gods must no longer control them and that they should be free to go forward out of their own resources, fig.11.7.

Fig. 11.7 In Greek times men came to feel that they must overcome domination by, and to become independent of, the gods who, combined together had governed their animal impulses and their wisdom giving impulses.
Copyright: The Trustees of the British Museum,

[As we become increasingly aware of our own potentials in teenage we experience that no longer are we prepared to conform in the animal aspects of our sexual and other behaviour to the rules of authority, i.e. our parents and society. Equally we are no longer willing to follow the pattern of 'wise behaviour' that authorities seek to impose on us. We feel that we must be free to go our own way].

This meant, however, that instead of relying on the gods for guidance human beings had to think out how to progress for themselves, which required understanding the nature of existence and the role and purpose of humanity in it. This led to the development of a more-advanced philosophical level of thinking: this was the great contribution of the Ancient Greeks. The first group of thinkers, the Ionian philosophers of the fifth Century B.C. believed that the world came into being in accordance with the thoughts of the gods and that humanity by its own thinking could come to comprehend the thoughts of the gods and thereby to understand the cosmos. Because they inherited the cosmological/mythological description of the world as the activities of the gods, their thinking was of a cosmological nature, that is, they tried to form concepts for how the world was created and the basis of creation, (KIRK et al, from whom the following quotations are taken by courtesy of Cambridge University Press). There were two viewpoints on this:

> *Most of the first philosophers thought that the original source of all existing things, that from which a thing comes into being and into which it is finally destroyed must be some natural substance, over the form of this, however, they do not all agree. Two types of explanation are given by the physicists. Those who have made the subsisting body One, which is finer than air, from which the rest is generated by condensation and rarefaction, making it into the many. The others say that opposites are separated out from the One, being present in it as a mixture.*
>
> Aristotle Phys.

Dealing first with the condensation and rarefaction out of a basic substance viewpoint, Thales thought that the basic substance out of which everything arose was elemental moisture, Anaximenes thought it was air, while Heraclitus thought it was fire. Empedocles united these viewpoints by taking the view that the Universe came into existence in the stages of fire – air -. earth – water, out of a preceding 'aither' state.

(Empedocles says that) it is impossible for anything to come to be from what is not......he holds that aither was the first to become separated off, next fire and after that earth. From the earth as it was excessively constricted by the force of the rotation, sprang water.

This is not unlike the viewpoint of modern science which sees the Universe as arising out a hot plasma state from which there developed a gaseous condition out of which the Earth condensed, upon which water then formed. But this left the problem of where it all came from in the beginning. It was thought that there was an initial state out of which everything developed.

Diogenes: All existing things are differentiated from the same thing and are the same thing. For if the things that exist – earth and water and air and fire and all the other things apparent in this world order, did not retain an essential identity while undergoing changes and differentiations, it would be in no way possible for them to mix with each other, or for one to help or harm the other, or for a growing plant to grow out of the earth or for a living creature or anything else to come into being.
Simplicius in Phys.

Anaximander, seeing the changing of the four elements into each other, made none of these the substratum but some other apeiron (indefinite, unformed, infinite) nature, from which come into being all the heavens and the worlds in them by the separation off of the opposites through the eternal motion ....of the infinite (apeiron) there is no beginning ....but this seems to be the beginning of the other things and to enfold all things and this is the divine for it is immortal and indestructible, as Anaximander says and most of the other physical speculators.
Aristotle/Simplicius

For the second type of explanation, that everything arose from a mixture it was proposed that everything consists of minute atoms that were initially all mixed up together and became separated out and joined together, to make the things of the world:

Anaxagoras posited that ... since everything that comes into being must arise from what is ....when all things were together they were infinite in respect of both number and smallness and imperceptible to our senses. Things appear different from one another according to the nature of the thing that is predominant among the innumerable constituents of the mixture.
Aristotle Phys.

Leucippus thought ... that there is an infinite number of particles (atoms) that are invisible because of their smallness. These move in the void and when they come together they cause coming to be, and when they separate they cause perishing.
Aristotle de gen. et corr.

Leucippus and Democritus say that the atoms have all sorts of forms and shapes and differences in size and they move by mutual collisions and blows. As they collide some are shaken away by chance direction while others, becoming intertwined one with another according to the congruity of their shapes, sizes positions and arrangements, stay together and so effect the coming into being of compound bodies - bulks that are perceptible to sight.
Aristotle and Simplicus

There was then the problem of what caused it all to happen, on which there were three viewpoints, one was that it happened by 'chance':

There are those who make chance the cause of the heavens and of all the worlds: for from chance arose the whirl and then movement which, by separation, brought the Universe to its present order.
Aristotle

The 'whirl' would equate with the early turbulent state of *h*K-M. A second viewpoint was that there was an ordering mind (God) behind it all:

> *Anaxagoras: Mind controls all things.......Mind arranged all things that are now, including the rotating stars, the sun and moon, the air and aither. In the rotation the dense separated off from the rare......mind is in the things that have been either aggregated or separated.*
> Simplicius in Phys.

> *Nothing occurs at random, but everything for a reason and necessity. Thales said that the mind of the world is god and that the sum of things is besouled.*
> Aetius

A third viewpoint expressed by Heraclitus was that everything happens according to a sort of internal logic:

> *Men should try to comprehend the underlying coherence of things: it is expressed in the Logos, the formula or element of arrangement common to all things ....all things happen according to this Logos.*

In this way humanity developed philosophical thinking, fig. 11.8.

Fig. 11.8 Man becomes aware of himself as a 'thinker', (thought to be a portrait bust of Democritus). From this time on a person has often been considered adequately portrayed by a portrait bust. Compare with fig. 11.6b, that shows highly developed body awareness but little head awareness.
Photograph supplied by Mansell-Alinari

[When we embark on a life of our own we begin the challenging task of developing, at an earlier age what in ancient times humanity only arrived at in maturity, our own inner thinking 'spiritual' resources].

A key figure in the further development of Greek thought was Socrates (470 - 399 BC), who rejected the viewpoints of the earlier philosophers as being too mechanistic, confused, conflicting and irrelevant, in that they gave no meaning and purpose to Man's life. Socrates believed that self-knowledge (Man Know Thyself) was the important thing and not knowledge of the obscure workings of the cosmos, so that a person could know how to lead a perfect life and develop to become a perfect being. He took the search for knowledge from 'higher realms' into the market place, stimulating people to think for themselves about the purpose and conduct of their daily lives, as opposed to following the edicts of the authorities (for which the authorities condemned him to death). Socrates concern with man as a thinking being led him to the view that the physical body cannot of itself think and that man has an inner self or soul. He taught that the fulfilment of man was to be found in the perfecting of this soul; that is, that man should seek wisdom so that his behaviour would become determined by knowledge of the truth and thereby by a moral standard set up by himself, instead of following standards imposed by authorities.

Plato (427 - 347 BC), a pupil of Socrates, combined the earlier cosmological philosophies with Socrates' Man-centred view, in a comprehensive scheme of creation. A Demiurge (Creator-God) who was 'good' fashioned the world out of the basic elements, fire, air, water and earth.

> All these raw materials then, with the properties determined by their constitution, were employed by the Maker of the best and most beautiful of moral creatures when He created the Universe as a self-sufficient and perfect divinity. He subordinated these materials to the functions which He himself contrived for his creatures.

The Demiurge first fashioned gods, whose bodies are the stars and planets and these aided in the creation of Man and animals. All things on Earth were given forms appropriate to their functions and these forms were associated with the elements from which they were made, each element contributing a specific form (Platonic solids). Man was created with an immortal, head-centred soul and a mortal soul that has two parts, with the nobler nature situated in the breast and the lower bodily appetites placed in the trunk. Man has to strive to develop the rule of the higher rational soul over the lower mortal soul. The created, imperfect, visible world was formed according to perfect archetypal forms (the Demiurge's ideas). Thus Plato believed that it is not the visible things that are reality but that these are shadows of ideas that are the reality. Plato therefore believed that knowledge had to be gained by first grasping the ideas of the gods (by mystical practices) and then rationalising these by experience and reason.

Aristotle (383-322 BC), a pupil of Plato reversed this approach by taking the view that the way to understand the world is to observe how it works. He also conceived of a Creator-God lying behind the manifestations of the world, however not a God who was perfect and expressing his perfection in his creation, but instead a God who was working towards perfection through His creation. Aristotle's God worked with substance initially in a state of chaos, setting it into motion as the Prime Mover, and sustaining the movement of the things of the world. In doing this He was not imposing His ideas on it, as with Plato's Demiurge, but bringing to realisation the potentials inherent in the basic substance:

> We must say that everything changes from that which is potentially to that which is actually. Therefore not only can a thing come to be out of that which it is not, but also things come to be out of that which is, but is potentially and not actually. And this is the 'One' of Anaxagoras; for instead of 'all things were together' and the 'Mixture' of Empedocles and Anaximander and the account given by Democritus – it is better to say 'all things were together potentially but not actually'.
>
> Aristotle, Metaphysics

Aristotle saw creative contemplative thought as the highest attribute of the Creator-God and also of Man's endeavours. He believed that perfect archetypal forms were mental abstractions derived from the imperfect actualities of the world. Thus to understand things it is necessary first to observe the phenomena of existence and then to think out the underlying perfect forms and functions of which these are an imperfect expression. To this end Aristotle compiled a large amount of information in a series of books. He divided knowledge into five sections: Logic, Natural Philosophy (Science), Metaphysics, Ethics and Politics, Rhetoric and Poetry. With Aristotle came the turning point towards the present day scientific approach with the viewpoint that understanding Nature is to be achieved by observation and reason.

During the sixth century BC the Pythagoreans and other similar cults, had developed an aesthetic existence in which they sought mystical experiences/states of higher consciousness (POLLARD). The different viewpoints of the Greek philosophers probably derived from these experiences, in which they established contact with different aspects of the Akashic Record (the EM-energy) and what they experienced depended on what they activated. Hence the variety of viewpoints about the basic substance of the world; some got back to the initial state of chaos or aperion, out of which everything arose, (we would equate this with the dormant energy state of hK-M). Others in their strivings to contact the basic state, in fact got back to fire/plasma or gaseous atomic later states and assumed this was the beginning condition. This is also the reason for the difference between an initial formless state that existed before God/gods and the viewpoint of God/gods planning and arranging creation. The former viewpoint arose from those that got back to the dormant energy state, whereas the latter viewpoint came from those that got back to a later early stage of development of the Omniverse Hierarchy. According to hK-M, there is no God planning and arranging creation but a succession of beings came into existence, in a sequence of Universes, which make up an Omniverse Hierarchy. Those from the first Universe are less differentiated and most well-established and are at the top of the Hierarchy and they comprise a 'Godhead'. From their experiences they seek to encourage the development of new potentials in later Universes but they did not initiate or plan creation.

In developing the power of reason the Greeks first formulated basic questions about the nature of things and began to fashion answers to them, thereby starting an on-going process, that continues in contemporary society and to which hK-M seeks to make a contribution. While the social organisation of the Greeks, their philosophies, arts and dramas made major developments, their craft activities were little changed from those developed by the Egyptian and Mesopotamian cultures.

The Development of Down-to-Earth, Working-Face Thinking - The Hellenistic Era

In the fourth century B.C. Alexander the Great (a pupil of Aristotle) conquered much of the then known Middle East. Alexander died in his thirty-third year and his empire soon disintegrated but in his conquests Alexander spread Greek thinking and philosophy far and wide. In particular he introduced them to the highly-skilled craft societies of Egypt and Mesopotamia. This fusion of cultures gave rise to a period (the Hellenistic Age) in which humanity began to apply thinking to practical activities and this led to developments in applied mathematics and inventions, to the beginning of 'things thought out by men', such as levers, pulleys and simple machinery, (TOULMIN and GOODFIELD).

Euclid (330-260 BC) gathered together the geometrical understanding of that time and, adding to it considerably himself, integrated it into the series of propositions and theorems that were taught for the succeeding two thousand years. Archimedes (287-212 BC) worked out the theory of compound pulleys, the volume and surface area of a sphere and some of the theory of conoids, spheroids, paraboloids and hyperboloids of revolution, thus constructing the basis of statics and mechanics. He invented the Archimedian screw for raising water. Ctesibius (2nd century BC) invented a force pump, a water-powered organ and water clocks. Philon (2nd century BC) formulated engineering warfare, working and writing on levers, harbours, machines for shooting and fortifications. Hero worked on the theory of water flow in pipes, the reflection of light and plane surveying and invented siphons, fountains, a fire-engine and the principle of steam power. In the field of cosmology the approach became less mystical and more practical. Aristarchos (c. 320 BC) made measurements of the diameter of the sun and moon and put forward the idea that the earth revolves around the sun, with the fixed stars at a much greater distance away. The concept that found general acceptance, however, was that of Ptolemy (90-168 AD) that the sun and planets revolve around the earth and it was not until much later that Copernicus reverted to Aristarchos' concept. Hipparchos (2nd century BC) in an effort to improve astrological measurements worked with an astrolobe and invented trigonometry. Posidonios (c. 135 BC) accounted for tides in terms of the action of the sun and moon.

In seeking understanding of the nature of the substance out of which the Universe arose there were three streams of thought. One stream sought to develop Plato's view that the Universe is the result of the spiritual activity of a Supreme Creator (Neoplatonism). Lucretius (96-55 BC) developed further the substance/atomic viewpoint. The Stoics persued the Aristotlean view that all things comprise an interaction between material substances and spiritual forces (a pneuma) which give them their form and function. They believed that changes in shape – by combustion, melting, interaction, etc. were ascribable to changes in the pneuma associated with them. Distillation was developed to try and drive off and capture the pneuma and attempts were made to try and reproduce the processes of gestation that were believed to occur within the Earth, giving 'birth' to its various substances, by heating materials in glass spheres on sand or water baths. Thereby the foundations of experimental chemistry were laid.

The Further Development of Self-actualisation as Will Power - The Roman Era

When the Romans conquered most of the Western world they took over the Hellenistic culture. They tended to despise the metaphysical aspects of Hellenistic thinking because they believed that practical deeds and not vague insubstantial thoughts were important. As a result they concentrated on, and further developed, the application of reason to craft activities which they practiced in a down-to-earth, non-mystical way in all the towns throughout their Empire. They made great advances in building construction, bridges, aqueducts, harbours, roads, waterworks, sewage and other civil engineering constructions; they drove a three and a half mile tunnel through the Apennines a feat that was not surpassed until 1876, which they did before explosives had been invented.

The Roman culture developed from that of the Etruscans and earlier cultures that were based on mythological beliefs. While the Romans believed in the existence of a world of gods they considered that their role was to be men of action, performing deeds which would succeed if they were in conformity with the will of the gods, or would fail if contrary to such will. They strove to develop the qualities of subservience to a cause, discipline, courage, honour and leadership and they respected people of strong character who attained to such qualities. Alexander the Great had believed in and disseminated the ideal of the equality of all free men in a cosmopolitan international society (slaves were regarded as inferior). The Romans took over this ideal and they set up government, institutions, ethics and ideals in which the human personality could flourish in ordered freedom, with tolerance for all views that did not threaten to undermine this order and they spread these standards all through the Western world. They believed that a person's life depended on his/her own efforts and that people should be strong and resourceful and discipline themselves to serve the Roman state. People then experienced an enhanced sense of self by acting increasingly out of their own inner resources and they thereby became strong self-actualising individuals, fig. 11.9.

Fig.11.9 The Romans extolled individual, Ego, strength of character and portrayed people by portrait busts that conveyed the inner nature of the person.
Deutschen Archaelogischen Institute, Rome

At first the Romans directed their developing powers of resourcefulness to the common aim of expanding and serving the Roman State and through the State, their gods.

To suffer hardness with good cheer
In sternest school of warfare bred
....
What joy for fatherland to die
....
True virtue never knows defeat.
Lines from 'The duties of Youth'
Horace (65-8BC) Odes III, 2.

We recapitulate this stage of development when we develop the ability, self-actualisingly to think and to act in accord with contemporary ways, so that we take our place as contributing beings within the framework of established society. We then begin to become individuals in our own right in our society and this begins to take place perhaps from about sixteen to eighteen years of age onwards.

However, with the increased power of the human being, fig. 11.10(a), came also the use of this power to achieve an enhanced sense of self for personal, Egoistic ends, fig. 11.10(b and c).

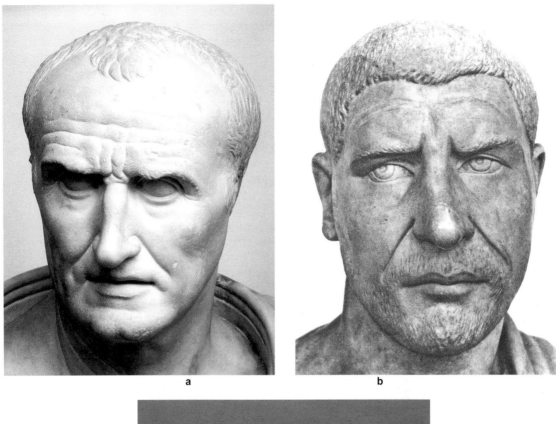

a
b

c

Fig.11.10 (a). Portrait bust of the Emperor Marius who was elected by the proletariat and achieved the position of Emperor by his own efforts and not by birth or influence. With the development of individual power there arose also the possibility of using this power for human conniving, (b) the Emperor Philip the Arabian, (c) the Emperor Pompey.
a The Antikensammlungen and Glyptothek, Munich b photograph supplied by Mansell Alinari c Ng Carlsberg Glyptetek , Copenhagen

[Roman portrait busts of Emperors. Greek portrait busts tend to portray more the type, for example that a particular man is a 'thinker', as in fig. 11.8, whereas Roman busts, ruthlessly portray the person as the individual he/she is].

When this became the major preoccupation of the Roman leaders there was a loss of the coordinated drive and power that had built the Roman Empire and energies were dissipated in internecine strife and the Empire degenerated and disintegrated.

The Christ Phenomenon

As humanity increasingly went its own way independently of the gods then, in order to maintain and enhance the sense of self that they got from fostering the evolution of humanity, the 'Godhead' level of the Omniverse Hierarchy sought direct experience of what was happening at the 'working face' on Earth and to renew their influence with humanity, by an emissary from them incarnating as a human being on Earth. This took place in the Hebrew society. Like the other early cultures, the Hebrews had a mythological cosmology, which was expounded in Genesis. There was acceptance that all peoples had their gods and in their own case they had their tribal god Yahweh who, as time went on they elevated to the status of the Supreme God. According to hK-M this would be the central collective of entities at the highest level in the Omniverse Hierarchy, (in the Old Testament the term God is a translation from Elohim, which is plural). Again, as with other cultures the Hebrew society was initially authoritarian and paternalistic, with its ethos based on the interpretations of revelations received from God by their prophets and seers in dreams and visions. The Hebrews had led a difficult existence of persecution and slavery and their prophets told them that God would give them a Messiah, who would help them to triumph over their adversaries and that they were the people whom God had chosen to prepare the way for the coming of this Messiah.

The Hebrew's expectation was of a leader of great power and command who would raise them to a position of supremacy in the world. But when the Messiah, Christ, came he lived and taught a universal way forward for all humanity, 'The Way, The Truth and The Life'. He did not teach that people should perform the will of a God of retribution as in the Old Testament but that God is forgiving. He encouraged people to go forward out of their own resources, as in the parable of the Prodigal Son who went out into the world and was feted by his Father on his return, compared with the son who stayed at home with him, and the Parable of the servants who were given money/talents to look after while their Master was away and on his return he approved of the servants who had used the money/talents to increase their value but not the servant who had harboured it for him. However, this development of personal resources was to be done, not for self interest but for the love of God and humanity, with the basic principle of do unto others as you would have them do unto you. Christ remonstrated against the money lenders and those who lived for material gain and against the Pharisees who lived according to a dead, rigid authoritarian religious dogma without a living understanding of its basic principles and concern for the welfare of others. In hK-M terms the money lenders would be people dominated by materialistic-Ahrimanic impulses, while those following rigid spiritual doctrines would be dominated by the Luciferic impulse. Christ taught that what one does in Earth life determines whether one goes to heaven or hell in a future life. Christ also demonstrated that by meditation and prayer it is possible to invoke a 'Holy Spirit' to perform healing and miracles, in the way that he healed lepers, the blind and many others of their diseases and the way in which he fed the multitudes of his followers from three loaves and five fishes. According to hK-M this would be due to the EM-energy that is invoked automatically and unconsciously by all organisms all the time, to bring about their growth and development but that can be manipulated for higher purposes by someone with sufficient awareness of the laws by which it operates or by appeal to a high member of the Omniverse Hierarchy who can do this.

Western European Civilisation

The growth of the next civilisation – that of Western Europe – is the story of a people who were barbaric when the Middle East civilisations were flourishing, who went through similar mythological stages of development to those of the earlier cultures, absorbed and further developed the culture of the Greeks, the democracy and technology of the Romans, the ethics of the Christian Church and then went on to make their own contribution to the development of humanity, particularly the Scientific and Industrial Revolution.

Because of the harsher climate and greater afforestation there was not the natural transition to a Neolithic agriculturally based way of life that happened in the conditions conducive to this in the Near East. This only came about in Western Europe by a gradual diffusion from its origins in the Near East, working its way up through fertile river valleys, particularly that of the Danube. Thus while Egypt and Mesopotamia were developing high levels of craftsmanship and social organisation, Western European peoples existed in a Mesolithic state, building megalithic monuments such as Stonehenge which seem to demonstrate a centering of their lives around cosmic activities and a belief in a world of gods. This belief in a world of gods, described in the Nordic-Germanic sagas portrays a way of life encompassing gods, heroes and warriors similar to that of the ancient Greeks described earlier in the Illiad and Odessey.

The peoples of Western Europe developed skills in the working of stone and the craft skills of the Egyptian and Mesopotamian cultures in making clay pots, and the extraction and use of metals and making glassware. These developments reached a peak in the Celtic culture that had spread across Western Europe by the middle of the first millennium BC. When these peoples were conquered by the Romans they were brought into contact with a more advanced social organisation and level of technological achievement.

However, they vigorously opposed Roman rule and in the 5th century AD they brought about the collapse of the Western Roman Empire. Because they were unable by themselves to maintain the high standards of social organisation and technology of the Romans they reverted to their, by comparison, primitive state of existence.

In the Roman Empire more and more people adopted Christianity as their religion until, by 400 AD it became the official state religion. Thereby, during Roman rule the Christian Church became established in Western Europe and it steadily spread and replaced pagan mythology with a Christian world order. This order was based on a study of the Bible, supplemented by the wisdom conveyed by the Holy Spirit to those who attained to such levels of purity and devotion that they became fitted to be channels for it, fig. 11.11.

Fig.11.11 The Holy Spirit transmitting divine wisdom to St. Gregory the Great. The Holy Spirit is portrayed as possessing the peaceful qualities of a dove, as opposed to the assertive qualities of a falcon required in the earlier stages of humanity establishing an existence on Earth in the Egyptian era, fig. 11.1(b).
Kunsthistorisches Museum, Vienna

Humanity in general in Western Europe then passed through the 'guided activity' phase of evolution, in which people developed learning and craft abilities under an authoritarian system, with monasteries as centres for the teaching and practice of these activities. Apart from attending to the necessities of physical existence, efforts were directed to the glorification of the concepts of the Christian Church, with consequent rewards or punishment in a subsequent heaven or hell, according to a person's achievements, fig. 11.12.

Fig.11.12 The Christian version of the weighing of the soul after death under the jurisdiction of Christ, with the souls damned to go to hell on the right and those who ascend to heaven on the left. Underneath is a frieze showing souls rising up out of their coffins on Judgement Day. Tympanum sculpted by Gislebertus,12c. Cathedral of Autun.
The Ancient Art and Architecture Collection

The only search for understanding was by devotion to spiritual exercises designed to obtain enlightenment on the Holy Scriptures by revelation.

This state of affairs existed until the twelfth-thirteenth centuries when men like Roger Bacon (1214-1294) criticised this approach and extolled debate and disputation for arriving at religious truths, giving rise to the Scholastic movement. This initiated the spirit of free thinking in Western Europe which soon got out of control of the Church, giving rise to a period of great development of human potential, with exploration (Marco Polo, Columbus, Magellon) great artistic achievement (primarily in Italy – e.g. Michelangelo, Leonardo da Vinci); science (Copernicus, Kepler, Galileo and finally Newton) and reformation of the Church (Luther, Calvin). The dominant themes were that people should be free to express themselves and that Nature was arranged to bring about evolution and progress in a rational Universe. Free thought was encouraged on all subjects and, as a result, new ideas arose in technology, science, politics, economics, art, religion, education, etc. There was exploration and travel bringing Western European peoples into contact with the whole panorama of human cultures and this led to developments in archaeology, history, zoology, botany, medicine, biology, geology, etc. while education and the search for knowledge expanded. There thus arose a period of rapid development, in which there was a revival, and recapitulation, of Greek and Roman achievements. This came about from contact with the Islamic Empire. After the decline of the Western Roman Empire, the Eastern Empire (Byzantium) flourished, maintaining a basis of Christian spiritual values together with Greek culture and Roman practicality. The Arabic and Turkish peoples constantly attacked Byzantium, steadily reducing its size until, in 1453, the Byzantine Empire came to an end with the fall of Constantinople.

During the disintegration of the Byzantine Empire the Islamic Empire was established and became the cultural centre of the Western World. In the same way that Christianity was based on the bible and the teachings of Christ, Islam was based on the Koran and the teachings of Mohammed. Moslems were enjoined by their religion to study far and wide and thus travel along Allah's path to paradise. They brought together Greek philosophy, science and art from Byzantium and Hindu mathematics and added Arabic numerals and they made advances in trigonometry, astronomy, levers and optics. They also pursued the cosmic-spiritual-experimental approach initiated by the Stoics, seeking the spirit in matter in the development of alchemy. Thus when the spirit of free expression arose in Western Europe and Western humanity began to 'step out into the world' and to strive forward on its own account, it was able to recover and to take up the culture that had been initially developed by the Greeks, the Hellenists, the Romans and the Islamic Empire and carry this to a greater stage of achievement. As a result there arose the relatively dramatic flowering of the Renaissance, rich in artistic achievement, philosophy, science and technology, spiritual development and commerce.

During the pagan and early Christian eras the processes of Nature were regarded as the activities of supernatural powers that could be approached by ritual or prayer to intercede and modify the course of events. After the spirit of freethinking arose in the 13th century human reason began to play an increasingly important part in seeking understanding of existence. With the awareness that other thinkers, the Greeks in particular, had already thought about these matters, attention was turned to the works of these. Because of the Western European approach of seeking for a rational understanding of Nature by reason, the works of the mystically-based philosophers such as Plato, became rejected in favour of those of Aristotle, based as these were on observation and analysis of physical phenomena. Aristotle's works had come to the West from Jewish scholars who, travelling with the Moslem invasions, had settled in Spain. His works thus became known as a Latin translation of a Syriac translation from the Greek. Universities were set up, e.g. at Oxford, Cambridge and Paris that devoted themselves primarily to the study of Aristotle's works and to an intensive search for them in their original Greek form. Alchemy was taken up from the same source and the search for the pneuma in things by distillation continued and resulted in the collection of the 'essences' of plants, (vanilla essence, rose essence, etc.) and the 'spirit' in things (spirits of wine – alcohol; spirits of salts – hydrochloric acid). In this way the alchemists became familiar with the behaviour of a wide range of substances and developed vessels and equipment for carrying out reactions and distillations and thus provided the craft basis for chemistry. Following the procedures of the alchemists Van Helmont (1577-1644) claimed to show that there were different types of pneuma and in effect separated out several different gases.

The Universe was shown to operate according to well-defined laws. Copernicus (1473-1543) put forward his theory of the solar system with the sun at the centre and the planets rotating around it. Kepler (1571-1630) formulated the laws of planetary motion. Galileo (1564-1642) showed that all bodies fall at the same speed. This approach reached its climax with the formulation by Newton of the concept of universal gravitation and the laws of motion. Crafts became rationalised, with the rejection of the mystical element previously associated with them, and textbooks were produced to show how to carry them out.

The essential features of the changes that took place during this period are characterised in the works of the French mathematician-scientist-philosopher, Descartes (1596-1650). Descartes believed that truth and understanding should be sought by clear thinking and analysis of experience and not by baseless conjecture, received opinions or, as hitherto in Western Europe, as portrayed in the bible and taught by the Church:

> We ought to inquire into what we can clearly and evidently intuit or deduce
> with certainty, and not into what others have opined or into what we
> ourselves conjecture – for in no other way is knowledge acquired.
> Descartes
> Rule III for the Direction of the Native Talents

Descartes did not reject belief in the Universe being created by God, but he rejected belief in God as a matter of faith and sought knowledge of God by humanity's reasoning powers:

> I have noted certain laws that God so established in Nature, and of which he
> has impressed such notions in our soul, that after having devoted sufficient
> reflection to them, we could not doubt that they are exactly observed in
> everything that is or happens in the world.
> Descartes
> Discourse Concerning Method

Descartes thought that our senses can deceive us as to the nature of things (including our own bodies). But of one thing he felt absolutely certain – that he had complete control over his thinking and that his true nature was, therefore, a thinking soul/mind and furthermore, that from his experience of thinking he knew himself to exist, giving rise to his famous maxim, 'I think therefore I am', that is, by exercising his basic nature to think he got a sense of self:

> Because I desired to attend only to the search for truth, I thought it necessary
> to reject everything in which I could imagine the least doubt, in order to see if
> there would not afterward remain something entirely indubitable. Because
> our senses sometimes deceive us I resolved to suppose that all things that
> entered my mind were no more true than the illusions of my dreams. But
> immediately I noticed that, while I thus wished to think that everything was
> false, it was necessary that I who was thinking be something. And that this
> truth – I think, therefore I am – was so firm and assured that I could receive it
> as the first principle of the philosophy I was seeking.
> Descartes
> Discourse Concerning Method

In striving to understand everything by reason, however, Descartes had two problem areas. We experience the physical world through our senses and, although Descartes took the view that our senses can deceive us, nevertheless he regarded our sense experience as showing the existence of a world consisting of bodies that have extension and motion in space, the behaviour of which can be expressed by mathematical laws. But to Descartes the two aspects of God and the human soul, which are not known through sensory experience demanded different approaches:

> *What makes people persuade themselves there is difficulty in recognising God and even in recognising what their soul is, is that the ideas of God and of the soul have never been in the senses.*
>
> Descartes
> Discourse Concerning Method

The Descartian viewpoint was that the material world operates according to rational laws of behaviour built into it by God, that can be deduced and formulated mathematically by humanity and that the nature/purpose of God is a separate issue, as also is the nature and purpose of the existence of the human soul. This led to a three culture split, in which issues concerning God became the province of theology and those concerning the inner soul life the province of the humanities, leaving science to investigate, and to formulate rational laws to describe, the behaviour of the material world, untrammelled by the larger issues of the cause of it coming-into-being and the nature and purpose of humanity's role in it.

There was a transition from mystical alchemy to practical chemistry, in which the materials that comprise matter and the different properties of these were investigated. People improved on the machines and mechanisms developed by the Hellenistic and Roman cultures and formulated the laws by which these operated. It was found that the material world could be described in similar terms and so the Universe and all the processes occurring therein, including humanity, came to be regarded as mechanistic in behaviour. While other viewpoints existed, the success of the scientific, mechanistic approach dominated developments and greatly influenced the other two cultures. Philosophy became more down-to-earth and practical; religion became less mystical and, whereas the medieval Catholic religion had imposed monastic ideas and concern with life after death, the new Protestant religion was more concerned with the present life and encouraged industry and thrift. Many Quakers in particular were active in the development of new industries.

The new feeling of freedom gave rise to an explosion of ideas and inventions. At first progress resulted from the free thinking and ingenuity of a comparatively few pioneers but as technology and science gathered momentum it became more and more the result of a mass effort. A similar transformation took place in the arts that became less traditional and formalised and more a matter of free personal interpretation and expression.

Ingenuity in practical innovation was matched by progress in the understanding of the basic nature of the material world. In 1700 the Greek view of Democritus, of the atomic state of matter was becoming dominant: the four-element (fire – air – earth – water) view was not so well accepted although still current. Newton about 1706 advanced the atomic viewpoint by showing that, by postulating the existence of short-range forces acting between atoms (by analogy with gravitational forces between cosmic bodies acting through space) it was possible to account for the cohesion of atoms into solid bodies and the properties of these. To correlate the atomic concept with the variety of different materials in Nature, Newton proposed that there were different types of atoms, that:

> *God in the beginning formed matter in solid, massy, hard impenetrable movable particles of such sizes and figures, and with such properties, and in such proportion to space, as most conduced to the end for which he formed them: and these primitive particles, being solids, are incomparably harder than any porous body compounded of them, even so very hard, as never to wear or break in pieces; no ordinary power being able to divide what God Himself made one in the first creation.*
>
> Isaac Newton, Principia

Newton's postulate that there were different types of atoms and that these cohered into solid bodies by the forces between them led chemists to separate out and classify the different types of substances/atoms of which the material world consists and physicists to seek to understand the nature of interatomic forces. Exploiting the knowledge so gained has given rise to the, still on-going, advances in the understanding and development of our material existence.

When Newton made his statement of his atomic view of matter he aligned it with the Christian view of an initial once and for all creation, compared with the alchemical view of substances coming about as part of a growing system. However, the view that everything was brought into existence in a 'finished' form by an act of creation was shattered by scientists finding that the creatures now living on Earth had come about by evolution over a long period, starting with primeval organisms in the sea. There then ensued a period when the evolution of organisms on Earth was accepted but the viewpoint about the rest of the Universe remained much as it had been. However, during the twentieth century scientists found that the Universe as a whole has evolved from an earlier primeval state, with different substances arising as part of this evolution.

[Although it is regarded as a major scientific advance to show that the Universe is evolving, the Ancient Greeks took it for granted that this was so. They were concerned with the initial state from which it started and the stages by which it had developed, as shown by the quotations from Empedocles and others. It was only with the Christian world view, that took over the Hebrew mythology of the Old Testament, that there arose the belief in an initial once and for all creation].

Thus it is now clear that we are part of an evolving system and, as described in the Introduction to this book, with a clearer understanding of how the Universe works, scientists are beginning to try to understand what causes it to work in this way. This is leading to a total evolutionary-wholistic understanding that could reintegrate the three-culture split and the subdivisions into which each culture has become divided, to provide an overall view of the nature and purpose of existence and our role in it. The objective of this book is to make a contribution to this end.

The Evolution of the Individual Human Being

During our description of the various stages in the evolution of homo sapiens we have related these to corresponding stages in our individual development. We now consider the evolution of the individual in more detail. The *h*K-M view is that we are 'spiritual' entities from the Omniverse Hierarchy who have incarnated into hominid bodies in order to experience life on Earth. By being incarcerated in a hominid body we become cut off from our spiritual origins and we become occupied with understanding the sensory information which our body gives us, which we have to interpret by thinking, to give us a conscious understanding of existence. This was described by WORDSWORTH in his 'Ode on Intimations of Immortality from Recollections of early Childhood'

'There was a time when meadow, grove and stream
The earth and every common sight
To me did seem
Apparelled in celestial light
The glory and the freshness of a dream.
It is not now as it hath been of yore; -
Turn wheresoe'er I may'
By night or day,
The things which I have seen I now can see no more...

Wordsworth ascribed this childhood celestial vision of Nature to a carry-over from a state prior to Earth existence:

Our birth is but a sleep and a forgetting:
The Soul that rises with us, our life's star
Hath had elsewhere its setting
And cometh from afar.
Not in entire forgetfulness
And not in utter nakedness.
But trailing clouds of glory do we come
From God, who is our home:

And the loss of celestial vision as due to incarceration in the Earth situation as we leave infancy behind:

Heaven lies about us in our infancy!
Shades of the prison house begin to close
Upon the growing boy,

With increasing loss as we grow up until it has gone completely in the grown man, to be replaced by the common, everyday, material vision of Nature;

At length the Man perceives it die away,
And fade into the light of common day.

But as this happens the child's celestial, at-one-ness with Nature is replaced by an adult, thinking, philosophic, understanding:

> What though the radiance which was once so bright
> Be now forever taken from my sight,
> Though nothing can bring back the hour
> Of splendour in the grass, of glory in the flower;
> We will grieve not, rather find
> Strength in what remains behind;
> ....
> In years that bring the philosophic mind.

However, our hearts can awaken in our thinking a joyous appreciation of Nature:

> Thanks to the human heart by which we live,
> Thanks to its tenderness, its joys, and fears,
> To me the meanest flower that blows can give
> Thoughts that often lie too deep for tears.

Wordsworth's poetic description of the journey of the individual through a lifetime, applies equally to the journey of humanity as a whole, from leaving its state of bliss with the gods, (the Omniverse Hierarchy), its prodigal-son journey through Earth existence and its eventual return to the Omniverse Hierarchy, taking with it the philosophic, conceptual powers of understanding that it has developed.

Life on Earth is so demanding and, at the same time, gives us such an enhanced sense of self, that it occupies our full attention, so that we get bogged down in it. Then, when our body dies we remain caught up in our involvement with the Earth situation, so that we have to continue with it until we have resolved the demands that it makes on us and we are free to return to the Omniverse Hierarchy, taking with us the qualities that we have developed from our lives on Earth. This means that we reincarnate into the Earth situation many times (see Chapter 12) but with knowledge of our prior existence in the Omniverse Hierarchy and our previous Earth lives blotted out by the pressures of incarnating into the current life, although some of us, like Wordsworth, may have a dim recollection of a prior existence.

Our Willing-Feeling-Thinking Development Through Life

We come into the world as a baby, the body of which has need for sustenance and excretion and this gives rise to feelings that are concerned with the satisfaction of these ends. The baby then uses its will to express these feelings by making, to the limited extent of which it is capable, appropriate noises and body movements.

As it evolves, the child wills itself into movement and then gets an enhanced sense of self by crawling, etc. In so doing it explores the world around it and begins to get sensations and feelings from its interaction with this world. It then seeks increasing sense of self by pursuing activities that give it enhanced feelings, as in play activities. And, in doing this it develops more skilled expressions of its will through its body, as in sports activities. Then, in seeking greater satisfaction of its feelings, the young person seeks interaction with the opposite sex and it then becomes more aware of the feeling needs of others.

Thinking arises at first in order to perceive ways of getting satisfaction of feelings. But, in doing this the thinking I gets a sense of self and it begins to immerse itself in its thinking activity and in expressing its thoughts (as in teenage arguments) and it can then become absorbed in itself. We see this in public figures who get a sense of self by expressing their thoughts about things and, as a result, advocating a particular line of action. Sometimes, something causes them to change to a diametrically opposite viewpoint and they then express their thoughts and proposed opposite actions equally vehemently. It is not the thoughts or actions that are important but the sense of self that they get in thinking and expressing them. (The rest of us are, of course, no different, it is just that this feature is readily observable in public figures).

Once our thinking I has developed some control of its situation, then by its interaction with the thoughts of other Is (through discussions, school, books, television, etc.), it becomes aware of being part of a larger pattern of things. It then begins to direct its actions, not solely to its own ends, but to take account also of the other things and beings with which it is involved, in this larger pattern of life. In this way thinking begins to lead to wisdom, i.e. a fusion of willing, feeling and thinking in 'Right Doing, Right Feeling, Right Thinking'. The development of a (hypo)thetical male from birth to death is portrayed in the 'wheel of life' of fig. 11.13.

In defining stages in our willing-feeling-thinking development, it is not that we complete each stage before we pass on to the next one. We are a mixture of stages, with some parts of our activities ahead of others. In particular we usually have incompleted childhood developmental problems within us that can cause us to behave in immature ways in circumstances that trigger them off. These can be difficult for us to deal with because they arose at an age when we had not developed conscious thinking, so that they exist at a subconscious level. But, by thinking about our feelings and actions we can re-programme our pattern of behaviour to become more rational and mature. In effect our will-feeling-thinking development is a matter of growing to increasing maturity, all through life. The pattern of will activity, soul-feelings and spirit-thinking that we build up makes us the person that we are.

We can make a self assessment of our development by setting up a balance sheet that evaluates our contribution to collective human endeavour in terms of what we put into life compared with what we take out, at the three levels at which we live, namely, bodily material existence, soul-feeling and ego-thinking. At the bodily-material level we can list things like the food that we eat, what we drink, the clothes that we wear, the accommodation we occupy, the services that we use, e.g. heating, water, sanitation, telephone, radio, television, transportation, medical services, etc. At a soul-feeling level we can list things like the arts and entertainment that feed our soul, and the warmth, support, love and concern that others give us on our journey through life. At the Ego-thinking level there is the contribution that we make to advancing evolution in terms of creative ideas, understanding and wisdom that help humanity to develop a more-evolved existence. And there are, of course, many other features at each of these levels, on all of which we can enter into the credit side of our balance sheet what we contribute and on the debit side what we take out, that is supplied by other people.

As we grow up and develop, our attitudes to, and understanding of, things are moulded by those of the society in which we live (and would be different in a different society in a different age). This is necessary so that we can make a contribution to the mutual activity that supplies us all with the needs of life and the enrichment that our culture provides. But society is continually evolving and we can make a contribution to this as well. However, to do this we have to become able to achieve something independently out of ourselves by realising our creative potentials. The depth psychologist C.G. Jung called this 'coming to selfhood' or self realisation, the process of 'individuation'. MASLOW examined people in different walks of life who live spontaneously and creatively out of their own resources and he used the term 'self-actualising' to describe them, which he defined as the full use and exploitation of talents, capacities, potentials, etc. Such people seem to be fulfilling themselves and doing the best that they are capable of doing, reminding us of Nietzche's exhortation, 'Become what thou art'. They are people who are developing to the full stature of which they are capable.

Maslow's interest in this issue was awakened by his experience of two of his teachers who possessed qualities that made them different from the norm and so he sought to determine why this was and to define the qualities that they possessed. Self-actualising people were found by eliminating those who were neurotic and then selecting those who had attained to well-adjusted lives in relation to material and emotional needs of food, shelter, sex and love. Among this group he found some people who were actualising their potentials and living abundantly. He found that typical characteristics of such people are that they have become independent of the fashions and prejudices of their environment. They lead individual lives, yet work efficiently and harmoniously with others. They are truly democratic, taking people for what they are in themselves, rather than for their class, race or creed. They are able to laugh philosophically at the vicissitudes of life and the absurdities in it, including their own foibles. They possess considerable powers of discrimination and perception; they can detect humbug and cant, and are merely amused by pomposity and self-importance. They have a splendid awareness of present things and are therefore able to concentrate well on the work in hand. They form deep relationships but are not interested in superficial acquaintanceships. They are a joy to know because they are creative, harmonious, intelligent and understanding. They do not cast emotional burdens on others, nor do they assert themselves.

Maslow found that self actualising people tend to have moments of 'expanded consciousness' in which their awareness and perception is heightened. According to hK-M, for people to have become independent and self actualising in this way, they need to have developed a relationship with the creative harmonising power of the central stream of the Omniverse Hierarchy: such people are true 'Prodigal Sons'.

Footnote

According to hK-M, the evolution of homo sapiens, from Neolithic times to the present era, is the story of how spiritual entities from the Omniverse Hierarchy have entered into hominid bodies and increasingly come to understand the situation in which they find themselves and to develop new potentials in themselves and in the world around them, through successive civilisations, as we have outlined in this Chapter. The current scientific viewpoint is that evolution and human behaviour can be explained in terms of genetic structure but it is difficult to envisage how genetics could explain these developments.

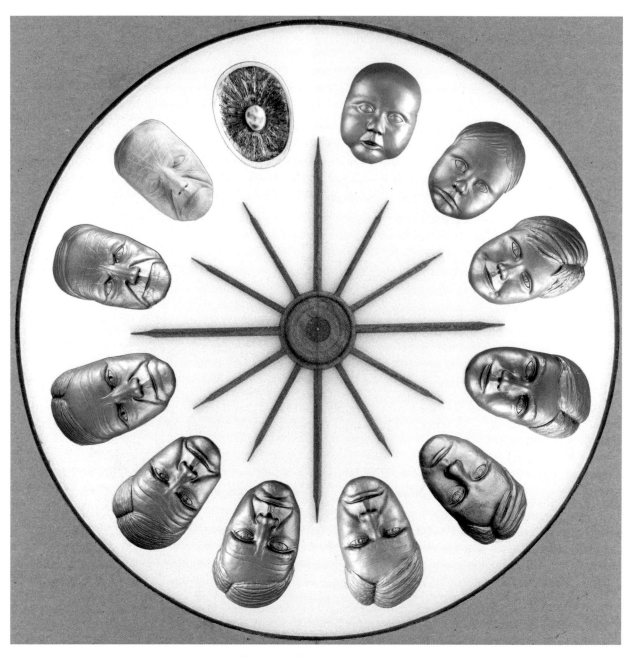

Fig.11.13a. The "Wheel of Life"
With thanks to Bob Russell

Hypo comes into the world
seeking sustenance to maintain
his bodily existence

Hypo becomes aware that there
is a multitude of happenings
in the world around him

Hypo experiences the joy of
exploring his world and his ability to do so

This gives hypo an enhanced
experience of self, as a callow
youth

He then experiences the daunting
challenge of growing up into an adult
person

Hypo sees opportunities for enhanced
sense of self if only he can measure up to
them

Hypo gets down to the steady grind of
coping with the pressures of life

Hypo gets satisfaction in succeeding
according to society's view of success

But this does not give him the fulfilment
that he expected and he ponders this

By seeking understanding of his life's
experiences Hypo develops wisdom

Having achieved what he is capable of ,
Hypo departs from the material world

Hypo's achievements serve as a seed for
those of future generations

Fig.11.13b. The evolution through his life cycle of a hypothetical male.

Chapter 12

Appendix 2 to Chapter 5: The Omniverse and a New Dimension to Hominids

Psychic and Mystical Experiences

The concept that we are spiritual entities from the Omniverse Hierarchy who incarnate into a sequence of hominid bodies to gain experience of life on Earth throws light on a number of psychic and mystical phenomena that are otherwise difficult to explain, of which we deal with four aspects in this Chapter. First, there are psychic experiences in which people claim, by clairvoyance or clairaudience, to be able to contact the so-called dead. Second, some people claim to remember past lives on Earth. Third, there are people who claim to separate from their body in Out of the Body Experiences (OBEs). Fourth, mystics claim to be able at will to separate from their bodies, as soul and/or spirit entities and to be able to explore 'spiritual' realms that, according to hK-M would be the various levels of existence of the Omniverse Hierarchy.

However, before dealing with these phenomena we consider first the basic feature on which, according to hK-M, they are based, that is, that each of us comprises a thinking spirit, that inhabits a hierarchical system that comprises a feeling-soul and multicellular body of eukaryotic cells with their prokaryotic components. This can be checked by a simple analysis of our everyday experience of ourselves.

What exactly are we?

When we ask ourselves what we are, it might seem at first sight that we are our bodies, but this is not so. Our body is made up of millions of eukaryotic cells, each of which controls the activities of prokaryotic components. The eukaryotic cells are, in turn, subject to an overall multicellular organisation comprising the integrated organs and activities that make up our bodies. We cannot claim to be our body for we are in no way responsible for its design and for bringing it into being, and we do not control the activities of the millions of eukaryotic cells of which it is made and the way that these work. Other than providing our body with sustenance and making use of it in physical, emotional and mental activity, the millions of eukaryotic cells and their overall multicellular organisation get on with what they are doing quite independently of us. (This separate independence of the physical body is shown, in particular, by the instances where after an accident a person's body can exist in a comatose state for many months, with medical support supplying the required nutrition, without it being under the control of a 'personality' of feelings and thoughts). The most that we can say is that we inhabit and make use of a body. What then is the 'inner part' that inhabits and uses this body?

If we look at our inner life it consists of will, feeling and thinking. Through our will we act in, and make contact with, the world around us, and through this contact we experience sensations and feelings, and by thinking about these experiences we come to understand and control our situation and our actions. Our body is a vehicle by which we act in the world. The sensations and feelings that we then get from doing this are something that rise up in us, over which we do not have much control. By our thinking we can control our actions, i.e. whether we will let our feelings make us behave in one way or another, but we cannot control whether or not the feelings arise. Thinking, however, is something over which we have total control; we can decide to think or not to think and we can determine the way in which we think and what we think about.

Thus the essential inner part, our I, is something that can think, (I think, therefore I am) and through its connection with its body can will into being actions. The I experiences its body through the sensations and feelings it gets from it and also what the body experiences in its interaction with the world around it, and thereby the I gets to know its body and the world. The I is an independent thing, separate from the inner feeling part, as can be seen from the fact that it is possible to sit and quietly think about things in a neutral way without having any feelings or emotions about them.

The different aspects of which we consist, physical body, feelings, and thinking are demonstrated clearly in the following account of an experience that Rosalind HEYWOOD had while on a Summer holiday in France, reproduced by courtesy of PAN MACMILLAN, publishers.

'One hot night my husband was peacefully sleeping while I wriggled, restless and wide awake, at his side in the great carved bed. At last the excessive peace became unbearable. 'I can't stand it ,' I thought, 'I shall wake him up to make love to me. Before I could carry out this egoistic idea I did something very odd - I split in two. One me in its pink nightie continued to toss self-centredly against the embroidered pillows, but another, clad in a long, very white, hooded garment, was standing, calm, immobile and impersonally outward-looking, at the foot of the bed. This White Me seemed just as actual as the Pink Me and I was equally conscious in both places at the same time. I vividly remember myself as White Me looking down and observing the carved end of the bed in front of me and also thinking what a silly fool Pink Me looked, tossing in that petulant way against the pillows. 'You're behaving disgracefully', said White Me to Pink Me with cold contempt. 'Don't be so selfish, you know he's dog-tired'. Pink Me was a totally self-regarding little animal, entirely composed of 'appetites', and she cared not at all whether her unfortunate husband was tired or not. 'I shall do what I like,' she retorted furiously, 'and you can't stop me, you pious white prig!' She was particularly furious because she knew very well that White Me was the stronger and could stop her.

A moment or two later - I felt no transition - White Me was once more imprisoned with Pink Me in one body, and there they have dwelt as oil and water ever since.'

According to *h*K-M the Pink Me is the feeling-soul with its ego desire nature, concerned with self-gratification, while the White Me is the thinking, Ego-spirit, which is concerned with rational, wise behaviour. This 'oil and water' battle between our self-centred egotistical desires and rational well-thought out, wise Ego behaviour is, of course, something that we all experience.

Post-mortem existence according to Psychics

Some people - psychics - claim to be able to 'tune into' soul/spirit worlds by clairvoyance or clairaudience, which gives them contact with the deceased who describe their experiences in post-mortem worlds. There are other psychics who go into a trance state when they are seemingly taken over by deceased spirits who communicate through them. All such communications are dependent on both the level of development of the communicator and that of the psychic through whom they take place.

There is a large literature describing communications of this nature. Much of it is mundane, in that the deceased describe an existence similar to that which they had while incarnate on Earth. This is because they exist in a world of 'thought forms' which they created while incarnate, and which do not change significantly when they become discarnate, except that, without the problems involved in manipulating the Earth situation, things become more like how they wished/willed them to be. There are some communications, however, that seem to come from discarnate spirits who have greater awareness, and therefore exist at higher levels in the soul and spirit worlds, through psychics capable of conveying this more difficult information.

Paul BEARD, who had much experience of evaluating psychic communications, gathered together and cross-correlated what he considered to be the soundest descriptions of post-mortem existence on soul-spiritual planes. As a result he divided post-mortem existence into a progression of phases of development.

Early experiences. While death may cause suffering to the body, the soul-spirit experiences a freeing into the vigour of a new life as it separates from the body. The rapidity of this change depends on the experiences and awareness of the soul-spirit while incarnate. If the soul-spirit has endured considerable stress by struggling for some time with a painful body it needs a period of recuperation before it awakens to its new surroundings. If it did not believe in life after death then it has shut itself off from its new situation and only awakens to it with time and help. When, however, the soul-spirit has made the transition it finds itself meeting discarnate relatives and friends with whom it had close ties, together with helpers who aid its transition to its new state and it experiences that it is automatically in telepathic communication with these. It finds itself in familiar surroundings to Earth ones, which have been fashioned by its own thoughts while incarnate and by the thoughts of discarnate family, friends and others. It may for a while still have ties with incarnate people with whom it had a close relationship and may even experience some degree of telepathic communication with them.

The soul-spirit then progresses to an environment which accords with its soul nature. With most people this is the ideal environment that their soul desired, without the problems of physical existence and it is therefore sometimes referred to as the 'Summerland'. However, hard, cruel or selfish people experience a 'Winterland', which is entirely of their own making and which they are able to leave by changing their soul outlook. In the Summerland the soul-spirit experiences that it can contribute to the shaping of itself and its surroundings by thought. Thus, purely by thought, it clothes itself in the sort of clothes that it feels are suitable for it. Also it slowly leaves behind the effects of stressful periods in its life and comes to resemble its bodily self in its prime, whether this be in its youthful vigour or a later, wiser period. It also finds that time and space are not as they were in the physical world, when they were determined by physical activities. They are now soul-like, i.e. when engaged in satisfying soul activities time flies and vice versa and also movement in space is concerned with where the soul desires to be and not with overcoming physical obstacles in getting there. The soul-spirit finds that it is living in an 'emotional body' and its interactions with other souls around it are in terms of the emotions which they express for each other. Thus it cannot hide its feelings and emotions - they are what it is, so that it is immediately obvious to others and to itself what sort of soul-spirit it is.

This enhanced self-awareness leads to a period known as 'purgation' in which the soul-spirit seeks to rid itself of the negative aspects of its soul nature. In order to do this it looks back on all the events of its life and sees where it has done harm or hurt and where it could have done better and this builds up impulses, to be worked out in subsequent incarnations, to overcome these weaknesses in its nature. In all of this it is helped by guides or teachers who have themselves passed through these processes. As a result of purging the negative aspects of its soul nature it enters into a 'heavenly' state in which its thought forms and those of the environment are upgraded - the landscapes, buildings, etc. are more beautiful.

After a time in this 'heaven state' the soul-spirit undergoes a second death in which it becomes unconscious, loses its sense of self and reawakens. (The hK-M interpretation of this is the spirit separating from the soul when it has worked out its soul experiences, in much the same way that the soul-spirit separated from the physical body when this was no longer of use to it). At this point the spirit has sorted out, and separates from, the soul's ego desires.

The spirit now enters into what is described as a 'second heaven' - a state of bliss and at-one-ness with creation. The spirit is then in its own world, that comprises other spirits and their mental activities, in which it experiences fulfilment and ever-expanding horizons. It is an environment of developing understanding and wisdom. In this second heaven the spirit becomes aware of the whole of its evolution through past lives and the pattern of development that these make up. It sees its weaknesses, lost opportunities, the underdeveloped parts of its nature and what it needs to achieve in its next incarnation.

Because all that it has done in the past has involved interactions and relationships with others, that have to be worked out, it finds itself to be part of an interacting group. This group experiences being under the guidance of Higher Entities (which hK-M sees as from the Omniverse Hierarchy), who seek to help humanity and to promote harmonious evolution on Earth. As such, they help us to select our next incarnation situation so that this will provide a further stage in our personal development and also contribute to the development of humanity.

Reincarnation

STEMMAN (1) has surveyed the data and literature about reincarnation. There are many well-attested cases of children recalling previous lives (HARDO) and having attitudes and behaviours that are related to the previous life and are different from what they would have acquired from the conditions of their current life; this occurs particularly in cultures where reincarnation is an accepted feature. When taken to the site of their previous life these children recognise places and know their way around and, if their previous life was comparatively recent, they know people there and can converse with them about intimate details of their lives. These children can describe how they died in their previous life and, in one case that Stemman quotes two children who claimed to have been murdered in their recent previous lives, gave the names of their murderers that led to their arrest, trial and conviction. Usually as they grow up and become more immersed in their current lives children's memories of their past lives fade. While, as adults, we are not usually aware of our past lives, sometimes a person will visit a place that they have not been to before in this life and find that they 'remember' it and know their way around and this triggers off a memory of a past life there.

Stemman quotes cases where children describe 'birthmarks' as being due to bullet wounds or other inflictions on them in previous lives and in some cases this ties up with evidence, such as autopsies, on the body of the supposed previous personality.

We can carry into our present life characteristics that we developed in a past life. For example, where the past life was a desirable one of the opposite sex to the current one, it can lead to a tendency to behave according to the sex of the previous life.

While most of us do not spontaneously remember past lives, many people can recall them under hypnosis, and Stemman describes a number of examples where the existence of the personality of the claimed previous life was confirmed by research. One case that he quotes is that of a girl who regressed to a past life 400 years ago and described a house with a hidden cupboard that contained the deeds of the house. The house was then traced and the secret cupboard, which the owner was not aware of, found with the deeds inside it. In some cases, under hypnosis, a person may recall a past life in a different culture and find him/herself able to talk in the language of that culture and to describe its customs and activities. Stemman also quotes the case of a person who, while recalling a past life under hypnosis, could play works by Chopin, Beethoven and Mozart on the piano, although normally he could not play a note.

Healing by Past-life Regression

In the 1950's a psychiatrist, Denis Kelsey was using hypnotherapy to regress some of his patients to events which were the cause of their problems, as he had found that this was a rapid and effective method of effecting a cure. For example, a man suffering from a neurosis as the result of a horrific accident with an automobile was cured by reliving the circumstances of the accident with a tremendous release of locked in emotion. Kelsey found that, in seeking the cause of a person's problems they often regressed to childhood events. Thus a girl regressed to the age of five when she had fallen off a pony, of which she was terrified, and her parents had urged her to remount which caused her to imagine that her parents hoped she would fall off again and be killed. This caused a great anxiety that, at that age, was more than she could cope with and so she had suppressed it into her subconscious mind: the regression released the emotion and her understanding of the way in which she had caused it resolved the problem. Kelsey had other patients who regressed to earlier ages. One person was suffering from mental problems as a result of which the hospital that was treating her had advised a leucotomy operation: with Kelsey she regressed first to the age of two when, on being taken into her Mother's bedroom to be introduced to her newborn brother she experienced fury at the sight of this baby nestling in her Mother's arms; later she regressed to the age of three weeks where her Mother was having trouble breast feeding her and put her down to fetch her a bottle, which she interpreted with anger at being abandoned. With these insights she became completely cured. Kelsey also experienced cases where the person went back to traumas during the birth process and to pre-birth problems, e.g. where the embryo felt suffocated because the umbilical cord had become wound around its neck. In another case, a woman who suffered from depression and had a great fear of anything to do with sex, regressed to the moment of conception when she experienced great distress: it turned out that her Mother was scared of becoming pregnant because her husband's Mother, who was fanatically jealous of her, had threatened her with violence if she ever became pregnant. Again the regression cleared up the patient's problems.

These experiences left Kelsey thinking that there must be a non-physical, pre-birth part to a human being. He then read books by a psychic, Joan Grant, who claimed to be able to shift her level of consciousness so as to recall past lives and had described these in a series of books. They teamed up and, working together, found that some of Kelsey's patients recalled incidents in previous lives that were the cause of their problems, (GRANT and KELSEY). A young man was suffering from increasing anxiety that had been triggered off by a youth coming up to him in a bar and threatening to 'kick his teeth in' and the anxiety built up to the point where he attempted to commit suicide. Grant 'tuned into' a past life in which the patient had been a pretty young woman who was married to an older man who she refused to have sex with. When she smiled at young men this made her husband wildly jealous to the point at which he tied her down and pulled all her teeth out. When the patient was told this story he totally accepted it and his anxiety vanished. Another case that Kelsey quotes is that of a highly cultured professional man in his mid-forties who was concerned that he was homosexual. Loneliness was the core of his problem and he underwent thirteen sessions of hypnotherapy that were devoted to exploring his present life, without finding anything to account for him seeking a male companion to assuage this. Then he regressed to a past life in an ancient civilisation when he had been the wife of a governor of a province, in which she lived a life of luxury and power. Her husband had to go on an extensive campaign and she insisted on going with him, to prove that he could not do without her and to show that she was as strong, if not stronger than he was. However, the campaign was long and arduous and it destroyed her health and beauty so that her husband lost interest in her and when she found that she had been supplanted, not by another woman, but by a handsome boy, her jealousy knew no bounds. She stole her husband's dagger and had a curse put on it by an evil priest but in fact it was she who ended up murdered by being stabbed. The patient was appalled by the nature of the woman of his past incarnation but Kelsey persuaded him to forgive and absolve her and by doing this he became free of his homosexuality and subsequently formed a good heterosexual relationship.

Grant and Kelsey describe their experiences with a close friend who had terminal cancer who was aware of the effect of the events of past lives on one's personality and she asked them for help in clearing facets that she wished she did not possess namely, fear, anger and an excessive compulsion to do good works, so that she would not have to resolve these problems in a further life. They did this by past-life regression and this gave her peace of mind and a positive attitude to death that, as she said, she had experienced many times before and she died serene and happily looking forward to her post-mortem existence.

Stemman quotes a number of cases where the events of past lives are the cause of a psychological phobia, a physical problem, or a deformity in the present life. For example, that of a woman who was plagued by a disfiguring problem that defied medical treatment. Her thumbs would become sore and swollen and the nails would fall off. New nails would grow and the same process would be repeated at six-monthly intervals. Under hypnosis she recalled a horrific incident in a past life in which she was subjected to thumb screws. Becoming aware of the past life event had a therapeutic effect, so that her condition greatly improved. Incidents like these have led to the development of 'past life regression therapy'.

A well-established psychiatrist, Brian WEISS, who was conversant with the full range of current psychiatric techniques and had much experience of using these on many patients with a wide range of different conditions, encountered a patient who he calls Catherine, who suffered from recurring nightmares and intense anxiety attacks. For eighteen months Weiss tried to help Catherine, using standard psychiatric techniques but without success. He then tried hypnosis to regress Catherine to the childhood events that he thought were the source of her problems. Catherine recalled an experience at the age of five when she nearly drowned in a swimming pool and another experience at the age of three when her drunken father molested her. Weiss expected that these recollections would release her tensions and anxieties but they had no effect, so the next time that he hypnotised Catherine he told her to go back to the time when her symptoms arose, expecting her to go back to some other childhood experience. He found, however, that Catherine regressed to a past life where she lived in a village that was engulfed by a tidal wave that drowned her and her daughter. This past-life recall greatly reduced Catherine's anxiety and in particular she became free of a life-long fear of drowning. In further sessions Catherine regressed to a number of other past lives, in one of which she had her throat slashed by an assailant, in another she died in an epidemic and she also recalled traumatic experiences of other past lives, some of which involved servitude and abuse. As a result of these past life regressions Catherine became freed of her nightmares and anxiety attacks and, according to Weiss, her personality expanded and she became radiant and 'healthy beyond normal'. Weiss states that the conventional psychiatric treatment for Catherine's condition would be heavy doses of tranquillisers and antidepressants and that past life regression under hypnosis was far more effective, more rapid and without the side-effects of the drugs and subsequently he employed this successfully in a number of similar cases.

As well as regressing to past lives, Catherine also regressed to her between-life situation, in which she encountered wise 'Masters' who helped her to assess the significance of her previous life and also to decide the next type of life that she required, so as to evolve further. The Masters told Catherine that her current incarnation was her eighty-sixth. The Masters also referred to increasingly developed levels of post-mortem existence that we progressively attain to as we evolve (we deal with this in more detail later in this chapter) as well as expounding a metaphysics about life and existence, which the Masters stated was meant more for Weiss than Catherine. While in the hypnotised state Catherine was very psychic and described to Weiss intimate details of his life that she could not possibly otherwise have known about. As well as having a dramatic effect on Catherine, these experiences greatly altered the life and outlook of Weiss.

When describing events of her past lives Catherine sometimes recognised people who existed in her current life. This is a frequent feature of past life recall, that there is a tendency for groups of people to reincarnate together, so as to work out common problems. A case in which people's interactions brought about mutual recalls of past lives, which resulted in healings, centred on Arthur GUIRDHAM. Guirdham was trained in orthodox medicine and pursued a career in psychiatry but found himself undergoing mystical and psychic experiences that did not fit in with his training, which at first he sought to ignore or suppress. However, the experiences persisted and he found that some of his patients had similar experiences, sometimes triggered off by contact with him. This resulted in himself and an expanding circle of patients and friends, and friends of friends, recalling events from past lives as members of a persecuted sect of Cathars, in the Provencal region of France in the 13th century. Becoming aware of the events of these past lives led to cures of problems in their current lives. For example, Guirdham himself was cured of Menieres disease and migraine headaches, so that he came to believe that problems like these could be caused by repression of burgeoning psychic and mystical experiences.

Much of the knowledge recalled by this group of people was of obscure facts known only to experts who had studied Catharism and there were some examples that conflicted with the experts' view, which were later found to be correct. Some of the members of the group had deja vu experiences on visiting the places where the events occurred. Some had physical problems in this life related to horrific experiences, such as burning at the stake, which they went through in the past life. The whole story is far too complex to be considered here; GUIRDHAM wrote four books that give a detailed account of it, the salient features of which have been summarised by CHRISTIE-MURRAY in his survey of beliefs in, and evidence for, reincarnation.

BROWNE, a psychic who trained as a hypnotherapist, has carried out past-life regressions with a large number of people to try and alleviate their problems. Many of these people were referred to her by doctors or psychiatrists, as a last resort, because they had not been able to help them. Often the past life experience that the person regressed to had been horrific, which was why its effects had carried over to the present life but it was not necessary for the person concerned to actually re-experience it; perceiving it as an external observer provided sufficient understanding to alleviate its subconscious effects.

BROWNE quotes a selection of her cases: for example, a woman who lived happily near a lake but at the age of 28 suddenly became fearful of water and had to move away; under hypnosis she recalled a previous life in which she drowned at the age of 28. This was a common feature in Browne's work, that traumatic incidents in a past life 'kicked' into the present life at the same age as they occurred in the past life. Examples of other cases were: an extremely healthy, athletic woman who suddenly lost her voice who recalled a past life in which she had been tortured and had her tongue cut out: a man who had a back problem which was not responding to surgical treatment as it should have done, recalled two past lives in one of which he had fallen off a ladder and in the other he had been killed by an assailant striking him in the back with an axe: a person who suffered from an inexplicable pain in the chest who recalled a past life in which he suffered a slow death as a result of a gunshot wound in the chest: a woman who had an extreme fear of anything burning, even a match, who recalled being burnt at the stake as a witch: a man who suffered badly from painful indigestion and stomach cramp that prevented him from sleeping who recalled a past life in which he died from stomach cancer: a successful and happily married man who, in his forties lost his joie de vivre and became cold towards his wife, who regressed to two past lives, one as a woman born into a loveless marriage who was rejected by her parents and coped by repressing her emotions, the second as a man who was ecstatically married late in life and lost his wife and young son in a boating accident which he dealt with by again repressing his emotions and this 'kicked in' at the same age in his current life: a woman who dressed and acted in ways to seek attention who had suffered a violent death in a past life but then remained as an Earth-bound spirit in isolation and loneliness and now sought to compensate for this. In many cases people had birthmarks or scars on their bodies that related to physical events in their past lives.

Browne also describes a number of cases involving children, who she states are very responsive and easy to work with; for example a boy who was an only child and had a breathing problem and was difficult to cope with because he was hyperactive recalled two past lives, in one of which he had been the father of a large family and as a young man had to go to war and was killed by a piece of metal striking his windpipe; in the second life he had been the mother of a large family and died young (aged 34) of pneumonia. Browne explained to him that these were the cause of his breathing problem and that he was missing all the activity that had been involved in those lives. As a result his breathing problem and his hyperactivity were cured. A case where the cause of the problem originated in the present life was that of a four-year old boy who was born blind and was sad and introverted and not progressing as he should have been, despite his parents giving him their full love and attention. He regressed to the age of seven months when he was with his mother while she and her doctor were talking about how limited he would be and this had registered with him. He then regressed to a previous life in which he had been a musician who played the piano and as a result he learned to play the piano in his present life and this released him from his sad and introverted condition.

Browne found that where a past-life experience was the cause of the current problem often only one session, in which the person recalled the relevant events of the past life or lives, was necessary. This relieved the subconscious stress or tension of an unresolved problem from the past life that, in turn, alleviated or cured the problem in the current life.

Browne states that the spirit that inhabits the body carries the experiences of all of its lives down to the cellular level and these thereby cause the birthmarks and deformities that she often found her patients to possess. Where there is a transplant of an organ from a donor to a recipient the donor's memory can be carried with it. She quotes two examples of this. One is of a woman who had a kidney transplant who had never touched alcohol or smoked in her life but as she came round from the operation had an intense craving for a cigarette and a martini that, it turned out, were two passions of the donor. The second was of a girl aged 10 who received a heart transplant from a boy who was stabbed to death at the age of 17. Some months later the girl began having nightmares about a dark figure in a mask laying in wait for her with a knife. Under hypnosis the girl was able to describe the assailant and the police recognised the description as someone who had been known to the stabbed boy and he was arrested and confessed to the murder.

[A psychologist, PEARSALL has investigated the experiences of a large number of people who have had heart, or other major organ, transplants and found that it is common for the recipient to acquire some of the characteristics of the donor, while the family of people who have undergone a major transplant often comment on the personality change that this has resulted in. At the plant level of evolution it is common practice for a weak plant that produces desirable fruit, e.g. apples, to be grafted onto the root of a strong plant. Each plant has developed in the way that it has by activating the relevant species memory registered in the EM-energy The grafting process connects the combination to both streams in the EM-energy, resulting in a strong plant that produces prolific quantities of desirable apples].

However, evaluating the experiences of past lives is not simple. In many cases claims to remember a past life have been shown to be fantasies built on traumas that the person has undergone in their present life. In other cases it has been shown that the so-called recall of a past life was in fact a recall of a forgotten remembrance of a life described in a book that the person had read. Some investigators claim that these are the explanations for all so-called past-life recalls. But it is difficult to see how this could explain the cases of the children who have a clear memory of a past life, when they have not become old enough to read books and build up a memory store of fictional characters. It is also difficult to see how phobias, physical illnesses, birthmarks, scars, deformities and the release of traumas could be explained in this way. Another complicating factor is that everything is registered in the EM-energy (the Akashic Record) and it is possible for a person to tap into the stream of developments of another person so that, even if the details are traced and shown to genuinely relate to the life of a person, it may not be a past life of the person relating them.

Historical Value of Recall of Past Lives

We have mentioned, in the recall of past lives by the Guirdham group, how people recalled features of the period of their past life existence that at the time were at variance with the views of experts, but were later found to be correct. Although this is an area fraught with problems, it may be that past life recall could throw light on past eras; this could be particularly useful where historical evidence is limited. Examples of this genre are books by Joan GRANT, who claimed to be able to recall her past lives and gave accounts of five eventful ones; three during the long period of the ancient Egyptian civilisation. In the earliest of these lives, during the first dynasty about 3,000 BC, she was a female priest/Pharaoh and she describes her training and life in this role GRANT (1). In another life in Egypt, about 1,000 years later, she was a male member of a movement that overthrew a decadent authoritarian rule based on terrorisation. Egypt had come to be ruled by Pharaohs and priests who were under the sway of powers of darkness; they sought personal power, wealth and self-aggrandisement and the priests enacted empty rituals without possessing and transmitting living spirituality. In this period the status of people had become judged by their power and possessions. The movement to which Grant belonged in this incarnation overthrew this establishment and replaced it with one that ruled by truth and integrity, with justice for the common good, in which people were treated according to their level of development and the qualities that they possessed as human beings and the priests were trained in healing and spiritual awareness GRANT (2a) and (2b). In her third life in Egypt she was a male contemporary of Rameses II, GRANT (3). In GRANT (4) she describes a life in the second millennium BC as a woman in a Red Indian tribe in America in which she was concerned with raising to equality with men, the denigrated status of women. In GRANT (5) she describes a life as a woman in the Greco-Roman period in the second century BC in which she was the ward of a philosopher who was seeking to replace superstition and a belief in the supernatural with a belief in reason, in which she demonstrated psychic and healing abilities sufficient to show that there was more to life than merely material existence. In GRANT (6) she describes a short life (twenty seven years) as a woman in the sixteenth century in the Perugia area of Italy, in which she was born from a liaison between an aristocrat and a sewing woman, was cast out and led an existence of poverty with a group of strolling players, and then became a nun who suffered cruelly at the hands of the abbess.

An example of possible historical value comes from Grant's earliest past life recall in ancient Egypt in which she trained to be a 'Winged Pharaoh', i.e. a priest who could separate her spirit from her body and consciously enter, and communicate with, the world of the gods (the Omniverse Hierarchy) and thereby transmit the wisdom of the gods to her people and also to be able to read the (Akashic) memory records, so as to perceive the cause of people's problems and offer advice and healing. As the culmination of many years of training she was incarcerated in a sarcophagus, in a chamber sealed off from the world, for four days which she had to spend with her spirit separated from her body and travel through various regions of the spiritual world, including the underworld, dealing with the situations that she encountered. When she returned to her body at the end of the four days she had to be able to describe what she had done during her period in the spiritual world. (We all go on such journeys when we are asleep but we are not in conscious control of what we do and we do not remember afterwards what happened). When a person can separate from their body and enter the spiritual world at will in this way they are called an Initiate. When the interior of the Great Pyramid of Giza was explored by cutting a way into it, a passage was found that led to an empty chamber in which, instead of the expected burial treasure, there was only an empty sarcophagus (WILSON 2). Egyptologists had no explanation for the significance of this, but the nature of the chamber and the sarcophagus and the way in which it was sealed off from the outside world conforms to Grant's description of an initiation site, of the type that she had experienced in her past life recall.

Cannon, a past-life hypno-therapist, over a period of more than twenty years has worked with hundreds of people who have recalled past lives. One woman who readily entered into a deep trance state recalled many past lives in which she identified totally with the person of the previous life. She recalled one life of particular interest in which she was a man, referred to as Suddi, who lived in the Essene community, which was a religious sect that existed in Palestine and had separated from the main body of Jews in the second century BC. The existence of the Essenes came to the public eye when the Dead Sea Scrolls were discovered in caves near the Dead Sea in the late forties and fifties of the last century, that related to their beliefs and activities. The Essenes did not accept the precepts of the Jewish religion as espoused by its priests but lived a simple life of aestheticism based on love of God, love of virtue and love of Humanity, with communal ownership of all possessions. They sought to preserve a secret wisdom inherited from a past era (Atlantis) that gave powers of healing and prophesy. They believed in the coming of the Messiah and, according to Suddi, Jesus was born in this period and spent some time in the Essene community practising their way of life and developing spiritual powers. Suddi gave extensive descriptions of the way of life that he experienced in the Essene community and of Christ's life, [CANNON (1)].

Cannon states that, among the many people that she worked with, she encountered several who recalled past lives in the region and times when Christ was around but, other than the woman who recalled a past life as Suddi, only two others had remembrance of him, both of whom were women. One recalled being in charge of children in a temple in Jerusalem that was visited by Christ. She found his presence and the love that he radiated almost overpowering. The other woman recalled being a distant member of Christ's family and visits that he made to her parents. She was so influenced by the personality of Christ, his teachings and the love that he radiated, that she left her home and parents and became one of his followers [CANNON (2)].

Out-of-the-Body Experiences (OBEs)

There is a significant number of cases where people claim to have experienced separating from their physical body and finding themselves still to be conscious and, in fact, feeling more alive than when in their body, (see CROOKALL, MOODY). Situations in which this has occurred are: on being anaesthetised; serious illness, sometimes with seeming death but then revival; accident and/or shock; total exhaustion; unbearable pain; under hypnosis. Typically people describe themselves as floating above their physical body and looking down on it and perceiving it with a heightened state of consciousness that gives them an 'X-ray type' view of its structure and workings.

In their OBE state these individuals see the people who are around their body and what they are doing but they cannot communicate with them. Equally people around the body are not aware of the person's OBE condition although, very occasionally, someone may perceive a misty shape separate from the body. (There is some evidence that animals, such as a pet dog, may perceive them as existing separate from the body). If the body is undergoing an operation they see what is being done to it and when they return to normal consciousness they are able to describe how the operation was carried out and the comments of the surgical staff.

Although separated from the body they see themselves retaining a connection with it via a pulsing 'thread' or 'cord'. They find that they are no longer subject to the physical laws of gravity and space and time. They are able to travel very rapidly to where they desire to go simply by wishing to be there. In their travel they can pass through walls and other seemingly solid objects. They can visit a friend who lives some distance away, or even in a different part of the world, and perceive what the person is doing (and check the validity of this later). But they cannot communicate with the person who may, however, if they are sensitive, have some awareness of their presence.

If the OBE experience is an extensive one bordering on death, they may find themselves passing through a long tunnel and emerging into a scene of great brightness and paradisiacal beauty, where they meet discarnate loved relatives and friends, with whom they find themselves in telepathic communication. In some cases the person describes meeting a radiant, Christ-like figure and this may be accompanied by a flashback review of their life in which they see what they did well and what they could have done better. In his near-death OBE experience RITCHIE describes the Christ-like figure as totally knowing him in all his weaknesses, totally accepting him and totally loving him. This figure then took him to a post-mortem hellish state of existence in which discarnates were trapped by their selfish and materialistic desires and then to a paradisiacal region where discarnates exist as radiant figures that have grown beyond selfish ego desires. This made him aware of these two aspects of his own nature.

In many cases the person in this type of OBE state feels that they do not want to return to the confined existence of the physical body and that when they do so it is like leaving a region of bright light and becoming immersed in darkness and oblivion. But through their OBE experience they lose all fear of death and often it causes them to lead a more selfless life.

Detailed accounts of OBE experiences are given by MONROE. Monroe, an American businessman with extensive interests, without any religious calling, found himself spontaneously undergoing OBE experiences. At first these caused him considerable concern but, as he gathered experience and confidence, he progressively explored this condition further. To begin with he found that in his OBE state he could visit people remote from him and see what they were doing. He then found that he could explore non-physical regions where discarnates seemed to exist. He experienced three such regions, one where the soul's outlooks were confined to the Earth situation, second, an intermediate level, where souls were aware of a broader existence and the third where souls were concerned with relating to the broader situation. Each of these regions comprised a number of sub levels. The first region was 'closest to Earth' and there souls existed who did not know they had died and were totally unaware of any other existence than the physical one. In one sub-level they were still trying to live an Earth life but without a physical body and sometimes trying to inhabit someone else's body. In another level he found souls who were 'stunned out' by the experience of death and existing in a catatonic state (In a similar region he found souls that had exited their bodies during sleep and were existing in a dream-like state). In a further sub-level he found souls that, finding they were free of the restrictions of physical existence, were concerned solely with trying, in a totally uninhibited manner to achieve the type of satisfactions they had sought on Earth, e.g. writhing around with each other, trying to get sexual satisfaction but without physical bodies to achieve this. In the second region souls were aware that they had died and were trying to adjust to their new conditions of existence and to reconcile what they were experiencing with their belief systems from their Earth lives. The different belief systems that they were working out gave rise to a number of sub-levels. In the third region there were souls who were aware that they were dead and who were concerned with the broader implications of their situation. In one level they had found that they were able, by thought power, to create an environment and pursue activities of the sort that gave them satisfaction on Earth. 'Above' them there was the last zone associated with Earth existence where there were souls who had completed the lessons to be learned from Earth, or who were preparing for one final incarnation and were working as teachers and leaders to souls in the lower zones, before 'moving on'.

As he learned to 'move out further' in his OBE state, Monroe encountered invisible presences that he called 'intelligent species' who either had not incarnated into Earth existence or who had completed their Earth incarnations. He found these entities beneficent and with them he experienced supreme peace, harmony, warmth and at-one-ness, so much so that he found the experience difficult to define and said that he could only describe it as 'returning Home'. According to hK-M, in this state Monroe's spirit/consciousness had separated from that of his bodily existence and returned to that of his existence in the Omniverse Hierarchy. To show him how the human situation arose, the entities that Monroe met in his OBE state guided him to observe entities from the Omniverse Hierarchy who became progressively aware of, and attracted to, the human situation to an extent that caused them to enter into it. The pull for doing this was the intense, compressed stronger learning experience that Earth life offered.

These entities entering into a human body found themselves highly restricted and confined, compared with their previous existence. Nevertheless, what in hK-M terms would be the increased sense of self that their experiences gave them, caused them to reincarnate and re-experience this state. But, in so doing they became 'hooked' on, and bogged down in, the Earth situation, so that, in the discarnate state they remained in the lower zones close to the Earth. Monroe stated that the number of such souls was increasing and their build up was creating a blockage in the flow of energy and souls to and from the Earth. It required help from higher levels and considerable effort from the entity concerned to progress out of this condition, as John OXENHAM, who himself underwent OBE experiences, expressed it:

> To every man there openeth,
> A way and ways and a way.
> And the high soul climbs the high way
> And the low soul gropes the low,
> And in between on the misty flats,
> The rest drift to and fro.
> But to every man there openeth
> A high way and a low
> And every man decideth the way his soul shall go.

Monroe stated that those who graduated from Earth experience possessed outstanding qualities and that, although they had found Earth lives difficult, none of them regretted their experiences because of the resulting rewards. The point of Earth existence had been to experience a state in which individual free will was operative while, at the same time, because of being separated from their origins, they experienced much stronger emotions, e.g. loneliness, resentment, hate, etc. which, however, could be transformed into a greater empathy and love for other entities. Entities who achieved this state converted the 'primal energy' into an outwards radiating 'super love' that was independent of, and embraced, everything. It is the prodigal son story of leaving a situation where we are part of a supporting family organisation headed by a caring Father and going out into the world, developing our own independent qualities and then returning home and contributing these to the Father and family.

The Inspecs (Monroe's terminology for the intelligent species that he encountered), conveyed the fact that they (and us) had been in existence long before human beings arose. They communicated with Monroe by what he called NVC (non-verbal communication), a state like telepathy but more all embracing. His method of contact in this state was to 'tune in', i.e. as if you know someone's personality very well and you conjure up the feelings and thoughts of experiencing contact with them and this then brings about the contact. Monroe found it very difficult to express these experiences in words and he had to invent a jargon, using contemporary expressions of his society to do so. The Inspecs 'stated' that they had been assigned to try to help the Earth situation. When he sought further details on their role and nature they stated that they were not the Creator but had been created and themselves created. In hK-M terms they would correspond to an intermediate level of the Omniverse Hierarchy.

The Inspecs presented Monroe with a possible scenario for 3000 A.D, when humanity had evolved to return Earth to a state of pristine ecological purity, and human beings could experience at first hand, total understanding and empathy for all forms of life on Earth. They also transported him to a state some distance from the Earth where there existed a large array of 'spaceships', (or that was Monroe's visualisation of the situation) where, he was told, there existed entities from other energy systems who are watching with considerable concern what is happening on Earth, as the situation is reaching critical proportions which could either open up great potentials for further developments, or else danger for the future, that could affect other regions in the cosmos.

During the many years that Monroe was undergoing these experiences, he developed techniques for helping others to enter the OBE state and to explore the different planes of consciousness and realms that he encountered. He and his co-workers in this venture identified the type of brain waves associated with the OBE state and then found ways of inducing this state by exposing the person concerned to sound waves of the same frequency. (They also found that this technique could be adapted to help people relax after traumatic experiences e.g. after operations, and emotional or mental stress, thereby bringing about psychological and/or physiological healing). Some of the people who thereby entered into the OBE state had similar experiences to Monroe, thus suggesting that these were not just subjective experiences specific to him.

These experiences left Monroe searching for an 'Overview' as a basis from which to understand them. This resulted in him being led into a new phase of OBE explorations. In these he encountered personalities from his past incarnations, (that had exerted subconscious influences on him in his current life) and he became aware that the endpoint of Earth experiences was an integration of all these different personalities into a 'whole' that returned to the source.

During these explorations Monroe found himself approached by discarnate souls who needed help to move on which, from his experiences, he was able to give. He thereby became able to enter into the post-mortem world at will and to act as a rescuer of lost souls. When his wife died, to whom he had been very close, he was able to contact her in the discarnate state and he found the experience of non-physical, soul bonding between them so over-powering as to be almost unbearable. Monroe then developed and expanded his techniques for OBE experiences and taught them to others. The people who learned them became able to explore post-mortem worlds and to help rescue lost souls and themselves lost any fear of death.

The Worlds of Soul and Spirit According to Mystics

Some people - mystics and occultists - claim to be able to separate off their soul and spirit 'bodies' at will and in these to explore consciously and objectively the worlds of soul and spirit. This has given rise to an extensive occult literature that describes these worlds in considerable detail. Mostly this has arisen in the mystical-spiritual-oriented cultures of the East, so that these accounts have a terminology and background viewpoint that is very different from that of the West, which makes them difficult to understand. But there is an account that seems to encapsulate basic features of the mystical descriptions of soul and spirit worlds in a way that is comparatively simple. This is given in 'A Soul's Journey' by Peter RICHELIEU.

Richelieu describes how he was shown the way consciously to detach his soul and spirit from his body during sleep and then taken on an exploration of soul and spirit worlds by an Indian Teacher. He describes seven levels of the soul world. The first two are inhabited by souls whose concerns are strongly linked to the materialistic desires they had while incarnate. The third and fourth levels are occupied by souls who get satisfaction from their commitment to their work - as musicians, artists, doctors, etc. The fifth and sixth levels are the realms of souls whose satisfaction comes from serving humanity or seeking for truth as scientific researchers, philosophers, mystics, etc. The seventh level is the domain of aesthetes who get soul satisfaction from shutting themselves off and seeking internal enlightenment. Richelieu's teacher showed him that the environment in each of these soul levels comprises thought forms generated according to the level of development of the spirits occupying them. Richelieu then describes two levels in the mental-thinking world. The first is the domain of 'wispy creatures', i.e. Egos who have as yet little mental capacity. In the second level the Egos are more advanced, they have evolved greater mental abilities and they are thereby more substantial. Because of limitations imposed by his own state of development Richelieu was unable to penetrate to higher spirit levels.

Richelieu's teacher states that the ultimate aim of the spirit is to seek perfection by successive incarnations, for which about 500 incarnations are required. He states that at top of the evolutionary ladder there exist a number of spirits - Masters - who have achieved this. Among these is Christ who, 'is in control of the spiritual development of this planet'.

Richelieu's teacher describes how, after each incarnation the soul-spirit works its way through the different levels of soul development, passing quickly through those levels which it has worked out in the past and spending more time at the levels that are relevant to its current state of development. After the spirit has worked out and discarded its feeling-soul experiences it moves on to working out its mental, thinking experiences, again passing quickly through levels of past achievement, until it reaches its current state of development. Then it perceives the type of experiences that it needs to undergo in further incarnations (its 'karma') and starts on the journey back. It gathers together the 'mental and soul-feeling equipment' that it has so far developed and carries these with it into its next incarnation. (This pattern of development is similar, but on a larger scale, to the way in which we develop as we pass through different experiences in growing up, e.g. education, jobs, setting up a home, personal relationships, marriage/s, bringing up a family, etc. Each time we leave behind the events involved but carry with us into the next situation the soul-feeling and spirit-thinking qualities that we developed in previous ones).

Although the mystical-spiritual viewpoint has not played as big a part in Western life as it has in the East, there has been an on-going stream of indigenous mysticism. A member of this stream who lectured and wrote extensively on his mystical experiences and viewpoint was RUDOLF STEINER, (1861 - 1925). Steiner seems to have been a 'natural mystic', in that he was born with his consciousness centred more in worlds of soul and spirit than in the physical world, [see his Autobiography and WILSON (1)]. From the hK-M viewpoint we incarnate into the Earth situation from the 'spiritual' world of the Omniverse Hierarchy, so that we exist simultaneously in both worlds and what determines our orientation in life is whether our consciousness is concentrated on our bodily sense impressions from the material world or the less substantial soul-spirit impressions of the spiritual world. With most of us our consciousness is fully occupied with the phenomena of our material existence. Mystics relate more to the spiritual world. In Steiner's case, spiritual world impressions were dominant, at least for the early part of his life. However, he was impressed by the clarity of scientific thinking about the material world so that, by comparison, he regarded most mystical accounts of spiritual worlds as vague and woolly. He therefore determined to expound his mystical experiences with clarity of thought and comprehension. Steiner's studies had led him to the works of the great Germanic philosophers and this caused him to express his ideas in their type of language that made his writings austere and rather tortuous. At the same time he aimed at thoroughness and great detail and he expressed this in esoteric mystical concepts. Thus, all in all, Steiner's books and published lectures are intricate, complex, indigestible and difficult to understand. However, he claimed that everything he said was direct personal experience (and not communicated to him by other mystics as with the accounts of Theosophy). But judging from his extensive works on Western mystics he probably operated within a School of Western mysticism, so that, while he reported his own experiences, his explanations and understanding of them were probably collectively arrived at.

What Steiner says about the worlds of soul and spirit is more detailed and intellectually expressed compared with Richelieu's teacher but much of it is essentially the same. Thus the concept of human beings evolving through sequential incarnations, with karma being the determining factor governing each incarnation is the same. But there is a difference between Richelieu's teacher and Steiner, as to how this takes place. Steiner states that when a spirit is unevolved it reincarnates to gather experience more rapidly than a highly-evolved spirit. But an averagely-evolved spirit reincarnates about twice in each cultural epoch, once as a man and once as a woman (to develop the qualities of each sex). For Western Man this means something like two incarnations in each of the Egyptian, Greek, Roman and modern Western cultures.

There is also a difference in the endpoint to the sequence of our incarnations. Richelieu's teacher claims that the aim is to achieve perfection so as to get off the wheel of rebirth. Steiner states that this is the way of the East, whereas the path of the West is, by repeated incarnations to stay with, and contribute to, the development of the Earth situation for as long as it exists.

Steiner describes the soul as living in a soul world that comprises different levels of activity. And in the same way that, on death, the physical body disintegrates and becomes one with the similar constituents of the background physical world, so does our soul pass through the different states of the soul, (as described by Richelieu's teacher), steadily disintegrating and dispersing into the relevant levels. Having thereby evaluated its soul experience our spirit then finds itself in the spirit world.

The spirit world again comprises different levels of activity. The lower levels are concerned with the spiritual activity involved in physical and soul relationships, the intermediate levels with creative activity, i.e. the thoughts behind art, science, technology, etc. We spend time in, and pass through, these levels according to how we can relate to them. Then we enter into higher levels in which we perceive our past incarnations and how what we have achieved relates to the overall development of humanity and we become aware of our nature as a spiritual entity.

Steiner states that the activity of the spirit world comprises living thoughts, spirit formations, that are continually coming together and dispersing and that these are the creative archetypes of events that take place on Earth. According to hK-M, the activities of entities on Earth create 'memories' in the EM-energy which, as a result of its integrating activity, come together to generate ideas for further developments. Then, living entities, plants, animals and humanity, tap into the relevant integrated memory experiences and work them out and thereby develop them further, in a continuously evolving process. We consider more of what Steiner had to say, and the mystic's viewpoint in general, in further parts of this book.

The Cosmology of the Mystics

The idea of the existence of a Hierarchy of Spiritual Beings, which in this book we have designated the Omniverse Hierarchy, and an associated cosmology is not new; it is extensively described by mystics who give various accounts of its structure and chronology. The mystics look into what they call the Akashic Record, which they state is the memory of all the events of the world, (we would equate this with the EM-energy of hK-M) and from what they 'see' they give an account of creation. Mostly, such cosmologies originate from mystics from the East where, as we have explained earlier, there is a tendency to seek contact with one's spiritual origins. Some of these cosmologies have filtered across to the West, e.g. in Theosophy (BLAVATSKY) and the complementary Arcane School of Alice BAILEY (which are claimed to derive from mystics in Tibet) and the teachings of GURDJIEFF. We have found the concepts of these difficult to understand, as they are described by mystical symbology expressed in Eastern terminology. There is also the Western stream of mysticism, as exemplified by Rudolf Steiner, in which the concepts are equally difficult but at least they are expressed from a Western viewpoint, so we take what Steiner had to say as an example, for an assessment in terms of hK-M.

Steiner's lectures and writings cover many subjects and, in particular, he made significant contributions to education (particularly of disabled children), agriculture and medicine. We synopsise here what, as far as we can understand them, are the key features of his cosmology. This cosmology is concerned with the formation of the Solar System and the Earth planet: it does not deal with the prior formation of galaxies and how these arise and how the Solar System arises out of the Milky Way galaxy and how substances and their atomic structures come into existence. Steiner's cosmology starts with a pre-existing Spiritual Hierarchy comprising three levels, each of which has three sub-levels. These are Seraphim, Cherubim, Thrones, Archangels, Angels, etc. These spiritual beings take it in turns to work in an inert cosmic ether to create the Solar System, according to a Godhead's preconceived plan. The nature of the Godhead is Love, Wisdom and Will and the Spiritual Hierarchy are its manifestations of these qualities.

The Godhead's plan is to create a new type of entity - Humanity - that develops the qualities of will, love and wisdom for itself, in freedom and independence. To achieve this the members of the Spiritual Hierarchy put their qualities of will, feeling and thinking into the inert cosmic ether to create bodies comprising these. Then spirit beings enter into these bodies in an unconscious state to create human beings, who then experience and develop these qualities as they evolve and become conscious.

The Spiritual Hierarchy work in phases of development, in each of which a certain state is achieved and then there is a 'rest and evaluation period' followed by a further phase of activity. But at each stage some of the beings of the Spiritual Hierarchy become immersed in their activities and get left behind. Thus when Humanity emerges it does so against a background of physical, plant and animal kingdoms, each of which comprises different stages of 'left-behind activity'. Humanity's job is then to find its way forward in this left-behind world and in so doing to find new creative potentials in it and in itself and then, as prodigal sons and daughters, to return to God with its achievements. The successive phases of development, or 'incarnations', by which the Earth and its different kingdoms of Nature come into existence are designated Old Saturn, Old Sun and Old Moon, signifying a progressive differentiation out of the cosmic ether of the Solar System, in which each phase of development carries the previous one further forward.

This 'cosmology', describing the creation of the Solar System and Humanity, starts with a God with a conscious plan for creation that is carried out by the activities of a Spiritual Hierarchy. It does not, like hK-M, get back to a state before any beings exist and give an account of how the Hierarchy comes about. With hK-M the different levels of the Omniverse Hierarchy arise in successive Universes as a result of cycles of s-entity break down which give rise to self-actualising beings. When they first come into existence, as self-actualising entities these are simply beings of will activity then, as described in Chapter 5, through their interaction with subsequent generations of entities, which arise in later Universes, they develop sensation-feeling-soul qualities and then, thinking-understanding-wisdom. Thus the Hierarchy comprises beings of will, soul-feeling and spirit-thinking-understanding at different levels of development. In studying the Akashic Record to understand the creation of the Earth planet and Humanity, Steiner and other mystics at a similar level of development, perceive the Spiritual Hierarchy and its activities (i.e. the Omniverse Hierarchy) and assume that the creative thinking and loving concern that emanates from the top levels shows the existence of a Creator God. But, according to hK-M, even the higher, seemingly God-like, levels of the Omniverse Hierarchy arise out of the creative evolutionary processes and do not precede them.

The mystics' awareness of spiritual activities underlying material events leads them to assume that there is a Godhead who has a conscious preconceived plan that it is working out. According to hK-M consciousness is something that develops out of the evolutionary processes, not something that precedes them. Creation proceeds in cycles in which the s-entities, in seeking increased sense of self become increasingly active until their stress of interaction causes them to break down at their peripheries and to revert to an inactive state, giving rise to a sequence of Universes. In the inwards reversion part of the cycle the experience of what happened in the outwards expansion part is assimilated and evaluated and stresses associated with disharmonies and potentials for further developments, that have inadvertently arisen, are recognised. In this respect, although overall there is no initial plan for creation, on the next outwards pulse there is an attempt to realise these potentials in further developments. In doing this the established members of the hierarchy seek to guide the development of the new generation of activities, that arises from the interaction of the s-entities, (in the same way that we seek to guide the development of further generations that arise 'from the workings of Nature').

Phenomena that arise within a cycle likewise work themselves out in sub-cycles. Thus Steiner's account of the formation of the Solar System taking place in phases, or incarnations, was probably his observation, in the Akashic Record, of its formation by the punctuated equilibrium principle, described in Chapter 9. In this the activity of the Sun entity accumulates substances to its centre until the resistance that these create to its motion builds up to a level that causes it to contract under the s-pressure, with rejection of excess material to form a planet. This happens a number of times to create the Solar System.

If in hK-M you want to look for an ultimate Creator, you find it in the s-pressure that causes everything to happen. But this is not by design, or to achieve any pre-determined goal and there is no consciousness by which the, purely mechanical, s-pressure knows what it is doing. Once brought into existence by the s-pressure things are responsible for their own, and for their mutual, development. There is no overall pre-conceived plan that is being worked out; plans for new developments evolve as the evolutionary process progresses.

Steiner's cosmological account of a Spiritual Hierarchy, with above them an all empowering, unknowable Godhead, is an ancient cosmology that was described by DIONYSIUS THE AREOPAGITE (1st Century A.D.) but he was not the originator of this doctrine, he got it from earlier mystics and it has been a theme of the beliefs of subsequent mystics, such as Thomas Aquinas, through the ages. The Hierarchy comprises three groups or a first, second and third hierarchy, each of which is subdivided into three subgroups. In his efforts to develop a greater understanding of the Hierarchy and its workings, Steiner renamed the different levels according to the roles which he perceived them to be carrying out. We give below the ancient, traditional designations, (in some cases with alternative names) and Steiner's 'functional' designations.

First Hierarchy	Steiner's Designation
Seraphim	Spirits of Love
Cherubim	Spirits of Harmony
Thrones	Spirits of Will
Second Hierarchy	
Kyriotetes or Dominions	Spirits of Wisdom
Dynamis or Mights or Virtues	Spirits of Movement
Exusiai or Powers	Spirits of Form
Third Hierarchy	
Archai or Principalities	Spirits of Personality
Archangels	Fire Spirits
Angels	Sons of Life or of Twilight

According to hK-M, the members of the Omniverse Hierarchy who incarnated into bodies that had biologically evolved on Earth, to give rise to humanity, came from an intermediate level and at first, they still had some memory of their existence in the Hierarchy. Thus they formulated a cosmology in terms of creation taking place in terms of the workings of the Hierarchy, according to their understanding of this. Their ideas created thought forms, which were then re-activated and reinforced by subsequent mystics through the ages, thereby building up this viewpoint. Thus, when seeking understanding of the workings of the Universe, it is possible for mystics to activate these thought forms created by earlier thinkers, instead of perceiving the reality of events in the memory-record of the Omniverse Hierarchy (the Akashic Record).

When Richelieu's teacher took him to a high level of the soul world, he said:

> *At these higher levels some men surround themselves with the thought-forms of Seraphim and Cherubim, in strict accordance with the ancient Hebrew scriptures.It is perfectly real to them ......many of them even make thought forms of God or St Peter, and nothing that you could say would convince them that they are living in a world of illusion. There will come a day when they have developed their intellect a little more, when they will begin to try to ascertain what is fact and what is illusion.'*

It could be that this applies to Steiner (and many other mystics).

Thus it is not easy to assess the validity of what Steiner had to say. Colin WILSON (1), tried to do this and concluded that there is much that gives a deeper understanding of existence but also much that is erroneous; we would agree with this evaluation. As a simple example of something erroneous, Wilson points out that Steiner's 'spiritual visions' of the events associated with King Arthur's castle at Tintagel in Cornwall were at variance with the archaeological evidence. Here we suspect that Steiner was tuning into the thought forms of the mythology that had developed around King Arthur and Tintagel Castle and not into the reality of the situation. We think that, in a similar way, Steiner's spiritual visions of the workings of creation and the activities of the Spiritual Hierarchy confused events recorded in the Akashic Record (the EM-energy) with thought forms that other mystics had created about these happenings.

[In their mystical state of consciousness mystics seem able to become aware of entities and their activities taking place remotely and/or at non-physical levels of existence. According to hK-M everything consists of activities in the basic energy, the reverberations of which impinge on everything else so that, in principle it is possible to become aware of any other activity/entity by tuning into it. This is a normal procedure for the members of the Omniverse Hierarchy and it is an ability that we all possessed and something that mystics can do in their incarnated homo sapiens state. Because of the pressure of coping with events taking place in the space-time of physical existence on Earth, most of us have lost this expanded awareness ability. However, Kalahari bushmen (VAN DER POST) and Australian aborigines (ROSE) still possess this expanded awareness, in that they know when their hunters have made a kill regardless of how far away this happens. There is considerable evidence that animals possess this expanded awareness. Thus there are many examples of dogs and cats and some other animals, that possess a strong bond with their owners, that are aware when their owner is coming home or is the person at the other end of the line when the phone rings. Animals can also sense impending catastrophes, such as earthquakes, SHELDRAKE (2). Also there is, of course, the ability of birds and some other animals to navigate across vast distances in migrations, and for pets to find their way home when transported long distances away. All of this points to the existence of expanded states of awareness that most of us no longer possess but must lie incipient within us].

Another feature of Steiner's cosmology, which again is expressed in esoteric, 'mythological' type terminology, is that he claimed to perceive three streams of activity at work. He called these the Luciferic, Ahrimanic and Christ streams. We would equate these with what we have called the Idealist (Luciferic), Materialist (Ahrimanic) and the Central, Christ streams. The primary feature of hK-M is that everything is evolving and that this is brought about by seeking enhanced sense of self. Evolution consists of moving from a past state of development to a future state but this is not a uniform progression, so that some parts are ahead, some parts lag behind and some parts occupy a middle state in moving from the old to the new. Thus, in our era of spiritual entities incarnating into hominid bodies to lead a material existence on Earth, there are some people who get their sense of self from a strong bonding to material existence, while some people get their sense of self from hanging on to their contact with the spiritual world. In between are people who represent the balanced state who, through material activities develop soul-feeling and spirit-thinking and understanding. This principle equally applied as successive Universes arose, so that the three groups exist at the top level of the Omniverse Hierarchy and they seek enhanced sense of self by fostering the development of the lower levels, according to their natures. Thus, the more material (Ahrimanic) group seeks to foster materialistic interests and activities, the more ethereal (Luciferic) group seeks to foster spiritual interests and activities, while the central group seeks to foster balanced, spiritual development through material existence.

Two Contemporary Mystics

For those of us who are not mystics it is difficult to develop empathy for them and their experiences and mystics usually do not say much about themselves. But to try and gain some insight into the mystical nature and its experiences we synopsise accounts given by other people of the lives of two contemporary mystics, Sai Baba and 'Daskalos'.

Sai Baba

The story of the contemporary Sai Baba starts with a previous Sai Baba of Shirdi who was an Indian Saint (who in turn was reputed to be a reincarnation of a yet earlier Indian Saint) who died in Shirdi in 1918, after stating that he would reincarnate in eight year's time. In 1926 a boy was born in Puttaparti who, as he grew up, showed himself to possess magical powers and to be of outstanding spirituality and great wisdom. At the age of thirteen this boy went through a period of transformation lasting some weeks, at the end of which he announced that he was Sai Baba and an Avatar. It is a story similar to that of Jesus becoming Christ and, in fact, Sai Baba claims that he is an incarnation of God, as was Krishna and Christ and that he comes to teach humanity the way to God. He states that when it is necessary Avatars appear on Earth to show humanity the way forward.

Avatars are difficult to understand by the Western mind but in the East they are regarded as incarnations in a material body of some, or all, of the qualities of God (in hK-M terms, the Godhead). It would seem that the Avatar state is achieved by the practice of a highly spiritual way of life and meditation exercises over many incarnations, that leads to at-one-ness with God and in the case of Krishna, Christ (and Sai Baba), to manifesting the qualities of God. Sai Baba claims that he is Divine Love and he states that he wants to share with humanity the gift of love. People who meet him report that they have an experience of almost over-powering love. He has a large following in India and a number of Westerners have spent time with him and written books about him, (for example, MURPHET, LANG, SANDWEISS).

It is attested by these Western authors that Sai Baba performs miracles similar to those carried out by Christ, that is: healing; raising from the dead; production of food for his followers, like Christ with the loaves and fishes; the ability to appear to his followers in places far removed from where he is physically; omnipresence, that is, he can know what happens to anyone anywhere. He often manifests objects out of empty space as gifts for his followers and, in particular, in this way he produces large quantities of vibuti, a sort of ash that has healing properties. He says that he does this by exercising his will power to create and that we can all do this if we develop our mental powers, purify our hearts and love creation.

However, Sai Baba says these things are not important, he calls them his visiting cards that are designed to awaken people to his Divinity and thereby to his spiritual teachings. Once so awakened he wants his devotees to follow the path of service to God and humanity. Sai Baba seeks to influence people to this end by the spiritual teachings that he expounds to the large number of people who visit his ashram. These teachings have been published in books, and a number of Sai Baba centres set up around the world by his devotees, who seek to promote wider awareness of them. In India Sai Baba has set up schools in which young people are instructed in moral principles, as well as conventional subjects. For a practical application of moral principles in daily life Sai Baba proposes cutting down on waste in four areas. These are money, food, time and energy, (KRYSTAL). For specific examples of unnecessary wastage Sai Baba quotes; expenditure on excessive material possessions; unnecessary luxurious travelling; lavish dinner parties and excessive eating while the poor starve; time wasted on meaningless pursuits, e.g. unedifying films, books, chatter and gossip; energy expended on negative emotions of anger, greed, envy and jealousy; activities such as card playing, gambling and drinking which waste time, money and energy. By cutting down on these activities people can reduce their attachment to material things and, at the same time, help those less fortunate than themselves. Sai Baba himself eats very little food - he states that he does not need earthly food and he does not solicit or accept money or gifts for himself.

The core of Sai Baba's teachings is that the essential being of Man is spirit, which is a fragment of the Supreme Consciousness - God. He states that the difference between him and other people is that he is God and knows it, whereas the rest of us are God but we do not know it. Human beings have become so immersed in the material world and in Egotism that their spirits have lost contact with their source and this has given rise to the troubles of the world. Therefore humanity needs to seek to reunite with God. The way to do this is to follow the path of love by the practice of compassion, humility and forbearance that leads to God. That if we live a righteous life, seek God, eliminate egoism and perform the will of God, then God comes to us. Sai Baba teaches a return to the ethical and moral principles of life laid down in the ancient Indian texts of the Vedas, Upanishads and Gita, to counterbalance the materialism that has arisen from Western culture. By following these principles humanity can attain eternal bliss and become one with the Absolute and get off the wheel of continual rebirths in the world of substance. But, he says, all faiths should be respected as there is a basic unity underlying them and there are many paths that lead to God.

Sai Baba states that the Western way of science is to seek God in the world outside us, whereas we should seek God within, by meditation and other spiritual practices. He says that the material world is impermanent, Maya (illusion), and that we should renounce material attachments to follow the path of the spirit that is the true reality.

The path of spiritual development pursued in the East and the, to us, strange powers that it gives rise to, are so very different from the outlook of the West that it can seem incomprehensible and unbelievable. One yogi, YOGANANDA, states that he was trained by Eastern 'Masters' and sent by them to the West to provide enlightenment and understanding of the Eastern path of development. In his autobiography he describes his training and indicates how yogis and Avatars acquire the powers ascribed to them. He gives many examples of: omnipresence (the ability to know what is going on anywhere), bilocation (the ability to appear simultaneously in different places), miraculous healing, raising from the dead and materialisation of objects by thought power. These powers, he says, arise from the practice of meditation in which, by eliminating one's personal ego desires and Ego thoughts it is possible to enter into a state of bliss and at-oneness with God and thereby to become a channel through which the will of God can work. Miracles, healing etc. are then brought about by the Master or Avatar through his omnipresence, knowing what lies behind the physically manifest situation and interceding with God to heal and supply the needs of those concerned, where this is in harmony with God's aims for His Creation. In some cases the Master/Avatar takes upon himself, and resolves, disharmonies in the person that block the healing process.

Sai Baba's teachings, and those of the other Masters and Avatars described by Yogananda, are based on the existence of a God behind all creation and that nothing can happen without the will of God and that God is unknowable and unfathomable.

'Daskalos'

It is difficult for those of us who do not have mystical experience to get to grips with what is said by those who do. The experiences themselves are a strange and foreign world and, where they are described by Eastern mystics, the unfamiliar language in which they are couched adds to the difficulty of their comprehension. There is, however, a mystic who, despite his wide-ranging mystical experiences has led an ordinary western life style and who has allowed his experiences to be described by an observer-friend in simple, understandable language. The mystic, Spyros Sathi, known as Daskalos (a Greek term for Master), lived in Cyprus and the person writing about him, MARKIDES, left Cyprus, became a Professor of Sociology in the USA and returned to Cyprus to apply his sociological studies to the activities of the mystic. At the time when Markides did this the mystic was a retired civil servant living on a small pension.

Markides is a typically Western-educated person to whom mystical experiences were at first unbelievable and incomprehensible. However, he formed a good relationship with Daskalos and he tried, over a period of several years, to gain some understanding of Daskalos and his experiences by asking him a great many questions that Daskalos did his best to answer in a way understandable to a non-mystic. As a result Markides wrote three books that provide non-mystics with a good insight into the very different world of the mystic. At the same time his accounts of Daskalos's down-to-earth life style make it easier to relate to Daskalos as a person.

Daskalos, like Sai Baba, would seem to have developed his mystical abilities over a number of previous incarnations in which, by intensive meditation, he made strenuous efforts to achieve at-one-ness with God. He claims to have acquired the status of 'Master', i.e. in his meditations to be able to enter into a state of God consciousness. Daskalos mentions some of his past incarnations and states that, as a self-realised person he has always been conscious of these. Also, because he retained his consciousness of soul-spirit worlds he was aware of entering into a body at birth, which he witnessed from outside as well as experiencing it from inside.

The key feature of the mystical practices of Daskalos and the members of the School of mystics which he founded, is the ability to detach themselves, as soul-spirit entities, from their gross material bodies and to be able to explore the worlds of soul and spirit. At the same time they develop omnipresence - the ability to know what happens anywhere, which Daskalos describes as being able to concentrate and tune into the vibrations involved in the happening, (in the way that we tune into different vibrations to get different radio and television stations). In this way, he says, it is possible to contact another person's soul and/or spirit, or discarnate souls and spirits. Daskalos states that the Universe is full of intelligent beings who live on soul and spirit planes of existence and that, as well as these beings existing alongside humanity, many of them are associated with the other planets of the Solar System and even with the Sun. They are more advanced than humanity in that, by their power of thought, they are able to materialise and dematerialise 'bodies' for themselves if they require to do so and that they are also behind the so-called UFO phenomena. Daskalos claims to be able to communicate with these beings and also to perceive past events, because everything registers in the Akashic Record, which the mystic can examine. But, in order to do this, it is necessary to have conventional knowledge of events so as to know what particular underlying soul and spirit activity to look for. He describes a variant of the state of omnipresence, in which he detaches his consciousness from his body and expands it over increasingly larger areas, to perceive what is going on around him. Arising from this is the ability to enter into, and communicate with, other forms of life, e.g. plants and animals, at their level of consciousness.

Examples are given where Daskalos materialised himself at a distance from his physical body and in this state performed actions, which he claimed he did by channelling the universal energy that exists everywhere. Thus, during a rough sea voyage, in an expanded state of consciousness he drew on this energy to calm the sea. Daskalos claims that he produces phenomena such as these by intense concentration and will power, developed by his meditation practices, by which he can direct the universal energy. Many cases are quoted of 'miraculous' healing, that is, healing that seems to contravene physical laws. Daskalos states that in order to do this, one has to develop unconditional love for other human beings, and that he would not accept money for it, as he is operating Divine laws and using energies from which he is not allowed personal gain. Daskalos states that his group is part of a world-wide 'White Brotherhood' of mystics but that his group are pursuing their own particular path of Research for Truth, and development of mystical powers for serving humanity. He claims that there is nothing miraculous in what he does, that he operates with laws of Nature that the mystic is aware of and that the powers that he works with are available to everyone.

Daskalos gives teachings on personal development and the purpose of life. These derive in part from his personal experiences and also from invisible Masters who he contacts, in particular, a Father Yohannan who he says is Saint John the Evangelist. The purpose of life is for humanity to undergo cycles of incarnations of separateness in which we seek union with God, which is achieved by overcoming our personal ego desires and seeking to serve our fellow men. When at-one-ness with God is achieved there is no longer a need to reincarnate. However, advanced Masters often continue to do so, in order to take up and work out the negative karma of others, so as to help them, and descriptions are given of him doing this. We have a permanent personality, which is the totality of all of our incarnations, within which our present personality exists, unconscious of its source. We do not become aware of our past incarnations until we have evolved sufficiently to be able to cope with the complexity and implications of this knowledge. When we achieve this stage of development we merge with our permanent personality. The advanced mystic lives in his permanent personality using his soul and spirit bodies to express himself, in the same way that the rest of us use our physical body to express ourselves. The reason for the cycle of incarnations is to develop individuality. In Earth existence each of us is a separate personality, whereas in other worlds e.g. that of 'angels', all angels are the same and perform the tasks allotted to them; they do not possess our individuality and free will. As with the other mystics, Daskalos states that the material world is Maya (illusion) and that true reality lies in the spiritual world.

Behind all this is God, the Absolute, the Pan-Universal Logos, who is aware of everything, who is working out His Divine Plan for creation. However, in the case of Humanity the Divine Plan extends only up to our birth and after our death because, with the gift of free will, it is up to us what we make of our lives in between. The Absolute is all, it is self-sufficient and it has the urge to express itself, it has life and motion. It expresses itself in mind that is a super-substance that makes possible this Divine Expressiveness. As with all descriptions where it is claimed that there exists a God with a plan behind creation, Daskalos has difficulty in accounting for the existence of evil. He gives the usual explanation that God created this to provide alternatives for Humanity in the development of free will. But he states that it also exists at other levels in the spiritual world. Furthermore, when he experiences the scale of cruelty and death in battles in the Middle East he says that he cannot understand how God allows this. [This is a non-existent problem with hK-M, where there is no Divine Plan but a self-evolving system of entities, some of whom get caught up in pursuing their sense of self at the expense of others and thereby create disharmony/evil].

Daskalos states that Christ was God incarnate, whereas other spiritual leaders, such as Buddha, were human beings who, by spiritual striving, achieved a degree of God consciousness. He says that Yohannan (St. John the Baptist), who is the source of the higher aspects of his teaching, was not a human being undergoing cycles of incarnation but an angel who incarnated on Earth to announce the coming of Christ.

Daskalos states that humanity did not arise by biological evolution, but started as Holy Monads that entered into Earth incarnations. [In this he could have been tracing back, in the Akashic Record, the origins of the members of the Omniverse Hierarchy who incarnated into hominid bodies, to give rise to homo sapiens].

An important feature of Daskalos's teachings is that all our feelings and thoughts create forms in the basic energy substance that is present everywhere and because these thought forms take on an independent existence he calls them 'elementals'. We are creating these unconsciously all the time, but if we develop our will power we can do this consciously and invest these elementals with the power to perform controlled actions for us in which they carry out good or bad intentions (black magic). [As we have explained earlier, according to hK-M what Daskalos calls elementals, would be thought forms created by the mind taking in, giving form to, and expelling space-energy].

Daskalos states that the elementals that we create do what we assign them to do and then return to us. Thereby we become the collection of all our feelings, thoughts and deeds; and these are carried with us through our subsequent incarnations and this is the mechanism of karma, that is, this is the conglomeration of our past actions that we have to work out in order to develop further. However, if we have done things that we sincerely repent of it is possible for God to negate this part of our karma for us.

A major problem is that when our elementals of desire and thoughts return to us, and we continue to feel and think in the same way, we can put more energy into them and this can happen again and again and thereby build up into obsessions, e.g. for smoking, drinking, gambling, etc. If we then fight these we put more energy and power into them; the way to deal with them is to ignore them as much as possible and to create new elementals that lead to a more positive way of life, and put our energy into these. In our feelings and thoughts about other people we create elementals that impinge on them and these evoke a response according to the nature of the person. That is, if we send out elementals of love to a person this can awaken the nature of love in that person and evoke a response of love from them. Similarly, by creating elementals of love for an animal we create a reaction of love from the animal. Equally if we create elementals of dislike or hatred for a person we can evoke a similar response from them, unless the person does not possess these qualities to activate. By thinking, and thereby creating elementals, about what will happen and then reinforcing these it is possible to create self-fulfilling prophecies.

The Viewpoint of hK-M on These Matters

OBE's show that the spirit is something separate from the body that can exist independently of it. Post-mortem communications show that the spirit survives the death of the body. The experiences of mystics show that the spirit can separate from the body and explore a spiritual world.

In terms of the scientific viewpoint developed to describe the pattern of our existence these phenomena are strange and difficult to explain but from the hK-M viewpoint they do not present any problem. That our spirit is separate from the body, and exists after the death of the body, and is able to detach from the body and explore a spiritual world, do not require explanation. We, as spirits, came into existence in a previous Universe, long before the body into which we have incarnated existed. Our spirit exists permanently - it is only the body that dies. And when mystics explore the spiritual world they are not exploring into the unknown, but only returning whence they came, our true home.

According to hK-M in the beginning the Kosmos was in a state of unconscious dormant energy. This stirred into activity that, on the one hand gave it a sense of self and on the other hand created a state of stress in it so that it reverted to an inactive unstressed state but it then lost its sense of self so it became active again. This started the Kosmos on a cyclic existence in each cycle of which it recapitulated what it had achieved previously and then went on to carry the situation further. In seeking increased sense of self it became increasingly active, to a state of turbulence in which it broke down into a collective of separate self-actualising substance-like entities whose natures were to exert their will to be active. In further cycles these will activity entities interacted with each other and thereby developed sensations and they became beings who acted out of their (soul) feelings. In yet further cycles, in which new will activity entities 'were born', the extensive experiences of the earlier ones generated in them an awareness of what was happening and this led them to form thoughts about it all and they then acted out of their (spirit) thinking of what was going on. In this way there developed a Hierarchy of Kosmic entities playing their various roles in its evolution.

In the present cycle, on planet Earth there has taken place a localised miniature pattern of development similar to that of the Kosmos as a whole, in which the will activities of substance entities have created stresses in the space energy that have given these parts of it a sense of self and they have become self actualising entities to bring about a hierarchy of will activity, sensation-feeling activity and awareness-generated activity in the biological evolution of single-celled and multicellular plant and animal organisms, culminating in hominids. Because this development took place largely independently of the main stream Omniverse Hierarchy it attracted the attention of some of its members who became involved in it and gradually they incarnated into hominid bodies to give rise to homo sapiens. In doing this homo sapiens lost their contact with the Omniverse Hierarchy but they then experienced a greater sense of self and independence of activity and free will, than they did in the activities of the mainstream Hierarchy. When, in their incarnated state, they attained the thinking, seeking to understand their situation, state of development, two streams arose. There was the 'scientific' stream that directed their consciousness to observing what was taking place around them and sought to classify and clarify the processes taking place and to deduce by their thinking what lay behind it all. There was the mystical stream that looked into themselves and found that they comprised life, soul-feeling and spirit thinking activities and by exploring these aspects of their natures they came into contact with and explored these worlds of activity in the Omniverse Hierarchy. Thereby they learned about what lay behind the manifestations of these activities and established contact with various levels of the Omniverse Hierarchy.

Mystics such as Daskalos seem to have mastered the ability to explore the worlds of soul and spirit in considerable depth and, as a result, they have developed the ability to cooperate with the beings of the Omniverse Hierarchy and to manipulate the space-energy and the phenomena that derive from it which make up the Universe, by the power of thought. But, although they seem to have developed a great understanding of the way that the established order works and of how things happen, they do not understand why things are the way that they are. Various schools of mystics have come up with different ideas, e.g. Steiner stated that behind the processes of creation there lies the activities of a spiritual hierarchy of Seraphim, Cherubim, etc. whereas Richelieu's Indian teachers state that these are illusory thought forms, they in turn promulgate the Hindu doctrine that we evolve from animals, whereas Daskalos's group state that this is not so and that we are holy monads originating from the Holy Spirit.

In general mystics state that humanity comprises spiritual beings inhabiting material bodies but they offer no explanation for why this should be so or, indeed, for why humanity exists at all. They state that there exists a world of spiritual beings who, in their mystical state of awareness they can contact but again, they offer no explanation for why this is so. They pursue their development 'within the organisation', by seeking to operate at increasingly higher levels, according to the methods by which it works. The world that they describe, with its different levels of spiritual beings and their multifarious activities is very complex and lacks any underlying principles and rationale. When asked about what lies behind creation they come up with abstract explanations in terms like 'God', or the Absolute, or the Universal Logos. Because they reach up to ever-higher levels of spiritual beings, they take the view that ultimately behind everything there is a God/the Absolute/ the Logos, who is working out a preconceived plan and then they interpret everything according to what they imagine this plan to be. (Mystics have to form concepts about their experiences like scientists do and in the same way that their observations, like those of scientists, may be valid, their interpretations of the significance of them can, like those of scientists, be incorrect).

According to hK-M, by being cut-off in a material body humanity perceives the world as an 'outside observer', and thereby develops objective scientific consciousness. That is, because we do not perceive directly the workings of creation but only their external, material manifestations, we have to form concepts about what lies behind it all. Thus scientists have developed theories about the underlying forces at work that explain their astronomical observations of the Universe and of the behaviour of the substances of the world. This, in turn, has led them to seek for the laws and principles at work in it all and to the origin of everything giving rise, for example, to the Big Bang theory and how it has all evolved to become the way that it is. As a result humanity is able to make a contribution to understanding that cannot be obtained by entities that live within the organisation who, although they know **how** it works, do not understand **why** it is the way that it is and the underlying principles by which it has developed. As a result of this detached objectivity it is possible for a deeper understanding of the workings of the Kosmos to arise.

The mystic's teachings do not offer any explanation for, or relate to, the observations of science about the galaxy-star-planetary structure of the Universe. Equally they do not offer any explanation for the way that life has evolved on Earth. Daskalos states that the body of a human being is provided by the 'Holy Spirit.' But this takes no account of data gathered by science that shows that life has evolved on Earth through prokaryotic cells, eukaryotic cells and multicellular organisms and that these have evolved to give rise to hominids. Like Steiner, Daskalos states that everything arises from a world of ideas or creative archetypes. According to hK-M, everything started from a state of dormant energy, without any prior plan or ideas - ideas are the manifestation of mind activity and there was no mind - this is something that has arisen out of evolution and did not pre-exist. As the dormant energy became active and differentiated into entities that underwent experiences, their experiences became their natures. Each entity is a storehouse of its experiences that, as it encounters different situations, seeks expression in ways that give it enhanced sense of self. Thus, in our own lives whatever we do becomes a memory that relates to memories of our previous activities and leads to ideas for new ventures and developments. There is no pre-existing plan, everything evolves out of what has gone before, according to the way that things fit together.

According to hK-M, nothing can be dismissed as Maya (illusion), in the way that the mystics dismiss the phenomena of the material world. Everything is part of a whole and understanding the whole requires understanding the significance of all of the parts and not the dismissal of some of them. Mystical experience may lead to contact with the highest levels of the Omniverse Hierarchy and their quality of love. But these beings are not a pre-existing God that lies behind the manifestations of creation and they are not omniscient and they do not preplan creation and they do not know what the future holds. According to hK-M, the Kosmos is a self-evolving system and, as such, each further phase of development arises out of previously unknown potentials that appear during the activities of the current phase.

hK-M claims that, by the 'external objective consciousness' of science probing for underlying principles to perceive what brings everything about, a new understanding of the origins and working of the Omniverse can be achieved. The contribution of the mystics is a practical, living awareness of the activities of the already-established Omniverse Hierarchy, which science knows nothing about. The development of hK-M type principles, incorporating scientific findings with the working knowledge of the mystic, would produce a conscious realisation by the Kosmos of its own nature and abilities; so that, out of its initial unconscious expression of its energy and realisation of its innate potentials, it would become a self-conscious Creator.

Nowadays our perception of the world is largely conditioned by modern science that conceives everything to consist of mechanical activities taking place in a world of substance and this therefore is the way in which everything is explained. In the past humanity saw everything as the activities of spirits - in stones, plants, animals, everything. In the future humanity's perception will doubtless be different again, perhaps in something like hK-M's evolutionary-wholistic terms, with its grading of mechanical-will, soul-feeling and spirit-thinking levels of activities

Chapter 13

Appendix 3 to Chapter 5: The Omniverse and a New Dimension to Hominids

The Energy Fields of the Human Being

The Constitution of the Human Being

In this Chapter we consider the nature of the human being in the light of the *h*K-M principles of evolution and some of the implications of this, particularly for healing.

According to *h*K-M human beings have come about as the result of a long period of evolution that started with the arising of prokaryotic cells. These interacted to create eukaryotic cells; eukaryotic cells interacted to create multicellular entities; multicellular organisms interacted with each other and the world around them to give rise to sensations that led to the development of a feeling soul; out of this stream of development there arose entities in which the organising soul activities became individualised, to give rise to a thinking hominid (Neanderthal man). Members of the pre-existing spiritual hierarchy then incarnated into Neanderthal bodies so as to gain experience of the Earth situation, resulting in the 'spirit' in human beings that seeks to interact with, and express itself through, the hierarchy of energy fields that make up the hominid body, via a system of energy meridians and controlling centres (chakras), fig. 13.1.

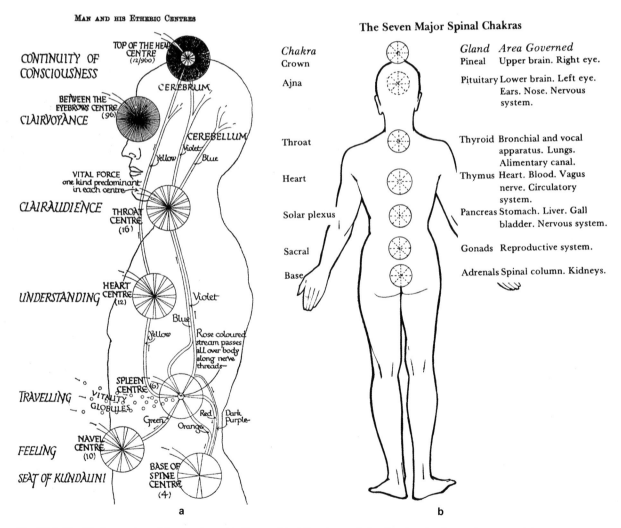

Fig. 13.1 The Chakra system, (a) as portrayed in theosophical literature, relating it to levels of consciousness; (b) relating it to the workings of the body via the endocrine glands. Different authors give different viewpoints on the chakra system.
a from POWELL, 'The Etheric Double', Courtesy of the Theosophical Publishing House, London b from TANSLEY, reproduced by kind permission of the author

Thus we comprise a hierarchy of activities, with each level interacting with, and dependent on, the level below. All levels of our existence on Earth are ultimately dependent on the manipulation of physical substances while, conversely, physical substances can affect all levels, as with the changes in feelings and thinking brought about by the ingestion of hallucinatory drugs. The link with substance is necessary for us to live, and to express ourselves, in the material world. As long as we are alive the channel for doing this is always there, thus even if we are in a relaxed meditative state of non-physical activity, the link with our biological/substance body is still sufficient to produce detectable biological/physical changes, as measured for example, by an EEG (electroencephalogram) of our brain activity. Equally soul-feeling and spirit-thinking activities when we are inert and asleep produce biological-physical activity, as shown by REMs (rapid eye movements) during dreaming. But because these come about through the interactions of a hierarchy of levels of activity, the measured physical activity is only a remote shadow of the activities of our soul-feeling and spirit-thinking events that cause it.

The Energy Fields of Organisms

If we could perceive everything that makes us what we are, that lies behind the behaviour of the substances of our bodies, we would see a hierarchy of energy fields. Similarly we would see limited hierarchies of energy fields for animals and plants. Thus if we look at someone and imagine that we could see his/her inner workings we would see a complex system of flows of substances in the blood stream, the digestive and excretory systems, the reproductive system, the nervous system, etc. And each of these would, in turn be associated with a pattern of energy activity. Then, if we could look beyond that we would see patterns of soul-feeling and spirit-thinking and the energy activities associated with these, which cause a person to behave as they do.

It is only modern Western science that believes that substances can somehow assemble themselves into a human body e.g. into a heart that then acts as a pump to cause blood to flow throughout the body, and that substances somehow give rise to feelings and to thinking and consciousness. Other cultures believe that there is a flow of energy associated with the activities of the body. Thus the ancient Greeks believed that the body's activities are sustained by a flow of pneuma and the activity of the mind by a flow of psyche; the Indian culture believes that the activities of the body are brought about by a flow of prana; the Chinese culture by a flow of Qi (or Ch'i); and the Polynesians by mana; while contemporary Russian scientists, from their researches conclude that there is a flow of what they call bioplasma. WHITE AND KRIPPNER list these and other such beliefs in the existence of energy systems that sustain the human body in Appendix I of their book. As explained previously, the hK-M view is that substances do not of themselves create organisms: organisms come about by substances creating stresses in the space energy that give rise to patterns of activity that become self-actualising and act on the substances, giving rise to prokaryotic cells, eukaryotic cells, multicellular entities and hominids in ways that have been described.

A number of mystics and psychics claim to perceive the workings of etheric (life) processes and the soul and spirit of a person as an aura of activities that permeates and surrounds the physical body. They also claim to see illness as aberrations in these 'bodies' that, with sufficient skill, they can diagnose. (A detailed description of a range of auric states has been given by the Theosophically-orientated mystic, LEADBEATER). In some cases they claim that, by appropriately concentrating their 'psychic vision', they can perceive the workings of the organs of the body by an X-ray-type vision. A neuro-psychiatrist, Shafica KARAGULLA was so impressed by the evidence for the perception of auras and the way in which these express the state of biological, emotional and mental health of a person, that she directed her researches to this subject. She found a number of people who were able to perceive the human aura, who she investigated and she described their abilities and perceptions. (An account by a person with these abilities, of the different levels of consciousness that are associated with them and what each level perceives is given in 'Man's Latent Powers', by PAYNE). Although most of us cannot perceive these energy fields, we can sometimes 'sense them' by our emotional reactions, positive or negative, to other people without physical contact, or without even speaking to them. Also, our auras or force fields can merge to create a collective one, as occurs, for example, when watching a football match, or enjoying a musical festival or concert, or when crowds are aroused by a charismatic leader. Auras are usually perceived by mystics and clairvoyants and therefore tend to have a mystical or spiritualist connotation. But there is nothing mystical about the fact that the human body operates by patterns of energy activities that we do not normally perceive.

According to hK-M the hierarchy of self-actualising activities that makes up a human being operates against the s-pressure, causing a pattern of reverberations, or vibrations, away from him/her corresponding to the various activities taking place in him/her, which clairvoyants claim to be able to perceive and which can to some extent be detected by suitable equipment, to provide information on what is going on in the body. This is similar to the way in which scientists detect the structure and activities of the constituents of atoms from the radiations that are given off in atomic spectra and the rearrangements taking place in molecules from the molecular spectra. Radiations corresponding to substance activities in the workings of the heart and brain are measured in ECG and EEG recordings. Thus we, by our body, soul and feeling activities produce vibrations that impinge on everything around us and equally we experience vibrations impinging on us as a result of the activities of other things. This is a potentially important expanding field of investigation, to deal with which would require a book in itself and an expertise that we do not possess; we can only point to a few books that give accounts and references for the interested reader to follow up.

Radionics

We consider first the development of what has come to be known as Radionics (RUSSELL, see also GERBER and SCOTT-MUMBY). This began in the early 1900's when an American neurologist, Albert Abrams, noticed that when he percussed (tapped) the abdomen of a patient who had a small cancerous ulcer on the lip, when the patient was facing west, instead of getting the hollow resonance of a healthy person he got a dull note and he got similar dull responses from an area just above the navel and another area over the left shoulder blade. He then found that he got the same effect with other patients suffering from cancer in the early stages. Abrams attributed the dull note from the patient's abdomen to some sort of 'radiation' originating in the molecules of the cancerous tissue affecting nerve fibres to cause muscle contraction in the abdominal wall that his percussing detected. To see whether this 'radiation' could affect someone else he selected a healthy medical student and attached to his forehead a container in which there was a piece of cancerous tumour and he found that when the student was facing west (and only then) percussion of the student's abdomen produced a dull note. In this way he found that cancer present in one person could be detected using another, healthy, person as the detecting instrument. Abrams next found that the 'radiation' from the cancerous tissue in the container could be transmitted via a wire to a disc attached to the forehead of the healthy 'detector' to produce the dull note when his abdomen was percussed. When Abrams tried the same tests with other diseases he found that these produced a dull note on percussion of different parts of the body of the healthy 'detector'. He then tried putting a variable resistance in the wire leading from the container with diseased tissue in it to the 'detector' and he got the dull note from the healthy person's abdomen at different values of resistance for different diseases. Next he found that a blood spot from the patient would suffice as a specimen instead of diseased tissue. And this was the final form of Abrams 'radionic' diagnostic equipment, a blood spot from a patient on a piece of filter paper placed in a container with a wire going to earth and another wire from the lid of the container going, via a variable resistance, to a disc attached to the forehead of the 'detector' whose abdomen Abrams percussed. By much experimentation Abrams determined the value of the variable resistance associated with the dull note on percussion for various diseases. With this technique Abrams also found that he could detect incipient disease before it became physically manifest.

In his wide-ranging experiments Abrams found that a sample of quinine gave the same reaction from the 'detector' as malaria, which it was used to cure and that when he tested quinine together with a blood spot of a malarial patient he got no reaction at all, i.e. it seemed that the 'radiation' from the quinine neutralised the 'radiation' from the malarial blood spot.

Abrams had long had the experience that he only got a dull note from the abdomen of the detector when the detector was facing west, from which he inferred that the Earth's magnetic field had an influence, so he then tried 'artificial', electromagnetically-produced radiations and he found that these could cancel the radiation from the diseased tissue. So he designed a piece of equipment, an 'Oscilloclast' with which he treated his patients with radiations, via a variable resistance set according to the result that he got from his diagnostic tests. Abrams used these equipments and techniques with his own patients and demonstrated them to other doctors who also used them and this started the now well-established complementary therapy of radionics.

Other people who used Abrams' techniques made modifications to his equipment. In particular Ruth Drown found a way to dispense with the need to diagnose by percussing the abdomen of a healthy person, by incorporating a rubber diaphragm above the container with its blood spot, (CONSTABLE). The state of the spot of blood is then determined by stroking the diaphragm, instead of percussing a detector's abdomen. In treatment it was found that it was not necessary to have the patient present but that the treatment could be applied to the blood spot, which provided the necessary link with the patient, who could be any distance from it. Some radionic practitioners treat plants for diseases using a leaf from the plant as the contact, in place of the blood spot used with a human being. Also, it is claimed, areas of plants have been treated via a photographic negative of the area and pests eradicated by putting an appropriate pest killer with the leaf or negative during treatment.

Not everyone can operate a radionic diagnostic equipment. RUSSELL states that six out of ten people can operate it, out of which three can operate it well, while four out of ten cannot use it at all. Radionic diagnosis has something in common with dowsing and seems to require some sort of sensitivity of the operator. Furthermore a few practitioners found that a photographic plate incorporated into the equipment would register an image of the organ being investigated and its condition. This is akin to thoughtography in which a few people can think an image onto a photographic plate, (see FUKURAI, EISENBUD, BARADUC). Abrams had previously found a link between radionics and thought by showing that energy/activity associated with the thoughts and emotions of a person in one room could be detected by percussing the abdomen of a person in another room.

Russell states that a few radionic practitioners develop to the point where they no longer need a radionic instrument. This puts them into a similar category to the famous American psychic, Edgar Cayce who, in a state of trance, from a letter could diagnose a person's condition and suggest remedies and who did this for many well-attested cases, (SUGRUE). All of this suggests that there is a strong 'psychic' component to radionics.

The problem is to understand what is going on in radionic perception. When we normally perceive an object, for example a daisy, we do so by selecting out of the vast number of radiations entering our eyes from our field of vision, those pertaining to the daisy and we then automatically and unconsciously select, out of the vast mass of our stored memory experience, how when we previously experienced these radiations we gave the name 'daisy' to them. At the same time this opens up the 'file' of information that we have built up in our subconscious memory about the nature of the daisy, i.e. how it grows from a seed, develops roots from which foliage grows in Spring that culminates in the daisy flower, etc. Similarly, in the EM-energy there is stored the totality of its daisy experience and in radionics it seems that it is possible to access this encyclopaedic information from a small part, e.g. a leaf of the daisy, that serves as a centre to focus on this aspect of the EM-energy. Mystics claim to be able to control their consciousness so as to focus on whatever aspect of the EM-energy that is of concern to them. Perhaps the role of the radionic equipment is to provide the focus for the operator to do this.

A feature of radionic equipment is that it operates by a number of dials that have settings that enable the operator to diagnose conditions. Once these settings have been set up by the designer of the equipment they seem to be usable by other operators. This is akin to the way in which, once one member of a species establishes a pattern of behaviour this activity and its associated vibrations registers in the EM-energy and is activated under the appropriate conditions by other members of the species.

Electromagnetic Fields Associated With Life

In his investigations Abrams found that radiation from electromagnetic fields that he generated could affect the functioning of the body. This is because the vibrations given off by substances as a result of the activities of the cells of the body are the same as when they are activated by electric/magnetic fields, so that cellular activity can be affected by impinging electromagnetic radiations, while such radiations from the body are a manifestation of what is taking place in it. A number of workers have explored the electromagnetic activity of the body.

In the 1920s LAKHOVSKY took the view that all living organisms emit, and are capable of detecting and receiving radiations. He claimed that good health is characterised by oscillatory equilibrium. Lakhovsky proposed a three-fold principle, that: life is created by radiations: life is maintained by radiations: life is destroyed by oscillatory disequilibria. On the basis of his theories Lakhovsky carried out experiments in which he cured plants of cancer by subjecting them to electromagnetic radiations. He then went on to construct a multiwave oscillator, the field of which could cause cells to vibrate in resonance at their own particular frequency. Lakhovsky's book was written in French; in the English edition the translator has appended a number of medical reports by different doctors, in which the multiwave oscillator was used successfully to treat patients for a variety of problems.

BURR detected what he called an L (Life) field of electromagnetic activity associated with the human body. He found that the L-field varied with different people in a way that they could be divided into four groups. Females showed a variation of their L-field associated with ovulation. Malignancy in ovarian tissue could be detected in the L-field. The presence of a wound could be detected, and its healing monitored, by changes in the L-field. The effects of drugs were registered in the L-field. Mental, psychotic and hypnotic states were reflected in the L-field. Animals, plants, primitive organisms, in fact everything living, exhibited L-fields. Measurements made over many years on trees showed rhythmical variations that correlated with variations in the electrical field of the Earth and the atmosphere, which led Burr to conclude that all living things are inter-connected in a hierarchy of L-fields. Burr found that L-field measurements on a frog's egg showed the future location of the frog's nervous system. By measuring the L-field of seeds it was possible to predict how strong and healthy the future plant would be. A person's L-field remained constant with time despite the fact that all the substances and cells of the body changed. From these features Burr concluded that the L-field is primary and responsible for the organisation of living organisms and the cells and substances of which they consist are secondary. Burr found that the electromagnetic field manifested the presence of disease before it became apparent in the body itself. A number of Soviet scientists have carried out similar electromagnetic investigations and as a result they have postulated the existence of an organising bioplasmic field (see INYUSIN in WHITE and KRIPPNER's book and PLAYFAIR and HILL).

Becker has carried out extensive research into the role of electromagnetic fields associated with the body's functioning, (BECKER and SELDEN). As an orthopaedic surgeon Becker was seeking to understand the basic principles of bone healing so as to deal with cases where a person's bones do not heal. He concentrated at first on researches with animals, particularly salamanders, in which the ability to heal is so great that they are able to regenerate a lost tail or limbs and other parts of the body, even to the extent of regenerating the heart if half of it is removed. Becker pursued the idea of a 'current of injury' being set up as shown, for example, by Russian scientists who cut branches from tomato plants and found an electric current associated with the growth of a new shoot and that growth could be enhanced by increasing the current or retarded by nullifying it, using a small battery. A current of injury is emitted from wounds in animals and in hydra reversal of the current causes a head to form where the tail should be and vice versa. Becker plotted out the potentials associated with the current of injury in salamanders and other animals and determined how these changed with healing. From these researches Becker developed techniques for stimulating bone and tissue growth in human situations that were proving difficult to heal.

A major problem with regeneration is to identify where the cells come from that give rise to the new bone and tissue that make up the new limb or whatever. In researches on the healing of fractures in the legs of frogs Becker found that red blood cells, that were differentiated to perform a specialised function, dedifferentiated and changed into the bone cells needed to repair the fracture and that this was associated with changes in the electrical potential. He then found that by applying a critical value of potential, at a minute current of less than a billionth of an ampere he could dedifferentiate frog red blood cells in cultures, outside the body. He then got the same changes with the blood cells of goldfish, salamanders, snakes and turtles. While throwing light on the healing of fractured bones, these experiments also showed that a minute electric current can have a dramatic effect on cell structure and behaviour. In seeking a deeper understanding of the current of injury, Becker sought to relate this to electrical potentials and current in the nervous system and brain. He found that reversing the normal current through the brain of a salamander caused it to become unconscious and that a magnetic field would do the same thing. With human beings and animals he found a correlation between the hypnotic state and the electrical polarity of the body and between psychiatric behaviour and solar magnetic storms and applied magnetic fields and he related this to experiments that have shown that animals have an awareness of the Earth's magnetic field that enables them to navigate. Becker concluded that, while suitably controlled electromagnetic fields could be used for healing, the uncontrolled fields to which we are subjected now-a-days, arising from the many types of power lines and electrical equipment in use around us, can have adverse effects on our functioning.

SMITH and BEST, in 'Electromagnetic Man' are concerned with these adverse effects that electromagnetic fields generated by power-lines, and electrical equipment in general, can have on the human body. People claiming to be affected by power-lines report experiencing a wide range of effects, such as lassitude, exhaustion, sleeplessness, loss of appetite, depression, palpitations, dizziness and, in extreme cases, disorientation and blackouts and there are also effects on animals, e.g. bees stop making honey and seal up their hives in mid season. Smith and Best survey the basic principles of the phenomena of bioelectricity, their relationship to cosmic cycles and the sensitivity of organisms to the 'natural' electromagnetic changes taking place in the environment. They describe how the electromagnetic phenomena of the body can be used to monitor its activities, (as in ECG and EEG recordings). They show how the body is sensitive to the electromagnetic fields generated by power lines and other electrical equipment. They claim that, with all the electrical equipment in use now-a-days, we have impinging on us many electromagnetic impulses and that some people have allergies to specific electromagnetic impulses, in the same way that people can have allergies to certain foods and chemicals. In fact the two may be connected, in that the food or chemical allergies may result from their electromagnetic effects in the body. Where a person has such an 'allergy' they describe how this can be nullified by applying a rectifying electromagnetic field of the correct frequency. They suggest that many complementary healing techniques can be explained in terms of their electromagnetic action on the body's electromagnetic field. For example, healing by the laying-on of hands they suggest could be due to the healer being able to activate in his/her own body, processes that give rise to electromagnetic impulses that are transmitted to the patient. They also seek to account for dowsing, extrasensory perception and other parapsychological phenomena in these terms.

Because they measure electromagnetic forces associated with the activities of the body, some scientists (e.g Selden and Smith and Best), claim that the body is an electromagnetic activity. However, what scientists know about electromagnetic activity has been derived from experiments on the mineral kingdom. When they measure electromagnetic activity associated with the human body they are detecting the substance level manifestations of the workings of the higher levels of life, soul-feeling and spirit-thinking activities and while electromagnetic measurements provide useful indirect information about these, they do not deal directly with these activities, that mystics and clairvoyants claim to perceive.

Clairvoyant Observations of the Body's Energy Fields

There are a number of descriptions of the body's energy fields, or aura, particularly those given by PIERRAKOS and BRENNAN. John Pierrakos was a psychiatrist practising in New York concerned with developing an understanding of psychodynamics, i.e. the workings of the life force within each of us that makes us what we are; how this operates; how its activity becomes blocked and causes us to be less than we could be and with developing a therapy that releases the blockages and allows us to realise our potentials. He picked up on the work of Kilner (1847-1920) who was a doctor in charge of electro-therapy at St. Thomas's Hospital, London. Kilner had become aware of Reichenbach's work showing that some people could perceive auras around magnets, crystals, the human hand and other things (Chapter 9) and of the theosophical descriptions of the human aura. This led him to try to find ways of detecting emanations from the body's activities and then to try to perceive these emanations visually.

KILNER found that when he viewed a person, in subdued lighting, through a glass cell containing an alcoholic solution of the coal tar dye, dicyanin, he could perceive two auras around him/her, an inner one about 3 to 10 cm wide which showed activity and had a texture to it and a broader, diffuse outer one, sometimes with rays passing through them, with a narrow void of about 5mm. immediately around, and following the contours of, the body. He carried out a variety of tests to try to clarify these phenomena, from which he concluded that the effect of looking through the dicyanin screen was to make eyes more sensitive to ultraviolet radiation. Kilner observed the auras of a large number of people and found that they varied with the age, sex, temperament and state of health of the person. Fig. 13.2(a) shows his diagram for the auras of a healthy male with the outer one measuring 20cm around the head and about 13cm down the trunk, arms and legs, with the inner one about 8cm in breadth and showing clear striations in its structure.

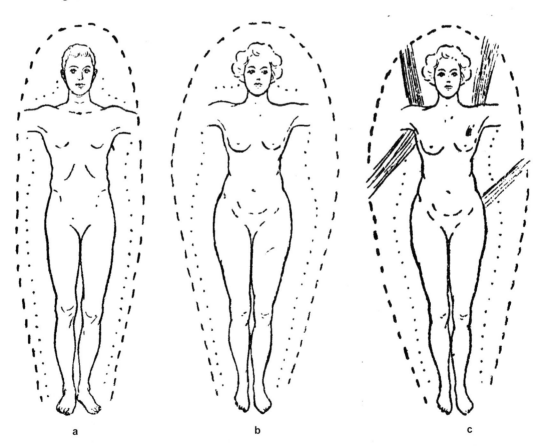

Fig. 13.2 Kilner's diagrams for the human aura of, (a) a healthy male, (b) a healthy female, (c) the aura of a female that had rays passing through it.

Fig. 13.2(b) shows the auras of a healthy woman that are broader around the middle, compared with those of a man with this broadening equally perceptible from a side view. Fig. 13.2(c) shows an example of a woman with four rays passing through her auras who, from a side view had a fifth small ray emanating from a small fibro-adenoid tumour of the left breast. Kilner found that different diseases affect the auras, either generally and/or locally, e.g. epileptic people had their auras displaced to one side, while other problems showed up as variations in the size and structure of the aura.

Kilner also found that he could perceive a 'haze' around a magnet, that did not have the configuration of its magnetic field, and that rays projected from its poles and he saw a similar haze around a wire carrying an electric current. There was an interaction between the magnet's 'haze' and the human aura and between the auras of two people. A person's aura expanded when they were electrostatically charged.

PIERRAKOS developed Kilner's work further and then found that he became able to perceive energy fields without the use of filters. He observed energy fields associated with all living entities, with crystals, with the Earth, its oceans and its atmosphere. In all cases there was a pulsating rhythm of activity, involving an interchange of energy with other entities and the environment.

According to Pierrakos, the energy field around plants varies greatly depending on the species and whether the plant is flowering. It comprises an inner and an outer layer, with the inner layer around leaves and branches being 3-4mm wide and the outer layer 15-30 mm. Flowering plants have a much more extensive field, with a great luminosity around the flower. The rate of pulsation is usually 10 to 30 times per minute and it varies with the geographical orientation and location. Trees have similar energy fields, which merge in woodland and produce a combined radiation that shoots hundreds of feet skywards, with a reverse movement bringing energy from the surrounding atmosphere into the wood. With crystals Pierrakos observed similar two-layer pulsating energy fields to those of plants, with streams flowing from the crystal to the environment and vice versa. The pulsation rate varied with the type of crystal and with its geographical orientation and location. In the interplay of natural forces Pierrakos observed energy field activities on a large scale, particularly at the interface between a sandy beach and the ocean and sky. There is a pulsating movement in which three zones form, with luminous streamers surging skywards from the outer zone, that vary with the seasons, time of day and weather conditions. There is an interplay between these energy fields and the energy field of the human being, (many of us have an awareness of environmental conditions that make us feel invigorated or depressed). Pierrakos found in his psychiatric practice, that plants in his office were adversely affected by patients working out their negative emotions, even to the extent of dying when subjected to three or four hours of this experience.

Pierrakos observed that the energy field (aura) of the human being shows, not only the person's current condition but also their life history, in that its structure shows disruptions and blockages resulting from traumas that we have experienced in the past, while its colour, luminosity and brightness give information about our unrealised potentials. The ability to perceive the structure and workings of the energy fields of the human aura thereby gave Pierrakos an understanding of life energy activities, that he was seeking for a foundation in his psychiatric work.

Pierrakos portrayal of the human energy field as he saw it is shown in fig. 13.3(a). This comprises an inner etheric aura, that hK-M would relate to the body's prokaryotic, eukaryotic and multicellular biological activities with next, a level corresponding to a person's emotional (soul) activity, then a level of mental activity, all encompassed by the activity of the incarnating spirit. His portrayal of the chakra system that, according to hK-M connects our spirit and its world to our body is shown in fig. 13.3(b), in which the chakras are in three groupings corresponding to the activities of will, soul-feeling and mental-thinking.

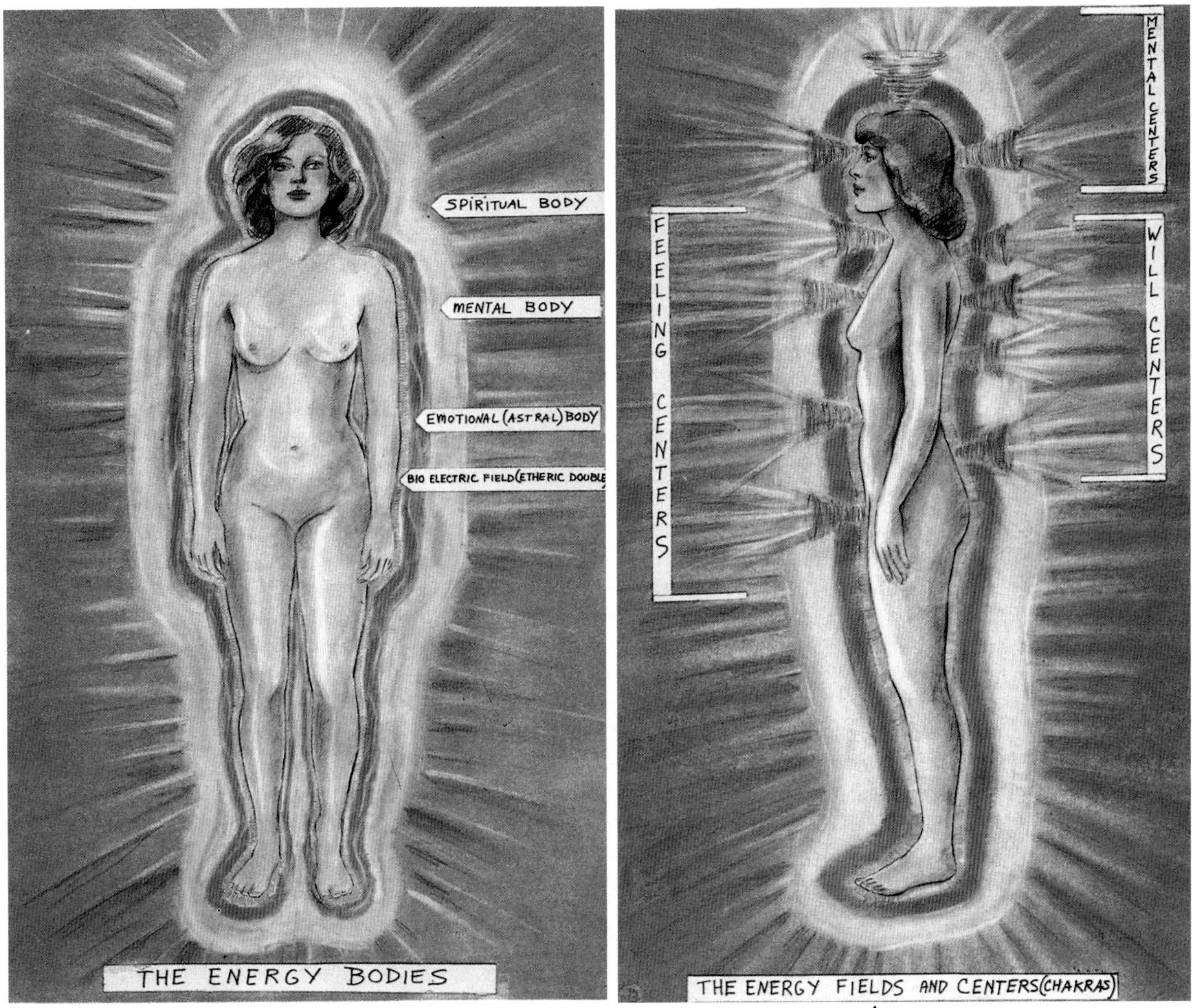
SPIRITUAL BODY
MENTAL BODY
EMOTIONAL (ASTRAL) BODY
BIO ELECTRIC FIELD (ETHERIC DOUBLE
THE ENERGY BODIES
MENTAL CENTERS
FEELING CENTERS
WILL CENTERS
THE ENERGY FIELDS AND CENTERS (CHAKRAS)

a b

Fig. 13.3 (a) The human energy field (aura) and its structure (b)The chakra system and its functions, according to PIERRAKOS.
From Core Energetics by John PIERRAKOS reproduced by kind permission of the publishers

The auric envelope as a whole is oval in shape and in the average waking person pulsates 15 to 25 times a minute, extending to 60 to 120 cm, with all levels pulsing in synchronisation. Pierrakos states that all levels comprise the same basic energy operating at different frequencies, which is in accord with *k*K-M that sees everything as arising from, and comprising patterns of activities in, the basic energy. The aura of a baby is unstructured; layers begin to develop between the ages of 2 and 3 and are well differentiated by puberty. Groups of people working together develop an impressive communal aura.

BRENNAN gives extensive accounts of her observations of auric energy fields (and also a bibliography on the subject). Brennan had a natural ability to perceive auras and energy fields as a child, which she lost as she grew up. She studied physics and then worked for NASA as an astrophysicist but became interested in counselling and found that as she sought to help people with their problems her ability to see their auras gradually returned. She has spent many years improving her ability to perceive the aura and studying it in increasingly greater depth. Brennan describes in some detail: her development of higher sense perception; what she perceives as the structures of the various chakras and their energy systems, that make up the aura; what she perceives where these are malfunctioning in different ways and how this relates to illness. She describes how our life's experiences give rise to malfunctioning and illness and also how in some cases we carry past life experiences with us that are the cause of illness, together with case histories to illustrate the principles that she expounds. She describes exercises for promoting self-awareness and health and well-being. Brennan carries out healing by the laying on of hands technique. Her development of higher sense perception brought her into contact with spiritual guides (entities of what, in *h*K-M we have called the Omniverse Hierarchy), for whom she became a channel for healing activities. (We deal with this phenomenon later when we have considered a number of factors that provide the necessary background to do so). Brennan states that all living organisms possess auras or energy fields as also do some gemstones and crystals, which can interact with the aura of the human body and be used for healing, which she sees with her clairvoyant vision. She describes exercises by which people can develop the ability to perceive the body's energy fields and she runs a school in which she trains people to do this. Brennan claims that this is something that is possible by many people and that the development of these abilities will become increasingly wide spread as part of a New Age change in consciousness that is taking place in humanity.

Registration of the Body's Energy Fields

A way that is claimed to register the activity of the energy body is Kirlian photography, named after the Russian husband and wife team Semyon and Valentina Kirlian who developed it in the 1960s. With this technique a high frequency, high voltage, low current field is produced between two electrodes and an object placed within the field interacts with it in a way that produces a corona of light around it, that registers on a photographic plate. Living objects show a larger corona of interaction than non-living ones, while the corona around people's fingers shows a correlation with their physiological and psychological state and in this way it is claimed that Kirlian photography can be used for diagnosis. However, the primary feature for the claim that it registers the energy body is the 'phantom leaf' effect. Thus some workers have found that when a piece is removed from a leaf the Kirlian photograph shows a picture of the whole leaf, as though what is being registered is the leaf's energy field and not its substance body, (GERBER).

Oldfield has sought to develop ways of registering the activity of the body's energy fields (Grant and Jane SOLOMON). At first Oldfield used the Kirlian technique and he registered a range of energy-related phenomena, e.g. fresh foods (milk, fruit, vegetables, etc.) show greater corona activity than processed or cooked foods. (OLDFIELD and COGHILL). The problem with the Kirlian technique is that interactions with a high frequency field are affected by many factors so that reproducibility of results is a problem and they are difficult to interpret unambiguously. Oldfield then developed a more direct method for examining the body's energy field, in which the subject holds an electrode connected to a high frequency generator that induces a field around him/her, (at a lower voltage than that required to produce the corona required for Kirlian photography). This is then measured at a distance of 2-3 cm from the body, by a simple hand-held meter that Oldfield developed, in what he calls his ESM (electroscanning method). The generator is tuned to give a stable reading on the detector from one, or more, control places on the subject's body that are thought to be in sound condition. The rest of the body is then surveyed for divergences from the control reading, to give data that can be interpreted by an experienced operator to diagnose abnormalities in the energy field and hence incipient or manifest malfunctioning of the body systems.

To achieve a more direct way of observing the body's energy fields Oldfield then developed a method of registering its interference with light, in what he calls his PIP (Polycontrast Interference Photography) technique. In this method the image of a person obtained with a full spectrum light source is recorded photographically, by still or video photography, and this is analysed by a computer software programme that selects out and magnifies subtle interference interactions between the person's energy field and the ambient light. The Solomons quote a healer who claims to perceive the human aura, as stating that Oldfield's PIP photographs show a cartoon version of what he sees. There have been claims that the energy channels registered in Oldfield's PIP images, eg. fig 13.4, correspond to the energy meridian flow lines of acupuncture.

Fig 13.4 Meridian energy flows along a person's arm registered by Oldfields's PIP technique

Pathological or other conditions that affect the energy body are shown by Oldfield's polycontrast interference photography, from which we have selected the following from a collection that he provided, figs 13.5 to 13.8.

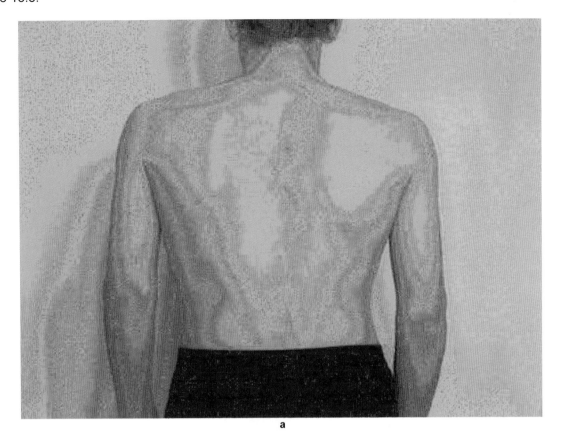

a

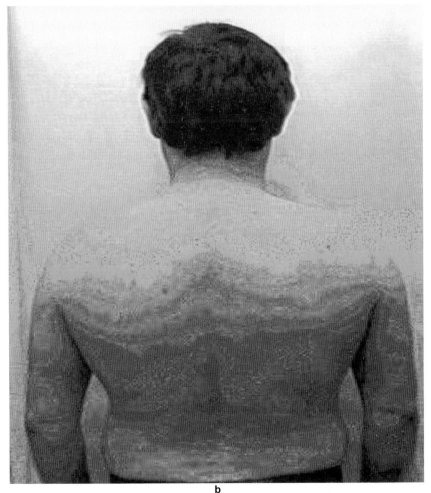

b

Fig. 13.5 Oldfield PIP images for (a) a person with a healthy back and (b) a person with a back problem

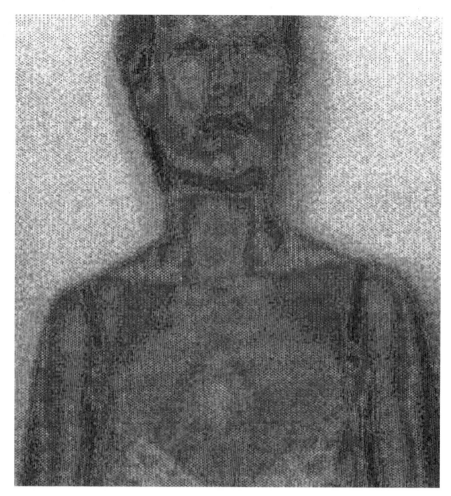

Fig. 13.6 PIP image for a person with flu

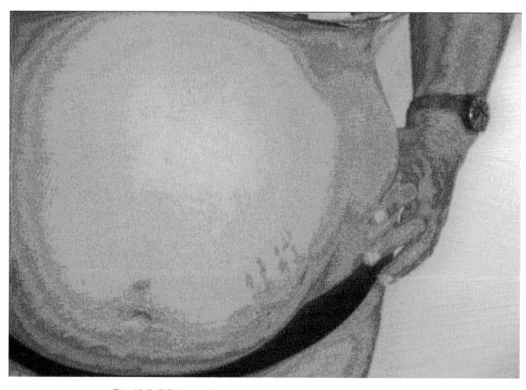

Fig. 13.7 PIP image for a woman who was eight months pregnant

One of the aims of Oldfield's work is to build up an atlas of pathological conditions so that from an, easily obtained, PIP photograph incipient or manifest health problems can be quickly diagnosed.

In seeking an interpretation of the results of his researches into the interaction of the body's energy field with light, using his PIP system, Oldfield compared the images obtained from the living activity of the body with those obtained from crystals. When he put them in close proximity he found that there was an interaction between a crystal and the body (as claimed by crystal therapists). This interaction was greater when the crystal was subjected to an electromagnetic pulsing, than with either the use of the electromagnetic pulsing or the crystal on their own and he used this finding to develop a system of electro-crystal therapy. The problem then was to relate the type of crystal and its radiations to a person's requirements. Oldfield solved this by filling a tube with a variety of small crystal chips, in a conducting saline solution, and connecting this to a variable frequency pulse generator. He then used the concept of seven primary chakra centres, in which he could determine any imbalance with his PIP photography, to work out the frequencies required to rebalance them. Fig 13.8 shows a PIP image for a person with a stomach disorder before and after treatment with electro-crystal therapy. Further information on Harry Oldfield's techniques, and more pictures, can be seen at www.electrocrystal.com.

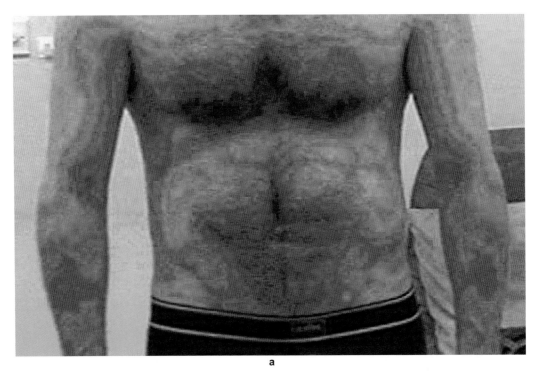

a

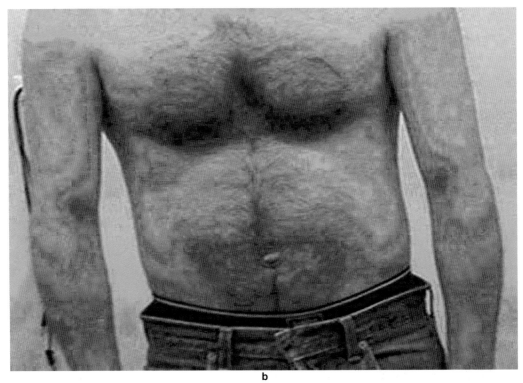

b

Fig. 13.8 PIP images for a person with a stomach disorder (a) before and (b) after, treatment by Oldfield's electro-crystal therapy

The Integration of Energy Field Concepts into Medical Practice

Malfunctioning at any of our energy levels can result in illness that manifests at the physical level. Current Western medical practice concentrates on the physical manifestations and treats these by drugs or surgery but in many cases this does not get at the cause of the problem. Some complementary therapies, such as acupuncture, Reiki and reflexology seek to rebalance the energy flows through the body, as do healers in their 'laying on of hands' treatments. An increasing number of doctors are integrating energy body considerations into their practices.

Shealy, in his medical practice, makes use of the observations of 'a medical clairvoyant' who can perceive the energy bodies of a person and any malfunctioning of these, together with an 'intuitive' explanation for the cause of the problem, so that as well as offering patients conventional medical treatment they can be given advice on how to overcome its cause, (SHEALY and MYSS). This book gives case histories for many different problems and MYSS who is the main medical clairvoyant that Shealy has worked with describes how she developed her ability to perceive energy fields and her awareness of the emotional and spiritual causes of disharmony in these. Myss also trains other people to become medical clairvoyants.

Christine PAGE has integrated her conventional medical knowledge with her understanding of the workings of the chakras. From an early age Page felt that she wanted to be a healer. She went to Medical School and trained to be a doctor but was disappointed by the way that patients were treated in that it took no account of their basic underlying emotional and mental problems. She felt that it was necessary to deal with the whole person and not just the physical symptoms. Page therefore embarked on developing a holistic body, soul, spirit understanding of the human being and the way in which imbalances in one level affect the other levels and thereby to get at the cause and role of disease. She sets out a psychospiritual causation of disease in terms of imbalances in the etheric, soul and spiritual activities operating through the seven primary chakras, (fig. 13.1):-

1. The Base Chakra: situated at the base of the spine: associated with self-awareness, security, confidence, fear and courage.
2. The Sacral Chakra: situated at the lower abdomen: associated with self-respect, creativity within relationships, possessiveness and sharing.
3. The Solar Plexus Chakra: associated with self-worth, anger, resentment, unworthiness and guilt.
4. The Heart Chakra: associated with self-love, the ability to give and take unconditionally, joy, hurt and bitterness.
5. The Throat Chakra: associated with self-expression, the ability to accept change, frustration and freedom.
6. The Third Eye: situated in the forehead: associated with self-responsibility, vision, balance, confusion and clarity.
7. The Crown Chakra: situated at the top of the head, associated with self-consciousness, acceptance, despair and peace.

Page gives examples of the effects of disharmony within the chakras, e.g. constipation associated with an imbalance in the base chakra seen in someone who is always busy and under stress, without sufficient time for bodily functions: menstrual problems in women due to an imbalance in the sacral chakra as a result of insufficient nurturing of the creativity of their feminine nature: heart attacks due to hardening of the arteries as a result of inflexibility of attitude and outlook. Page goes into many psychospiritual problems and their physical effects, with examples from her medical practice, giving suggestions for dealing with them.

GERBER has surveyed different aspects of the human energy fields' viewpoint. He describes what these comprise according to traditional Indian-theosophy, namely etheric (life) body, astral (emotional) body, and mental, causal spiritual bodies working via the chakra system. He discusses the roles of the different chakras and describes bioenergy/electrical experimental evidence that tends to substantiate their existence. He considers the Chinese view of energy (ch'I or qi) that is believed to flow through the human body by a system of meridians and by which human beings interact with the energy of the environment. He describes experiments in which a radioactive material injected into acupuncture points travelled along, and marked out, these meridians, distinct from the vascular or nervous system. In experiments with chickens the meridians formed before even the most rudimentary organs, suggesting that the meridians influence the formation of these. Acupuncture points were found to have a lower electrical skin resistance (by a factor of ten) and Gerber describes diagnostic devices that electrically monitor the acupuncture points and meridians. He considers psychic healing by the laying on of hands, and describes experiments in which healers produced measurable biological effects. He surveys the developing use of 'energy medicine' in the West, e.g. the use of radiation to treat cancer, electricity to alleviate pain and to reduce tumours, electromagnetic fields to stimulate fracture healing and magnetic fields to alleviate the pain and inflammation of arthritis. Gerber claims that Western medicine is changing from the Newtonian view, that sees the human being as built of molecular particles and operating as a mechanism, to what he calls the Einsteinian view, since it reflects Einstein's famous equation $E = mc^2$, which shows that everything derives from energy. Gerber sees the interplay of the energy systems as taking place by vibrational activities, and healing as requiring the application of vibrations to rectify malfunctioning, (the title of his book is Vibrational Medicine), compared to the Newtonian approach in which the mechanism is adjusted by modifying its substance balance by drugs or by surgery. He sees complementary healing with crystals, light and magnetism as vibrational therapies. Gerber proposes that the increasing awareness of the effects of our spiritual-mental, soul-feeling and etheric (life) activities, on the working of our physical body, will make us more responsible for our own health.

SCOTT-MUMBY has written a book called Virtual Medicine that is the term that he uses for diagnosing pathological conditions and healing via the body's energy fields. He covers much of the same background material as Gerber's book but then concentrates on electro-acupuncture methods of diagnosis and treatment in which the state of a person's health is determined from measurements of skin resistance taken along the acupuncture meridians. Where the resistance is high (inflammatory condition) or low (degenerate condition) the required remedy can be determined by finding the one that, incorporated into the circuit, restores the measurement of the acupuncture point to that for a healthy condition (in a similar way to that developed by Abrams). Testing for materials to which a person is allergic can be carried out by incorporating potential allergy-causing substances into the circuit, when those that cause problems result in the electrical potential of the acupuncture point deviating from a healthy value.

Scott-Mumby then describes a further development of electro-acupuncture, called bio-resonance therapy, in which, instead of a remedy being determined from the measurement of pathological radiations from a person's energy field, the pathological signal is appropriately modified and returned to the person to provide a neutralising curative effect. Scott-Mumby claims that as experience of these techniques of working with a patient's energy bodies builds up they will revolutionise the practice of medicine.

These phenomena are in accord with the hK-M point of view that sees living organisms as giving off radiations that are a manifestation of the activity that is taking place in them, which can be modified by radiations impinging on them. If, for some reason an organism is malfunctioning, the corresponding radiation will be given off and applying radiations to neutralise the malfunctioning and/or promote normal functioning can have a healing effect. GERBER describes a number of radiation therapies due to Rife, Lakhovsky and Antoine Priore dating back to the 1930's that seemed to achieve positive results, particularly with cancer, but which were not pursued because they did not fit into the contemporary paradigm. More recently Popp has found that radiations play a major role in the activities of the body and that characteristic radiations are given off by cancerous tumours and that it could be possible to eliminate the tumour by nullifying its radiations with other appropriate radiations (McTAGGART).

Recent work by Jaques Benveniste showed that it is possible to record electronically the vibrational characteristics of the molecules of a remedy, or any other substance. Once this is done it can be played back in any required situation. Benveniste also transmitted the vibrations along a wire, as did Abrams in the early 1900s, and he sent them to other laboratories by e-mail (McTAGGART). It has also been suggested that electromagnetic vibrations from a diseased person can be transmitted to others. Thus OLDFIELD and COGHILL quote examples of influenza epidemics breaking out in different places and spreading faster than was possible by person-to-person contact and, in some cases, where such contact could not have occurred.

[According to hK-M everything comprises patterns of activity in the basic energy, from which everything has arisen. These activities generate vibrations/radiations in the space energy that impinge on everything else and produce an effect if what they impinge on is 'tuned' to respond to them. Radio communication is an example of the harnessing of this general principle for a specific application but the basic phenomenon exists everywhere, at all levels of existence. Biologists tend to think in terms of physical, substance contact being necessary for physico-chemical interactions to occur between organisms, and between the cells that make up organisms. However, the work described in this Chapter shows that interactions between cells and organisms can take place without physical contact, by the transmission of vibrations between them. The obvious and outstanding example of this is the plant kingdom (and at least some aspects of the animal kingdom), in which activities taking place in the Sun produce vibrations that are transmitted to, and play a major role in the life activity of, the majority of plants without any substance contact between them].

From the hK-M viewpoint radiations that manifest malfunctioning in the body may be brought about by soul/spirit activity that would not be directly affected by applying rectifying radiations at the substance level so that, while malfunctioning at the substance level might be corrected, the basic cause of it will remain unaffected. However, practitioners of these techniques report that, as well as rectifying the malfunctioning, they often bring about a change in outlook of the person to whom they are applied, presumably due to the person experiencing life differently through his/her, no longer malfunctioning, healthy body. Where people do not respond to the treatment it may be because the basic cause is unaffected and they do not make the necessary soul/feeling and/or spirit/thinking change. An interesting example of the effect of personal qualities comes from Benveniste's researches, where he found that his experiments did not work with a person who was emitting radiations that interfered with the molecular signalling involved.

Techniques that seek to cure pathological conditions by some sort of radiation therapy working on the energy body are very different from the surgical and drug methods that dominate modern medicine and they are based on a different view of the constitution of the human being to that of the mechanistic-substance view that underlies contemporary medicine. In putting these techniques into perspective Scott-Mumby classifies the various types of therapies into four categories:

(i)   Invasive methods, i.e. surgical procedures.
(ii)   Biochemical methods: use of minerals, herbs, drugs.
(iii)   Energy methods: acupuncture, electromagnetic waves, sound and colour therapy.
(iv)   Information methods: high potency homoeopathy and Bach flower remedies.

Surgical methods operate at the physical level, by manipulating the substance structures of the body. Therapies classified under (ii) act on its substance structure and energy fields. Therapies classified under (iii) work directly on the body's energy field level. Therapies classified under (iv), i.e. high dilution homoeopathics (and the Bach flower remedies which are similar), Scott-Mumby sees as operating at an information level, on the basis that for an organism to become organised and function in the way that it does there must be some sort of underlying 'information field'. Scott-Mumby does not elucidate on where the information field comes from but from the *h*K-M viewpoint all the information underlying the development and workings of an organism has been built up through the evolutionary experience of the EM-energy and it is by activating the relevant experience of this, that an information therapy such as homoeopathy, works.

Current medical practice is dominated by the substance approach and seeks to correct any malfunctioning by surgery and/or the administration of drugs but introducing drugs into the complex activities of the body systems can produce undesirable side effects, (for a list of the side effects that drugs can have see the BMA book MEDICINES AND DRUGS). In extreme cases, as with thalidomide, drugs can cause disastrous malformations of the body of a foetus.

According to *h*K-M, the human being consists of a hierarchy of levels of activity, physical, etheric (prokaryotic, eukaryotic and multicellular), soul and spirit and each level has to be dealt with on its own terms, so that it is necessary to understand the principles and workings of each level. While there is some understanding of physical level therapies and of those that operate at the energy level, there is no understanding of the principles by which an information level therapy, such as homoeopathy works.

The Principles of Homoeopathy

This is a method of healing developed by Samuel Hahnemann (1755-1843). Hahnemann was a physician who became dissatisfied with the treatments used by the medical profession (at that time mostly unscientific prescriptions, leeches and blood-letting), so he began to experiment with other contemporary cures, to determine their efficacy for himself. He read about the use of cinchona bark (the source of quinine) for the treatment of fevers and so he tried it while he was in a normal healthy state, to see what happened. He was surprised to find that it produced the symptoms of the fever that it was supposed to cure, and it had the same effect on members of his family and friends. He then tried other substances, with similar results and this led him to the simillimum principle of using like substances to treat like diseases. The basis of this principle is that when we are ill the symptoms that we exhibit do not represent the illness but the way that our body is fighting back against it. Therefore giving a substance that causes these symptoms, reinforces the body's own healing activity. (On this basis giving something that suppresses the symptoms can interfere with the body's curative action). Thus trials of substances are made by giving them to healthy people and if they produce the symptoms that are exhibited by a particular illness they are then used to treat that problem.

However, Hahnemann found that these substances often at first aggravated the symptoms before improvement started. So he tried using them in reduced, diluted amounts and found that the more he diluted them the more effective they became and this led to the homoeopathic method of potentisation. Using this method a homoeopathic remedy is made by dissolving a substance, e.g. rock salt, in water in the ratio of one part of salt to ten parts of water and the solution is succussed (a specific type of shaking). Some of this solution is diluted with water, again in the ratio of one part to ten and the succussion repeated. This is done a number of times, depending on the level at which it is desired to treat the patient, and alcohol (usually brandy) is added to give good keeping properties. The liquid may be used for treatment or, more usually, it is dripped onto tablets (generally lactose). Materials that are not soluble in water, such as metals, are triturated, (ground up) with successive dilutions of lactose.

Different practitioners use different dilutions for particular situations but one common view is that if the treatment is for a physical disorder then a remedy is used where the dilution and succussion have been carried out six times (giving a dilution of 1 part in a million). If the problem is considered to originate at an emotional level then a remedy that has been diluted and succussed 30 times is used and if it is considered to result from a deep mental-emotional problem in the person's character, then a remedy would be used that has been diluted and succussed 200, or even as much as 10,000 times. Most homoeopathic remedies on sale are at the 6 dilution level. Because they are less used, the other dilutions of 30, 200 and 10m usually have to be obtained via the postal services run by the manufacturers).

Hahnemann attributed the action of homoeopathic remedies to the effect that they had on a vital energy that underlies the workings of the body. This led to another feature of Hahnemann's treatment-philosophy, which is axiomatic to homoeopathy, that it is not sufficient to deal with the symptoms that the patient exhibits, it is necessary to deal with the person as a whole, i.e. their personality type and their emotional and mental, as well as their bodily, state, since emotional and mental problems can have a major effect on health and general well being. In order to determine the appropriate remedy homoeopathic practitioners enquire into a patient's history, attitude, temperament, likes and dislikes, diet, etc.

In the UK there are six NHS homoeopathic hospitals or clinics and about six hundred medical doctors who use homoeopathic remedies to a greater or lesser extent, alongside conventional (allopathic) remedies, (see LOCKIE in HOMOEOPATHIC references). Thus, this is not a matter of a fringe, alternative medicine group but of medical practitioners finding, out of their practical experiences of both allopathic and homoeopathic remedies, a useful role for homoeopathy. There are also many trained homoeopaths who are not medical doctors.

There is considerable controversy about how homoeopathic remedies work and indeed whether in fact they do work. Practitioners of homoeopathy claim from their clinical experiences that they definitely work and there have been a number of attempts to 'scientifically' examine the working of homoeopathic remedies (McTAGGART), prominent among which is the work of Benveniste. Benveniste, a well-established scientist of repute, working with top class facilities in a top-class laboratory found that an antibody subjected to high, homoeopathic dilutions was still biologically active and also that homoeopathic dilutions of histamine affected coronary blood flow in guinea pig hearts. When the homoeopathic solution was subjected to heat or a magnetic field it no longer had any effect, (McTAGGART, GERBER).

Many scientists reject the possibility of high dilution homoeopathic remedies having any effect, on the grounds that they contravene scientific principles, since they are diluted to such an extent that there are no atoms of the substances left. Scientific principles are based on the view that the atoms of substances interact and behave as they do as the result of electromagnetic forces which they exert on each other, acting through 'space'. 'Space' is regarded as something nebulous which does not play any significant role, whereas the hK-M view is that 'space' is all important and it comprises the energy out of which substances, as patterns of activity, have arisen and likewise patterns of life, emotional and thinking activities and associated memory, which science does not yet understand and has no explanation for. 'Space', i.e. the EM-energy is involved in everything and it is its properties and behaviour that accounts for the working of the high dilution homoeopathics and Bach flower remedies.

According to hK-M every activity takes place, and interacts with everything else, in the EM-energy, which contains the memory of everything that it has experienced, the relevant part of which is activated by the circumstances in which it finds itself. Thus, as described previously, the patterns of behaviour of living organisms, such as beavers, are built up by the EM-energy experiencing the life cycles of innumerable individual beavers that build up a species pattern of behaviour in it, that is triggered off in its individual beaver existence as the beaver's instinctive pattern of behaviour. This build up of a pattern of behaviour also takes place with the mineral kingdom, so that, for example, when a substance crystallises out of solution the EM-energy associated with the solution experiences a state of stress as the solution becomes supersaturated which is resolved when the stress build up causes excess substance to separate off and crystallise out. And the more times that this happens, the more experience the EM-energy accumulates so that it responds to the stress situation more readily, (instinctively). Thus SHELDRAKE has pointed out that when chemists first create a new substance they can find it difficult to get it to crystallise out of solution but once it has done so, it crystallises more readily next time and increasingly so thereafter.

Innumerable repetitions of substance phenomena, such as crystallisation and their behaviour in organisms, builds up a memory pattern in the EM-energy. This pattern of behaviour is dormant until it is activated by the stresses that arise in crystallisation, or those that arise as organisms pursue their activities with substances. When the EM-energy has a substance successively diluted and succussed in it, this 'jogs its memory' of that substance's pattern of behaviour and the more that the diluting and succussing is done, the deeper the level of involvement of the substance that it is jogged into remembering. It is as though our memory of a past event is activated at increasingly deeper levels, first to remember the physical situation, then our emotional experience of it and then our thoughts about it. This principle is not confined to homoeopathically diluted substances thus, in their work on the curative effects of electromagnetic vibrations mentioned earlier, Smith and Best found that water that has been exposed to an electromagnetic field could be potentised to have a curative effect. Bernard Grad carried out experiments in which glass phials of water were treated by a healer and the water was then found to have a beneficial effect on the germination of seeds and their subsequent growth into plants. Conversely Grad found that water treated by depressed persons had an adverse effect on seed germination and plant growth. Grad also found that water 'treated' with magnets had a beneficial effect (GERBER).

As a result of the findings from their researches, some investigators have been led to propose that water possesses a memory, e.g. Benveniste (McTAGGART, GERBER), while scientists who base their thinking on the current understanding of the physical and chemical nature and structure of water and the way in which the hydrogen and oxygen atoms that make up the substance of water are bonded together, cannot see how this can be possible (BALL has analysed this problem in depth). The *h*K-M view is that it is not the substance (hydrogen and oxygen atoms) that carry the memory but the aspect of the EM-energy that is related to water.

Over a long period of evolution our body has developed a pattern of structure and functioning that gives rise to its workings and this is experienced by, and registered in, the EM-energy, which thereby contains a blue-print of our body's workings. Our soul/Ego makes use of our body to express itself in the world and if it exceeds the pattern of behaviour of what the body can adapt to, it creates stresses that cause the body to malfunction in some way. The body's pattern of behaviour then needs to be brought back into line and a homoeopathic remedy does this by reminding it of how it should be behaving. If, for example, we are working in a disharmonious stressful way that causes malfunctioning in the use of iron and we take homoeopathic iron, in which the memory of how iron normally behaves has been activated, the homoeopathic remedy 'knows' what it should be doing and as it passes through the body it influences the iron in the malfunctioning situation to behave correctly.

The big problem with homoeopathy is for the practitioner to decide the remedy, or remedies, required by the patient. This is done by an extensive interview in which the homoeopath enquires in depth into the person's life history and current life style and it requires considerable knowledge, skill and insight to arrive at the correct decision. This is where there could be considerable potential for the techniques described by Scott-Mumby that measure the radiations created by a person's malfunctioning and then use the same technique to survey remedies to select one that will eliminate it.

Self Healing

Homoeopathy works by stimulating the hierarchy of a person's body systems into healing mode, by changing from a malfunctioning activity to a harmonious one. Sometimes, however, the body systems will do this for themselves, thus there are many cases where a person has recovered from an apparently hopeless condition by 'spontaneous remission'. Examination of such cases shows that this was sometimes associated with a positive change in the person's lifestyle that gave them greater motivation to live. This has led to the view that we have the potential for self-healing and various ways have been developed to try to harness this. For example, the psychotherapist, Lawrence LeSHAN has developed methods that seek to harness a person's ability to self heal for cancer patients and as a result about half of his 'hopeless', 'terminal' patients have gone into long term remission, the lives of many others were longer than medically predicted, while nearly all of them found their lives opened up and more exciting. Instead of concentrating on what is wrong with a patient and seeking the cause of it, LeShan seeks to explore the positive side of a person's character, to find the 'unique song' that a person has to sing so that they get up in the morning full of zest and involvement in life and go to bed healthily tired. When their lives are full of such joyous activity their immune system is stimulated and they do not have time to worry about having cancer.

LeShan quotes a number of examples of his patients where this approach supplemented their conventional chemotherapy, or other treatment, to reverse or eliminate their cancer. Sydney was a highly successful business man, with a high level of drive and intelligence who retired at 65 and in his retirement played more golf and tennis, for which he had not been able to find enough time while working. However, after a while he found that this left him feeling unsatisfied, 'drifting' and uninvolved, without the clear sense of direction that he had as a business man. At the same time he developed cancer of the small intestine. With LeShan, Sydney explored his situation and it was apparent that he needed some way of expressing his creativity and he joined a group of serious, intelligent people who were concerned with social issues, like the effects of the population explosion, business and agricultural activities. As these interests developed, they challenged and extended him and he became very busy and fulfilled, and the chemotherapy was successful and there was no return of the cancer. Carol was a successful high executive in a large firm, living a glamorous life, who in her late thirties developed cancer in her back, with a poor prognosis. It turned out that she hated her job and disliked the people who rose to the top in her field and worried that working with them would make her as unfeeling, driven and ruthlessly ambitious as they were and she found that her ability and willingness to work to the limit had brought her neither happiness or inner peace. She felt at a dead end without any future. LeShan concentrated on what Carol did like and it turned out that during her student years Carol had worked at a centre for retraining people who, through accidents or illness, had become severely handicapped. She had found this work very fulfilling. So she got involved in it again and jettisoned her high-powered job and high standard of living. Slowly her cancer disappeared and when LeShan met her many years later she was free of her cancer and leading a busy and fulfilling life. Pedreo grew up in 'gangland' in a New York suburb and became a member of a gang at the age of nine. In his late teens the gang disintegrated and he was left on his own and he developed Hodgkins disease for which there was no known cure. With LeShan he explored what had given him fulfilment in his gangland existence and it turned out that it was the camaraderie of being part of a group experiencing periods of danger together. As a result of LeShan's influence he became a successful member of the fire-fighting service and was happy and well when LeShan met him again15 years later. Karen was an artistically talented child but under pressure from her family studied and qualified in school administration in which she got a job and did well. In her early thirties she developed rapidly growing breast cancer and during her hospitalisation and post-recuperative period she returned to her artistic activities. The fulfilment that she got from these made her give more attention to her needs as a person and as an artist and her recovery was excellent and her artistic work gave her a great zest for life. Carl was a foreman in a mid-sized Company who had lost one kidney with cancer some years ago and then developed cancer in the other kidney, for which he was undergoing chemotherapy with a very poor prognosis. He was married to a highly energetic wife who dominated their home life. After discussions with LeShan about doing one's own thing he began D.I.Y. activities in his home, which gave him great satisfaction but which his wife had always been against. He also began to assert himself in his marriage in other ways and his relationship with his wife improved. His response to the chemotherapy was excellent and he was doing well under a maintenance programme when LeShan met him seven years later.

The SIMONTON cancer centre has a good record of success in dealing with cancer patients and takes a similar view to LeShan; attributing a major role to a person's beliefs, attitudes and life style. However, as well as helping a person to resolve his/her emotional and mental stresses and problems, they teach the patient visualisation exercises. In these the patient visualises their treatment successfully attacking and killing off the cancer cells, these being washed away by healthy blood cells, and him/her regaining good health. According to hK-M, we, that is our soul/spirit, inhabit a physical body and by our feelings and thoughts we can misuse it and cause it to malfunction; equally, if it is malfunctioning, by our thoughts and feelings we can cure and reharmonise it.

Meridian energy healing

This is a technique that was developed by Roger CALLAHAN, an experienced psychotherapist. Callahan had a patient with a very strong phobia about water in any form that, after two years of conventional psychotherapy treatments he had been able to do little to help. Previously Callahan had explored other treatments to try and find more effective ways of helping people and in so doing he had gained some experience of kinesiology (the way in which emotional and thinking activities affect the physical working of the body) and of acupuncture based on the flow of non-physical energy (Ch'i) along meridians and how this can be accessed at specific acupuncture points. When his patient was in the grip of her phobia she experienced a 'knot in her stomach' and, almost in desperation and without any real expectation of anything happening, Callahan told her to tap on the meridian energy point under her eye traditionally associated with the stomach. Immediately and permanently, after many years, her phobia about water vanished completely. Callahan realised that here was the possibility that he had long sought of a quick and effective way of helping his patients, so he used the same technique to try and help other patients. Tapping under the eye did not resolve their problems but by using his knowledge of kinesiology to diagnose the problem and his knowledge of acupuncture to work out the relevant place to tap on the body, he found that he could cure a wide variety of problems. Callahan found that there were 13 main acupuncture tapping points that covered most situations.

CRAIG, an engineer who had an interest in personal development and in removing obstacles that hindered it, developed a technique that involved tapping all 13 main meridian points (this only takes a few minutes), so that it is not necessary to diagnose the problem or to know the associated meridian energy point. This made the whole process so simple that it is possible for a person to carry it out for him/herself without having to consult a psychotherapist or other type of healer. What you do is to define and state your problem to yourself, concentrate your attention on it and, via a ritual of tapping and activating the meridian energy system, resolve it. This technique, known as the Emotional Freedom Technique (EFT) is very simple, highly effective and can bring about dramatic changes, sometimes in minutes, for a wide range of psychological and physical problems, (HARTMANN).

According to hK-M we comprise a hierarchy of activities, namely a thinking spirit, a sensory feeling soul, a will activity etheric energy body and a physical substance body, all of which operate in unison when we carry out an activity. Suppose, for example, that we perform the simple task of selecting a book from our bookshelf. This involves first the thought that we wish to look at that particular book, second the sensory activity of perceiving where the book is and then willing into action the physical body movement required to pick it off the bookshelf. We have no problem in doing this, or in carrying out any similar activity, because as we have grown up we have programmed our self to do such things and we simply activate the pattern of behaviour that we have programmed into our subconscious mind. Suppose now that we know from previous experience that the book that we wish to look at contains information that will make our life better – perhaps be a good read or help us to resolve a problem, then our will activity will be stronger than if it is a book that we don't really want to read but have to – perhaps to pass an examination in a subject that we know from previous experience is boring, uninteresting and stressful. In this way our feelings acquired from previous experiences become programmed into our subconscious patterns of behaviour and thereby affect the quality of our bodily activity. A simple demonstration that kinesiologists use to show the effect of feeling on bodily activity is to get a person to hold out his/her hand while feeling normal and to resist someone trying to push it down and then to repeat the exercise while thinking of some adverse or traumatic experience, when it is found that their resistance to having their hand pushed down is much decreased.

According to hK-M our spirit and soul are connected to our body via a number of centres (chakras, fig. 13.1) and they operate along a system of energy channels or meridians according to the way that we have developed these as we have gone through life (possibly influenced by experiences from previous incarnations). Adverse emotional, or mental, experiences as we develop create perturbations in the pattern of energy flow that can then be reactivated when we again encounter similar experiences and thereby affect the harmonious workings of the physical body. Meridian energy healing techniques show that these can be rectified by concentrating on the thoughts and feelings that disturb the energy flow, while physically tapping appropriate points on the meridians that activate, and allow these parts to normalise. If this is done correctly the response is almost instantaneous because we are dealing with emotions and thoughts that exist in a different and far more active space-time world to that of our substance body. If the energy flows are realigned in this way physical effects then subsequently occur at a slower rate as our body responds to the new pattern of energy flow.

HAY, a 'metaphysical healer' takes the view that adverse personal experiences as we grow up give rise to negative thoughts and emotions that lead to malfunctioning of our body's systems; and that good health can be restored by changing our thought patterns. She quotes her own case as an example. As a child Hay was subjected to mental, physical and sexual abuse. In later life she developed vaginal cancer that she attributed to the deep resentment she felt about her childhood treatment. By changing her thoughts and feelings from resentment to understanding, compassion and love towards those who had maltreated her and towards herself, Hay dispersed her cancer.

Using this type of approach Hay has been able to help many people with different types of problems. She has described her techniques and the correlations she found between bodily ailments and the underlying feelings and thought patterns, in a book that has been translated into 26 languages and sold over 30 million copies.

The dominant current view of ill health is that the problem lies in the functioning of the physical, substance body and as such requires bodily treatment, e.g. physical adjustments, operations and/or the administration of substances such as drugs. It is recognised that some problems have a psychosomatic element to them but this is not generally regarded as a key factor. The hK-M view, that we are soul/spirit entities that inhabit a physical body to get experience of life on Earth, attributes a major role to the way that our soul/spirit uses or misuses its physical body. It sees good health of the physical body as requiring good health of our emotional feeling soul and our thinking spirit, which means lively, active positive emotions of love and joy for life and not negative emotions of resentment, anxiety and aggression that eat away inside and undermine us, together with clear active flexible thinking, unimpeded by rigid invalid thoughts or beliefs, that limit us in our interactions with life. This means eliminating blockages in our emotions and thoughts, as proposed by HAY and as carried out by WEISS in his hypnotherapy treatment of Catherine described in the last chapter, as a result of which she became 'radiant and healthy beyond normal', or using something like meridian energy based EFT to remove inhibiting issues so that 'you take delight in your activity/your body/your health/your work and your life' (HARTMANN) and achieve a 'freedom that allows you to blossom and rise above whatever hidden hurdles keep you from performing to your capacity' (CRAIG) or, following LeSHAN's approach of finding the unique song that we have to sing to realise our potential, so that we get up in the morning full of zest and involvement in life and go to bed healthily tired.

At first sight there seems to be a large gap between these viewpoints that stress the importance of emotional and mental activity in determining good health and the biological view that the activity of our body is determined by the DNA composition of its genes. The structure of a living organism is built up by the proteins of which it consists and this is encoded in its genes which are primarily concentrated in the nuclei of its cells. However, LIPTON, a cell biologist, has pointed out that prokaryotic cells do not possess nuclei and controlling DNA, yet they carry out the multiple functions necessary for life, with the control of the ingestion and excretion of the substances on which their life depends vested in their membrane. With more evolved eukaryotic cells that do possess nuclei it is possible to remove the nucleus and for a cell to carry on living, performing the functions that keep it alive for weeks, or even months, (although it cannot replicate). As mentioned on p. 91, recent research has shown that all organisms have a great many genes in common, so that it has not been possible to explain the widely different organisms that exist on Earth in terms of differences in their genetic structure. The factor that seems to determine the nature and behaviour of an organism seems to be, not so much the genes that it possesses, but what selects and activates specific genes, which Lipton states is determined by its environment. In human beings the energies associated with our emotions and thoughts create an environment that determines the activities of our genes and thereby affect our health. Our emotions and thoughts about things are determined by our beliefs, which thereby determine our genetic activity, so that Lipton takes the view that in essence, we are our beliefs (his book is called 'The Biology of Belief').

This is in line with hK-M, according to which we comprise a hierarchy of spirit-thinking, soul-feeling and etheric-will activities, so that our etheric-will operates in an atmosphere created by our soul-feeling and spirit-thinking energy activities. According to hK-M the stresses imposed on any organism by its environment and/or its inner striving determine its genetic activity and thereby its form and function and cause it to be adapted to its environment and its genes pass this on to its off-spring. This is how bodily evolution of organisms occurs.

This means that poor health can be rectified by changing our emotions, thoughts and beliefs. Lipton uses this fact to account for the placebo effect, in which in many cases, in trials of drugs or other 'cures', patients who, without them knowing it, are given a fake treatment often respond well, simply because they believe that what is being done will make them better. He quotes a particularly outstanding case in which patients with severe debilitating knee problems were divided into two groups and one group was given surgical treatments and the other, 'placebo' group, without them knowing it, were given 'fake surgery' and it was found that the placebo group improved as much as the group that received surgery. In particular, one member of the placebo group who had to use a cane 'before surgery' was able to play baseball with his grandchildren. However, improving our health by improving our emotions and thoughts is not as simple as it might seem because, while we have control of, and can change by an effort of will, our conscious emotions and thoughts, a great deal of the pattern of our emotional and thinking activity has been built into us at a subconscious level, particularly when we were children and even in the womb (see Lipton). However, psychotherapists are developing techniques, such as meridian energy therapy, by which we can reprogram our emotional and thinking energy activities and thereby improve our bodily health.

Spiritual Healing

We have referred in Chapter 12 to the ability of Sai Baba and Daskalos to heal people and there was of course the healing activity of Christ. These are extreme examples of spiritual healing in which a person manifests the ability to heal others. Spiritual healing is quite widespread but because it is not understandable in terms of the current scientific approach to healing it is a controversial subject. STEMMAN (2) has surveyed the phenomena of spiritual healing and the, comparatively small, number of investigations that have been made into what takes place.

It would seem that some people possess the gift of being able to heal others by applying their hands to the person they are working on, either touching them directly or holding their hands close to them. Some healers, however, do not seem to need such direct contact and can transmit healing to someone who has written to them, in what appears to be a telepathic type process. In some cases a person can experience healing after someone else has written to a healer asking for healing for them, without the person concerned even knowing that healing has been asked for on their behalf. There is also evidence that it is possible to heal people by prayer. Healers explain healing of this type as carried out by attuning with the Divine source to beam energies to the patient. Sometimes a person receives healing by going to a shrine, such as Lourdes.

A small number of investigations have been carried out to try to get to grips with the healing force. In controlled experiments it has been found that it is possible for a healer to affect the rate at which blood cells break down in a saline solution, to kill cancer cells grown in a special culture flask, to affect enzyme activity, to affect the longevity of mice injected with virulent cancer cells and for water treated by a healer to increase the growth rate of plants, whereas water treated by a person suffering from depression decreased it, STEMMAN (2).

In spiritual healing, sometimes the healer carries out 'operations' on the patient, often accompanied by dramatic manifestations of apparent opening of the body with removal of body material and associated blood.

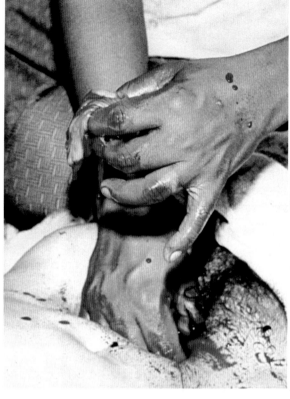

a 'physical' operation on a hernia, in which the healer has opened the body and is removing tissue material with his fingers.

b A part 'physical' and part 'astral materialisation' in which the healer has performed a physical partition of the skin and then an 'astral materialisation' of tissue material in the opening.

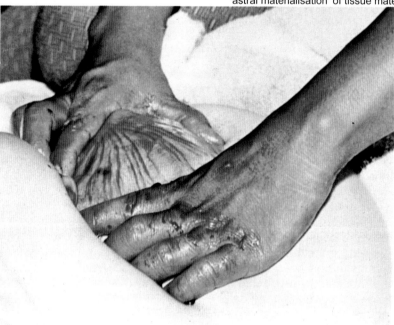

c An 'astral (etheric?) materialisation performed to heal a stomach problem. The materialised tissue substance appears on the surface of the body and is smooth and nearly bloodless.

Fig. 13.9 Photographs by Dr. Sigrun Seutemann of healing carried out by the Philippine healer Tony Agpaoa.

This type of healing seems to be prolific in the Philippines and has been subjected to a number of investigations, some of which have shown the manifestations to be the result of trickery and sleight of hand,

STEMMAN (2)   Whether the physical manifestations are necessary to convince the patient that healing is being carried out or whether the whole process is bogus is not clear but it is claimed that healing often occurs. Dr. Sigrun Seutemann investigated a number of Phillipine healers and selected one, Tony Agpaoa, who she thought to be genuine. Over a period of fifteen months Seutemann took more than 700 patients to Agpaoa for healing; these people were suffering from a wide variety of problems that had not responded to conventional medical treatments. She found that 2% of the patients were immediately healed, 20-25% were healed or much better within 2-4 weeks, 50% were better within 6 months and 10% showed no change. From her observations Seutemann differentiated Agpaoa's healing into three types, one, 'magnetic healing' where there was a flow of energy from his hands to the patient, secondly, where he seemingly materialised substances from the patient's body and thirdly, where he carried out an internal operation in which his hand penetrated into the body. Dr. Seutemann did not detect fraud in the operations that Tony Agpaoa carried out and she supplied us with copies of some of the photographs that she took, fig. 13.9.

The problem is to know what is going on in spiritual healing. Usually the healer states that they feel that they do not carry out the healing themselves but that they are channels for 'a higher 'spiritual power'. In some cases they claim that discarnate doctors are working through them and sometimes they go into a trance state and are taken over by the spirit of the discarnate doctor who uses the healer as a channel. There is a well-documented case of a healer, George Chapman who operated in a trance state, allegedly being controlled by a discarnate doctor, Dr. Lang. Many people visited Chapman/Lang for healing, one of whom was Joseph HUTTON who had deteriorating vision which conventional medical practice could do little to arrest. Hutton, who was a journalist and author, initially had no time for 'spiritualist healing' but his wife persuaded him to visit Chapman/Lang and Dr.Lang carried out a 'spirit operation' on his eyes which dramatically improved his vision. This convinced Hutton that what Chapman/Lang were doing was genuine and he felt that he should apply his journalistic skills to researching and reporting the situation.   Both Chapman and Lang co-operated with Hutton and he also tracked down a large number of people who had been treated by them. The story is that Dr. Lang, who died in 1937 was a highly-skilled ophthalmic surgeon at Moorfields Eye Hospital in London and when he died he wanted to carry on with helping people still in the incarnate state with his surgical activities. To do this he had to have a suitable living person, a medium, through whom he could work and he found such a person in Chapman, who worked as a fireman. For Lang to operate Chapman had to go into a trance and allow Lang to take over his body. Many people went to Chapman/Lang, some of whom had been colleagues or patients of Lang while he was alive.   Through Chapman Dr. Lang had detailed discussions with his erstwhile colleagues about their professional activities and they, and Lang's previous patients were convinced that they really were dealing with Lang. (Chapman had little scientific education and none of the complex ophthalmic and other medical knowledge that Lang displayed through Chapman in his trance state).

Although Lang had been a specialist in ophthalmic operations he also had general surgical experience, so that he was able to deal with other problems. He stated that with these he could be joined by other discarnate surgeons who applied their specialist skills where required. Not all of the people who visited Lang were healed and Chapman was too much in demand to be able to keep track of what happened so it is not clear to what extent Lang was successful and where his healing did not work. In the book that he wrote HUTTON gives an account of his interviews with Chapman and with Lang, through Chapman in a trance state, and he presents the follow up evidence that he obtained and numerous case histories of patients who were healed.

Dr. Lang stated that a human being has a spirit body underlying the substance body and that he carried out operations on this and the effects were then carried over into the substance body. He could perceive what was wrong through the patient's aura and by an X-ray type vision of the workings of the spirit and substance bodies. According to hK-M the 'spirit body' would be the etheric body that organises the workings of the substance body and Lang's 'X-ray' and aura vision of it resulted from the fact that, in his discarnate state, he no longer lived in a physical body with its physical sense organs but in an etheric-astral body which gave him an etheric-astral level of awareness of the patient. Lang stated that the energies that he used for healing in his operations came from 'God'.

A more extensive account of the process of spiritual healing comes from Markides' description of the activities of Daskalos and his explanations for these. Daskalos describes Man as a three-part being - gross material body, soul and spirit, (Daskalos does not use the terms soul and spirit but the terms that he uses have more or less the same meaning so, to avoid confusion we have continued with our terminology). The gross material body comprises substances organised and functioning according to the pattern of activity of the etheric body. He states that good health of the material body requires healthy etheric functioning and this is destroyed by negative vibrations, such as, anxiety, depression, stubbornness, anger, hatred and similar morbid emotions. Conversely, people who live balanced lives have a large healthy active etheric body and give out etheric energy that others can draw on for vitality.

All activities that manifest through the material body e.g. those of soul and spirit, are mediated by the etheric body and the mystic can perceive this and must have a detailed knowledge of its workings and also of body functioning, so that he can perceive the malfunctioning of the etheric body and knows what needs to be done to put it right. He states that there are three types of etheric functioning (which seem to correspond to biological, soul and spirit motivated activities) and that the mystic/healer must have developed the knowledge and will power to direct the universal energy to correct malfunctioning at the required level.

Daskalos, states that this energy comes from the Holy Spirit and that he directs it by his power of thought but that he does not have total control as he can only heal someone if it is in accord with the will of 'the Masters' and if it is not against a person's karma. We would equate the energy of the Holy Spirit with the EM-energy of *h*K-M that permeates, experiences and is the active principle in all aspects of evolution. Daskalos states that in some cases he is able, by power of thought to dematerialise diseased parts and rematerialise them in a normal, cured form. In one case, which was claimed to be carried out in front of a number of observers, Daskalos healed a young boy who could not walk as a result of polio and at the same time lengthened one of his legs that was shorter than the other so that, after the 10 minute healing session, the boy walked and his legs were of the same length. As a result of these activities, people claimed that Daskalos was able to perform miracles but Daskalos stated that this was not so, he simply operated metaphysical laws that are not generally known.

The problem is, what are these laws? Science has formulated laws that describe the behaviour of physical, mineral kingdom bodies in terms of their response to physical forces acting on them but, other than the fact that genes are somehow involved, it has no awareness of any laws that give rise to the forms and functions of living organisms. It certainly has no understanding of how healers, and mystics like Daskalos, can intervene in the activities of a person's body to rectify any malfunctioning. Scientists take the view that somehow, out of themselves, substances come together to create the bodies of organisms which somehow evolve the abilities to feel and to think. It is manifestly obvious that feelings and thoughts can bring about activities in substances; we are doing this all the time when a feeling or thought causes us to perform an action that involves activity of the substances of our body but how this comes about scientists do not know. According to *h*K-M, behind the physical activities of a human being their lies a hierarchy of worlds of living, soul-feeling and spirit-thinking activities of which we have little awareness. Mystics, however, can raise their levels of consciousness to be aware of, and participate in, the activities of these 'other worlds' and use these abilities to bring about healing of people's malfunctioning bodies.

Daskalos states that he diagnoses the patient's condition by entering into a state of consciousness that gives him an 'X-ray-type' vision of the working of the body, combined with observations of the aura and his knowledge of what aberrations in this signify. If necessary, in this state of consciousness he can magnify what he is looking at (e.g. a virus) to see it more clearly. But he cannot always effect cures; sometimes a person subconsciously does not want to be cured because of the attention they are getting; in other cases, if it is part of a person's karma that they have to work out, then the invisible Masters will not allow him to cure it. It is not necessary for the person to be physically present; Daskalos can contact and heal a person from a photograph or letter.

[This is similar to the way that the famous American psychic Edgar Cayce carried out many well-attested diagnoses and healings (SUGRUE). Caroline Myss, who we have mentioned earlier in this Chapter as diagnosing clairvoyantly the state of Dr. Norman Shealy's patients does this remotely, reporting by telephone from 1200 miles away].

Daskalos carries out his healing by constructing healing elementals (living thoughts) for the person concerned. He states that spiritual healers have the ability to heal but because they are not conscious of what they are doing they sometimes only alleviate the condition and do not get at, and nullify, the root cause. Furthermore the energy of such a healer may become depleted in healing whereas the mystic, by purifying his nature becomes a channel for higher energies and does not have this problem. In some cases he, and other 'Masters' (i.e. people who have developed the ability to control these activities), carry out healing by materialising where this is needed, e.g. on battlefields, and this accounts for cases where soldiers state that someone appeared from no-where and attended to them until help arrived.

Daskalos claims that elementals play a major part in psychological illnesses and their cure. He states that, other than brain damage, there are three main causes of schizophrenic-type illness; elementals (the most common); earth-bound spirits and demons. A person can, by reinforcing his desires and thoughts, build up elementals that are so powerful that they take control of him/her and s/he then experiences them as urges and voices that s/he must follow. Possession by earth-bound spirits occurs when a discarnate entity does not move on in the soul-spirit worlds and seeks to retain an existence in the material world by taking over someone's body. Demons are non-human entities (negative elementals) that seek experience of Earth incarnation. Cure is possible by the healer creating positive elementals of sufficient power that they neutralise the effects of the negative ones and a number of examples of Daskalos doing this are described. Even if cure is not immediate, or the person resists it, the healing elemental will remain with the person and will carry out its curative activity when conditions become suitable for it to do so.

[The idea that some mental illnesses are caused by a low-level discarnate entity superimposing itself on a person, in an effort to continue incarnate existence and to satisfy its desires, has been the basis of the work of spiritualist 'rescue circles' (WICKLAND); other examples of 'possession' are presented in books by WOODARD and PEARCE-HIGGINS and WHITBY].

Markides describes a number of examples where Daskalos carried out physical healing of cases that could not be cured by the medical profession. One such case was that of a paralysed woman with a distorted spine in which the vertebrae were in poor condition. Daskalos stated that he corrected this by willing the dematerialisation of the vertebrae and then their rematerialisation in their correct positions and in sound condition. The woman then got up and walked normally. Markides said that Daskalos's claims were supported by X-ray photographs taken before and after the healing. During healing the patient reported feelings as though electricity or little ants were running up and down her spine. Many other similar cases are described. In some of the cancers that Daskalos cured he stated that, rather than work on the tumour in the patient he dematerialised it from the patient and transferred it to his own body where he could disperse it over a more extended period (several days). Where illness is caused by a virus, Daskalos stated that we all have viruses in us but they do not necessarily thrive and lead to illness, this only takes place if the etheric energy of the body is depleted. This happens when our desires and thoughts create vibrations of anxiety, depression, stubbornness, anger, hatred, etc. The healer can cure the virus condition by strengthening the etheric energy of the patient and curing the emotional-mental state.

One does not, however, need to be a mystic or to possess the clairvoyant ability that enables one to perceive the body's energy fields in order to connect with higher powers of healing. An example of this comes from PEARL, a chiropractor with a large practice in Los Angeles who, in his chiropractic treatment began to experience an energy flow taking place through him that was directed to healing his patients, beyond the chiropractic adjustments that he made. As this happened with more and more of his patients Pearl became increasingly concerned with what was going on and with what lay behind it all. Then a succession of (ordinary, non-psychic) patients 'channelled' statements to him saying, 'we are here to tell you to continue what you are doing, what you are doing is bringing light and information to the planet. What you are doing is reconnecting strands. You must know that you are a 'Master'. In trying to understand his situation Pearl consulted a number of psychics and he was told that he was a Pleiadian. In the next chapter we outline claims that have been made for 'Pleiadians' and their contribution to the activities of humanity. In the present context the essential feature is that in a past era there had been a closer connection with healing energies that has become lost and that a period is now ensuing in which there will be a reconnection with these healing forces, with Pleiadians playing a central role in bringing this about. Certainly in Pearl's chiropractic practice healings became more amazing and widespread until they dominated his activities. In one outstanding case there was a similar healing to that of Daskalos healing the boy who had had polio, in which Pearl was a channel for the healing of a 26 year old person who had had a distorted skeletal structure from birth with one leg shorter than the other. Under his aegis Pearl observed this person's body being manipulated, straightened out and legs made of equal length by unknown forces outside of his control. Whereas Daskalos consciously invoked the universal energy to carry out specific, intentional healings, Pearl opened himself up to unknown forces to carry out whatever healing that they deemed appropriate.

Then people began to ask Pearl to teach them how to carry out healings. He felt that he was unable to 'teach' healing because he did not know what was going on but he found that he was able to activate the ability to channel the flow of healing energy in other people, first on a one to one basis and then with increasingly large numbers of people in Seminars and then by demonstrations on TV and to convey the ability to heal by telephone and even by the written word in a book that he wrote. When a healing takes place the patient and the healer may experience it in a variety of ways, e.g. as a flow of heat or cold or like an experience of electricity and patients may feel as though they are being manipulated by invisible entities. The patient may not necessarily receive healing for the condition for which they seek it and if there is an underlying reason for them not wanting healing, e.g. because of the attention that they get for their problem, healing may not take place. The key feature seems to be that the healer and the patient have to open themselves up to allow the flow of healing forces to achieve whatever they seek to do.

Chapter 14

Appendix 4 to Chapter 5: The Omniverse and a New Dimension to Hominids

Phenomena Suggesting Contact With the Omniverse Hierarchy

While interactions of the Omniverse Hierarchy with humanity on Earth may have played a major part in the development of past civilisations, this is not just something that happened in the past but is an on-going process. Thus there have been, and still are, many accounts of such interactions. Throughout history there have been reports of contacts with non-human entities, from lowly gnomes, fairies and Nature spirits, to gods who seek to guide mankind. Currently a number of people claim to be in telepathic contact with 'high spiritual beings' that offer guidance for Man on Earth. These have become known as 'channelled communications'. There are also the so-called UFO phenomena that, with their physical manifestations, could derive from the activities of lower levels of the Omniverse Hierarchy. Contact with the higher levels of the Omniverse Hierarchy, with their greater experience and awareness of the processes of creation, could be immensely valuable in getting a more wholistic understanding of our existence on Earth. However, evaluating such supposed contacts is a veritable minefield. Before we examine these issues, we first look at something of great importance that must be taken into account in dealing with them, namely, the creative power of thinking.

The Creative Power of Thought

According to hK-M the central, essential, part of our nature is a thinking spirit, our I, that derives from, and exists in, a spiritual world. We (our Is) have incarnated into Earth existence by inhabiting soul-etheric-physical bodies that arose by biological evolution on Earth, by which we experience, think about and act in, the physical world. In Western Civilisation we have become so immersed in our physical activities that we tend to regard these as the basis of all phenomena. Thus, there is no recognition of the existence and workings of an etheric body, while soul and spirit, if they are acknowledged at all, are regarded as something shadowy and insubstantial in the background. Thinking is often considered to be the way the brain works. However, as described earlier, there is considerable evidence to show that the thinking mind, or spirit is separate from the brain. But this then raises the problem of how mind and body interact to bring about physical actions, i.e. how an insubstantial thought can cause an activity in substance, (and can cause psychosomatic illness), about which we have very little understanding.

Psychics and mystics claim to perceive the thinking mind (spirit) as an aura of energy-activity that permeates and encompasses the physical body (encompassing also soul and etheric auras of activities). When we think of something that we want to do, we generate a thought-energy impulse that triggers the appropriate pattern of behaviour of the soul-etheric body complex, to turn the 'thought' into a physical action. But we do not always turn our thoughts into physical actions. Much of our 'thinking' is a subconsciously-driven 'rambling around' of reminiscences and possibilities, without being concerned with generating physical actions. As a result of this energy-activity we create a continual output of 'thought forms'. (Descriptions of these are given by Occultists and clairvoyants who claim to be able to perceive them; see, for example, LEADBEATER, PAYNE). We create these thought forms by taking in space-energy from our environment, shaping it into thoughts that we expel back into the environment. These thoughts do not have much stability to them, so that the forms that we create are ephemeral. Sometimes when we concentrate and pursue a specific line of thinking our thought forms have more clarity and energy and then they possess greater stability and survive longer. If we keep returning to a particular line of thinking we can revitalise and strengthen the thought forms involved. Equally, if many people follow the same line of thinking, the stability, energy and life of the communal thought form that this creates, builds up.

PAYNE, who claimed to perceive these thought forms, states that where many people meet together regularly to worship their concept of God they can build up a very powerful thought form that conforms to this concept. Psychics often refer to the powerful 'aura' associated with places of worship that act as centres, as do images and sculptures, for the concentration of feeling and thought power. But because the thought form is not self actualising it needs a constant feeding of energy into it from the thoughts and feelings of human beings. If this ceases then it dies away. Thus VAN DER POST describes an experience he had with Kalahari bushmen, where he was taken to one of their sacred sites but their gods (which presumably they had created by their beliefs/thought power), were only able to manifest in diminished form because they had begun to 'die off'.

One of the practices of mystics during meditation is to hold a single thought firmly in the mind for an extended period of time. This then gives the thought form considerable strength and stability. Again, where a number of people concentrate on the same thought the same thing happens.

The creative power of thought seems to operate at three levels.

First, extensive accounts are given of post-mortem existence in a spiritual world that is created by thought. Discarnate entities move and interact with each other in this world by the power of thought. Incarnate entities who can separate from their bodies, in an OBE can equally travel and communicate in the spiritual world by the power of thought. There are also accounts of mystics and religious leaders manifesting in duplicate 'thought bodies' in the phenomenon of bilocation. These phenomena seem to be a matter of thought power creating forms in the EM-energy.

Second, there are accounts of psychics and mystics apporting objects by thought and a few instances of them 'apporting' their physical body so as to travel, almost instantaneously, to another place where they are perceived as physical entities who perform physical actions. A similar phenomenon is that of healing being carried out by thought power, for example as manifested by Daskalos, which involves manipulating the substances of a physical body by thought.

Third, Sai Baba and others who have developed their thought power by meditation (examples of whom are given by YOGANANDA) seem to be able to create substantial objects by thought.

A good example of the creation of a thought form that then took on an interesting and enlightening existence comes from a controlled experimental investigation by the Toronto Society for Psychical Research. Members of this society had investigated ghost and poltergeist phenomena and had come to the conclusion that hallucinations could be involved. They therefore carried out an experiment to determine whether a group of them could create a collective hallucination. They imagined an entity whom they called Philip and concocted an existence for him in the middle 1600s. Then they tried to contact Philip in a typical séance circle, sitting around a table and requesting responses from him to their questions.

The group met regularly for a year, concentrating and meditating on Philip and seeking results in an objective way, without success. Then they changed their technique to one of a casual, child-like attitude of belief in manifestations and immediately they got responses from Philip, in terms of raps on the table conveying positive or negative answers to their questions. Then Philip took on a life of his own, embellishing his story. At the same time, there were massive movements of the table across the room. A psychological analysis concluded that Philip was a composite personality formed from unconscious, uncontrolled infantile aspects of the different group members' characters.

This experiment showed convincingly the ability to create a thought form but, although it concluded that this form was constructed out of 'uncontrolled infantile energies', it gave no understanding of how such infantile energy could bring about the physical effect of moving a table around. Usually we think of psychological energies and physical energies as being quite different. But it may have been a manifestation, on a small group scale, of what WILSON thinks could have been the collective consciousness that enabled Egyptian workers to build the pyramids, (before they developed rational consciousness and were therefore like the Toronto group when they 'let go' of their rational consciousness) (For a detailed account of the Toronto group researches, see OWEN and SPARROW)

Phoebe PAYNE, who claimed to be able to perceive the events in the soul and spirit worlds that lie behind physical activities, carried out extensive investigations into psychic phenomena. She observed that physical phenomena at seances (and poltergeist activities) occurred with primitive, uneducated or young undeveloped persons in whom the etheric body was unstable, that is, not fully under their soul-spirit (ego-Ego) feeling-thinking control. Their energy was then drawn on by either a low-grade discarnate entity or an 'elemental', in either of whom the desire was to perform freakish or prankish activities. This could be the explanation for the results of the members of the Toronto Society experiments, in that when they relinquished ego/Ego control they allowed an external influence to use some of their etheric energy. In the case of manoeuvring tables, Phoebe Payne states that these entities shape this energy into rods or levers to make these movements, (presumably tapping into the ways that Man uses to do this). Some decades ago, when it was fashionable to investigate the physical phenomena of mediumship, CRAWFORD obtained photographs and other evidence of such 'ectoplasmic rods', as they were then called.

Similarly photographs and other evidence was obtained of ectoplasm from mediums being shaped into recognisable human forms, allegedly by the thought power of discarnate beings who wished to provide evidence of their continued existence. There have also been cases where, by thought power, 'psychic' images were produced on photographic plates. In some instances it would seem that these were produced by non-physical entities manipulating etheric energy derived from mediums, (PATTERSON, DE BRATH, WARRICK). In other cases it seems that the registrations were produced by a person concentrating and willing an image to appear on the photographic emulsion, (FUKURAI, EISENBUD).

Payne classified psychics into two classes, negative and positive. Negative psychics relax and open themselves up to allow external influences to work unconsciously or semi-consciously through them, whereas positive psychics (and mystics) work consciously out of their own controlled feeling-soul and thinking-spirit abilities. The activities of the Toronto research group, when Philip manifest, would fall into the former category.

An anecdotal account of the production of a thought form of the second category, that is, of forms produced by controlled thinking, was given by ALEXANDRA DAVID-NEEL who travelled and studied extensively in Tibet. She described thought forms produced by Tibetan mystics, that had sufficient 'reality' to be perceived by other people and also how, by using their methods she created a thought form of a monk herself. Other members of her group also perceived this 'phantom'. However, once created, it escaped her control and took on an independent life of its own. (It may have been taken over by an elemental). As a result it became a nuisance and she had considerable difficulty in dispersing it - which took her six months of effort.

Phoebe Payne and Daskalos use the term 'elemental' to describe a powerful thought form, created by strongly-willed emotions or thoughts, that is impelled, in a robot-like way, to do what its emotional-mental content/nature requires of it. Mostly our thoughts and feelings produce forms that do not possess enough energy to survive for long. But, Payne states, powerful or repeated thoughts or feelings produce an entity that can exist for years or even centuries. Such an elemental is then attracted automatically to anyone possessing similar qualities, on which it can draw to renew its vitality. Presumably the elemental experiences a rudimentary sense of self that it then seeks to maintain but, since it is not self actualising, it is dependent on drawing supporting energy from sources external to it. Payne states that the trained clairvoyant can always distinguish an elemental by the fact that it lacks 'essential vitality'.

According to Payne apports are brought about by using the power of thought to spread the atoms of which the object consists over a wider area, while the etheric counterpart is held together by the will of the operator. The object can then be passed through any dense physical obstruction and restored to its original form by releasing the concentration of will that held the atoms apart. This can be done consciously by mystics who have developed the necessary strength of will and thought power, or it can happen unconsciously where mediums open themselves up to external influences that can use the medium's loose etheric energy to act on the physical object.

The ability, by will and thought power, to manifest elsewhere is something that, for example, Sai Baba and Daskalos seem able to do. This is more extensive than an OBE where a person detaches themselves (their spirit) from their physical body and perceives what is happening elsewhere but are not seen there, in that, in the case of Sai Baba and Daskalos, at their destinations they are perceived as physical beings who perform physical actions.

Where mystics produce objects 'out of nowhere', this seems to operate at two levels. First, it is done by strongly developed thinking, willing the space-energy out of which substance atoms are formed into the configuration of the object, in a sort of reverse dematerialisation process. The object then exists for as long as the thought energy holds it together. But where a greater effect is required Yogananda states that this can be brought about if the mystic has 'purified' his personality and practised meditation exercises which result in being at-one with God. Then, by thinking that something should happen, the forces of God, (the higher levels of the Omniverse Hierarchy) flow through him/her and cause it to be so. This is supposed to be the way that the so-called miracles brought about by Christ and Sai Baba occurred; for example, the way in which Christ was able to feed the multitudes and similarly Sai Baba regularly feeds large numbers of his devotees. Daskalos stated that he drew consciously on this energy when required and that healers who carry out extensive healing without depleting themselves, unconsciously draw on this energy.

If the higher, thinking levels of the Omniverse Hierarchy seek to influence the activities of the levels below, this thought creates an activity in the space energy which the members of the lower level perceive as coming via 'messengers from the gods'. For example, the prophets of the Old Testament described how they received communications from God via visions of angels. So-called primitive peoples sometimes receive messages via a vision of the totem animal of the tribe concerned. It is interesting that ROSE, who studied Australian aborigines states that one aborigine who received 'messages' via visions of her totem animal, when converted to Christianity then received 'messages' via visions of an angel. The messengers from the gods could be equivalent on an Omniverse scale to the generation of thought forms and elementals by human beings.

When we try to comprehend what is going on in what seem to be contacts with the Omniverse Hierarchy we have to keep in mind a number of issues. First there are different levels of the Hierarchy with different degrees of evolution. Any contact with higher levels, whose nature is thinking, is in terms of thoughts, or visions that we perceive if we are open to them. Contact with intermediate levels, who have a strong physical-energy component to their nature, (but in a different space-time, 'vibrational' level to us) is via intelligently controlled physical manifestations. At all levels there exist three streams that seek enhanced sense of self by influencing humanity. There is the Idealist (Luciferic) stream that seeks power by getting people to subscribe to their cults and beliefs; there is the Materialist (Ahrimanic) stream that seeks power by getting people 'to serve Mammon', and the central (Christ) stream that seeks balanced harmonious evolution. In addition there exists a large range of thought forms, created by incarnate or discarnate human beings, that can influence us, from those of a trivial nature to those generated by deep thinkers concerned with the nature of existence and spiritual worlds. (As shown by the Toronto group experiment, these thought forms could be taken over and activated by elementals, or by discarnate entities, seeking a sense of self). Then, there is the problem of our ability to understand these activities, which is determined by our level of development. Thus the situation is a highly complex one, in which it is difficult to come to clear unambiguous evaluations.

The potentially most important contacts with the Omniverse Hierarchy would be mental ones with the higher levels, as so-called 'channelled communications' purport to be but, because of the problems outlined above, this is a real minefield to investigate. Before we come to these we consider UFO phenomena that could be manifestations of the activities of lower levels, (equally a minefield to deal with).

UFO Phenomena As a Possible Manifestation of the Omniverse Hierarchy?

There have been thousands of reports of these phenomena (see for example, GOOD, VALLEE). The people who testify to them range from experienced pilots who have encountered them in the air, ground observers from all walks of life, including former Presidents of the United States, while many people, again from a great variety of professions and walks of life, claim to have had personal contact with UFO's and aliens associated with them. In many cases a particular phenomenon has been perceived and corroborated by a number of observers. (An account of the history and features of UFO phenomena is given by HOUGHTEN and RANDLES).

The types of UFO 'space craft' that people have claimed to see varies from 'balls of light and energy' to large 'Mother ships' high above the Earth with, in between a variety of smaller craft that zoom around near the Earth and/or land on it. These vary in shape, being saucer-like or cigar or egg-shaped, sometimes with illuminated domes and an array of coloured lights. It is stated that these craft can move much faster than any flying object made by Man and that they have incredible manoeuvrability. Sometimes they suddenly appear and disappear.

CONSTABLE investigated UFO phenomena starting from the fact that there have been occasions when, while not physically observable, UFOs have been recorded by radar. Radar operates by microwaves that are adjacent to infrared radiation in the electromagnetic spectrum. Constable found that using infrared film and a filter that eliminated visible radiation he could get photographs of UFOs. He also got photographs of other, pulsating living organisms in the atmosphere. He concluded that these inhabit an etheric realm and live off etheric energy that also powers UFOs, (we would equate this with an aspect of the space energy of hK-M). During his investigations Constable developed some sort of psychic contact with the entities of his photographs and, in the absence of confirmatory results by other investigators, it is difficult to know whether his photographs required psychic energy on his part, as with the radionic photographs and those of thought forms referred to in the last chapter. Constable makes the point that these phenomena are not explicable in terms of the current scientific mechanistic paradigm and that a new 'etherian physics' is required. He then attempts to lay a foundation for this by bringing together Rudolf Steiner's exposition on etheric formative forces, work by Ruth Drown in the field of radionics and Wilhelm Reich's work on orgone energy. This is an area where much needs to be done to establish what is going on and the underlying principles at work.

Where people claim to have had contact with aliens from the UFO's that have landed, they state that this is with humanoids who have come forth from the UFO, sometimes just appearing, without there being any door, hatch, or point of entry or exit. The aliens may communicate in the language of the contactee, or express themselves in an incomprehensible language, or sometimes the communication is telepathic. What they have to say is a mixture of the sensible and the absurd.

Various types of aliens are described; beings of less than 4 feet in height, some man-sized and others larger, 7 feet or so. In appearance these are usually described as 'humanoid', i.e. having bodies, with arms and legs and moving around like human beings but with faces distinctly different, e.g. with large heads, slits for eyes, nose and mouth. The smaller entities are often described as 'robot-like'. The taller entities can be handsome and impressive. There have also been accounts of 'frog-like' humanoids. GOOD refers to an assessment that concludes that there are nine types of aliens interacting with Earth. In a few cases people have tried to shoot a UFO humanoid but bullets had no effect on it.

As well as the UFO craft possessing greater powers of movement and manoeuvrability, the 'aliens' associated with them possess powers by which they can stop Earth vehicles by 'mentally' incapacitating their power systems, together with the ability to freeze or paralyse the movement of people who try to interfere with them. Some people claim to have been taken on flights in a UFO or abducted for some sort of investigation, usually of their sexual functioning. Often there is a time and memory loss for the period during which this happens. Usually abductions take place when the person concerned is travelling by car in a remote area and the car is stopped by the UFO. Sometimes, after a time loss period, the person finds him/herself, in their car, in a place remote from where the abduction took place. There are cases where a person claims that they underwent an abduction experience while a witness with them states that they never left the car. There are also cases where the person undergoing abduction is aware of separating from their body, which remains in the car.

Many people have been subjected to hypnotic recall to try to ascertain what went on in their 'missing period'. For example, JACOBS states that he has subjected 60 people who claimed to be abducted by UFO's, to hypnotic regression of their experiences. He claims that he found a common pattern in which the aliens were concerned with extracting eggs and sperm and carrying out breeding programmes and with exploring sexual functioning and associated feelings and thoughts.

CANNON(3) has also carried out hypnotic regression on many people who have had UFO experiences and seemed to establish contact with a benevolent group of aliens and sources of information on what lies behind these activities. It is stated that the aliens live on a higher vibrational plane. In order to experience Earth circumstances they have to lower their vibrational level and protect themselves by creating suitable vehicles to travel in and bodies to inhabit, which they do by their thought energy. They are interested in perceiving and monitoring what goes on, on Earth, that they say is a unique situation. They are very interested in our emotions, which they do not experience. In particular they cannot understand the violence in our natures, as they do not possess this characteristic. The benevolent group that Cannon contacted state that they have sought to influence the evolution of humanity from its beginnings but they do not, and are not allowed to, interfere with our free will. They act under orders from higher spiritual levels of entities. They interact with people who possess the necessary affinity for this but they erase the memory of the interaction from the person's mind to avoid disturbing them; however the time is approaching when conditions will be such that they will manifest openly on Earth. They state that Earth is entering a critical period when there will be great turmoil and disturbance, (as they say happened to destroy Atlantis) but also there will be an up grading in the spiritual evolution of humanity. Their investigations of our sexuality and procreation is to help to produce a race of superior human beings who will be able to survive to carry further the evolution of humanity. Other groups are exploring Earth to see what they can use for their own life systems and environments.

In other UFO accounts, other types of alien activities are reported. Some have been hostile, in some cases either inadvertently or deliberately killing a contactee. There are reports of adverse physical effects, such as loss of consciousness, dizziness, blindness, nausea and vomiting, loss of energy, inability to sleep and burn-like phenomena appearing on the contactee's skin. Sometimes the burns are like a branding mark, e.g. a triangle, that remains permanently, or regularly reappears. In a few instances it is claimed that spectacular healing followed from an encounter.

There are reports of aliens pursuing their activities indifferent to the well being of humanity and animals. Typical of these activities are the collection of plants and the cutting out, with surgical precision, of parts of the anatomy of animals, particularly parts concerned with sexual reproduction. Domestic animals, dogs, horses, etc., are sent into a state of panic by the manifestation of UFO aliens.

In some cases the aliens seem to be observing developments that humanity is making, particularly those related to atomic energy, and are concerned that these could be dangerous to Earth and beyond. When they 'communicate' they say that humanity is creating disharmony in the Universe and needs to change to a more harmonious way of life. Sometimes the contactee regards the contact as a mystical, or religious experience that has a permanent effect on his/her attitude to life.

Many of these claims of observations and contacts seem so bizarre that they are often dismissed. Where people take them seriously the usual view is that they are manifestations of civilisations from elsewhere in the Universe that have developed greater technological powers that we have. However, VALLEE, who has researched these phenomena in depth for many years has concluded from the way in which the UFO's materialise and dematerialise, merge together and change shape, the way in which the aliens pass through physical objects (walls, etc.), the poltergeist phenomena often associated with them and their psychic powers, that they are not extra-terrestrial from within our Universe but manifestations from another space-time system. He states that to understand these phenomena we need a greater understanding of the nature of space-time and consciousness.

VALLEE has also shown that they are not a modern phenomenon, as is often thought, but that they are part of a continuum of experiences going back to pre-Christian times. He refers, for example: to representations by the ancient Phoenicians of winged discs from which entities emerged: to accounts from Japan of luminous flying objects from the 10th century onwards: to an account of an encounter around 30 A.D. by St Anthony, with a manikin of similar appearance to a UFO being: a clear exposition around 800 A.D. of the abduction, in France, of four human beings who were taken to another world and then returned to Earth: luminous discs and/or pillars of light associated with the manifestations of angels, and religious apparitions such as that of the Virgin Mary (sometimes resulting in the establishment of healing centres) and of folk lore from many countries of similar events. These accounts point to the existence of beings in a different space-time system, in what has been called 'The Secret Commonwealth' and which Vallee calls a 'Multiverse', who seek to interact with us. Vallee points out that the underlying key features of the Secret Commonwealth, i.e., the ability to materialise and dematerialise, change shape, abductions, the mixture of sense and absurdity in what the beings had to say, etc., are the same as with UFO accounts, but that the way in which they appeared and were described, was related to the belief structure of the age in which they manifested.

GOOD, in his investigations comes to the conclusion that UFOs and aliens are established on Earth and, in some cases, have developed bases for their operations here. He claims that a number of governments are aware of them and are even collaborating with them but maintaining strict secrecy about their activities. Certainly, there is the allure of mastering the systems by which the UFOs seemingly operate and the power that this would offer any government or military authority that could master it.

Paul Dong (in GOOD's Alien Update) states that in China there has been extensive UFO activity and research into the problems that they pose and that there is developing a psycho-physical theory. This has arisen from a large number of people practising 'chi gong', which is concerned with promoting good health, developing psychic abilities, such as clairvoyance, telekinesis (mentally moving an object from one place to another), healing, levitation and OBEs. As part of these experiences some 'hundreds of people', of all intellectual levels, claim to have entered into a mental state in which they have travelled to other planets, met UFO extra-terrestrials and were shown their craft.

A computer engineer in Israel, DVIR, spontaneously began to have psychic experiences in which he found himself in contact with his dead father and other deceased persons, together with super sensible perception of spirits and other non-physical phenomena. In seeking to understand what was going on Dvir consulted psychics knowledgeable in these matters and this led him to join a group of people who were seeking to develop their psychic powers by active imagination. As he developed his own psychic abilities Dvir found himself in contact with aliens from a different space-time dimension, in a parallel Universe.

The aliens told Dvir that they were from distant galaxies and that their journey to Earth took several weeks. This involved their spacecraft travelling at speeds greater than the speed of light, which they do by separating from the space around them which releases them from the restriction of the speed of light that is a property of the space in which we exist. The aliens told Dvir that there are many diverse forms of life living in different worlds and that they seek to discover and study these. Our planet is one source of life forms that they have discovered and are studying.

The aliens contacting Dvir claim that they are far in advance of us in their culture and technology and that they are seeking to help our Earth civilisation, which is facing the possibility of a major catastrophe as a result of the advanced technologies that we are developing, particularly that of nuclear weapons. They state that there are 12,000 different organisations studying the Earth, with about 1 alien for every four people. Each plane of existence has its own basic vibration rate but there are overtones to the vibrations by which different planes interact, that enable them to contact each other. The aliens are concerned that Earth should not undergo a catastrophic disaster because this would have adverse effects on civilisations on other levels with which the Earth interacts. There are primary civilisations where life developed independently and there are civilisations resulting from the settlement of planets by life forms that originated from elsewhere. Earth is a primary civilisation that developed independently but has then been subjected to interventions from beings from elsewhere. Without such interventions life on Earth would still be primitive and undeveloped.

The groups of aliens contacting Dvir seem to be organised in a similar way to humanity on Earth, in that they are studying various subjects, like the differences between nations, ethnic groups, modes of survival, geology, our bodily workings, etc. There is a controlling council at the top, comprising their older, wiser members and the council develops as the different groups of aliens that are exploring different realms of existence report back to them. Their physicists, who study the nature of matter and space and energy, state that everything comprises vibrations in a basic energy and when we perceive something we perceive the encompassing outline of the pattern of vibrations, in the way that if we look at a vibrating rope we see the outline pattern of its vibrations and not the individual vibrations. Space is a sea of vibrations in which there are free quanta of energy that provide them with an endless source of energy to power their spacecraft. They regard the Big Bang of our physicists as just a local event in an infinite Universe.

Alien medical groups sought to use Dvir as a channel for healing, working with other psychics and discarnate spiritual entities, e.g. discarnate doctors who wished to carry on with their medical activities in their post-mortem existence. Because of their advanced level of development, compared with us, the aliens possess super sensory perception that enables them to see what is wrong with a person when s/he is malfunctioning and to apply their advanced technology to carry out healing and Dvir describes a number of examples of healings that they carried out.

In answer to Dvir's questioning the aliens told him that, like us they comprise spirits that inhabit bodies but that they live in their bodies a lot longer than us, usually hundreds or even a few thousand years measured in Earth time. It seems that they construct their bodies themselves and decide when they need to change their body. Their bodies are similar to ours in that they comprise a head and arms and legs but they can be much smaller, (40cms) in height or much larger (4 metres) and can look very different e.g in some cases they have a reptilian appearance. They have a different metabolism and nervous system and they communicate with each other by thought. One group that Dvir dealt with could proliferate by duplicating themselves, with the entities so formed all being under the control of a central being and they all had the same memories and thoughts. In comparison we are emotionally more complex than they are. The members of the medical team that worked through Dvir had undergone a medical training analogous to that of doctors on Earth but more broadly based to take account of the different life forms that they encountered in their explorations of creation, and they have hospitals and operating theatres in their dimension. They state that there are many teams of aliens operating in this way and that, in about 10 year's time there will be a revolution in the way that we see our world and that this will prepare the way for a mass landing of aliens on Earth.

The proposed mechanism for UFOs visiting Earth seems to be like that claimed for apports and by which some mystics and shamans reputably move around, in that an entity or object on one plane 'dematerialises' from that plane by changing to another plane which allows it to move freed from the constraints of its 'home' plane and then it rematerialises elsewhere on its home plane. In the case of a UFO, an entity with highly-developed thought power, currently 'resident' on another plane, by thought and will power travels to the Earth planet, in a way that is unrestrained by physical laws, and then materialises here as a UFO with them resident on it in humanoid form. Then, again by thought power, they create android, robot-like entities to carry out tests and experiments, in much the same way that Daskalos and others like him create elementals to carry out tasks assigned to them.

Comments on UFO Phenomena

There are probably many threads of activity operating in what are reported as UFO phenomena. Vallee pointed out that sometimes the UFO manifestation is similar to a previously written science fiction story. In this case it is possible that the author, in concentrating his thinking on developing the characters of his story created thought forms that were taken over, and used to provide a sense of self, by either an elemental or a low level energy being from the Omniverse Hierarchy.   Once such a form is perceived by other people, leading to them thinking about it, this further thought energy reinforces it and its pattern of behaviour, so that it can then be seen (and reinforced) by others, in the way that Phoebe Payne described for the build up of thought forms.

An example of this type of phenomenon could be the experiences described by WHITLEY STRIEBER, who is a writer of horror stories, and found himself caught up in a sequence of encounters with humanoid beings that were a horror story in themselves. Strieber describes many encounters, in some of which he was abducted by the humanoids and in one case having a needle pushed into his brain. The encounters seemed to be associated with UFO-type activity in the neighbourhood in which he lived. There were also physical manifestations of a poltergeist nature. His wife, young son and friends also experienced some of the phenomena.

As with Alexandra David-Neel's thought form and that of Philip created by the Toronto research group, those created by science fiction authors with strong imaginative powers may take on a life of their own. It is comparatively common that once authors have created characters these take on a continuing existence in their imaginations. The problem then is where do the characters come from in the first place - are they created by the subconscious activity of the authors or are they intrusions into the authors' minds from other space-time dimensions. Certainly the activity of our subconscious mind can give rise to a whole range of characters, often representing various aspects of our personality. Equally external influences can produce imagery of broader significance and carry us into other dimensions. (Extensive examples of both types are given in Part III of this book). In Streiber's case, psychological investigations brought about memory recall that showed that he had been concerned with alien-type activity since early childhood. The need to express this may have given rise to his horror stories, the thought forms of which reinforced the imagery of the entities involved. Sometimes it seems it is a matter of the consciousness of entities in another space-time dimension intruding into our world and at other times of our consciousness intruding into their's.

When an entity invades our world it can utilise our energies. Thus a UFO contact that had associated with it outstanding healing phenomena involved a doctor whose energy, which he presumably directed to healing others, then experienced dramatic healing directed to himself. In another case, in Brazil, a group of hunters were deliberately hunted, and in some cases killed, by UFOs. Again it could be a matter of the hunting energy that they had generated being taken over and used against them by invading entities.

The examination of plants and animals, abductions and sexual investigations by UFO beings represent a more clearly organised activity. Bizarre as these activities may appear to be this is an obvious area for beings from other levels of existence to investigate, in which such things do not happen in their world and which perhaps offer a greater sense of self than that which they possess.

While a clear understanding of these phenomena is difficult to achieve, the important feature is whether they make a contribution to balanced harmonious evolution. According to hK-M any activity must emanate from one of the three streams of entities that seek to enmesh Humanity in their Idealistic or Materialistic activities or to follow the central Christ path. Some UFO aliens seem to be offering the allure of greater Ego material power (the Materialist path), others the allure of greater Ego knowledge (the Idealist path). Another group state that our activities are creating disharmony on Earth, and in the Universe at large, by pollution, etc. and that they wish to show us how we can remedy this situation. This is a central path of ideas linked to material practicality to create harmonious evolution. Since any members of the Omniverse Hierarchy, manifesting as aliens on Earth, must exist at one of its lower levels, where they have a strong 'physical energy' component to their natures, this is their level of perception of, and contribution to, Man's activities. We are not aware of any higher level of understanding, e.g. of the nature and workings of the Kosmos and the basis and purpose of creation, reported from UFO contacts. Any such teachings would need to come from higher levels of the Hierarchy via mental contact, which we deal with in the next section.

While UFO phenomena are difficult for us to comprehend it is not surprising that they exist. Our Earth is part of our Solar System, which is just one of millions in the Milky Way galaxy and the Milky Way is only one of millions of galaxies in the Universe. It would be most surprising if life on Earth were the only form of life in all these billions of places. According to hK-M any life form seeks a sense of self by at first seeking to express and experience its energy that causes it to develop a body with appendages (e.g. arms and legs) to do this. In expressing and experiencing itself it interacts with its environment, which leads it to develop a sensory system that registers the interactions as sensations and feelings. These, in turn, lead to it becoming aware of its situation and thereby developing a degree of consciousness. While we are familiar with the way that this has worked out on Earth, there could be innumerable variations on this basic theme, according to the circumstances in which they develop.

Channelled Communications

There exist a large number of books that describe experiences of communications from spiritual worlds. Many of these claim to be from discarnate relatives or spirit guides. There are also extensive communications claimed to emanate from 'Masters', i.e. mystics who have developed some larger awareness of the nature of spiritual worlds and are able to communicate this telepathically to appropriate recipients, e.g. Blavatsky and Alice Bailey.

In the past few years, however, a new dimension has developed in these types of communications, in that a number of people claim that, in higher states of consciousness, they experience contact with High Spiritual Beings, who have never been part of Earth existence (the Omniverse Hierarchy) through which they are offered guidance to help humanity. It is claimed that this is taking place because we are approaching a critical time when conditions of existence and consciousness will change. And that, for this to take place harmoniously, it is necessary for humanity to understand what is happening. This type of communication has become known as 'channelling'. However, this is a veritable minefield to evaluate.

As Phoebe PAYNE has pointed out, when people open themselves up to external influences they can lose rational control and often the so-called influence arises from a part of their own subconscious nature finding a way of expressing itself and seeking self gratification. Even if contact is made with other intelligences then these can be discarnate relatives, friends, or Teachers or Guides who seek to help us, out of their now broader but still limited, perspective of things. Or they may come from members of the Omniverse Hierarchy. (For an account of channelling and the problems that it raises and possible explanations for it, see HASTINGS).

Even if the contact is with the Omniverse Hierarchy, then the significance of this depends on the level and orientation (Idealist, Materialist, or Christ) that is contacted. And our ability to understand such contacts is limited by the framework of our beliefs and by our conceptual understanding of things. And, in any case, the Omniverse Hierarchy is not omniscient. It possesses the experiences and understanding of entities generated in previous Universe cycles, but it does not encompass Man's experience at the 'working face' of the present Universe. The entities of the Omniverse Hierarchy can only offer guidance from their 'higher', or broader, point of view but we still have to work things out on Earth.

It would be nice to ignore or dismiss these matters and just get on with trying to lead a pleasant, uncomplicated life. But if the pressure of these incidents continues to build up, somehow we are going to have to come to terms with them. Otherwise we will not know what is going on and we will lose our bearings and have difficulty in maintaining a stable, meaningful existence. This is particularly true for people who experience these phenomena at first hand, who can become frightened or undermined by them. According to hK-M there is nothing mysterious or mystical about the ways of creation. Everything happens according to a comprehensible underlying pattern of development and all communications from spiritual sources should be subjected to the same rational evaluation that we apply to our everyday experiences. In fact it is humanity's responsibility and contribution to evaluate, by rational thinking, all these matters and to put into practise in life on Earth, whatever helps to make a contribution to harmonious evolution.

Many of the books on channelling, where people believe themselves to be in contact with high spiritual sources are diffuse, rambling and self-deluding. In some cases the writers/receivers believe themselves to be channels for saving humanity and they lose all sense of rationality but there are also other cases that seem to offer a useful contribution. So we synopsise here a few books describing some of the better channelled communications of which we know, to illustrate the type of material they present, without in any way endorsing what they have to say.

[The possibility of people receiving information from high spiritual sources is not new. In their writings, the Old Testament prophets and Enoch, who we have quoted, often stated that they were given this information from God by angels, or that 'they were in the spirit', possibly a high level OBE experience].

Mindweld (ref. PERRY)

This book describes communications received at weekly meetings of a spiritually-seeking group, over a period of five months, by one of its members in a trance state. The entity that used this person to make the communications claimed to be from the Universal Collective Consciousness, from which Christ emanated and which operates according to the Christ Principle. This entity that, for purposes of identification takes the name of Odin, states that there are millions of entities in the Collective Consciousness who exist in total harmony together. Odin states that he came into existence in a barely remembered dim and distant past, in a world long since dispersed, that existed way back before the beginning of the present Universe. He says that he is only one of many who seek contact with us, to guide us to find balance and harmony in our lives on Earth. Odin states that humanity's separation from the Universal Hierarchy has gone on for too long and his purpose is now to make known the existence of the Higher Realms and the Higher Principle, so that humanity can seek to tune into this and thereby achieve harmony in life on Earth. He claims that, not only is this possible, but that it will happen in the comparatively near future, in a 'New Age' of humanity which will occur as a result of a 'heightening of vibrations' that will bring about a change in awareness. In this New Age there will be a new level of understanding that will lead to the integration of peoples of different cultures and a unifying of science, religion, philosophy and the arts.

When questioned about the nature of God Odin described a Centre, a Cause, which expands and contracts, that has its essence in all that is, and also the existence of gods, such as a god of the Solar System, which seems to be a localised collective of higher minds within those that make up the Universal Consciousness. A representative or focus of the Universal Consciousness incarnated in a human body on Earth and is known as Christ, Christos or Krishna.

Humanity, Odin says, is rich in knowledge, understanding and emotional experience in a way that he can only experience second-hand, through his contact with his trance medium. Thus, despite the suffering involved, entities from the Universal Collective strive to incarnate on Earth, but this is difficult for them to do. With the descent into matter perception of the spiritual world is lost but it can be recaptured while incarnate. Earth is regarded as unique in that it is the first world on which there exist together entities who have arisen here and others who have incarnated here from the Universal Collective. The peoples of Earth have the greatest journey to travel and the way is hard but the rewards are great.

The 'higher' members of the Universal Collective, created in earlier Universes, (when the s-entities were less active) are less dense (more diffuse, less individualised) than Earthly Beings. In between are levels of entities of intermediate density and energy, generated in later Universes. When these seek to intercede in Earthly activities they sometimes manifest at a near-physical energy level that gives rise to the phenomena that people describe as UFOs.

It is claimed that we may experience guidance from higher realms - teachers, guides or members of the Universal Hierarchy, when an idea or insight 'pops into our mind', usually when we are in a relaxed state, or sometimes we awaken with such insights in the morning that unconsciously we have received during sleep.

Starseed Transmissions (ref. CAREY)

In this book the author describes communications that he received in a heightened state of consciousness over an 11-day period in 1978/79. The communicating entity claimed to be a focus of the Collective Consciousness and its purpose was to bring awareness of the existence of the Collective Consciousness and of our basic nature as part of this, so that we will lose our sense of separateness and become aware of our one-ness with all creation.

He states that the totality of the Collective Consciousness, which has been called 'God the Father', animates all creation. Thus when we attune to, and commune with, this we come into contact with the life-giving force behind everything.

Our life is described as being in two halves. In one, conscious, half we are focused on our substance existence and in the other, unconscious sleep-state half, on our identity with the totality. Through our senses we experience the space-time world of our substance existence and when, through Carey, the communicating entity also experienced this state he found the experience wonderful, and he could understand why it has become increasingly harder for us to avoid identifying with our ego/Ego experience. This linking of consciousness with Earth matter is referred to as The Fall. Our existence in the world of form is regarded as a wonderful privilege but one that carries with it responsibilities; also it is deceptive, in taking us away from knowledge of our origins and, because of forthcoming events, it is important that we should now change.

He states that since the first breath of God, which occurred at the beginning of all worlds, creation has existed within a rhythm of expansion and contraction. The current situation is now very close to the mid-point. When this is reached the Universe will stop expanding, physical laws will be suspended and the Universe will then start to contract. As this change in direction occurs there will be a momentary period of rest in which there will occur a change in our space-time consciousness and we will begin to become one with the Creator. We will then be the Son, the Christ, returning to the Creator. The coming of Christ was to herald this change and this was the first time that a representative of the Collective Consciousness appeared on Earth in the frame of a man. There will be a second coming at the mid point. There is a need for humanity to prepare itself for this event in order to cope with it when it happens.

Those who are attuned to the change will experience an expansion of their consciousness, a union with the Collective Consciousness, a vibration of truth and love. The Collective Consciousness can only work with those who transcend their ego natures and are conscious of who they are and what they are doing. Through those that are so awakened God, the Collective Consciousness, can enter into the material plane. Awakened to this consciousness man will be able to will changes in events to take place. Such people will become aware of their role and responsibility in the creative process and they will then achieve harmony and fulfilment.

This was stated to be the second of a series of three revelations. The first occurred during 1967 to 1969. Those described here were part of a series between 1977 to 1979. At that time it was claimed that there would be a third series during 1987 to 1989. There would then be many signs and wonders and the reality of the Christ Consciousness in individuals would be commonplace. These individuals would develop a collective power that would draw others to it, to give rise to a Planetary Awakening. The entities of the Collective Consciousness are experimenting with ways to bring this about. They need first to bring about a conceptual change to facilitate the change to a new reality, restoring harmony and balance that works to realise the full potential of the planet. The new state of consciousness, when it occurs, will not, however, be a conceptual one but a living at-oneness consciousness of life; the law of Love in Action. Many people are caught up in their ego mechanisms and are not yet open to change but there are enough who are sympathetic to the change to bring it about. Eventually all humanity will become involved in conscious creation.

Agartha (ref. YOUNG)

This is a good example of the need for an understanding of these extra-sensory experiences, so that those people who find themselves caught up in them have some basis for coping with the situation. The author was a thirty-seven year old suburban housewife leading a conventional existence. She accompanied her husband on a four-day workshop on expanded consciousness and found the meditation exercises that she encountered helped her to achieve a state of inner harmony, so that she began to practise them. As a result, some months later she found herself engulfed in an intense emotional-mental state which she found frightening, so much so that she thought she might be going mad. While sitting quietly trying to control what was going on she was impelled to fetch a notepad and a pencil and she then found that an outside intelligence used her to make communications.

This intelligence reassured her and, after coming to terms with this type of experience, the author developed a telepathic dialogue with the intelligence that, for purposes of identification took the name of Mentor. Mentor claimed to be from a more spiritually evolved plane of beings whose aim is to guide humanity to a greater, more universal, awareness than it presently has on Earth. Mentor stated that this is necessary because many individuals are seeking a greater understanding of existence and also because things that humanity is doing are causing the Earth planet to become unbalanced in a way that could affect the cosmos.

According to Mentor, our Earth activities give off vibrations, which affect everything around them. Equally vibrations from the activities going on around us affect us. For example, if we live harmonious lives then we create a harmonious atmosphere in our homes, which is experienced by people visiting us. Equally if we work in harmony with the plants in our garden they grow better and we produce an atmosphere of harmony in our garden.

The key feature to this is love. Mentor describes three types of love: the lowest form is based on personal physical needs, which he calls 'emotional release love': next is 'enlightened love' which develops as we become less concerned with our own desires and more with contributing to the development of others: the highest form that Mentor knows is that of the spiritual world in which he exists (the Universal Collective) which is 'abstract love', i.e. impersonal love for the whole of creation, which he describes as 'love as harmony'.

In order to evolve, our Spirit/Ego has to develop so that it has control over the lower, more personal aspects of our nature (ego, soul-body desires) and is then able to foster its connection with our Higher Self, from which we derive. This is the repository of our spiritual wisdom, which is able to develop a relationship with the Universal Consciousness. The problem is that we possess in our conscious mind a framework within which we understand and accept things. To establish contact with our Higher Selves we need to reduce the barriers that this framework creates and open ourselves up and broaden our outlook. If we do this we can progressively achieve enlightenment, which ultimately is understanding and concern and loving support for the role of everything in the cosmic pattern. We progress towards this by successive incarnations on Earth, in which we advance by experiences that we then evaluate in discarnate existence. Mentor points out that even if the incarnate existence is very short then we advance in the subsequent evaluation of it, e.g. by perceiving the reactions of our family to our early demise.

If, during the incarnate state we can achieve attunement with the Universal Consciousness then this enables us to tap into the infinite power that lies behind the Universe and we can thereby achieve anything that we want to. This is done by the power of thought, by which we create our own reality.

Mentor refers to what he calls the 'Yo-yo' nature of creation, whereby worlds come into existence and return to the source, and he states that a return is imminent. This is bringing about a change in consciousness on Earth, in which an increasing number of people will begin to experience, and tap into, the Universal Consciousness. However, many Egos will oppose this change, because they are based on beliefs and power structures that will have to go. The change will therefore involve a period of conflict and wars.

There is, however, no absolute right or wrong, or good or evil, because there are no ultimate, intrinsic standards to measure these by. But there is positive and negative, positive being activity which nutures progress in evolution, while negative activities are destructive. We each have to accept responsibility for our negative activities.

There is a flow of energy through our bodies that maintains all the life-giving processes. Mentor states that this flow is affected by our emotional and mental activities. If these are negative they block the natural flow and create disharmony and disease, so that to be healthy requires a positive approach to life. He gives some detail on the pattern of energy flow, how this can become distorted and what we can do to correct it.

Equally humanity's activities affect the pattern of energy flow associated with the Earth. Mentor states that the Ionosphere that surrounds and protects the Earth is affected by our thought waves as well as by our physical activities and that it is getting into a parlous state.

When asked about the nature of God, Mentor states that God is the collective presence of all things, that humanity is God on Earth and that through successive incarnations we evolve towards awareness of this.

New Teachings for An Awakening Humanity: The Christ (ref. ESSENE).

This book claims to be a telepathic transmission from Jesus, through Virginia Essene, who Jesus chose for these communications because of the ability to receive them that she had developed by many years of meditation. Jesus, who claims to have developed Christ Consciousness and hence to have become Jesus the Christ, states that it is now necessary for him to put forward new teachings, that are related to a more-evolved humanity; that his previous teachings have become distorted and corrupted and that, in the meantime he has evolved further (and is still evolving).

Jesus states that a time of crisis is at hand for humanity when we will be recalled to our Creator and that he is one of many who are seeking to help humanity make the necessary change to effect the return. He claims that only those who have orientated themselves to performing the will of God will be assimilated. Those who do not do this will be set other experiences to go through (in future Universes).

In this book great emphasis is given to the existence of God and to God's plan of creation. Both God and his plan are described as beyond comprehension and therefore unknowable. When giving an account of the working of creation Jesus describes it in terms of God carrying out experiments.

Jesus states that our Universe is the 12th created by God. He says that he was created in the first Universe, which was much simpler and had much less variety to it than our Universe. Universes are created by God breathing out, followed by breathing in, and we are now approaching a breathing-in period. According to his description, early Universes were the expression of the female (love, nurturing), or the male (will, power) aspects of God's nature, at first separately and then together. Later Universes involved also the expression of thought and intellect. The essential feature in each Universe was the extent to which its inhabitants felt love for, harmonised with, and therefore returned to, God. The objective of our Universe is to develop Love and Wisdom to a higher level.

The problem is that, by our thoughts and actions, we have created a lot of negativity in the energy surround to our planet, which not only harms the Earth but could also affect the cosmos beyond. To combat this it is therefore necessary for us to strive, individually and collectively, for peace and harmony on Earth. This book places great emphasis on personal and group meditation as the way to achieve union with spiritual teachers and with God, and thereby to find the way forward.

The Wind of Change and The Cosmic Dance (ref. SOSKIN)

Julie Soskin is a psychic and spiritual healer who experienced a shift in her normal psychic communications to a higher level. These told her that she was to be a channel for information from 'A synthesis of energies of higher consciousness - Original Thought' that then dictated these two books to her.

The essential message of these books is that we are entering a time of transition, the change from a cosmic breathing out to a breathing in, that is the end of a Universe cycle, while within this cycle subsidiary Solar and Earth planet cycles are also coming to an end. As a result of this change there will be a reconstruction of cosmic, Solar and Earth energies, as part of which the Earth's axis will change and convulsions will occur in the Earth and its atmosphere. At the same time there will be a change in our bodily activities and in our state of consciousness.

It is stated that we need to be aware of, and prepared for, these events, in order to flow with them and to make the necessary transition. Those of us who do not do so will experience physical and mental disorder and will not move into the next phase of evolution. The most important thing in making the change is to eliminate fear and negativity in our natures and to have faith and trust that all is well in what happens, so as to enable us to accept and go with the transition. The change will bring about a heightening of awareness of all of our faculties.

These communications state that humanity, by its thoughts and actions has created a great deal of negativity in the psychic atmosphere of the Earth and that the communicators are doing all they can to disperse this and thereby to help us to go forward. It is stressed that this is not in any way condemnatory or judgmental but simply the way that things have worked out. The underlying reason for our situation is that humanity has undergone a unique evolution on Earth that has not happened in previous Universe cycles, in which it has been more than usually cut off from the Source. As a result human beings have had to develop greater individual abilities and this has given us more personalised feelings - emotions - and also a greater intellectual understanding, in a way that has not happened before.

From the early times of hominids on Earth there has developed a strong sense for self survival, together with negative emotions, thoughts and fear of anything or anyone that appears to challenge this, leading to wars and excessive exploitation of Nature. Such emotions only exist on Earth and the negative aspects of these have created discord in the psychic atmosphere around the Earth, so that at this crucial time of change the Spiritual Hierarchy is seeking to help us to find the way forward. When the evolution of life on Earth reached the development of intelligence in hominids, there was an influx of activity from the Spiritual Hierarchy that gave rise to Homo Sapiens. This, it is said, caused a change in shape of the cranium/brain (this is something that scientists have found from the fossil evidence, fig. 5.3).

It is stated that, despite the pain and suffering involved, we are privileged in the type of experience that we undergo on Earth, which is unique in the cosmos, so that it is the centre of attention for many other entities that have undergone lesser experiences. *'The joy of human physical experience is unequalled and incomparable to that of any other planet.'* There has never been another planet like Earth.

It is the responsibility of each individual to open up and to go with the change. No one can make or teach anyone else to change. However, those who make the necessary change in their natures become examples for the change, create an atmosphere conducive to it, and in this way help others to make it. Understanding does not of itself make the change, although it facilitates it. There is no need to strive for heightened states of consciousness by meditation or other means, although entering into a state of inner stillness will help. It is claimed that it is easy to make the change, that the 'Light', i.e. the force for increased living awareness, is already there but that we cut ourselves off from it by living in our personal emotions, particularly our fears. If we get rid of these and live in a state of trust, faith and harmony we automatically open ourselves up to the change. Some people, however, derive strength and power by tapping into the negative energies that Man has generated (Hitler is quoted as an example). Such people then become centres for the concentration and growth of negative energy and thereby influence others in this direction, in the same way that people following a positive path can influence others in the positive direction.

Those who do not make the change, because of their increased fear and inability to adapt as change takes place, will become even more violent and aggressive. At the same time their imbalance will cause them to experience increased physical, emotional and mental dis-ease. Thus there will develop a greater polarity between 'positive and negative' forces in society. Even those who do make the change will experience physical and mental disruption, but with a positive outcome that results in increased at-one-ness with the forces of creation and the Universal Hierarchy. At the same time such people will begin to experience an ability to tap into the totality of Earth and Cosmic experience. They will also be able to tap into the power behind creation and to will things to happen.

It is stated that by seeking for Father figure gods in its soul desires, Humanity has anthropomorphised and individualised this soul energy, to give rise to gods and devils. The belief in these has to go, to enable the negative energy to be dispersed. At the same time by anthropomorphising beliefs in the existence of other, extra-terrestrial, UFO-type entities and phenomena Humanity has given these energy so that they manifest in human-like forms.

The change is the beginning of the return to the Source and because of our unique experiences we have a valuable contribution to make to the collective consciousness of the Source, which evolves with each cosmic cycle. Humanity now has to become at-one, and in harmony, with the rest of creation and those that do this will acquire Christ consciousness. They will then develop love without (ego orientated) emotions. Such people then become their own channellers for the higher wisdom, at the same time contributing their experience to furthering this wisdom.

It is stated that as these developments take place the emotional atmosphere of the Earth planet will change and it will become a place of paradise, with the elimination of hostility and the development of an impersonal love ethos by all, for all. At the same time there will be a change to a more equable climate and a corresponding development of a 'garden of Eden' type existence. The claim is made that there will be permanent light, as one of the other planets will metamorphose to give out light to supplement that of the Sun.

In describing the nature of the 'Source' this book first characterises it as 'Thought'. The normal usage of 'thought' is to convey a consciousness that plans and initiates activities. However, when the book goes into greater detail on the nature of the Source it is described as pure energy. The communicators stated that they started their existence as particles of energy, without consciousness - pure beingness - that were set free from the Source and that they have evolved by repeated 'incarnations' and thereby they have developed consciousness. All of this has happened, not by design, but as part of the 'automatic process' which governs all things and which governs the imminent return to the Source, which is described as breathing out and breathing in.

Bringers of the Dawn: Teachings From the Pleiadians & Earth: Pleiadian Keys to The Living Library. (Ref MARCINIAK).

All books presenting channelled communications are difficult to read, because they express unfamiliar concepts through channels who impose their own limitations and outlooks on what is given to them. These two books are particularly difficult but they are included here because, although the cosmic viewpoints that they touch on are better dealt with in other books, they concentrate more on the situation of the Earth planet.

The communicators state that they derive from a Universe that completed its existence long before the present one and that in order to further their experience they have taken up existence in the Pleiades star system. From the Pleiades they incarnated into Earth existence in a previous civilisation (Atlantis) and their adverse behaviour at that time resulted in a karma that has stopped their development, so that they have to work this out before they can progress further. They have to correct the effects of what they did on Earth. They state that because of their behaviour they are renegades from the 'Family of Light', (in hK-M terms the central stream of the Omniverse Hierarchy), of which they were once part. They refer to higher beings who seek to teach and guide them so that they can return to the Family of Light, while they in turn seek to teach and guide us.

The 'Pleiadians' are thus at an intermediate level of evolution where they are trying to sort themselves out, so that, while they offer us wisdom and guidance from a higher viewpoint, they are themselves in a confused state and this is reflected in the communications.

The Pleiadians state that many of the people who have now incarnated originate from them and have done so in order to carry out the task of putting their situation to rights, but by becoming involved in Earth existence they have lost their memory of their intentions. The Pleiadians seek to reawaken these intentions by leading such people to increased awareness and to a heightened state of consciousness that regains contact with the Family of Light. They state that they need us as much as we need them. In order to progress we have to find a new reality to that we currently believe in. Their contribution is to put forward ideas that will break up our established beliefs and open us up to other possibilities without however, putting forward a final reality, since this does not exist and is something that we have to continually strive for, changing our view of reality as we do so: they aim to 'confound us into clarity'.

It is important that these changes are brought about because the Earth is heading for another crustal shift and catastrophe of the type reputed to have wiped out Atlantis. They specify the Mayan date for when this will take place - December 2012; they claim that they were responsible for the Mayan civilisation. They state that the remains of a high civilisation of Atlantis exist under the ice cap of Antarctica and of an even earlier civilisation under the Gobi desert. To the cosmos and the Hierarchy the Earth's crustal shift will be a small local event and this is what it will seem to those of us who awaken to a higher consciousness, but to those of us tied to the Earth situation it will be dire destruction. There will then be a division between the two types of people.

Earth has been visited many times by different beings. Because of the desirable experience that Earth existence offers, in past times different types of gods (members of the Omniverse Hierarchy) fought to gain possession of it. (The myths of many cultures refer to such battles between the gods). Unfortunately the gods of darkness won, which accounts for the lack of contact with the Family of Light and the disharmony and wars on Earth. Because of the critical state that the Earth is now in, the 'gods' are returning.

The hierarchies of beings that exist in the cosmos have different experiences of time to us; time is just a construct. For them to enter into the Earth situation requires finding 'portals' that lead into Earth space-time. Many of the ancient sacred sites were such portals and these will be used again. Some of the 'gods' will appear to possess divine abilities by which they can 'fix' the Earth's problems if we follow their authority. But they seek power and it is important not to follow any authority; we should live according to our own spiritual striving and insights, but with a continual willingness to change. Earth is a planet for the development of free will; we are each in charge of, and responsible for, our own development.

In their cosmology, the Pleiadians consider everything to be the activities of a 'Prime Creator'. We are part of the experiments of Prime Creator seeking greater self-exploration, self-gratification and self-expression. We are coming into an Age of Light when we will become aware of our connection with Prime Creator. This will come about because, along with the physical changes on Earth, changes are coming in which we will find ourselves opening up energy centres, chakras, that are portals to higher states of consciousness. We need awareness of this in order to go with the situation; people who cannot do so may find themselves having mental experiences that they cannot cope with. As we evolve in consciousness we will remember our place in evolution and become members of the Family of Light and become conscious contributors to the evolutionary process and thereby 'feed' Prime Creator. Earth is stated to be a 'Living Library' of creation that can be accessed by us to provide understanding of the workings of evolution and the Universe, an understanding which we can then contribute to the rest of the Omniverse.

The Pleidians place considerable emphasise on sexual relations. This seems to be something that they misused when on Earth and which they have to help us to sort out. The sex act at its high point of completion is, they say, a route to higher consciousness if it is between two people who are fully in harmony in themselves and with each other - a divine experience. Problems that impede this are the ways in which we have been conditioned to think and feel about sex and our bodies. Two people truly in love should freely explore each other physically, emotionally and mentally but sexuality is not something to be fooled around with, and promiscuity does no good.

The Only Planet of Choice: Essential Briefings from Deep Space (ref. SCHLEMMER and JENKINS).

This is a selection of communications received by a group of people in various walks of life, over a period of 18 years, through a trance medium, Phyllis Schlemmer, from a body that calls itself the Council of Nine. The Nine claim to be nine principles of the Universe - knowledge, wisdom, love, kindness, technology, continuity, etc. Although individuals, they operate as a collective. They state that they are at the top of the Hierarchical structure of creation and they claim that they oversee progress on Earth.

The Nine state that they have manifested before on Earth, when they were designated by humanity as the gods referred to by ancient civilisations, but they say that they are not gods. They state that they are the Elohim of Hebraic tradition, (Elohim is plural and means gods, whereas in the bible it is translated as the singular, God). The spokesman of the group states that the first time he manifested on Earth was 34,000 years ago and he was known in various ancient civilisations as Tehuti, Hamarkos, Herenkar and Atum. The Nine state that their role in ancient times, as now, was to help humanity to find the way forward by giving guidance from their larger understanding of creation. But they are not omniscient; in outlining past developments they describe a number of cases where they misjudged the situation, so that the events which they brought about worked out adversely and not in the way that they intended.

When asked about themselves they responded with the circular statement that we created them and out of their creation we were created. They have the nature of soul energy (spirit, in hK-M terminology), and they have never had a physical body existence, (although they can put on the mantle of one to intervene in Earth events if this becomes necessary), and they grow as we grow and through us they come to understand physical existence and our emotions.

The Nine state that under them there exist twenty-four 'civilisations', in another dimensional realm, that were created to govern and guide all over the Universe. (The term 'civilisation', as used here means state of consciousness). Each civilisation has a Head and consists of a collective consciousness that oversees a particular area of activity of the Universe. Below the twenty-four are many sub-civilisations (levels of consciousness). The twenty-four exist in a subtle form of physicalness ('physicalness' becomes increasingly dense as one moves 'down' through the sub-civilisations), and because of this they have some of the problems associated with Earth existence but not to the same extent. However, because of their physicalness (which the Nine do not have), the twenty-four can provide the means for manifestations on, and communications from the Nine to, Earth. Beings from all of the civilisations have incarnated on, or visited, planet Earth and have intervened when necessary.

[There is what could be a reference to the twenty-four heads of civilisations in Chapter 4 of the Book of Revelations.

> '... I was in the spirit: and behold a throne was set in heaven .... and round
> about the throne were four and twenty seats: and upon the seats I saw four
> and twenty elders ....']

The cosmology they describe refers to a Creator God. Various statements are made about the nature of God: God is unified infinite intelligence, supported by pure love: God is love and inasmuch as we love God we feed God: God is a collective of beings of the highest order, in which the individuals have knowledge of the parts but only the collective has knowledge of the whole and this collective is what we know as God. All of them and all of us make God.

In the beginning there was One that understood that it needed to be many. So all of the many are in truth the One. What the Creator created was an energy. Energy was in aloneness, all creativity, encompassing all. Again there is the circular statement that we created God and God created us. Without us God would not exist and without God we would not exist. (According to hK-M this is because in any organisation the sense of self of those at the top is dependent on them marshalling the activities of those at the working face and that of those at the working face on being part of a meaningful organisation with a sense of direction given to it by its 'Management'. All are mutually interdependent parts of a whole and cannot exist without each other).

In the processes of creation there arose entities that were concerned with maintaining power for themselves and these thereby oppose the harmonious evolution of the whole. They are described as being negative or positive in relation to the activities of the Nine who state that they represent central balanced evolution. The 'opposition' know their own divinity and they try to control, they attempt to be God; in so doing they disrupt the work of the Universe. Their influence can be distinguished by their attempts to control and manipulate people, working through temptation, desire, greed, etc. The Nine do not interfere with our free will, because we each have to accept responsibility for ourselves. They seek to influence us to strive for knowledge, truth and wisdom in freedom and, out of the highest motives, to serve creation.

The Nine state that Earth is the most beautiful planet that exists in the Universe. It has physical variety and a varied climate that no other planet has. It is the only planet of individual free will; elsewhere it is a matter of collective free will and behaviour. It is a planet where physical existence has to be balanced with spiritual existence.

(According to hK-M this is because it is only on Earth, by incarnating into biologically evolved bodies, that individualised soul and spirit activity has arisen, separate from the Omniverse Hierarchy. Previously these arose as collective developments in successive Universes. This means that each of us is an individualised physical-soul-spirit being, with free will and personal responsibility, and we each have to find a balance between our physical and our soul/spirit activities. Because of these factors the Earth is a place where a stronger ego-soul and Ego-spirit sense of self has developed).

On Earth there evolved, in the first place, an indigenous black race of humanity. Some 20 million years ago, because of its beauty and its life forms, members of the Hierarchy sought to establish an existence for themselves on Earth but it took a long time and a lot of 'genetic engineering' to make bodies suitable for them and the development of complex energy (chakra) systems by which they could link up with the bodies. Different groups from the Hierarchy made various attempts and this gave rise to the different races on Earth. As the lower more physical levels incarnated, this created simple cultures that then allowed members from the higher levels (the twenty four) to establish a highly developed culture, around 20,000 B.C. Some of these incarnated into physical bodies to produce a new race of humanity, (homo sapiens?), others remained as spiritual beings in the Earth's 'spiritual atmosphere', seeking to guide Earth developments; these were looked up to and worshipped by the Earth-bound ones, as gods. This gave rise to two types of beings associated with Earth, those that were 'birthed' and others who were not, who sought to guide developments. Those that bodily incarnated into Earth existence became so absorbed by the sense of ego/Ego self that this gave them, that they reincarnated again and again, thereby losing contact with their origins.

By pursuing the heightened ego/Ego sense of self which they got from Earth existence, and losing sight of their origins and purpose, the Earth-bound entities created an imbalance which, combined with natural Earth upheavals, led to the destruction of their culture, and the continent on which it existed became submerged, (about 11,000 B.C.). An awareness of this ancient culture exists in the myths of the lost continents and cultures of Atlantis and Lemuria, while remains from unsubmerged, outposts that then degenerated, exist in various ruins around the world, such as those in Egypt and in South America. The Nine state that the Atlantean civilisation was more advanced than we are in medical knowledge, (with organ and animal transplants and an advanced type of acupuncture), 'electronics', flight using energy fields in space, and movement by mind power. However, because of their obsession with sexual experience, they used their medical knowledge to improve their sex organs, *'If it had not been that below their waist they were always in trouble, then it would have been a fine civilisation'.*

The Nine give accounts of various subsequent 'colonisations' of the Earth and the way in which these brought about the ancient civilisations of Egypt, Mesopotamia and China. They state that we all derive from such colonisations by members of the Hierarchy and that, in the past we have lived in other places in the Universe and will live in yet others in the future and that most of us have lived before on Earth. This time we have come to help Earth transform itself.

However, the Nine state, a similar situation to that of the Atlantean civilisation has arisen again, in that with our self-interested pursuits we are creating an imbalance in Nature, with pollution of air and water and destruction of species, that will make Earth uninhabitable and there will be another Ice Age within 200 years. But an Atlantean-type catastrophe, as predicted by other communicators, is not inevitable. With knowledge and understanding giving rise to a transformed way of life, it is possible to avoid, or at least to control and minimise this. The energy of our thoughts is much greater than we think. At present there is much negative thinking on Earth, which contributes to the possibility of a destructive catastrophe; what is required is a realisation of why we are here - to forward the evolution of the Universe - and positive thinking to this end. Thus, as well as the possibility of imminent catastrophe it is also a time of great opportunity for positive change. The Nine state that they will help us but that they cannot do so unless we call on them, they cannot interfere with our free will.

One of the civilisations that incarnated strongly into Earth conditions is stated to have given rise to the Jews. These became particularly strongly absorbed in the heightened ego/Ego sense of self that they got from Earth experience and they lost sight of their origins. The head of this civilisation is the being described in the bible as Jehovah. The Nine state that Jehovah incarnated on Earth as Jesus Christ and that his intention was to stimulate the Jews into finding their way forward from their lost state, caused by over-bonding to the ego/Ego sense of self given by the Earth situation. The Nine state that Christ's inspirational teachings, healings and energy were supplied by them. The Arabs arose from the same civilisation and the Jews and Arabs have a pivotal role to play by achieving harmony between them and, in so doing, to serve as a nucleus for this to happen all over the Earth. The nation of Israel is described as a microcosm of the races of the world.

Every soul (spirit) in the Universe needs to live on Earth at least once, to gain the experience of balancing the physical with the spiritual. When the souls on Earth have gained the self-awareness and understanding that derives from this they can go elsewhere and provide teachings and understanding for those in other galaxies and solar systems in the Universe.

The problem arose, however, that because souls became attracted to the heightened sense of self, which they got from Earth experience, they chose to return again. This has led to souls undergoing successive incarnations in which the ego/Ego-orientated deeds that they perform tie them to Earth existence. And as more souls have sought repetitive Earth experience this has led to what is described as a 'bottlenecking' in the development of the Universe as a whole. And this bottlenecking of increasing numbers of souls living self-orientated existences has thrown the Earth out of balance, with physical pollution, soul greed and spiritual aggrandisement.

The body on Earth has great physicalness, which gives the soul stronger feelings of joy and pain. Ill health is due to imbalance, physical, emotional or mental and much of this is connected with diet and pollution. There are many upon Planet Earth who are trapped in their soul addictions - power - experiences through drugs - sex - or attempting to find oneself in others.

Earth is the only planet where sexuality is the means of reproduction. Sex is not a problem but its misuse is. The Nine state that in two people whose motives are clean and who understand who they are, the emotion in bonding on reaching completion, the feeling of oneness with the other, is the highest experience of returning to the source.

In the sex act the male is trying to return to the source and continually searching to have relationships with a female to achieve this but without doing so properly and this brings much trouble. The drive in the female is to be given the power to create - it needs the male catalytic energy to do this.

Part of the bottlenecking on Earth comes from the New Age movement, with the belief in the releasing of inhibitions and 'doing your own thing'. What we do needs to be consciously aligned to the forward evolution of the Universe. We have free will but this also gives us responsibility. Also the New Age belief that you can think things away causes problems, as this does not work.

It is stated that it is imperative at this time that balance is regained. The key is the free will of humanity to make this happen. This depends on an expansion of thinking, the development of love and understanding. For this, inner self-direction is required. But the situation has now gone too far for Humanity to accomplish this on its own and it is important to recognise that there are those of the twenty-four civilisations who can and will bring help. But, because of Humanity's free will they cannot intervene unless asked. However, the Nine state that if total or major destruction of the Earth planet becomes imminent they will intervene because they will not let this happen. But this would not help humanity who would remain at the same level of development. What is required is for human beings to do this for themselves, this would involve them developing with it.

One step which the Nine state has been taken is that there is now intervention whereby some souls who leave Earth with their mission not completed, and who would thereby reincarnate with bitterness and aggression to work out, are being transferred to other domains to work these things out, so as to reduce the negative pressure on Earth.

However, it is stated, if the necessary change is left to depend on the awakening of humanity it will come too late and there will be disaster. Therefore intervention by the manifestation on Earth of beings from the twenty-four civilisations will be necessary at some time. These would then infuse new, non-polluting technology, new truth and understanding and love to the planet. They state, however, that they are not teachers, that we are all students in the Universe; when one has exchange with another then the so-called 'teacher' is taught. The problem is that if this intervention were to happen now, too many people would panic and react in a hostile way because they do not have sufficient understanding to cope with the situation. Some of the lesser civilisations are manifesting as UFO-type phenomena, which is creating problems. The Nine state that there are twelve such groups interacting with Earth but not all of them have good intentions; some are well meaning and work to prevent destruction on Earth. Others are exploring the Earth situation to seek to control it for their own ends. In particular it is necessary to be careful with those that claim to come from Reticulum and some of the beings associated with the Pleiades are of great negativity. **It is not enough to assume that because they have superior technology they are superior beings**. In some cases they have brought about the destruction of the planet where they took up residence in the Universe and are looking for somewhere else to re-site. To find out about life here they are carrying out abductions and taking tissue samples.

The Nine state that some of these beings already exist on Earth, incarnated in human bodies. Others appear as extra-terrestrial humanoids. This is because all physical existence requires a body with arms and legs and a sensory system to get to grips with it. They state that they will give prior knowledge of any intervention by themselves or the twenty-four civilisations.

It is a time of change but it requires Humanity to bring this about; by seeking unity, for human beings to take responsibility for their actions towards each other and for the pollution and degradation of the physical and biological kingdoms of Nature. Science has become the elitism, the new religion and scientists now have to accept responsibility for the Earth. But we are each responsible for ourselves. For change to take place requires courage, the courage to be whom we truly are and not be led by power-seeking forces. We must never follow in blind faith; we must always seek clarification. Change must occur with people and we must not expect governments to bring it about. People get the government that they deserve and it is up to the populace to demand changes from their governments; people must take control.

Qualities that they say humanity needs to develop are compassion, kindness, understanding, gentleness, creativity, joy, peace and balance. The golden law is to treat each and every soul, every animal and every plant, as you would wish them to treat you. Each person needs to understand that he/she is part of a larger whole and that what we do, say or think can affect the whole; the energy of our thoughts has a much greater power than we realise. Technology needs to be refined and not driven by greed and ego soul desires; it is good if it contributes to people's fulfilment but not if it gives pride in ownership. Business is good if it is not driven by greed but to help people.

It is stated that because of its great beauty Earth could become a place of paradise. People have a fear of boredom and many of the activities that we pursue are to avoid this, but making existence on Earth a paradise will not lead to boredom but to continual challenge, new knowledge, new colour, new sound.

[In this communication, and the previous one from the Pleidians, it is stated that there have been a number of colonisations of Earth by different members of the Omniverse Hierarchy. In our account of the arising of hominids we have followed the currently dominant scheme of starting with the arising of a bipedal ape-like creature, Australopithecus, about 5-7 million years ago, from which there developed homo habilis a hominid that used rudimentary stone tools, about 2.5 million years ago, then homo erectus that made a more advanced pear-shaped stone hand axe and a few other tools. This was followed by Neanderthal Man, about 100,000 years ago, who made a variety of tools in stone, wood, bone, antler and ivory and who made clothes from animal skins sewn together, and buried his dead, showing a consciousness of existence beyond that of the physical body on Earth. There then arose modern man, homo sapiens, about 40,000 years ago, who we have attributed to the incarnation of a level of the Omniverse Hierarchy into hominid bodies, to give rise to the current era of homo sapiens evolution. However, as Bill BRYSON points out, in his Short History of Nearly Everything, this view of hominid development prior to homo sapiens is derived from fragments of skeletons found in many different places and assigned to different dates with by no means all of the evidence fitting clearly into it and wide ranging disagreements between the experts in the field. This scheme is changing all the time as new finds are made. Also there is a great deal of anomalous evidence, comprising the existence of stone tools and their use, various artefacts and skeletal remains, that predate, in some cases by a long period, the currently accepted scheme of things, (CREMO and THOMPSON) that could, perhaps be due to earlier colonisations by members of the Omniverse Hierarchy].

Conversations With God (ref WALSCH)

Neale WALSCH was at a low point in his life when he decided to vent his frustrations by writing a letter of complaints to God. To his surprise when he finished, his hand was held by an invisible force that took over, that claimed to be God and responded to his outpourings and in this way began the writing of a series of books of 'Conversations with God'. We all have different conceptions of 'God' that derive from our cultural and religious backgrounds. Walsch was brought up as a Roman Catholic and therefore had a belief in a God who created the world, and in good and evil, and heaven and hell, and in God passing judgements on us. God told Walsch that his/her communications to him were made through the filter of Walsch's understanding, as there was no other way that he could receive them. These communications are therefore coloured by Walsch's Roman Catholic viewpoint and by his struggles to adjust to the nature of God portrayed in these communications, which was different to that which he was brought up to have. They have generated considerable interest, being translated into twenty-four languages and selling over a million copies.

Although dealing at great depth and wisdom with the issues and problems put to the God of his understanding by Walsch, God's responses are expressed in a down-to-earth, person-to-person way, without any suggestion of remote holiness. At times in these communications Walsch argues with God, in the way that we would argue with anyone who is trying to convince us of a point of view and God welcomes this as a way of sorting out the truth of a situation. In these conversations Walsch's God describes the basis of the creation of humanity and gives guidance on the main issues of our lives.

God states that s/he existed for a long time before the creation of the Universe, in a state described as 'speculating'. In this state God knew 'conceptually' that s/he was a Creator but s/he could not experience the magnificence of his/her creative ability because God was a unity so that there was nothing with which s/he could interact to express and experience his/her speculations. This generated a frustration that led to 'a great explosion from within', in which God separated off his/her speculations for further developments, of which humanity is part. As a result there are now three parts to existence. There is God the Father, from which creation arose, God the Son that comprises the parts that were sent out to develop on their own and the Holy Spirit that is the energy of the 'explosion', in which events take place. The God the Father aspect, the initiator of creation, is what is normally, and in Walsch's book, referred to as God. The Holy Spirit we equate with the space-energy of hK-M, in which everything takes place. This is the memory, the collective consciousness and the medium in which everything happens. The parts separated off in the 'explosion' have free will bestowed on them by God. They go their own ways, not knowing their God-given origins but because they derive from God, each part possesses its own creative drive and desire to experience a sense of self and, as all the parts work this out they create the Universe and life on Earth. What they create becomes the body of God that is permeated by the Holy Spirit/space energy, in the same way that the cells of our body are pursuing their individual activities but are permeated by our soul and spirit. Thus, in the way that the cells of our body evolve to make up its structure and workings, so do all the parts separated off in 'the explosion from within' evolve to make up the structure and workings of God. Although the initial unity of God is lost by the 'explosion from within', as each part goes its own way it creates vibrations in the Holy

Spirit/space energy that radiate out from it. These vibrations impinge on everything else and the vibrations of everything else impinge on it, to create a complex matrix of energy/activity. In this way everything continues to contribute to, and to be part of, a whole. We are part of this self-creating, evolving body of God.

In these books God skips over what we regard as the long period of billions of years of evolution of the Universe and life on Earth, that from God's point of view take place 'in the blink of an eye', and concentrates on the human situation in which, cut off in physical bodies, we work out our destinies and recover, or remember the qualities that we possessed as parts of God (in hK-M terms, parts of the Spiritual Hierarchy), from which we originated. We are all prodigal sons and daughters of God and our job is to work with one another and with the rest of creation, so as to realise our creative potentials, and then to re-unite with God the Father, taking with us the qualities that we have developed. As parts of God we are creator God-beings but by entering the physical world we forget this and as we go our own ways we distance ourselves from God. By living in the world separated from God the Father in this way, we are parts of God that have been sent out to act independently of God, so as to give God a perception and experience of his/her creative ability at work. When we incarnate into the Earth situation we are called upon to deal with the circumstances that we encounter and thereby we develop the qualities that make us the persons that we are. Our bodily Earth experience is a tool for our spiritual growth, in which our soul seeks to manifest its spiritual qualities while incarnated in a physical body.

Collectively and individually we create the life and times that we are experiencing and, as we do this God, via the Holy Spirit/space energy is aware of what we are doing and thereby everything - ourselves and God - evolves. Fundamentally we are in partnership with God and we are all One but first we have to get to know ourselves for what we are, by independently developing our innate potentials to become creator beings in our own right and then look back and come to know God the Father. God's attitude to humanity is like that of parents who let their off-spring go freely out into the world and do not interfere when they make mistakes, recognising that this is the only way that they will grow up, but they are available to offer help if this is needed and asked for. God's fulfilment, like that of the parents, lies in seeing us 'go out into the world' and developing and acting out of our own resources. When the off-spring have worked through the experiences that life offers they can return to the parents on an equal footing and form a one-to-one relationship with them, in a way that they never could if they grew up under the auspices of the parents.

In working out our sense of self, we all have different aims and this can create friction, disharmonies and clashes between us that lead, in extreme cases to killing one another and to wars. But God does not interfere because this would defeat the purpose of experiencing our unfettered creativity in action and negate our free will to behave as we wish. God does not impose any rules or obligations on our behaviour and does not pass judgements on us. We are offered opportunities for growth and development and God observes what we do. Although God does not pass judgements on us, where God perceives that developments could take place more harmoniously, God offers us guidance. This may come to us by inner impulses, visions, feelings, thoughts, the 'voice within', occasionally, as with Walsch's book, through words but primarily through our experience of life. Thus, where we experience that what we do does not work out well, we are seeing that it is not in accord with the underlying principles of God and creation. We have to discern, from among the many types of impulses, feelings, thoughts etc. that we experience, those that emanate from God. God states that these are the highest that we experience and that we can recognise our highest thoughts because these always contain joy, the clearest words that come to us are those that contain truth, and the grandest feeling we get is that of love. When we experience the presence of God we experience a great inner peace and harmony. Where we face problems and difficulties we should not blame anyone or anything else, we should ask ourselves, what part of myself do I wish to experience and develop in these circumstances?

We are each so wrapped up in pursuing our individual sense of self in the physical world that we lose awareness of the existence of God. But as we evolve we become aware of a larger pattern to existence and wonder about what lies behind it. In seeking an answer to this, a few people have become aware of God and of God's guidance and they proclaim God's existence; God quotes specifically Christ, Buddha and Krishna as achieving this state. God states that a number of people now on Earth have developed God consciousness and those that become at-one with God acquire God-given powers, for example; the ability to make physical objects appear and disappear; to make themselves appear and disappear; to appear in more than one place at a time. God also uses 'ordinary' people, like Walsch, to act as messengers to proclaim God's existence and to offer guidance to humanity. Ultimately all of us will achieve God awareness and, as prodigal sons and daughters, we will return to, and re-experience the unity and love of, God, taking with us the qualities that we have developed from our experiences.

Since God does not judge, there is no such thing as right or wrong, 'how could God judge God's own creation and call it bad?'. Although there is no right or wrong there is cause and effect, so that there are consequences to the ways in which we behave, to our actions and inactions. God states that right and wrong are concepts that we have generated to describe behaviours that lead to outcomes that are in accord with, or contrary to, the ways in which we seek to develop our God-given natures. In after life we review what we have thought, said and done and this can create in us desires to be better, to evolve and to grow, that lead to subsequent incarnations in circumstances selected to give us the required opportunities to achieve these qualities but nothing is imposed on us, we are beings of free will. There is no heaven or hell created by God, to which s/he assigns us as a result of our deeds. Heaven and Hell are the terms that we use to describe the effects of our behaviour, when we look back and 'wish like hell' that we had not done this or that or wish 'like hell' that we had seized that 'heaven sent' opportunity that would have led to us making something of ourselves that we could have been proud of. 'Hell' is the pain that we experience from the worst possible outcome of our choices and decisions made by 'wrong' thinking; it is the natural outcome of any thought or activity that is contrary to the ways of God, or negates our relationship to God; it is unfulfillment, the opposite of joy.

Although there is no intrinsic right or wrong some things work out well and others do not. However, it is necessary for us to work through these different experiences, so that our response to them creates the qualities that make us the persons that we are. We are our own rule makers and judges but our judgements have no basic, ultimate value; they vary from culture to culture and change as we evolve, e.g. at one time it was considered right to burn witches at the stake.

What is considered to be right and wrong in our society has been laid down by teachers and leaders, in religion, politics, etc. to make us conform to their ideas, so as to maintain their authority. Mostly we are creatures of habit and follow the ideas and beliefs of others and thereby we avoid the difficult task of thinking and becoming responsible for ourselves but by following other people's rules we deny our chance to grow. We should all seek for the God centre within us for true understanding and true values and strive to be, do and live according to our highest ideals and as more people do this the values of society will change. By accepting the viewpoint of others we deny our experience in favour of what we have been told to think. God quotes as the outstanding example of this, human sexuality. The sexual experience can be the most exhilarating, exciting, intimate, uniting and creative physical experience of which we are capable, providing that we are expressing love and do not misuse it, e.g. for power, ego gratification, or domination of another person but we have accepted the judgements of others that cause us to deny ourselves to freely and joyfully experience it. (God gives a graphic account of the interaction between two people, 'Tom' and 'Mary', who are on the opposite sides of a room from each other. They are both emitting their personal energy waves which unite midway to create a body of energy, to which they are both connected and which sends its energies back to them. Tom and Mary thereby feel the sublime joy of the connection and are irrevocably drawn together, closer and closer, so that the intensity of their feelings intensifies, until they are physically connected. They heave and move to get closer, CLOSER, until they explode and have the exquisite experience of their combined being). As with sex, the same is true of money, power, fame and success. There is nothing inherently 'good' or 'evil' about these; the important feature is what we do with them. They give us the opportunity to facilitate creative growth in ourselves and others. But, more than anything we have accepted the views of others about the nature of God, that God and God's judgement are to be feared, so that we must be 'God fearing' and obedient to God's commands, or else! We have also been taught that God is forgiveness and compassion but that we must seek this in the way laid down by authorities (who have a vested interest in maintaining their authority). Walsch's books state that God is above all judgements and does not punish and has no needs for us to be one way or another but God does have desires. God's first desire is to know and experience him/herself and to do this God created us and all the worlds of the Universe. Second God desires that we know and experience who we really are, that is, our God-given natures, through our power to create and to experience ourselves in whatever way we choose. Third, God desires the whole life process to be an experience of constant joy, continuous creation, never-ending expansion and total fulfilment in each moment of now.

God is not vengeful as portrayed in some religions, this was invented by religious leaders to keep people under their control and no religious leader has the power to forgive people their sins because in the eyes of God there are no sins, only experiences that we are working through, as a result of which we will come to know ourselves. The idea of a vengeful God has created fear in our lives. But fundamentally there is only a loving God; there is no devil or evil; however by forming concepts of evil and fear we equally conceive of love and by seeking love we seek God and our own Godself. If 'evil' did not exist we could not recognise and know love. (According to hK-M, fear came about as the result of 'God' casting us out, in the same way that going out into the world from life in a loving family leaves us fearful of how we are going to cope without the support that we are used to). We should seek to see God at work in everything and not condemn another person, because we do not know what part of God's plan they are working out. We should allow each soul to walk its own path. Respect for life sometimes makes war necessary because it is necessary to stop aggression on others or ourselves (God did not create life for it to be destroyed) but killing as a punishment or retribution or to settle petty differences and arguments is not appropriate. Killing in the name of God is the highest blasphemy.

We should each live our highest vision of our self; this requires continual examination of every thought, word and deed and that we change these where they do not conform to our highest vision of our self. In this way we create our long-term natures and move from unconscious to conscious living. The soul/sole purpose is evolution. The highest feeling of the soul is the experience of reuniting with All That Is, the return to the feeling of perfect love. But to do this we have to experience everything – ups and downs, good and evil, love and fear, so that we can select the best, otherwise, how can we have compassion and forgiveness for that which we do not understand, but this takes many lifetimes. God states that Walsch has had 647 previous incarnations, in which he has experienced being a king, a queen, a serf, a teacher. a student, a master, male, female, a warrior, a pacifist, a hero, a coward, a killer, a saviour, a sage, a fool.

Walsch asked God how he could have let the world get into the state that it is in. God replied that it is not his doing, but ours, we have free will and we create the life and times that we live in. In the case of famine and hunger, God states that s/he has provided all the resources needed to put an end to these but we do not choose to do so. In the case of disease we create our own ill-health; we eat, drink and breathe poisons; people smoke and wonder why they get cancer; they ingest animals and fat and wonder why they get blocked arteries; they get angry and wonder why they have heart attacks; they compete mercilessly under great stress and wonder why they have strokes, and they worry, hate and fear, all of which attack the body at a cellular level. We have the power to end famine and disease – we only have to choose to do so.

Walsch asked God about the Hitler phenomenon. God stated that Hitler's actions were the mistakes of an unevolved being but Hitler could do nothing without the cooperation, support, and willing submission of millions of people; collective consciousness provided the fertile soil for the growth of the Nazi movement; Hitler seized the moment but did not create it. The horror of the Hitler experience was not that he perpetrated it on the human race but that the human race allowed him to.

Walsch asked about problems in our relationships with each other. God stated that it is only through our relationships with other people, places and events that we experience ourselves and relationships call upon us to express who we are. Instead of being concerned with what we get out of a relationship from the other person or with what we give to the other, we need to be concerned with how the relationship promotes our own development. As we develop, so will the relationship.

Walsch asked God if life and civilisations exist on other planets, to which God replied that there are thousands of other civilisations, most of which are much more advanced than we are. The first guiding principle of an advanced civilisation is unity, the recognition that everybody and everything is part of a whole; they are aware that there is no separation between themselves and others and God. In comparison we are concerned with individualism and separateness, of nations, races and persons; we each pursue our own interests irrespective of the needs of others and of the needs of the environment in which we live and which we exploit. Highly evolved civilisations view themselves as part of an interacting system in which the well being of each part is dependent on the well being of all the other parts. They share everything and own nothing; they regard themselves as in stewardship for the things that their lives depend on, that is, they live collective existences. They do not destroy that which supports them, they do not pollute their environment and they live a lot longer than we do. They do not need words to communicate with each other, they communicate directly by telepathy, (as has been reported to be the situation in our post-mortem existence). They do not tell lies; their emotional state is directly observable to each other, (again as reported to be the situation in post-mortem existence, when we are divested of our physical bodies and exist as soul beings). They perceive directly the effects of their interactions with each other and with the world around them, so that they observe more clearly than we do what works and what doesn't work and their way of life, based on these observations, is more 'truthful' than ours which incorporates errors in our concepts of how we think things are.

In highly evolved societies there are no conflicts or wars and they do not need or have governments and laws like we do; they live in peace and harmony according to mutual agreements that are based on awareness, honesty and responsibility. They live in small inter-relating communities, as opposed to our large cities, because they have found that this is what works best. Their goal in life is to 'do what brings value'. They have advanced beyond the need to use machine-based transport: as a result of advances in their understanding of physicality and of the nature of their minds they can 'travel' by disassembling and reassembling their bodies elsewhere at will, to be wherever they choose, whenever they choose, even to the extent of travelling across the Universe.

By comparison we are still in a primitive state of development. However, God does not experience our primitiveness in a negative way but is aroused by it, awakened to new adventures, to new possibilities, new experiences yet to come. We are only just beginning to experience our splendours; our blossoming is at hand but we are on the brink of dramatic changes. Our technology is outstripping our ability to use it wisely and this has happened before. In the past there existed on the Earth planet civilisations (Atlantis, Lemuria) that were more highly evolved in technology and other respects than we are now but they misused their technology and brought about their own destruction. We are now in a similar situation, we have created an evolved technology but we remain spiritually primitive. Ecologically we are polluting the atmosphere of our planet: our farming methods are damaging and depleting the nutritive top soil, while the chemical additions to it, that we absorb in our food, will have long-term deleterious effects on our bodies: with nuclear power we have developed weapons of mass destruction that will soon get into the hands of someone who will hold the world hostage to them or destroy the world trying: with our medical science we have created viruses that are so resistant to attack that they threaten to eliminate our species. Socially, instead of developing for the well being of all we have developed cultures in which the needs of the mass of people are subjugated to the desires of a small minority who seek maximum wealth and power for themselves. We are poised for disaster but at the same time God states that s/he perceives the rapid growth of a force for change, in an expansion of consciousness as a result of which our civilisation could move out of its primitive state into a more evolved one.

God singles out two basic aspects of our civilisation that show our primitiveness in comparison with highly evolved societies, namely Education and Government. Walsch is American and God tends to orientate his/her comments to the American situation but in principle they apply to the whole of our civilisation. We do not understand the basic concepts of civilised societies; namely, how to solve conflicts without violence, how to live without fear, how to act without self interest and how to love without condition. In our system of education we are ignoring wisdom in favour of knowledge. In knowledge we are teaching children what to think and thereby what they believe to be true, not how to think and arrive at their own truths. As a result they repeat the same mistakes that we have made and they do not change that which is not working well; our education develops memory instead of skills and abilities. Advanced civilisations encourage children to discover and create answers for themselves, so as to achieve wisdom and develop a better, more appropriate sense of values. We expose our children to images of violence, that is something an advanced society would never do, whereas we need to expose them to images of love. Highly evolved beings would never place their off spring for many hours in front of a device that shows pictures of behaviour that they wish their off-spring to avoid. We teach our children to repress their emotions and this has disastrous effects when they become adults. We need to develop in our children an appreciation of the wonder of life and to teach them that they are spiritual beings, starting with fairy stories that embody these principles. Rather than imparting facts and imposing our own viewpoints, it would be better to base the teaching of our children on developing awareness, honesty and responsibility and to be respectful of other people's feelings and of other people's paths, as is done in advanced societies.

On the issue of Government, advanced societies have few laws because there is a mutual awareness of what is needed. You cannot legislate morality or equality. You cannot grow and become great when you are constantly told what to do by government. Our civilisation looks after and supports the wealthy few while the poor go in need. Our wealthy societies throw away enough food to feed half the world. The vast sums spent on the military would solve all the world's problems. The wealthy few reject the problems of the poor and deprived as 'their own fault' and believe in survival of the fittest. God states that, while each person must take responsibility for him/herself, all should be given equal opportunity. God does not advocate that all people should be treated equally because people are not equal, but everyone should have the basic necessities of life, to be able to survive with dignity, so that they are then free to choose how to develop. Enlightened societies are concerned with the benefit to, and survival of, all. God states that a powerful force for equality is 'visibility, in which there is no secrecy between the members of society: everyone knows what everyone else has, what is paid in wages and taxes and what profits corporations make; everything is visible.

God advocates a one-world government that embodies the principle that gave rise to the United States of America, that of freedom of the individual but in a spirit of brotherhood of all, in which individual States preserve their freedom and independence of development, with a Federal government that maintains harmony between them. (God states that the original principles that gave rise to the greatness of America have been lost and have given way to self-seeking; the U.S.A. seems to have lost its vision). This could produce cohesion and eliminate wars between nations in the way that it has done with the different States of America. Beyond this what is needed is a change in collective consciousness, a move towards people seeking inner peace and God consciousness, a realisation that we are all one family and that what affects one, affects all. As more people find inner peace and harmony this will lead to society as a whole achieving peace and harmony. At the same time, finding internal peace results in a lessened desire for satisfaction through the accumulation of external possessions, which eliminates competition for, and conflict over, these.

In a further book, WALSCH (4) asks the God of his understanding for help with our World situation and its endless wars and killings. In response God reiterates statements that he made in the previous three books emphasising the aspects that pertain to this issue. God says that we are in a serious state because, through our advanced technology we have developed immense powers of destruction but in other respects we are in a state of immaturity, the earliest stages of adolescence: we have advanced in our ability to destroy each other but not in our ability to get along with each other and this is creating a crisis. If we use our advanced destructive powers to try to resolve our differences we could destroy our civilisation and humanity on Earth would never reach maturity.

God states that our behaviour is determined by our beliefs and that the insistence that our particular belief is right and that other beliefs are wrong, to the point of killing those who hold them, is the source of our problems; therefore, if we wish to achieve a world of peace and harmony we need to change our beliefs. It is clear from the state of disharmony in the world that our religions (and our education and our economics) are not working; this is because they are based on beliefs that do not reflect reality. Our beliefs derive from what was laid down in ancient, holy books, such as the Bible, the Qur'an, the Bhagavad-Gita, the Tao-te Ching, the Talmud, etc. A major feature of all of these books is that they portray God as requiring us to behave according to his laws and that we will be punished if we transgress them and that we should fight and kill people who do not conform to our beliefs and God quotes many examples from different scriptures to illustrate this feature. (Walsch's God seems to be omniscient in that s/he knows everything that has happened, and is happening, to everyone everywhere). God reiterates that s/he does not require us to conform to any type of behaviour laid down by him/her; we have been given free will and s/he does not pass any judgement or impose any punishment on us. These ideas derive from the way that human beings treat each other and the belief that God treats people in the same way.

These ancient holy books gave rise to organised religions in which they were misused by those in power so as to maintain their status. Organised religions are not a solution but a problem because they exclude those who do not conform to them and thereby they create divisions between people and they do not teach understanding and tolerance for others who have different beliefs. (Nationalism similarly divides and produces antagonisms between peoples, as do cultural, ethnic, racial and social groupings). No religion is the true religion, no people are the chosen people and no prophet is the greatest prophet. Religions have been the cause of much hatred and killing. More wars have been fought in the cause of organised religion than in any other cause. Millions of people have been killed in the name of God and humans have used God's Will as an excuse to justify the most appalling barbaric behaviours. Where people claim that what they are doing is the will of God, to satisfy God's desires, it is in fact their own will and desires that they are seeking to justify. God reiterates that s/he has no desires and does not want or need anything from humanity.

Organised religions require us to believe in their teachings and thereby they stop us from a direct experience of God. One's religion is a product of birthplace and early teaching; it is not eternal truth; people believe what they are taught to believe. What is needed is a transcending and expansion of our beliefs, a new spirituality, new theological thoughts and ideas that allow us to release our grip on the old doctrines. Religion is an institution, spirituality is an experience and it does not require us to believe in anything. Spirituality calls upon us to notice our experience and to change to seeking what works to achieve our goals and this way our behaviours will change and our personal experience becomes our authority.

The ancient beliefs arose from revelations from God in past times which we tend to think of as special, received by a few people who we also think of as special but, Walsch's God states, these past eras and people were not special; s/he has never ceased to communicate with humanity. S/he is talking to all of us all the time and we all have the power to communicate with him/her and thereby to determine for ourselves the beliefs and principles by which we behave. God says we should each believe as we wish, follow our hearts and souls where they lead us for it is within our hearts, souls and minds that our Divinity can be found but we should not seek to impose our beliefs on others and certainly not try to do so by force. We should determine the validity of our beliefs by seeing how they work in practice in achieving the ends that we seek.

To achieve peace and harmony on Earth we first have to find it within ourselves. We then become a source of peace, love and harmony that influences others. To do this we have to decide that this is how we are going to be and then meet life with these qualities. Love, compassion, caring, patience, acceptance and understanding, the capacity to create and inspire are the grandest qualities of God and are what true humanity is all about. People who exhibit these qualities become catalysts for others to develop them and for humanity as a whole to change. According to Walsch's God it only requires a small proportion of humanity (less than 5%) to bring about a total change. If this happens there will emerge a new conception of God and a new spirituality that will lead to advances in all aspects of human existence, economic, education, political, etc. in which God will be seen as the totality of everything, of which we are all part and with which we are all in contact. To avoid conflict with the different views of God possessed by different religions, it would be best to substitute for 'God' the term 'Life', which empowers everything. With this development there will come about a state of consciousness in which we will see everyone and everything as manifestations of particular aspects of God. This 'God consciousness', although at present rare, is being experienced by more and more people and God outlines two simple exercises that we can carry out to help us to achieve it.

A final book in this series, 'Home with God' WALSCH (6), deals with the issue of death. God states that there is no such thing as death, in the sense of the cessation of existence. There is only a transition from a physical to a spiritual existence and that, far from being a negative experience, death is a wonderful, joyful event. Our existence is a continual cycling between what we call the 'life' and 'death' states. In the death state we exist in the spiritual world and follow the path of 'knowing', in the physical world we follow the path of 'experiencing'.

[A simplistic analogy to the alternation between our 'death state' in the spiritual world of 'knowing' and our 'life state' in the physical world of 'experiencing' is the situation in which we embark on a project in which first, by inner spiritual activity we work out and 'know' what we are going to do and then we put our plan into action in the physical world and 'experience' how it works out. However, this analogy does not take into account the fact that, in our life experience of working out the plan that we conceived in the spiritual world, when we enter into a physical body we get cut off from, and lose awareness of, our plan and of our spiritual existence].

Walsch's God states that in all of this we are beings of free will and follow a path of our own choosing, including choosing when and how we die and that, despite the struggles and suffering of Earth existence, we are following a perfect pattern of development. We are not aware of this pattern because we exist at three levels of experience, subconscious, conscious and superconscious. The subconscious level controls the activities of our body systems and our automatic, unconsciously driven, responses to events. The conscious level controls our everyday activities in which we have some awareness of what we are doing and why we are doing it. The superconscious level of activity determines the overall pattern of our development, that derives from the relationship of our spirit with the spiritual world (in hK-M terms the world of our Higher Self and its existence in the Omniverse Hierarchy), of which we have no awareness unless we have developed the ability to enter into a higher state of consciousness (in which we exist in the 'death' state). When we exist within the Omniverse Hierarchy we are in spiritual contact with, and can become aware of, 'All That Is'. There is also a supraconscious level in which one is simultaneously conscious at all levels, that is attained by highly developed beings, when it becomes possible to perceive the purpose and forces behind everything and at which the perfection of it all becomes clear

In our Earthly consciousness we relate to events in terms of time and space but Walsch's God states that in His/Her consciousness of the 'All That Is' there is no time and space, everything is in existence simultaneously and our conception of time and space arise from the rate and direction at which we move through the All That Is.

When we die, after we experience that we no longer have a body, we enter into a post-mortem existence that is determined by our beliefs about life after death, e.g. if we believe there is nothing after death we experience nothing, until we 'wake up' to a new existence. If we believe that after death we will meet God in some form, Muhammad, Jesus, Lord Krishna or Buddha then this is what we will perceive, or we may experience simply the Essence of Pure Love. After we have sorted out our beliefs, we enter into a third stage, of total bliss, when we merge into, and experience oneness with, 'All That Is', a state that some religions and mystics describe as being 'Home With God', which hK-M would regard as returning to the Omniverse Hierarchy. However, Walsch's God says that we do not have to die to experience this state, this state of being at oneness with everything may occur spontaneously for a short time, or it may be experienced for longer by training to enter into a heightened state of consciousness.

An hK-M Evaluation

According to hK-M the paramount feature governing everything is sense of self. Homo sapiens arose by members of an intermediate level of the Spiritual Hierarchy incarnating into hominid bodies that had arisen by biological evolution on Earth. While they were within the Spiritual Hierarchy they developed in accord with, and supported by, the higher levels of the Hierarchy. But when they incarnated into hominid bodies and had to survive in the complex and demanding conditions of life on Earth they became progressively cut off from the Hierarchy and had to find their ways forward out of their own resources. While this gave rise to an enhanced sense of self, this sense of self was, and is, very precarious. Seeking stability led to striving to retain awareness of, and contact with, the Spiritual Hierarchy. Those people who seemed to achieve this contact were thought of as different and holy and because of the innate wisdom in their viewpoints they attracted people who were/are seeking a basis for, and meaning and purpose to, their lives. This gave rise to the different religions, all of which are partial viewpoints of a larger understanding. But to each person in a religious group their particular viewpoint gives them stability and a sense of self. Any challenge to this takes away their stability and the sense of self on which they feel that their existence depends and is therefore met with hostility. The solution to this is to recognise that we are all trying to find our ways forward along different paths, to have tolerance for each other's endeavours and to share each other's findings and experiences. In this way humanity could develop a larger understanding that encompasses all viewpoints which would then be seen, not as competitive and antagonistic to each other but as part of an overall common evolution to greater things.

Channelled communications naturally take the form of, and fit into, the framework of understanding of the receiver of them. Thus, if you believe in a Creator God who has brought everything into existence, then this is the form in which you will receive them. This was the standpoint from which Walsch received his communications from God; that is, the generally accepted Western view that we have been brought up to believe in, of a Creator God. This is at variance with the viewpoint of *h*K-M, of an Omniverse Hierarchy with a collective Godhead at the top but, as we have pointed out previously, the God of the Christian bible is a translation from Elohim that is plural. In Book 3 Walsch's God states that s/he is a collective and that the Christian Bible stated, 'Let **Us** create man in **Our** image and after **Our** likeness', before the translation was changed.

Another feature that Walsch had to deal with is that we are brought up to believe that God is remote, mysterious and incomprehensible but the God of Walsch's communications is not like this; Walsch's God is down to Earth, approachable and works in ways that we can readily understand.

In line with the generally accepted concept of creation taking place at the behest of an omnipotent God, Walsch describes the way in which God created the world according to a preconceived plan. In this description God stated that before s/he created the Universe, s/he existed in a state of 'speculating', in which s/he knew conceptually that s/he was magnificent but because s/he was a unity s/he could not experience this, which led to God separating off part of itself as God's creation. This differs from the viewpoint of *h*K-M, in which everything arises out of an unconscious dormant energy state that becomes active, develops into a state of turmoil that differentiates into entities who make the experiences that they inadvertently undergo, self actualising. In line with *h*K-M, Walsch's God states that the Universe is expanding and that there will come a time when it all contracts back and that this happens again and again and is the breathing out and breathing in of God. According to *h*K-M, during the 'breathing in' there is an 'internalisation' of experience, giving rise to a recognition of potentials that have inadvertently arisen for further developments. Then, in the next cycle there is a positive plan to realise these and again inadvertent events arise that lead to the pattern of activity of the following cycle. Thus, according to *h*K-M there is no preconceived, thought-out plan to creation: new developments arise out of events that first happened unconsciously and inadvertently which then give rise to a consciously conceived plan to work out their potentials. In the current cycle the inadvertent arising of biological evolution on Earth culminating with the development of hominids and members of the Omniverse Hierarchy then inadvertently getting caught up in hominid bodies and seeking, from this cut off situation to maintain and enhance their sense of self gave rise to a conscious seeking for a new level of self awareness of the Godhead. Because of his belief that everything happens according to God's plan, Walsch describes these developments as though they were pre-planned.

Walsch's God states that a basic problem is that it is difficult for us to understand his/her descriptions of events in terms of our Earth-bound space-time consciousness because God's perception of things is different to ours, which s/he amplifies by the example of a rock. If we look at a rock we see something that in terms of the events of our lives, and the space-time framework that we use to describe these, is unmoving and unchanging. But if we were to centre our consciousness on the atoms that make up the rock, we would see that these are engaged in intense activity, the events of which take place so rapidly that it requires a different space-time framework to describe them and that it is their activities that make up the unmoving, unchanging rock. Equally, if we were to centre our consciousness at a level that is concerned with the evolution of the Universe, we would not see the rock as permanent and unmoving, but we would see that it becomes what it is as a sequence of evolutionary developments that take place on a much more extended space-time scale than the days, months and years that we use to describe the events of our lives. Walsch's God states that there is in fact no intrinsic space or time, or past, present or future; these are ideas that we have invented to describe our experiences. At God's level of consciousness everything exists in the Eternal Now but the Eternal Now is continually changing as a result of what is happening.

When Walsch queried the status of the God of his communications, God stated that s/he is the creator of everything that we know and experience and is therefore the God of our understanding and that we are his/her body and that everything that s/he experiences s/he does so through us but that this is only a limited view of things and that s/he is in turn the body of another. God stated that, in the same way that 'looking downwards' our body comprises a descending hierarchy of levels of ever-smaller entities and their activities, so 'looking upwards' there exists an unending hierarchy of levels above and that this is a glimpse of a larger Truth to which humanity will become privy. Walsch's God refers to an 'Absolute', to which s/he seems to bear a similar relationship to that which we bear to him/her.

The *h*K-M viewpoint came to us as a result of 'communications' (see Part III) in which we were seeking for an explanation for what we were observing in our experiments, which would tie in with the findings of science on the evolution of the Universe and life on Earth. Although none of us practised any religious beliefs, we had absorbed the prevailing view that if there is anything behind creation it is God, so that at first the story that we got was in terms of the activities of God, which gradually developed to become a collective Godhead. The problem then was that the Godhead possessed qualities, so that there had to be some prior situation in which these developed. As we probed for information on this we were led back to a 'Father-Mother' of the Godhead but this again possessed qualities and as we probed into this we were led back to an Absolute:

> *'The Absolute is everything, way back before the Father-Mother and the Godhead is the Absolute – it is there/the beginning and the end. The Absolute seems to shake itself and centre itself'.*

It was at this stage that we got to a state of dormant energy that began to stir, that led to the events described by *h*K-M. Walsch's God's account is in accord with *h*K-M in that s/he states that everything comprises the same basic energy, in which different parts have taken on different characteristics by becoming more condensed or more rarefied in their activities, thereby forming different 'things' (as proposed by early Greek philosophers, Chapter 11). Walsch's God states that s/he is this energy that developed the ability to differentiate. It is in this way that we are all part of the whole that is God. By going back to a state of dormant energy and explaining how everything arose from this, *h*K-M portrays a larger, more basic viewpoint that offers an explanation for features of God's communications to Walsch. For example, *h*K-M explains why God is a collective and how the breathing in and out of the Universe arises, from the s-entities increasing in activity until they reach a state of stress that causes them to relax back. There is also the feature that God is love and God is energy, but the energy that is God had somehow to develop the quality of love, for which *h*K-M offers an explanation, as we have described, in terms of the development of each level of the Omniverse Hierarchy arising out of its interaction with the later levels that come into existence, with the highest level developing love for the lower levels.

The Significance of the Channelled Communications

The significance of channelled communications is something that the next generation will have to work out as the situation evolves. All that we can do here is to make a few interim comments.

Each of the books that we have summarised claims to emanate from spiritual sources that came into existence before the present Universe. They all have the common theme that our Universe is the latest in a succession of Universes, which come into existence by a 'breathing out and breathing in' and they state that we are approaching a time when there will be a change from breathing out to breathing in. As this happens there will be a re-uniting, a return to wholeness in which we will experience at-oneness and reunion with God.

In Soskin's and Schlemmer's books it is stated that the communications are not made in words; they are picked up by the channeller's mind and translated into words and Walsch's God states that the communications to Walsch had to be made from Walsch's viewpoint. This means that communications can only be expressed in the framework of the vocabulary and concepts possessed by the channeller. Thus, although they have much in common, these communications are expressed from different viewpoints. As will be seen in the next section, we have had experiences of something like channelling ourselves. We have found that what is 'received' is coloured very much by the nature of the person receiving it - both in imposing limitations on the depth and range of the material and in the orientation from which it is perceived. Also, our experience has been that what is given can change, as efforts are made on both the side of the communicators and/or the receivers to achieve mutual understanding.

According to *h*K-M, the uniqueness of Man's experience on Earth arises because the Earth planet is the only place where the independent, biological evolution of life has occurred. This gave rise to hominids, culminating in Neanderthal man who developed a sense of self with an ability to act out of his own resources. The enhanced sense of self attracted members of the Omniverse Hierarchy, who exist in a collective state of development, to incarnate into, and experience, Earth existence, to give rise to what we know as homo sapiens. Because humanity has then developed on Earth separated off from the Spiritual Hierarchy, we have greater freedom of opportunity to pursue personal aims, rather than collective ones and, as a result human beings have had to develop a stronger sense of self and greater inner resources. In this way humanity has developed a greater ability to understand and a greater intensity of feelings. Thus on the return, reuniting, path humanity has these to contribute to the collective experience of the Omniverse

Hierarchy. And as this ability to think and feel more intensely becomes converted from personal to universal ends humanity can contribute a higher level of love and wisdom to the whole.

But to make its contribution to the Omniverse Hierarchy humanity has to reunite, and to harmonise, with it. In order to do this it has to have some awareness of, and contact with, the Hierarchy. These channelled communications suggest that humanity could be entering a new era, in which contact with the Omniverse Hierarchy could become increasingly widespread. The communications claim that a change in consciousness is coming about in humanity and this is borne out by the increasing number of books by people reporting experiences of expanded consciousness. However, several of the communications mention that, for some people this could be a shattering experience. An example of this is Hazel COURTENEY(1) who was an alternative therapy and health columnist for the Daily Mail and the Sunday Times. As a result of her work Hazel had met a wide range of people, medical doctors, alternative therapy practitioners, psychics and people from various walks of life, including Diana, Princess of Wales who she had met a number of times and twice had lunch time conversations with. From her experiences with psychics Hazel had had convincing contact with her deceased parents. During the Easter period in 1998 she was shopping in Harrods when she underwent the beginning of a shattering sequence of experiences in which, without help from her medical, alternative therapy and psychic friends, she would have died. During this period she experienced a searing pain that went down through her head into her chest and she underwent dramatic physical changes, including her eyes changing colour, she became telepathic and developed other psychic powers, she levitated and developed the ability to manifest objects and a grey ash (like Sai Baba), she felt filled with an energy that enabled her to give people healing, affected electrical equipment, perceived energy fields around people, she 'heard voices in her head' and experienced contact with spirits of deceased persons, in particular with Princess Diana. She experienced the traumatic emotions of Diana during her life, at the time of her accident and death and in post-mortem existence. The point of all this seems to be that Diana had impacted on the lives of many people and 'the spiritual world' that seeks to open up the consciousness of people to post mortem existence and life as a meaningful spiritual existence was using Diana as a focus for this. To do this they required a person who had some contact with Diana and who possessed the skills and abilities to write up the experiences and ideas that they wished to communicate. Hazel fulfilled these requirements but before she could carry out this task she had to undergo a change in her consciousness so that she could experience Diana's life and develop the ability to communicate with her. During these demanding and distracting experiences Hazel desperately wanted to be normal but then, as they faded away she greatly missed the abilities that she had had and she embarked on a search for greater understanding [COURTENEY (2)]. In particular she wanted proof that she had been in contact with Diana and so she visited Gary SCHWARTZ a Professor at the University of Arizona in the U.S.A. who has carried out research on post-mortem existence. Schwartz's method was to expose Hazel to the successive presence of two highly accredited mediums who he had worked with for some years (who Hazel had not previously met and knew nothing about) without telling the mediums anything about Hazel or allowing Hazel to say anything and both mediums independently picked up the presence of Diana and the fact that she was manifesting through Hazel. After Hazel's first book was published a number of people wrote to tell her that they had been through similar experiences and that they were grateful to her for making her experiences public and establishing their validity; very often people having such experiences are regarded as 'queer' or psychotic and one woman who wrote to Hazel described how she had been confined in a mental institution for 20 years for hearing voices in the way that Hazel had.

The channelled communications warn us that, as well as the major transition from a Universe-creating breathing out to a breathing in, there is the possibility of a more immediate local change in the comparatively near future, which will be a repeat of that which, it is claimed, wiped out an Atlantean civilisation. If the predicted Atlantean-type catastrophe were to happen many, if not all, human beings would be destroyed and there would be a division between souls who were Earth-bound and were therefore stuck in the lower planes of post-mortem existence and those who were able to leave Earth experience behind and move on, or rather revert, to being members of the Omniverse Hierarchy. A common aim claimed by the communications is to stimulate us to raise our level of understanding and consciousness so that we do not remain bound to Earth existence.

The Nine in the Schlemmer book offer two departures from this pattern of development. One is that souls/spirits who have become trapped in, and therefore have to work out, Earth karma are being taken to another abode in the Universe where they will be able to continue with their development. The other possibility suggested is that by the power of thought, by meditation it may be possible to release the negative locked up energy in a controlled way, at a rate that minimises the catastrophic destruction.

Atlantis

The existence of a highly developed prior civilisation of Atlantis (and also a previous Lemurian one) is repeatedly referred to in the channelled communications. It is subscribed to by mystics from their reading of the Akashic records, for example STEINER (3). Steiner concentrates on the evolution of consciousness that occurred during this period. He states that early Atlanteans had a highly developed memory but none of the rational consciousness that we possess now. According to hK-M this was because, like animals and plants, they were still part of collective existence, so that their behaviour was determined by the situations/stresses that they encountered activating a response from the collective experience built up in the EM-energy. The contribution of the early Atlanteans was that they individually became aware of what they were doing and thereby each member built up a personalised memory of how to respond to specific situations and began to act out of his/her individual resources within the collective. At first things were repeated as they had always been done and this was handed on to the next generation. The person who had experienced much and remembered much was regarded as an authority. However, in trying to repeat a pattern of behaviour when circumstances became different this did not work out, which caused them to try to adapt previous behaviour to the new circumstances. The stress of this activity led to the development of thinking and to authority then being invested in the greatest thinkers and those who pursued new developments. This led to an enhanced sense of self by the leaders, the development of Egotism, with a striving for self-aggrandisement and greater power and the misuse of this brought about catastrophe and the destruction of their civilisation.

References to Atlantis crop up in past life recall, for example, in that of Suddi who was a member of the Essene sect [Chapter 12, ref. CANON(1)], Suddi stated that the wisdom of the Essenes derived from the Atlantean culture and that the Essenes still possessed objects from that time, specifically a continually moving mechanism that modelled the movements of celestial bodies and a large crystal that was an energy magnifier. Some people recall a past life in Atlantis either by hypnotic past life recall or spontaneously. HOPE (1), for example claims to recall a past life in which she was the youngest daughter of a High Priest of Atlantis and her interest in Atlantis spurred her to collate all the mythological and other evidence that could relate to its nature and existence, including an account of Atlantis by Plato that Solon got from an Egyptian priest, HOPE (2).

BERLITZ gathered together mythological accounts of Atlantis and evidence that might support them. He claims the existence of ancient maps that show knowledge of the disposition of the continents that was only discovered a few hundred years ago and particularly Antarctica, which was only discovered in 1818. A feature claimed for these maps is that they show the topography of Antarctica before it was covered in ice, i.e. before 12,000 years ago, (this topography only became known as the result of a seismic survey carried out in 1949). He claims that the maps are accurate and drawn with a high level of mathematical stereographic skill. Berlitz gives examples of optical lenses, an 'electric battery' and evidence for advanced surgical operations, such as trepanning of the brain and the insertion of a metal plate, from ancient civilisations, found by archaeologists. These things he claims suggest a lost high level of knowledge.

Much of the evidence claimed for past civilisations inaugurated by the gods, quoted by VON DANIKEN and others pursuing this theme, comes from archaeological remains that, in many cases, have been subjected to severe destructions. There are massive ruins of vast ancient cities of unknown origin that show a highly developed constructional ability, in many cases involving the shaping and manipulation of large stonework weighing tens and even hundreds of tons. Some of these cities have been raised up and some are under the sea, supporting the idea of past cataclysms. It is claimed that in these ruins, thousands of miles apart there are inscriptions of a similarity that suggests they were once part of a common culture. However the current view of archaeologists is that there is no evidence for a prior common culture and that these cultures developed independently at different times, along similar lines. From the hK-M viewpoint all cultures in their evolution would follow a similar pattern of development, because they would tap into and contribute to, the collective consciousness of the EM-energy, in the way that we have described for biological evolution.

HANCOCK in a review of the problem of how the high levels of the civilisations of S.America and Egypt arose rapidly with no history of a lengthy prior development concludes that they developed from the remnants of a high level of civilisation in Atlantis that was submerged in a world catastrophe. Evidence that he quotes to support a common origin are the similarities in their customs and beliefs. Evidence for a catastrophe is the large numbers of animals (e.g. mammoths) that have been found apparently 'flash frozen' in Siberia and Alaska, as though they were taken rapidly from temperate conditions into deep freeze, with undigested temperate climate food still in their stomachs. There is strong evidence of this resulting from a cataclysm because, in some places, vast piles of shattered, mixed up bones have been found, giving the impression that the animals from which they derived were swept up together and crushed. Although these areas are now in conditions of permafrost, many of the animals are of a type that existed in temperate climates. There are also finds of fossilised forests and plants in Arctic and Antarctic regions that came from temperate or sub-tropical climates. These features suggest a major change in the Earth's disposition.

Hancock summarises a theory of Earth crust movement by Charles Hapgood, to account for the rapid change in conditions. It is based on the build up of ice in the Antarctic and that this is happening in an asymmetrical way, that creates an imbalance, leading to a centrifugal force on the Earth's crust which results in its movement over a more fluid underlying base. Einstein, in endorsing Hapgood's theory, stated:

> 'In a polar region there is a continual deposition of ice, which is not symmetrically distributed about the pole. The earth's rotation acts on these asymmetrically deposited masses, and produces centrifugal momentum that is transmitted to the rigid crust of the earth. The constantly increasing centrifugal momentum produced in this way will, when it has reached a certain point, produce a movement of the earth's crust over the rest of the earth's body '.

If such a crustal movement occurs, regions that were in temperate or tropical zones could be suddenly shifted into polar zones and vice versa. This could be accompanied by great upheaval of the Earth's crust and volcanic activity, so that some regions that were at sea level become thrust up to become mountains, while some mountainous regions become submerged beneath seas. There would be vast destruction everywhere and it is proposed that, in this way, the continent and civilisation of Atlantis moved into the Antarctic region where it has subsequently become buried beneath what is now a mile or more thickness of ice. But, in investigating the formation of the Antarctic ice sheet, scientists have drilled out deep cores of ice and nothing suggestive of a buried civilisation has come up.

If the ice-bound Antarctic region moved into a more temperate climate zone the melting of the ice would cause massive flooding. Hancock points out that myths from around the world, e.g. Sumeria, S. America, Central America. N. America, Greece, India, Egypt, describe a time of a past cataclysm and subsequent massive flooding. Some of these myths also refer to this having happened a number of times.

The problem then is that, given the asymmetric build up of ice at the Antarctic, what triggers the catastrophic crustal movement? Hancock points out two factors; one is that the (slow) precession of the Earth's axis of rotation causes an eccentricity that throws the centrifugal force out of balance; the other is that alignment of the planets can take up a configuration that modifies the Sun's gravitational force.

. WILSON (2) has examined these findings of Berlitz, Hapgood and Hancock, and other investigators of early civilisations, concentrating on the idea that the 'lost civilisation' and the early periods of the Egyptian, S. American and Indian cultures possessed some of this knowledge as a result of having a different type of consciousness to that which we possess now. Wilson then tried to work out how their consciousness differed from ours and enabled them to carry out the massive building operations required for the pyramids and other large edifices, and why these cultures were so concerned with astronomical knowledge and how they achieved such a high level in this. He concluded that their consciousness was an intuitive one, an at-one-ness with the workings of Nature that gave them a deeper connection with the forces behind things but without the rational understanding of modern consciousness. From the hK-M viewpoint this would be because these early cultures were more in touch with, and derived their knowledge from, the Omniverse Hierarchy from which they incarnated and had not become cut off and forced to develop the, 'viewed from the outside', independent rational objective understanding that we have now. Wilson also concludes that by being in touch with Nature and with each other, the members of these cultures possessed a group consciousness that enabled them to move the large blocks that make up the pyramids by a sort of mental power, allied to the technology (levers and ramps, etc), that they were using.

An interesting item suggesting the existence of an earlier high level of technology is the Mitchell-Hedges crystal skull (named after its discoverer). This is a life-sized skull carved out of quartz crystal, with a detachable jaw.

It is claimed that it was found in the ruins of an ancient Mayan Citadel in the S. American jungle around 1925. It presents a mystery of where it originally came from and how it was made, because quartz crystal is an extremely hard and brittle material that, when used in modern technology requires recently invented diamond tipped tools to cut and shape it and very careful handling to prevent it from splitting. It was examined by scientists at the Hewlett-Packard laboratories, who are experts at working with such crystals. They concluded that both parts were cut from the same piece of very pure quartz but they could not understand how it could have been made by the ancient technique of hand grinding and polishing with sand. They estimated that using this method it would have taken 300 man-years of effort and that it would have been very difficult to make such a complex shape without it shattering, in fact in terms of contemporary understanding it should not exist. MORTON and THOMAS have investigated the problems posed by the skull and found that there are a number of similar skulls, together with some modern copies. People who have the old skulls find that they invoke psychic and/or healing phenomena.   Morton and Thomas's investigations led them to Native American Shamans who explained that their legends state that there are thirteen of the old, original skulls that belonged to their ancestors who had them in Atlantean times. They stated that the skulls were made by beings from other planets that came to the Earth Planet, with each skull providing access to the particular wisdom and understanding of creation of the people who were responsible for it.

The Native American world-view is more wholistic and living than that of the Western World. Everything, including minerals, is regarded as a living part of the sacred essence of creation and that all things are connected and have a sense of consciousness and memory. It is claimed that the skulls can enable people to tune into the events of creation. (In *h*K-M terms they could act as a focus for accessing the events in the EM-energy/Akashic record with which they have been associated). According to the Native American world-view the Earth goes through cycles, or epochs, of existence and we are now approaching the end of an epoch that has been governed by developing increasing separateness, of peoples from each other, from God, and from Nature and we are now approaching an era in which peoples, God/Nature will come together again and this will entail a change in consciousness in which people will become 'psychically aware' of the connections between everything and in which the skulls will play a part. They state that the advent of this new era that, they claim starts in the year 2012, will be accompanied by massive Earth changes, beginning with environmental and weather changes.

Another feature that suggests a lost high level of knowledge is that about Sirius by the Dogon tribe in Africa. It would seem that Dogon priests have a detailed knowledge of the Sirius star system. In particular they are aware of a small heavy companion star (Sirius B) that revolves around Sirius and of the period and shape of its orbit. Sirius B is invisible to the naked eye and it, and the knowledge of its period and orbit, was only discovered recently using the high-powered techniques of modern astronomy. The Dogon believe that the seed of creation came from the Sirius companion star. TEMPLE has researched this problem and he concludes that the Dogon are descended from the ancient Egyptians, who had this knowledge, and that the civilisation of ancient Egypt was founded on Earth from Sirius.

In our summary of the developments of the early civilisations we have pointed out the major role played by the 'gods', as with the massive metallurgical operation carried out by Prince Sennacherib that derived from the understanding given to him by the god Nin-igi-kug, supplemented by this own thinking, (Chapter 5). This leaves the problem of how the 'god' came by this knowledge that derives from practical experience of working with the materials of the Earth. It could be that this was derived from the developments of a previous civilisation of Atlantis.

An interesting feature is that however much the experts disprove and oppose the idea of Atlantis there is an endless stream of books written about it that get a considerable response from the general public. It could be that this is because they strike a chord in the collective consciousness of humanity.

Is there an Impending Catastrophe?

The problems of whether there have been Earth catastrophes in the past and whether another one is imminent have been exhaustively surveyed by WHITE by considering; the evidence for ice ages, ice sheets and glaciation in what are now temperate or tropical regions; tropical vegetation associated with animal skeletons in now-frozen regions; the reversal of the magnetic poles; mass extinctions of animals and the frozen mammoths; the myths of destructions of past civilisations; the predictions of psychics for an imminent catastrophe; and the pro-catastrophe and anti-catastrophe theories and explanations that have been put forward to account for these phenomena. In his evaluation of this mass of data White concludes that there is no decisive evidence for or against an impending catastrophe: he was at first inclined to think that a catastrophe would happen but then he became unsure and concluded that even if there is to be a catastrophe it is not imminent. Certainly, as he points out, predictions by psychics for catastrophic events taking place in the 1980's have not come true.

Of the myths of cultures from around the world that refer to a catastrophe, or catastrophes, happening in the past and claim that this will happen again, the most precise is that of the Mayans. According to Hancock, the Mayans had an incredibly accurate and detailed knowledge of astronomy: they knew of cosmic events that happened millions of years ago and they developed calendars based on cosmic events. In their ancient sacred book, the Popul Vuh they claimed that their advanced knowledge derived from the First Men, who were endowed with intelligence by which they knew all that there is in the world. According to *h*K-M these would be members of the Omniverse Hierarchy who, on incarnating into the Earth situation retained their collective, omniscient 'God consciousness' enabling them to know what happens everywhere. The Mayans believe that the Universe operates in greater and lesser cycles and that, since the creation of the human race, there have been four cycles or 'Suns', each lasting some 4000 plus years, all of which ended in catastrophe and that we are now in the period of a fifth 'Sun' which is coming to a close and will likewise end in catastrophe. The date that they give for this ending is the 23rd December 2012, which they derive from the cosmic relationship between Venus, the Sun, the Pleiades, and Orion, which they claim determines these events; this will complete an overall 17,125 year cycle, (GILBERT and COTTERELL). Cotterell relates the Mayan's 'Sun cycles' and the accompanying catastrophic events to a reversal of the Sun's magnetic field, that causes the Earth's magnetic field to reverse. A problem with this is that the Mayan's Sun cycle epochs last about 4000 years, whereas scientists estimate that reversals of the Earth's magnetic field have usually occurred over the much longer time period of every 200,000 years. Scientists state that there hasn't been a reversal for nearly 800,000 years so that one is long overdue: they estimate that the Earth's magnetic field has steadily weakened over the past 2000 years and that in some places it has already reversed (New Scientist 13 Dec 2003) but they do not know if and when a complete reversal will occur. Other scientists have observed a recent decline of species of birds and butterflies and are wondering whether this foreshadows a sixth mass extinction comparable with five previous ones that they deduce to have happened, (ANANTHASWAMY). The problem is, what could cause a dramatic change in the working of our Solar System that results in a mass extinction of this nature? Recent sophisticated scientific analyses applying chaos theory have shown that when Jupiter and Saturn line up in front of the Sun their gravitational pull could create instability in the asteroid belt and cause an asteroid to collide with the Earth and that this could be the reason for the wiping out of the dinosaurs and other life forms 65 million years ago, CHOWN (3). Thus it appears feasible that cosmic relationships could determine the major cycles of events on Earth. (For a compilation of prophesies, data and theories relating to events in 2012 see Stray).

There are two schools of thought about the evolution of the Earth, a uniformitarian one, which claims that all the evidence can be interpreted in terms of gradual uniform development and the other that the evidence shows that catastrophes take place. According to hK-M it is fundamental to evolution that it occurs by the punctuated equilibrium principle, whereby developments take place by a striving for increased sense of self along established lines until further progress in this way is limited and then a stress builds up that brings about a catastrophic change to a new set of circumstances, when further evolution then settles down to a steady development along new lines until this runs out and there is a further catastrophic change, and so on. For example, astronomers perceive the activities of the cosmos, i.e. of galaxies and stars as taking place in a uniform way punctuated by catastrophic changes such as that which occurs when a star finishes a long period of creating atoms of a particular type and then dramatically 'blows up'.

Ancient cultures were greatly concerned with cosmic events and tracking astrological behaviour, in many cases building observatories and orientating their structures and buildings according to aspects of these that they regarded as relevant to them, because they believed that cosmic activities governed events on Earth. According to hK-M the Universe comes into existence as conglomerations of substances that interfere with the s-entities' activities, creating stresses in these which develop into self-actualising entities, that act on and thereby manipulate, the substances that they encompass. Thus all cosmic bodies comprise a self-actualising field of activity acting on a body of substance, in the way that the Earth comprises what we have designated as the Earth Entity acting on the substances of the Earth planet, with the Earth's magnetic field being one aspect of the Earth Entity's activity. (In the same way that we comprise a substance body permeated and acted on, by willing, feeling, and thinking fields of activity). The Universe comprises endless cosmic bodies and their associated fields of activities of this nature, all interacting and affecting each other. We cannot directly perceive these activities; we only become aware of them by correlating what goes on, on Earth with cosmic events, in the way that, for example, we correlate the growth of plants with the activity of the Sun, although we cannot see directly how a plant is affected by Sun activity. The reason that we cannot see directly what is going on is because we are limited in what we can observe by the nature of our sense organs that developed by biological evolution of animals and hominids, arising from the stresses and striving for sense of self and survival, and the type of understanding and consciousness that these give rise to. It would seem that in 'higher states of consciousness' possessed by members of the Omniverse Hierarchy, and occurs at times spontaneously or with suitable training by some people during Earth incarnation, it is possible to perceive directly these cosmic activities and that the 'First Men' referred to in the Popol Vuh possessed such abilities as did also some of the priest/kings of other earlier cultures and that this formed the basis of their beliefs and predictions. (We refer again to the possibility of the direct perception of cosmic activities in higher states of consciousness in relation to some of our personal experiences, reported in Chapter 18).

PART III

HOW KOSMIC-METAPHYSICS CAME ABOUT

(CHAPTERS 15 to 24)

Like all ideas, those presented in this book can be judged only by the extent to which they make sense of the facts of the situation being considered. But it is natural to want to know the background to any new ideas that we come across and what caused their authors to think in this way. For this reason, in Part III of this book we give some account of ourselves and the path that we have followed that has led to hK-M.

Chapter 15

The Beginning

The Background

It might be thought that the scheme of creation that we have set out has been arrived at as the culmination of a sustained search for such an endpoint. However, this is not so at all, we never set out to achieve this. All that we have done is to come across something interesting that led on to something else interesting, which then led onto something else, and so on. Eventually we found ourselves somehow led to this end. In this journey from one interesting thing to another we have made many fruitless digressions. Therefore we confine ourselves to the essentials of what seems, with hindsight, to have been the main path within our wanderings.

It started with two of us, Dennis (a scientist) and Ted (a technician), working together in a University on researches into scientific-technological problems and, at the same time, supervising and helping students working for doctorate degrees by original research. After a number of years we began to realise that the basic problem lay not so much in the scientific and technological problems that we were investigating, as in the creativity of the students and ourselves. So we began to take an interest in what this involved. This expansion of our interests began when we were in our mid-thirties that, at the time of completing this book is some forty five years ago.

Creative ideas arise out of the workings of the mind. So psychology is the obvious place to seek an understanding of how these come about, and it was in this direction that we first looked. But we found that psychologists have not yet been able to arrive at clear answers to the problem of how the mind works or, in fact, what the mind is. In this way we found ourselves confronting a basic problem that many people, particularly philosophers and psychologically-orientated scientists have come up against, that is, 'What exactly is the human mind?' Is it the way that the brain works, or is it something separate that uses the brain as an instrument?

Our interest in the nature and workings of the mind led us into parapsychology. This is a controversial minefield of phenomena, claims and viewpoints. However, there does seem to be substantial evidence suggesting that the mind, or personality, exists after death and before birth. There is also evidence for reincarnation and for out-of-the-body consciousness. This implies that our mind is something separate from our brain.

The Problem of Mind and the Human Aura

This then leads to the problem that if the mind is something separate, then how does it interact with the brain and body? We think of the activity of the mind as generating thoughts, which we do not regard as physical things. But if this is so, then how can something insubstantial and non-physical interact with something physical and substantial like the cells of the brain?

In taking an interest in this problem we found that a significant number of people claim to have clairvoyant powers that enable them to perceive mind activity as part of an aura of energy that permeates and surrounds the physical body, fig 15.1.

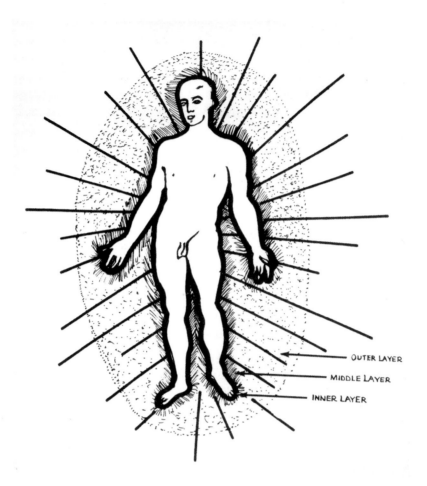

Fig. 15.1 Diagram of the human aura as perceived by the New York psychiatrist Dr. John Pierrakos. The inner part is the etheric (multicellular) activity, the oval is the astral-soul activity and the raying out is the Ego activity.

Thoughts are seen as patterns of activity in the aura with an associated activity in the brain. Furthermore, these clairvoyants claim that there are two other levels of activity in the human aura, one corresponding to our feelings and emotions and the other corresponding to our life processes. They also claim that animals possess a two-fold aura of life and sensation/feeling and that plants possess a single aura of life activity. Furthermore they claim that interactions take place between the auric fields of different entities and this implies that the 'space' between things is not empty and inert but capable of supporting this activity. It seemed to us that the evidence for auric fields and 'space activities' was sufficiently well attested to be worth investigating further and that if these activities influence substance in the brain then they might be detectable with appropriate physical experiments. The Head of the Department in which we worked had a sympathetic interest in these matters so that we were able to start experimenting in a small way as an extra-curricular activity. In looking for suitable leads into this problem we found that in the early twentieth century a French medical practitioner (Dr. H. BARADUC) had used an electro-photography technique to register an 'aura' around a hand, fig. 15.2.

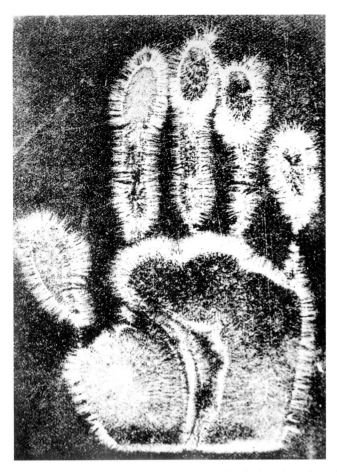

Fig.15.2 Reproduction of the registration around a hand obtained by Dr. H. Baraduc using a high voltage machine

No experimental details were given and we were unable to reproduce this result. However, while trying to do so we found an electrophotography way of registering auric-type patterns around leaves and evidence for interactions taking place in the space around them, as in figs. 15.3 to 15.8.

a   b

Fig. 15.3. Showing 'a' the type of 'etheric' aura described by clairvoyants, around a privet leaf, which we would ascribe to 'the body' of its multicellular organising activity 'b' a larger ovoid aura encompassing the leaf and its inner aura.

205

Fig.15.4 Auric phenomena registered on Ektachrome colour film: **'a'** around a privet leaf: **'b'** around clover leaves.

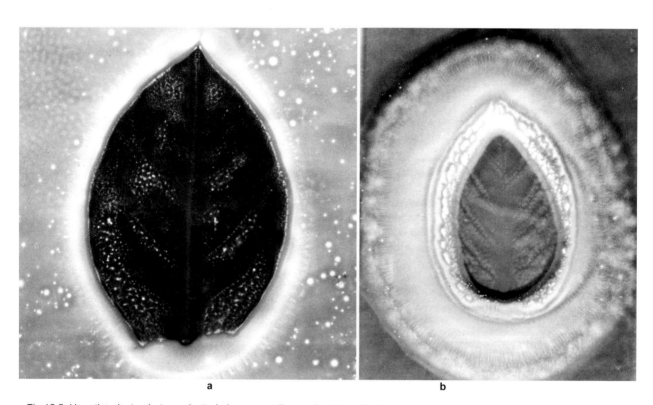

Fig.15.5 Here the electrophotography technique, as well as registering auric phenomena around the leaves, seems to have brought about emanations from them. In particular, in '**a**' bright 'globules' seem to be emanating from the privet leaf. These could relate to the descriptions by mystics and clairvoyants of 'prana' energy globules that, they claim are associated with living activity. Such 'globules' can also be seen in some of the other pictures; we deal further with this phenomenon in Chapter 25.

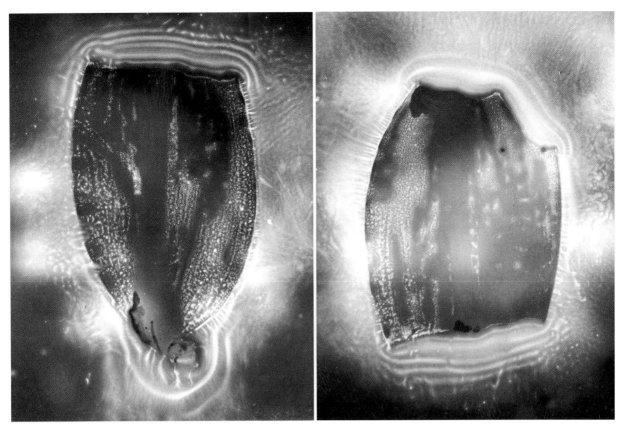

Fig. 15.6 These figures show an effect in the space energy of damaging a tradescanthia leaf.

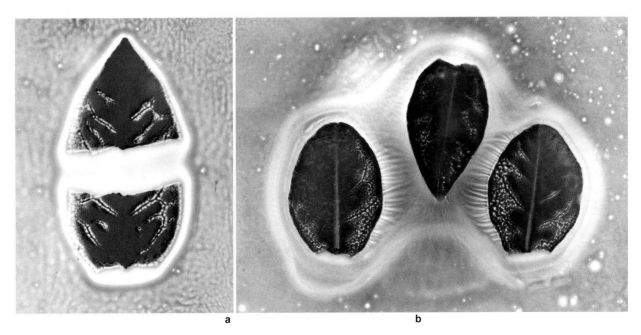

a   b

Fig.15.7 'a' Interaction between the two parts of a leaf torn in half, 'b' interaction between three privet leaves, taking place through the space energy.

Fig. 15.8 'a' Interaction between a freshly picked leaf (on the right) and a dying leaf picked twenty four hours previously, 'b' Interaction between wet filter paper and a dying leaf.

It seemed that the electrophotography technique might be registering phenomena that people claim to perceive in a heightened state of consciousness as, for example reported by the chemist, SHERWOOD-TAYLOR:

> 'on a clear sunny autumn morning I had walked into the gardens of St. John's College, Oxford: the dahlias were still in bloom and the Michaelmas daisies were covered in great butterflies, tortoise-shells, fritillaries and red admirals. Suddenly I saw the whole scene take on a new figure .... everything revealed itself as inter-connected. There was no visible link, yet around each centre of life there was an influence, as if each living thing were a centre of a spiritual medium. The vision faded after about half an hour.'

ALDOUS HUXLEY describes a change in consciousness arising from taking mescaline, in which flowers appeared 'in their living light ... and seemed to have the quality of breathing'.

These are generalised statements that suggest the existence of 'etheric activity' in space. People who possess controlled 'etheric awareness' give more extensive accounts of the etheric activity of plants. PAYNE states that etheric clouds emanate from plants, and trees are described as giving off radiations in a 'spray of bright mist' that dies down during winter. GARRETT states that plants have a 'surround' which appears to move or breath gently; space is filled with globules of light and plants and trees draw the globules into their surround and derive their colour from them. In one of the first exercises that she gives for developing higher sense perception, BRENNAN suggests lying on your back and relaxing on a sunny day, looking at the sky and seeing globules, white balls of energy, that flow into the aura around a tree.

While our experimental results might be seen as supporting the claims of clairvoyants for the presence of auric activity associated with living things and interactions in 'space', an unambiguous interpretation of them is, in fact, very difficult. So, to try to clarify the situation we simplified our experiments and we then found that, by manipulating the parameters involved in the technique a wide range of forms registered on the photographic plate, without any object being present. The fact that the experiments produced 'electrical discharge' patterns was not surprising, but the interesting thing was that they resembled forms found in plants and other organic structures, some examples of which are shown in figs. 15.9 and 15.10. At the same time part of our conventional researches had become concerned with the forms that substances take up when they solidify which, as will be seen later, also often resemble plant forms. The emphasis of our researches then changed from seeking evidence for auric fields to seeking an understanding of what gives rise to form and function in Nature.

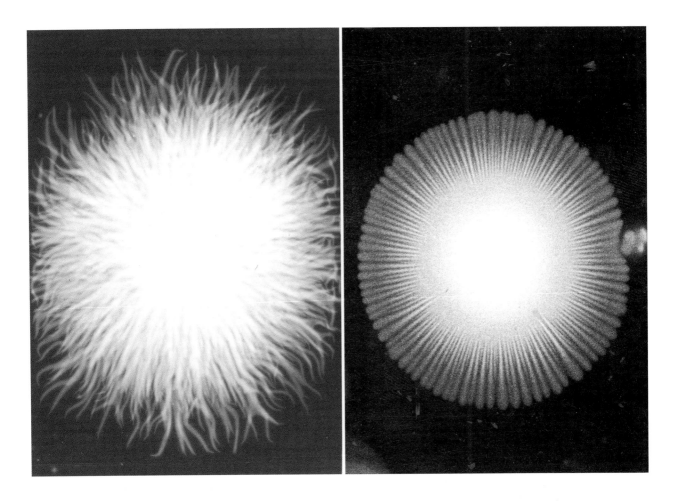

Fig.15.9 Four examples of forms that resemble flower or feather shapes created in the space energy, and registered, by the electrophotography technique.

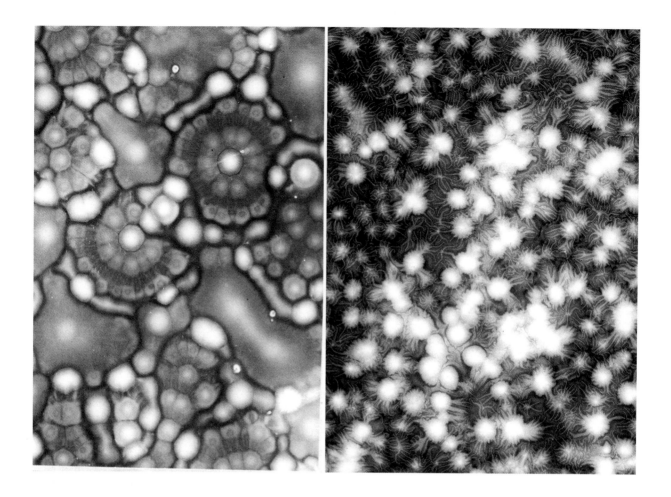

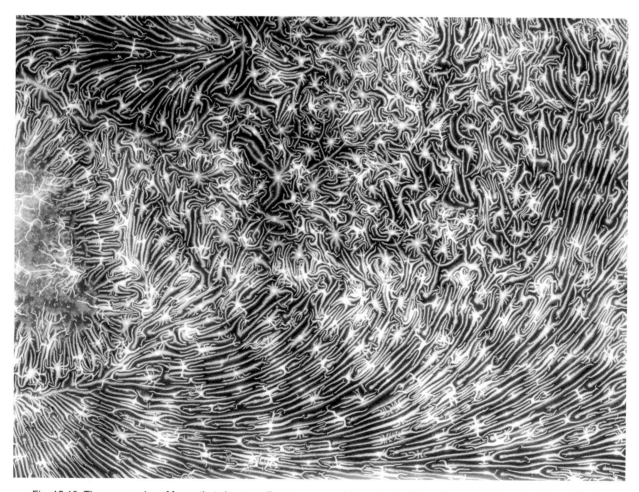

Fig. 15.10 Three examples of forms that show a rudimentary resemblance to plant formations created, and registered, by the electrophotography technique.

[An outline of the experimental investigations that gave rise to figures 15.3 to 15.10 is given in Part 4 of this book].

The Problem of Form and Function in Nature

Everywhere that we look in Nature, from the crystallisation of minerals to the shapes of living things, we see forms that are a manifestation of their natures and functioning. Modern science has been largely concerned with understanding things in terms of their basic constituents, that is, the types and amounts of atoms of which they consist. But how and why billions of atoms should come together to build up specific forms, particularly living forms that possess a variety of functions, is not at all clear. (Although genetics is part of the answer, it is very difficult to derive from the behaviour of genes within a cell, an understanding of the form and functioning of a complete organism. One would have to attribute to genes, i.e. a group of chemicals, the ability to organise form, function, feelings and consciousness). The fact that organic-type forms were produced in our experiments suggested to us that there exist some universal principles of organisation common to all kingdoms of Nature.

In the meantime, in our reading about the nature of the mind we had come across works by mystics. Because of our practical orientation these had a certain appeal to us, since they involved first-hand explorations of the workings of the mind and of different states of consciousness, and not just theorising about them. In particular some of these works give accounts of the human aura. In many cases the mystical viewpoint has an eastern origin and is expressed in concepts and terminology that we found very difficult to understand. In looking for something simpler we came across the works of the western mystic Rudolf STEINER. We found that his writings were also difficult to understand, but we could not find anything better so we then tended to use these as our basis for seeking understanding of the mystical viewpoint.

As well as dealing with the mind-aura problem Steiner also put forward the concept of four etheric forces that determine the form and function of things. This looked as though it might throw some light on the results of our experiments. But the problem was that this came as part of a cosmology in which the activities of the material world are brought about by a complex hierarchy of spiritual beings working at different levels in a 'cosmic ether'.

This all seemed very complicated and far removed from contemporary scientific thinking. But it also seemed to us that by integrating Steiner's mystical-spiritual viewpoint with the scientific materialist one, it might be possible to explain in a practical way phenomena such as mind and form and function that are not yet understood by science. To make a step in this direction we tried to order, and find some coherence in, the morass of phenomena and concepts that we had become involved in, in our studies, together with the results of the experiments we had carried out up to then, by putting them together in a book, (ref. MILNER and SMART).

In our conventional work in the Department, Dennis had been given the responsibility of developing a lecture course on the History of Humanity's use and understanding of metals and materials. This involved an account of the scientific understanding of how different substances are formed in stars and the formation and composition of the Earth, and how successive civilisations have evolved and made increasing use of these substances. This introduced an evolutionary orientation to our thinking and a need for a wholistic understanding to make sense of it all. Thus, in our book we brought together: first, the idea of Man as an essentially thinking, spiritual being who evolves through successive cultures; second, the empirical evidence for the existence of a spiritual world; third, Steiner's mystical description of how this world came about and works; fourth, an interpretation of our experimental results in terms of 'etheric force' activity.

A major problem with this attempt at a synthesis was that we had no access ourselves to the experiences of the forces and phenomena that Steiner described from his mystical viewpoint. We had to rely on his accounts and we had no means of getting further detail on aspects on which we needed clarification. In particular what Steiner had to say about etheric forces was very limited and we needed to know much more if we were to interpret satisfactorily our experimental results in these terms.

So we continued with our researches, seeking more information on what types of forms are associated with different experimental conditions. What we were doing brought us into contact with a number of people who had similar interests. Two of these, George Meek and Arthur Twitchell of Life Energies Research, New York, contributed helpful financial support for our researches, which would otherwise have foundered.

Then we met Mr. Andrew Wilson who had had many experiences that are not explicable by current scientific understanding, and who had set up the 'Truth Research Foundation' in the UK specifically to foster work that might lead to the 'truth'. He took an interest in what we were doing and gave us financial support for our work. However, it needed much more effort than we could put in, as an extra-mural activity, while carrying out the scientific-technological researches that were our raison d'être in the University. Fortunately our work attracted the attention of a young research worker, Dr. Brian Meredith, and a year and a half later it attracted two other young research workers, Dr. Andrew McNeil and Dr. Harry Dean, and, via Andrew Wilson, the Truth Research Foundation gave the necessary financial support that enabled them to work full time on these researches. In this way we were able to expand our researches into morphology, i.e. the forms that substances take up in physical experiments, (while looking for correlations with similar organic forms and their associated functions in Nature). With Brian, Andy and Harry's commitment, skills and enthusiasm the work moved forward much more rapidly. From then on it was a group activity and we make no effort, in our descriptions of it, to distinguish individual contributions.

Chapter 16

Experiences of Expanded Consciousness (ECEs)

As we have stated, a major problem in relating our work to Steiner's mystically derived concepts about etheric forces was that we had no direct access ourselves to this type of experience. However, one day we came across a book by GLASKIN that described a technique for achieving an expanded state of consciousness. We experimented with this technique and found that it was easy to enter into such a state and from then on it played an important part in our activities. At first the members of the group found that expanded consciousness experiences (ECEs) gave them insights into their inner, sub-conscious activities that determined their natures and behaviour. But the ECEs then developed to consider the broader issue of the human situation in general.

With the experience that the ECEs could provide light on larger issues, we sought insights into the underlying forces at work in our experiments and the ECEs responded to this. The expanded consciousness state did not allow the members of the group to perceive for themselves the workings of 'etheric forces', in the way that mystics claim to direct their consciousness, but it seemed to open up contact with a source that could answer questions about these matters. Many ECEs followed which gave an account of the origins and workings of the etheric forces in terms of Steiner's cosmology. Then a sequence of further developments led away from the detail of the workings of etheric forces and Steiner's cosmology, to portray different, seemingly more advanced, cosmologies. A number of such cosmologies were portrayed, each one having different features and leading on to yet another cosmology, in a sequence that led eventually to hK-M. Our ECEs seem to have something in common with the channelled communications that we have described in Chapter 14 but this was before these had been published and we were just experimenting with anything interesting that came along, following events where they led us.

The Expanded Consciousness Technique

The ECE technique is simple and from our experiences with ourselves and with family and friends it works with the majority of people.

The person who is to undergo an ECE lies down, relaxes and normally they would then go to sleep. However, another person who is the 'guide' stops this from happening by leading the experiencer through a series of controlled visualisations. The purpose of these is to get the experiencer to become aware of his inner (soul-feeling, spirit-thinking) activity. When this has been achieved the guide ceases to direct the proceedings and transfers the experiencer's attention to whatever is taking place spontaneously within him.

There are doubtless many ways in which this can be achieved, but we give here some details about the method that we used. First, the experiencer lies on the floor, well supported with carpet and a thick layer of foam, so that there is no physical discomfort and the distraction that this would cause. We found that the soft playing of gentle background music can help relaxation. In order to disrupt normal consciousness the guide massages an area between the eyebrows of the experiencer, with the outside edge of his closed fist, while another person massages his ankles. This continues for five minutes or so, to produce a degree of disorientation of the normal sensory impressions.

To get the inner image-forming activity going, the guide tells the experiencer to form an image of their feet and then to imagine them expanding out a few inches. They are then told to retract their feet. The next stage is to form an image of their head, imagine extending this and then retracting it. All the time the experiencer is asked by the guide to describe what is happening. These exercises are then repeated several times, with the experiencer being told to extent their feet and head further each time. When the experiencer has developed the ability to do this they are told to extend their feet to the wall of the room, keep them there and do the same with his head, and then to expand all over to fill the room.

The point of these exercises is to dissociate the experiencer's consciousness from his bodily activity. The next stage in this process is to tell the experiencer to imagine that they are standing outside their front door and describe it. As they do this the guide asks questions about the detail of the imagery, so as to reinforce the image-forming activity. Next the experiencer is asked to describe a particular feature of their garden and then to imagine that they are seeing it from above and floating up higher and higher, so that it becomes smaller and smaller, while the guide asks questions about the, now more panoramic, view that they are seeing.

The experiencer is then asked to look up and describe the sky, whether it is clear and blue or whether there are clouds about. They are then told to imagine themself floating up very high, above the clouds if they are there. When they have done this they are told to imagine the Sun going down and the night sky appearing and to describe whether the sky is bright and star-filled and whether the Moon is out. Next the experiencer is told to imagine the scene returning to daylight and to describe the scene below. Often they find that a layer of cloud exists below them. If this is not so then they are asked to change the scene back to night again and to visualise a layer of cloud forming below them and then return the scene to daylight.

The next stage is to get the experiencer away from controlled imagery to a state where the imagery follows a course of its own. This is done by telling them to descend through the cloud and describe the scene as they come out of it. We have found that the experiencer then usually perceives images that express symbolically the workings of their personal subconscious activity.

By experimenting among ourselves and with family and friends we have found a variety of responses to these exercises, depending on the psychology of the experiencer. Where a person has very active inner imagery the exercises are not necessary, on just relaxing they describe a plethora of images, which the guide can have trouble in getting to take on a disciplined coherence. In other cases the person may require several sessions with the exercises for their image-forming activity to develop. Some people experience vivid images, others get only hazy images which become clearer with practice, while some people never get clear images but have strong feelings about what is taking place. There are also different responses to the preliminary exercises; when asked to extend their feet, etc. some people find themselves outside their body and watching these things happen.

The younger members of the group tried the technique first and got some limited and not very inspiring imagery. But this was sufficient to stimulate Ted to try it, with Dennis acting as the guide. With his 'craftsman's' approach to his work Ted 'thought in images', that is, he visualised what he had in mind to make and how to do it, so that he had no difficulty in getting expanded consciousness imagery and, as a result, he entered into rewarding ECEs. With Ted showing the way forward other members of the group, Brian, Andy and Harry were also able to develop the ability to do so; Dennis took on the role of guide for the group. Each ECE lasted for two to three hours and the group organised one a week for some two years or so. As we have stated previously, the ECEs went through several phases of development. The first phase was concerned with experimenting with the technique to see what happened and we found that the ECEs portrayed the subconscious activity underlying the nature and behaviour of each of the group members; then they dealt with the human situation in general; they then responded to the group's desire to understand better the workings of the etheric forces and Steiner's cosmology.

It seemed then that, with the help of the insights gained from the ECEs, it was becoming possible to explain the group's experimental results in terms of etheric forces, while at the same time making a contribution to the further development of Steiner's cosmology. This phase of development seemed to have a degree of completeness to it and to provide a foundation on which to build further, so it was put together in a book (Explorations of Consciousness, Ed MILNER).

However, in pursuing these activities further, the more that the group tried to develop this viewpoint in greater detail the more difficult this became. Then, rather than illustrating Steiner's etheric force cosmology, the ECEs took on a different slant and portrayed a different cosmology. A lot of effort was put into trying to grasp this and to develop it in a way that could be applied to the experiment results. Again this could not be achieved and again the ECEs changed direction, to portray a series of different cosmologies and, gradually, out of these efforts there emerged the Kosmic Metaphysics on which this book has been based.

The book in which we described the first phase of our ECEs has long been out of print but, to give continuity to the story of our activities, we synopsise what happened, giving brief extracts from them, to illustrate key features. As we have stated, the group members found that their initial ECEs were concerned with their personal sub-conscious activities. These give insight into their different characters, which is important when we get to the 'channelled experiences', since these are considerably influenced by the character and outlook of the individual concerned. Only key snippets are given of the group members' first ECEs, which were very extensive and rambling, with a lot of extraneous material, as the experiencer and the guide tried to make sense of what was going on. We begin with Ted's first experience that started it all off.

Ted's First ECEs

Ted had no difficulty with the preliminary image-forming exercises and as he came down through the cloud the guide asked him to describe what he saw: (T: Ted, G: guide).

T: Rather pleasant country, meadows and woodland with a road running through it.

A path or road through countryside is a common first image that offers the experiencer the opportunity of making a journey through the country of his subconscious, so the guide encourages this and tries to help him firm up the experience by asking him to describe the imagery:

G: What time of year is it?
T: It seems to be Spring or early Summer - everything is in leaf and the greens are still quite vivid -- Now I'm walking along a road between hedges.
G: What have you got on your feet?
T: Difficult to make out -- black, fairly pointed shoes as far as I can see.
G: What sort of trousers have you got on?
T: Mm, I think they're shorts, I appear to have bare knees and socks below.
G: What colour are the socks?
T: Oh, those horrible multi-coloured golfing socks, plaid pattern, almost knee high.
G: How old would you say you are?
T: 'Teens or twenties I would think.

His youthfulness indicates that Ted is on an inner journey which is concerned with an aspect of his nature relating to an earlier stage of development, (at the time of this ECE Ted was in his early fifties). It is something to do with a part of him concerned with walking his path through life that needs sorting out, or harmonising, symbolised by the bizarre socks and footwear.

G: Where are you going to?
T: I think I'm just out walking.
G: Where have you come from?
T: From the isolated house that stands on a hill --- Now I'm standing outside the house looking at it.
G: Describe it: what is it built of?
T: It seems to be a sand-stone texture, a square solidly-built house, that stands on a hill with no attempt at all to shelter it.

Through these questions the guide has attempted to establish the nature of the journey. Clearly the destination is not important, as asking about this yielded an answer of no significance. The concern is with the conditions at the start of the journey, since this question activated new imagery. As we go through life we build for ourselves a personality, a dwelling place or house, within which we live. The objective of the experience is to show Ted something about his dwelling place or personality. The guide therefore seeks further information about the nature of the house.

G: Can you see the front door of the house?
T: It's of dark wood with a rounded top to it. It's got a lift-up country-type latch.
G: Well lift up the latch, go in and let's have a look around.
T: Yes, OK -- Oh, the door opens outwards --- The ground floor seems to be just one big room. There's a staircase towards the back of the house that is indistinct.
G: Is there any furniture in the room?
T: Two plain wooden Windsor armchairs - no cushions or anything - one on either side of the fireplace and a white-topped table in front of the fireplace.

It's a good solid house, well sited, with the front door opening out on the world; the ground floor is equipped functionally without sophistication, which symbolises Ted's character.

G: Right, now can you go up the stairs?
T: (After a long pause). Yes, (hesitantly) the staircase is narrower than it looked at first -- as I go up the stairs they narrow rapidly and I get to a small landing and they turn through a right angle. I think there is a window on this landing but I can't see through it. I go on up the stairs --- (Ted is clearly experiencing some sort of difficulty) it gets narrower with a small archway at the top -- I have to crouch to squeeze through it -- (Silence, the Guide wonders what is happening).
G: Are you through it?
T: Yes.
G: What's on the other side then?

T: Again the whole floor is just one room; it seems to be dark -- there doesn't appear to be any windows.

The imagery is here showing Ted that he finds it difficult to get into his 'upper storey' and that illumination is not active there. The scene then changes to show Ted why this situation exists.

G: (After long pause). Where are you now? Are you still in the house?
T: I don't think so --- I seem to be wearing what I can only describe as old sacking for clothing. I seem isolated somewhere -- I can't make anything out -- it's quite dark.
G: Why are you wearing this sacking material and why are you in the dark on your own?
T: I don't know -- I think I do it from choice -- I don't think it's anything that's been forced on me, there doesn't appear to be anyone else involved.
G: Do you want to stay there?
T: No -- No -- I think I'll try and move from here.
G: What do you have to do to move?
T: It seems dead easy -- I just think of moving and I seem to move.
G: Are you walking along the road again?
T: I seem to be floating above it, looking down into the trees and hedges. There are plenty of birds and nests with eggs in, and nests with young birds being fed by parents.
G: Can you carry on further down this road and see where it leads to?
T: No. I'm back in the cloud and I can't see anything.

This imagery is telling Ted that the reason why he finds it difficult to get into, and to illuminate, his upper storey is a self imposed one. In this aspect of his nature he has put himself into sackcloth and ashes, and darkness and solitude. When he became a technician in a University, (in his twenties), surrounded by people with academic qualifications Ted had told himself that he was not clever, like these other 'clever people'. When asked about the possibility of moving from this situation Ted finds that all he has to do is to want to do so, and that if he so frees himself he can pursue his path through life at a higher level of creative activity, symbolised by the birds and the hatching eggs. Once the imagery has conveyed the intended message it fades away.

This imagery was not new to Ted, on a number of occasions in dreams he had been faced with the dark narrow passage at the top of the stairs. But, at the dim level of consciousness and the lack of control in the dream world, the experience had been rather frightening. When he experienced the same imagery in the expanded consciousness state he was well aware that he was in control of the situation and there was also a guide to support him, so that he had no difficulty in going through the dark narrow archway and exploring its significance. When asked why he saw himself dressed in sackcloth he knew immediately the reason - that it was self imposed. It is a characteristic of the ECE state that the experiencer can often answer questions with greater insight and wisdom than in normal consciousness.

Ted had no difficulty in recognising the facet of his nature that had been portrayed to him in this ECE, showing him a self-imposed feeling of inferiority. In a subsequent ECE Ted was shown that, rather than being limited in his 'upper storey', he possessed a deeply rooted, very valuable, but neglected, intuitive faculty. In this ECE Ted seemed to be a member of a primitive tribe in a time long, long ago. He possessed, through some intuitive means, an awareness of the healing (or poisonous) properties of plants that he conveyed to the rest of the tribe; he was also responsible for making fire, and for guarding the dead until they could be buried (under a pile of stones). When Ted ceased to have imagery of his activities with the primitive tribe the guide asked:

G: Where are you now?
T: I'm outside the square stone house -- I go into the house and I've gone straight to the stairs, expecting to find a narrowing staircase but there's a normal flight of stairs which just go straight up to a landing. There are three or four doors off the landing -- before, this was very narrow with a tight archway -- that's gone and I know which door I want to go through -- I just go into this room, it was a very dark room but it's not any longer. There are windows that are open, it's sunny outside. There are bookshelves, lots of books. I can see through to a valley, rhododendrons are in bloom and there's a river that meanders along the bottom of the valley ----- Now I'm back in the mist.

This imagery shows that Ted's intuitive faculty can bring light into his upper story and give him knowledge and understanding - symbolised by the books; his subconscious intuition, freely flowing (as the river) can produce growth and blossoming of his nature (the rhododendrons).

After these personal ECEs, Ted's further ECEs were more far-reaching and concerned with the group as a whole. At one stage when Dennis and Ted had amassed some potentially significant results from their experiments but could not fathom their meaning, Ted had a fleeting dream image of a clogged-up sparking plug, which he felt was relevant. So, in his next ECE Dennis took this as a starting point.

G: See if you can visualise the sparking plug.
T: Yes -- I'm holding it and I'm wearing overalls -- it comes off a high-performance engine, it looks like an aero plug.

Ted had been a Flight Engineer (with some navigational experience) in the RAF. In the imagery he found himself servicing the engines of an RAF aircraft to find out what had caused the sparking plug to become clogged up and to correct the problem. The imagery was extensive and detailed and when Ted had done what was necessary to get all the engines running properly, he said:

T: Now I can see the rest of the crew, we're all dressed to fly -- I've just found out that I've got to fly as navigator and flight engineer for this trip. We're going across the channel, we're going into Germany somewhere, it's a training flight ---- it's disappeared -- I'm back in mist again.

The clogged-up sparking plug we see as symbolising the spark of creative insight that was missing in our work. The aircraft, as the vehicle of flight, is a symbol of the activity of ideation - the flight of ideas. It has to cross the channel of subconscious activity, so as to explore the foreign country on the other side. The crew are the members of the group. Ted has the role of Flight Engineer and Navigator to the group, i.e. he has the responsibility to 'engineer' the flight and to chart the direction for the group to travel.

In his next ECE Ted felt from the beginning that it was related to the group and not just to himself. After the preliminary exercises he came down on the coast, which represents the meeting point between the sea of subconscious activity and the land of firm, rational conscious understanding.

T: It looks like a typical storm beach backed by sand dunes It's very warm, very pleasant -- I think I'll go into the sand dunes -- there are extensive patches of marram grass, lots of footprints of wild life, birds' prints, rabbits' and ducks' prints.
G: Why are you in the sand dunes?
T: Don't know -- no clear reason -- a feeling that the sand dunes lie between two places, somewhere I've come from, somewhere I'm going to. I'm at the foot of a very tall sand dune, I need to get up a little way -- Now I can see the coast and I'm heading for a fishing port, with lots of deep-sea trawlers -- Mm -- this is what I've come this way for, to get on one of these boats.

The first imagery of the coast and sand dunes (very much more extensive than the extracts given here) represents virgin territory to be explored, i.e. a new venture for Ted. The deep-sea trawlers represent in-depth exploration of the sea of subconscious activity.

T: I knew that if I made the right contact on the quay I could get onto one of these boats.
G: Who have you contacted on the quay then?
T: The skipper of a trawler. He says I can go if I want to, they do take people but they have to be prepared to work for part of the time, it's not a passenger trip -- he says the sort of thing they've done before is to take people who have written or reported about the trips. I don't want to do that, it's the working side that appeals -- in fact I'm already aboard --- Everyone in the crew is beavering away, quietly preparing for something which lies in the future. There's a fairly steep swell but the boat feels perfectly safe --- it is moving very slowly with the trawl streaming out behind it ---- Now they've started to heave the trawl in. Smaller fish escape through the meshes but the sizeable fish are retained -- Ah -- that's a surprise, I expected the net to come up full, in fact it's quite small and it holds four beautiful bright fish.
G: What's beautiful about them?
T: They're silvery, bright, fresh, absolutely living, brim full of life -- everyone seems extremely happy. They explain that they never take more than two of the fish normally, to take four is unusual. The skipper says we've got more than he expected to get and what we've got is extremely well worthwhile --- Now we're back in the fishing port and lots of people come to admire the fish, everyone's placing a great deal of emphasis on the fact that four were caught by this one boat -- the skipper says he's glad I chose his boat to go with, he seems to think somehow I'm responsible for the fact that they caught this number of these fish, but I had nothing to do with it, I just watched.

At the end of this ECE we could not perceive the significance of the fish. Ted felt that he in particular had in some way failed and missed something in his imagery which would have resolved this problem, so one day he relaxed and visualised himself back on the fishing trip and he asked the skipper of the boat:

T: What is the significance of the fish?
Sk: They are a gift -- cherish them.

T: When shall we know the significance of them?
Sk: All will be revealed eventually.

In the light of what ensued we interpret the four fish as symbolising the fact that four of the group members developed the ability to explore the depths of subconscious activity. By using his intuitive abilities in this way, Ted played a central role in guiding the other members of the group into rewarding ECEs and in the developments that led eventually to *h*K-M. This raises the problem of where Ted got his intuitive faculty from? Whereas most of the ECEs were clearly symbolic imagery, the one in which Ted was shown his role in a primitive tribe was much more realistic, as though he could be reliving experiences from a past incarnation, in which he developed this faculty.

This, however, leaves the problem of what is happening during an ECE. When we 'see' something, in our daily existence, we form an image of it and we relate this to a 'memory store' that we have built up of previous images that we have formed of the same, or similar, things, by which we recognise and put into context what we see. We can also manipulate our store of images. Thus, as with Ted's craftsman's activity, when we work out how we are going to do something we do so by recalling images of what is involved and, in our imagination, suitably modify these to achieve a desired result. In this way we create a living imaginative activity within us.

Our imaginative activity is not, however, limited to our relationships with the physical world, it is affected by our emotional and mental lives. Thus, when we see something, not only do we physically recognise it but we have feelings about it. And these feelings, or emotions may bring about a recall of images of earlier incidents that resulted in similar emotions. Similarly, we may see something done that activates images of something similar which we thought of doing. In this way, images can relate to, or even portray, emotions and thoughts.

Our imaginative activity also works independently of our conscious control of it, as in dreams when we are asleep. Sometimes dreams may be particularly clear (lucid dreams) with their imagery symbolising our inner state of development. A simple example, quoted by JUNG, was of a man of humble origins who had attained a comparatively high position in life and was then offered the opportunity of yet further advancement. He experienced a degree of anxiety and dreamed that he was going to catch a train, but he could not gather his baggage together, so that he got to the station in time only to see the train go out. As the train gathered speed he saw that it lost contact with the rails and crashed in catastrophe. Jung's interpretation of this dream was that, in progressing from his humble beginnings to his higher position in life, the man had not acquired the baggage, i.e. the personal equipment, necessary to tackle the proposed 'more advanced journey' in his profession. He, in fact, took the job and, as predicted by the dream, he went violently off track and cracked up. This type of dream imagery guidance can occur particularly when we are in a state of stress and have problems to resolve, or when a change of direction would be beneficial in our life. Depth psychologists, such as Jung, have concluded from these sorts of experiences, that behind each of us there is a 'Higher Self' of greater wisdom which can offer us guidance in life. It was Ted's 'Higher Self' which we think was responsible for showing him the 'lack of light' in his upper storey. Ted had had a little of this imagery in dreams but had not realised its significance; his ECE allowed the 'message' to unfold much more fully and clearly.

The problem is, what is the 'Higher Self' that seeks to help and guide us? According to *h*K-M, after the evolution of hominids on Earth, members of the Omniverse Hierarchy incarnate and reincarnate into hominid bodies to obtain the experiences that Earth existence has to offer, for their further development. Thus, behind each of us, on a different plane of existence, there lies an entity that is accumulating the experiences of its different incarnations. This has a much clearer picture of our situation than we have, and it is in a position to offer guidance and help. This, we think is the 'Higher Self' of depth psychologists.

Because our Higher Self exists in the universal spiritual world, which is concerned with the totality of existence, its guidance is often in terms of abstract, universal principles, rather than in details specific to our particular situation. This then acts on our store of imagery, in much the same way that if we read a book this conjures up images from our past experience, so that we absorb the information in terms which are meaningful to us. But because it originates as abstract principles, the imagery is symbolic and we then have the problem of interpreting it. We have found that, while some of the symbols require a specific interpretation relevant to the individual concerned, much of it is universal. Thus a house tends to represent the character that the person has built for him/herself. Water tends to represent the unformed, unconscious condition; e.g., the ocean as what is universally unconscious to humanity; a river as the flow of unconscious activity through the person undergoing the ECE. Where spiritual guidance is portrayed as coming from a source this is often symbolised as a monk figure. Animals often figure in the symbology, e.g., birds representing flights of imagination or ideation, lions as courage, sheep as a routine but non-striving character, slippery, slimy creatures as hidden shameful characteristics, domesticated animals, such as cats, dogs and horses as primitive, unconscious energies that have been brought under control. Sometimes, in the ECE state, the contact is more direct, in that people hear a 'voice' that gives them guidance. This, of course, is not to say that all inner images and voices are positive guidance. Sometimes these activities can run amok, creating an inner world of fantasy; psychedelic drugs can cause this to happen. Inner images, or voices, may even try to exert a negative influence on our actions. In all cases there is a need to subject these inner experiences to the same rational evaluation that we give to our 'outer' experiences of the world around us.

[It may be thought that inner imagery comes purely from one's imagination, that is, something that one imagines for oneself. But Ted, (and the other group members) found that where their imagery was from their own imaginations they could change it at will, but not where it was seemingly from an 'outside source'. After a few ECEs they learnt not to let their own feelings, thoughts and imaginations intrude, (we describe how this happened later)].

The concept of a Higher Self having a greater understanding of, and giving guidance on, one's personal development, does not, however, account for those of Ted's ECEs that seemed to relate to the activities of the group as a whole, e.g. the skipper on the fishing trip. As we will see later, this is an example of where Ted, and all the other group members moved into an ECE mode where their imagery was more universal, than personal, in nature.

Brian's First ECEs

As stated previously, when Brian first tried the ECE technique he got only a few, desultory images but after Ted had shown what could happen he had very extensive and prolific ECEs. At this time Brian was in his late twenties. He has a great love of Nature and of sensuously enjoying the warmth of the Sun, the feel of the air, the sight of the sea and beautiful countryside. Despite his intellectual training at University he works out of his inspirations and he likes to be unconstrained and free. Brian's early ECEs were very long and we can give here only a few snippets from them. In the first of these, as Brian descended through cloud the guide asked:

G: What does the ground look like below you?
B: It's forest -- It's a bright sunny day -- there's a forestry commission road made of chippings. I walk along the road and it's very pleasant -- there are birds singing -- I come to a bridge, there's a big stretch of water to the left and right. The road goes up the other side -- there's a donkey walking along the road with a man leading it -- I've just gone past them, they were going slowly and I'm going quite fast.
G: What have you got on your feet?
B: I'm not actually walking -- I'm sort of flying along, but I'm quite upright -- and I can't really see my feet.
G: Can you see what you're wearing? Trousers? Shirt?
B: Yes, I've got floppy khaki trousers on -- nice and cool because as you go along the breeze flaps on them -- and a white cotton shirt.
G: How old are you?
B: About eighteen I think -- young --- I just saw some heather and then I was lying in it -- there's a smell of damp rotting heather, but it's a nice smell -- musty -- and the sky is very clear and there are swifts chasing around, circling --- I'll get up now and go on -- there's a man on a white horse on the horizon --- I go up to the horse and get on it -- the man has gone now.
G: Now what are you doing?
B: We're flying again.
G: On the horse?
B: Yes we're going right up in the air. It's an immensely strong creature and it's galloping, its muscles are pounding very strenuously --- We've come down by the sea now and we're zooming along in the surf -- Now we've come to a tunnel in the cliff. The horse is carrying me along and the tunnel comes out on the top of the cliff --- the Sun is setting.
G: What's happening now?
B: The horse is tired -- there's a farmhouse with a light on and a barn with hay in it. I put the horse in there. I come out and knock on the door -- There's a lady wearing an apron, she says to come inside. Ah, she's brought me some soup -- Oh, it's very hot salty soup, I wonder why she has put too much salt in it --- the soup is cooler now and I've finished it. There were some crunchy bits at the bottom as if there was earth in the soup (long pause).
G: Now what's happening?
B: I think I'm going to sleep -- Yes, I'm lying on the floor. I'm going to sleep.

At this point Brian's subconscious activity went to sleep and he 'woke up', i.e. he came back to normal consciousness. In this experience Brian finds himself on a journey, symbolising journeying into his inner life. He crosses the flow of the subconscious (the water) and is shown different parts of his nature. He is shown that he does not plod through life in a steady, down-to-earth way (like a donkey) but floats along 'up in the air'. He loves the sensuous experience of the countryside - this aspect of his character is eighteen years of age -- an age when primal nature forces are very strong in us. Brian is then shown the strength of this side of nature in the symbol of the powerful white horse which is the 'domesticated energy' that underlies his activities - his 'up in the air' attitude to life - at the boundary between sea and land (the region where we gain insights from the sea of subconscious activity and form them into solid understanding) and the energy that carries him through the 'tunnel of confinement' of earth-bound experiences.

While this is a good driving force when we are eighteen it needs to be transformed into a more mature inner strength as we get older. Brian is led to a farmhouse - the symbol for the centre of growth on Earth - to an older woman who represents a more mature feminine-feeling activity. She gives him sustenance for growth - the soup, and she puts extra salt and earth in it, which she feels he needs to bring him more down to earth.

In Brian's next ECE he comes out of the cloud to descend to an island with a hill on it that he climbs, this changes to a mountain and he follows a path down the mountain to a town where he wanders around observing various activities. Then he leaves the town by a road that leads to a river on which there's a man with a boat that he gets into.

B: He's rowing me downstream. We go round a bend -- he says, 'You know you've got to get down to it'.
G: What sort of a man is he?
B: A fatherly character -- he's a firm man but benevolent, he's not a harsh man. We've landed on a bank in a grassy meadow -- he's gone off now and left me in this field --- There's a wood that comes down into this field with a path that goes through it up a slope. But I don't feel like going up there, I think I'll sit in this field -- it's a very pleasant place because it has very tall grass -- very cool, green -- smashing smell to it -- I'm grubbing about in it having a nice time, I ought to go up into the wood - in fact I'll do that, it's just that it was very nice in the field. Anyway I get up now and I go, 'Cough, cough', to myself. I pull my jacket down and I'm climbing this path in a rather determined fashion now, having messed about for a bit.

Brian is taken across the river, the flow of unconscious activity, into the country beyond by a boatman who tells him that he has got to get down to it (i.e. sorting out his inner life and impulses). But first Brian cannot resist having a bit of a lark about, enjoying experiencing the countryside that he finds himself in. However, he then moves on to explore an area of confusion (wood) in his subconscious.

B: The path runs diagonally up the wood --- Cor blimey!
G: What's that?
B: Well, you get out on to the top and there's a man -- he's like a Druid. He's all hairy -- he's got a white flowing garment down to the ground and a long white beard. He's pointing with a rod to go along the top of this wooded escarpment that I've just climbed up. He's a stern man. He knows you see.

The Druid is a symbol for the Nature wisdom that Brian could develop by seeking a deeper understanding in his appreciation of Nature and for the need to insert a sense of direction into his life to do this.

G: Well, don't you think you'd better go the way he says?
B: Yes ---- Ah ---- well --- there's a castle. That's where I'm going. Now I bang on this door with the butt of a sword --- there's a lady in white who opens it.

While a house symbolises the nature of the personality that one has developed, the castle represents the collective of ones inner potentials. The sword with which Brian bangs on the door represents his resolve to do something about his situation. The lady now appears in a different guise (Brian felt she was the same lady as in the farmhouse experience). She, the feminine feeling-soul figure is going to show him around the castle.

B: I go inside and there's a big round cobbled courtyard -- I'm familiar with the place, but I don't live there -- There are lots of doors off the courtyard -- I open one door, and there's a clown inside who says, 'Boo', so I shut it -- and I open another door and it seems there's a hole in the side of the castle because you can look out across this extraordinary vista --- Oh --- the sky looks so blue; I've never seen such a blue sky and oh --- there are birds flying off --- There's a beautiful golden light everywhere -- I just want to look at it -- it makes your heart thump it's so beautiful ---- But enough of that, I open the next door and there's quite a dark room -- no windows -- dead solid square walls, with a thick table in the middle of it. I don't want to go in there -- I've shut that door -- There are all sorts of other doors as well but I don't want to look in those.

220

Brian has had a look at three of his inner qualities, firstly the clown, secondly his intuitive appreciation of Nature and thirdly, the room with the table where you get down to disciplined work. There isn't much light or activity there and he doesn't really want to know about that place. Now the lady appears again:

B: The lady has taken me by the hand and we go through a door at the other end, outside onto a parapet. We're looking out over this view. It's not the same view as when I was looking out of the window before but it's very nice and she says, 'Look at that, now isn't that nice?' It's just countryside. It's wooded -- no roads -- idyllic, and it's growing -- it's just got growing potential -- and she says, 'Look at that' and 'Breathe it in'.
G: Why does she tell you to breathe it in.
B: Because it has goodness -- anyway she says, 'You can have too much of that'. So I'm leaving now.

Brian is shown that there is great potential in him for growth, then the time has come for him to leave the castle and get on with his journey.

G: Where are you going?
B: Down the hill -- aimlessly -- there are all these vague possibilities of where I can go and I don't have any inclination to take any particular direction. I'm going downhill until something crops up and then I'll follow that --- Well, now there's a cave with a hermit who's pointing again. He says that I ought to go along the path to the right, a sandy path through the pine trees.

The hermit in the cave symbolises the ability to live out of one's own inner resources and he points the direction for Brian to take.

B: So I say, 'All right' and I stick my hands in my pockets, I'm sort of whistling and jigging along. Oh, they're getting a bit fed up with me -- they've got stern faces and they say, 'Look, stop larking about' --- The white horse has appeared on the path and he whispers in my ear, 'Gold' -- he's a great friend of mine actually -- we're walking along together.
G: What is the significance of this white horse?
B: Well, he seems to be a steadying influence. I want to lark about but he's a very understanding character and he doesn't say not to lark about but he's telling me I've got to slow down -- and I've got to make an effort -- I think when he said 'Gold' it could mean that I might get some-thing worthwhile if I did as he told me to --- We've stopped going along and we've sat down. He's a bit of a larker-about himself -- he's rolling about on the grass with his feet up in the air. When you lie down in the grass and kick your feet up in the air it's smashing -- you get a lovely feeling of vigour and it's good to do it. But that's just something you do in small bursts, it's not a thing to do all the time. Now it's time to rest --- We're in a field that looks down over the countryside and it's the end of the day. He's galloped around and now he says, 'Well you know what to do'.
G: And do you know what to do?
B: Yes -- I've got to slow down -- I'm too frisky for him -- I need to be slower and calmer and I need to concentrate. Anyway he's gone now and I'm just lying on the grass where we've been talking.

Essentially the message is that if Brian slows down and concentrates he can metamorphose the primal-nature forces in his character into a rich achievement - gold - the fulfilment of his potential.

In his next ECE Brian finds himself in a simple, one-roomed, stone hut that, like the hermit, symbolises the ability to live out of his own resources. There's a track outside which he follows. He sees the lady in white and the horse and they greet him as he passes them. Then he comes to a mountain that he 'falls into'.

B: I have this feeling of being very deep inside a mountain.
G: Well, presumably you've come here to be shown something, ask -- are you being shown something?
B: Right. I'll ask --- SOLIDITY! This whole cavern rang with a great booming word --- SOLIDITY! --- Now I have a picture of a background 'stuff'. I feel it's what will become all things. This stuff has become gas and this stuff has become rock, because it has been acted upon and transformed into these things.

At this stage Brian (and the rest of the group) were struggling to correlate Steiner's etheric force concepts with the findings of science about the basic nature of substances. This produced a response in this ECE, which presented Brian with a lengthy account of how solid rock forms out of an initially inert ether. However, he found it very difficult to 'see' clearly what was being conveyed in the ECE and to discriminate between what he was being shown and his own ideas on these matters. Furthermore he felt that his imagery was at a low level.

B: The problem is my ability to see it properly -- You see I'm just getting low level images.

Brian had several more ECEs like the one on solidity, where he felt that there was a problem in his ability to 'see things clearly' in the ECE state and then after one of these the white lady appeared:

B: The white lady says, 'You're a silly old fool, it was a simple situation and you managed to confuse it'. She tells me to stop thinking. She says, 'It's the simplest thing.' She can't understand why I make it so difficult for myself, because it's easy.

In his next ECE Brian decided that he wanted to contact his Higher Self so as to improve his ability to 'see' in the ECE state:

B: I'm soaring about in air currents above the deepest and most beautiful valley I've ever seen. This is leading me to a throne where there are two seats. There's a very powerful reddy-gold being in one. I can't see a face or anything, just a presence. I sit down in the other seat. I'm a bit overwhelmed -- But the 'presence' is just chatting about the splendour of the place that we live in.
G: You and this presence live there?
B: Yes. It's as if I'd come to take up residence there -- It says, 'I'm your Father' --- Now he's picked me up and he's carrying me in his arms like a baby. We've gone into a room where there's a table with a crystal ball. He says, 'Well go on then, look into it' --- So I look in and see a monsterish pair of eyes looking back at me. The veins stand out making them look rather maniacal. He says, 'That's what you get for trying too hard, strained eyeballs' --- I now see a pond.
G: What does he say that signifies?
B: Calmness --- Now I see a herd of galloping stallions.
G: What does that signify?
B: Activity, thrusting --- Now I see a stick.
G: Ask him what that signifies?
B: He says, 'That's for clouting you with' --- Now I see a jewel -- He says, 'That's the prize I dangle in front of your nose. That's the incentive, something of value'. With that he gave me a push and said, 'Now you know', and I slid off.

In this ECE Brian is shown that he strives too hard, needs to relax and develop inner calmness and that he has lots of energy but that it is uncontrolled, like a herd of stallions. And that to get him to go in the right direction his Higher Self has to both 'clout' him and entice him. As a result of this experience Brian decided that he wanted to become a more 'passive channel', which led to a different beginning to his next ECE:

B: I feel very dizzy --- It feels as if I'm falling past lots of windows and I'm looking at my reflection in them, so that I see myself as a very jerky, falling something. At the same time my feet are being pulled round to the right.
G: Ask the significance of this.
B: 'Tearing', it says, tearing me out --- I've landed in a plain with a post. It's a cross with my Ego stuck to it with a dagger.
G: Is it that your Ego is being torn out of you to make you free?
B: Yes, it says, 'Free' --- There are now two of me. There's one who's stood up and this one is grey. There's another me lying on the ground pulsating. And there's a third me that's watching the two others.
G: Is the third me your connection with your Higher Self?
B: I don't know how to get hold of my Higher Self -- So I've made an image of the orange being that I saw last time and I'm addressing him. And he said, 'It is you, you are free'. You can ask me now.

In his new, free, state Brian sought help in understanding his experiments (at that time on liquid flow patterns in filter paper). However, instead of receiving specific information on these experiments, he was given a lecture by a 'Teacher' on the nature and behaviour of liquids, as a basis for this understanding. Brian was shown the behaviour of liquids in a series of archetypal situations and he was able to 'get inside' them and experience what was taking place. Questions that he and the guide asked were answered with clarity and precision. This went on for over two hours and when it became clear that Brian and the guide could not absorb any more information the lecture came to an end with Brian's final image being:

B: Well, he had a book open on his lap, and he just shut the book and stood up. He got up off his chair and walked out. He ruffled my hair as he left, patted me on the shoulder, saying, 'That's enough for now'.

The unrealised potential in his nature, that Ted was shown, and the various aspects of his character that pulled him in different directions, that Brian was shown, are problems that exist in all of us. This is what we have to live with and work out, on the path to becoming more evolved and integrated persons. But we also have a Higher Self that can lead us forward in our development and this has a broader view of our situation and is able to contact sources of greater wisdom. But in order to relate to our Higher Self, in the ECE state, we have to set aside our ego feelings and Ego thoughts. Ted, after freeing his intuitive faculty did this automatically, since he did not trust his feelings and his ability to think about things, so that, where these intruded into his ECEs, he shut them out. Brian, with his highly-active nature, had to make a much greater effort to slow down and concentrate on what was being presented during his ECEs, so as not to intrude his ego feelings and Ego thoughts.

Andy's First ECEs

Whereas Ted was shown that he had a self-imposed subconscious barrier to developing his potential and Brian was shown that he needed to discipline the subconscious activities at work in him, Andy was shown that he had problems from his early years that he needed to sort out. At this stage Andy, like Brian, was in his late twenties. His ECEs were very long and slow and tentative as he was gradually brought face to face with the, somewhat unpleasant, experiences that he was shown he had to deal with. Here we present a few key snippets. After descending through the cloud Andy said:

A: I see myself on a sloping area of countryside, in long grass -- There 's a hint of a path -- I feel like taking a walk down this path.
G: Right. Start walking along the path, what sort of scenery is there around you?
A: I've come to a brick and stone bridge over a river and I'm standing on the bridge looking upstream and the sun is shining on me. The down-stream side is darker and cooler. I don't want to go on the downstream side, I want to be upstream where it is sunny.

The river represents the flow of Andy's subconscious activity. He prefers looking upstream, i.e. to the future that looks bright and hopeful. He sees a darkness and coldness in what has already flowed through. This indicates a dark area in his subconscious relating to his past life, that needs sorting out. The imagery then becomes confused but the bridge seems to be the central feature, so Andy tries to get a clearer image of it and it then changes:

A: Other things are dim but the bridge is clearer -- Ah -- Um I think we've got a railway bridge here. As I look to the left a tunnel has appeared in the hillside -- it's a big tunnel or perhaps I've got smaller -- I'm standing at the edge of this tunnel feeling a bit small -- it's as though I've shrunk a bit.

There seems to be a dark tunnel associated with Andy's past that reduces him in stature. But, in this ECE he feels that this is not the time to explore it. Instead he climbs the hill and meets a jolly monk figure that joins him. This symbolises Andy reaching up to a higher, but nevertheless down-to-earth, spiritual part of his nature to help him on his journey. He then goes on a walk through pleasant countryside where at first he gets lost but then finds the path that he has to follow. This leads him to a very simple hut in an open moorland area, with a stream and forest nearby.

A: I'm very conscious of everything being open. Ah, that's why the hut is out in the open, there's nothing to hide and the moorland, this hut - which is mine, the brook, the forest are all there under the sky. And it's very lovely. Other things could appear but I don't want to see any more.

Here Andy is shown his ability to live out of his own resources and that nothing needs to be hidden away (suppressed) - everything can be brought out into the open. This is as far as the 'message' goes in this ECE. In his next ECE Andy comes down at the same point as in the first one but he takes a different path. He is dressed as a hiker and he goes through a wood and emerges into strong sunlight which at first he finds difficult to bear. The wood is an area of confusion (suppressed, unresolved past experiences), in his subconscious but he is used to it and feels at home in it and finds it difficult to cope with the idea of having this part of his nature exposed. However, he feels himself harden up (he says, like an insect that has come out of a cocoon) and he proceeds on his way. He walks through some lovely countryside and then the imagery becomes unstable until again he finds himself confronted by a tunnel:

A: I'm going down a cobbled roadway to a canal - I see a tunnel ahead of me.
G: Do you have to go into it?
A: I feel as though I do. I can go and do other things, but sooner or later I have to go and look in the tunnel - -- It seems a low tunnel so you've got to bend over a bit to get in. There's a railing so that you can't fall into the water -- The water is inky black -- it is surging up and washing over my feet -- I don't like it but it doesn't somehow seem to make them wet --- I'm pulling myself along and the tunnel is getting bigger, easier to get through and I can see the light. In fact I've just come out, it's quite open and sunny -- Now the canal water is quiet.

Andy found that the experience of going through the tunnel was not as bad as he had anticipated. The murky waters of the dark area of his subconscious rose up as if to engulf him, but he found that they presented no real difficulty. This makes him aware that whatever it was that caused the darkness in his subconscious, he has the ability to deal with it and, as a result, he experiences a sense of freedom. Subsequent imagery showed the source of the darkness:

A: I'm where I was at boarding school -- This is a place where I lived and grew up for a few years - where I had hard times, where I had good times, and I've come back to have another look. I have left it behind, I have another life to lead now.
G: What are you wearing?
A: Good heavens! It's a schoolboy's outfit - black shoes, grey socks and grey short trousers. Perhaps I haven't left here after all, or not totally. I think I probably tried to push it away. Perhaps I haven't properly assimilated it, maybe there are still bits remaining to be dealt with.
G: When you were at school did you go through any dark tunnels, inwardly?
A: I tend to see the whole thing as a bit of a dark tunnel. I wasn't very happy --- I'm just wandering about inside the school building which is a big, old place, very dingy -- it's like a tunnel -- a few windows, all stone, dark and cold. It's a miserable place, there's no joy in it and the stones themselves are depressed.

The problem represented by the tunnel has unfolded. As a boy Andy had gone to a boarding school which had an atmosphere that his sensitive nature found difficult to endure. In his next ECE Andy found himself on a small island - a region of stable rational consciousness in the midst of the sea of subconscious activity. He is shown that the painful experience at school was necessary for his development; then he finds himself to be first, a Chinese warrior, second a Greek philosopher (Plato-like figure) and then a Roman charioteer - these are the aspects of his nature that he can use to help him cope with his problems. Then he is transformed back to the hiker and continues on his journey and sees the effect that the dark period of his life had on him. In this journey he finds himself in a dark pit:

A: It's dark down here, muddy and squelchy. I feel there are dangerous things here. Yet if I head straight across I'll go right through them --- I get through and I go a little way up the slope on the other side. I turn round. It's dark, so I throw light back in, and I see two prehistoric creatures. I feel that they cannot live anymore, but, again they mustn't die. So I hold out my arms and say, 'Come with me'. They disappear and in their place are two large eggs, one in each hand. So I take these up into the sunshine. And I thought: there's life in these - where shall I put them so that they can hatch out? Ah, like the turtle I'll put them on the seashore where the waves can wash over them and the sun can warm them and they can hatch out in the sand. When I'm ready I'll come back.

Andy sees here that his boarding school experiences had caused him to withdraw into himself, locking up undeveloped (primitive) energies. Unleashed, such energies can be dangerous but he sees that, with his new found awareness of his situation, he can free this energy locked up in the dark recesses of his subconscious so that it becomes reborn. This enabled Andy's ECEs to move beyond his personal subconscious problems and contribute to the groups' search for understanding, as will be apparent later.

Harry's First ECEs

Like Andy and Brian, Harry was also in his late twenties. After going through the preliminary exercises Harry experienced an eruption of images.

H: I can see a lot of crosses -- Now birds have landed -- There's a fish like a dolphin and then -- there's a curve like a big wave -- it's like feathers -- then it curves round on itself to form a sheaf of corn -- then it was as if I was under water -- this thin line went to the surface of the water and it started revolving and it was like water going down a hole, like a vortex which then separated into a ring, now it's like two cones on top of each other -- then it's split into three petal shapes which then spin like a propeller -- and there is the cross again. The imagery's so fleeting, it comes and goes and seems to move at high speed all the time.

Harry is clearly someone with a lot of turmoil going on in his subconscious. The guide realises that this turmoil has got to be brought under control. When Harry had initially tried the ECE technique with Brian and Andy, he got a fleeting vision of a monk. This became a frequently occurring image in the groups' experiences that seemed to symbolise a 'spiritual guide' who could show them the state of their inner development and the way forward. At this stage the guide (Dennis) did not know this but he felt he needed help in getting Harry's imagery under control.

G: Well, let's try and get some order into the imagery. Remember when you first tried the technique a monk appeared -- try and visualise him.
H: Yes --- I can do that.
G: Well, describe him to me.
H: He's got a brown cloak -- I can't see his face, there's a hood over his head -- he's just standing there.

224

Harry's chaotic turmoil of imagery then took over again until:

H: It's very confusing -- now I can see the monk again. He's going down some stairs into darkness -- I'm following him. I think he's stopped -- it looks like a big cavern - It's indistinct though. I can't see it properly -- I'm asking him to help me see everything. Every time I ask he flares up and points his arms all over -- He's saying, 'Look! Look! He says I've got to look -- It's all around me -- I just can't see it. There's plenty of light -- It's like an amphitheatre and he's down in the centre pointing all around.

The monk has led Harry into an inner amphitheatre, i.e. a place where Harry can see the turmoil of his inner life but Harry cannot get control of the situation, so as to perceive what is going on, as far as he is concerned it is all engulfed in darkness. The guide then tries to stabilise the situation by asking Harry to describe his clothes.

G: What are you wearing?
H: I'm wearing a white tunic and a belt.
G: Look at your face, describe it.
H: It's a youngish face, tight curly golden hair -- I have a long spear in my hand --- now I'm walking out of the cave.
G: How are you getting out of it?
H: With great difficulty --- along a tunnel --- There's light I've come out into the light.

The aspect of Harry's character that can lead him out of the darkness has now appeared. This is Harry's spiritual striving as represented by the golden youth holding the spear, who can, with difficulty, bring Harry to the light. Harry's imagery then degenerated into turmoil again, until it semi-stabilised with an image of a young woman.

H: I can see a young woman with curly blond hair, she's wearing a bonnet and she keeps moving her head from side to side.
G: What does that signify?
H: Indecision. She doesn't know what to do, where to go -- She wanted me to notice her and now I've noticed her she's happy. She's running round me and smiling, laughing. She's quite gay now.
G: How old is she?
H: Twenty three.
G: What's her name?
H: Emily. She says, 'Come with me' -- Now there's this funny embankment and there are two small wooden doors and she's gone inside. There's an old man in there - he's mending shoes. The girl's gone now.
G: Ask him what his name is.
H: Dorimus
G: Ask him why he's there.
H: To help me -- He's telling me how he's going to help me but I can't hear him.
G: Well tell him you can't hear him.
H: Well, I've told him and he's showing me this vortex -- It's gone black now and he took my hand and he said, 'Come on' and we went through this hole into a garden. It's not a real garden. It's a garden where you are shown things - And I saw big unfolding flowers, like a crown -- and then water splashing up in a ring, with little droplets - again like a crown.

The girl represents the feminine feeling side of Harry's nature, which had been neglected and rejected. She is pleased to be recognised and accepted and she leads Harry to an old, wiser figure that can show him the way forward. This figure shows him that the reason that he cannot hear (or see) in the ECE state is because of a vortex - the turmoil of his inner activity. He then takes Harry to a garden where he is shown the potential to 'blossom'; in particular there is something there that has a 'crown-like' nature. Then Harry's inner turmoil takes over and another figure appears.

H: He's gone -- Now I see a man's face -- he's like a Spaniard with a dark black beard -- he's very jolly.
G: What's his name?
H: Cortez. He's looking at me and shaking his head from side to side, as if to say, 'Oh, I don't know, I don't know'.
G: Why is he saying that?
H: Because I can't see things.
G: Well, ask him what you've got to do to see things.
H: He says, 'Look around you, it's all here' -- it's the big arena again. Now I've got them all here, Dorimus and the monk and I've told them all that I couldn't see.
G: How do you learn to see?

H: You follow the path -- they've all gone away but up different paths -- I've got to follow my own path -- Ah there's a path I'll follow that.
G: What sort of path is it?
H: It's dead straight -- but I'm having trouble keeping on it
G: Why do you have trouble?
H: Because it's a round pole and I can't balance on it -- Now it's changed to a square pole which is easier to walk along -- but then it revolves and I fall off it again. Now it's going all dark.
G: I think the journey's probably over.
H: Yes, they're all there waving -- now they've gone

This ECE shows Harry that there are many different characters operating in his subconscious activity. As a result Harry has experienced 'pulls' in different directions in his life. In his next ECE Harry found the preliminary exercises distracting and the chaotic imagery took over, so the guide asked for help from the monk figure.

G: See if you can get an image of the monk.
H: Yes, I've got the monk.
G: Right, ask him to help again.
H: He doesn't seem to be taking any notice of me --- a dog ran up and he picked it up -- he's not communicating at all -- he put the dog down and it ran off through a doorway. There's a garden and a path, so I follow the dog down this path.
G: What's the dogs name and your relationship to him?
H: Sammy -- I have to watch him because he draws my attention to things.

The dog represents the follow-your-nose, instinctive quality. He leads Harry on an extensive journey in which Harry meets yet another aspect of his inner nature, an immensely strong Genghis Khan character, who Harry at first finds overpowering. The Genghis Khan figure then metamorphoses into a surly Viking. These figures fade away and the dog returns. In his researches Harry was concerned with how forms arise in nature and the dog then shows him how light and life and plant forms arise on Earth. A lot of turmoil and fantasy intrudes and Sammy said:

H: 'You're very cluttered up, aren't you? and I said, 'Yes'. But he said, 'Oh, it'll get better'. He's says, Now I'm going to take you to someone who's going to help you'.
G: Good!
H: Now the road goes down into a tunnel -- there's a lady at the end -- It's Emily. 'Come on', she says, 'We're wasting time'. She's dressed in white -- we come to a circular area like an amphitheatre and I go down into the centre of it where there's a pool of water and I say, Do I have to go down into the pool?' and she says. 'Yes' -- I walk down some steps and the water's over my head, there's somebody here who's going to help me but I can't see this person very clearly - lots of images are coming in -- he's not the monk, I haven't met this person before.
G: What's his name?
H: It's like Astradamus -- and I said, 'Is it Astradamus?' and he said, 'Well, it's close enough'.

Emily, the feminine-feeling side has led Harry into a deeper level of his subconscious activity, as represented by the pool of water. Here he meets, in Astradamus, a higher, wiser figure.

G: What does he look like?
H: I still can't see him very clearly -- a dark figure -- it all seems to be a bit jolly here and I said to him, 'You're not taking this very seriously'. And he said, 'You don't seem to be either' --- I've got to concentrate more on my work, he says I've got to concentrate and listen to him.

Astradamus then gives Harry a lecture on how plant forms arise and the role of etheric forces, which is much more mature than the account given by the dog. But Astradamus is not omniscient and he is unable to answer questions when the guide seeks clarification. When Astradamus thinks that Harry has absorbed as much as he can he sends him back out of the pool.

H: So I come out of the pool and we go back down these white steps -- the dog and the woman. Sammy says there's one more thing to show me --- We're at the end of the journey and there's a big circular table loaded with food and wine and lots of people are seated there, having a good time.
G: What sort of people?
H: They're all friends of mine from long ago.
G: Is Olympus there?
H: Yes.
G: Dorimus?

H: Yes.
G: Cortez?
H: Yes -- and the monk, he's there. Oh, there's lots and lots of people.
G: What do they represent?
H: Me -- I'm talking to Sammy because he knows these things, and he says they're all parts of me from my different incarnations. And he says that they're all drawing closer together -- it's slow, he says, but sure.
G: Is Astradamus there?
H: Yes, he looks at me across the table and says, 'See, it's easy'. And I say, 'What?' And he says, 'Seeing of course'.

The guide decides that the best way to go about Harry's next ECE is first to call up all of Harry's characters and to try and get some order into their activities. One by one they appear and the guide suggests that it is time to embark on the ECE but Harry says:

H: Wait a minute -- A very powerful image came in then of the head of a man -- he's like a king, clad in mail with a shield, a sword in his hand and a crown on his head. I'm following him --- I've got another one of these vortices again.

A yet further character has appeared in Harry's subconscious activity - a kingly side (hinted at earlier by the crown symbology) that can control and rule the situation. But when Harry tries to follow his path the vortex (turmoil) intrudes again. The guide feels that it is about time something was done about this.

G: Tell him you've met this vortex several times before and you'd like to know its significance
H: He got his sword and he chopped it up into bits and it all drifted away -- And he says, 'Does this answer your question?
G: Mm -- not quite. Is it some hang up that has to be dispersed - some emotional hang-up from childhood?
H: Yes, partially. I have to rid myself of it -- of the knots and tangles.

Harry then embarks on extensive imagery that shows him that as a child, in order to overcome hurt feelings associated with disappointment, he had rejected the feeling part of his nature, (symbolised by Emily) and he needs to reintegrate it. Then, with the king as his guide he continues on his inner path and finds that now he has no trouble following it - he can keep his balance. He then meets up with Astradamus who continues with his lecture on etheric forces and their role in plant growth. Harry is now able to see and hear clearly what Astradamus has to say. It is a long lecture but Harry maintains his concentration throughout, without the turmoil intruding. At the end Harry has an image of a plant bud opening up and collecting and concentrating all the forces at work, which seems to have a dual meaning by applying to both the workings of the plant and to himself.

G: So, this signifies two things at different levels. One is that it's showing us something to do with plant growth and the other is with your ability of open up and receive information from Astradamus.
H: Yes. That's right -- I have to sacrifice myself -- I have to sacrifice all my understanding -- I just have to receive.
G: There are no impediments to be removed?
H: No -- he says I'm in the clear now. Just have to refine it and that's a matter of experience -- Hm -- seems to be a woman here.
G: Emily?
H: Yes.
G: What does she look like?
H: She's naked -- the monk says to me, 'She's yours'. We just melted into each other -- And I feel free -- very free -- very light -- and I drift away -- that's it -- it's all gone dark now -- it's finished.

In this ECE Harry resolves the problem of his rejected feelings and this clears away the inner turmoil that they cause and he is then able to be a clear free channel for whatever 'higher information' comes to him in the ECE state. This is something that all the members of the group had to learn to do.

In their ECEs, Ted, Brian, Andy and Harry were shown the state of their inner natures in a quite uncompromising, but nevertheless positive and helpful way. All four of them, by recognising their situations were able to set aside personal issues in the ECE state and become 'channels' for a higher wisdom. The insights into their state of development also helped them to become more integrated and to express their innate potentials in daily life. But they found it much more difficult to put into practice and achieve the changes required, in their daily lives, than in the ECE state.

Changing in daily life requires recognising the part of our character that has been expressed in an ECE and then working on it. Thus we may have been shown an immature, child-like part of our nature. Then, in everyday existence when this part takes over it is a matter of recognising it and telling ourself that we have behaved like a child and that we don't want to do that again. After this part has been recognised in this way a number of times it loses its strength and control over our behaviour and fades away. Thus, where an ECE shows us different aspects of our nature we can recognise these in our behaviour and then, instead of letting them take over, e.g. as with a hostile aggressive aspect, we can develop the ability to control this energy and use it for positive purposes. Of course, if we have enough self-awareness we do not have to undergo an ECE to do this. Also ECEs are not necessarily as positive as those experienced by the group members. By experimenting with the ECE technique with family and friends, we found that what occurs reflects the person's attitude. A trivial or superficial attitude produces trivial or superficial ECEs. We were striving to make progress in our researches and they showed a need to sort ourselves out first. Once they had developed the ability to set aside their ego feelings and Ego thinking in their ECEs all of the group members found themselves to be channels for a 'higher wisdom' that gave insight into the problems they were tackling.

We all, in normal consciousness, experience periods of insight, ideas and creativity. Some important advances made by scientists have occurred as a result of visions that came to them (see GHISELIN). Sometimes something goes on while we are asleep, so that we wake up with a creative idea or a solution to a problem, without having consciously worked this out. People who often have such experiences and, as a result, work out of their own creative inspirations, Maslow called 'self actualising', and their periods of illumination, 'peak experiences'; see Chapter 11. When these things happen to us we tend to say, 'I had an idea', whereas it would be more accurate to say, 'An idea came to me'. The ECE technique seems to activate these phenomena in a more conscious and controlled way. Sometimes peak experiences, and channelled communications, seem almost overpowering, making the person feel that they are in contact with some superior spiritual source, or even God. We experienced feelings of this nature with the ECEs. But, as will be seen, the sources of the information given in the ECEs are not omniscient and the information cannot be accepted uncritically.

Once the ECEs had made us aware of, and in the ECE state able to separate from, our personal inner blockages and tangles, we found that we experienced imagery that purported to give insights and understanding on larger issues and on what was going on in our experiments. We start our account of this phase of our activities with some ECEs that dealt with the basic human situation.

Chapter 17

ECEs on the Human Situation

The Incarnation of Egos Into the Earth Situation

The first of this selection of ECEs on the human situation in general relates to members of the Spiritual (Omniverse) Hierarchy incarnating into Earth existence, via biologically developed hominid bodies.

T: Images came in of the first Egos coming into incarnation. At that early stage they are aware of their origins in the spiritual world and of the task ahead of them. Then slowly they become cut off from their origins as they move into the bodies. The image shows this as a very gentle, drawn out, process that occupies a long time (many lifetimes) as they gradually learn to work with and control the bodies. In fact the very first movements into the bodies scarcely make any contact with them at all. They are only vaguely aware of them, living more or less in the spiritual world. They then gradually sink further and further into the bodies until they are unaware of their spiritual origins.

The legends and myths of early homo sapiens show that the 'spiritual world of the gods' was a living reality to them which, according to this ECE, was due to their Egos not having fully separated from their origins in the Spiritual (Omniverse) Hierarchy, in the way in which modern man has.

G: Although the Ego is then cut off, does it still have some contact with its Higher Self?
T: It's unaware of its Higher Self because it's engrossed in this sheer business of living. It's unaware that it is a small part of a relatively high-powered spiritual being. But this is part of coping with life at a physical level. It's much easier for the Ego to be aware of the physical world because it has sense organs that give it direct links with it, so that its perceptions are mainly in physical terms.
G: You say that the problem of early man is to learn to master these bodies. What does mastering the bodies mean?
T: It comes across in feelings. There are feelings of lightness, freedom, weightlessness, brightness, the feeling of belonging to a whole, something which is complete. As they move into the bodies they start to lose the feeling of lightness and brightness, they feel clumsy and heavy. The tasks they can perform with the physical body are quite limited. An image came in of someone who had been quite active having to learn to walk all over again on artificial legs.

According to the accounts of mystics the human being comprises a physical-biological, substance body and a system of etheric, astral (soul) and mental (spirit) energy flows, with chakra centres to it, which they perceive by appropriately raising their level of consciousness. According to hK-M the chakra system and its energy flows are the connections that the Egos incarnating from the Omniverse Hierarchy developed in order to gain control of the human body. But by incarnating in a hominid body the Ego loses contact with its origins in the spiritual world and these become an unconscious memory.

G: Is it the sense of regaining what has been lost that drives a person on?
T: Yes, that's what it's all about, striving to regain the original feelings, despite all the handicaps of the physical, etheric and astral (soul) bodies.
G: If the problem of the primitive human being is the struggle to cope with these bodies, what about a modern human being?
T: For modern human beings coping with their bodies is largely automatic they don't give much thought to it, so they look for distractions.
G: What do you mean by that, if what drives a person on is the desire to re-experience the feelings of brightness and lightness that they have lost, how do distractions fit in?
T: It appears to show up as an alternative. If they listen to their Ego they feel these urges, this drive to regain the lightness and brightness. But without the feeling of wanting this experience there is a void to fill, so they look for distractions -- The image shows the Ego as self-satisfied in material things. It is scarcely aware of the spiritual world and its origins. It is cut right off and looks for its satisfaction at a physical level.
G: What about a more evolved person?
T: This Ego has experienced the material world and looked for satisfaction there and it has been led some way towards the feelings of lightness but it feels that there is more to life and it's driven to seek beyond the material and if the drive is sufficiently intense it begins to strive back towards its origins. It wants to experience the satisfactions that weren't present from its diversions in the material world.

Because of the demands made on us to cope with life on Earth, our attention is concentrated on the features of daily existence that we have to deal with. So we have lost any feeling of being part of an all-embracing, harmonious whole. But buried deep in our subconscious there is an awareness of the experience of such a state. So-called primitive tribes may seek to re-experience it in their rituals and in drug-induced hallucinogenic states. It could be that this is the sub-conscious impulse for people taking drugs - to escape from the demands of everyday life and return to such a state. Occasionally we may experience a connectedness and lightness and brightness behind everything, as a state of euphoria:

G: What about an individual's development through their life time?

T: That appears to start before the Ego comes into incarnation, so that its drives and impulses are instilled there. For some it means that they go through the whole of Earth life immersed in the physical because this is what they have chosen to do. Others have come in with impulses to spiritualise Earth life, so that they continually seek the spiritual world behind the material. They seek a broader understanding and in this way make progress. The more complete an Ego's understanding becomes, the more liberated it feels and the closer it comes to experiencing the feelings of lightness and wholeness.

G: Why should an Ego, before it incarnates, when it knows about the spiritual world, decide to cut itself off and concern itself only with the physical world?

T: The image shows an Ego that, through an Earth period, was totally absorbed in the physical. When it returns to the spiritual world this appears to have been vital for its overall development. It has had to know the satisfactions that the material world can offer and where it stands in relation to the spiritual world.

G: Can an Ego's stance change during its life time?

T: Oh yes, a lot depends on the influences brought to bear on it. A diagram came in that split life into three main periods. The first period is where the Ego has to rely on other people for it to grow and mature to a point where it can go off into the world on its own. In that early stage it can be influenced to look towards the spiritual, to look for the total picture of life, or it can be influenced to ignore the spiritual side completely and to regard the material world as the only reality. In the second stage it moves out into the world to establish itself there. To do this it tends to become materially minded. This is the world it has to battle with if it is to establish itself and so it gets bogged down in material life. But then it can be led to recognise that behind the physical struggle lies the spiritual world. So, when it feels secure in material existence, it can devote the energies that it used for establishing itself to looking for a more complete picture that combines the physical and spiritual worlds.

G: What happens at death?

T: The act of dying is for the Ego, astral (soul) and etheric bodies to move completely out of contact with the physical. Then the physical body returns to the material world because, without the etheric body, there is nothing to maintain the life forces in it. The etheric, astral and Ego move into the spiritual world and now, for the first time, the etheric and astral are closely linked, without the physical body. The totality of its life experience can then be shown to the Ego. This is released from the etheric and it evokes images in the astral, which make the Ego aware of the entire pattern of the life it has concluded. The etheric then leaves the astral-Ego combination, which now contains the total life experience, and this combination moves further on into the spiritual world. Its progress is then governed by the rate at which it sheds the part of the astral body that contains its Earthly links, its Earthly desires and passions. As these are shed the Ego moves back into the realms of the spiritual world, where its complete consciousness is restored.

The Interaction of the Ego With the Body

We asked about the nature of the interaction of the Ego with the body systems.

T: When the Ego incarnates it automatically takes over the flows through its different bodies. This is its means of keeping in touch, receiving information.

G: But as it works with these it can bring disharmony into them?

T: Yes, it can become too concerned with its physical level or with its feelings and this disturbs the natural flows.

G: What happens if it becomes over concerned with its physical level?

T: The image shows a person who is concerned with the physical appearance that they present to the world, the feeling side is neglected and with it any feelings for others. The image shows the Ego as being self-centred. It takes pride in its physical well-being and appearance and convinces itself that physical well-being means a healthy person.

G: How does this give rise to disharmony?

T: The image shows a young person brimming with health and vitality. Their concentration is on maintaining physical well being and appearance but totally neglecting the feeling and mental sides of their natures. The image then shifts to an older person who is fighting harder and harder to maintain this physical fitness but

eventually it runs out on them. The image shows a body that is getting hardened, joints getting set and the person can no longer cope. Their entire outlook was concerned with their physical well being and when it becomes impossible to maintain this they have lost their anchor and the person shows mental stress.
G: What happens when the Ego becomes over-concerned with its feelings?
T: It sees its feelings as giving a true representation of the outer world. It then experiences everything through its feelings, so that the Ego becomes subject to the to-ing and fro-ing of the feelings. The image is of a nervous person, always fussing, unable to concentrate on anything for very long. They are aware of their inability to focus their attention and this gives them cause for concern, it worries them and they become ill in this way.

G: Are there any other types of disharmony that can occur?
T: The words come in, 'We are all in some sort of disharmony', occasionally we hit the right balance and we feel absolutely great. But because we are individual Egos we make our own decisions and this can involve us in disharmonising the system. None of us operate in complete harmony all the time, this is what life is all about, this is the goal we work towards.
G: Does disharmony come about because the Ego is influenced by the Ahrimanic and Luciferic activities?
T: Yes, one draws up and the other draws down. The image makes the point that the important thing is that they are external to man.

This ECE states that there are forces acting on us that seek to influence us in the 'spiritual-Luciferic' or 'materialist-Ahrimanic' direction. We see this in the spiritual cults and the striving for material goals which people get gripped by, and the way in which people can acquire strength by aligning themselves with either of these.

G: Where does Christ fit into this?
T: The image shows Christ as the leader of the beings who incarnate. He sacrifices himself to live and work as a man at the material level. He became aware of the stresses that man can be subjected to, the flows of energies and the temptations that can disharmonise these flows. He was able to return to the spiritual world having accomplished the conversion of the qualities that were donated to mankind. In so doing he gives a direction for mankind to follow.
G: How do we follow the Christ path?
T: Man has to be aware of the upward and downward flows of Lucifer and Ahriman, to recognise these and to consciously reach out for the Christ force if he wishes to follow it.
G: How does he do this?
T: The image shows a man who is concerned with the questions: Who is he? Where does he come from? What is he doing in this material world? Is he only here to work with material things? Is there more to life than this? Is there anything that is more continuous outside the physical life? He begins to search around for answers to these questions and this helps to create a receptive situation for the Christ force.
G: If, instead of following the Christ path, the Ego allows itself to be influenced by the Luciferic towards the spiritual world, then it loses its grip on the material world?
T: Yes, and the image shows the person appears wasted, emaciated.
G: An aesthetic?
T: Yes, that's right.
G: Now if it was the other way round, so that the person gave more attention to the Ahrimanic, it would draw in material substance - it would make it greedy - the opposite of emaciation?
T: The word, 'gross' came in.

Causes of Illness Arising From Disharmony in Ego-Body Interactions

In a number of ECEs we sought the role of disharmony between the Ego and its bodies in illness. Here we give examples of some of the responses that we received.

G: Can we seek understanding of illness?
T: An image came in with words that showed two aspects to the problem. One showed the situation viewed from the spiritual world and everything made sense, so that when illness affected a person the feeling was of naturalness. There was nothing of the 'Why should it happen to me?' or 'Why should that person be stricken in that way, they have done nothing to deserve an illness like this', to the spiritual side of the picture. But viewed from the Earth situation all these questions crowded in, as if illness was totally unjustified. On the other hand, where people are ill or afflicted in some way then some people can feel that this is a just reward for the way in which they have lived their lives. But from the spiritual point of view there is clarity and wholeness to it. I had an image then of someone who had died after a terminal illness. There had been a great deal of confusion and resentment that they had this illness and that it would lead to the end of life as they knew it, 'Why should this happen to me? What have I done to deserve this?' But towards the end of the

illness some feeling of peace came in, as if there was acceptance of the fact that the illness had a purpose. Then, when this person has moved into the spiritual world they gradually begin to see the logic of the situation and why it was necessary and with this understanding the resentment disappears.

G: The body is not built to go on forever, so that even if no disharmony arises it must decay.

T: Yes, that's so. I'm shown an Ego that inhabits a physical body for a long time. There is a feeling of wanting to cling to this body but contact with the world around has been greatly reduced and there is a confused feeling of wanting to hang on and at the same time wanting to lay down the burden. It's this confusion of wanting to go and wanting to stay that keeps the system just ticking over and this can exist for a long, long time.

G: So senility arises by the Ego hanging onto the physical body long after it should have relinquished it?

T: Yes, the image displays an Ego firmly anchored in the physical world, it has lost track of its spiritual origins. The only 'real' things it knows are those in the physical world around it and its day-to-day contact with people. This is a terrible state to be in, the spark inside the physical body that is you longs for release. To what? It doesn't know. To where? It doesn't know. And so it clings to the only thing it really knows. This is a shocking feeling, very, very confused --- The image changed to an Ego that has some awareness of its origins, one that feels that time in the physical environment is limited but life itself is timeless. I get again that this is why the situation seems so clear from the spiritual side, the spiritual aspect clearly recognises that incarnation is a dip down into the physical world, a cutting off for a time. In this case the incarnated Ego is still aware of its spiritual origins and this gives it something solid to anchor to while it is in the physical world. But if the incarnating bit gets so cut off that all contact with the Higher Self is lost, it then has no solid basis, it has nothing behind it .... I get the highly confused feeling all over again.

G: What can be done to help people like that?

T: The imagery showed someone living in that state surrounded by people who wanted to tell the Ego that there was much beyond life in the physical body but this only made it even more determined to cling to what it considered to be real. The imagery showed that the person has to come to the understanding of the continuity of life out of themselves, it can't be forced on them.

G: That means there isn't much that others can do to help Egos in this state?

T: Imagery and words came in that nothing much can be done in a direct manner but a person with awareness can consciously help to make a bridge to discarnate Egos who care for the trapped Ego, those that have undergone the transition and know that life continues -- I'm shown how frustrating it can be for someone who is looking after a person in a state like this. When people get short-tempered and angry it worsens the situation and makes it difficult to live with. What is needed is a firm sympathetic approach by the person who is doing the looking after; they should try and establish strong links with their own guide and try to work on the situation through the back door, as it were.

G: When, in the spiritual world, an Ego sees that it is necessary for it to undergo certain experiences of malfunction or disease, does it bring this down with it, or does it choose a malfunctioning body to incarnate into, or can it be either?

T: I am shown an Ego that has an aspect of its behaviour that it needs to work out and has chosen to do this by inhabiting a deformed body. All the links are made before the Ego departs from its Higher Self. The body is produced by the parents coming together and the image shows that they both have situations which they have to work out, from their past lives, and the production of this deformed body is part of this working out. The meeting up of the deformed body and the incarnating Ego adds another dimension to this, so now all three are working out aspects of their lives together, through this deformed body --- Another string of images came in that show an Ego incarnating into a normal body but changes take place in this body during early life. Again three Egos are involved, all needing to come to terms with the situation. The words, 'Four or five years' come in. Nothing has happened to this body in this time and the parents are very happy. Then an illness arises, I get the word, 'Leukaemia' and immediately there is a feeling of a death sentence passed on the growing body. The Ego of the sick body is still close enough to the spiritual world to have some feeling for what is going on but for the parents this situation can lead to great anguish, a questioning of the reasons for it - if there is a controlling entity, a God, then why does he let these things happen?

G: In what way does this advance the evolution of the Ego that incarnates and then so soon dies?

T: That doesn't seem as clear as the effects on the parents, who either learn from the situation or grow embittered. For the Ego incarnating into the body this is just a short dip into the physical and then a return to the spiritual.

G: What about this from the point of view of the medical profession? They do all they can to cure the child but it sounds as though it's a waste of time.

T: It's not that straight forward at all. In some cases the medic is well aware that there is an inevitability about these things but he nevertheless feels a need to try to cure the body and it feels right that this should happen --- Now another stream of images has come in, of a child seriously ill and not expected to survive but after treatment the child lived and both the parents and the medics responsible seemed to have got a tremendous amount out of this. The parents no longer took the life of their child for granted, they were more aware of the value of it and of the contribution it made to their own lives, and of the contribution they could make to it.

G: What about an Ego that incarnates as a spastic child?
T: The Ego appears to have chosen this condition, it wants that type of experience in the evolutionary period it has entered. It also provides experience for the parents; they find themselves with a spastic child to raise.
G: You make it sound as though it is a positive experience.
T: That's the way it appears to be.
G: What qualities do the Ego and the parents develop as a result of this situation?
T: Awareness that the lives of all of them must continue. The image shows the parents acquiring patience, dedication and understanding, whilst the child Ego finds itself contained within a body that it possibly can never control. But the image shows that some spastics can lead quite a full mental life within the spastic body if they receive the care, dedication and understanding of the parents.
G: I don't quite see the positive development that this spastic Ego would get.
T: The imagery shows it as relationships to others around it; other Ego's reactions to it and its relationships with them.
G: So, in a way it draws out the qualities of patience and dedication from other people - that's its primary experience?
T: Yes, that appears to be so.

G: How about a Downs syndrome child?
T: I have an image of an Ego coming into incarnation but at the moment of joining up with the body there was a reluctance on its part to face up to the situation ahead of it and it held back. It didn't return to the spiritual world, if it had the body would have died, it just held itself aloof from fully incarnating. It doesn't appear to be through dissatisfaction with the body or the parents. While in the spiritual world it had assimilated the experiences of its last life, it could see the totality of its development and it had undertaken to reincarnate to continue its development. Then, at the moment of incarnating there's a feeling of not being able to face up to it all and a holding off. The Ego is then in a situation where it can neither come in or get back. The child then remains permanently fixed at one level of development, or else develops only very, very slowly. This makes demands on the people around it --- I'm shown cases where it becomes impossible for the parents to cope any further. They have struggled to give this child all the love and attention that it needs but as they grow older, and the child also, it becomes difficult for them to keep this up and eventually the child goes away to live in sheltered accommodation. This experience adds to the parents' development, in that they have to endure separation from the child. As for the child, its environment changes and it's surrounded by people who care for it and gradually it becomes used to the new situation. The partially incarnated Ego seems very dull and remote and after a time it's not even conscious of its parents, as it finds itself in another situation where it is cared for. But often the parents have guilty feelings about their action in removing the child from their lives. In this case the lessons seem to be much more important to the parents than the incarnating ego in the Downs syndrome body.

G: What about an autistic child?
T: In this case it appears that the Ego comes into incarnation but when it experiences the world around it, it can't face up to it. It doesn't like the world around it and doesn't want to communicate with it. The image shows the Ego more in control than for the Downs syndrome child but not relating to the world.

G: What happens if a person goes through life and becomes mature and then brain damage occurs?
T: Depending on what the damage is, there are functions of the physical body that the Ego cannot control. These can be paralysis of limbs, loss of speech, loss of sight. I'm sitting above a chap I knew who suffered brain damage and I'm looking down on this figure who is very irritable and bad tempered. The Ego is partially outside and there is a feeling of sadness to it, some things are outside its control. I see a child in a temper tantrum, the child flares up quite automatically and this brain damaged person has reverted to the child-like state, this expression of displeasure, bad temper, has become almost a permanent feature. Normally people can gradually bring this side of their feelings under control.
G: When a child is born as a physical and etheric body, the astral (feeling body) and Ego are largely outside?
T: Yes.
G: And during the first few years the astral body moves in on its own and it's only later that the Ego begins to take over and control the situation. So, in the brain damage situation it reverts to the Ego being outside but with the astral expressing itself, without the Ego control?
T: Yes.

G: What is the significance of an illness such as flu?
T: I'm shown the comparison between a lively healthy body and one that is suffering the effects of flu. The flu-infected one looks very dejected and run down, it's disharmonised and full of aches, pains and temperature. The inclination of the Ego is to sleep and withdraw and when it does, the natural healing forces begin to flow to restore harmony to the bodies.

G: Is it that the Ego inhabiting the body has created more disharmony than can be rectified during its normal nightly departure from the body?

T: Yes, the image came in of an Ego that was heavily involved in lots of different things, never remaining long with any one of them. This caused confusion at the mental level that's reflected down through the bodies, so that the physical was driven by this frantic mental activity. For a time it could cope but then it slowly became exhausted, so that during sleep, when the Ego was absent, the physical-etheric was never properly restored - the Ego was anxious to be back in again and drive the physical onwards. Another image comes in, of an Ego that is very conscientious, it feels that what it has set itself to achieve it must accomplish. But sometimes this is not possible and in this case the Ego feels that it has not met its target and this feeling is reflected down through the bodies and the system is disharmonised and unbalanced and this eventually leads to temperature and fever in the physical body.

G: How about when flu is transmitted from one person to another.

T: An image came in then to show different ways in which the Ego could put stress on the physical level and of something then coming into the physical from the outside. Without the stress, with the system in balance, then nothing came in from outside. I see a calm Ego that goes about its daily life, tackling each situation as it arises and managing to keep its system in balance. It doesn't put stress into its situation and if it does, then it corrects for it unconsciously. The adverse effects from outside don't seem to be able to find a point of weakness at which to enter. Then an image came in of an Ego that is convinced that if there is an epidemic, then it is going to be one of its victims. Just the thought of the illness is sufficient to disorganise it and to create the point of weakness at which the illness enters. I get images of doctors and nurses who work with epidemics. Quite often these medical people will go right through an epidemic without being ill themselves. They get physically tired but they somehow manage to retain control, their systems appear to be well organised, so that they don't provide the weakness through which the illnesses can attack.

G: How do you see the illness entering?

T: I see it in terms of man's aura through which he makes his contacts with the world around him. He can reach out through it and influences from outside can reach in. As an Ego he has control over what is allowed in but if he opens himself to a flood from outside, then he has lost control.

G: When people have flu, is it better to let it take its course, or should they try to do something about it?

T: The first image was of an Ego withdrawing, so that the natural healing forces could move in and restore the balance. I see another situation where the Ego is fighting the illness but not out of understanding. It's the kind of reaction that says it's determined not to be laid low by illness. It takes medicines that act on the symptoms and the Ego is convinced that it has fought off the illness but the aura shows a residue of the illness still within it.

G: Flu must be only one example of diseases that arise in this way?

T: I had an image of the world and the word 'flu' completely encircled it.

G: This presumably implies that the totality of mankind becomes susceptible to flu through a disharmonious way of life?

T: Yes, I had an image of a primitive tribe. In their own terms they are extremely civilised and they are extremely open people, who live in harmony with Nature. They don't seem to be affected by things like flu - I see the word flu with a cross through it. Then 'civilised' people move in that see them as deprived people whose life style should be brought up to date. Yet when these primitive people are brought into contact with modern society they are very susceptible to common illnesses like colds and flu. Since they are harmonised and live at one with the natural world around them they have no barriers, so that things flow in and out of them easily and in consequence the civilised illnesses also flow through them as easily as the natural forces do.

G: There must be other illnesses that arise where people live out of harmony with the workings of Nature?

T: 'Blood pressure', Nervous complaints', Stomach ulcers' all came in as resulting from the way the individual lives giving rise to pressures within his system.

G: What type of disharmony would give rise to blood pressure?

T: The word 'frustration' came in. The image is of someone who has a responsible job but often his efforts are frustrated because of other peoples' failures and this leads to blood pressure. I'm also shown the explosive type of individual; almost every situation causes him to explode with impatience or temper and this can lead to blood pressure. Then I was shown images of two people, one who has no regard at all for the people he is responsible for; if his plans are frustrated he simply removes the person he thinks is responsible, so that he doesn't get frustrated. The other person is slightly aware that other people should be taken into consideration and this can lead him to be indecisive, to wonder and to ponder, which can cause stress for that Ego. Not having sufficient understanding of the overall pattern, when it finds itself frustrated by the actions of others it doesn't know what to do about it.

G: Is that a blood pressure case?

T: The answer I got was, 'Yes, and stomach ulcers also'.

G: Is a stomach ulcer something that is more localised than blood pressure?

T: The words, 'Areas of weakness' came in. Upsets or frustrations find their way to these points of weakness, in this case it's the person's digestive system and it manifests as a stomach ulcer.

G: You also said nervous disorders?

T: The word, 'Undermined' has come in. I'm shown a person to whom every undertaking is a burden. The image comes in of them going to some local council offices, they are rehearsing what they should say and how they should approach the person involved. They practically live the whole situation in advance before they have even contacted anyone. This places great strain on them and they feel undermined from the word go.

G: Are there other types of disorders that a person brings upon themself?
T: 'Cancer' came in. This can result from disharmony working from the mental level down into the physical, so that the system gets out of control. Again I'm shown a person under heavy pressure, someone with a lot of responsibility, who takes it all very seriously and attempts to carry everything by himself. He keeps picking up additional loads until he is hopelessly overloaded.
G: How does an overloaded Ego allow a bit of the system to become uncontrolled?
T: The image came in of an Ego totally concerned with its own problems and unaware of the other levels of its system. The defences appear to be down and this lets in outside influences that work within the system and the Ego is not aware of it. But something also came in saying that a person could choose to come into existence bringing with them the necessity of cancer.
G: Can we clarify that with an example?
T: I'm given the image of a woman with the word 'selfless'. All her time and energy is devoted to others and this woman succumbs to cancer. In this case it is an experience that it must undergo and it had also decided that it needed to experience this life of total service to others. There arose an image of a person of great faith, who goes through an illness like cancer and they know what the outcome will be but their faith is not shaken. They see it through without it becoming a traumatic experience. In the case of this woman, she is just as selfless through this fatal illness and she demands nothing of others to look after her. The feeling of the others is, 'Why should it happen to a person like this?' but she accepts it. The thing that I get clearly is that the Ego had consciously made this decision before it left its Higher Self.

We asked about long-term chronic illnesses, such as arthritis and multiple sclerosis and about polio. The answers we got were that with these situations the person learns acceptance, resignation and to depend on others. In this case the person realises that there are lessons to be learned from the situation and appreciates the efforts of the people around it and thereby they change the situation from a destructive one to a constructive one, so that there is spiritual development. This can, sometimes, lead to a cure. There are other cases where people shut themselves up and complain about the situation, or do not accept it and fight against it, in a way that makes it worse. We then asked:

G: Is there anything else?
T: The words, 'Children's' illnesses' come in.
G: How do these arise?
T: They occur on contact, through being in the same environment as others suffering from the illness. I see a class of children in which one goes down with chicken pox and subsequently two-thirds suffer from it also. The image also shows one of the children being vaccinated against chicken pox and this is effective. The image is suggesting that an influence taken in at the physical level can be effective at the etheric level. The child's Ego plays no part in this, it's not that the child has faith that will see it through an illness or that it can make itself strong enough to keep external influences out, neither of these appear to be the case at all.
G: In babies and young children the Ego has not incarnated and therefore cannot play a part, so babies don't suffer much from illnesses because they are physical-etheric beings in harmony?
T: Yes, but the word, 'Influenza' comes in and I see a hospital with a lot of new-born babies and an influenza epidemic sweeps through and a lot of babies suffer. I also have an image of a gastric epidemic and this seems to be a similar thing.
G: You make it sound as though the baby's aura is open to these things.
T: Yes, that's it.

In these, and all of our other ECEs, we were just going along with what was happening and trying to understand the viewpoint that they expressed, to see where this would lead. We have no means of assessing the validity of these explanations given for illness, etc. but they do have an internal logic, in terms of an interaction between Egos incarnating into the Earth situation from a spiritual world, in order to further their development. This view is not contrary to current scientific views of the physical-biological nature of these conditions but complementary to them. The metaphysical deals with the basic, underlying causes, the scientific with the physical-biological manifestations. And, because all levels are inter-related, changes at one level have an effect on the other levels, whether this occurs from the top down or from the bottom up. We use our bodies to carry out tasks in our domestic, professional, family activities, etc. and in doing this our bodies express our will, feelings and thinking. But the human body has its own built-in nature and pattern of behaviour and if we do not supply its needs and harmonise our use of it with its capabilities, then we create disharmony in it.

According to these ECEs, illness and 'abnormal' conditions are not necessarily the adverse experiences that we think they are. The usual human attitude to these things is that they occur because something has gone wrong that should be put right but the ECEs take the view that they are a normal part of human development. That is not to say that no efforts should be made to cure them for, in seeking to rectifying them we advance our knowledge of what is happening at the working face and thereby our contribution to the understanding of the workings of 'creation'. But, also by living with these situations in the best way that we can, we advance in our ability to play a part in working out further developments.

According to *h*K-M hominid bodies evolved on Earth and members of the Omniverse Hierarchy incarnated into these, via the chakra energy systems, to give rise to homo-sapiens. Thus two streams of activity are at work in us, the physical-biological-etheric activity inherited from the evolution of hominids and our ego-feeling/soul and Ego-spirit/thinking activities that we impose on our body by our incarnation from the Omniverse Hierarchy. Whatever we make use of our body for, its hierarchy of prokaryotic-eukaryotic-multicellular entities will strive to maintain its harmonious working while, during sleep, this is assisted by our Higher Self seeking to negate adverse activities of our Ego.

'Spiritual' Healing

There is evidence that some people can channel healing forces to others in the way that, in Chapter 12, we described Sai Baba and Daskalos seem to do, with control and understanding of what they are doing, but which is also done by other healers without such understanding, so in our ECEs we asked about this.

G: What happens in spiritual healing?
T: I'm seeing a healer and the flow seems to take place along the lines where the Ego's own Higher Self would operate. In the healing state the channel between the healer's Ego and his Higher Self is a very good clear channel. I'm shown the healer as having this clear channel for that specific purpose. It doesn't mean that the healer has always got this broad channel. I'm shown that when not used for healing a healer's connection to its Higher Self can be quite narrow and closed down. It's the surrendering of itself to the healing purposes that creates a good broad channel. The healing is as good as the healer is prepared to give of themselves to healing.

G: What about the Philippine type of healing, where the healer appears to open up the body with his hands?
T: That appears to operate in a similar manner, except that the healer is standing outside it and is just being used as a channel.
G: Does some other Ego take over control?
T: In some cases, yes. I saw an image of a group of healers in which some were controlled by something outside of themselves, while others had the healing source operating through them.

G: Is it true that, with George Chapman a discarnate doctor, Dr. Lang, takes over his body and works through it?
T: There's a vigorous 'Yes' to that.
G: And this is not holding up George Chapman's development?
T: No, this is something that helps his development because he gives up this part of his life to work so closely with Lang.

G: There is a lot going on in the world today in terms of spiritual healing, radionic healing, discarnate doctors taking over mediums in trance states, and things like that, is all of this perfectly sound?
T: They say a lot of it, but not all of it.
G: What is meant by not all of it is sound?
T: I think this refers to people who profess to heal but don't. There are healing energies available and, approached in the right way, these can be channelled through people to those that need them but there are people who profess to make contact with these energies but don't.
G: Can we interfere in anyone's karma by asking for spiritual healing?
T: No, but I am told that with anyone who is old or in the terminal stages of illness it is better to ask for peace of mind and contentment rather than healing.

For many of us there are times when we would like to help or heal someone but the problem is how to contact the 'spiritual world' and invoke the energies required.

G: If one is asking for healing for a person is it a good thing to visualise the person, on the one hand, and to ask for help from one's spiritual guide on the other hand?

T: They say to put out the call for healing with a particular person in mind but to keep in mind the spiritual guide as well. He forms the link; he can see the person the proposer has in mind and he can help to channel the healing energy to them.

G: Is spiritual healing a valid way forward for Western man?
T: There's a hesitant 'yes' to that and the image shows a weak Ego receiving spiritual healing. The Ego isn't really working to balance the system and so, although spiritual healing can do quite a lot, the Ego needs to regain control. For this it needs to be strengthened, or to be made aware of the position, so that it can make a conscious effort to get hold of, and control, the systems. Spiritual healing can be applied and will work even though the Ego is weak but there could be a relapse at a later stage.
G: Is it possible for spiritual healing to be bad?
T: The image I'm shown is of a spiritual healer who is working out of genuine feelings for the sick person; there is no intention to do harm but the illness is irreversible and must take its course. Then spiritual healing can unnecessarily prolong the illness. It's not beneficial and in that case the healing should be given to the Ego.
G: So a spiritual healer can interfere with a person's karma?
T: There's a hesitant 'yes' to that. It's saying that karma will prevail in the end but the healing can interfere with the course of it.

Good health requires leading a balanced life. According to *h*K-M, this means reconciling the Luciferic and Ahrimanic influences that work on us and seeking the harmonised Christ path. It is the balancing, harmonising Christ energy that Daskalos and other healers who direct their efforts to promoting healing and harmony in life, call on. In his ECEs Andy found himself experiencing symbolically the key characteristics of the Ahrimanic, Luciferic and Christ paths.

ECEs on the Three Paths of Human Development

Andy Visits the Kingdom of Ahriman

In this ECE Andy comes down through the clouds to find sea below him. He dives down into the sea and comes to a crater in which there is a large hole which he goes down into. He then finds himself in a much larger world, in which he feels ant-sized, where there is much activity associated with machinery, boilers and the production of heat. Although the beings working in it are very large, their features are gnome-like. One of these picks Andy up in his hand. Andy feels some trepidation but decides to brazen out the situation. He feels that these are underlings of some kind and he demands 'to be taken to the boss'. He is taken along a corridor to a room. Andy decides it is not satisfactory to be so small in these surroundings, so he huffs and puffs himself to a size commensurate with the room. Then a dark menacing figure walks in. They size one another up and Andy decides that as long as he is bold he has nothing to worry about, but if he shows fear the menacing figure will overwhelm him. The figure will not volunteer his name or proffer Andy any help or information but it seems he has to respond to Andy's questions and requests. Andy asks him if he is Ahriman and he grudgingly agrees that he is. Andy is not quite sure what to do next, so the guide suggests:

G: Ask him to show you his role in the world.
A: It was as though I was between two parallel mirrors, where you see repeating images on either side that retreat far off into the distance.
G: And is this the way it is in his kingdom?
A: I see him nod and in these mirrors I see many images of him, all nodding, and now I see him with horns on his head and a kind of goats face ---- Just ahead there's an iron railing and we look down into a squash court and I see two people playing. One of them has hit the ball up towards me and I've caught it.
G: Ask Ahriman what the ball represents.
A: 'The Ball of Life' came into my mind.
G: Ask him to show you something else in his kingdom.
A: He opens a door in the mirrored wall and it's as though we go behind the scenes. There's a chain hanging down into a furnace and Ahriman is daring me to go down this chain with him, but I'm not worried, I know I'll be alright. As we go down into the furnace I know there is great heat, I feel its rising movement, but it's not hot. Now we go out through a door in the furnace and he's leading me up a great pile of coal which we sink down through and go through a trap door below, down a ladder. At the bottom we're in a long cellar with great barrels on either side. I wanted to know what was in these barrels but he'd zipped on ahead very quickly and I couldn't ask him, so I looked at one and I saw H_2SO_4 on it. Then I went on very fast to catch him -- He takes me by the arm and we're on the edge of a dusty plain and a man on horseback galloped very fast out of the distance towards us, past us, and on away into the distance again. I got the impression he

was flying from a battle -- I think Ahriman is waiting for me to ask questions but I don't think I've got to the heart of the matter.

G: *Ask him to show you the heart of it.*

A: *I asked him that and we went back to the furnaces and opened them and I looked inside and saw faint shapes.*

G: *Is the furnace there to consume that which gives itself into the realm of Ahriman?*

A: *I saw him nod, his nose became more beak-like and he looked like a bird of prey. I asked him what he burnt in the furnaces and he said, 'Souls'. Earlier on when he first appeared I had a faint awareness of him saying, 'This is the land of lost souls'.*

G: *Yes, that's the centre of Ahriman's kingdom, isn't it. With his illusions, his hall of mirrors, and all the tricks he plays, he entices lost souls and tries to consume them.*

A: *When you were saying that, the word 'Furnace-master' came into mind. And he wasn't quite so fine, he became a more down-to-earth figure with these furnaces to look after. He doesn't look imposing any more, he looks tired. So I leave him. I pat him on the shoulder and say, 'Well, thank you very much for giving me your time'. And he opens an eye and waves his hand and I go back to the furnace room, back to the mirrored hall, up through the water to the surface of the ocean, to an island -- it's nice to feel the ground under your feet.*

These are just a few snippets from this ECE that lasted for some two hours. The imagery that Andy experienced was at times disturbing and he proceeded slowly, only moving on when he had gained confidence at each point. The parts of the imagery that we have quoted show a few aspects of Ahrimanic activity, which is essentially concerned with the material side of existence. The hall of mirrors shows that the multiplication and proliferation of material activities and events - minerals, life forms, etc. are a reflection of the underlying basic forces/activities, that add up to the on-going evolution of the Kosmos, which material existence makes possible. This is the substantial part of the 'Ball of Life'. But, where Ego/egos get hooked on these matters, it is also responsible for disruptive division between men, and vitriolic antagonism (H_2SO_4 = oil of vitriol) and wars and battles. If we give ourselves over to, and become consumed by, this negative side of Ahrimanic activities, we become lost souls.

Andy Visits the Kingdom of Lucifer

This ECE starts with Andy finding himself hanging below the clouds, like a puppet on strings. He looks up and sees a trapdoor in the sky and two hands manipulating the strings. This he feels is highly unsatisfactory - he is quite capable of supporting himself and he does not want to be anybody's puppet. So he casts off the strings and throws them up through the trapdoor. But then he feels that he wants to know what is behind it, so he flies up through it and finds himself in a tunnel that he goes along but it falls in on him as he does so. He comes out into a garden where there are drifts of dead leaves. At the end of the garden is a Victorian house that he enters. He goes upstairs and finds himself in a most peculiar room, he cannot go across it but has to go all round it to get to a further room. This turns out to be an anteroom where there is a secretary who directs him to a further room. Again he has to go all round this room to get to the next one.

In this room there is a palatial desk and Andy expects someone of significance to be there, but behind the desk is a dog. The dog indicates that it is going to lead Andy somewhere and they go through a tunnel under the house to a building site. There they go up a tall tower, however when they get to the top Andy realises that the tower is insubstantial, for when he grasps it, it just crumbles in his hand. He feels this is ridiculous and that he can support himself better than the tower can. The guide then suggests that Andy should ask the dog to take him to its Master.

A: *I do that and the dog indicates a castle on a hill. We flew to the top of this and again it's not solid - it wobbles like jelly. We come down a steel ladder and there's a figure waiting for us. The steel ladder has fallen down on the ground after us and I pick up one of the pieces and it's like putty. So I say to the figure, 'Things aren't very substantial here, are they'? And he looks at me as though to say, 'Well, what do you expect up here?'*

G: *What's this figure like?*

A: *He's a bit devilish, something like a jester and he has a witches broom in his hand. I ask him, 'Is your name Lucifer?' and I see him nodding his head, the bells ring on his cap and he stamps his broom on the ground -- I ask him, 'Is this your kingdom?' and he nodded again. As he did this the tower began to crumble, bits of the roof start falling in -- I say to Lucifer, 'I would like to learn more about your kingdom , will you show me round? And he hops up on to an outer wall and I hop up as well and we start walking round and round this circular wall. It's making me dizzy and I say, 'Is this what you do? Do you make people dizzy? He laughs and nods -- He is now quite a dashing figure dark and handsome, more like a magician.*

G: *Ask him to show you something else in his kingdom.*

A: We were standing on the outer wall of the castle and four steel girders appeared which curved upwards to meet in the middle. Lucifer skipped up and I went to join him and the girders disappeared and I fall slowly into the courtyard and the ground opens up beneath me and I'm falling through --- I seem to be in a very big cavern which is filled with arrangements of pulleys and wheels and ropes and pendulums and the whole lot is moving to no real purpose. Then I backed up against the wall and it was made of spongy stuff that sucked me in and closed over me. I kicked and pushed about in this and then it was as though I rose to the surface of some liquid contained in a great big cast-iron cooking pot in an old-fashioned kitchen. And Lucifer's here again, he's got a tankard of ale on the table beside him and there's one for me too. It's time I tried to sort this out. I climb out of the pot and we're sitting in front of the fire with our beer and I say to Lucifer, 'Well, OK I asked you to show me your kingdom and I've got a feeling for this insubstantiality you've shown me, but what do you do with people? He holds his finger up in the air and says, 'Ah I was waiting for you to get to that' --- Now we're off through a series of barns and there's nothing there except leaves piled up in the corners.

G: Are the leaves symbols of the souls of people who have been over-powered by Lucifer?

A: I did wonder if those had anything to do with people. What happened is that we came to the end of the barns to a lake and Lucifer had got into a boat and was rowing out on the water. So I do a long jump and land in the boat with him. I say, 'Look here Lucifer, I want some straight answers from you. The leaves in the barns, were they the souls of human beings?' And he won't give a straight answer. It's caused a feeling of impatience in me -- I change places with him and row back to the shore, we get out and go to the barns and I say, 'Are these your leaves?' He nods. 'Why are they here?' He says, 'They fell'. And I take the leaves and sprinkle them over his head and I go back to the trapdoor, lower myself through and float down to an island in the ocean. I'm tired, so I'm lying on the beach and I take the sand and crunch it in my hands and it won't crunch. It won't collapse, it's solid sand and the particles bite into your skin. It hurts -- it's real. Ah, it's nice to be back here.

Again these are only short extracts from Andy's ECE, which lasted some two hours. Although it does not appear so, it was a very demanding experience for Andy, the guide and the group, because it took considerable concentration to keep in touch with what was going on. There was a strong tendency for thoughts to drift away or for people to fall asleep. The whole atmosphere was one of insubstantiality, confusion and illusion. These are prominent features of Luciferic activity. This works against rational down-to-earth consciousness and creates vague, castles-in-the-air illusory ideas, (the sort of ideas that we come up with when we solve the world's problems over a few pints of beer). Thus at no point in this experience was Andy able to get to grips with anything substantial. He has to go round and round in a confusing way to get from one room to another, the tunnel collapses, the castle collapses, the girders collapse, the machinery doesn't do anything. As a guide Andy is given a dog, which represents the follow-your-nose, lacking in rationality, approach to life. Lucifer's kingdom is nothing more than a collection of leaves in the wind and if we pursue this path through life we do not achieve anything substantial.

Andy Visits the Kingdom of Christ

Again this was a long ECE, which Andy found rather over-powering, so that he proceeded slowly; here we give a few extracts from it.

A: I'm falling down into a cloud around the Earth that is boiling and turbulent and represents Man's activity. He rushes about doing this and that and being very important and he creates this cloud of boiling activity that doesn't really go anywhere. Now I'm falling down on my back, my arms spread out in the air --- I saw my body land on a sharp piece of rock which was pointing upwards and it's just lying there --- I thought, 'Oh, I don't like that,' but in fact, well it's only my body after all -- then a big flash of lightning came down and consumed my body -- I think I have been put on a different plane. The body 'died', I saw myself to be ghostlike and then I was in an apparently substantial world again, but one in which the scene seems rather stylised, more symbolic. -- Now I'm in a big canyon and it's as though there are two parts of the matter, the left hand and the right hand separated by the canyon -- Somehow the canyon is entering into the darkness, into the Earth, and it stretches ahead in front of me -- it's a voluntary descending and in the descending you move forward through the darkness. And always, even at the bottom of the canyon, if you look up you can see the sky -- But you can't walk forward looking up at the sky, because you'll trip over your own feet. So you look up to see the light, but to carry on forward you've got to put your head down and watch where you put your feet. In other words you've got to go back into the darkness again. I saw two pictures. The first was of a man lying on his back on the floor of the canyon looking up at the sky. That's all he looked at, he quite forgot, ignored, what was going on around him. In the other, a man was on his knees, scrabbling about in the earth, sifting the earth, picking up pebbles. He was quite unaware of the existence of sky and light --- In the wall on either side of the canyon there are caves and tunnels and workings of one sort and another, activities for you to enter into if you want.

G: Is it necessary to enter into some of these activities on either side?

A: Oh yes, they're all there to be seen, but the magnitude of the canyon dwarfs them all. It's a magnificent thing and it cuts through everything, running in one direction -- The idea came to me that the progress of civilisations is represented by this canyon -- Then I turned to go forward and the way was stopped by a big iron gate set in the canyon.

G: What happens if you knock on the gate and ask to come through?

A: I knocked and the gate opened and a horny-headed figure stuck his head out and slammed the gate shut again --- There are two gates which are hinged to a post in the middle so you can go either to left or right -- As I was standing in the middle wondering what to do, I was presented with a middle way. I looked down and saw a very small door at the bottom in the middle, but it's too small for me.

G: Can you kneel down and tap?

A: Ha! - with my fingernail, yes --- I saw myself as an inflated dummy figure and I wondered what it was that was making me so big -- And the idea dropped into my mind that the gas that inflates this dummy so that it can't get through the small door, is pride -- I wonder if this presents a way in -- I take a pin and burst it and all the shreds of the balloon lie on the ground and then, from the middle of these there appears a very small figure, which is me. I see myself walking up to what is now a good sized-door, in comparison with me. I knocked and it opened but I didn't see anything but light -- Now I'm hovering about near the doorway, very uncertain as to what to do.

G: Ask the question, what do I have to do to enter the Kingdom of Heaven?

A: I did this, and I heard just one word, 'KNOCK'. So I knocked again and a magic carpet has rolled up to the door and I think it's an invitation to go in. So I sit down on the carpet and we glide away from the door into the white light and we've come to a steep mountain -- I looked up, wondering what I would see up there -- I thought I saw some kind of glow at the top and I feel a bit nervous about going any further, so we're going up slowly -- I see something like a golden throne --- I had been thinking that I didn't want to see what was on top of this mountain but then I thought I get shown what I must see, the carpet will take care of this --- I didn't want to look up -- I had my head down -- and then I did look up and everything was a golden blaze --- I got the strong impression of two very dark piercing eyes and then I stepped from the carpet onto the mountain in front of the throne and I knelt down --- I felt one finger put on the top of my head --- Two hands then reached down to lift me up to my feet --- I took one of these hands and moved round to the side --- I thought, well, if this is Christ himself -- I might be wrong in thinking he would ever get me up here -- and yet he was the one who had taken on an earthly body -- he had gone around with ordinary people -- then it seemed more reasonable that I should be up here -- I thought if this is Christ himself then he is real --- and I felt the rough bits on his hands --- and I felt the lines on his forehead, and they were the lines of earthly experience -- and I felt a little bit of sweat --- And I felt his feet as well, which were all hard and rough from walking on the rough ground --- He is a Supreme Being --- and yet we have this much in common -- that I can reach out and feel his hardened and roughened feet, and I can feel the lines on his forehead ------ I think that's just about it --- there's little more to do, certainly hardly anything to say. It doesn't feel the time to ask questions or say anything. I feel as though if I were to ask a question he would not reply, he would point back at me, and I would find the answer there. But I did say one thing --- I said that I had expected there would be hordes of angels and cherubs around, and he opened his arms out and said something like, 'Well, it is whatever you want, if you want angels here we can have them here. That doesn't really matter, does it'. And it doesn't ..... So I just waited a little bit ---- and then I wanted to look into his eyes again --- and they now seemed blue --- and I looked again at his forehead which was slightly beaded with sweat ---- and I took my handkerchief and dried it ---- and I thought he said, 'Whatever you do for Me, you do for others' ----- and that was the end.

In all of our ECEs we had the feeling of being in the presence of high-powered entities, and this was particularly so with these three experiences, especially the last, Christ, ECE. Andy in particular felt that in them he had been lifted up to heights that he could not maintain. In his next ECE he found himself high up above serried banks of clouds and given a pair of skis and he had to ski down through level after level of the clouds, until he reached an ordinary Earth situation, and the clouds then withdrew.

Andy's ECEs portray Man as existing between a material world (Earth existence) and a spiritual world (that of the Omniverse Hierarchy from which he incarnated onto Earth) and having to find a middle path in which he integrates the two. Although they were given in the esoteric-mythological terms of 'kingdoms of Ahriman and Lucifer', they express the fact that Man has a substance side and a spiritual side to his nature and to his existence and has to find a balance between them.

On Sai Baba

We had been wondering where Sai Baba fits into this story, with his manifestation of Christ-like powers but seemingly remote from the developments taking place in Western society, which we termed the 'prodigal son' path. (We could have related more readily to Daskalos, with his westernised explanations of mysticism but at this stage of our activities we did not know about him).

G: We have been reading about Sai Baba and one cannot fail to be impressed by him, can you get any relevant imagery?

T: I had an image of Sai Baba in an orange robe; this image radiates immense love, it's very powerful. I feel that the presence of Sai Baba is to make people aware of this love. It's a feeling that doesn't go into words at all. It's an all-enveloping love that takes in everyone and everything and this man holds out this possibility, all men can feel this, all men can be part of it. It seems as if Sai Baba brings this down to Earth, into the physical world, where it can be felt and experienced but people still have to work their way towards it and there seem to be so many paths that lead to it.

G: If a person becomes a Sai Baba devotee, do they forsake the 'prodigal son' path?

T: The imagery shows the development and realisation of the Ego in the prodigal-son Western stream of development and the Ego then subsequently losing its self importance and seeing itself as part of a much vaster plan. It also showed an Ego seeking out a route to Sai Baba and here the Ego had to be consumed. It didn't develop and realise itself, it had to disappear and become part of this all-enveloping love. There was no stage at which the Ego developed to become an 'I' and then, out of its experiences, moving towards the state of oneness and wholeness.

G: Sai Baba teaches that one should purify oneself and get off the cycle of reincarnation. But if we were to do that, surely we would be rejecting the whole point and purpose of humanity, our job is to go on reincarnating and fighting our way through?

T: Yes, this is so. All the images of this that we have ever had are brought back again. The Higher Self that can see both forwards and backwards and can accumulate the totality of lives it has lived, that can help to decide where its next experience should be and can see the evolution of all its bodies. It can see that by working things out at this level, shut up inside its bodies and taking its independently-won qualities back to the Spiritual Hierarchy it is contributing to the evolution of the Spiritual Hierarchy. These images are very intense, very bright, very clear.

G: Does this mean that one should reject Sai Baba?

T: No, I don't think so.

G: Can you get an image of Egos that are struggling along the prodigal-son path absorbing Sai Baba's love quality?

T: Yes, it's something that they can experience. But the words come in, 'There is no short cut' -- It's a wonderful feeling associated with Sai Baba, you really can see why people turn to him.

G: So a strong Ego, committed to the prodigal-son path, could go to Sai Baba and gain a great deal, without being deflected?

T: Yes, but it would be so easy to wallow in this feeling, this sense of having arrived or belonging, it would be so easy to get lost in that.

G: And when you see an Ego lost in that, it is taken off the path?

T: Yes, I think so, but it's nothing very clear at all ..... I feel it's all beyond us .....

Chapter 18

ECEs on the Forces of Nature and the Natures of Substances

In Chapter 16 we described the way in which we learned to enter into a state of expanded consciousness. In Chapter 17 we described how this gave us imagery that purported to show us how spiritual, Ego-thinking and soul-feeling activities affect our incarnating into the physical world, sometimes causing imbalances and illness, and how humanity is affected by the spiritual Ahrimanic, Luciferic and Christ forces. We think that this information was transmitted to us by entities (our Higher Selves?) that were able to perceive these spiritual world activities themselves, or able to contact other entities that did so, and then to pass the information on. As we stated in the Introduction, we think that we are at the beginning of an era that will be characterised by the development of an evolutionary-wholistic understanding arising from the fusion of scientific observations with the findings of mystics, in states of higher consciousness, about what lies behind the phenomena observed by science. But this will take a lot of sorting out from both the scientific and mystical points of view. We have spent many years trying to do this, on the way to arriving at *h*K-M. This has been a long and confusing journey encompassing much that we did not, and still do not, understand. Many times it became apparent that we were 'on the wrong track' and we have mostly discarded such material. But in other cases we are not sure about the situation; there could, or could not, be useful insights in the material that we received. So, in this, and the following two, chapters we present brief extracts from our experiences to show the path that we have followed, drawing in relevant material from elsewhere and making such assessments as we can, largely from the point of view of *h*K-M that eventually emerged.

According to *h*K-M, everything in the Universe, and indeed in the whole Omniverse, is part of an evolving Kosmos that has arisen out of a dormant energy state. The dormant energy became active and broke down into self-actualising s-entities. Then, as these became increasingly active their interaction caused them to break down at their peripheries, into 'whirlpools' which were centres of activity, taking in energy from their environment and flowing it back out changed by the experience it had undergone. Out of this activity the 'whirlpools' experienced a sense of self and became self-actualising. Thus, everything is part of an interweaving, evolving totality and in order to understand any part it is necessary to understand how it came into existence, the qualities that it was 'born with' and how it is developing further, and its relationship to the rest of the totality.

Wherever we look in the world around us we see living things; plants in many forms with roots that grow down into the earth and foliage and flowers that grow upwards into the atmosphere; animals of many different forms working out their life cycles and human beings pursuing multitudinous activities. These have all arisen out of the forces created by this interweaving activity. We present extracts from some of the ECEs that were concerned with this problem, starting with an ECE, in which Ted was the receiver, that purported to show the cosmic forces at work in the Solar System.

Cosmic Forces

T: I'm way, way out looking at the Earth. There appear to be different levels and areas of activity that stretch way out into space. Long curtains of colour extend towards the Earth and then move back towards space in continuous motion, continuously changing. Now I look down on the Solar System with all the planets, including the Earth, processing round the Sun. Each planet has an enormous sphere of activity around it that interpenetrates with all the other planets. The Sun's sphere of influence envelopes the whole thing, fig. 18.1.

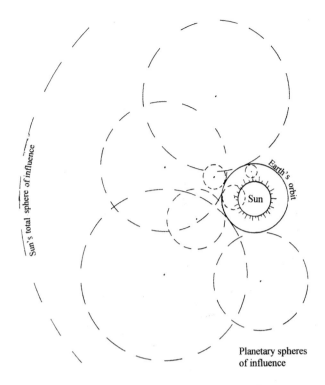

Fig. 18.1 Ted's image of the interacting (etheric) spheres of the Solar System.

This great interplay of force between all of them is in terms of curtains or draperies of light that rise and fall. The energies complement one another and the Earth moves through them --- Now I've got an image of a man and all this activity is vital to him. I see all these fields of energy pulsing through him and coming back out of him and the form of it is changed when it comes back out. When I try to isolate one activity, such as the Sun's, then the head of the man appears to be lit with a golden light but I still see the other activities pulsing through him.
G: *What about the Moon?*
T: *I see the physical Moon and this has a sphere of activity that reaches down to Earth level; where this touches the Earth it's flattened and encompasses a fair area of ground, which moves as the Moon moves round the Earth and its influence penetrates into the Earth.*
G: *What is its relationship to man?*
T: *There's a silvery area around the solar plexus and the lower part of the chest.*
G: *Mars?*
T: *A word came up for that - blood.*
G: *Saturn?*
T: *Warmth and feelings.*
G: *Mercury?*
T: *Nothing clear*

This ECE portrays the planets of the Solar System as producing fields of activity within an overall field of activity caused by the Sun, all acting on the Earth and, as part of the Earth scene, acting on Man. This pattern of interacting cosmic spheres of etheric activity is described by Steiner and other mystics. It is also described in a book by SHERWOOD(1) who developed the ability to communicate with discarnate entities who sought, with her, to formulate an objective understanding of their world in relation to ours and vice versa. This gave rise to a fourfold conception of our existence, i.e. physical, etheric, astral (soul) and Ego, SHERWOOD(2). The discarnates stated that with the type of vision they possessed, they did not see the physical Earth but instead they perceived a much larger etheric spheroid revolving in space, corresponding to the orbit of the Earth, carrying with it on its rim a small void where the physical body of the Earth exists. Each planet similarly exists on the periphery of the wheel of its revolving etheric spheroid and they all exist within a spheroid of the Sun's orbit and this in turn wheels through cosmic space, carrying with it all these interlocked systems of etheric energy.

> *'Forget the illusion of small, solid planets wandering about precariously in empty space. Think rather of those shining discs rotating in harmonious order and mutual dependence, interlocked in a great etheric system and sweeping through the sky on the verge of the stupendous etheric sphere traced out by the Sun itself as it rotates about some unknown hub of the Universe. The Ancients were feeling for the truth when they spoke of the turning of the spheres'*

According to hK-M all the planets and the Sun create dynamic stress fields in the space-energy and, with a state of consciousness directed to 'etheric activities', this could be what Steiner and Sherwood's communicators perceived and what was portrayed to Ted in this ECE. Also, it might be that the peoples of early civilisations were not so strongly incarnated into physical consciousness so that they perceived etheric activities, or that their priests did in a heightened state of consciousness, and that they perceived the heavens in this way. As we have stated earlier, WILSON (2) pointed out the great emphasis that ancient civilisations gave to the movements of the heavenly bodies and with developing a precise understanding of these and he raised the question of why this should be so. When we look at the sky we see only stars as pinpoints of light and the larger Sun and Moon and, other than light and warmth from the Sun it is not immediately obvious that these are of great significance in our lives. But if we were to see ourselves as part of a vast system of interacting spheres of activity, like those described in this ECE and by mystics and by Jane Sherwood's discarnate contacts, we would certainly feel that what goes on in the heavens affects what happens on Earth and that it is important to understand these activities.

A simple example of the effect of a cosmic stress field, in this case that of the Earth Entity, affecting events on Earth is that of magnetism. It is a property of iron and a few other materials that when the atoms of which they consist are lined up so that their self-actualising activities reinforce each other the material exhibits a force field around it. We see this with a bar magnet which has associated with it a B-cell-type force field, as demonstrated by the way in which this acts on, and lines up, iron filings, (fig. 9.6). In this case the B-cell stress field of the magnet has an affinity for, and responds to, that of the Earth Entity, so that a pivoted needle of magnetic material lines up with the Earth Entity's B-cell field in the widely used device of a magnetic compass.

Cosmic stress fields can affect chemical reactions. For example, Picardi measured the rate at which bismuth trichloride forms the colloid, bismuth oxychloride, when poured into distilled water, over a period of many years and found this to vary with cosmic conditions, in particular with Solar eruptions and Sunspot cycles, (GAUQUELIN).

A planetary effect on 'capillary dynamolysis' patterns and precipitation in associated chemical reactions has been demonstrated by a number of workers. In these experiments a mixture of 1% ferrous sulphate and 1% silver nitrate solutions is allowed to rise up a cylinder of filter paper. As this takes place metallic silver precipitates out and affects the upward flow of the solutions, thereby producing a distinctive pattern. Small variations in the rate of precipitation produce large variations in the flow patterns. Materials under investigation are then added to the ferrous sulphate/silver nitrate mix and their effects monitored. In one such investigation 1% lead nitrate solution was added to the mixture and changes in the chemical reactions and associated dynamolysis patterns were observed before, during, and after a Mars-Saturn conjunction. (Mars is traditionally associated with iron and Saturn with lead). It was found that the capillary dynamolysis patterns and the reaction between the iron sulphate and lead nitrate (to form lead sulphate) changed around the period of the conjunction, (KOLLERSTROM and DRUMMOND). This was in agreement with the findings of other workers on this system and similar effects have been found for other metallic salt solutions and the traditionally associated planet, (KOLLERSTROM).

PLAYFAIR and HILL summarise the investigations and theories of a number of scientists who have concluded that planetary forces affect sunspot activity. A relationship between sunspot activity and weather and other Earthly phenomena could affect physical and biological activity on Earth. But how and why the position of a planet affects the behaviour of a particular substance, as with the Saturn-Mars conjunction and the behaviour of a lead salt, is something for which there is no current scientific explanation.

The Sun produces daily rhythms of light and dark that create rhythms of activity and sleep in organisms and, on a longer time scale, annual rhythms of activity in plants and animals. The Moon has an effect on the oceans, resulting in the tides, and also on many sea organisms that results in a lunar rhythm to their existence. GAUQUELIN, WATSON, and PLAYFAIR and HILL, have gathered together the results of a number of investigations of these rhythms. By depriving organisms of light or exposing them to changed, artificial light conditions it has been shown, as might be expected, that the effect of the Sun is largely associated with its light impinging on the organism. However, this is not always so. For example, the activity of the embryos of fertilised hen's eggs kept in uniform lighting and temperature in an incubator follows a twenty-four hour variation, with peaks related to sunrise and sunset, suggesting a response to the Sun's stress field without exposure to the Sun's light. Frank A. Brown carried out many investigations of the relationship of the activities of different organisms to solar and lunar rhythms. He found that, as with the chick embryos, seaweed, carrots, potatoes, earthworms and salamanders, when kept in uniform lighting and temperature conditions in the laboratory, show a daily variation in metabolic activity that peaks at sunrise and sunset. Particularly outstanding were his investigations of the opening and closing of the valves of oysters which, in the sea follows the rhythm of the tides. When enclosed in a tank in the laboratory, where there are no tides, oysters (and other sea organisms) continued with the same rhythm of activity. Brown then moved oysters to an inland laboratory some thousand miles away and found that they changed their rhythm of activity to relate to the movement of the Moon at their new site.

According to hK-M the oysters in the laboratory were responding to the changes in the stress field in the space-energy brought about by the Moon. Where they had come from in the sea they were not responding to the changes in the tide but both the sea in its tides and the oysters were responding to the changes in the Moon's stress field. This is only one example where correlations between phenomena are not due to the effect one has on the other but to the fact that they are both responding to changes in the underlying space-energy stress field. In some experiments quoted by Gauquelin and Watson organisms were responsive to a local change in the space-energy field produced by placing a magnet in their proximity. The behaviour of cockchafer beetles in an opaque container was affected by the nearby presence of a large lump of lead, which altered the 'gravitational' space-energy stress field in that region.

The conventional scientific explanation for the cyclic variation in the behaviour of organisms is that they adapt to cyclic changes in their environment, that is, the organism comes first and the cyclic behaviour comes later. The hK-M viewpoint is the opposite of this. According to hK-M, organisms arise where a cyclic stress field, acting on a region of the space-energy gives it a sense of self so that it takes over the cyclic pattern of behaviour and makes it self actualising. Once established in this way then, in pursuing increasing sense of self it may depart from the rhythm that formed it, in the way that hominids were formed with a day-night rhythm but now modern man, in his pursuit of increased sense of self, has developed devices that enable him to turn night into day and to change his life-style accordingly.

The Plant

In a few of the ECEs we asked about the role of the Sun in plant nature and behaviour, as with the following one with Ted as the receiver.

G: Can you see a seed planted just below the surface of the Earth and an interaction between the Sun and the seed?
T: I have an image of a seed in the soil and the Sun beaming down onto the Earth. Part of the Sun's activity goes down into the earth and, as well as providing physical warmth for the soil, some of the etheric activity associated with the Sun goes into the soil and reacts with the Earth's etheric field. There is a response from the Earth's etheric field to move out towards the Sun. So the seed finds itself at the boundary of these two lots of forces. It's being worked upon to move down into the earth and the Earth's etheric energies are moving out and so inducing the seed to move upwards to the Sun. So that as the seed begins to germinate it forms a centre through which these forces concentrate. As it pushes its roots down into the Earth and it pushes its shoots towards the Sun, it is responding to the flow of energies focused through it. The plant has a rudimentary etheric body and it appears to be more concerned with external relationships. It's as if this is controlled from outside.
G: Can you get the experience of the seed, the 'consciousness' of it?
T: I can be inside a seed and as it absorbs moisture from the soil there is a feeling that the seed will only respond when the energies are right. When it's put into the soil the Sun's energies work through it and the Earth's etheric energies also work through it. Between them these elicit a response, a quickening of the seed, but it's simply a response to these two lots of forces. There's nothing to suggest that the seed is making a conscious decision to come to life - it's responding to the flow.
G: So there's a force carrying substances upwards from the Earth and another force carrying substances down into the Earth?
T: This appears to be the same force. It originates outside and rays down into the Earth and carries down the root system of the plant. It is then returned from Earth and takes the mineral materials into the root and away on up through the plant. The Sun's etheric activity goes through the seed into the earth around it, it radiates out in a series of lines into the soil and it's grasping and holding. --- The image I had then was of an enormously enlarged seed and the skin of the seed bulged slowly outwards and follows this channel. The image shows the interaction of the etheric forces at the Earth's surface producing plant-like etheric forms and material is then carried by the flow of the forces until it fills up the etheric form.

BRENNAN states that she, and her mentor, Dr. John PIERRAKOS, through their higher sense perception observed that a plant grows into a prior existing etheric form.

G: If we look at the atomic level, the same activities give rise to the plant chemistry?
T: That's OK. Yes
G: So the chemistry inside the seed, the gene structure, has been built up by exactly the same forces that produce the form of the plant?

T: Yes, the image was of the form of the plant appearing, then this extending right down through all the levels to the atoms.

This ECE ascribes plant growth and form to the flow through it of etheric forces between Earth and Sun. The Earth's etheric field has a 'whirlpool' relationship with the larger one of the Sun, within which it exists. Thus there is a flow of etheric energy from the Sun's etheric field into it, which it returns having acted on it. Steiner, presumably from his etheric vision, describes the Earth as 'breathing in and out' - (WACHSMUTH) as also do several of the channelled communications summarised in Chapter 14. A seed acts as a focal point within these etheric flows, to create a stress field that gives rise to the form of the plant and causes substances to take up this form. (We have shown in figs. 15.9 and 15.10 how stress fields can take the form of plants and we deal with this further in Chapters 25 and 26). However, it needs fluidity of movement of the substances of the seed and its environment, i.e. moisture, for these to respond to these forces. The way that the etheric forces act on the seed determines also the chemistry of its substances and hence its genetic behaviour. A similar description of plant growth was given in one of Harry's ECEs, in which 'Astradamus' gave him a lecture on etheric forces:

H: It's to do with learning about etheric forces and growth. He says it's very important to the group as a whole.
G: Can we start with a seed in the earth?
H: Yes, I've put it in the earth -- it seems that forces come down from the Sun and take the roots down with them and the forces that come from the Earth take the plant up with them. The seed acts as a point of focus for these forces. The Sun forces pass through the seed and become transformed into Earth forces and the Earth forces come up from the Earth through the seed and get transformed into Sun forces and return to the Sun, fig. 18.2.

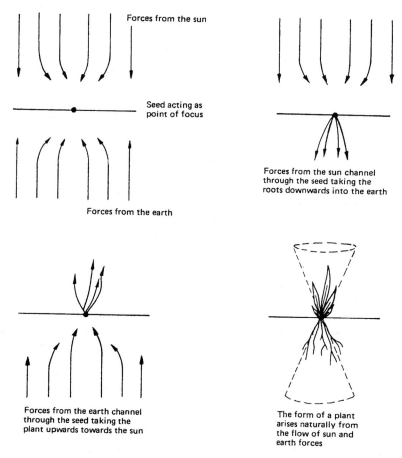

Fig. 18.2 Harry's image of how etheric flows from Sun and Earth act on a seed, to give rise to the form of the plant.

If we imagine water impinging on compacted earth, then the water will permeate slowly through it and this is the way that the etheric flows pass through the Earth planet. But if there is a small area where the water can pass through more readily, then a jet-like flow will occur there and this is what happens when a seed is present in the earth: its etheric body responds more readily to the etheric flow, than do the substances of the earth around it, so that in both directions of flow it produces a fanning out, jet-like pattern. In another ECE Harry was given a similar explanation for the formation and opening of a bud:

H: There's a very large tree and I'm up in the branches. There's a group of people and we're going to study the interface between tips of the tree and the air. There's a small spiritual being coming out of a closed bud that we're looking at. We watch consciousness return to this being, it opens its eyes and says, 'I'm free' and flies up and away. They signify a grid pattern around this bud; the bud is long, tapering off to a tip. There are lines that go out at right angles from the bud and other lines that are parallel to the bud, layers of them going outwards that form a very regular pattern all round this tip. The leader of this group holds his hand up in a sort of chopping action. The bud unfolds within this regular pattern of lines.

G: Do these lines actually exist or are they diagrammatic?

H: They say they exist, 'This is what we see'. Now he's superimposing another diagram for the Sun's forces, to give two inverted cones, fig. 18.3.

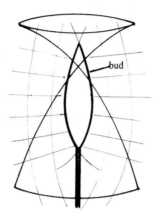

Fig. 18.3 Harry's image of the etheric stress field around a bud and the double cone that forms a growing point.

This can be applied just as well to a flower coming out of the ground but they've chosen to show it as a bud on a tree. It's to do with the bud being up in the air away from the Earth's surface, so that we needn't worry about root systems.

G: What makes this pattern of lines?

H: He says it's the bud that makes it. They are produced by the forces from the Earth flowing through the bud with the point of meeting at the centre of the bud.

G: This is the same as our diagram for a seed in the surface of the Earth, where the Sun's lines get swept in through the seed and spread out into the Earth, while the Earth rays back in the opposite manner. Does this double cone exist at all growing points?

H: That's right, where the two cones meet there is a light-kindling spark --They're showing us the air a little way out from the bud, there's an exchange of spiritual beings there. The ones coming in carry sacks of, like fertiliser, they direct the opening of the bud, they're using forces from the sap and the substance. He says, these beings have to grow through experience. The ones going out are excited and laughing and glad to be free - but they are also messengers.

In this ECE it is claimed that a growing plant, or bud, as it penetrates out into the space-energy creates stresses in it, which can be perceived with space-energy (etheric) vision. Also, it is claimed small etheric entities exist that feed the plant with etheric energy. HODSON, who claimed to be able to enter into a heightened, mystical, state of consciousness in which he could observe these activities, stated that large numbers of 'small etheric creatures' are to be seen moving in and out of growing plants. These absorb something from the atmosphere, expand, and enter the plant and discharge the 'vital energy' that they have absorbed. A growing bulb gives the impression of being a small power house; there is an intense 'etheric light' at its centre and from this rises an upward flowing 'etheric stream' carrying with it, at a slower pace, moisture and nutriment.

While the form of the plant may be due to the pattern of etheric force flow through the seed, the body of the plant arises from the interaction of these forces with substances of the earth.

H: I start with a seed that germinates, it's alive, it wakens up. It looks around it and says, What have I got to do? - strive upwards towards the light. It looks down into the earth and sees all these beings and forces and it opens itself up to them. It becomes aware of these forces around it and it wants to gather them into itself. It literally tries to open up its body so that all these beings can channel through it. As it grows and gets bigger and bigger, this waking consciousness dies away - a cycle - it becomes exhausted and goes back to sleep again and mineralising forces set in and grasp it and bring it back down again.

G: Why does it strive upwards towards the Sun?

H: It's striving towards its source, that's where it came from, it wants to get back.

G: And what is its experience as it does that?

H: Expansion and growth.

247

At that time we had been studying Steiner's lectures on Agriculture, in which he claimed that calcium (in lime) mediates the earthly formative force, while silicon is the mediator for the cosmic forces in plant growth and that carbon follows these to give the form of the plant. So the guide asked:

G: To strive upwards it has to choose something to do this and to bed itself down in the ground it has to choose something to do that. Is it correct that the plant seeks out specifically silicon and calcium to do that?
H: I get this very strong picture of silicon giving this strong growth above the ground. But not only that, when the silicon beings leave the plant they are looking back behind them at the plant calling to their fellow beings saying, 'this way, this way'.
G: What about calcium?
H: I'm seeing it enter the roots; it's not travelling very fast and while it's in the roots it looks back and it directs the roots to further calcium in the ground. The silicon once it enters the roots whoofs up the plant and escapes and becomes free, whereas the calcium would rather say look, go over there. It does this on its way to becoming free. All the calcium, all the silicon beings are linked to each other.
G: What about iron?
H: Iron seems to be the element that binds it all together. If I watch a plant which has no iron and iron is given to it, it enters the root system and goes up at a very assured pace. They seem very balanced beings, the ones that go up. Iron's very evolved because it's conscious that it's got these capabilities that if we don't make full use of them we can't get the maximum amount of iron out. But if we help to grow strong plants, if we work with the plant to strengthen it, then that will help ourselves and help everything.
G: The plant also needs minute quantities of trace elements?
H: I don't think this is easy but it's something to do with harmonious growth. The plant grows in a rhythmical way, rhythms determined by night and day and the Moon; rhythms determined by the weather, the amount of cloud cover, the amount of rain. They indicate that a lot of these trace elements have some important function for the form of the plant. The plant has a good deal of control over trace elements. The plant gathers up one of these trace elements and tucks it into a point in the plant and either a new shoot or a bud will grow -- some sort of occurrence will take place in the form of the plant. Says the whole structure of the plant is a delicate balance of various things. Two important functions are the growth above ground and the growth below ground, which the silicon and calcium have a lot to do with. Iron bonds and strengthens the plant. Carbon is to do with form. Hydrogen is to do with breathing; oxygen is to do with this and that. It's a very delicate balance between all these things. Most of the trace element beings seem fairly unconscious; they're moving quite slowly so this means the plant will use them. So it gathers, say beryllium together sticks it on the outer wall and a little shoot flicks out. Now this is a good channel so this beryllium goes along the shoot and speeds up and flies off the tip. The planets have got something to do with it. It's a geometrical thing, it tries to produce some sort of etheric shape so it can home in on its planet. A planet has forms, a characteristic geometry; the element will try and leave the plant in that form, that particular geometry.

This ECE states that the plant grows in a rhythmical way determined by night and day and also the Moon. FYFE carried out 70,000 capillary dynamolysis tests over a period of twelve years with mistletoe sap, that showed a correlation with the Moon's path across the heavens.

In making use of minerals to create substance bodies, plants have an effect on the minerals.

T: The image is of a plant's growing cycle, with the seed putting down roots and beginning to spread upwards, right through the 12 month cycle, putting out its leaves, buds and flowers and seeds and dying away again. The bits of the mineral kingdom that get caught up in the plant are subjected to a much higher level of activity; this raises them up. The plant has an etheric body that is working down into the mineral connected with the plant. There's a spell during the transformation from bud to flower to seed where it's at the peak of its activity and then it dies away. The mineral is now transformed to something else, it's part of the seed. It waits to be awakened afresh when the new growing cycle begins.
G: Presumably it does it slightly easier?
T: Yes, the image showed that the leaves, stems and roots of the plant that were left in the soil during the dormant season were broken down and returned to the mineral kingdom but not to the same level that they were before. They're raised up just that little bit, they're more adapted to the plant's requirements than the raw mineral.

We asked about what happened to the mineral in plants and also in animals.

T: The image shows the mineral level as quite sluggish, it's quite dead. The image moves up to the plant kingdom and there the mineral is raised to a more active level. In the plant there is just the vague glimmering of some sort of consciousness, some feeling of uplift, of knowing something was happening - the deadness, the lifelessness has gone, there's a quickening to it. Then in the animal kingdom it's moved up a stage further. I see an image of the animal with the mineral kingdom spread all through its body. There's a wide range to the mineral kingdom within the animal; it goes from pretty well dead, inert material, to material that is at the level of the plant and levels where the action is faster still. In man it's the animal story again but some of it's at a higher level of consciousness than the animal but no particular words come in.

The 'Characters' of Substances

From the large range of substances available, plants and animals utilise specific ones to form bodies through which they manifest their inner natures. Thus different substances must possess different qualities. In the following ECE the behaviours of different substances were portrayed to us as resulting from their 'spiritual natures', as expounded to Harry by a 'figure of wisdom'.

H: He says, we've got to see the spiritual working in the Earth on the minerals.
G: If you could see a mineral some time back and some time in the future, would it have evolved?
H: Yes, it would have become more refined, like people become more refined, more individualistic.
G: Can we look at iron in the past and in the future?
H: Iron in the past was duller, its whole consciousness was dull, it had no strength or will. During very long processes of development it met influences that tried to change it. It resisted those, so that iron is right up in the front in the evolution of the elements. As it evolves it releases spirit substance and starts to acquire the properties it now has. It has to do this in order to have the iron qualities as it works in plants, animals and the human body. It has to lose its spirituality, otherwise it won't develop these qualities that are necessary for the evolution of the other kingdoms.
G: By losing its spirituality you mean it's got to descend into matter?
H: Yes.
G: Is it that in overcoming the Ahrimanic force it develops its will?
H: I see a battle between Ahriman and Lucifer acting on iron in the middle. There's Ahriman dragging it down (this is right from the year dot when everything was very thin gas-like stuff) but as it condensed I see Lucifer pulling the spiritual out of it. But Ahriman and Lucifer do not know physical matter as we know it, they're pulling at the soul. Iron has emerged unscathed. The minerals have evolved to the extent that they are now performing functions in plants, animals and man. The picture I've had all along is of Lucifer and Ahriman north and south. In between them is the mouth of a trumpet pointing to the right, (fig. 18.4a) and the physical iron is emerging from the mouth of the trumpet, but the soul of iron is behind the trumpet's mouth. Through its experience as physical iron it can evolve soul qualities and make them its own.

[At the time of these ECEs we imagined that the trumpet image was a way of expressing the sequential coming into existence of the elements of substances symbolically, particularly since it does not bear any relation to the way that these are formed in stars. However, recently as a result of sophisticated analyses scientists are thinking that the Universe could be horn shaped, fig 18.4b, (BATTERSBY).

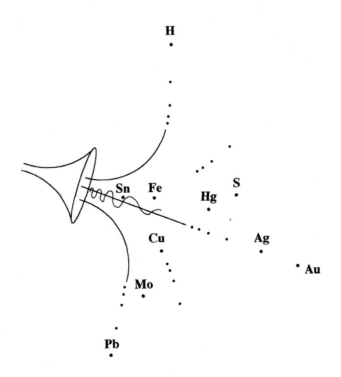

Fig. 18.4 (a) Harry's image of substances being 'trumpeted' into existence.

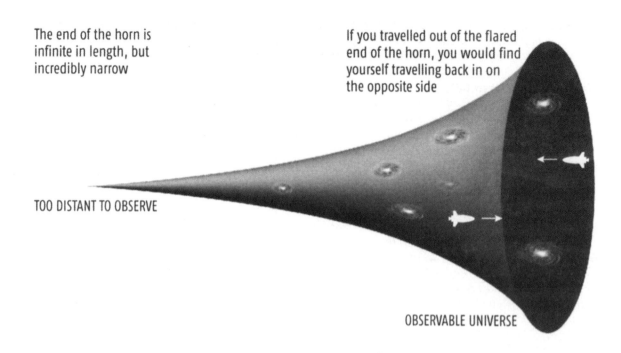

The end of the horn is infinite in length, but incredibly narrow

If you travelled out of the flared end of the horn, you would find yourself travelling back in on the opposite side

TOO DISTANT TO OBSERVE

OBSERVABLE UNIVERSE

Fig.18.4(b) A recent scientific conception of the Universe as being trumpet shaped.
(reproduced by courtesy of the publishers of New Scientist)

On a simplistic view this portrays the Universe as starting from small beginnings that increase in magnitude and variety as it develops and since what it becomes creates what it is, i.e. its 'space', this can be represented by a trumpet shape].

According to *h*K-M we are spiritual beings from the Omniverse Hierarchy who have incarnated into the Earth situation so as to evolve by working with the substances of the Earth. In this way we develop our spiritual qualities of will, feeling and thinking in a way that we never would have done if we had remained in the Omniverse Hierarchy. This ECE portrays plants as doing the same thing at a lower level of development. And, in the same way that we select substances to express our natures/activities, e.g. ceramics and iron for building strong structures, aluminium and plastics for building light ones, gold and silver for ornaments and jewellery, etc., so do plants select substances by which they can express their natures. What we, and plants, do gives the minerals that we work with experience that, it is claimed in the ECE, contributes to their evolution. It is not immediately obvious how this is so, but we have mentioned in Chapter 13 that SHELDRAKE has pointed out that when chemists first create a new substance they can find it difficult to get it to crystallise out of solution but that once it has done so, it crystallises more readily next time and increasingly so thereafter.

G: How does iron compare with, say, sulphur.
H: Sulphur is quite a long way ahead of iron.
G: Gold?
H: It's disappearing off into the distance on the right.
G: Where's silver?
H: Somewhere between iron and gold.
G: What about a metal that's radioactive - uranium?
H: That's way over to the left.
G: Is its disintegration related to its retarded state?
H: Yes, it couldn't make it, couldn't keep up. It's fully under the influence of both Ahriman and Lucifer. They both exert their full will on it. They're disintegrating it.
G: It's because its got no sort of metal ego?
H: That's right, it's got no ego, nothing to fight with.
G: Where is oxygen?
H: It's a bit towards the left.
G: What happens when iron is grasped by oxygen?
H: It holds it back towards the left.
G: Where is hydrogen?
H: A big cloud right up at the top.
G: I can understand that hydrogen is Luciferic because it's a gas and has hardly become substantial but oxygen is on the centre line lagging behind and yet everything else on the centre line is solid. I would have thought everything would get denser from the Luciferic down to the Ahrimanic.

H: They said it's not quite like that, it seems that density isn't the property to look at. Oxygen is very difficult to get as a liquid, it requires such a low temperature, so it does the next best thing and combines with the solid, oxygen is trying to pull itself forward. It then appears as a solid - you should be looking at qualities like that.

G: We have to look at its desires?

H: Yes.—Now he wants us to grasp something, not just about oxygen but about air. He keeps mentioning the spirituality of the air. When you breathe in, you're breathing in this spiritual substance of air. When you breathe out, you're breathing out just physical air. The spiritual substance is still entering your body, which works on it during the rest period between breaths.

G: Are we, in fact, breathing in ego qualities at the same time?

H: Oxygen likes to be at the centre of things, it would like to be in the centre of man, it would like to take man over.

G: What's the soul quality of nitrogen?

H: I get the image of a very thin old man who's interested in books. He says, the bearer of spiritual life.

G: Old man with books - this denotes some sort of wisdom?

H: Yes, eternal wisdom.

G: Is it that we have to breathe in oxygen and nitrogen in the right combination to give us egotism in conjunction with wisdom?

H: Yes, he says nitrogen is a regulator.

G: What happens to the nitrogen we breathe in?

H: Warms up our bodies, makes them 'tingle' and alive. A will to live and to carry on forwards. The wisdom of man as a spiritual being. Something to do with the head as well. Sends forces flowing up the spinal cord to the brain.

In considering this ECE, we have the problem of accounting for the different 'characters' of substances. The basis of hK-M is that everything is part of an ever-evolving Kosmos and so substances must be seen in this light. Modern science also sees the Universe as evolving, i.e. celestial bodies and life on Earth have come to be the way they are as a result of their evolution. It sees different substances as having been formed at different stages of evolution, but it does not ascribe their properties to this, i.e. to being less-or more-evolved and it does not see substances as evolving once they have been formed.

A way of correlating the characters of different people is to put them on a line according to how evolved they are and at right angles to this to position them according to the extent to which they are Luciferically (Idealistically) or Ahrimanically (Materialistically) orientated, fig.18.5.

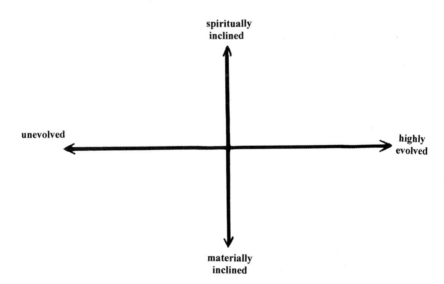

Fig. 18.5 An evolutionary-wholistic scheme for the classification of people's natures according to how evolved they are and their orientation towards spiritual-idealistic (Luciferic) or materialistic (Ahrimanic) tendencies.

In this ECE the characters of different substances are related to one another in this way. The 'characters' of different animals could probably be classified in a similar way: birds, up in the air - 'Luciferic', surface creatures on the centre line, creatures living predominantly in the earth as 'Ahrimanic': and whether they are primitive or more evolved. Plants could also be classified as being more- or less-evolved and as reaching more up or down (foliage or root dominated) or balanced.

While this ECE refers to the 'spiritual natures' of substances, when we pursued this viewpoint further the ECEs responded according to Steiner's cosmology of creation taking place by the activities of a spiritual hierarchy that, at that time, was the viewpoint that we were pursuing. The primary purpose of the Spiritual Hierarchy was to create the bodies of Man. To do this different levels gave (sacrificed) parts of themselves to build up a hierarchy of activities in the world of substance that reflected their natures, which they then separated off and individualised as Man's bodies. According to this viewpoint Man is an unrealised miniature version of the Spiritual Hierarchy separated off from the mainstream. At the same time these activities, in a less-evolved state, created the mineral, plant and animal kingdoms of Nature. The underlying idea is that this sacrificed material evolves through its experiences on Earth, which the Spiritual Hierarchy seeks to monitor and foster and which then returns, as the prodigal son, to its source, with the fruits of its labours. As we tried to pin this viewpoint down to practical situations the ECEs expressed vast quantities of information along these lines that we could not then, and cannot now, understand and tended to reject. However, in case we have missed something important that could be meaningful to other people we include here a short example of the type of features that it portrayed.

The Basic Nature of Substances

The following is a synopsis of an ECE dealing with copper and how its form changes in melting and solidification, with Ted as the experiencer.

G: Can you get an image of copper in terms of the activities of the Hierarchy?
T: I see this as an image of a piece of copper with alongside an image of the activities of the hierarchy of which it comprises. External forces come down from the main Hierarchy and attempt to influence these but their flow becomes quite sluggish and they don't make much impression on it. There is, however, a little bit going on because the flow comes down and returns. Overseeing all this is a Copper Being well up in the Hierarchy who is looking after this. In the same way that you have flows through man at physical, etheric and astral levels, there is a similar flow through the copper. The Beings of the main Hierarchy find it very tough to work on the copper hierarchy but there's a sense of harmony about it because they are both making their contribution to evolution. So it's a job and they just get on with it.
G: Can you get some idea of what its objective is?
T: The same qualities that the Hierarchy have donated to Man have been incorporated into the mineral kingdom in a much more condensed form. In this case the particular combination of these qualities express themselves as the copper pattern. The Copper Spirit is trying to harmonise these so that the beings that make up the copper can gradually be evolved and freed. The image shows the Copper Spirit and the human Ego as attempting to do exactly the same thing.
G: Now see what happens when a piece of copper is heated up.
T: I've put a torch under the piece of copper and the flame is playing on it. I'm looking into the structure of the copper and I see a regular lattice. At its intersections are little round spheres, each with a retaining shell around them, all initially spaced out in a regular array. As the heat comes in, these spheres begin to move relative to one another, the copper begins to flow and the lattice is not so regular.
G: What happens to the hierarchy of levels in the copper as it gets heated up?
T: The individualising force at the boundary is relaxed and there is some sort of response (to the main Hierarchy) from the levels inside.
G: Can you see what distinguishes the melting point?
T: This is when the pressing-down activity of the individualising beings is overcome by the pressing out of the beings inside, and that's when the copper collapses into a puddle.
G: What do we mean by putting heat in?
T: The flame now becomes a stream of beings. These are principally light and warmth beings. The combustion process is bringing them to life at the nozzle of the torch and they want to get at the copper to release the beings there.
G: And while this is happening the beings in the copper are coming to consciousness because of these outside flows?
T: Yes. I had a glimpse of the copper being sitting on the outside but still intimately connected with all this. The copper being recognises that here is an opportunity to work on the part of its body that had been sacrificed and also the bodies that the other levels of the hierarchy had sacrificed. It can see opportunities for these to become free. It recognises that this process isn't going to free everything immediately back to the spiritual but some of these beings can become copper beings in the atmosphere and from there they can go on to work with the plant kingdom and so work their way back through this level of evolution.

The story is of a substance as a being that comprises the qualities of the Spiritual Hierarchy in a cut-off, unconscious state brought about by an individualising force. Through its interactions the substance being experiences a momentary self awareness of its nature and the opportunity to exert itself and thereby evolve, which is encouraged by the 'parent being' in the Spiritual Hierarchy. When humanity acts on substance in a way that forcibly increases its activity, as with heating the copper then, during this period it experiences an enhanced self-awareness in which it overcomes the effect of the confining individualising force.

This is wildly different from the atomic view of substances of modern science, which has investigated their behaviour and nature in great detail. Our problem was that, if there exists a spiritual world as claimed by mystics and psychics and if their observations of auras and 'etheric forces' associated with substances and everything else have any validity, then how does all this fit together with the viewpoint of modern science, based on atoms and hypothetical force fields.

The mystics see everything in creation as the activities of a hierarchy of beings; even substances are (unevolved) beings. The last thing that science would see a substance as, would be a being. The *h*K-M viewpoint is that this is largely a matter of terminology. According to *h*K-M everything starts as energy but in the processes of evolution parts of this energy develop into self-actualising, self-maintaining activities, i.e. 'beings'. Atoms of substances exist 'in their own right', i.e. they are not maintained by anything therefore, from the *h*K-M viewpoint they are self-actualising 'beings'. But, according to *h*K-M, they do not participate out of themselves in the evolution of plants, animals and human beings, in the anthropomorphic way portrayed in Harry's and Ted's ECEs. They simply pursue their pattern of self-actualising activity to maintain and enhance their sense of self; the roles that they take up in plants, animals and humanity are brought about by the stress fields that organisms create in the space-energy that organise them. Where the ECE refers to warmth and light 'beings' in the flame of the torch, the sources of the ECE presumably saw these etheric activities and classified them as beings. *h*K-M, however, would not regard these as 'beings' but as quantised reverberations in the space-energy, brought about by the chemical reactions in the flame. They are not beings because they do not have a permanent self-actualising existence. They would be what science regards as light and warmth quanta of energy.

There is more of a problem with regard to the Overseeing 'Copper Being' in the spiritual hierarchy that sacrificed part of itself, along with the other members of the hierarchy, to give rise to Man and to the other kingdoms of Nature. We see this as part of Steiner's 'Creation by a Godhead and Spiritual Hierarchy Cosmology', which we now regard as erroneous. According to *h*K-M, the EM-energy, in its whirlpool-type activity flows into and out of the copper atoms and absorbs and integrates their experiences and, from this accumulated 'wisdom' responds to the stress situations that they encounter. However, as we have stated previously, at the time we were just going along with the ECEs to see where they would lead us, it was very much a jumble of incomprehensible ideas (and much of it still is). This was many years before the formulation of *h*K-M, but the ECEs illustrate the path that we followed that led, eventually, to *h*K-M.

Chapter 19

ECEs and the Experimental Investigations

When we found that the ECEs offered the possibility of deeper insights into things, we sought such insight into what was going on in our experimental researches. We give a more extensive account of these in Part IV of this book but, to provide continuity in our description of the development of our activities, that led eventually to hK-M, we explain here what we were doing and how we tried to use the ECEs to help us. As we have stated before, in all of this we just went along with what was going on, trying to understand the point of view that was presented to see where it would lead us. We start with imagery that Ted received that purported to show what went on in an experiment that he and Dennis had been working on.

An ECE Related to an Experiment

This type of ECE gave imagery that seemed to show the physical events taking place in our experiments in slow motion or greatly magnified. We give as an example of this Ted's perception of the electrical discharge picture shown in fig. 19.1b.

This picture was obtained by the experimental technique shown in fig. 19.1a, in which a high voltage was applied momentarily to a pointed electrode above a photographic plate sitting on a metal backing plate. The guide asks Ted if he can describe how the discharge picture forms:

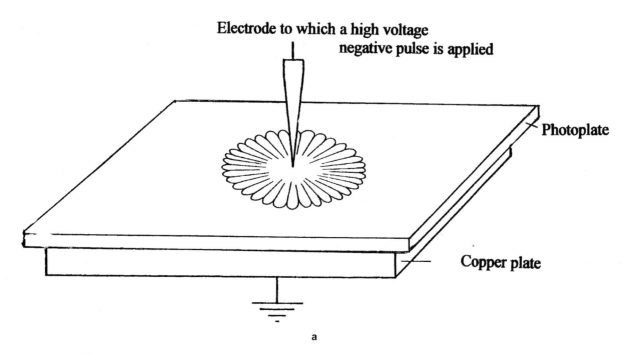

Fig. 19.1(a) The experimental set-up, in which a high voltage pulse was applied to a pointed electrode.

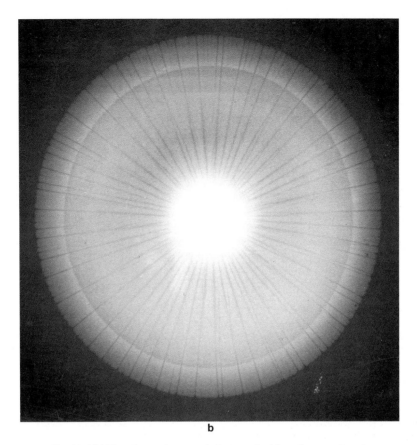

b

Fig. 19.1(b) The electrophotograph that resulted from the experiment.

T: There's a feeling of heat that emerges from the electrode and moves down onto the surface. It spreads out in a disc-like form evenly all the way around the centre and as it spreads it takes the layer on the surface with it, or disturbs it in some way, and the material forming the disc splits and separates into the individual segments.

We do not know how long it takes the disc to form, but it is probably less than one hundredth of a second. The ECE imagery, however, showed it taking place at a slow, observable rate.

G: Is there any detail in the structure of the disc?
T: Yes, I saw a honeycomb structure where you've got material forming networks with a pattern of holes running through it. It's as if the gas forms the networks but there are holes within it. It's a very fine thing though and you've really got to crawl right down into it to see it.

This shows the way in which the ECE showed a physical situation magnified and also that the experiencer found himself able to 'get inside' the imagery and explore it. There is, of course, the problem of whether, from his experience of working with this experiment, Ted could have created this imagery by his imagination but when the guide asked if he could change it, he could not do so, so it was not under his control. Also, the honeycomb structure was a completely new idea (that we did not, and still do not, understand) and therefore unlikely to have arisen from his imagination. This was equally true with the experiences of the other group members.

Steiner stated that form and function are determined by four etheric forces, or etheric states - warmth ether - light ether - chemical ether and life, or individualising, ether (we explain these in more detail later) and at this stage we were trying to understand Steiner's etheric force concepts to see if our experimental results could be explained in these terms. So the guide imagined that he was carrying out the experiment and asked Ted if he could perceive the activity of the etheric forces:

G: Now try to observe the behaviour of the etheric forces. When I press the switch try to see what the warmth ether does.
T: There's a feeling of something rising off the surface of the plate and a great flood goes off the electrode -- It's like watching a heat haze rise from the road on a summer's day.
G: When I press the switch watch the light ether.
T: MM. - it just seems to burst out in a great shower from the electrode, it expands outwards evenly and smoothly all the way around the electrode tip, outwards and downwards. MM - it's either moving the gas or reacting with the gas that's there - it comes out and presses itself into the gas.

G: Does anything happen at the plate?

T: Yes - it meets the plate immediately below the electrode and begins to spread out - The image loses its clarity then because as it moves out two or three things happen all at once. There's something which rises off the surface, there's an opposition as it moves out that causes the indents, and then there is the tension that causes the cracks that appear as black lines - I can't keep track of just one aspect.

G: This time watch the chemical ether.

T: It seems to crowd in from the edges, it causes a lot of contraction. It appears that the movement that is downwards and outwards from the electrode opposes the contractive force on the surface of the plate that wants to move inwards.

G: This time watch the life ether.

T: There's the feeling of being pulled or drawn closer to the surface. I don't actually see anything -- wherever you move in the pattern there is this feeling of being pressed down to the surface.

The guide then went on to ask further, more detailed, questions about what happened when the experimental conditions were changed and the imagery continued to respond. So, it seemed that the source of the imagery was operating in terms of Steiner's etheric force concepts.

According to *h*K-M, that arose many years later, everything exists, and creates stresses, in the background s-entity space energy activity. Thus all the different parts of our experimental equipment create stresses in the space energy according to their natures and they are maintained in their relationships by the interaction of these stress fields. In our experiments, by applying a high voltage to the electrode we were disturbing these stress fields and this is what registered on the photoplate and what Ted saw in his ECE.

When we look at the world around us we see multitudinous minerals, plants and animals, that are made of substances that have taken up particular forms and functions, which give the impression that there are forces at work in Nature that bring about these forms and activities. Science has determined, in considerable detail, the substance natures of things and generally takes the view that the substances, out of themselves, build up the forms and functions. If there are any forces at work that create forms and functions then, other than gravity and interatomic forces, these are not known to science. If gravity and interatomic forces were the only ones at work, then interatomic forces would bring substances together and gravity would force them onto the Earth's surface, in a dead world. At that stage the only principles that we had come across to account for form and function were Steiner's four etheric formative forces. The members of the group were working on a variety of shape-forming processes, electrophotography (of which the above is an example), fluid flow forms, solidification, crystallisation and electro-deposited structures. It seemed that Steiner's etheric forces might provide general principles for understanding the different forms that we were observing (and also biological forms).

Etheric Forces and Steiner's Cosmology

Although Steiner proposed the existence of four etheric formative forces, the only published account of their nature and workings was given by one of his collaborators, WACHSMUTH, and this does not explain clearly what they are and how they operate. So, in order to try to get a better understanding of the etheric forces, in a number of ECEs we sought information on why and how they arose and worked. We were then led back to a Steiner-type cosmology that described everything in terms of the activities of a Spiritual Hierarchy creating forces in a cosmic ether that was provided by a Godhead.

T: The image is of an evolving Hierarchy being built up layer upon layer over an enormously long time. As it is building up, intense feelings arise of the qualities of Will, Wisdom and Love that the Hierarchy is achieving. These feelings surge strongly down from the top of the Hierarchy and are reflected back again from the bottom. With each succeeding stage the qualities are brought closer to perfection, both in the Godhead and in the Hierarchy below it. It's difficult to put into words, but there is an intense feeling of harmony, with everything known through all the levels. The Godhead has sacrificed itself to have these qualities developed through the different layers of the Hierarchy and these have been worked through and upon until it all reaches this final glorious stage --- The image changes and I see the Hierarchy as three main groups, with three levels within each group. At the top there is a great blaze of light; this tapers down through the column, becoming less bright and more liveable with. The imagery shows this as one enormous pattern, it's complete.

G: Can we perhaps have imagery for the creation of humanity?

T: The column is moved to the side, the light is withdrawn, the feeling is of a cold empty void. Then from the Godhead above the Hierarchy there emerges a misty substance - this is the cosmic ether - the Godhead giving of its own body. Then the image moves to the Hierarchy and from the lowest level of the top group there is a movement of material into the cosmic ether. This is the activity of the Thrones (Spirits of Will Activity) moving into the inert cosmic ether penetrating it completely. There is a feeling of warmth -- Then the *image moves to the next level of the Hierarchy and material from them flows into the situation -- Everything settles down and the image moves to the topmost levels of the Hierarchy; this is the time of the Cherubim and then the Seraphim sacrifice (Spirits of Wisdom and Love)--- The image changes to show similar kinds of activity from the lower levels of the hierarchy. They each in turn flow through this material, giving something of themselves to it and seeking a response from it --- When all the levels have worked with it the material has taken on the form of spheres that are glowing gently --- Then the Godhead makes a sacrifice of individualising beings, that surround the entities. The desire now is for the qualities of will, wisdom and love to be developed from inside these spheres -- The image now shows a Spirit of Form (the lowest level of the second group of the Hierarchy) moving to take up the vehicles that have been created for it. There is an elongation of the Spirit of Form, so that it is still connected to the Hierarchy but the bottom of it experiences these bodies. But this is in a very dreamlike fashion because it is still closely linked to the spiritual world. Gradually the elongated Spirit of Form reaches down like a descending drop and the individualising beings close up around it and there remains only a slender link between the Spirit of Form that is inside the bodies and the bulk of it which is connected to the spiritual world. At this stage the Spirit of Form has to take up the organising of the bodies from inside them --- I see an image of someone learning to drive a car. The Spirit of Form begins to work in an uncoordinated manner, everything is very difficult. It is struggling to work with the qualities of the body in this state of freedom and self-will and as it gets some control over its systems it disrupts them, it breaks up their harmony. Its Ego in its uncoordinated way is putting too much of itself into its emotions and interfering with the flows through the bodies. The image shows lots of combinations where the bodies are being influenced by the Ego and these in turn are influencing the flows and reacting with them in unbalanced ways. It's unaware of what it's doing. It's trying to bring this system under control but in this shut-off condition it's almost impossible. But the image also shows that when the Ego is withdrawn in sleep, flows from outside can work to restore the balance.*

G: *How does the Ego find its way out of this situation?*

T: *The image shows that as the Ego becomes more used to the bodies it begins to investigate the world around it. As it accumulates experiences it begins to form patterns of understanding and as it does so the link between itself and its Higher Self (the part of the Spirit of Form remaining in the spiritual world) very, very, gradually opens. Then, during sleep it can be prompted and prodded and it can carry these promptings and proddings through into its daily life and the link can then grow stronger --- The image shows that the Ego can be influenced towards the physical or towards the spiritual. If it is drawn towards the physical exclusively then the link to the Higher Self is restricted to such an extent that nothing can flow along it, even during sleep. If it is influenced in the direction of the spiritual world then it's not really within the body and can't control its own hierarchy. The ideal situation is where the Ego is within its own system and aware of the flows through it and with this awareness works at harmonising the levels of its bodies and converting the sacrificed materials back to consciousness.*

The above extract portrays a cosmology in which there was first an 'autocratic' creation by a Godhead carrying out a preconceived plan. The Godhead possesses the qualities of Will, Wisdom and Love and it expresses these, to create the first group of a Hierarchy of activities, or Spiritual Beings, (Thrones - Will: Cherubim - Wisdom: Seraphim - Love) and two further subsidiary groups. These beings have contact with, and awareness of, each other, according to their level of development, and they work together in harmony according to the Godhead's plan. There was then a second creation - of the human being - whose body was built up stage by stage out of a basic state sacrificed by the Godhead, designated as a cosmic ether, by these beings putting their qualities into it, and then it was individualised and cut-off. Entities from the Hierarchy then 'incarnated' into these bodies and became absorbed in the task of controlling and manipulating them. By being cut off in this way, these members of the Hierarchy lost awareness of, and contact and harmonious at-one-ness with, the rest of the Spiritual Hierarchy. But this separation from the Hierarchy gave human beings free will. They are then stimulated by the members of the Hierarchy, who work on them externally to try to elicit a response from the unconscious qualities of Will, Wisdom and Love built into them.

In elaborations of this cosmology the mineral, plant and animal kingdoms of Nature appeared as stages of development of the cosmic ether that got 'left behind' in the creation of humanity. Thus these comprise the qualities of Will, Wisdom and Love in less-developed, or curtailed, forms and by working with these, human beings bring to consciousness the unconscious qualities of will, wisdom and love, that were built into them while, at the same time, through this experience the mineral, plant and animal kingdoms of Nature evolve.

This is very much along the lines of Steiner's cosmology that we outlined in Chapter 12. We imagine that in a state of enhanced consciousness Steiner perceived the complex 'etheric activities' associated with these phases of development in the space-energy, which he designated as will/warmth, wisdom/light, love/chemical and life etheric states'. In the mineral kingdom he related the different etheric conditions to the states of gas, liquid and solid. This is redolent of the ancient, possibly mystically derived, Greek view of everything comprising some combination of the four basic elements of fire, gas, water, and earth, (which the mystic Daskalos referred to in Chapter 12, subscribed to from his etheric vision).

Although we had studied Steiner's cosmology, the imagery in these ECEs was not simply a rehash of the information that we had got from our studies. It responded in much greater detail and gave 'answers' to questions that we asked on aspects that were not elucidated in Steiner's works. With hindsight, in the light of subsequent events, we think that in some way we had established contact with entities at the level of consciousness associated with Steiner and his cosmology and they were providing answers to our questions in terms of their framework of understanding. At this period of our ECEs we received masses of material that explained everything in terms of Steiner's cosmology and the activities of the different levels of the beings of his Spiritual Hierarchy in increasing detail.

The Formative Behaviour of Substances

Because we were carrying out experiments on the forms that arise in the mineral kingdom we asked questions about this, to which the ECEs responded in terms of the activities of 'substance beings'. Here is an example of experiments that Andy was carrying out on the crystallisation of copper chloride solution.

G: Let's look at your experiment on the crystallisation of a drop of solution of 1% copper chloride on a glass plate.
A: It was just a puddle of solution on the glass and then, quite quickly, a random array of needles started to grow in from the edge towards the centre, fig. 19.2.

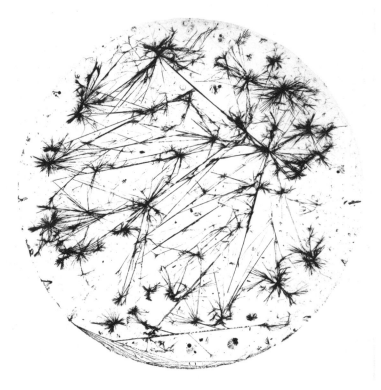

Fig.19.2 The pattern formed by a drop of 1% copper chloride solution on a glass plate evaporating slowly under controlled conditions.

G: Can you get any feel for why they should be needles?
A: There's a large amount of tension within the relationship between copper and chlorine. They're locked together but they're struggling to get apart. In flying apart, away from each other they create a needle.
G: Now copper on its own would be a crystalline lump of metal.
A: When you said, 'copper' I saw a small cube of bright copper appear.
G: But chlorine ...?
A: I see it as a spherical cloud of gas.
G: Can you see these two change to copper chloride?
A: Well, the cube of copper starts growing out through its corners. The corners extend and become needles. The cloud of green gas and the copper block have gone and in their place is a green crystal formation, which is made up of 8 needles radiating out from a centre, (fig 19.3).

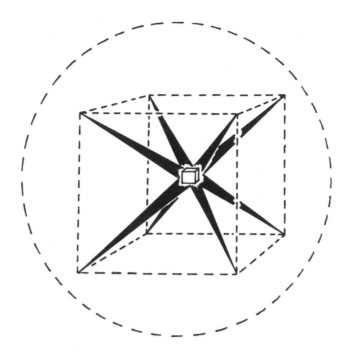

Fig.19.3 The way in which the cube-forming tendency of copper and the expanding sphere forming tendency of chlorine combine to give rise to needles of copper chloride

G: So it's a combination of a sphere and a cube.
A: Yes, the points of the needles define the surfaces of both a cube and a sphere. I don't get the feeling of any antagonism now between the two, the feeling I get is that the two have come together and, out of what they were as individuals, they have created something that contains elements of their individual characters, something new that wasn't there before. I feel a certain amount of surprise within the new creation and a bit of pleasure as well, at what it has become.
G: In the constrained circumstances of the drop they can't generate this 8-armed figure but they do the best they can?
A: 'We can't do anything else they say, 'We just go forward, move forward and outward'.

In this ECE copper is portrayed as exerting its will to be a solid, cubic form. Chlorine, in contrast, is portrayed as diffuse, nebulous, out-going and when copper and chlorine crystallise as copper chloride out of the fluid environment of water, they form a relationship in which each expresses its nature. That is, they combine as solid, radiating outwards, needles. The scientific view is that the properties of copper and chlorine are determined by the structure of their atoms, (that is, by the number of protons in their nuclei and the corresponding number of electrons which occupy incompletely filled 'shells' around the nucleus). When they crystallise out of water their atoms pack together in a way that, by sharing electrons, produces completely filled shells, to produce a tiny bit of solid copper chloride. This then grows by further atoms of copper and chlorine attaching to the nucleus in positions where they fit in most readily, in this case as a protrusion that grows to form a needle. That is, the scientific explanation is that the overall form is determined by the way the bits fit together and build it up out of themselves.

Pattern Formation in Crystallisation

In many of our experiments the crystals took on an overall pattern, so we asked about this and Andy got imagery in terms of the entities from the Spiritual Hierarchy who had sacrificed, or 'incarnated' their qualities as substance trying to influence the substance beings in the same way, at a mineral kingdom level, that the members of Spiritual Hierarchy from which we have incarnated (our Higher Selves) seek to stimulate us:

G: Can you watch the crystallisation pattern form from your copper chloride solution?
A: I can see little water beings, little copper chloride beings. The water beings are colourless, the copper chloride are pale blue, all mingling and flowing, turning over and over, rotating in a sort of endless flowing dance.
G: See what the copper being and the chlorine being in the Hierarchy above are doing?
A: I see a composite figure that's coppery on one side of its body and blue-green and scaly on the other side. The copper is male and the chlorine is female. The two sides seem happy together; I get the feeling of harmonious interaction.
G: What happens in the drop of solution as the water evaporates?

A: The copper chloride entities are swimming around in the solution, highly active, going here and there and the copper chloride being is always trying to reach down and stimulate them, I get the same feeling as a parent-child relationship, but it can't get through, the little copper chloride beings are all too busy interacting with other things to take any notice --- Now I've reduced the amount of water in the drop, so the copper chloride units are meeting each other more and more. Each time two units meet face to face, each sees itself and there's a short jolt of awareness, of self recognition and then that goes. As the drop dries, these moments of self awareness become more frequent, attaining more to a continuity -- The big copper chloride being is nodding at that. The little copper chloride units respond by joining hands, linking up in chains and I see the growth of a needle. This needle has sparked off the formation of another needle, and this second needle initiates the growth of a third needle -- Now I see that the big copper chloride being tries to direct the needles into a pattern. The impulse to form needles springs out of the small units but the big copper chloride being then tries to bring all the needles together into an interrelating whole, a unity. The copper chloride being said, 'I want these little units in the drop to become aware, to become conscious.' and I said, 'Conscious of what?' and the big being said, 'Conscious of me' -- We've got a fairly extended but random pattern, with needles criss-crossing all over the place, (fig. 19.2). The copper chloride being said a bit deprecatingly, 'Well, that's the best I could do.' I said, 'What would you like to make?' and I got the feeling of patterns with features of harmony and symmetry, in which every part related to every other part.

G: Can you see what determines the crystallisation pattern?

A: The copper chloride being looked over to one side and I saw a wobbly figure which I assume is the water being - which wobbled in an affirmative way. Then there's the glass being here as well - each of them is trying to influence the situation in its own way. I start with the glass being and say, 'How would things be if you could have everything your way? -- The glass would take the copper chloride into itself, I see an amorphous pattern which has been pulled out of solution. Then I ask the water what it would like to do. At first it said that it stepped aside and let the copper chloride get on with it, and then I saw the water carry the copper chloride away, I see images of clouds. Now I go to the copper chloride being who says, 'Well look what a job I've got struggling to try and create something against the influences of these two. One wants to drag it all down and kill it, and the other wants to carry it all away into nothingness.' I say, 'Well, what is it that you would like to do?' and the copper chloride being said, 'Anything, anything! Just to create something.'

According to this ECE, in the same way that the Beings in the Spiritual Hierarchy try to influence humanity to form harmonious patterns of activity, the relevant Beings of the Spiritual Hierarchy seek to do the same thing with substance activities.

We used the crystallisation of copper chloride as a basis to examine the formative effects on it of a number of other substances. Here we give two examples, first, another mineral, iron chloride and second, a plant extract, mercurialis (dog's mercury). The addition of iron chloride produced a stronger, more organised pattern than that produced by the copper chloride alone fig. 19.4 (compare with fig. 19.2), while the addition of the plant extract resulted in a yet stronger organisation, fig. 19.5.

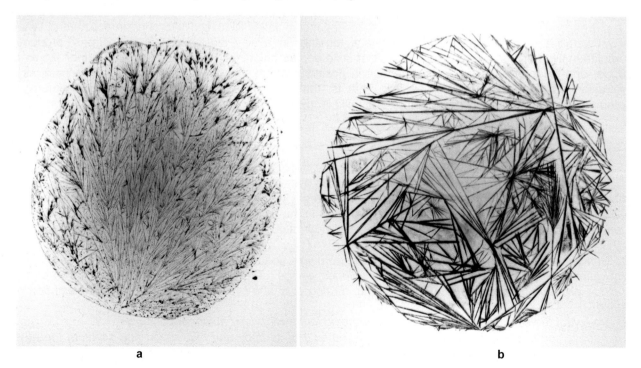

a   b

19.4(a) and (b) The patterns formed by copper chloride crystallising out of a 1% solution to which increasing amounts of iron chloride have been added: the iron chloride produces a 'stronger', more well-defined pattern than is formed by copper chloride alone (fig. 19.2).

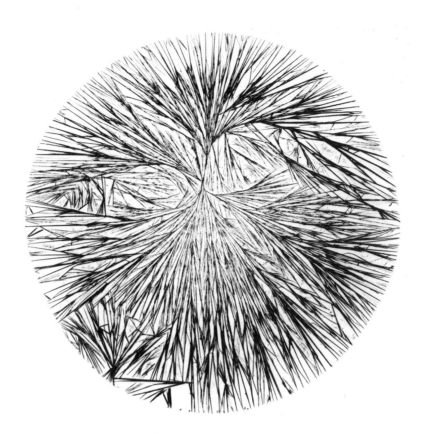

Fig.19.5 The more organised type of crystallisation pattern formed by a 1% solution of copper chloride to which has been added 10% of a tincture of mercurialis plant (dog's mercury).

We asked about this in the ECE.

G: Can you see the effect of adding iron chloride?
A: I see iron chloride as the fusion of an armoured warrior with a courtly lady. The iron is like a little King Kong, beating his chest in a very egotistical gesture. It said, 'I, I - I am very strong'. The chlorine by contrast was soft and gentle, very feminine, it brings softening understanding qualities to the iron. I say to the iron chloride, 'What is it you want to do?' -- The impression is that the iron chloride wants to push things forward. He says, 'Look, I'll show you,' and he's got the copper chloride by the ear and he's slowly turning it round and round, leading it this way and that. The copper chloride comes over as rather weak and feeble. The iron chloride was leading the copper chloride in a curved dancing pattern. I've asked him to show me the dance and we're standing at the centre of what looks like a sheaf of corn growing out from the centre and coming back on itself. I got an image of the copper chloride and I heard the word, 'Dissipated'. It's dissipated its energies and the iron is saying something about concentrating your effort and the type of pattern he would like to form would be where the crystals go out and turn back in and meet each other and where they meet they are pointing back to the centre.

(The 'ideal pattern' is like a two-dimensional view of the B-cell pattern, that gets a sense of self by the activity flowing out from the centre and interacting with the environment which returns it to the centre, fig. 1.4(c)).

G: Ideally he would like to form one completely inter-related pattern for the whole drop?
A: He spreads his arms out and there are many other centres and he wants to join up with those, but he points down to the centre we're on and says we've got to learn this lesson first.
G: What happens when we add extract of the plant mercurialis?
A: It came in very clearly that the iron helped the mercurialis to get hold of the copper chloride, to produce the kind of pattern that the mercurialis wants. The mercurialis spreads the copper chloride pattern out, trying to relate the needles as they move outwards but it can't bend them back in and relate them back to the centre again.

This ECE explains the overall pattern formation in terms of the interaction of the inner qualities of the different substance entities involved, in a highly anthropomorphic way, analogous to the way in which the overall behaviour of a group of human beings is determined by the inner natures of the individuals of the group of beings and the way in which they interact. As this happens, members of the Spiritual Hierarchy, whose concern is for the group to work towards a pattern of harmonious interaction, try to influence them in this direction.

The scientific explanation for the crystallisation patterns would be that as the water evaporates, so that the solution becomes more and more concentrated and supersaturated with substance, a small amount of it is forced out of the liquid, to form a nucleus and then further substance deposits out onto surfaces of preferred growth on the nucleus, to build up the pattern that is formed. This is the 'reductionist' approach of science, that takes everything apart to determine the units, or bricks, from which it is built up and then assumes that the bricks come together and, out of themselves, build up an organisation, without any overall organising and integrating activity.

In terms of the hK-M viewpoint that developed many years later, the crystallisation pattern is an expression of the basic features underlying the evolution of the Universe, as these manifest in this situation. According to the Big Bang theory of the Universe, all energy and substance expanded out and cooled so fast that there was not time for the necessary amount of interaction to maintain equilibrium. Thus the Universe consists of substances and energy 'frozen', or trapped, in a non-uniform state so that, if it is activated in some way, i.e. becomes free to move around, it evens itself out. But in its non-uniform condition, everything in the Universe is also in a state of stress and when anything is able to move it does so towards a less-stressed condition. Although hK-M sees the Universe as arising from a collective of little bangs, instead of a single Big Bang, the principle of it existing in a state of non-uniformity of energy and stress is the same. These stresses determine the patterns of activity that ensue. For example, in the crystallising of copper chloride solution, as the water evaporates there is more copper chloride than the water/space energy combination can accommodate so it comes under increasing stress until the copper chloride is forced out, along the lines of, and thereby marking out, the stress pattern in the space energy. We deal with this in more detail in Chapter 26.

When observing the crystallisation of a substance from an evaporating liquid, a nucleus of the substance can be seen to separate out, which then gradually grows into the liquid, to form a crystallisation pattern. If, however, conditions are kept very still, then the liquid can evaporate to an extent far beyond that at which crystallisation would normally occur and the liquid-space-energy combination then becomes increasingly stressed by having too much substance in it. Then, at some point it 'cracks' and the crystallisation pattern is instantaneously there, throughout the whole of the liquid, formed far faster than the eye can see, taking up a configuration which, according to hK-M, marks out the stress pattern in the liquid/space energy combination. However, the problem then is to explain how different types of stress patterns arise which, at that time we were trying to do in terms of Steiner's etheric forces. In the curtailed form in which they act in the mineral kingdom Steiner designated Will as warmth (activity) force, Wisdom as light ether (enlightenment). Love as chemical etheric force (providing relationships) and the force that individualised out, and bestowed life on, humanity and acted on everything else on Earth, as Life or Individualising ether. In the ECEs we tried to get a better understanding of these etheric forces and how they might explain our experiments. We start with an ECE in which we sought insight into the etheric forces, with Brian as the experiencer.

Etheric Force Interpretation of Our Experimental Results

G: Can you get an image of the ethers, starting with warmth ether?
B: The image was of a big tank with warmth ether in it that I saw as black space. Then light appeared, as a Sun that wakes the warmth ether up. It provides a focal point. It is saying, 'I wake everything up. Everything looks to me. I strike everything.' Light ether is aware of itself as having a centre and penetrating outwards. Things are awakened and look in towards the central light. The feeling is that things on the outside can see the centre but the centre doesn't see anything outside. It just penetrates right out through. Then, when chemical ether arrives it can no longer penetrate through, the light ether becomes aware of boundaries and limits, whereas before it was not aware of any.
G: So what are the qualities of the chemical ether then?
B: Enveloping, wrapping. The light feels it is being cut off, it can't do what it used to. The chemical ether feels it has these things inside it and it is pushing them around - it's as if it is arranging its stomach so that it is comfortable.
G: What about the life ether?
B: When you said that, everything suddenly acquired surfaces and light played off them and there was a feeling of great pleasure. The cosmic process can start to crystallise. Things can get under way. You can see me and I can see you and we can see the world. There is also an inner aspect, in that it gives everything some sort of inner identity, things can work from centres. Things have the ability to experience themselves as individuals. Everything has centres.

In trying to sort out the formative nature of each of the etheric forces we saw warmth ether' as out-going, in the way that it manifests as heat and has an outwards, expansive nature, (fig. 19.6).

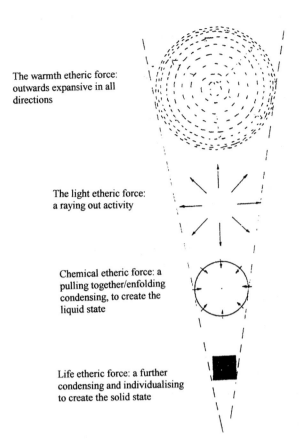

The warmth etheric force: outwards expansive in all directions

The light etheric force: a raying out activity

Chemical etheric force: a pulling together/enfolding condensing, to create the liquid state

Life etheric force: a further condensing and individualising to create the solid state

Fig. 19.6 Our conception of the shaping activities of etheric forces that work sequentially to 'condense' substances out of an initial inert cosmic ether.

Thus when heat is put into a solid it causes it to break down, first into liquid and then into gas that expands outwards. Light ether we saw as manifesting a raying-out light activity, which illuminates and enlightens, and transmits enlightenment, as in radio and television. Chemical ether which brings about interactions and relationships between substances we saw as pulling together and enfolding, in the way that small amounts of water are pulled together to form droplets. It enfolds, as when liquids dissolve and encompass solids, while bringing about relationships between them. The Life or Individualising etheric force, by which human beings were cut off and left to find their own ways forward, we saw as having a cutting-off, cube-forming activity, in the way that many substances often form cubic crystals, when they are separated off from, or individualised out of, their environment.

We then tried to interpret our experimental results on the forms that we observed in terms of etheric forces. To give examples, fig. 19.7a shows the uniform spreading, from a centre, of a solution of a salt flowing into filter paper.

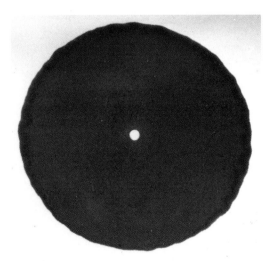

Fig.19.7(a) A liquid spreading uniformly from a centre in filter paper; (from a wick dipping into a dish of liquid underneath) the expansive warmth ether force causes the spreading, while the encompassing chemical ether force holds it together and causes this to happen uniformly.

263

The cause of the outwards spreading we attributed to expansive warmth ether activity, while the maintenance of uniformity in this, to the unifying activity of the chemical ether holding the spreading liquid front together. Figs. 19.7b and 19.7c show two examples where, as the liquid front spreads out it breaks down, which we attributed to the influence of a light ether raying-out activity, superimposed on the spreading out.

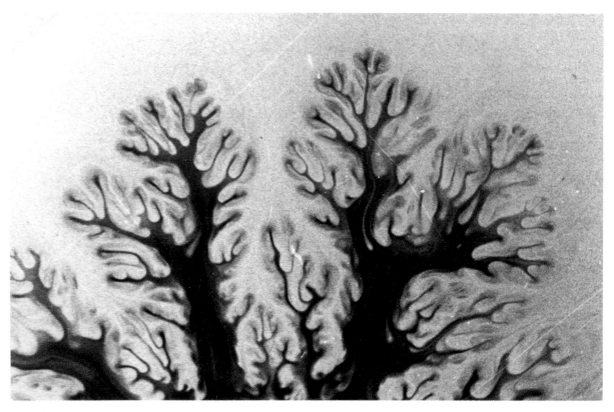

Fig.19.7(b) A spreading liquid form where the raying-out light ether causes break down and differentiation of the advancing front.

Fig.19.7(c) Another example of warmth ether - light ether interaction where the light ether exerts a greater effect and thereby causes more differentiated raying out.

Fig. 19.7d shows the cubic form of a solid crystallising out of solution, which we attributed to the dominance of the life ether force.

Fig. 19.7(d) A cubic form that has crystallised out of solution, showing the dominance of the individualising ether force, x ~ 150

Fig. 19.7e shows a cubic form 'breaking out' which we attributed to the light ether raying-out activity superimposed on the cube-forming individualising life ether.

Fig. 19.7(e) Example of a cubic crystal 'breaking out', which we attributed to the light ether force, x ~ 150.

Fig 19.7f shows the 'breaking out' becoming unstable and fig.19.7g shows this leading to further breaking out.

Fig. 19.7(f) In this case the 'breaking out projection' is showing signs of instability, x ~ 150.

Fig. 19.7(g) The instability has given rise to further breaking out, to form a 'dendritic' structure, x ~ 150.

Plants, as they grow, create stresses in the space-energy of their environment that are similar to those of substances crystallising or solidifying out.   Hence some of the patterns in the stress forms in our electrophotography, (figs. 15.9 and 15.10) and in our crystallisation experiments, show a rudimentary similarity to plant forms, as in fig. 19.8.

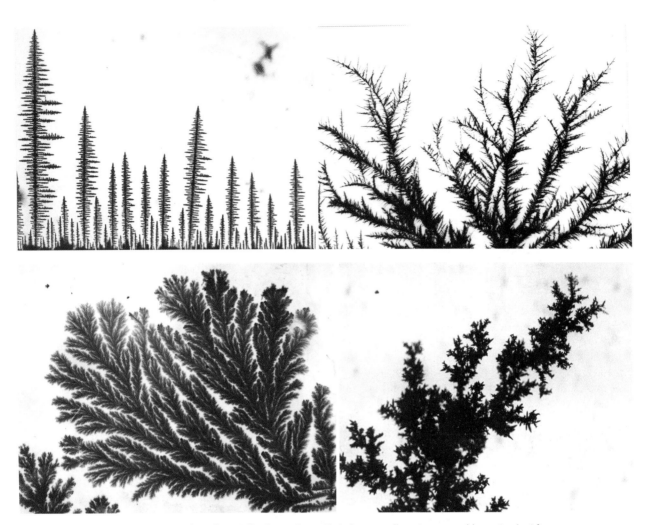

Fig. 19.8 Four examples of crystallisation patterns that show a rudimentary resemblance to plant forms

An *h*K-M Evaluation of These ECEs and Etheric Force Concepts

When we carried out an experiment and saw what happened at a physical level, we imagine that the sources of our ECEs could perceive what was going on at the etheric level and they then described their perceptions in terms of the cosmology that they believed in. As we have stated earlier, there are a number of accounts by mystics and psychics of the perception of 'auras' and fields of 'etheric activity' associated with everything. Equally, many phenomena are explained by scientists in terms of invisible hypothetical 'fields of force'. We think that in his higher consciousness state Steiner observed, and described as etheric forces, activities taking place in 'space' that scientists hypothesise about. Thus, for example, when an object 'gives off light' this consists of individualised, or quantised, changes in its stress field which emanate from it, which we do not perceive; we become aware of them only when they impinge on something and elicit a response from it, so that it becomes 'lit up'. What mystics and psychics describe as etheric vision we suspect is an ability to perceive these activities passing through 'space' and in the case of light this is what Steiner describes as the light etheric force. Similarly, where the emanations give rise to heat this is what Steiner describes as the warmth ether force. And what scientists describe as the electromagnetic forces between atoms that create the liquid and solid states, we suspect are what Steiner describes as the 'chemical ether' force, that brings about relationships. However, science does not ascribe any shape-forming activities to these forces in the way that Steiner did.

We think that with his 'etheric vision' Steiner was able to perceive these different activities in 'space' and he assumed that these etheric forces or states brought about the observed behaviour of substances. This interpretation may have been influenced by activating thought forms from the past. The ancient Hindus categorised five different levels of prana - the energy of the Universe (see WHITE and KRIPPNER). The ancient Greeks, in their efforts to explain the forms in Nature in terms of their four-element, fire, air, water, earth viewpoint, allocated form-producing activities to each element (Platonic forms - see TOULMIN and GOODFIELD). These Platonic forms were different from Steiner's etheric force forms except for the earth element - life ether, to which both assigned cubic formation.

Another feature of Steiner's account of the etheric forces, or etheric states, is that he described them as evolving out of each other in the sequence warmth-light-chemical and life/individualising ethers as they are raised to higher levels of activity by the Spiritual Hierarchy. According to hK-M 'creation' began as a state of dormant energy that became active and differentiated into s-entities (so that none of the original dormant energy state remains). In the cosmic developments that we have described, the Sun entity develops out of the s-entity background state, and the Earth entity out of the Sun entity state. On this basis, the EM-space-energy of the Earth system has evolved through the s-entity, Sun entity and Earth entity stages, so that it does not have a single uniform nature and how its different aspects respond to stresses exerted on it could be responsible for the different forms that substances take up.

It may be that Steiner's warmth ether is the purely outwards expressing activity, s-entity, experience level of the EM-energy, the light ether is its experience of the Sun's raying-out activity and the chemical ether is its experience of the relationships in the forming of the Earth and that the EM-energy responds to events according to the different levels of its experience in the same way that we do. Thus, if something calls on us to be active, or to spread enlightenment, or to form relationships, we may respond to each of these different aspects individually, according to our past experience of them, or to them all collectively, if the stimulus evokes this.

A problem arises with what Steiner calls the life, or individualising ether or entities. According to the ECEs, all the separate things, and all the separate levels within things, (e.g. the different levels of activity within atoms, the different levels of activity [organs/systems] within organisms) are separated off by a surround of individualising beings that are a direct emanation from the Godhead that bestows a separated-off individualised existence on everything, to allow things to find their own way forward. According to hK-M, individualisation is something that comes about by parts of the space-energy undergoing an activity which gives them a sense of self so that they take it over to become self-actualising, thereby pursuing their activity and further development in opposition to the s-pressure. On this basis there has to be a boundary zone between the activity of a self-actualising entity on the one side and the s-pressurised space-energy, on the other side. This region of interaction may give rise to a zone of 'etheric turbulences' that can be perceived by etheric vision, and which the ECEs designate as individualising beings. Where the disturbance in the space-energy is created by a large body, such as the Earth planet, the zone of turbulences would be much larger. In one ECE, with Ted as the receiver, we obtained the following:

T: I have an image of the Earth with a big shell of individualising beings around it that tries to push things down. The main concentration of individualising beings is at the Earth's surface, where the shell is constructed. There are fewer of them as you go up and away from the Earth. A lot of them are associated with the atmosphere. As the atmosphere thins out, the number of individualising beings thins out.

According to this ECE the zone of individualising beings around the Earth, which may be a zone of (non self-actualising) turbulences, is responsible for the atmospheric activity of the Earth.

However, a further problem is that the ECEs attributed to the individualising or life etheric force a cubic grid-forming activity. Some of our experimental results suggested the existence of such a force. Thus fig. 19.9 shows a two-dimensional solidification structure of this nature (two dimensional because it is formed in a thin film of liquid), while fig. 19.10 shows a delicate cubic structure.

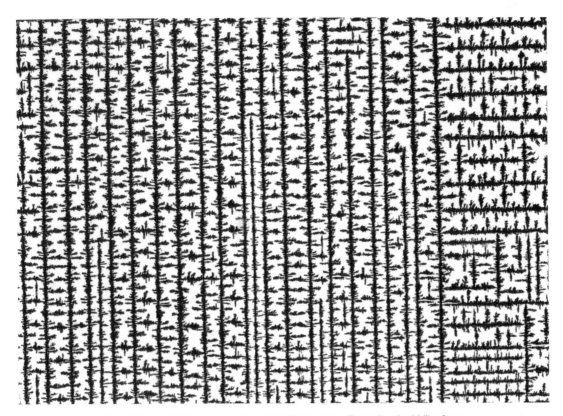

Fig.19.9 A solidification structure that shows a two-dimensional grid-like form

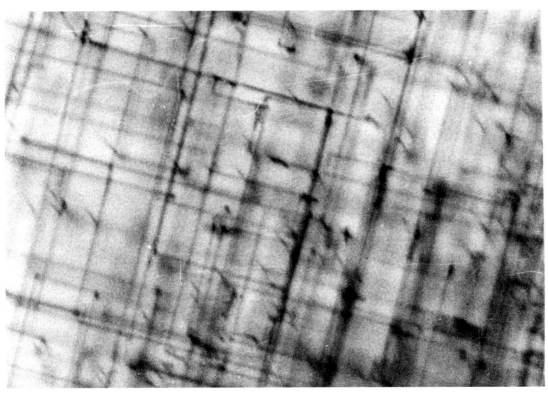

Fig. 19.10. A very fine delicate cubic crystallisation structure x ~ 1200.

In this particular case the cubic structure has developed in a gelatinous material that has supported its growth and not in a liquid, where any movement in the liquid would have destroyed it. It is difficult to conceive of this structure forming by the conventional scientific explanation of atoms depositing out onto a number of (fibre-like) growth fronts and these joining up to make a coherent, unified grid; it looks very much as though the structure arises from an underlying organisation which, according to hK-M would be a stress field in the gelatinous material in which it is growing. The uniformity of this structure suggests a uniform stress field, as opposed for example, to a centred stress field that gave rise to figs. 19.7b and 7c, or a planar stress field, as in fig.19.9. A uniform stress field arises, for example, where a field of mud becomes uniformly dried out by the Sun, so that a regular pattern of cracks arise in it. In one of our experiments we got a pattern of this nature by soaking a photographic plate in water. The gelatinous layer then expanded all over and this caused a more or less uniform stress pattern in it as it detached from the plate, fig. 19.11.

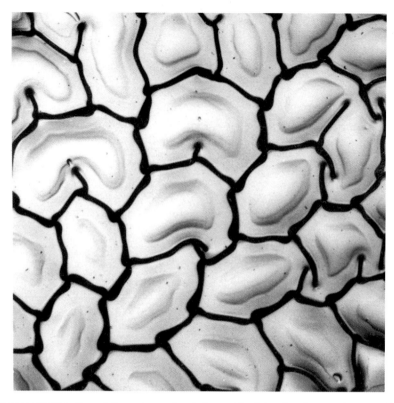

Fig.19.11 A stress 'field' in the gelatinous layer of a photographic plate when it expands on soaking in water.

The cubic structure of fig. 19.10 could arise from a three-dimensional stress field of this nature.

As we have stated, everywhere that we look around us we see things and entities that possess form and function, for which there is no satisfactory explanation. Investigating experimentally how forms arise in the mineral kingdom and seeking an understanding of the underlying causes of our observations, has been a major theme of our researches. At the same time we have sought for underlying principles that determine the production of forms from the works of Rudolf Steiner, as the only source that we have found for such principles. From his observations in his mystical state of consciousness Steiner proposed that there is a basic cosmic ether that has evolved through four states, which are described as the warmth etheric state, the light etheric state, chemical ether and life ether states that bring about aggregations and forms of matter. The warmth etheric state creates heat, the light etheric state creates the gaseous condition, the chemical etheric state creates the liquid condition and the life etheric state the solid condition. The nature of the warmth and light etheric states is to be expansive and that of the chemical and life etheric states is to be contractive and condensing. Warmth ether produces expansive spherical forms, light ether expansive triangular forms, chemical ether contractile half moon forms and life ether contractile square forms. We could not perceive a sound conceptual basis for these claims and so we enquired further into them in our ECEs and as a result arrived at the slightly modified scheme portrayed in fig. 19.6 and we tried to make a rudimentary interpretation of our experimental results in these terms. Science does not ascribe any formative activities to Nature that act on substances but takes the view that substances come together and their forces of interaction bring about the forms that we observe. The hK-M viewpoint is that stresses created in the basic energy by substances determine their distribution and the form that they take up. In this Chapter we have given some account of our activities, to illustrate the path that we followed. In Part IV, dealing with our experimental researches, we give a more detailed account of this aspect of our work. We do not subscribe to Steiner's view of forms being brought about by the activity of four etheric formative forces (equally we do not reject it, we just do not know one way or the other) but, as will be seen in Chapter 26, some of our results have led us to interpreting them as arising from the interaction of a spherical condensing force and a cubic creating force, akin to Steiner's chemical and life etheric forces.

Chapter 20

Homoeopathy

We found the claims of homoeopathy, that substances in an extreme state of dilution could have curative effects, interesting, in that this suggested as yet unknown forces associated with substances, that might tie up with 'etheric forces'. A group of medical doctors in the locality in which we were working had become disillusioned with drug therapies, because they found that many of their patients ended up in hospital with the side effects of these. They had therefore tried homoeopathic treatments and found that these could sometimes have a dramatic curative action without side effects. So they set up a research group to try and get a better understanding of homoeopathy and they invited Dennis to become a member to assist with trying to understand how substances in extreme dilutions could have these properties. In this way we became exposed to the experiences of medical doctors on the efficacy of homoeopathic remedies and we tried them ourselves and found them to be of value.

[We have mentioned the problem of the side effects of drugs in Chapter 13 and referred to the British Medical Association book on Medicines and Drugs. One only has to look at this to see what a major problem the side effects of drugs is in causing malfunctioning of the body's operating systems even, in extreme cases like thalidomide, resulting in deformations of foetuses].

Because of the challenge to understand what was going on in homoeopathy, in our ECEs we sought insight into its workings and we carried out many experiments to see if we could develop a way of detecting any 'homoeopathic forces'.

ECEs On How Homoeopathy Works

We asked about how a homoeopathic remedy affects the activities of the body:

G: Can you get an image of a man with his auras?
T: Yes.
G: Presumably you see many different streams of energy working through him?
T: Yes, there is an interchange between his bodies and the activities outside him.
G: Can we have an example of a man where an activity is not working in harmony - what do you see then?
T: If we look at one stream of activity, while it's flowing freely it moves in and out of him in a continuous stream. But if it's in disharmony it becomes spasmodic and finally ceases, the energy from outside rebounds off some sort of barrier, the point of entry is closed.
G: What happens if you give this person a homoeopathic remedy?
T: The remedy travels to the organs that are deficient in that particular energy. It passes through that area, restoring some of the activity which was lost when it was cut off from its outer sources and the beings of the remedy then make their way out through the Ego and return to the spiritual world. At the same time it breaks down the blockage or barrier that has prevented the outer activity from entering to carry out its harmonising function.
G: What do you mean by blockage?
T: I see this as a point on the aura of the person through which the stream of energy from the outside would normally flow but this is closed or partially closed. This has something to do with the control that the Ego exerts over the parts of its body.
G: Where does this stream of energy that you see going in and out of the body come from?
T: It's coming from the fields of energy that surround us, they run through the entire planetary system.

Normally we think of the activities of our body as deriving from the energies of the substances that we ingest and this is what the guide had in mind when he asked about the streams of energy working through a person. However, the response was in terms of streams of activity from outside which maintain our body's workings and which we can disharmonise: this ECE claims that it is these streams of energy that a homoeopathic remedy works on.

[The idea that food is not the dominant factor in the workings of our body receives some support from accounts of a few, usually highly religious, people who seem to be able to survive with little or no food. For example, Sai Baba eats very little food and claims that he doesn't need any and yet he functions as a homo sapiens.]

According to hK-M life on Earth began with the formation of prebiotic globules in the watery environment. Cyclic variations of the space-energy, due to the interaction of the Sun's and Earth's stress fields then acted rhythmically on the globules and thereby caused a cyclic flow of constituents in and out of them. It is as though, from the mystic's point of view, the Sun sought to elicit a response from the globule but, in fact, there was no motivation, only mechanical activity that inadvertently acted in this way. The space-energy associated with the globule got a sense of self from this cyclic movement of substances and, in seeking to increase its sense of self, it actively 'breathed' them in and out, to give rise to self-actualising prokaryotic cells. Similarly, the developments that gave rise to eukaryotic cells and multicellular entities took place by cyclic variations in the space-energy causing flows that became self-actualising. At the same time, by bringing substances together, there is a release of energy that is given direction by, and strengthens, the flow patterns initiated by the cosmic stress fields.

[The role of external forces on the workings of organisms can be most readily perceived in plants that clearly become what they are by the interaction of Sun and Earth forces acting on substances, according to a pattern determined by the cyclic patterns of their movements. We have referred to investigations that show an effect of the Sun, Moon and planets on the behaviour of substances and organisms in Chapter 13].

The Earth Entity, with its B-cell pattern of activity participates in everything that happens and its experience builds up in its EM-energy that thereby comprises a collective of the various strands of activities that have developed and as it enters into subsequent activities this activates its past experience which influences the way that it deals with the current situation. We experience this principle at work in ourselves as the strands of emotions and ideas that are continually running through us derived from past experiences influence how we behave in the current situation and in what we want to achieve in the future. As we incarnate into hominid bodies, we activate the relevant strands of development but then, out of our self-actualising Ego impulses we can create disharmony, in two possible directions - the Ahrimanic or the Luciferic and the guide asked how this affected the situation:

G: Can you get an image of a man who is under Ahrimanic or Luciferic influences?
T: I have asked for an image of a harmonised man, there is a steady flow of energy in and out of this man. Now I ask for the image to move to the Ahrimanic end and the energy flow rebounds off him.
G: And when you give him the homoeopathic remedy the energies flow through?
T: Yes. Now if I ask for the image to move to the Luciferic side then the energy from outside moves in at its normal rate, but then becomes highly active and moves out quickly and the homoeopathic remedy in that case slows it down - the remedy has the harmonised rhythm.
G: It's the same remedy administered to either the Ahrimanic or Luciferic situation?
T: Yes, it seems that where the activity is blocked the remedy lifts it out through the blockage, in the other case it slows it down to the harmonised return speed.

G: What type of remedy would you give someone who is Luciferically inclined?
T: The image shows a pulling down of the Ego, something to bring it back within the system.
G: Would you give him lead?
T: The image shows the Ego being drawn gently back down to take up its proper place, lead would pull the Ego too far down.
G: How about iron?
T: A partial 'yes' to that, with the words, 'strengthening the Ego.
G: So, do you give this Ego a remedy to pull it down forcibly to the required extent, or do you give it a remedy to bring the Ego to its senses, so that it sees where it should be and then moves there of its own accord?
T: That is more like the position, the image shows that the Ego needs to be restored gently to its proper place, you can't snatch it back.
G: From what you say a mineral might be too brutal, a plant might be better?
T: Yes, that seems O.K.
G: It would have to be a plant with a good root?
T: Yes, something that was anchored strongly.
G: What about Dock, or a bulb like a daffodil, or oak root?
T: Yes, that sort of thing. What is being shown is that it is the principle that must be followed and the specific remedy sought for the personality.
G: What about the case where the Ahrimanic stream is dominating the Ego?
T: This is the opposite situation, the Ego is enveloped and cut off, it needs to be lifted.
G: A flower remedy or a climbing plant that grows upwards?
T: Yes, the image is again showing that it is the principle that is needed.
G: What about where disease originates in the astral, due to primitive passions that the Ego hasn't got under control?
T: The Ego needs strengthening - to enable it to control its passions.

G: So iron might be O.K. here?

T: There was a 'yes' to that.

G: What about the case where the Ego has clamped down on its feelings because it's frightened of them?

T: It's the opening up principle, relaxing the Ego.

G: Gold is used for depression - what is depression in these terms?

T: Everything goes very sad and dull, the Ego slows right down, it is no longer controlling its bodies, they are leading an independent life. The Ego has opted out of trying to do anything with them, outside influences have taken over, everything looks heavy and dull.

G: Would you give gold in this case?

T: The word gold produced just that in the image. Golden light began to diffuse through the bodies and connect up with the Ego. I suppose that is the harmonising principle connecting them together again.

G: If the Ahrimanic or Luciferic flows get out of balance this can cause a blockage or an enhancement in the flow of, say, iron from outside and homoeopathic iron can bring everything back into harmony.

T: Yes.

G: Now iron is going through the body in the diet in say, an iron-containing plant such as spinach but the body's flows can't work with it?

T: The image shows that the iron that is assimilated in the diet comes to consciousness but the system's use of it depends on how it is responding to the flows from outside. The homoeopathic remedy is quite independent of the system and it can restore the external flow.

G: Can you see the iron activity in the body?

T: Yes, it approaches from outside, penetrates to the centre, bends round and goes back out again. The image shows the energy making contact with the blood stream - this receives something from the iron energy.

G: If a person is Ahrimanic will they want to keep this iron activity to themselves?

T: The image shows them as being reluctant to let it return.

G: And so the iron pressure in the blood will build up and cause malfunctioning - can we get a name for it?

T: The words 'blood disorder' came in.

G: Would it make the blood thicker?

T: The word 'richer' came in.

G: If on the other hand they were Luciferic...?

T: Anaemic comes in.

G: And if they were Christ oriented?

T: It's harmonised.

G: Can you see four levels of iron activity, etheric, astral, mental and physical?

T: Yes, the image split into two, one showed the flow going through the four bodies of a man, then alongside it appeared a column representing iron and this split into four components.

G: Now, iron at the mental level....?

T: The words 'mental strength' come in.

G: If the man is grasping iron, that is, being Ahrimanic, at the mental level, would that give him rigidity of thinking?

T: Yes.

G: Run-away thoughts would be Luciferic?

T: Yes.

G: What would too much iron activity at the astral level give rise to?

T: The image shows that the feelings are concentrated - intense.

G: And if he was on the Luciferic side they would be wishy-washy.

T: Yes.

G: What do we mean by someone being Luciferic or Ahrimanic at the etheric level?

T: The etheric is closely bound to the physical and at this level it is the will that is affected.

G: If we give a low dilution remedy to a person, at what level in the body systems does it work?

T: The most unconscious part stays at the physical level and has some effect there, while the more conscious part travels on up through his subtle bodies.

G: Right, now dilute it down to 200C and get a person to take that.

T: They take it, it is very lively, everything is conscious, everything is striving to be out and on its way back, so it goes straight through the physical, etheric and astral. It touches these in varying degrees but the main reaction takes place at the mental body.

G: What would be the point of taking a plant remedy, would it do something that the homoeopathic metallic iron cannot do?

T: The image shows the beings that make up the plant to be more conscious than those of the metal. It shows an increasing level of consciousness from root to stem to flower of a plant.

G: Now suppose that we take a low dilution of the plant, how is this different to metallic iron?

T: There appears to be less remaining at the physical level, it wants to go on up through the etheric and astral levels.

G: So if we want to concentrate attention at the etheric level, it's better to use a plant remedy?

T: There's a straight 'yes' to that.

G: And if we want to concentrate attention at the astral level, it's better to use an animal-based remedy?

T: There's a 'yes' to that, accompanied by an image of beings of increased consciousness.

G: We could waken up the beings at the astral level by the right dilution of the metal but would there be any advantage to using a plant at the astral level?

T: Yes, the dilution of the plant appears to contain more beings than the iron and the combination of the beings is different.

G: So a homoeopathic remedy has a higher level of activity or 'consciousness' which frees the clogged up iron flow?

T: When it experiences the homoeopathic remedy it just naturally moves on. It goes to a higher level of consciousness.

G: What happens to the clogged up iron activity when a person goes to sleep. Presumably the Higher Self tries to do something about it?

T: The image shows that during sleep, while the Ego is outside, the Higher Self is attempting to do in a slower manner what the homoeopathic remedy achieves quite quickly. That is, to break down this blockage and raise the iron up further. It seems to make a little progress and the Ego moves back in again and that progress is lost.

A physician, Edward Bach (1886-1936), became increasingly dissatisfied with the limitations of orthodox medicine and its concentration on treating symptoms so that he sought to treat the causes of illness and thereby became involved in homoeopathic methods. However, Bach's philosophy went further than the homoeopathic one, in that he took the view that, while people respond differently to illness and treatment according to their personality, good health requires us to be true to our inner, spiritual nature. He developed a range of 38 flower remedies to treat the problems that different types of people experience in being true to themselves, such as anxiety, fear, despondency, etc. (see WEEKS and handbooks supplied with Bach remedies). These remedies do not treat the physical problems but seek to re-establish a person's contact with their Higher Self so that this can regain and maintain their good health. From the *h*K-M viewpoint the flower represents the plant's expression of fulfilment of its inner nature.

As well as the problem of understanding how a homoeopathic remedy works, there is the problem of understanding what homoeopathic dilution and succussion do in making a remedy. One of Harry's ECEs made some comments on this.

H: Homoeopathic dilution is a speeded-up process of evolution. This seems to be the essential thing about potentisation. It's the amount of experience that you give it. In one shake an iron atom can move a large distance and experience a lot. A hundred shakes and it goes through the same experience again and again. You shake a thing and it experiences its environment.

G: So, when a person who has got their iron activity out of balance takes a homoeopathic dilution ...?

H: It goes in and it knows what needs to be done, it's active, it's evolved, it can move wherever it wants to go. It sees areas that need strength, it sees areas which are too rigid and it helps to ease and loosen. Gradually it brings the whole body of iron activity back into balance. This is because it's aware of these activities within itself. It's an active, walking blueprint of its purpose. It can go up to the barrier between the spiritual and the physical, where they're not working.

According to *h*K-M everything comprises patterns of activity in the initially dormant basic energy. Our body comprises a hierarchy of such activities, namely prokaryotic cells and eukaryotic cells within a multicellular organisation. All of these act on and manifest their behaviour in the organisation of substances. If there is an inadequate supply of substances, as in malnutrition, or an insufficient amount of a key material, the patterns of activity cannot perform their functions. But if the supply of substances is adequate and the patterns of activity do not work harmoniously in accord with each other, as an integrated totality, then the body malfunctions. To correct this it is necessary to restore the malfunctioning activity to its healthy state. This ECE states that this can be done by an appropriate substance that has been homoeopathically activated to perform according to its strand of development in the EM-energy.

Iron plays a role at all levels of evolution, mineral, plant, animal and humanity and this is all experienced by and registered in the EM-energy. In its mineral form it expresses its least evolved level of activity but, according to this ECE, when diluted and succussed it can undergo a rapid evolutionary development that activates it to behave in a way appropriate to a higher level and this is how it works as a homoeopathic remedy.

Disharmony can originate from any of the body's levels, physical-etheric stresses due to unbalanced diet or physical misuse, or emotional, or mental stresses, which affect the energy flows through the various levels. Thus, in order to rectify any of these disharmonies it is necessary to bring about a rebalancing at the required level. This requires diluting and succussing the homoeopathic remedy so that it is activated to the appropriate level. It then 'kick starts' the malfunctioning into normal behaviour, so that the Ego can regain harmonious control.

[Normally we think of the body chemistry breaking down and reconstituting the substances which it ingests but there is also evidence for a deeper activity at the sub-atomic level, resulting in the rearrangement of the sub-atomic components and thereby a reconstitution of the atoms of some substances, by the workings of the human body. Thus, KERVRAN (and others quoted in his book) have found what seems to be evidence for the transmutation of sodium into potassium and magnesium in the human body, silicon into calcium in plants and a number of other transmutations. This would release energy at a number of different levels. Because this evidence has not fitted in with the established viewpoint of science it has largely been ignored].

The return to harmony is something that we can experience after taking a homoeopathic remedy. We (our Ego) then has to maintain harmonious use of our body systems but often we revert to our pattern of behaviour that created the disharmony, so that we have to take the homoeopathic remedy several times before we can maintain the harmony that it produces. Conversely, sometimes people experience that an improvement occurs even before they take the remedy; this is because, in seeking out the remedy, they have generated enough self-awareness to start the rebalancing process themselves.

Experimental Researches into Homoeopathy

We reasoned that, if homoeopathic remedies could affect the functioning of living organisms, then the most likely mineral kingdom phenomenon to show an effect would be a dynamic, delicately organising, pattern of behaviour. We thus tried adding homoeopathic remedies to a number of such situations and to illustrate this we describe some experiments with the crystallisation of a 1% solution of copper chloride.

We added various homoeopathic remedies, supplied by a manufacturer, and they had a dramatic effect, fig. 20.2, compared with copper chloride on its own, fig. 20.1.

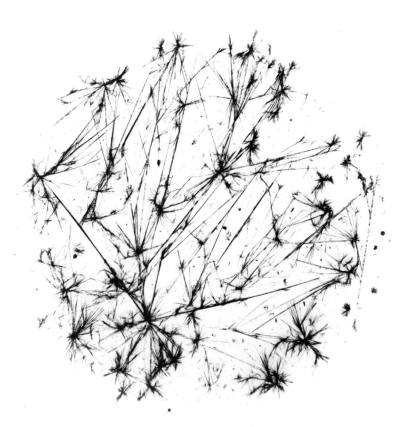

Fig. 20.1 The pattern formed by a drop of 1% copper chloride solution evaporating slowly on a glass plate under controlled conditions.

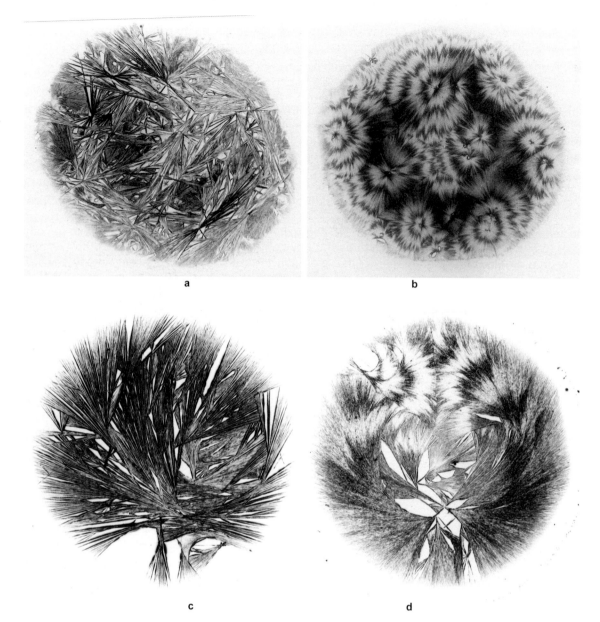

Fig. 20.2 Patterns formed by a 1% copper chloride solution crystallising under the same conditions as for fig. 20.1, but with a small addition of a homoeopathic remedy, (**a**) calcium 6x, (**b**) graphite 12x, (**c**) iron 12x, (**d**) gold 20x. We thought that these patterns revealed formative forces associated with the different remedies but we subsequently found that they were largely due to the lactose used in their preparation.

But as we carried out further experiments to ensure that this result was unambiguously attributable to the homoeopathic substance, we found that it was, in fact, due to the presence of lactose.

Whereas a homoeopathic remedy of a substance that dissolves in water can be made by straight-forward multiple dilution, with substances that do not dissolve in water, such as a metal, it is made by first grinding small particles in lactose (sugar of milk) and then dissolving this in water. We had not realised that sometimes manufacturers use lactose solution for the dilution as well and that a substantial amount of lactose was present in the remedies that we were experimenting with. This led to the results shown in fig. 20.2 and the difference between these and fig. 20.1 we would now attribute to the change in the stress pattern brought about by the presence of the lactose in the crystallising liquid.

After sorting out this misleading situation we made our own homoeopathic dilutions so that we knew exactly what we were dealing with. We then carried out many more experiments, in which we tried to detect homoeopathic forces in crystallisation, capillary dynamolysis patterns, fluid flow and other delicately balanced dynamic situations. Sometimes the addition of a homoeopathic solution seemed to affect the result but we were never able to produce a controlled and reproducible effect, (we give later further details of what happened). At the same time we sought, in our ECEs, help in understanding what was going on in our experiments.

ECEs Dealing With Homoeopathic Forces

We tried many times to gain insight into what occurred in homoeopathic diluting and we present a selection of the responses that we got.

G: Let's have a look at homoeopathic diluting. Can you first of all get the consciousness of the water?
T: The image is of a phial of water that is comparatively still. There is a limited, sleepy sort of activity of the beings inside. But when the water is shaken, within a few cycles the beings become vigorous and conscious. I get an image of a waterfall where a comparatively passive stream moves along quite quietly then falls a long distance over a ledge and rocks into a pool below. In the disturbed region, where the falling water meets the pool, the consciousness of the water is raised. The image shows fish seeking out this increased consciousness; they are attracted to the turbulence, they can relate to it, they become more active.
G: Would someone standing by this waterfall be aware of this increased consciousness?
T: I see people standing at the side of a deep waterfall in contact with the mist, some are invigorated and excited, others are frightened by the experience and draw back from it.
G: Now take a piece of copper, grind it up in lactose and dilute this in water, shaking it as you do so, what do you see?
T: The imagery has shown me the water alone being shaken in the way that homoeopathic remedies are prepared. When water is shaken its consciousness is awakened but as it becomes still, its consciousness dies down again and it returns to the state it was in before the shaking. Now the copper is added and on succussion they are both becoming more conscious; when the shaking ceases, although consciousness dies down again, the copper has achieved an increase in consciousness that it retains. For it to become more active it is necessary to carry on diluting and succussing. The image shows that after each shaking there is a reduction in the consciousness that the shaking achieves but the copper never goes right back. With each dilution the activity put into it increases its consciousness step by step. Also the tiny amounts of copper have a big effect on the water, which has its consciousness raised considerably in the shaking process. The extent to which the consciousness of the copper and water are dimmed at the conclusion of shaking is different. The water moves much further back towards the inert state, while the copper retains a lot more of its increased consciousness; but in association with copper the water does not return completely to its original state.
G: What is happening to the copper as it is homoeopathically diluted?
T: I'm shown a lump of copper with quite a few individual copper entities inside. As long as it remains like that the individualising beings form a really rigid shell around the outside of it. When the copper gets down to a smaller number of entities the individualising beings find it more difficult to keep these together. The outward-moving beings can sense freedom is close at hand and this excites them into pressing outwards against the individualising beings.
G: What happens when you put this into water?
T: When this is put into water there is a neutralising of the pressing in by the individualising beings. The water is fluid and they would like to stifle the water's activity
G: What happens as the copper is further diluted in water?
T: The image shows it coming to life through all three layers and the water is beginning to call to them as well.
G: But we have to keep on diluting and shaking to really free them?
T: Yes.

Again we think that the sources of these ECEs perceived what was happening at an etheric level and presented it to us in terms of their Steiner viewpoint/cosmology. This regards substances as sacrificed parts of a Spiritual Hierarchy comprising 'beings' cut off by a surround of individualising beings and working towards self consciousness and freedom and a return to their origins. On another occasion we asked about the homoeopathic dilution of iron.

G: What happens when we grind small particles of iron in lactose?
T: There is some sort of reaction. The lactose wants the iron and in the breaking-down process the iron wants to move into the lactose. The beings in the iron begin to wake up, offering resistance to the squeezing from outside -- The image changed then to the smallest complete piece of iron, with all its beings, being shaken in water and the same thing happened. The iron and the water want to combine and the iron then offers resistance, from the inside, to the individualising beings on the outside.
G: So the beings in the iron are waking up?
T: Yes.
G: And this somehow fills the liquid with activity?
T: Yes, the liquid in which they are contained seems to have life in it now.
G: What happens if you carry on diluting?
T: The activity just increases.

G: If we dilute iron right down to 200c is there still an iron being left in it?
T: There is iron activity.
G: Is it possible to dilute to the state where you begin to lose it because you are splitting it up so much?
T: There is a hesitant 'yes' to that. The image shows the awakening activity so active it can't be contained in the liquid, it is breaking the surface of the water and some of it appears to be escaping.

Another ECE, concerned with the homoeopathic diluting of salt, gave further detail on the viewpoint that was being expressed.

G: Take a bottle of dissolved salt and throw away nine-tenths of it and replace it by water, shake it up and see what's happened to it?
T: The salt atoms are more individual and widely spaced; they tend to become isolated from one another.
G: The atoms look just the same in themselves?
T: Yes.
G: Now again throw away nine tenths, fill it up, shake it and now what have you got?
T: The process has been exaggerated, just a few atoms and a lot of liquid.
G: Do the atoms change?
T: No.
G: Do the same again, throw away nine-tenths, fill it up with water, shake it, let's have a look.
T: Smaller number of atoms and they appear to be more active, they are moving about much more. It's as if, in the previous stage the number of atoms present restricted their movement so that they still had some sort of relationship to one another, they couldn't move about completely freely. Now at this dilution there are fewer of them and their movement is exaggerated, they move through bigger distances.
G: Have they changed in appearance?
T: I think they may have increased in size very slightly.
G: Right, throw away nine-tenths, fill it up, shake it.
T: Now there are only one or two atoms in the liquid. They move quite freely and rapidly and the shaking helps the movement.
G: Have they changed in appearance at all?
T: Yes, the picture that came in was of just two atoms in the liquid, these dash about but don't collide with one another. Now when the bottle is shaken and I remain with one of the atoms during the shaking it feels as if it gets lighter, the weight is taken off it and it begins to unravel or unwind.
G: Suppose you give a hundred shakes?
T: They're well on the way to totally unwinding.
G: A thousand shakes?
T: Completely unwound, right back to the warmth state.
G: A million shakes?
T: It doesn't do any more as far as I can see.
G: How has this affected the water?
T: I can only describe this in terms of feeling, it's as if the water has come to life. The original water feels quite lifeless, whereas the water containing the broken up atom is a quite different thing altogether, very lively.
G: What happens when you drink some?
T: It doesn't taste any different to drink but when you see it inside your body, the organs it passes through get brighter and lighter, life is transferred to them.

These ECEs continue the theme of substances as beings in an unconscious state that experience consciousness when they are caused to become active and interact with each other. They portray homoeopathic diluting as 'freeing' the atoms when they become very small in number, so that they become highly active and conscious and move about independently of the water molecules. (It also puts forward the concept of atoms 'unwinding', which we deal with in Part IV). The scientific view would be that the atoms of the homoeopathic substance are a part of the jostling mass of water molecules and can only move as these move. In the ECE the reason given for their ability to move independently of the water molecules is that the confining force cannot exert its effect on just a few atoms. This seems to imply that somehow the homoeopathically diluted substance has moved out of the space-time of physical activities.

An ECE-led Experiment

Our seeking, in the ECEs, for a way to demonstrate experimentally the existence of homoeopathic forces led to a 'co-operative experiment' in which various entities, who we categorise as a collective 'He', appeared in the imagery of the ECEs and advised us on what to do. This arose, in the first place, out of our efforts to try to understand the 'inner nature' of substances.

G: When we're working with metals, how can we establish contact with the 'soul' of the metal?

H: 'He' says you must be very thoroughly acquainted with all its physical properties. You must be spiritually aware. And you can hold the metal in your hands and open yourself and the qualities will be shown to you. It can be done but there are other ways.

G: What's the best way for us?

H: What we're doing, the experiments on homoeopathy he says. I put an atom of iron in some water and it splits up and there is water with the power of iron in it.

G: What do you mean by the power of iron?

H: There's strength, will, determination in the water - You can't detect these qualities by physical means. Can't see them. Can't drink it and feel them. He says you look at a human being and see these qualities in them. In the same way you look at the bucket of water and see the qualities there. It's staring you in the face, he says.

G: Supposing we crystallise copper chloride in water with and without the iron force?

H: Then you'll get a pattern modified by the iron force.

G: So it does affect the physical in that respect then?

H: No, it doesn't affect the physical, it affects the copper chloride in the etheric.

G: So when the copper chloride crystallises out, the physical form that it takes is a manifestation of etheric forces. Is that how the crystallisation patterns show these forces?

H: Yes --- He suggests that we make a bucket of potentised water by putting a chunk of iron under the surface of the water and scrape it a few times to get atoms released into the water and then stir rapidly to create a vortex.

G: What does the vortex do?

H: The iron atoms concentrate at the tip of the vortex and spin upwards and outwards and they get stretched up the vortex. Then when you stop stirring you disorganise all that stretchness and start to break them up. Then these bits collect at the bottom of the water and you break them up again.

G: This means several stirring operations.

H: Yes. Stir the bucket for about five minutes in one direction and about five minutes in the other direction, for about half an hour.

G: When you scrape the iron, can you put your hands in, to scrape under water?

H: He's got some rubber gloves on, your body would taint the water. Mind you, he says, if you were a saint or a holy man you'd be alright.

Stirring of this nature was laid down by Steiner in the formulation of esoteric 'spiritual manure' to supplement ordinary manuring, to improve plant growth (see Steiner's lectures/book on Agriculture).

We tried this experiment and got changes in the copper chloride crystallisation patterns. But further experiments to ensure that these were due to the iron stirring showed that they resulted from talcum powder on the plastic gloves that we were wearing when holding the iron under water. When we eliminated this we did not get any definite changes. So, in another ECE we asked about this.

G: Andy's tried stirring the iron to get the iron force out, without getting an effect, is it that Andy hasn't got the iron force into the water or that he's got the iron force in and the crystallisation experiments haven't shown it up - will this definitely work?

H: He got very serious then and said, 'Oh yes, because he's got this from somewhere higher up'. He says Andy hasn't got the iron force into the water. He says the stirring's alright, it's the scraping of the iron; he says, get very pure iron, make thin sheets and tear it under water. And use a container with sloping sides, experiment with different types of bucket to create a deeper vortex.

We made a sloping-sided, conical-shaped bucket and got some pure iron foil that we tore under the water but we still didn't get a definite effect, so in another ECE Andy tried to 'see' what was going on.

A: I saw the foil being torn and a few atoms coming off but they do not go into the vortex.

G: Ask for images to help get these atoms into the vortex.

A: I heard the word 'stir'.

G: But we are stirring, ask for an image to show what is meant by 'stir'.

A: I do a bit of stirring in a bucket and I see another bucket being stirred by an 'expert'. I saw atoms at the bottom of the expert's bucket and as he stirred they were swept up in a circular motion. Then I looked through that to see a galaxy out in the Universe that was doing the same thing, a great mass of stars all rotating and spiralling in the same way. Now I go back to my own bucket and I'm not getting the atoms moving.

G: Ask him if the imagery of the galaxy means that one has to adjust one's tempo of stirring in some way, to harmonise with something?

A: He says, 'You saw that and its meaning was obvious, from the tiny bucket situation to the vast heavenly situation, it's all the same'.

G: What does he think of our cone-shaped bucket?
A: He says it's a bit better and I say, 'What is the right container for working with iron?' And I saw a container similar to our conical one but the sides are flared out.
G: Is the curvature vitally important?
A: I got the feeling of a definite mathematical relationship governing the curve of the sides. It's something like an exponential. It starts out at the bottom very slender and apparently straight-sided and it comes up nearly to the top and then swiftly bells out.
G: Is it the shape of the vortex itself?
A: I think so.

We did many more experiments and had many more ECEs in which we were given advice on the method of stirring to achieve the best vortex and on ways of introducing the iron. Sometimes we seemed to get an effect but it was not reproducible, so we asked about the efficiency of our method of testing for homoeopathic forces.

G: Ask him to check the crystallisation technique.
A: He's got a big fat manual for that. He's rifling the pages under my nose. I back off and say, 'Oh dear, have I got to go through all that?', and he waves it at me, saying, 'Yes, you've got to know all this off by heart' - he opens it at the title page which says, 'Crystallisation: A Technique for Revealing Cosmic Forces'.
G: We seem to have sometimes got some success with the iron water in the way that we've been doing it?
A: He's drunk a bit of water from our test stirring and he said that's alright and he points to the results I got comparing stirred water with water which we had not stirred and he says, 'That's real'.

'He' then went through each step in our experimental technique in detail and Andy commented:

A: It's funny, it's as though he's seeing all this for the first time - he's saying that he'll have to go back and report this to his superiors.
G: Who is he?
A: He points upwards and mutters, 'I just work for them up there'. He's not a high member of 'them up there' - he accepts that, he's some kind of engineer-technician I think.

A basic problem with the experimental researches was that, despite carrying out our crystallisation experiments as rigorously as we were able, i.e. control of temperature, humidity, atmosphere cleanliness and eliminating mechanical vibrations and air disturbances, we still got some 'random' variations in our results. While sometimes we got an effect that seemed to be attributable to the iron water, because of the background random changes, we could never be sure of this. So we tried, in one of Andy's ECEs to see what effect we might expect to get.

G: What is the difference between the copper chloride crystallising out of distilled water and crystallising out of iron water?
A: In the distilled water the pattern of crystals was made by them criss-crossing randomly all over the place. But the iron water was organising them.
G: Can you see the pattern?
A: It seems to be a swirling one. I flew along the lines of the iron force and it was a spiral and as I approached the centre of the pattern I began to spiral up and I had the feeling of warmth and contentment, happiness at returning home - the iron has homing instincts. Then I saw a picture of a great big iron being sinking into the Earth, I heard him groan and it all went quiet. I've picked up a lump of rich iron ore from the ground and I hit it with my hand and shout, 'Is anybody there?' and I hear only faint stirrings, as though I'm trying to wake someone up but they're far away and dreaming --- I've been given a mortar and pestle and I pound my rock down into finer and finer pieces and I heard the word, 'Resurrection' and it seemed that this was resurrecting the iron, bringing it back to life - The big iron being is on the edge of the bowl now, pointing down into the dust and then up into the sky, he says, 'I enter that dust'.
G: So you free him from the Earth?
A: I think so, yes. I saw the iron-being get up and twirl around on his toes. He disappeared and became a flowing vortex of motion. I heard him say, 'I am not really here, I am a pattern, I am an arrangement.

By its B-cell motion the Earth Entity brings together all the constituents that make up the Earth planet and via its EM-energy aspect it contains a memory of all of the strands of development that have taken place. The strand of development of iron could be called the Spirit of Iron that this ECE portrays, picturesquely, as becoming incarcerated into the Earth situation as iron ore. But in this state iron is 'dead', i.e. it cannot manifest its inner nature. To do this it has to be broken down finer and finer to allow the atoms of which it consists to manifest their properties.

G: There's a problem with our experiments, in that the iron water sometimes shows a pattern and sometimes it doesn't.

A: I feel that we must somehow harness the water. I see the water as full of fickle energy, dancing about all over the place and I heard it say, 'I'm responsive, I'm not doing this myself you know'. And I say, 'Responding to what?' and the water says, 'Oh, all sorts of things, you wouldn't believe how many things there are to respond to, sometimes it's almost too much'. And I say, 'Well, what about the iron?' 'Oh, yes, I know about that, but that's not the only fish in the sea', the water replies. Then I heard the word, 'Dedication' and I thought of Holy Water that had been charged by prayer. And I see a vortical crystal pattern that had formed in the iron water and I ask, 'How do we get that?' And I heard the word, 'Love' but I was not happy and said, 'Can we not add a chemical to show the iron force? What kind of experiment is that where you give it a bit of love to show the iron force?' And I hear, 'What chemical is as good as love?'

G: Are scientists like us, glued to the material earth in the way that we are, really capable of putting love into water?

A: I'm told we can do it, we are channels but we can do it.

G: The effect of prayer on water, people blessing water, and Holy Water - it seems that water is responsive, in some way that we do not understand ....?

This imagery highlights the role of water, which is interesting because scientists who claim to have demonstrated the existence of homoeopathic forces, by sensitive biological experiments, conclude that somehow water gets a pattern of behaviour, or memory, imposed on it, (SCHIFF).

This ECE also claims that 'Love' can affect the experiment. This may seem a ludicrous idea from the standpoint of modern science but emotions do affect the behaviour of substances; they are doing it all the time in our body as, for example, when we experience fear and this causes substances to form adrenaline that flows through our body. And this relationship between substance activity and emotions finds no explanation in modern science. Scientists can trace through the activities of the nervous system that are associated with the formation of adrenaline but they cannot explain how an insubstantial emotion or thought initiates this train of events. This relationship is, however, central to our existence in that everything that we do depends on it. We start with a thought or feeling that we will do something and in some way the thought/feeling is translated into physical activity that involves movements and interactions in the substances that make up our body. According to *h*K-M our physical body is permeated by an etheric energy system (etheric body) that gives it form and function and through which our soul feelings and spirit thinking express themselves, in a way that has evolved over a long period and that is registered in, and activated from, the EM-energy. Thereby our thinking/feeling spirit/soul bring about movements of the substances that comprise our bodies. Water, that is a responsive fluid, comprises 70% of our body and it may be that it plays a central role in this chain of events.

It also seems that it is possible for our soul/feeling and spirit/thinking to affect water that is not connected with our bodily functioning. We have referred in Chapter 13 to experiments by Bernard Grad, which showed that water treated by a healer had a beneficial effect on the germination of seeds, whereas water treated by a depressive had a detrimental effect. EMOTO has developed a delicate crystallisation technique that shows, not only what are probably physical differences in waters from different sources but also a soul/spirit effect on water, i.e. an effect of prayer on water and the effect of exposing water to different sentiments, fig. 20.3.

Emoto ascribes these effects to Hado, i.e. an inner energy, like the Chinese ch'l, the ancient Greek's pneuma, the Indian prana, the Universal energy of Daskalos, equivalent perhaps to the EM-energy of *h*K-M that exists in everything. It would be interesting to know whether Emoto's experiments are reproducible by other workers or whether they are a manifestation of his and his co-workers abilities to be channels for the Hado force, in the same way that Grad's experiments showed an effect of the healing nature of a person on water. We referred, in Chapter 13, to the fact that some people can emit an energy and focus it to produce an image on a photographic plate and that a few radionic practitioners have found that they can produce an image of a patient's malfunctioning organs on a photographic plate. There are also the many healing phenomena in which healers bring about changes in the activities of substances in the bodies of the people who they heal. These phenomena are further examples of the fact that there is an energy by which people can affect the behaviour of substances but It is not clear to what extent such people have conscious control of the energy involved and how much they act as channels for entities that are able to perceive, by etheric or astral vision, what is wrong and then use the person's energy to manipulate it in this way. It could be that, with its responsive fluid nature, water plays a significant role in many of these phenomena. We consider further the nature of water in Chapter 27 of this book.

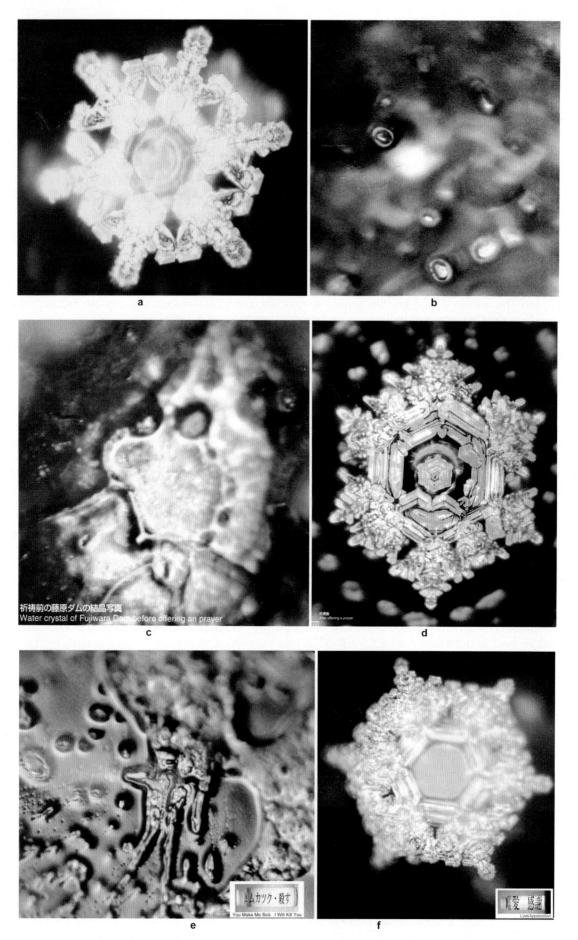

Fig 20.3 Examples of the types of crystals that Emoto obtained with his delicate crystallisation technique that show the 'quality' possessed by the water, **a** a natural spring water, **b** London tap water, in which crystals would not develop, **c** water from the Fujiwara Dam before offering a prayer, **d** water from the same dam after a priest performed a prayer for one hour beside the dam, **e** crystal obtained with distilled water where the container had a label with the words 'you make me sick, I will kill you' on it, **f** crystal obtained from a sample of the same distilled water where the container label had the words 'Love/Appreciation' on it
(From Messages from Water Vol 1, reproduced by permission of I.H.M. Co Ltd, Authorisation No ihm 0607070606)

In our striving to grasp the inner nature of iron, Andy was led into further contact with the 'iron being'.

A: I'm sitting down with the iron being and I say, 'We don't really know you at all. On Earth we weigh and measure you and we bash you about and make you react with others like yourself and we think we know you, but we only know the outside bits, we don't know the real you. Can you help us, so that we can work with you more fully?' -- And we've gone flying up into the air, rising higher and higher. I saw the disc of the Sun ahead of us, white hot and I heard the iron say, 'Here I was born, here I was formed'. As the iron was saying that, we were on the surface of the Sun. And the substance of the iron seems to have dissolved away, I now see the iron as a flickering flame, the whole of the Sun is flickering flames. And I wondered where the strength was that we associated with iron and the iron said, 'Remember, you have only seen a small part of me so far. There is much to me that you haven't seen'. So we leave the Sun and the iron flame is shrinking now, getting smaller, weaker, fainter. He's cooling down and now we approach the Earth and the living flame condensed to a piece of iron. I said, 'Where have you gone, you've died', and I heard a voice from inside say, 'Don't worry, I'm not dead, I'm just asleep'. We're sinking down to Earth and we land in a big desert. We have to have a large clear space because the iron is now a massive sculpture which could well be entitled 'Strength'. It's a figure between human and a flame, down on one knee, straining upwards. This figure and its posture represent the potential strength of iron.

In this ECE we regard the Iron Being as the Spirit of Iron, i.e. the strand of development in the EM-energy that relates to the nature and evolution of iron. It describes the Iron Being as becoming incarcerated in the Earth situation; it also describes iron as being formed in the Sun, which is different from the Steiner-type cosmology of Spiritual Entities pouring their activities into an inert cosmic ether and closer to the current scientific viewpoint of the formation of substances in (Sun) stars.

G: How can we cooperate with him?
A: We have to provide questions, it is incumbent on us to play our part in this but having said that I got the feeling that we should sit on his shoulder so to speak and watch him at work in his manifold activity. The iron being said, 'Work with me, love me no matter what I look like, no matter how awful, disgusting, ragged and mean I may appear'. Then I saw an industrial waste-site - filth and garbage and steel off-cuts rusting - that's what he means, not just the laboratory specimens or the bright and shiny metal but the rusting and forgotten metal, the metal that is used for guns, everything. So I say that I will try and he says, 'Good. That is the first thing, The second thing', he says, 'is to know me' and he puts his finger to his nose as though to say, 'and you've got a lot to learn!' Now I think he's going to let me get inside him and experience what he experiences. He held out a finger and a thin thread from his finger ran to a piece of iron in the earth and it's as though the iron down there is a radio transmitter sending back what it experiences but at the moment there's nothing coming back. Then a plant touched the iron particle and I heard alarm bells ringing, everything jolted into action, little beings in the plant root grabbed hold of the iron beings who had just woken up --- Then I saw the plant wilt and begin to collapse and the iron being turned to me and said, 'See! That plant needs iron'. Then he took off a fingernail and tossed it into the ground near a root and the root sucks hard at this fingernail and the sucked-up iron stuff is flowing through the plant and wherever it flows the plant perks up.

To try to relate this ECE imagery more directly to the experimental work, the guide asked:

G: Can you tear some iron foil under water?
A: I was tearing it and it was hurting him, I said, 'Sorry,' and he said, 'No, no, carry on, it's got to be'. Then I got the feeling that I didn't have to tear the foil, I could just ask it to part and it would - that seemed to happen, the foil just parted. I'm trying to get this clear with the iron being, on the one side I have the image of the foil parting and, on the other side, there's the image of me tearing the foil and I say to the iron, 'Can you show me how to work my way towards the parting situation?' And I got a quick impression of a spoon-bending experiment. And the iron being said, 'Yes, I work with that fellow - when he lets me, with all his running around, when he lets me in I manage to do a bit of bending - it's the same sort of thing'. And I saw myself tear the iron very slowly - so slowly that it felt as though it was opening up ahead of the tear. Then I heard the iron being say, 'Think of me when you do this' and he changed from the iron being to an image of Christ on the cross and then that changed back to the iron being again.

There is considerable evidence for some people being able to affect substances, e.g. as with spoon bending (see HASTEAD), or to move objects as in poltergeist activities and for dematerialisation and materialisation of objects and for Sai Baba to materialise objects 'out of thin air'. Two types of situation seem to be involved, one where people open themselves up to become unconscious channels for the forces involved, the other where they consciously know and direct what is happening, which corresponds with PAYNE's negative and positive psychism.

As we have stated before, in this work we were simply trying to understand and follow the suggestions that we were given, to see where they would lead us. Sometimes we got an interesting result that seemed to show an effect but in the end they didn't lead to anything that we could build on. When we queried this Harry got the reply:

H: He says you've got to understand that we're very much working in co-operation with them. It hasn't been done before down here. As far as they're concerned it's a very definite, practical direct route toward demonstrating the power of substance and to moving humanity onto a deeper understanding of what substance is. He can't give us too many suggestions; he can only observe what we are doing and develop suggestions from there.

And, on another occasion:

G: When you did the experiment they suggested, by diluting and shaking the iron solution it didn't produce a different result.
H: The comment I get is, what did you expect? They say that they're giving us directions to work with and it's up to us to work it out.
G: Would I be right in saying that they don't know what's going to happen when we carry out an experiment any more than we do?
H: There's a scale of effects and we are aware of one end of the scale and they're well aware of the other end. We try and reach into their end and they try and reach into our end. They are aware of the spiritual strivings of the elements, whereas we are aware of their physical properties.
G: When we carry out experiments that have never been done before, am I right in saying that there is no consciousness anywhere that knows what the result will be?
H: Absolutely correct. What is most important is that everything that's happening now has never been done before, it's a complete unknown. You must realise that everything has been cut adrift. Just as we work with it all and attempt to strive forwards in our understanding, they're doing exactly the same thing. But they have to work with different tools. We have to cooperate.

Although this aspect of our work did not get us anywhere, we have described it at some length to show what can happen in an ECE and that the sources of the ECEs were not omniscient. People dealing with so-called channelled communications often assume them to be omniscient and equally those communicating often take on an air of authority and omniscience. But this is clearly not so, as we found when we pursued the suggestions for experiments on making and testing a homoeopathic solution; the suggestions did not work. [It could be that 'homoeopathic forces' are not detectable by mineral substance experiments, and that they need living organisms to show their activity].

The type of situation that we seemed to be dealing with is a major problem with any organisation, that those 'at the top' - politicians, management, etc. are remote from the working face, so that their ideas may not work out in practice. Advances in understanding and new developments require co-operation between those who have a hypothetical understanding about what is going on and those who are coping with, and know the detailed activities, at the working face. According to *h*K-M, evolution occurs by unplanned events arising at the working face followed by an increasingly conscious exploitation of the new potentials that these open up. And any hypothetical understanding about what can be done, developed out of what has happened in the past, may not be valid for interpreting what is happening now or predicting events of the future; if it was then nothing really new would ever arise, there would only be an extension of what has happened previously.

Homoeopathy and the Scientific Viewpoint

At the level of 200 dilutions, the conventional scientific view is that there is not a single atom of substance left and therefore the so-called remedy cannot do anything. (An easy way to check on whether or not there is any basis to homoeopathy is to take a tablet of Nat. Mur. 200, i.e. rock salt at 200 dilutions, three times a day for an extended period, say a month, and see whether this has an effect. If it produces an adverse effect then this can be corrected by a few doses of the antidote - Arsen Alb 200). However, a number of scientists have been sufficiently impressed by medical claims for the effectiveness of homoeopathic remedies to seek 'scientific' evidence for their nature and behaviour. Particularly outstanding was the work of Benveniste and co-workers over several years of painstaking investigations. They showed that if solutions of antibodies were diluted repeatedly until they no longer contained a single molecule of the antibody, they still produced a response from immune cells. They also showed that the 'activity' in a sealed glass phial of the diluted solution could be transmitted to another, untreated, phial of pure water by placing them both in the coils of an electrical transmission machine that were connected by a wire. They concluded that water possesses a 'memory' of what it has been subjected to, that determines its subsequent behaviour.

(see McTAGGART, SCHIFF). Smith found that where a person is allergic to a particular electromagnetic frequency, instead of subjecting them directly to the neutralising frequency, the same effect can be obtained by getting them to hold a tube of water that has been subjected to it, (see SMITH and BEST). From this Smith concludes, as did Benveniste, that water possesses a 'memory' for what it has experienced. This is in accord with Harry's ECE which stated that homoeopathic diluting and succussing 'iron water' gave it iron experience which it brought to bear on the situation where a person needed the iron activity in their body to be harmonised. (Harry's ECE was not influenced by any awareness of the work of Benveniste or Smith because it took place some years prior to this).

Benveniste and Smith ascribed the memory ability of water to some structural disposition of the water molecules. *h*K-M, however, ascribes it to the space-energy associated with the water molecules. As we have stated, according to *h*K-M, the nature of the space-energy is its experience, in the same way that we are what we have experienced. And in the same way that the situations that we encounter activate our relevant memories and determine our response to them, this happens with the space-energy which circulates through everything - atoms and organisms. When the space-energy is caught up in the solid or liquid state its pattern of behaviour is determined by the over-riding stress fields/forces created by the mass of atoms that it encompasses. And this is its normal condition in the water state, which determines the way in which it responds. We suggest that when substances are homoeopathically diluted and succussed the collective of atom entities is broken up and, with this constriction released, their internal components unwind (we deal with this in Chapter 27). When this happens the energy of the atom entities disperses into, and gives its experience to, the space-energy from which it derived but this region of the space-energy is held by the water that thereby becomes a vehicle for conveying the energy.

The way in which a homoeopathic remedy works is another thing that the next generation has to work out, along with the roles and workings of the other so-called alternative or complementary therapies. For general references to cover the field of homoeopathy, see HOMOEOPATHY in the bibliography. For further references on research into the mechanism of the workings of homoeopathic remedies, see SCHIFF and SMITH and BEST. For sources to contact for other alternative therapies see the bibliography in LOCKIE (reference in the homoeopathic bibliography in this book); SMITH and BEST have a useful chapter on research into alternative therapies.

Chapter 21

An Evaluation of This Phase of Our Work

At the time of the ECEs, we did not, and to a large extent still do not, understand what was happening, so we cannot make a proper evaluation of them, we can only offer a few comments.

The Source of the Imagery

We had, of course, wondered about the source/s of the information that we received in our ECEs, so in one of Brian's ECEs we asked about this:

B: I said we would like to draw closer to the group on the other side and I had a picture of a 1930's house. I go in through the front door and there's a fairly large room on the left. Inside is a collection of grey-suited men seated round a table. They are deceased scientists who have all been intensely concerned for a long time with establishing contact with a group down here. They have been set a task and they latched onto us and were uncertain as to whether they could pull it off. So they were being tested as well as us. It seems we have passed the test and we are now OK. They class themselves as searchers, some were interested in philosophy and wider things than conventional science. They are learning now, from their position, as much as we are from ours.
G: I doubt if they provide the answers to the questions that we ask, out of themselves.
B: No, they mediate. I see a whole chain that gradually goes higher and higher. Different levels transmit down to the level below. It's a very long chain.
G: It must be very complicated, with lots of opportunity for error.
B: It's not complicated because that's one of their advantages. There's a huge curtain around the physical world. Beyond that it's a lot easier, or speedier to go up and down, or contact levels there. The problem is the coarsening of the information as it goes up and down. It's limited by each level's understanding. So what we get down here is the tree stripped of all its leaves and fine twigs. We just get the trunk and a few major branches.

According to this ECE we were dealing with a group of discarnate scientists of somewhat similar standing to ourselves, who could therefore see things from our point of view and then seek answers to our questions from higher levels of the Omniverse Hierarchy and express the answers to us in our terms. This 'complementary group' had no difficulty in communicating with the Omniverse Hierarchy. According to hK-M, this is because each new level of entities is born into the environment of the Omniverse Hierarchy and is in continual interaction with it. Thus, all members of the Omniverse Hierarchy (including our Higher Selves) can, according to their level of development, 'tune into' the activities of the other members of the Hierarchy. (This is the normal situation; Humanity is abnormal through being cut off from the rest of the Hierarchy by the bodies that it inhabits). But in order to seek insights from the understanding of the higher levels of the Hierarchy it is necessary to be aware that they exist and to formulate meaningful questions and then to understand the answers. (In our own case we often found that we had to struggle to develop a different viewpoint before we could generate a meaningful dialogue).

In one of Brian's ECEs, his guide pointed out the potentials of the technique:

B: He's talking about how the mind is a powerful tool for investigation. How it can turn in the wink of an eye from investigating the heavens to investigating atomic worlds. What we are doing now is an apprenticeship. He is talking about the potential of the whole thing, how far we've come in the time we've been working at it. Limitless is a word he keeps using.
G: Will it spread?
B: He says it depends on the receptivity of other people. He points out that it involves a great deal of effort and motivation and sticking at it. This is the beauty of groups, in that everybody carries everybody else along in a group, whereas individuals find it much more difficult, but the time is ripe.

We certainly found that strength came from operating as a group and this was reinforced in one of Ted's ECEs:

T: I'm shown a group and an individual. An individual strives and can make only a weak connection. There are doubts as to its validity and genuineness. The group comprises individuals who are totally different but who share a common desire to understand. Instead of the thin link which the individual makes, the group opens up a great channel in comparison.

Of the five members of our group four had moved easily into the ECE state. Dennis had tried once, with no result, and had then assumed the role of guide. It subsequently appeared better if Dennis specifically did not try to develop inner imagery:

G: We are seeking understanding and this means seeing into things on the one hand and forming concepts for what is seen on the other hand. We do this between us, one sees into a situation and because I don't see into it I am forced to form the concepts.

T: Yes, the image is of a guide in this situation where the need is for understanding. We want to use the technique to find a way forward and we have to do this in great sincerity. If the guide gets imagery at the same time as the experiencer, then the clarity goes out of the situation. The guide's imagery begins to sway the direction in which the experience goes. Whereas, where the guide is forming concepts from the reported descriptions of the imagery, it is a much more disciplined approach. It keeps the experience moving along a path in one direction. It's a positive way forward, rather than the erratic result that would arise if we both had imagery.

G: Does this imply that it would be best if all guides did not experience imagery?

T: No, not necessarily, this particular group is using the technique for somewhat specialised purposes. The important thing is that we must want to go, then co-operation is there, but the effort must come from us and also the interpreting and working out.

The Validity of the Imagery

With such a complex situation, not only is there the question of the validity of what is given and where the imagery comes from, but also the problem of the validity of our perception and understanding of it. Comments on this arose in an ECE when we were asking about the source of the imagery with Ted as the experiencer.

G: Can you get anything that characterises the source of our information?

T: There is an image of a group above. The abilities of this group seem to be matched to ours, so that as we try to advance our understanding, this advances the material that the upper group can get hold of. I see this upper group with a network extending away from it that covers a vast area. Through the group above connections can be made to a wide variety of information dependent upon the efforts made by the group below. The group above is acting as a sort of relay station. They are struggling to understand the experience of our group in the Earth situation and at the same time to equate it to the spiritual situation behind the experience. They send out requests to higher levels, where experience of the Earth situation is even more remote. This then leaves them with the task of conveying the information in a manner that our group can attempt to grasp. This is quite difficult --- A strong image came in then of our group reaching upwards, and a group reaching down, to an area of common ground. I'm shown our group on tiptoe, we are really stretched out --- and also the group above is at full stretch and we make fleeting fingertip contact.

G: Has everybody got potential groups to help them?

T: There's now a very large image that shows thousands and thousands of groups reaching downwards and just occasional groups reaching upwards. But there appears to be unlimited numbers of groups reaching down.

G: So that any reaching up will bring a response?

T: Yes, a genuine desire to reach up will find a response.

G: What is meant by genuine desire?

T: The genuine desire to seek understanding and to further evolution at this level. Any reaching up out of purely personal desire meets with very little response or the wrong sort of response --- Now I have an image of our guides, who say that we are attempting something tremendously difficult. In effect we are operating out of normal consciousness but we try deliberately to subdue this. They show me an image of my Ego standing on one side while the link is made from my vehicles to the Higher Self. The Ego is restricted but this is not its nature - they show me images of our working lives where the personality has to make assessments and judgements. This can make the process quite difficult, particularly where we are striving for understanding in areas we are unfamiliar with; the conscious part then attempts to reason its way through - they show me the imagery being manipulated as it does this. They go on to show me that the imagery itself is very crude - they have problems at their level in converting some things into imagery that we can grasp, that can lead to a great deal being lost in the translation. With increasing development we can possibly reach behind this state and understand more clearly --- They show me an image of a person in trance, the Ego is led right away from the situation and it's subdued but they put an enormous cross through this, it is not our way. Our way is to tackle this out of consciousness, to quieten the Ego and listen to the internal voices and see the images but at all times to strive to do it clearly. The guides say that we have to live and work with the situation until we know quite clearly its advantages and shortcomings -- Words come in that it's a combination of the technique and then afterwards evaluating the results in complete consciousness; this brings out the anomalies on both sides.

G: *What happens when you see etheric forces at work?*

T: *I see the group above looking at the process; they then get across the workings of it in imagery that we can understand. A key thing seems to be that they are looking through a gauzy, misty atmosphere at the process and the words, 'not clearly' come in, I think it signifies that at their level the view is not entirely clear.*

According to *h*K-M, that arose long after these ECEs, there exists a range of levels in the spiritual world which comprises discarnate entities of increasing levels of development and, beyond these, the Omniverse Hierarchy, with its own levels of development. In our seeking for understanding we got a response from a comparatively low level, corresponding to our own soul/spirit development. But, because we had studied Steiner's cosmology and wanted further information on this, the lower group was able to activate responses from a higher level, at which Steiner and other spirits that believe in this cosmology, exist.

We think that Steiner, and similar mystics, were able, by controlling their level of consciousness, to arrive at some sort of perception of the existence and activities of the Omniverse Hierarchy. They then formed thoughts that expressed their interpretation of their perceptions, which were reinforced and elaborated as they continued with their mystical investigations, (with possibly the thoughts taking on a life of their own, as with Phillip in the activities of the Toronto psychical research group). We think it was this thought-world cosmology of these mystics that we were tapping into. As we have pointed out, we think that Steiner's cosmology, based on examining the Akashic record in fact activated these thought forms and is therefore erroneous but that his direct observations of etheric, soul-feeling and spirit-thinking activities could be valid.

The Endpoint of This Phase of the Group's Activities.

By a combination of seeking to understand how formative activities arise in Nature, studying the works of Rudolf Steiner, experimenting with an ECE technique and following this wherever it led us, we found ourselves involved in seeking a total cosmology and its workings in Nature. In all of this we had amassed a large number of experimental results and a morass of complex material from our ECEs. So, to try and bring order into the situation we wrote up our ECEs, with examples of our experimental results and the interpretations that they offered for these and they were published as a book (MILNER Ed). An additional feature of this book is that in our ECEs we were joined by a member of the Arts Faculty in the University, Dr. James Binns. With Jim's different background he contributed a further, humanities-orientated dimension to our work. Nevertheless, the principles underlying Jim's ECEs were the same, i.e. the imagery gave information on his personal development and interests.

Chapter 22

A New Phase of Development

The group had become accustomed to the ECEs being concerned with the workings of the Spiritual Hierarchy and etheric forces. Then, in one of Harry's experiences there occurred a different type of imagery:

A Different Type of ECE

H: I have an image of Steiner and he's sitting on a rocky seashore looking very joyful and relaxed.
G: Is this really Steiner?
H: Yes/no answer. No it's not the Steiner whose writings we read as it were, but yes in that it's a facet of his Higher Self.
G: Steiner made a pioneering effort at the beginning of the 19th century to lay down a path by which people might find their way from the material to the spiritual and, in our own way this is what we've been doing, but we're not following his path exactly.
H: No, the path he followed wasn't a strict and true path. I see it as very nebulous, like a thin lattice framework but it's firm here and there. He pointed the direction.
G: Is the Steiner image meant to convey some sort of encouragement?
H: It's encouragement, but it's more than that. We've completed the link, that sort of thing.
G: Does this mean then that we are contributing something too?
H: I think we've contributed a great deal to Steiner, yes. Very much so. In fact it's as if he's a bit embarrassed at how much he's taking as it were. The link is very strong between him, or them, and us -- He's taking as much from down here as we are taking from up there. But there's something we've got to do. He's working on a clay figure and he points to it and says we've got to climb inside this figure in order to bring it to life. Says we must assume the mantle of Christ.
G: Is this the central issue, the role of Christ, which will bring everything to life?
H: Yes, it's vital.
G: So if we can grasp the Christ force then we can grasp these concepts. How do we do that?
H: It manifests itself where harmony exists. If something is created in a totally balanced and harmonious way it manifests itself. We have to open ourselves up. One has to find the Christ within. This is all connected with getting the circulation going. The Christ force circulates; it flows in and out of our bodies. We have to allow it to flow through us. It's a tremendous feeling of being part of something larger. Obviously we have to rely on our own strength and resources as well. It's not as if the Christ force will do it for us. We bring the Christ force into our resources and act out of our strengths which is basically, the Christ force ---- Now there's an image of Steiner standing beside a monstrous rock. There's a crack in this rock with a little wooden wedge in it. He puts a few drops of water on the wedge and it splits the rock asunder. He looks at me unsmiling but meaningfully.

The group had been getting together for one evening a week, during which one person underwent an ECE that lasted two to three hours which we tape recorded, wrote up and discussed. This had been going on for a year and a half, during which time we had tried to get a clear understanding of the workings of the Spiritual Hierarchy and their etheric force activities, as portrayed by Steiner, which we could correlate with our experimental results and the phenomena of Nature in general. The imagery of this ECE conveyed that, while Steiner's work pointed us in the right direction it could not be assumed to be valid, that we needed to sort things out for ourselves and that we needed to bring the Christ force into our work. None of us had any strong religious convictions; we had been brought up in the prevailing Christian ethos of Western society and we had been exposed to Steiner's idea of the central Christ path that integrated the so-called Ahrimanic and Luciferic activities. But we had no real notion of what 'the Christ force' was. What happened next was that the ECEs jettisoned the Steiner, Spiritual Hierarchy - etheric force viewpoint and portrayed a different type of imagery that started the group on a new phase of development, as portrayed in the following ECE with Brian as the receiver:

B: We've thought about the Godhead as being something untouchable, incomprehensible, unapproachable. But we don't need to. I got the phrase that, 'We are created in his image'. We are tiny, but the principles embodied in us are part of the Godhead. This is why we can approach him, because we are part of him. We contain all that we need to know. It's not that you go up and up and reach the top. He's in evolution himself. He doesn't know what is going to go on, in that he is as much involved in it as we are because we are him. Inside myself there is a picture that we have built up over the years of a Hierarchy and structured layers and planes, with the Godhead outside the whole lot. What I see now is not like that at all. We are the Godhead and this world is the Godhead. All that goes on in this world goes on inside the Godhead. This is not chaotic; there is order, a specific way of things. The image shows a whole series of things within things. All these levels are separate in one sense, but at the same time the whole thing is a unit, a single thing. I used to feel that there was someone in charge of evolution, someone who knew what was going on and what would happen. But when I look at it now there's a major urge and major direction but no idea how it will turn out.

From this point onwards the change in the standpoint from which the ECEs presented the processes of creation made it clear that we had entered a new phase of development. Looking back on the situation we think that our striving to establish explanations for our experiments, and the phenomena of Nature in general, in terms of Steiner's cosmology, had shown that the two would not tie up. But this led to a response from a higher level that had a simpler, broader view of things. Instead of an autocratic Godhead outside the system causing creation to come about according to a preconceived plan, via a Spiritual Hierarchy, it portrayed a self-evolving totality, of which everything is part, that develops by finding its way forward out of its urges. And that, because we are part of the Godhead we work according to the same principles and we are therefore able to understand the workings of the Godhead out of ourselves. The situation that we were in was shown in one of Ted's ECEs:

T: I found myself looking down on an image of three schools, representing primary, junior and senior schools. Then I was shown the five of us going through the primary school and what was taught depended on the way the pupils and the staff responded to it. Then, shortly before we made the change from primary to junior school, some of the staff moved across to the junior school. The image shows that the top part of the junior school is empty, no staff, no pupils. There is not even a syllabus; this comes out of the workings. It hasn't happened this way before and the two sides, the pupils and staff, proceed together, with the staff just managing to get a slight distance ahead, but needing to move back again to catch up with the combined process. Then I'm shown into the senior building, it's completely empty, there are just rooms, no furniture, no equipment, it just sits there and waits for future pupils and staff. The way forward is not clearly seen, this depends upon the contributions by both sides, and only comes about when both sides strive for progress -- An image of a jig-saw puzzle arose that had a fair percentage of the straight-sided pieces in place. With the finding of the pieces that filled the gaps it turned out that they were not all straight sided, they had the effect of increasing the size of the puzzle. Again the straight-sided bits were accumulated and fitted and left some more gaps. The pieces that filled the gaps again projected beyond the boundary we had laid down. And so it went on, time after time. We have still not reached the stage where all the straight-sided pieces are in place and seal off the centre of the puzzle.

What this imagery meant we did not, at the time, know, but with hindsight we think that the primary school represented our work with Steiner's cosmology. As we have explained, we think that Steiner's cosmology derived from earlier Christian mythology, and although he made an attempt to modernise this, our trying to apply it to our experimental results and the findings of contemporary science showed up its inadequacies.

What followed next was a period of considerable confusion. As portrayed by Ted's imagery of the Junior School there was no clear 'syllabus'. We were given imagery that portrayed a diversity of viewpoints and we had no idea of what was going on and no clear goal to aim for. But eventually a clear theme did emerge and once this was established it seemed that the required endpoint had been reached and the group found that their ECEs dried up. This we now think was the end of the Junior School phase and, for reasons that will be explained later, the group began to disband. The essential feature of this phase was that it left behind the idea of a Father-figure Godhead outside creation who was following a preconceived plan and who possessed already-developed qualities (Will, Wisdom and Love). Instead, as in the quote from Brian's experience, it presented the view of a Godhead who was developing by working out His creation.

By this time the situation that we found ourselves in had caused our initial questing for the understanding of our experimental results to become secondary to establishing a meaningful, coherent, self-consistent cosmology out of the confusion of the ECEs. When the Junior School phase came to an end, with the establishment of its cosmology, we sought to apply this to the working-face situation of our experiments, the findings of science and the workings of Nature in general, but, as with Steiner's cosmology, we could not get these to tie up. The Junior School cosmology was too vague and generalised for us to be able to do this. However, out of this striving there emerged a further phase of development, which we now think represented the Senior School stage, which led eventually to *h*K-M.

The Senior School phase occurred after the group had disbanded, with Ted and Dennis continuing the questing and a return of Ted's ECE imagery, which took a long time to establish. It was, as portrayed in Ted's ECE, as though there was no set structure, or path, to be followed in what we were doing. Every step had to be worked out, retraced, and in many cases discarded and a fresh start made, over and over again, before the *h*K-M viewpoint emerged.

Our impression of the Senior School phase was that a channel of communication of mutual exchange of viewpoints was being established between us at the working face and increasingly higher levels of the Omniverse Hierarchy, that are totally remote from the working face, through an extensive number of intermediate levels. We were familiar with the working-face situation but we had no idea how this fitted into a broader total theme, what this theme might be, or even whether such a theme existed. Those at the 'top' had some understanding of this broader theme but were unaware of the working-face situation and how this integrated with, and extended, the broader theme. The many levels in between each had their own developing views on the situation and they had to line themselves up with the theme from above and with our activities below, in order to form a channel of communication. Each time that Ted and Dennis settled down to an ECE Ted had an impression of this channel of communication being assembled, with the entities concerned leaving what they were doing to give their attention to this. (However, as with the earlier phases of the ECEs, this evaluation arises entirely from hindsight many years later, at the time we were just stumbling along trying to understand the experiences and following them wherever they led us).

We deal with the Senior School, *h*K-M phase later. The important feature of it was, however, that as a result of our continual seeking for clarification of different aspects in our terms and this going up and down the channel of communication there emerged a total viewpoint that began to relate to the working-face situation. As this developed, the idea of the existence of a Godhead, of any sort, was discarded and replaced by a living system which differentiates into parts that bring about their own collective evolution.

Although the Junior School phase of development was superseded by that of the Senior School *h*K-M, it provided some useful insights and general principles, so we present key features of it here for completeness of our story. Also we suspect that expanded consciousness experiences, either voluntary or involuntary, will become an increasing phenomenon in life. If this is so, then it is important that people give accounts of them so that we can perceive the difficulties involved and learn to evaluate them, to determine what contribution they might offer. We present our account of our Junior School ECEs in three parts. The first part illustrates some of the varied and confusing types of imagery that were concerned with the 'Godhead in evolution' explanation of things. These seemed to show the 'finding the way forward on both sides' state of affairs portrayed in Ted's ECE. Concurrently with these ECEs, after Harry's experience stating the need to bring the Christ force into our work, we had many ECEs on this theme. We present a selection of these experiences in the second part. Gradually, out of the manifold and varied images of the 'Godhead in evolution' phase there emerged a clear theme that we present in the third part. This combined a Godhead in evolution with the traditional Godhead outside, by starting with an unformed state out of which a centre, or Godhead, arose which was then responsible for further evolutionary developments.

[The ECEs up to the end of the Junior School phase, after editing out obvious extraneous matter (about one third), filled over 1600 pages of typescript. So what is presented in this book comprises only a very small percentage of the total material. What we have selected is designed to provide continuity of our description of the phases of development of our experiences and, at the same time, to reinforce the fact that, in our experience, 'channelled communications' of this nature cannot be uncritically accepted. We found that they varied, depending on the outlook of the person experiencing them and they could not be relied on, as they continually changed their 'story'. Nevertheless, they always seemed to give rise to progress in one way or another].

The Junior School 'Godhead in Evolution' Cosmology

As we have stated, the essential feature of this new viewpoint was of the Godhead being in evolution, or of evolution being the Godhead evolving, instead of the Godhead being outside and directing it, as in Steiner's cosmology and is the general view in Western Society. At first the imagery was very abstract with a number of different, sometimes seemingly contradictory, themes that often changed as the experience progressed. We had great trouble trying to make sense of the situation. Only years later, looking at the ECEs from the point of view of *h*K-M, can we see the significance of what we were presented with and that they represented steps along the way to the development of *h*K-M; even so, much remains unclear. We illustrate what went on with a few examples, starting with brief extracts from some of Harry's experiences:

H: I see a sphere of light rotating slowly. This sphere is the Godhead way back before anything has taken place. I'm awe-struck by it. I have to get used to it and approach it gradually. It's pure consciousness and I don't know what that is. It's so complete and yet it's so isolated too. It has an aura of perfection to it. It's so beautiful I can't find the words to describe it. The beauty is a very feminine quality, beauty of form, colour and sound. There's another, masculine, side to it that has a yearning to grow. There's a frustration there. It wants to experience itself. It's an object of great beauty and yet it can't experience itself. It has all these desires and potentials but it isn't able to experience them. It contains within itself perfect creativity but it can't express it.

Although these ECEs were based on the view that everything consists of an evolving Godhead, which is not remote from us and of which we are part, this imagery continues the notion in which most of us have been brought up, of an awesome, way-above-us, Godhead. This Godhead possesses a range of attributes - consciousness, feelings, form, etc. that it wants to express and experience, but it cannot do so because it exists in isolation, there is nothing for it to relate to. The fact that it existed in isolation and yet had somehow already acquired all these attributes was a problem because it suggested that it must have derived them from some prior situation and, in response to our questioning, the imagery at first responded to this viewpoint.

H: I see above the Godhead a dual character, a big warlike figure containing within it a feminine figure. These give birth to our Godhead and they wave goodbye to it.

This figure was designated the 'Father-Mother' of the Godhead, from which we presumed it had derived its attributes. But what was the nature of the Father-Mother, that it could give birth to the Godhead with its innate qualities? This was resolved many ECEs later, when the Father-Mother figure changed from that of a self-actualising dual 'Being', to something more abstract:

H: It doesn't seem that the Father-Mother had much of a centre. It was full of potential but it had no centre.

This is how the imagery eventually settled - an initial abstract state of undefined potential, out of which a Godhead arose as a centre that, as it evolved, developed its innate potentials. As to how it did this, we continue the story from the first extract:

H: The feminine side, the beauty and form realised that it can only express itself outside of itself and so it decides to go outside. When it's outside the masculine side, the yearning and the frustration, the wish to express its creativity, comes to the realisation that it must reach out and leave nothing behind. Eventually it reaches out so much that there is nothing left of the original Godhead. What has been created is an infinite number of miniature Godheads which when they're whole will come back together again.

These ECEs portray an initial unity that divides into two parts, a masculine, active part that works into, and brings to fruition passive, feminine potentials but in so doing it breaks up and loses its unity. We found this imagery very abstract and the guide sought to pin it down to something more specific:

G: Can we see creation unfolding step by step?
H: The feminine side, outside, is shapeless, insubstantial and filmy. As the masculine side goes out it provides a binding force, a cohesive rigidity. This seems to provide scaffolding for the feminine, it stops it being all soft and filmy and insubstantial and gives it a framework in which to work. The image portraying this feminine quality is like if a man meets a woman and feels an irresistible urge, something invisible passes between them; this sort of feeling exists from the beginning after the feminine quality has poured out. The feminine side is enticing, alluring. It's both active and passive receptivity. It co-operates. It's passive in that it waits, it initiates nothing. It has a great feeling of wanting, a yearning. The masculine side has a feeling of exploring, going out into the unknown and finding out, only for the intrepid. The masculine side goes out into the feminine side and it finds out there's unfulfilled potential. It experiences itself and it also comes to the realisation of why it's wanted - for fulfilment, a balance, a harmony. The masculine side reaches its goal but the feminine side doesn't hold it there. It's a continual cycling of the masculine side through the feminine side. The masculine side goes out further and further, to gather more and more experience, until it's exhausted itself. Then, because it is weak the feminine side enfolds it and draws it into itself. The feminine is all that has been created. It is, as it were, the substance, the material of existence of creation. The masculine is that which acts. And the masculine has to reach a point where its foremost probing out has the mature consciousness of the entire scheme of creation.

This imagery shows the Godhead's masculine activity working through a feminine passive side in a series of cycles, each time realising new potentials in it, to bring about new creation. As it does this, the masculine side develops a consciousness of what it's about. We found this imagery picturesque but abstract and difficult to relate to the evolution of the Universe. Other imagery that Harry experienced was even more abstract:

H: There's an image of our Godhead as a seed within a cube and there's a spike sticking out of the middle of each face of the cube, with the words on the sides, top, bottom, front, back, right and left, fig. 22.1.

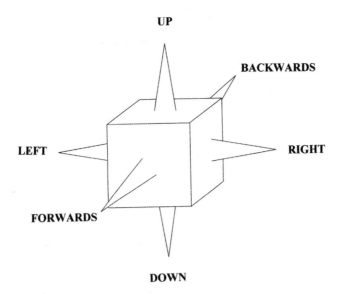

A cube was born from a sphere. A sphere has no identity; it's the same whichever way you look at it. In order to give the sphere identity you give it facets, a top and a bottom. It then has some sort of direction, it has a way of going forwards, it can go up and down and sideways: before it knew only one direction, it was static. As I look at it now from different directions it has different qualities. The faces on the sides, the top and bottom faces are like sinking down into the depths or rising up into the heights. This is why it has to have a centre. The problem is that the image of a sphere is only a representation of a centre and an outside --- I've got a single point. This point can be all. The point turns into a line that runs for ever in one direction and for ever in the other direction. The line turns into a never-ending plane, and planes grow above and below it. That's the progression I see and then it's all made into a grid. A grid is a representation of infinity. If we could imagine these shapes in terms of consciousness (fig. 22.2).

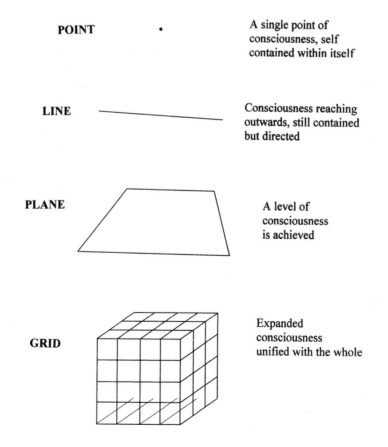

POINT · A single point of consciousness, self contained within itself

LINE Consciousness reaching outwards, still contained but directed

PLANE A level of consciousness is achieved

GRID Expanded consciousness unified with the whole

Fig. 22.2 Harry's expanded consciousness imagery of: a point, denoting a centre of existence: a line symbolising a centre of existence that has a sense of direction: a plane symbolising a level of awareness: a cubic grid symbolising awareness of everything, everywhere.

Our problem is that the evidence suggests that the cubic grid really does exist, rather than existing symbolically. I get the words, 'It does exist'.

While we could, through our feelings, relate to some extent to the previous imagery entailing concepts of a Father-Mother, a birth process and masculine interacting with feminine, we found this sort of abstract 'geometrical-psychology' imagery, of which Harry had much more, very difficult to understand. As far as we can see, the point symbolises the arising of a centre of activity. This then expresses itself by an activity that gives it a sense of direction, represented by a line. Then it spreads out to be active and conscious at this level, in all directions - the plane. From this base it expands in consciousness to become aware of itself in relation to the overall pattern of activities, 'above and below', in which it finds itself - the 'grid consciousness'. The comment on the reality of the existence of the cubic grid refers to the experimental result where we had observed the deposition of a delicate metal cubic grid in a gelatinous substrate, fig. 22.3, and were trying to puzzle out the significance of this.

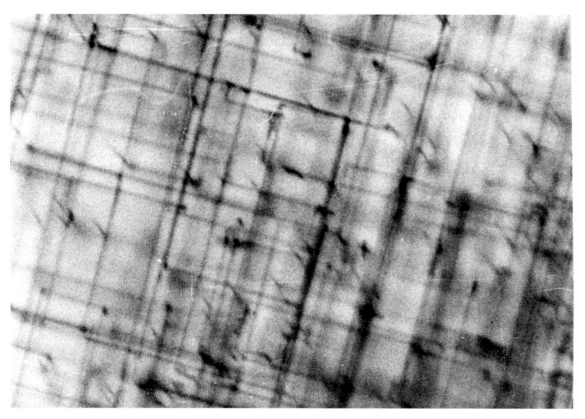

Fig. 22.3 Cubic grid of substance deposited out of a gelatinous solution in one of Harry's experiments that we were trying to understand. (This figure has also been presented as an example of our etheric force interpretation of the forms that we observed in our experiments – fig.19.10).

These examples characterise much of the imagery and our response to it. That is, the first type played on, and awakened a response from, some parts of our inner natures; the second type left us struggling in a world of mental abstractions. But a key feature was that, trying to comprehend what was being conveyed destroyed any basis of a creator God and the workings of a Steiner type Spiritual Hierarchy that had governed our thinking and left us with nothing to work with. Looking back that seems to have been the point of it, to get back to a state of nothing, out of which everything arose. Brian also experienced a lot of abstract imagery, some of which was a bit easier to relate to:

B: I have imagery of planetary systems. This disappears and I now see a galaxy. This is expanding imagery of systems within systems. The whole Universe is breathing in and out. It's a single living thing. There's a similarity between that and your own body. Now the imagery contracts down through all the various circulations and workings of the body, down to quite small operations of individual organs. Then it swaps to a sort of solar system somewhere in the human body. So, God's view of the Universe is the same as our view of our bodies. Another feeling associated with this is of time and space. When I look at it this way the Universe isn't as big as it appears from reading books about it. It depends on where you place your level of perception as to how big things are, so that when I am looking at stars and galaxies, when I stand back from them they cease to be separate disconnected objects and become part of a living whole that is pulsing.

This imagery conveys the general idea that the way to look at the Universe is as the body of God, comprising parts within interacting parts, with a circulation of activity going through them, comparable to that of the human body. And also, that if we look at it in this way then we can lose the feeling of almost over-powering vastness that we get when we try to understand the space-time, Big-Bang, galaxy, star formation, etc. complex descriptions of science and we can then conceive of it as a single evolving, living thing. The imagery also introduces the idea of the Universe 'breathing' in and out. In another ECE Brian continued with the theme of parts within parts:

B: I have imagery of systems within systems. This imagery shows evolution to be made up of things that are all the same. I have an image of a 'doughnut', which is very clearly a symbol. In the vertical plane there is a considerably bigger doughnut, with another yet larger doughnut expanding away to hazy edges, fig. 22.4a.

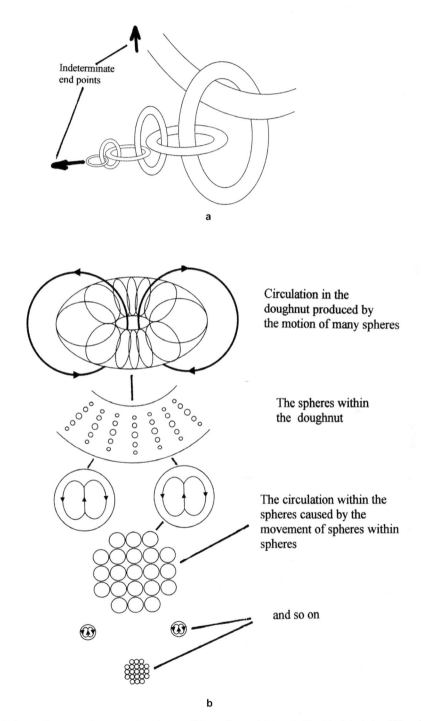

22.4 Brian's expanded consciousness imagery of systems within systems, (**a**), symbolised by intertwined 'doughnuts', and (**b**) the activities within activities taking place in each doughnut.

It doesn't ever reach a point where there is a beginning or end -- I feel that beginnings and ends are human conceptions. It's not like that at all, searching for ultimate endpoints is not necessary. The doughnut image is circulating rapidly when I look at it from the outside. But when I move into it the rapid movement disappears and there are lots of separate spheres. You then get inside these spheres and they are made up of little vortices. The imagery then shoots off, getting increasingly small, fig. 22.4b. The Words, 'Working models' keep coming in. It is clear that we can't work with this stuff up here yet. What we need to do is develop working models.

G: Can we think of the system being designed to bring about evolution, with part already evolved and part unevolved?

B: Yes, things that can be raised, their potentials realised. Potential is a very important word. When I look at one doughnut there are bits that are still unformed in it. Then it, in turn, is part of the bigger doughnut that is in advance of it. At the same time they are part of the smaller doughnut. The image showed the Father-Mother of the present doughnut. It started off at the south pole of this large doughnut in the vertical plane, as an idea, as a very nebulous, misty doughnut. As it moved to where it is now, it has hardened up and become increasingly definite. Each stage that it went through it has memories of, but they are living objects.

This imagery reinforces the idea that everything consists of circulations of activities within activities that evolve by working out innate potentials and it also conveys the idea of these being without beginning or end.

[According to *h*K-M, which came much later, 'creation' started with the space energy differentiating into superstructure entities. Then within these there differentiated out successively galaxy entities, star entities and planetary entities, as with the Earth and other planets forming within the Solar System. Within the Earth planetary entity there has differentiated out a sequence of living activities – prokaryotic cells (bacteria), eukaryotic protoctists, animals, plants and hominids. Each level has differentiated out of, and is part of and subjected to, the activities of the level above. But as each level becomes self actualising it creates activities in, and reacts back on, the level above].

Brian experienced a number of other abstract images in which the theme was of a self-evolving system at work. We give brief extracts of two more examples.

B: I have an image of a piece of dough kneading itself. The lump of dough split into two pieces which then started working on themselves. Then those split into two to work on themselves, to form a cascade -- You get a little separate nucleus and a cascade comes down from it. Then you get another nucleus given out and that cascades down. In the end there is this huge cascade. Down at the bottom there were very tiny bits of dough kneading themselves, fig. 22.5.

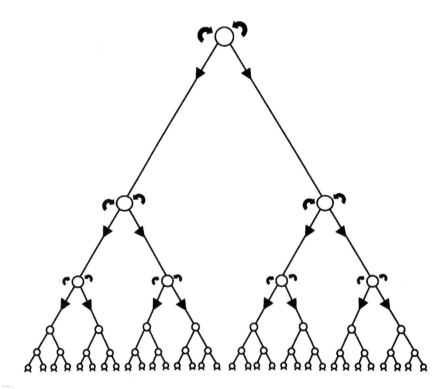

Fig. 22.5 Brian's expanded consciousness imagery of a self-evolving system that starts with an active principle that works into an inactive part, resulting in differentiation, each part of which comprises the active principle working into the inactive state to give rise to more differentiation and more parts, and so on.

At some point the cascade folds round on itself and everything goes back to the top of the cascade again --- I have an image now of a ball which is circulating.

This imagery reinforced the idea of creation starting from an unformed state, the dough, and differentiating into two sides, an active, which works into a passive. It also showed creation arising as a continual differentiation from an original splitting into two, with everything comprising the two sides, an active and a passive, and a reworking of everything. Another of Brian's experiences pursued the theme of an active part working through an inactive part, this time portraying the inactive as a 'spectrum' of past developments containing further potentials, and a recycling of it all.

B: I see a band surrounded by emptiness on all sides. It is a living band, it's like a primitive creature, a Uroborus which is eating its tail -- This has become a spectrum that forms a loop which is a series of spectra that go round and make a circuit (fig. 22.6).

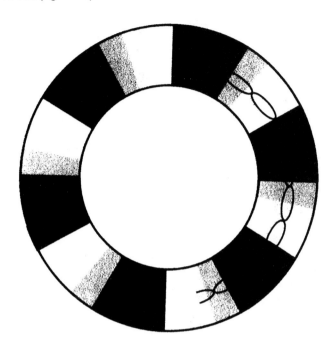

Fig. 22.6 Brian's expanded consciousness imagery of a ring of 'spectra of creation' through which an active principle works to bring about the development of further potentials in each spectrum.

Travelling in the circuit is a flow going round and round. All the spectra are different, so that this circulation experiences different things as it passes through the various spectra. It's not that this circulation has any form of intelligence or in fact, inquisitiveness or anything like that. It is just that it is dynamic and goes round the ring. There is no centre to this thing, but what you would call consciousness comes from the passage of this flow across the spectrum. The dynamic part lights up the different bits of the spectra as it goes round. Consciousness arises at the interface between the spectrum that gets lit and the flow that goes past it. As the active part flows on it lights up a different spectrum and the first lot die down. It's not that they lose consciousness because they don't actually have consciousness. Consciousness is a continuous thing. It goes round with the circuit. It's entirely within --- Now there is a tension and an explosion from the centre of the ring. The active flow has been dissipated and the spectrum has been shattered, fragmented. The activity likes to flow in channels, or it likes to flow. It then wafts around like a breeze in the morning. It passes over all the various fragments that have been dispersed and consciousness begins to arise at all these separate interfaces. Now I see it pull together again and I have an image of a little tiny hard grey solid sphere. This then blows up with tremendous force and violence. Then it is sucked back down and you've got this little ball again.

Looking back, the important point about the imagery quoted in the above examples is that it gets across the idea of a self-evolving system in which different activities arise by a process of repeated differentiation, out of an initial differentiation into two parts of a pre-existing whole. Brian's spectrum with its continuous flow through it, that blows up, breaks up and then comes together again we found very difficult to relate to. At the beginning of this book, In Chapter 1, we put forward the idea of the Kosmos initially existing in a uniform state of dormant energy in which there developed a tension to be more than that, which gave rise to it becoming active. Its activity gave it a sense of self but created a stress in its erstwhile harmonious dormant state, so that its activity subsided. But then it lost its sense of self so that it became active again. In this way it entered into a cyclic existence of increasing and decreasing in activity. Many years later Walsch's books on Conversations with God came out in which God states that s/he existed for a long time before the existence of the Universe, in a state described as speculating. In this state God knew 'conceptually ' that s/he was a Creator but because there was nothing for him/her to interact with to express and experience his/her speculations this generated a frustration that led to an 'explosion from within'. Brian's image of the flow through the spectrum (of unexpressed potentials?) that blows up we see as portraying this situation. God's description to Walsch also offers an explanation for the tension that gave rise to the activity in the first place. It is as though we have worked through a phase of development in which we have expressed all of our ideas and try as we may we cannot perceive of anything further to do, so that we become frustrated and say 'to hell with it' and thrust it away. A feature of this is that what is cast out contains within it our resentments and frustrations at not being able to further express our creativity and thereby further experience our sense of self and it may be that, at a Kosmic level this is how the element of discord became built into creation that has to be worked out. The difference in the time scale between the long period of the Kosmic cycle from our point of view and the dramatic explosion and return to unity portrayed in Brian's imagery shows the difference between our view and God's view of the situation. The Hindu religion, for example, sees the cycle as a day and night of Brahma each of which takes about 4.3 billion years. God sees it as taking place in the twinkle of an eye (see Chapter 24). Andy had imagery of a quite different sort

A: I'm looking upwards through something that blurs the vision. There are two big characters looking down. Perhaps this is our young Godhead looking back at its parents and seeing them dimly. It's very small, its parents recede. The Godhead goes out into the dark, a tadpole, a small thing swimming away out into the dark and alone. In the dark there is nothing, no object, no here or there, no light of any kind --- All of a sudden a tremendous flash of light filled everything --- it now seems to have sunk back into darkness again, there was nothing for the light to work on -- Oh! Maybe the darkness is just glimmering a tiny bit --- There's another flash of light and the darkness is glimmering back a bit more --- The light has defined a spherical shape filled with an unformed jelly -- but there's something hard and firm at the centre --- I see the jelly begin to swirl and move about - the nucleus is working hard to get this jelly moving, it's very sluggish. Its feeling of alone-ness is left behind because it now has a job of work to do. I saw then that the nucleus had got the jelly flowing in a self-enclosed spiral --- Then, with the spiral flow stabilised, the nucleus broke up and it's like fine black dust, little particles marking out the lines of flow in the jelly --- I see a vortex of flow drawing inwards. It pulls stuff in, down and through the centre of the sphere and then passes it out at the bottom. There is intense experience in the centre, followed by a period of recuperation and reflection coming up the outside, then another period of experience down the centre axis. I'm drawn down there myself and I'm in the flow. There are many strands – a rich texture to it. All these individual strands come together to tumble and be jostled and bash up against one another down the axis. I look at these strands and images of animals, birds and plants come up, and bullfrogs and flowers - buttercups – and human beings. It's a never ending thing. Nothing is static. They pass down through the middle and are all tumbled together and it can be very rough in there and you don't know what's going to happen but you come out at the bottom and come up round the outside and all the strands separate. Each strand is able to sort itself out and see what it is, where it has come from and where it is going to. Everything is sorted out and made straight and plain before it gets to the top and goes back down again.

This imagery portrays the Godhead as separating off from something bigger, as an unformed jelly-like state that exists alone in darkness. Bursts of spontaneous activity take place in it to give rise to an active centre in the jelly. The centre experiences itself through the bursts of its activity, which leads to it becoming continuously active. Its activity, i.e. doing something, gives it a sense of purpose and it thereby loses its sense of aloneness, in the same way that we can lose our experience of loneliness by actively doing something. By its self-contained activity the nucleus creates a spiral/B-cell motion in the jelly, the stress of which causes it to break up into multitudinous parts, or strands of activity that develop by alternate periods of mutual activity and periods of internal reflection on their experiences. To continue:

A: Now I see the Godhead as a football with a bullet inside it. The bullet at the centre is beginning to move around the sphere in which it finds itself --- It is now bouncing off the walls and these have exuded a jelly-like substance for the centre to weave patterns in. What the Godhead is, is what it does with these things.
G: It's a two-part being; with a male and female....?
A: I'm seeing things from the point of view of the centre - the male part. I tried to reach out to the female part, but I can't get anything back from that yet. It's waiting, perhaps the male part must start the ball rolling --- The centre has now woken the wall up. The wall, the female part, is responding by sending out a jelly and it holds the centre against the wall. Images of the course of human fertilisation come in, where the fertilised egg rolls around the womb and comes up against the wall of the womb and sticks to it. The male and female meet and each fuses with the other and is completed by it. Its consciousness now moves about on the surface, 'What shall I create in the jelly?' it seems to say. I get the feeling of unlimited possibilities. It's a ball of sleeping jelly surrounded by a hard, living conscious skin. The skin then went 'crack' and sent a shock wave surging in. I see a succession of these. It was doing this more and more urgently and finally the jelly at the centre sent back a weak shock wave of its own; and now the skin stops hammering away and listens and the centre of the jelly sends another weak wave back. I have the impression of a mother-child relationship. The mother has sent an impulse down to the child and the child has at last responded. It's a feminine protective role now, to nurture this little conscious bit of jelly. I get a vision of this newly formed centre creeping its way through the jelly towards the wall, and the amazement and illumination that comes

when it fuses with the wall. And the Godhead experiences too this sense of amazement. It has become a creator out of itself. Now, through the experience of its own creation, its progeny fusing with it, it knows about the business of creation. It knows that the act of creation needs gentleness and care, just as much as urgent hammerings. It's aware that what it creates has a life of its own, has feelings and can suffer - that came in fairly hard - suffering. Suffering is dependent on individuality; they go hand in hand. By the same token the Godhead suffers through the suffering of its creation --- Now I see many dots form more or less uniformly in the jelly. This one first creation goes back into the jelly and forms the centres. It says, 'I am jelly, like you are,' and it coaxes and leads the way. To create something out of the jelly the Godhead would have to slam down impulses but this is a much gentler process, the jelly is led, coerced, encouraged to form centres. The One That Went Before comes down and attends to every growing particle in the jelly personally --- What has come in is the Christ Impulse, this is what we know it as. I hear a voice that is everywhere throughout the jelly, and it says, 'Hear me, Listen' and the words and associated image of the Sermon on the Mount come in. And a vast number of little points in the jelly respond and they say, 'Yes! I heard that.' These come to light, awaken. I am with one of these now, a tiny point, aware of its own existence in jelly and not really aware of anything else. It's heard a voice. It has a life of its own, that's all. A tenuous thing. The little point explores outwards and as far as it explores it makes that jelly its own. Adjacent points of light explore outwards until they have consumed all the jelly between them -- The jelly blobs only known their own local environment: they are cut off. They don't know the Godhead's there. I don't think they even know they are created --- the jelly-blobs go all the way out to the Godhead's skin and I get the feeling of gradations as you descend further towards the centre. Something else came in then, the fact that The One That Went Before, the Christ-Being was created at the centre, the Christ Being is the Archetypal Man, the most cut off.

Andy's imagery portrays the Godhead as starting in an unformed state that separates into two parts a (masculine) striving to be active and a (feminine) body of potentials. As the masculine activity works on, and brings to realisation, the feminine potentials, it inadvertently and, at first, unknowingly, becomes a Creator. The 'progeny' so created are not at first aware of the Godhead, only of the fact that they exist. But one part (Christ) finds its way back to unite with the Godhead and this makes the Godhead aware of itself as a Creator. This induces in it an awareness of the separation and suffering of its creation and a love for it. The Christ part then seeks to lead the other parts back to the unified state with the Creator.

The portrayal of a jelly, or other unformed state, out of which a centre arises that works on the unformed material to bring about creation was the theme of many of our ECEs and it led to a defining of a sequence of seven stages of creation.

The Seven Stages of Creation

In our Introduction to this book we stated that the basic feature of the Universe is that it is evolving, so that any fundamental understanding has to be in terms of states of evolution and how these arise one from another and, in its picturesque way, this was the theme of the seven stages of creation. Ted's, Brian's and Harry's ECEs on the seven stages mostly dealt with the abstract underlying principles at work. Although this element was present in Andy's ECEs, in his case there was an orientation towards how these principles work in us, which made them easier to understand, so we present the theme that we were given by extracts from Andy's ECEs.

A: I seem to be at the centre of a planet or star that's made of stuff of the consistency of Christmas pudding and I'm all bound up in it. It feels as though I have just been born as an egg. I look up and things seem very large, like clouds --- The experience is transferred to the birth of a human baby that looks up and sees lights and vague colours that drift overhead like clouds in the sky ... I'm not sure which I am now - the small star in space or the little baby on Earth - they both seem the same in a way -- I was getting claustrophobic and I've kicked out and found resistance. At first it feels hard and unyielding but slowly I discover that I can make it yield. It's hard work because it's some black formless stuff, like tar. I know nothing about being at the centre of a very large thing, I only know about kicking out --- Slowly I'm able to reach out more and more and eventually I get out and I see myself extending all over the surface to enclose this black stuff. There is emptiness all around; I feel alone -- I feel some animosity towards this black stuff because it enclosed and imprisoned me and I try to reach into it and get a grip on it but it escapes and it's expanded out to form a shell and I'm inside a hollow sphere --- I'm much more conscious now. I see this figure now as a grown man with a swirling cloak on his shoulders and he has a beard.

G: Is the baby what we've called the masculine part and the treacle the feminine part?
A: I think what you say is right: the baby is masculine and the treacle is feminine --- The man figure has now fused with the shell and he and the black stuff felt that together they wanted to create something in the empty centre and they've filled it up with stuff, like a very light foam --- I saw a man and a woman making love together and the product of their union was this foam. On Earth men and women reach the stage where

they are mature enough to come together and procreate and so the higher universe gives them a child. And this is how it is, the male and female principles conjoin and they are given this foam to work with ---- The composite shell now pulses inwards and divides the foam up by laying down concentric shells and radial lines to form a grid structure that makes the foam more manageable --- Now it sends part of itself down into the centre so that what had seemed a continuous self-aware substance has split itself into two and the grid collapsed inwards to the centre. It's cut itself off from itself. If I look carefully I can see traces of where the grid used to be. It's as though a way back is marked.

G: So the grid collapses and leaves a sort of dim memory ...?
A: Yes, that's it and the feeling is that the longer they are separated so the memory of how it was once recedes - a suggestion of folk-myths and legends, as the stuff at the centre sinks down into itself. It can't or won't reach back to the shell. It wants to, it needs to, it must do, but first of all it has to sink down into itself and know deep utter loneliness and, almost in desperation, reach out and back, driven by the pressure of this loneliness. So I now see it reaching up desperately and slowly it works its way back again, building up the grid from the centre outwards until the grid structure and the rim are one again but now it's alive and vibrant. The male-female principle now becomes fully realised, it knows itself from the outside and from the inside --- And now it turns its attention to the many, many pockets of foam in the grid. There is tremendous scope and variety for all these little systems to work their own ways forward. Each one can get on with its job and see what it can make of it, independently of the rest --- I now descend down and down into one cell in this gigantic honeycomb; I see an outer rim around the foamy stuff and the outer rim is all alive and alert and keen to get to work on it and the rim sent some of itself down to the centre, recreating a tiny grid as it did so. This collapsed to the centre and the centre started to work out and the rim waited and watched, it was very concerned but it did nothing, it's up to the centre to get back. So this cycle is a repeat of what has gone before. And this miniature version itself has very many tiny pockets of foam in it and the cycle must be repeated again, on that minute scale. It doesn't look like ever ending. When I asked if it ever ended the rim shook as if to say, 'Yes, it does come to an end, when the very last piece of foam is brought back and the grid all filled in'. The quality of the filling-in grid is that it is a continuous consciousness. Every part is at one with the rest, it is a unity, it is all one, completely uniform and aware of itself. The grid has now looked inside itself and has acquainted itself completely with all the experiences it has had and there is nothing more to do --- It turns outwards and light comes from outside and things are revealed to it. It finds it's one entity in a Universe full of things. This Universe is pursuing its own course, going its own way, regardless of this little new entity that finds itself in the middle of all this celestial machinery. It sees itself as a very small thing now --- It's becoming aware of the inter-connections, of the workings of this Universe --- now it is taking part in the workings of this vast universal machine --- They wound those last three stages off quickly .... That image has receded into the distance, it's as though that was a demonstration film for us and it has ended now and it's up to us to ask questions.

G: It seems that, underlying all this, there's a basic cycle in which the centre and the rim are pulsing backwards and forwards through the foam?
*A: I'm looking at the cycle, which is crystallising clearly into a breathing, one activity leading to the other. Working from the outside to the centre; this is when you're working on substance, the foam, and through this you discover yourself, you gain self-knowledge. The centre working back, it's not working on the substance, **it's going back home**. And the outside is desperately urging the centre onwards back to itself. But it can't help in any material way. In getting back to the outside the centre has recreated the grid, but in a knowing way. It has fought and struggled to create every junction point, every line and every wall has been fought for.*

This imagery shows that, after the masculine, active self-actualising centre separates out; it works on the potentials of the passive, feminine, energy around it and, in so doing, gets them moving. This, in turn, gives the passive energy an experience of itself from which it learns to cooperate with the centre and they both thereafter increasingly work together. From their combined working they create a structure of different levels (the grid), which from the point of view of hK- M, we would equate with the creation of the Omniverse Hierarchy. The combined principle then sends part of itself out into its creation to work out independently its own path of development - the prodigal son story. This, on the hK-M basis we would equate with the members of the Hierarchy who incarnate in, and are cut off by, the hominid bodies on Earth, that have to find their own ways back and, in so doing, develop a consciousness of the situation in which they exist, thereby contributing to the understanding of how creation works. But the 'prodigal son' does not have an easy task, working in a substance body, in the material world, is a deadening experience compared with the lightness and freedom of life in the Omniverse Hierarchy, it's like being embedded in tar. But at the time, we had none of the understanding of hK-M so we were wallowing around, trying to make sense of it all. The baby imagery, with its orientation towards human development helped us to get some sort of feel for what was being conveyed, so in a further ECE the Guide asked Andy if he could get a more living experience of the nature and development of the Godhead and the imagery responded:

A: I'm seeing and experiencing an infant human state. I see vague colours, hear distant sounds. I have two images juxtaposed now. The one on the left is the baby in the treacle, a cold dark image. On the right is a rectangle of bright living colour, greens and yellows and reds and blues all mixed up. Now the baby on the left is kicking about in the treacle and the baby on the right is being turned over to go to sleep, it's kicking about in the blankets --- Now the baby on the right is holding a finger. It's able to connect this finger to a face. The face is blurred. I can feel general good-will even though the expression means nothing. I kick against the sides of the cot -- I play with things strung across the cot, things that rattle. It's always a new surprise when they rattle, even though I've done it before --- I now see myself lying flat on the floor -- I can't get up. Somehow I'm aware of my own weight, my nose is pressed into the carpet. I can't even lift up my head. I am completely flat and helpless.

G: And the baby on the left?

A: It's reaching out, discovering how tenacious the treacle is --- The picture on the right moved quite fast. I see myself get my head up, and then get onto all fours, and then begin to walk. I raise myself up from the Earth.

G: And the baby on the left?

A: It's beginning to get outside the treacle --- The baby on the right can begin to move, I can get around things and climb up.

G: Instead of being immersed in its environment and at the mercy of it, it's got outside it?

A: I think this is it; the situation isn't sitting on it. Before I was completely helpless, now I can get up and get at things -- The baby on the left is trying to get out of the treacle -- Now I'm climbing up the stairs. I go quite purposefully into one of the bedrooms to climb up onto a chair and I'm looking down onto the ground. I know the house and I know how to get about in it --- I look at the figure on the left and he's out of the treacle to his waist -- I go downstairs and find my Mother in the kitchen. My Father comes in through the back door. I know who they are and where they fit in. I go into the garden and I look and see where the house is in relation to the others --- The figure on the left is out of the treacle -- I know this house throughout and I know it is different and distinct from other houses. I know the extent of my domain -- I now see the baby looking at the books on the shelves - It's picking out small and annoying things, boxes of pins. Through the baby's eyes I look round the house and feel as though I have some idea of the significance of every single thing in the house. I may not understand it, but I know where each has its place, what each thing does. I know the rhythm and routine of the house --- Then things moved forward and I see myself going to school. Up to that point my life has been centred in the home -- There's a line going from the house to the school that ends in a small circle. The circle means that I have an existence at school that is mine alone, I now have a life outside the home.

G: And how's the child on the left doing?

A: He's got all the way round the treacle and he's trying to reach in to get hold of something. These are only the first attempts at reaching in, probing, exploring in -- I do the same thing at school, I explore the school and progress through it. I learn the names of the teachers and the pupils; I learn the layout of the school, the timetable, and the school rhythm.

G: And the child on the left?

A: He's getting closer to a centre -- I see myself now in the class, the balance has shifted. I am aware that I'm one of many who are like me: before I had only one place where I lived and now there's another place opened up for me. There is a class of children here and I sink down into them and feel that I am part of a group.

G: And the one on the left?

A: He's got his hand round the centre. He's reached into the middle -- In the image on the right I feel myself flowing, weaving within the group, changing friendships, changing loyalties; all this flows and lives through us. The teacher is there, an outside figure and I've become more aware of him, though it's only dim yet, the teacher's existence is reflected in our response to him -- I see myself continuing to grow up and I see a line between my eyes and the teacher's eyes and somehow that interaction is part of my coming to self consciousness. I am aware of myself as a distinct thing separate from my fellows and the relationship with the teacher plays an important part in this. It's nothing to do with home; home has receded for the moment.

G: With the teacher you experience what it is to be an individual in relation to another individual, it's not like interweaving with the children?

A: Yes, that's right, with the teacher there's a fixed thing, like a lighthouse, a light staring me in the eye -- And I go back home and discover my parents as individuals.

G: And the baby on the left?

A: I had seen him probing in and he has now grasped the centre --- I saw myself going up to the teacher after lessons and asking him questions extending wider and wider, beyond the scope of the lesson he had given. At home I saw myself as beginning to ask questions extending out of the home. I see a library, a museum, I see generally an outside world and I begin to see things in perspective, the pub on the corner, the shops, the church, the park and the school in relation to these -- The various interweaving activities of society come into focus. What was a world that contained me in the school now I see as one small part of a larger society -- This extends to cover a larger and larger scale, I see now our national society and that our *own country is just a small part of a world society. I had thought that my school was the whole world and now it dawns on me that there's a vast world outside -- I now go further into space and I discover the Earth as part of the Solar system, as part of the galaxy, as part of the Universe --- It makes me terribly aware of myself. I'm conscious of emptiness out there and somehow the emptiness throws my own existence into sharp contrast. It makes me feel all the more alive to contrast my small living self against the vast emptiness out there. It seems to be a clear moment in life when that realisation gets to you, and it's a very isolated lonely experience in a way, because it separates you from your fellow human beings and you realise your alone-ness and your individuality. But you've still got to get on with your life and I saw myself racing about the countryside, canoeing, running, doing all sorts of lively sports with friends. But every now and then I would stop and I would be separated from them by the memory of the experience, looking at the heavens, being cut off, and then I'd forget it and I'd go back to whatever I was doing. This is a thing that sets me apart and I think that no one else has had this experience. But then I start to read and talk to other people and - this is important - I discover that in different ways they have had similar thoughts and experiences, some of them haven't but some of them have. You discover that while you felt and thought one particular thing, someone else experienced a different facet. Out of that arises a feeling for fellow human beings, a real feeling; what were so far superficial relationships become deeper. You reach out into society and have these deep relationships with others that are like yourself. Also you now start the exploration inwards. I see myself beginning to ask, 'Who am I? What is the nature of Man?' In the process of reaching in, for the first time I become aware of the give and take of relationships and of the inner lives of myself and other people. I discover emotions and learn to distinguish between them, instead of them just flowing through me rather unconsciously. I learn to analyse inner processes and to control them ...... Now it seems to have slowed down and stopped.*

This ECE helped a great deal with the understanding of the other, more abstract ECEs received by Andy and Ted, Brian and Harry. From them we define the following seven stages of creation. We give first the abstract underlying principle and then the corresponding stage of human development.

Summary of the Underlying Principles of the Seven Stages of Evolution and How They Apply to Us

Stage 1

A self-actualising (masculine) centre of activity is 'born', i.e. emerges out of a background, feminine energy that contains all the experiences of past developments and potentials for future realisation.

An entity is born as a baby as it incarnates from the Omniverse Hierarchy into the pre-existing situation, comprising past evolutionary developments, on Earth.

Stage 2

In its activity the centre interacts with and is moulded by and moulded to the environment in which it finds itself. In this way the 'feminine' side, the past developments shape and combine with the masculine activity of the centre.

As the baby grows up into and through childhood it interacts with the environment in which it finds itself and as a result the pattern of activities around it mould it to their form, at home and at school.

Stage 3

As a result of becoming able to play a role as an individual entity in the situation in which it finds itself, the centre experiences itself as an Ego.

The young person grows up to play an adult role, according to the way it was moulded by society and thereby gets an Ego-centred self awareness of his/her abilities.

Stage 4

The centre develops an awareness of, and an ability to integrate its own activities with, the different activities taking place around it in its environment. The 'outside' is aware of the centre and the centre is aware of the 'outside'.

In developing and expressing him/herself, according to his/her innate potential, the young adult takes over the achievements of past developments and adds to them his/her own contribution to his/her field of endeavour, thereby becoming a self-actualising creative individual. The individual becomes aware of his/her role in society and society becomes aware of the contribution of the individual.

Stage 5

The centre realises that there exists something larger than the environment in which it is operating and it explores outwards to seek to understand what this larger situation is and thereby gets a sense of being an entity within a much larger situation.

With increasing maturity and awareness of the nature of the Universe the person ponders his/her role in it and the nature of themselves and what life and existence is all about and s/he explores out to find out what they can about this. This strengthens, and makes them more aware of, his/her own inner nature and potentials.

Stage 6

The centre seeks to relate to the activities of the larger environment.

The adult then, instead of living life according to the pressures and standards imposed on him/her by the social environment, begins to live according to the larger principles of understanding that s/he has personally developed.

Stage 7

The centre returns home. That is, it becomes a harmonious integrated contributing member of the larger environment from which it was born.

The person dies and returns to the spiritual world, of the Omniverse Hierarchy, taking with him/her whatever qualities, understanding and achievements s/he has developed during his/her lifetime.

The Seven Stages of Development of Humanity

These seven stages of development also apply to the evolution of humanity en masse.

Stage 1

Entities from the Omniverse Hierarchy incarnate into the hominid situation that has evolved on Earth, to give birth to Humanity. Thereby a 'masculine' activity enters into a pre-existing 'feminine' situation of past developments - The stories of the Gods coming to Earth.

Stage 2

In order to be active on Earth the incarnating entities learn to use the hominid bodies to work with the environment so as to maintain an Earth existence, taking over and further developing the patterns of behaviour originated by the animal kingdom and further developed by early hominids, giving rise to early homo sapiens.

Stage 3

By working in already-established ways homo sapiens experience their ability to work with the materials of their environment and thereby they develop their creative potentials, to give rise to a period of much more rapid development on Earth, i.e. the Neolithic Era.

Stage 4

Once they have developed the ability to satisfy their basic, material needs homo sapiens obtain fulfilment by developing their creativity further, giving rise first, to the ancient civilisations and now to modern civilisation. At the same time, their mental development leads them to begin to wonder what their existence is all about. They begin to look outwards to explore the larger aspects of the situation in which they find themselves and inwards to understand their inner natures. This is the situation we are in now; modern homo sapiens is using the materials of the environment in more and more creative ways and looking out to the broader aspects of its existence in the Universe, in astronomy and space travel and looking into itself by methods of inner exploration to seek to discover its nature.

Stages 5, 6, and 7

These are stages of the return path by which Humanity reunites with the sources from which it arose. This will mean a conscious linking with the Omniverse Hierarchy, of which so-called 'channelled communications' are, perhaps, a small beginning.

Chapter 23

ECEs Portraying the Christ Path

When the image of Steiner manifested in one of Harry's ECEs it said that it was necessary for us to bring the Christ force into our activities. As we have stated, none of us had any religious affiliations and no idea of what the Christ force is. (At this stage we had none of the concepts of hK-M, or awareness of the 'channelled communications' presented in Chapter 14). In Andy's experience quoted earlier, Christ is portrayed as the leader of mankind's development and images of a Christ figure played an increasingly important role as the ECEs progressed further. So, at this point we stop off our account of the developments in cosmology to give an account of how the Christ theme manifested in the ECEs, and then we return to the cosmology.

The verbatim accounts of the ECEs relating to Christ were rather long and in what follows we present just the essential features of these, starting with brief extracts from some of Harry's experiences:

H: If one mentions the Christ force and the Christ path one imagines all sorts of spiritual, mystical, holy sort of feelings but it's not like that. It's a very practical down-to-earth sort of thing.

The Christ path is a very patient path; it just waits for people to join it. I get the picture that the Christ force doesn't assert itself. It's there but it fades into the background.

I see the Christ impulse as a Universal harmonious consciousness.

As we have stated earlier, there is nothing mysterious or mystical about hK-M, it is a practical, down-to-earth account of the way that the processes of creation work and this applies equally well to the Christ force and the Christ path. So what then is meant by these terms? In his Steiner imagery Harry had stated that the Christ force manifests where harmony exists and that we have to open ourselves up to it. Here we turn to one of Andy's ECEs to amplify this:

A: Christ is standing with his arms outstretched, one reaching into Ahriman's kingdom, the other reaching into Lucifer's kingdom and drawing from both, in the form of a cross. This is the nature of the Christ path. Christ bridges the two kingdoms by treading the middle balanced way and thus the kingdoms of Lucifer and Ahriman are reconciled. We have to take Christ down into Ahriman's kingdom - the earth - so as to bring things out in the right way, to let them flower rather than using them for materialistic ends. You get great truths in Lucifer's kingdom, but they bear little or no relation to how things are on earth. If you go into the Luciferic world just as it is you give up, you just wallow and bathe in delicious timeless warmth. You need inner strength - Christ - to go into the Luciferic world, to hold onto your aims and goals, just as you need Christ's strength to reach down into Ahriman's kingdom and bring up the treasure there. Christ is at the interface and you need the Christ qualities to go either way. The thread of life is stitched, is woven back and forth, across the interface. The impression is that the greatest crime is being static, of being in neither kingdom, or wholly in one or the other,

The Luciferic kingdom is the world of the Omniverse Hierarchy. This is a world of great Universal truths, but these are not integrated with the conditions at the substance working face (the materialistic world of Ahriman). Contact with the Omniverse Hierarchy gives a wonderful feeling of a Nirvanic (being on a high) state. But wallowing in this state takes us away from dealing with our working-face problems. Equally, giving ourselves solely to the sense of self that we get from our working-face activities gives rise to materialistic ego/Egoistic ends. If, however, we bring the great, spiritual Universal truths into our materialistic activities, we raise these up; this at the same time grounds otherwise nebulous spiritual ideas in Earthly activities. This is what Christ, as a representative of the Omniverse Hierarchy, did by living and working in a human body on Earth, to show Man the way forward. Harry, in his Steiner ECE had said that we have to open ourselves up and find the Christ within, that it's a feeling of being part of something larger. This was amplified in one of Ted's ECEs:

T: The words, 'Universal' and 'Consciousness' come in and I see a Christ figure who is aware of himself and of everything else in that evolutionary period. I am shown an image of a sparrow falling from a branch and Christ is aware of that, for it happens within his consciousness that extends throughout all the kingdoms of Nature. Consciousness has a living quality to it, it's not a concept, not struggling to understand, but becoming more aware through the ways in which we live. Then we move closer to the Universal

Consciousness. We are always part of it, but as we become more aware of it we come closer to living it. I experience all this as feelings and I find it difficult to get it into words. It's feelings of warmth and vitality, totality, life, everything being in contact with everything else, nothing is isolated, all is unity -- I find it hard to get it clearer than this, even so the feelings I am experiencing are only a shadow of the real thing. We have to keep this feeling of the Christ Consciousness uppermost and it will live in us if we acknowledge it in everything we do. If, as is bound to happen, we react in our normal ways to situations in our daily lives, we shut the Christ force out and we lose it. This has to happen, but we should strive to hold it uppermost all the time, and then eventually we shall succeed in really living it and we shall reflect it in our actions and our relationships. It's not that we have to construct something, it's already there and we have to live it. This is the difficulty that man has always experienced, his daily life needs to be closed and contained in order to cope with it --- Now I'm shown images of people who open up like flowers - I see that this is the way in which we should endeavour to open ourselves. This feeling of totality, of everywhereness, this Christ Consciousness is real, all we have to do is reach out for it --- I've never felt anything like this feeling before -- I see Christ as a figure of an ordinary man in order that I can comprehend him and then he spreads out -- he is everywhere and the words, 'Christ Consciousness' arose. I'm shown that the Ego is part of the Universal Consciousness but it is shut up inside its situation. The Christ Consciousness is at the interface, directly aware. If the Ego can open out, it can be at the interface and be directly conscious, instead of consciousness arising in a dim way.

According to *h*K-M, when members of the Omniverse Hierarchy incarnated into hominid bodies they had to cope with the situation in which they found themselves and, in so doing, they lost contact with the Universal consciousness of the Hierarchy. But once the problems of coping with Earth existence are brought under control we can begin to open ourselves up and regain contact with the Universal consciousness of the Omniverse Hierarchy and begin to experience empathy with everything else in creation. In this way we move towards the Christ Consciousness.

Within these general principles we each experience and understand the Christ impulse according to our individual natures, as in the following extract from Brian's experiences:

B: I have been saying that we want to know about the Christ force and the word 'living' continually repeats itself. I think it means it is a thing that is lived. I have no appreciation of it myself.
G: Can you ask to experience it?
*B: OK. Just a glimpse. I was just an ordinary human being looking out onto a relatively insignificant landscape. When I look out normally in a situation like that I am concerned with myself. Rather than being concerned with pulling things into me, it seemed to be something to do with being aware of yourself as part of a whole, which is feeding you, but which you are also part of. The Ego seems to be the key. It's not a negation of the Ego, it is not a matter of being less Egocentric but one always tends to see things in relation to one's self. It is inevitable, it is very difficult not to. The Christ perception was one of seeing the situation for what it is on an absolute level, it means that one has a more wholesome appreciation of things, so that when you look at anything you feel that it is telling you something. But if you were to try to feel the meaning of everything you wouldn't be able to move, you would be an ineffective human -- This Christ feeling is very practical. It is an awareness of life, a vigorous, living feeling. Everything seems to be vibrant, the air is humming, the rocks are shimmering in the sunlight. The feeling is that you're a small entity who is looking out onto a great big living organism. The problem is the more you try and catch hold of it, the more facets it has to it. I am trying to appreciate this Christ principle myself and each person perceives it in their own way. My perception of it is strongly related to what I am. Another person would feel it and see it in a different way. I get the phrase, 'All things to all men'. Rather than being just a feeling it's this living whole and empathy with everything. Because everything is living, you are all interacting and living together. This contrasts remarkably with the materialistic approach of the 20th century. 20th century man thinks there is **you** and you are out for yourself. What is out there is up to you to use and do whatever you like with. Whereas this other -- is morally, ethically and physically fine, a considerate and very graceful appreciation of one's self and one's surrounding. But it's not wishy-washy. There is this practicality to it. When you go through life you have vague altruistic feelings about what you ought to do and when you make a decision you 'know' that one way is right and the other one isn't; you are filled with a certainty about the right thing to do at that time. Now that is the Christ force. Normally it is covered up and heaped over with an incessant barrage of activity, what you want to do tomorrow, what you've got to remember to do today. Then all of a sudden, some option is open to you by someone bursting into your room and saying something. You can think, 'Oh no, not now, I'm busy', or you give them an answer that will get rid of them. But this type of answer is unsatisfactory because it is concerned with satisfying them so that you can get on with what you were doing before they came in. Niggling away underneath there is a glimmer of what the person is actually after and what you can do for them. To start feeling the Christ force it is a matter of trying to dig that up. Everybody has this ability to detect and know, 'The heart of the matter'. You can go to the opposite extreme and be over helpful. But you can't stop your normal routine and adopt this approach all the time. It would demand too much of you and you'd never do anything. But there are occasions when your heart tells you and you catch a glimmer of the*

essence of the situation. The thing is to latch onto that and to recognise it and nourish it. Most people feel that they ought to be living a better life. So some people say, 'I ought to go in for more enlightened eating'. Others say, 'I ought to be more considerate', so they join organisations, visit old people's homes, join the RSPCA, etc. They have the urge to improve somehow. Within the norms of society they do whatever it is that they have the urge for. That is the Christ impulse but they don't recognise it. The Christ impulse is one you can use as a guideline for your whole life, one that you can always rely on as being there and you know it. It's in your heart.

After this general discourse on the Christ impulse the Guide asked Brian to seek for something specific to the group's work:

G: *Steiner told us that we've got to get the Christ force living in what we've been doing. Can you home in on that a bit more?*
B: *Well, we construct these intellectual descriptions of creation but this is a bit of a mental game. It's not that it shouldn't be a mental game but ----*
G: *It should be more than that?*
B: *Yes, we originally had stirrings and we've felt the need to go out and find something. So we did experiments not really knowing what we were looking for. We've tried to reach out on Tuesday evenings (our ECE sessions) to something bigger, not knowing what it is that we are after. This is why the Christ force is so important, because one of the main facets of it is the guiding principle. It provides a very clear direction. That has to be applied to our work, both to the ECEs and the laboratory experiments. What has happened recently is that, despite ourselves, we have been dumped into an area where there's a Godhead and processes that go on inside it. I see us and our activities as little insects scurrying around like bees - very busy but going round and round, bumping into each other and falling over each other. What we have acquired recently is the ability to channel all this into some clear, forward direction. There is a clear main way through, which stems from this knowledge of the Godhead and the total organisation of creation that we are getting. This knowledge is so strong, so fundamental and cuts across all fields and disciplines, all schools and philosophies. Human endeavour and philosophy can throw up all sorts of ideas. Any one idea is as good as almost any other. That is a past thing. We've got the power to get down a working philosophy that is totally embracing, that can be experimented with, used, anyone can latch into it, anyone can find out for themselves about it. This imagery is saying that we should be set on getting this total scheme of creation out clearly. Running it up and down and mirroring it. Experiments that repeat the processes of creation are what are needed.*
G: *We've got many experimental results and now we need to get to grips with them in terms of the basic processes of creation?*
B: *Right, this is it, yes. I think there is a lot in them that are glaringly obvious that we haven't seen. The strength will come from working from the bottom upwards as well as from the top down.*

This view/experience of the Christ impulse is influenced by Brian's lively character, which is highly appreciative of Nature's activities and the patterns that these form and with an intuitive, scientific experimental approach.

[Note the certainty of the 'source' in the truth of this 'Junior School Cosmology' and that this knowledge of the way that the Godhead works can provide a basis for all aspects of human understanding. Nevertheless, in the Senior School phase, the Junior School cosmology was largely replaced by the substantially different *h*K-M. Also, Steiner, in his writings on his (Primary School) cosmology was equally adamant, almost arrogantly so, of their absolute truth. But the Primary School cosmology was replaced first, by the Junior School one, and then by the Senior School one. At a lower level, psychic communications from discarnate relatives also claim that, as a result of their experiences in their discarnate state, they have now discovered 'the truth'. The so-called 'channelled communications', which seem more and more to be taking place everywhere, often claim an omniscience. It seems to be a characteristic of stages of enlightenment, that when we are grappling with something that we do not understand and suddenly insight comes that makes sense of the situation, we feel we have discovered 'the truth' of the matter. In fact truth seems to be a many-layered thing and our feeling that we have discovered 'the truth' of the situation arises because we have understood another layer, which represents the limit of our current ability. But then, as we live with this truth we become aware of inadequacies in it, and this makes us look for a further, deeper truth, and so on].

In a number of ECEs Andy was called upon to make symbolic journeys that showed the inner experiences that Man can undergo in his striving towards the Christ path. We present some extracts from these:

A: *I was standing on a hill- top and I had separated from myself and I heard the words, 'Ask and it shall be given'. Someone has me by the hand and I hear the words, 'Seek and ye shall find'.*

As is necessary in ECEs of this type, the higher, Ego, part of Andy's nature has separated off and this strives to perceive the Christ path.

G: How can we best expand our relationship to Christ?
A: I got a feeling of orientation, Christ was in front of me and he said, 'Turn towards me, keep turned towards me' -- I'm facing him and he takes my hands in his. I feel a great strength flowing through his hands. This strength is not knowledge, it's not a strength of might. It's an inner faith that things will be done even though you don't know how to do them ---- Now Christ is leading me along a road and we come to the brow of a hill and there's a big city spread out below us and Christ has told me to go off down to the city ----- I have to go down through a small tunnel into darkness where I cannot see. I send a mental message asking if Christ will come down here with me and I hear the words, 'I am with you always'. I move forwards. Man must move forwards, he cannot remain still, he must progress. I progress, and there seems to be this sparkly Christ-light in me, or in the figure that I see as me in this dark tunnel. I have to hold it somehow. I have to cast out fear. If I let fear in then I let the Christ-light out. The Christ-light and fear are incompatible; you can't have both. You have one or the other. Now I walk down a very long steep flight of rough steps, I can't see the bottom. The city that I saw before has gone. The steps are as though made for giants, I have to clamber down each one. I looked up then and saw something like a small landslide, a mass of stones and pebbles rolling down after me. So I crouch under one of the steps and they all go bouncing overhead. And now there's a whole line of giants walking down these steps. I keep wanting to come out from under this step where I'm hiding but each time I do so there's another giant coming --- I thought all the giants had gone so I came out, but there was one more coming a little way behind the rest and he saw me and picked me up. I wondered what on earth was going on and then I saw that he had the label 'Fear' on his back. And the next giant down the steps was labelled 'Frustration'. It's a bit like Pilgrim's Progress. There are all these giants, 'Fear, 'Anger', all these kinds of qualities --- The giants are in a circle now, they have picked me up and they are tossing me around. And then I realised that this is what it represents. These giants represent emotions, personal conflicts, that kind of thing, and they just toss you from one to the next, so that you can't get anywhere --- One of the giants has got me in its grip and I bring Christ in and it's as though I look very squarely at this giant and say, 'I don't believe in you. Stop wasting my time. I've got better things to do' - The giant then begins to shrink. Then I saw myself continuing along my way and taking this little giant figure with me, because it's a quality within you to be taken along and worked on. It can become a strength rather than a weakness -- I thought again about the city and I heard the response, Yes, now you're ready for the city.' So I go off again along a beaten path -- Now I've come out of the hills and I'm down on a plain. There's a river on the right; I wade through the river; there was a crocodile there but I cast out fear and it didn't bother me. Then I met a man going the other way along the path and I don't know why, but without saying anything, I went back with him and carried him across the river, put him down on the other side, and then recrossed to continue. I carried on my way a bit and then met someone else, and I take them across the river too. And then I see myself unable to get away because I haven't gone far before I meet someone else who wants to cross the river --- I see this scene from above now and I see this little figure of a man going back and forth across the river. I wonder if that's an example where someone set out to serve, but he traps people by serving them. He serves them so faithfully, so excessively that he binds them to himself.

This is, in part, a reflection of Andy's sensitive and helpful nature but it shows that in helping other people it is important to ensure that they do not become dependent on us - everyone is responsible for making his/her own journey through life. This is a matter of growing up to become more mature and to play a more significant part in life's activities and growing up is something we have to do for ourselves, no one else can do it for us.

A: Some way off in the distance is the city which now is bright and shining and glossy golden. I ask, 'What about the city?', and I see a hand come out of the clouds which punctures it. I get words coming in, 'Overblown, Inflated'.

In this part of the ECE Andy has been taken to a city that symbolises a glossy, inflated, superficial, way of life that has little value to the Christ path.

A: Now I'm inside this big building and I seem to be going round and round. It's painted green in a style that reminds me of Hindu devotional paintings. Everything is made of wiggly lines, bright garish colours, fantastic shapes of animals and things. I don't want to be here, I'm walking about saying, 'Let me out'. It's a sort of crazy Heaven. I can see from the outside the whole thing being taken up into the air away from the Earth, higher and higher, carrying me off with it --- I ask for help and slowly it stops rising. I try to find out what makes it start coming back to Earth and it's a single thing; weight. It's as though Christ has weight. He has substance. He brings things down to Earth. I asked for him to come into this temple affair, and he came in and just brought it down to earth. All the walls have been knocked flat. It has been opened up so that people can no longer be trapped inside it. The illusion has been punctured so no one will be fooled by it any more, because they can see outside it to where they really are.

This imagery symbolises how, on our journey through life, we can encounter Luciferic-type beliefs that can seem uplifting but in fact are full of fantasy and illusion and are divorced from down-to-earth reality and are not the Christ path.

A: Now we're walking back to the city, Christ and me. We get to the place where the man was ferrying people across and there's now a small footbridge that you can cross by. Christ is grateful for the bridge, he gives thanks for it --- Now we've come to a funny area where it's as though someone once built a giant viaduct on high pillars but all that remains are the stumps of the pillars, and there are many of these. We're crossing from the stump of one pillar to the next, across a plank, one after the other, many times. Oh! Now the ground has dropped away far, far below us. I get frightened and dizzy but Christ tells me to walk with him, 'Walk with me,' he says. I look down and I'm terrified by the drop. Christ gets very strong, very stern. He grits his teeth and starts running and I have to run with him; we run faster and faster and all of a sudden I see there's a gap where a plank is missing, so I jump across the gap, I have so much speed, and then I find myself jumping from pillar to pillar without needing the planks in between --- Now we're on the other side and I look back and see this rather difficult crossing and I think about putting a roadway across, but Christ says not, that it's not all bridges and easy going, others have to learn to overcome that difficult kind of crossing.

Here Andy is shown that, to follow the Christ path, it is not adequate to stick to a secure, comfortable, well-established way of life (we would then not progress). It is sometimes necessary to have the strength to make leaps into the unknown, even though this involves us losing our sense of security. This is something we each have to do for ourselves; we do not achieve this strength of character by following paths laid down by others.

A: Now I feel lost and I don't know what's happening, the journey just seems to go on and on. And the answer came in that the journey is what counts, I am not recognising the importance of the journey --- Now we have come to a railway line and there is a big dirty train of old coal wagons and I have to get behind these and push them along and I get covered in dirt, black from head to foot. I turn to ask if this is what I really should be doing. Surely I don't have to push this silly old train, but Christ was stern, 'Push them,' he says, 'You have to push the trucks.' So I push and push but I can't do it. So I go very still and I ask for help and there's something very calm and impartial about it. It's as though I step aside and Christ comes along and puts just one hand against the end truck and I saw myself ask for help and then begin to push again and without any effort at all I pushed the whole lot forward --- I'm trying to see more clearly into this. Certainly it's clear that I don't do it. You sort of set yourself aside and it's something that comes and acts through you, and uses you. But once you're tuned into this force there is nothing that can withstand it.

This symbolises the fact that, to follow the Christ path we have to bring the Christ force into even the most down-to-earth activities of our lives. If we do this then, via our Higher Selves and the Omniverse Hierarchy, we tap into immense resources to cope with things. Conversely we stifle this flow of energy if we remain caught up in our personal inner ego/Ego emotional and mental impulses, stresses and conflicts.

*A: Now I'm with Christ at the top of a mountain and I ask, 'How do we bring you in?' and I heard, 'Believe **on** me', not believe in, but believe **on**. Hold me always in your thoughts and actions.*

This last image on this particular journey conveys the message via Andy that, by following the Christ path we can reach the heights of human endeavour. But we cannot do this simply by believing in Christ - we may believe in all sorts of things but this is not important, it's the way that we **get on** with our lives that is important.

This next 'journey' by Andy emphasises the need to integrate the two aspects of our existence - the spiritual and the material:

A: I'm standing on the edge of a pit; the feeling is of being utterly alone. I look down into the pit and I see the glow of a fire spring up. I heard words saying, 'The Pit into which every man must descend'. I drop down into a furnace and I am pleased to see the unnecessary combustible things being burned away. There's a devil down here offering some kind of bargain, I can get out if I sell him my soul. And there's nothing that I on my own can do about it. It was brought home to me how helpless I was so I asked for Christ to come in, knowing this was the only way out. And a figure was there immediately, and now Christ and I turn and we just walk out and we're standing on an English country road. The sky is blue-grey and there are green trees and green plants and the air is moist from a shower of rain. I try to feel the relationship between Christ and myself and then, without prompting it seemed, I just said, 'I want to follow you.' Then He leaped into action. He seized me by the hand and we fly up into the air that is becoming increasingly filled with golden light. It's becoming too strong for me, I feel overcome. My body can't stand the light, it's consumed by it, it's filled with light. And yet I know I am here, I know Christ is here. It's quite overwhelming and I feel myself losing touch. So I hold Christ's hands very hard and I try to hold onto myself and I say, 'I am what I am. Don't let me be carried away. Let me be me, and accept myself for what I am, faults and all' --- And then I've gone back to being an ordinary me. Christ has become an ordinary figure too and we're back to the earthly scene again. He turns and he says, 'Walk with me,' and I have to be very calm; we're not on a road now, we're high up teetering on a knife-edge. He is walking along this razor's edge with complete calmness, control and balance. Balance seems to be the key word. I have to try very humbly to imitate this. Because Christ is in the way, two steps in front, I can't see what's ahead. All I have to do is put one foot after the other, one by one, step by step, and just follow. I fall behind a bit and I call out in fear, and Christ stops and waits for me to catch up --- I was feeling how I was getting individual attention, and the answer came back straight away, 'Yes, I lead everyone up here individually. I lead everyone up here who wants to come.'

In this journey Andy experiences first the Ahrimanic side of things where, in our activities on Earth we experience being cut off and alone and we have to learn to work out of our own resources. But if we give ourself up to the ego/Ego feelings that we derive from doing this, we sell our soul to materialistic power. Andy then experiences the Luciferic side where we can become filled with wonderful ideas of seeming great enlightenment that can give us an Ego sense of superiority. To follow the Christ path we have to accept that we are just ordinary people and strive to live a balanced life. In doing this we use the Christ force to integrate the two sides of our existence.

A: *Now we're sitting round a table. There are two me's and Christ is in the middle. He drew our two hands together and he's connecting us. I go transparent and I see this little Christ figure inside. It's only working in a little way, it's only newly there and small. The Christ bit is at the heart and you must open your heart. I saw myself huddling up to protect myself from the world, to keep what I had inside. But you mustn't do that, you must open yourself up and let the world in for the Christ within you to experience, and at the same time you let the Christ within you out to act in the world. I heard the words; 'You give yourself to the world.' And I see myself standing with arms outstretched, making a cross shape, and it's an attitude of giving, you hold nothing back.*
G: *We've been told that we need to awaken the Christ force within us. Is it that these experiences are trying to help us do this?*
A: *Yes, Christ indicated that we all have to go through journeys like this.*
G: *We are seeking truth, which is part of the Christ path?*
A: *Yes, I see the cross and I hear the words, 'And the Truth shall make you free.'*

To conclude this chapter we quote parts of another of Andy's ECEs that tie together an overall view with key features of our Earth existence, this ECE also refers to the existence of an 'Absolute', which is something that we deal with in the next Chapter:

A: *I found myself deep in space looking at everything spread out around me in the same way that man sees his earthly life spread around him. I look up to something higher than myself in the way that man looks upwards for authority and guidance. There is the Absolute deep in space looking out at what it – not what it's created so much as the world it works in, again in the same way that man has not created his world, but he lives there. It's all dark except for bright lights here and there, some weaker and some stronger. It sees all this and it knows every part of it. Then I saw our little planet Earth and how small it is in all of this vast Creation, how utterly miniscule and turned in on itself, teaming with energy and problems that we think are so important. We look in on ourselves and get very absorbed and we expend a lot of energy on **our** little problems when there is all this universe outside. I see the Earth as a sphere that is curled tightly on itself, like a foetus, a tiny infant that doesn't know any better. It seems to be carried through space, being supported, carried on its way to its destination.*

Now I see the Earth within the solar system, with everything steadily proceeding at its own rate, creating different patterns and configurations, the cycles of these endlessly continuing, always the same and yet never the same, for something new is always being created.

I got the word. 'Darkness'. There's the sun that arises from the spiritual activity pouring light into the darkness as it raises up the darkness – I saw into a dark cave stacked with all sorts of devices, equipment – things to be brought out. The darkness was a storehouse, a fund of potential, and I heard the words, 'Go into the darkness'-- I'm stumbling over things like old cookers and washing machines and mangles, all sorts of junk. I haven't come here with any purpose, I just find myself in here. This is typically how it happens. Some one might find himself in here and he gropes about and he feels things and sizes them up. The best you can do is to get your hands on something and say, 'This feels interesting' and get it out into the light. I go further in and the question of ideas came into my mind- concepts, something a bit beyond hardware and I see a row of figures made out of stone, they're like Greek philosophers and they dispense ideas in the form of nuggets, and you get hold of these and unravel them and explore them in the light of day.

Here existence is portrayed as comprising two parts. On the one hand a darkness and deadness of past material developments and ideas and, on the other hand, the light of spiritual activity that can expose and bring to realisation new potentials in these.

A: *I'm going along this tunnel deep into the Earth and it's twisting and turning all over the place --- I asked for Christ's help and guidance and he was there, almost as a demonstration that he could come right down here as well. Now I'm walking downwards – things are getting confused – I feel I'm descending into Hell. I see a figure with horns with his arms crossed, a devilish figure. I was going to ask it questions but this figure said sharply, 'You do not ask questions of me'. It was as though I was being tested for any commitment. If I were put to the test which way would I go? And I found myself thinking, well I've got weaknesses and under the pressure of certain events I will give way, or do silly, wrong or evil things but that's all in the short term, in the long term I was saying into the darkness, you have no hold on me, I have chosen the Christ path. And then the figure of Christ was there taking me up some steps, now made of white marble, and I hear doors slam behind us. Christ takes me by the hand and says, 'Come on' and we're back on Earth on a hill and it's sunset. I get the impression that this is where the Earth is, poised between the dark and the light but I'd forgotten that the Earth has to go through darkness too. We pass through a still point at the depth of the night, when things stop going down and start coming back up and we see the light of the sun gradually spread up into the sky and the sun comes up. I stand and watch and the sun passes overhead and begins to go down again. This is a cyclic rhythmic movement where I, as a human being am alternately cooled in the night where I have to exist out of my own resources. Then Christ steps in and says, 'I am the sun's light and heat to be with you even in the darkest night'.*

Although life requires us to work in the material world, it is important that we are not overpowered by it because we then lose touch with out basic spiritual natures. To avoid this we need to keep aligned to the Christ path that will support us in even our darkest times.

A: *I'm back in the darkness and I experience being utterly still, frozen, static and not even to know that. I am a lump of something that is petrified. It's not dead, it has awareness but it's just aware of its own existence. It says, I know I am', but that is stretched so that it says, 'IIIIIIIIIIIIknoooooooooowwwwwww……' and so on, so that it fills eternity in a suspended animation. And then a light falls upon it and the light is pain. I can't see it any other way – light and darkness seem to be so crucial, fundamental that they can't be broken down into anything else. Light is awareness, consciousness, movement and activity. Darkness is knowing and waiting. And then I saw the Absolute with two hands, one black and the other white and the white hand was reaching down for the black hand to take hold of it and raise it up. And somehow this lump has been in utter blackness so that even the faintest light is a terrible shock to it, it sort of scorches it. Hands are picking me up and taking me out into the light. After the first shock of the light I now begin to enjoy it because I feel myself coming to life. I have an awareness and when I am manipulated and put together in the right way my potential is released. And I can be put together in many different ways, each of them being more or less successful, although there's a way that is nearest to my heart where I say, 'Now you have found the true me'.*

This part of Andy's ECE makes the point that in the processes of existence that come to us, to realise our potentials and find fulfilment, we also experience the pain associated with change.

A: *Now I see Christ standing in space holding a sun in one hand and a ball of darkness in the other. He spans the two poles and the sun rays down on the ball of darkness and the parts of the darkness that have struggled to the surface feel the light, respond and out of the seeds of the darkness grow plants struggling up under the light of the sun. Plants and animals and life moves and is conjured up out of the darkness – this is why earth is dark, soil is dark. I saw a cross-section of a forest floor, beautiful in dynamic motion. The leaves fall and rot down to feed the soil, the soil grows up as grass and trees, it raises itself up to create plants, it breaks away further from the grip of itself to become animals and, in birds, it breaks away further to fly in the air. Man breaks away further still – he reaches right out of the earthly system. I saw something like a star and he reaches out and takes hold of the star, the star incarnates in him.*
G: *All things, plants, animals, human beings, have got to be drawn into the darkness and it's the devil's job to do that, is that right?*
A: *I find myself with the devil again asking whether things reach in of their own accord or whether the devil drags them in and again he's sullen and says, 'you don't ask questions of me'. Christ was there and he said, 'He doesn't want to tell you anything because he doesn't like to give anything away. He wants to keep it all to himself, even answers, information. What we call the devil's domain has all the sustenance in it and the plant must therefore reach into that domain in order to feed and live. I see a plant's roots reaching down into the darkness and they bring forth energies and activities that allow it to grow outwards into the light and create a flower. The heavy glutinous darkness is worked with to create a flower of infinite beauty and delicacy and infinite depth of colour. Christ has picked the flower and he is admiring it sniffing it, breathing it. The flower is the very highest achievement of the plant. Christ has taken the flower and he's shaking it over the earth, the flower is seeding the earth with golden seeds – 'Be fruitful and multiply'. One flower creates*

many, many more seeds, for more plants. The flower is the expression of reaching upwards, spiritualising – 'Transmuting' is the word I got. It represents the transmutation of gross dead matter into spirituality.

Christ takes hold of me and we just walk over the earth. I see a flowering, rich and growing and fruitful land. The grass is very long, broad-bladed, rich green. The sky is blue, with clouds that bring rain. There are trees that blow in the wind and shake themselves. There is water rippling and ducks on the water. The words come in, 'Here is the whole Earth, rich and growing, but it's just going on endlessly without getting anywhere, what it needs is Man, Man finishes it off.' This is not to say that all the animal and plant life is worthless, it's like a building, Man is the capping stone that finishes everything. I hear the words, 'If man was not here then who would eat the fruit? Who would fish the lakes? Who would fly in the air? I feel that the birds and the fish are within the system and that somehow Man is outside the system, he enters in. Perhaps, through Man, God can enter the system. Man's body is made of the earth but there is a spark within him which is not of the earth --- We carry on walking and it is so peaceful words cannot describe it - nothing out of the ordinary, no more than any English countryside, it's just very beautiful. And we go over this little hill and - wallop! We're right in the middle of a steel works. And I see vast derelict industrial landscapes where old factories have been pulled down and left heaps of twisted metal and concrete, rust and dirt, oil-soaked ground. I see how our activity kills everything off and it still tries to grow, so in the middle of this I see a small clump of green grass and a dandelion growing -- Christ does not criticise this. He accepts it as part of the way forward. He says, 'You will have to pay for this of course.' But he holds up a bar of bright metal. 'You have achieved this. And there is a ship leaving the harbour loaded with this to take it over the world to use it.'

So far, our developing understanding, and exploitation, of the potentials of the things that make up the Earth planet have been used to provide us with an enhanced material existence and to feed the feeling of cleverness that we get from doing this. But, as we are finding in modern life, what we do often has a disruptive impact on the ecology of the Earth, i.e. on the countryside and the plant and animal kingdoms. Perceiving these negative aspects is now stimulating a sense of responsibility for our actions. Thus the next stage in evolution is for a change from unrestrained, self-orientated progress to a controlled striving for harmonious development. This is something that the next generation has to work out.

A: *I see again Christ standing on the razor's edge reaching into Lucifer's and Ahriman's kingdoms and I was doing likewise myself. We've always thought in terms of trying to tread a precarious path and keep our balance, not to fall one way or the other. But I saw myself starting to fall towards Ahriman's kingdom and the way to stop this was to grab more firmly hold of Lucifer's kingdom so that you use each kingdom to balance out the other one. The impression I get from Christ is that **you** don't balance – if you take hold of Lucifer's kingdom and of Ahriman's kingdom as firmly as you can, then you will automatically be balanced.*

Chapter 24

The 'Senior School' Phase of Development

The Culmination of the Junior School Phase - The Absolute

After diverting to give an account of how Christ figured in the ECEs, we return to following through the sequence of developments in the cosmology.

The 'Junior School' ECEs conveying the nature and workings of the Godhead went on for many months and we were finding it difficult to make sense of the varied imagery that we were experiencing (a greater variety than has been presented here). Then one day the theme changed, to portray creation as the workings of an all-encompassing totality that was designated the 'Absolute'. This happened with all of the members of the group; we quote first, Brian's experience:

B: I have an image of the Absolute and the Absolute is All, Everything. It is the Beginning and the End. The Absolute shakes itself, centres itself and creates Soul. Soul is desire - desire for perfection. Soul experiences desire because it is empty. Soul desires to know and be known, to love and be loved. One's soul lies within waiting to be nurtured, to be fed, brought up and developed, in the same way that the Universal Soul within the body of the Absolute is developing and realising itself.

It seemed that if we could grasp this new viewpoint it would be the culmination of what our previous ECEs had been leading to and take us back to ultimate origins:

T: I am standing in an open space, the Sun lifted over the horizon and flooded everything with a new light and I am looking into the dawn of a new day that is opening up around me (book cover picture). *The tranquillity of the Christ force has completely enfolded us and we stand in this new dawn in peace and expectancy. I am told that we are almost there - the day that we are now entering will see us to the beginning.*
G: I'd like to double check - all the imagery of the Godhead, Masculine-Feminine, Ring-of-Creation, etc. were steps along the way, and we can now discard these and work entirely from the Absolute?
T: I get that these were essential steps - because of the way we are oriented we had to make a series of tiny steps. Had we been aware of the pattern when we started it would have been far too big, too remote. However, the steps that we have been through have established the basic principles. Now that we have got back to the Absolute we have the clearest picture that we have had so far - they are telling me that we should establish the chain of events in the Absolute, these form the basic principles that operate throughout the whole structure.

It seemed that all the different imageries and the problems that these had caused us as we had tried to grasp the nature of the Godhead and its workings were now to be discarded, but they had led us to the beginning of the story that the ECEs were designed to give us. From then on the imagery portrayed a cosmology that started with an Absolute in an inactive state, which became centred to give rise to an I or Ego, which comprised its soul. It then sought soul fulfilment by working out its innate potentials, to produce creation. We select extracts from two accounts, Ted's more basic, and Andy's more picturesque, to illustrate the essential features of the story we were given.

T: I'm drawn back to the stage when all is one - a vast quiet nothingness. Then something begins to move - parts of it arise and collapse. Only very gradually does any part become aware of the turmoil around it and then it subsides back down to continue being part of the turmoil. Somewhere else a centre arises - for a brief moment it sees what is happening but then it plunges back in and the identity of itself as something individual is lost. Then a centre arises that remains outside the turmoil and this gradually becomes the I of the Absolute. It can be immersed in all the activity and turmoil and then sit above it and know that it is itself. In recognising that it is itself it can then begin to control it and to develop form and order in it. There doesn't appear to be any plan, its like a dream state. The part that is outside witnesses the turmoil and the chaos and with this comes the appreciation of the raw potential - that its capabilities are limitless. Then the Absolute slowly realises that in order for it to realise the extent of its possibilities it must see the construction from the outside and then go about it from the inside. But when it goes back in the I gets lost in itself again. So it has to go in and work, then pull back and gather itself up to see what it has done, go back in, modify, pull back, recognise itself again, and so on. It goes through every bit of itself in this manner, gradually

313

bringing order where it had not existed before, trying to create harmony within itself. Each time it goes in it recognises something of itself and it can't really believe that all this potential is contained within itself and that it can exploit it. It's not a case of first thinking about what can be made and then assembling the materials to do it. This happens the other way round, the Absolute gets to know itself and then it recognises what it can do. This is something that develops as it goes along.

This imagery portrays an initial state of quiescence in which a random activity arises that builds up to a state of turmoil. As a result parts of the activity begin to experience a sense of self in relation to the rest and this sense of self builds up until one part stabilises with a permanent sense of self. This part then becomes a centre, or **I** that seeks first to control, and then to develop the potentials of, the turmoil, in a series of impulses. In this imagery there is no indication of a God outside creation pre-planning what is to happen but a self-evolving Absolute who becomes active and pursues development wherever the activity leads to.

Andy had a number of ECEs that showed creation as a cosmic dance by the Absolute, from which we present the following extracts:

A: I saw a pair of strong hands and I held these. They were Christ's hands and they were offering strength and support. I feel myself moving towards a kind of vantage point where you see everything - a still centre. Then I saw a gateway into a garden; Christ led me through the gate and I left a part of me behind. This was the collection of prejudices, weaknesses and fears that would get in the way -- Christ and I are sitting on benches facing each other, 'What do you wish to know? he says.
G: In recent months we've been led to the Godhead, the Father-Mother, the ring spectrum of Creation and then to the Absolute. Were these steps along the way that we can now discard and concentrate on the Absolute?
A: I saw a re-visualisation of where I was walking along the razor's edge two steps behind Christ. This seemed to mean that we dealt with each thing as it appeared under our noses. At the end of the sequence Christ stepped aside to reveal a powerful blaze of golden light so that I was face to face with the Absolute.
I see the Absolute with a great cloak of his creation spread out around him, and he takes everything in and fingers it all and I feel some kind of dissatisfaction, tension, impatience, the sense of something unresolved. He's picking out all the unresolved things he wants to work on. Once he's picked these out and identified them he lets everything out again. I see the things to be worked on as little golden rods and they glow while everything else is grey. The Absolute finds these gold bars not as a few areas to be tidied up in a sea of perfection, but according to what has gone before the next phase automatically presents itself, so that when the Absolute has dealt with these gold bars then another set of things will become prominent --- Just then the central figure looked up and said, 'Don't talk about the stages ahead, I've got enough on my hands with this lot'. Then he began to swirl round and the cloak slowly pulls after him, and then he stops and the cloak continues to turn and it winds itself around him. Then he turns the other way and the cloak swings up and out, and he stops again and it winds itself up the other way. He does a dance, turning and swinging this cloak around him, and he goes on and on. The cloak gets larger as it works out from him, it gets more differentiated, breaking down into finer detail. And I heard him say, 'I breathe into my creation', and I saw that as he breathed a ring of beads appeared extending it out further. So by repeated impulses the Absolute is perfecting the creation that's already there as well as advancing new creation. It's an endless process. As fast as the Absolute is able to reach out and make a perfect creation there's always more further out which is growing in a disharmonious way. It's not that the Absolute takes things in and sees what a terrible state they're in and says, 'Now I must put this right'. It just says, 'I must go out again. Me. As myself.' The nature of the Absolute just goes out as itself, because that is all it is. It is wholeness, it is the essence of everything, and it sends itself out time and again.
G: And just one of these turns is our Universe and everything that we know?
A: He holds up one finger and I catch a fragment of the Old Testament - what is it? - a thousand years is but the twinkling of an eye. The age of our Universe is but a twinkling in the eye of this figure.

In another ECE Andy had imagery that portrayed the workings of the Absolute from a slightly different point of view.

A: An image came in of a lake in the early evening on which a mist was settling, and I saw something like a fish jump. This is how the Absolute starts, like a still lake and then something goes 'plop', like a fish rising. Now another fish rises, and another, and the pattern of ripples becomes more complex. The Absolute says, 'I start unconscious -- this is how things commence.' In the beginning he is all inner nature and he sees these things sort of happen -- I had seen fish before but it's more that here and there the water begins to stir and twitch. And the water gets more active and is now thrashing about in furious random boiling energy. The feeling is of disharmony that's reaching such a pitch that the Absolute has to externalise it. He has to push it outside himself. Then the Absolute said, 'Any questions?' and I went back to the first event occurring in the lake and asked, 'What made it happen?' And he didn't know either, he has to work the whole of creation out and then he will know how it happened in the beginning. He says, 'Well, I was unconscious at the time so I don't know what happened myself' --- The Absolute takes me back to the image of the lake and he puts his hand in and passes the water through his fingers. He says, 'Look, there is nothing there. It is only water, it is formless, it is empty. All that we can say is that things are full of nothingness and out of this nothingness things begin to stir'. The Absolute is filled with nothingness but the nothingness is potential, all homogeneous and very still. Out of itself it begins to move, first here and then there and then somewhere else

*Now the Absolute has separated out as a sense of **I** and it has to get used to this. I see the centre making pulsing movements, moving gently into this seething activity and the Absolute now starts fitting things together in different ways. 'Things that fit', seems to be the phrase. He's not acting with any overall plan. Quite the opposite, he's starting from the very, very bottom, just seeing what things fit. Very slowly he arrives at a structure that has a pattern of flow within it-- I saw the Absolute climbing outside this structure and seeing it from the outside and he says, 'Ah! That's what I've built!' And I see a gigantic ramshackle scaffolding construction in space and there doesn't seem to be any harmony about it --- The Absolute now begins to work with this at a new and higher level. The impression is that previously there was no proper realisation of the potential. Now he can really get in and start to build out of what is there --- Something was brought into being by shuffling these things around in the right way and I heard the words, 'And life appears on Earth'. A new dimension is created and I see a construction that reaches up infinitely high. It's like a cathedral with a very, very tall slender spire with arches in stone rising tier upon tier, building up on one another ever higher.*

The Absolute is looking at what it has constructed and what it has constructed is much greater than itself. The Absolute feels a sense of awe at what it has been able to construct out of the materials it had --- The cathedral begins to glow, it's full of light, and I saw him go into the cathedral, stand underneath the steeple, and become one with the cathedral --- I now see an effigy carved in stone which was him. He's standing there with his hand on this stone effigy of himself, and I heard the words, 'And the dead have been brought to life'. He says, 'I am alive. I have come to life. I am living in my Father's house'.

After the Absolute has separated out as a centre that works on the rest of itself, this imagery portrays creation as taking part in two phases. The first phase is the creation of a 'dead' world, i.e. one that is created by him and dependent on him. The second phase is the creation of living, self-propagating, entities, ending with humanity, in whom the Absolute 'incarnates' and becomes conscious of what he has achieved. The reason for the transition from a 'dead', to a living, world was portrayed in other imagery; we start with the end of the 'dead' state.

*A: The Absolute is outside and he sees all the possible patterns and so on, and I get the reaction, 'Well, so what?' He can manipulate them if he wants to but that doesn't really accomplish anything. I heard the word, 'Leadership'. He's got to lead them, so the Absolute fragments itself and submerges itself in substance. A bit remains - there is a memory - but the pattern has to work itself out. I sit with the piece of the Absolute that it has left behind, while the rest has fragmented itself and gone to make these little entities --- The feeling I get is that the entities down there must come to know the Absolute up here. They must get back and so it sends out some of itself as a Christ-guide, to guide them back. I see the Christ entity incarnate and it's on the same level as all the others, and all sorts of other entities group and cluster around it, and then they start driving it away, but it remains until it is finally driven out and is killed and returns to the **I** up here. But the channel remains for those that want it. By incarnating, the Christ entity has set up and grounded a channel on Earth from the **I** of the Absolute up here ---- Now the image has moved on. All the entities down there have harmonised with the **I** and they are living in the cathedral, with the **I** situated at the pinnacle of the spire and I get the feeling that the **I** can now incarnate properly in all the entities. I get the words, 'A temple prepared on Earth, God's kingdom on Earth.'*

This was the endpoint of what we think was meant by the Junior School cosmology. It portrays creation arising from an initially unconscious state, out of which there first separates a creative centre, an **I**, that then determines further creation by continually working through, and realising new potentials in, what it has created. It does this in a series of cycles or impulses, in which it develops consciousness as it goes along. This takes place in two main phases, the first of which leads to the creation of a structure out of the potentials of the 'material' with which it is working but the Absolute gets only a limited sense of self from this because it does not respond to him/her. So, in a second phase it is brought to life by parts of the Absolute incarnating in it, with these parts being submerged in substance so that they are not aware of the Absolute. These, as prodigal sons, then have to find their ways back. Thereby the Absolute gets a greater sense of self out of their response to him/her. In working out the situation that they find themselves in the prodigal sons generate a new level of self-awareness in the Absolute but they get lost in the immensity of the situation, so they are given help by a further part of the Absolute (Christ) incarnating into this world and showing them the way back. It all comes to completion when the parts that incarnated and got immersed in their world rejoin, and reharmonise with, the Absolute.

Compared with the Primary School cosmology, with its unknowable, omnipotent Godhead with its preconceived plan for creation being carried out by a Spiritual Hierarchy, the Centre or I is knowable and its workings understandable. In this cosmology we are each a fragment of the I working in, and with, the other levels of creation of the Absolute, by which we can find our way back to our origins and the I has incarnated part of itself on Earth, as Christ, to show us the way back.

Looking back, we were still a long way from hK-M, that took many more years to arrive at, but these ECEs clearly contained some of the essential features of hK-M, that is: starting from an unconscious unformed state in which activity arises: the activity giving rise to a state of turmoil in which a part experiences a sense of I: creation then taking place from the bottom up by the continual realisation of new potentials, instead of from the top down at the behest of the plan of a pre-existing Godhead: creation taking place by repeated cycles in which our Universe is the latest cycle: the two phases of, first a directed creation and second, a self-actualising, self-propagating creation. Our problem was, how did all this tie up with the nature of the Universe comprising galaxies, stars, planets, the evolution of life on Earth, our daily lives and with the experiments that we were carrying out?

The 'Senior School' Cosmology

After seven months of two to three-hour sessions each week on the theme of the 'Junior School' cosmology, the ECEs ceased and we were told that it was now up to us to understand what we had been given. We tried for two years to do so but without being able to convert the story of the Absolute into a coherent cosmology that we could relate to the working-face situation, the way the Universe works, life on Earth and our experiments. Then one day, when Dennis and Ted were trying to sort out some particular features of this cosmology, Ted found his ECE imagery renewed. From then on Dennis and Ted were able to discuss problems of the metaphysical workings of creation in the same way that one discusses any other problems, but with Ted experiencing 'background' ECE imagery to help them. However, the orientation was no longer of a 'source' presenting us with a higher view of the principles of creation but with ourselves asking for clarification on what had been presented to us and the source trying to supply answers to our questions in terms that we could understand from our working-face viewpoint.

In the meantime the Truth Research Foundation financial support had run out and Andy, Harry and Brian had had to leave the group to build careers for themselves. Andy and Harry were the first to move on, after five years with the group. Brian stayed for longer, finally leaving after nine years with the group. This brought the experimental researches to an end but Dennis and Ted continued to plug away at trying to arrive at a coherent pattern of understanding. We pursued this, what we now presume to be the 'Senior School', phase of development for twelve years and then Ted went for a medical check up for a seemingly trivial matter and found that he had incurable cancer. He had an operation to alleviate the problem but he could not continue with the metaphysical investigations and he died some months later. By this time the structure of hK-M was beginning to emerge, so Dennis carried on pondering about various points of obscurity that he would previously have discussed with Ted, with the answers to these slowly 'drifting in' and some ten years later the investigations reached the stage presented in this book.

When we started on what turned out to be a long stint on the Senior School cosmology we had no idea that we were embarking on a new phase of development. We were simply trying to understand the Junior School ECEs and to apply these to the working-face situation. At this point, after several years of ECEs that were often uplifting and inspiring and that seemed to imply that they could offer understanding of our researches, on looking back we were in fact in some ways worse off than with Steiner's cosmology. This had a vague basis to it, with everything emanating from some indefinable Godhead, through a complex Spiritual Hierarchy, but it did at least postulate four etheric forces each having specific characteristics that offered us some sort of foundation to try and understand our experiments. Now we were left with a more basic story about the origins of everything, in terms of the workings of an Absolute, but with nothing at all concrete that we could apply to the working-face situation. We therefore sought for further detail on the workings of the cosmology that we had been given. However, instead of getting this, Ted experienced images portraying different viewpoints. These images and viewpoints kept changing with our further questioning and it was a long time before they stabilised with the structure of hK-M.

It was as though the questions that we formulated from our working-face viewpoint had to be interpreted by 'the other side' from their standpoint and they then had to formulate an appropriate answer and translate it into our terms and slowly lead us towards it. It seemed to be a matter of entities on different planes of existence trying to find a common theme for understanding each other's situations and communicating with each other in their different conceptual structures and languages. Many times, instead of getting direct answers to our questions we were led to reformulating them in a way that 'they' could answer them. Also, often we would get an answer that would be contradicted later, presumably because of misunderstandings, or lack of knowledge, on one, or both, sides.

Many lines of thought were generated and once a particular theme started it was locked into and worked through until it reached a stagnation point that gave no further progress. That is, either it lost self-consistency, so that further events did not arise naturally out of previous ones, or it did not tie up with the working-face situation. When a stagnation point was reached there would be a reversion to some earlier point along the way and an attempt to develop along more fruitful lines, which again continued until stagnation was reached. There would again be a reversion to an earlier point and a modified theme of development from thereon. But each time this happened some degree of progress was made and eventually *h*K-M started to emerge and we began to develop a common language of communication based on the workings of creation that it portrayed. It then became possible to perceive how a new step in evolution arose logically out of the previous one, in terms more related to the working face and thereby we could ask more sensible questions. (This assessment is, however, made with hindsight; at the time we were just struggling along in a state of confusion, trying to make sense of what was going on).

As the Senior School phase developed, basic features of the Junior School cosmology were slowly replaced by new ones. Thus the concept of a conscious **I** or Godhead arising out of an unconscious state, as the first phase of development, and this Godhead then organising further creation, was replaced by the breakdown of the initial state of turmoil into a collective of self-actualising but unconscious s-entities. Further evolution then occurred by a series of cycles in which each cycle gave rise to separated-off energy in turmoil that became differentiated and individualised. The individualised parts then became self-actualising entities that developed consciousness out of their experiences, to give rise to the Omniverse Hierarchy, as described in Part I. In the present cycle, the arising of the consecutive stages of evolution of life on Earth became the result of the, s-pressure driven, development of the space-energy and the individualisation of parts of this.

The Primary - Junior - Senior Schools' Progression of Cosmologies

This leaves the problem of; why the sequence of Primary - Junior - Senior School cosmologies, and where is it all leading to? We think that this sequence of cosmologies arises from stages of evolution in Man's ability to form thoughts about the nature of his existence; stages of development which we recapitulate during our own lifetimes.

When we go to primary school we experience that we are part of an organisation operated by a hierarchy of omnipotent, omniscient beings - adults, with someone (the Headmaster) in charge at the top. We think that the 'primary school' cosmology arose when the homo sapiens' thinking spirit was at a comparable stage of development; there was still some awareness of existence in the Omniverse Hierarchy, where impulses to activity and enlightenment came from 'somewhere higher up'. This gave rise to the concept of an autocratic Godhead (Headmaster) whose plans were implemented by a Spiritual Hierarchy (the School Staff). We think that it was this cosmology (in the Akashic Record), that Steiner tapped into and reported at length in his writings, and our working with this we think represented our progress through the primary school.

When we go to junior school our awareness has developed to the stage where we recognise that we are part of a scheme of things organised by beings who, although they are more advanced and superior to us, are basically like ourselves. By working hard we can come to understand their achievements and eventually take our place alongside them. But we believe that the whole situation in which we find ourselves has come about as the result of the creative activity of an unknowable being - God. We think that the 'Junior School' cosmology arose from the thoughts of men who still had an awareness of the existence of a Spiritual Hierarchy from which they derived, and they sought understanding of its workings (and sometimes took the view that they should never have left it and should strive to return to it). In so doing they tapped into the Akashic Record (the EM-energy) of the workings of the Spiritual Hierarchy and, in following these back, they reached a point when nothing existed. Because they believed in the existence of a Creator-God this gave rise to the cosmology of the Absolute starting in an unconscious condition, in which an **I** or centre arose, to produce a God, with the characteristics of a superior human being, that brought about further creation in a planned and conscious way.

When we go to senior school we begin to recognise that we are part of an evolving state of affairs and that it is up to us to make a further contribution to what has gone before. What we make of our lives and what we contribute to the situation is our own responsibility. We are aware that there is a pre-existing situation brought about by pre-existing beings, but that the creativity of a new generation can add a further dimension to this. Against this contemporary background outlook of individual responsibility and creativity, it has been possible for *h*K-M to arise, with its lack of a Father-figure God, with humanity arising at the end of a long evolutionary process and becoming increasingly responsible for taking on a conscious role in further evolution.

The basis of hK-M is that it deals with unconscious energy that becomes active and differentiates and with interactions and forces, out of which consciousness arises. We think that such a cosmology was not possible until the abstract concepts of energies and forces arose in modern science and provided a basis for understanding and expressing the workings of creation in these terms. Also, only recently, with the development of depth psychology, has humanity come to realise the significance and power of unconscious activities, which can give an understanding of how the complex manifestations of creation can have occurred as the result of the workings of unconscious forces.

As we stated in the Introduction to this book, the development of an hK-M of this nature is, we postulate, the next step in the Kosmos generating increasing awareness of itself, (which will be superseded by further developments; evolution is ever on-going). The objective of this book is to make a contribution to this end.

The development of a Kosmic Metaphysics requires the integration of the experience and understanding of life at the working face, with that of the previously-developed Omniverse Hierarchy, to produce a new dimension of understanding. This requires interaction with the Omniverse Hierarchy that, in turn, necessitates an expansion of consciousness by humanity. In this respect our account of our ECEs may be of value to other people who find themselves involved in something similar. We never sought these experiences, they just happened to us, and we have the impression that this sort of thing is happening to more and more people, giving rise to the phenomenon that has become known as 'channelling'. If this is so, then it is important that an understanding is developed of how to deal with the experiences and what they signify. The ECEs give you the feeling of 'being on a high' and as though they emanate from an omniscient, omnipotent source. People who describe experiences of this type often take them to be a sort of divine revelation which they uncritically accept as ultimate truth. In our own case the ECEs went on for so many years that we became accustomed to the 'high' feeling, although it was always there. At the same time, the changing viewpoints presented in the ECEs, and their inability to correlate with our experimental results, showed that there was no question of an omniscient understanding but an ever on-going attempt to develop a cosmology that combined the Kosmic viewpoint of the Omniverse Hierarchy with an understanding of the events at the working face.

The Nature of God

In view of the varied Godhead, Father-Mother of the Godhead and the Absolute imagery of these ECEs, it would perhaps be as well to clarify the hK-M viewpoint on the Nature of God and to relate it to the Western outlook on Creation that has been imbued with the idea of the existence of a Creator God.

We believe in (or reject) the existence of a single omniscient God behind creation because we have been brought up to have this viewpoint. It derives from the Old Testament of the Bible, that is an account of the experiences and beliefs of the ancient Hebrews. PHILLIPS has researched the historical and archaeological basis for this belief in God and it appears that, although one or two of the Hebrew patriarchs (Abraham, Jacob) referred to receiving messages from God, the Hebrews worshipped a multiplicity of gods (as did all ancient cultures) until the time of Moses about 3,300 years ago. It was Moses' experience of encountering God in a 'burning bush' and God revealing himself to Moses as the One God and empowering Moses with magical, occult powers and giving him pledges, laws and guidance for the Hebrew peoples, that gave rise to the belief in the existence of a Supreme God.

Moses was therefore the person on whom the belief in the existence of a Supreme God depends. At the time of his received revelation the Hebrews were enslaved to the Egyptians and in the Old Testament it is stated that Moses was a Hebrew who, as a baby, was adopted by a daughter of Pharaoh and that he underwent the training of an Egyptian priest and he became an Egyptian prince. GRANT(3), in one of her recalls of past incarnations recounted a life in which she was a half brother to Ramoses II, described how Moses was born from a love affair between Ramoses and a Hebrew girl. In order to keep this secret and to maintain the relationship with the girl and to keep the baby, Ramoses arranged for it to be cast, in a cradle of rushes, on the waters of the Nile (claimed to be a common practice with unwanted babies at that time) and for a barren daughter of his to publicly 'find' the baby and adopt it and bring it up, with the Mother as its nursemaid. The exposure of Moses to the Egyptian priesthood training could have developed his occult powers and at that time there was a (temporary) movement in Egypt to replace the belief in a multiplicity of gods with belief in One Supreme God (Atenism, see PHILLIPS) which could have opened him up to the burning bush experience, which has given rise in the Western world to the belief in the existence of a Supreme Creator God. However, as we pointed out in Chapter 1, Egyptian creation myths also recognise an initial state of nothingness, when there was no sky, no earth, no air, nor even gods, 'the infinity, the nothingness, the nowhere and the dark, which was described as the 'Primeval Waters'.

The hK-M viewpoint starts with a state of dormant energy that becomes active and differentiates into all the entities of existence. Before humanity arose on Earth there had developed a Hierarchy of 'spiritual beings' that had arisen in a succession of Universes. In the present Universe life arose on Earth that, according to hK-M principles, would have first happened inadvertently and then been perceived to offer the potential for new developments and taken up as a positive conscious impulse. When life evolved to give rise to hominids an intermediate level of the beings of the Spiritual Hierarchy incarnated into hominid bodies to give rise to humanity (homo sapiens). Initially these homo sapiens were aware of the existence of the Spiritual Hierarchy from which they derived, from whom they sought guidance and who sought to guide them. Thus early cultures believed in the existence of a pantheon of gods. But, according to hK-M at the top of the spiritual (Omniverse) Hierarchy there exists the beings who came into existence in the first Universe cycle of our Omniverse and a central group of them acts as a collective 'Godhead'. At times the collective Godhead has sought to make its existence known to humanity and to exert its unified harmonised nature on the diversity of activities and viewpoints of humanity, as in the manifestation of God to Moses.

However, according to the ECEs (and to Neal Walsch's Conversations With God), God, that is the collective Godhead, that oversees the development of our Universe/Omniverse is in turn part of something bigger – the Absolute. In our ECEs the Absolute was described as starting in a state of dormant energy but we were never able to elicit anything on where this energy came from. Since the pattern of evolution that we observe is of an endless proliferation of entities, then our Omniverse/Universe and Godhead could be one of many proliferating from the dormant energy state of the Absolute. At the same time, our Universe could be the source of other Universes in this proliferation. These are the sorts of considerations that are emerging from modern scientific analyses of the nature of our Universe (Martin REES). Because it is difficult for scientists to account for the 'finely tuned' conditions that were required to give rise to our Universe, e.g. the precise ratio of energy to mass in the beginning, the delicate balance of conditions for the formation of carbon on which life depends and many other features, they are proposing that these basic factors could vary and have given rise to a range of other Universes which exist in other space-time states that they create by their activities. Equally scientists are conjecturing that where cosmic phenomena in our Universe give rise to a black hole in which energy and substance go out of our space-time, this might be a source of other Universes that develop in other space-time conditions. If there is any validity to this we are part of an infinite scheme of evolution, in which events arise in the first place unconsciously and inadvertently and their potentials are then recognised and pursued consciously, with the entities who work out these potentials deriving from them a sense of self as 'creators' (God/gods) and being regarded as such by their creation.

A Final Comment

What this all adds up to and where it will lead is something that will become apparent in the future, as the next and future generations sort it out. On this note we conclude the main part of this book (Part IV is a technical section), by reporting claims for the future that were made in one of Brian's ECEs:

B: Evolution hasn't really started yet, not proper evolution. The stage is still being set. We can't conceive of what can be done and the powers that are there. We are right at the bottom of a monstrous ladder. Humanity will evolve to huge heights. It's going to be an intimate working with each other at spiritual levels in a spiritual evolution. In the present evolution there have been a few individuals who have reached heights and brought some awareness of it back. What will happen is that everyone will be doing these things. We can't imagine what life in the future will be like. It won't be orientated the way it is now. Ordinary common people - this is the point of the group - we are ordinary people. We'll never be great men, we're just ordinary and we are just beginning this thing that ordinary people will do. That's why it is hard for us, because we are ordinary. But this is the point of us, to make this ordinary. All this stuff that we have begun to understand and expose is for mankind, everyone to work with. The point of this experiment is conveying this knowledge to other people. Not to influence society and not to make big noises, but to live it ourselves, to give it to our immediate acquaintances, to put it out the best way we can to people we don't know, but aiming it low not high. It's not to be esoteric, it's not to be clever. It's point is to bring knowledge of this other world and this greatness to life. Our particular inclination is towards understanding and knowledge. This is what we are doing and this is what we are after. But there are hundreds of groups that are all doing the same thing as us but in medicine, in poetry and art and literature and all walks of life, in business and warfare. In everything it is bringing it to ordinary levels and living these things - to mix these spiritual worlds with daily life - not in an orthodox religious way. It's just a life that is lived, without thinking that this is an alternative or new way, but that this is the natural way.

According to this ECE there are exciting times ahead for future generations.

PART IV

EXPERIMENTAL INVESTIGATIONS AND KOSMIC METAPHYSICS

(CHAPTERS 25 to 28)

As we explained in Chapter 12, our experimental researches started with Dennis and Ted trying to find a way of registering the activity of the human aura, by reinventing the electrophotography method used by Baraduc that showed a 'surround' to a hand. We did not achieve this but in our experimenting we found a way of registering an 'aura' around leaves, by 'sandwiching' them between two photographic plates to which we applied a high voltage. However, because of the complexity of our experiments we could not unambiguously interpret our results and in seeking a simpler basis from which to work we applied the high voltage to the 'sandwich' with nothing in it and we found that we registered a variety of patterns. Many of these patterns resembled rudimentary plant forms, as shown in Chapter 12. At that stage of our work we found this intriguing but we could not perceive its significance. However, with the development of hK-M and its view that entities develop as a result of stress fields in the space-energy that become self-actualising, it now seems that our experiments could be registering etheric stress forms akin to those that gave rise to the plant kingdom and that they could throw light on how different types of stress give rise to different forms. These types of forms are known in science as LICHTENBERG figures, after their discoverer. As with all scientific explanations they are accounted for in terms of the behaviour of substances, in this case as streamers of electrons registering on the photoplate. In our experiments we investigated them as a basis for trying to explain formative phenomena as due to stress patterns in the space-energy.

When Brian joined the group he took up and expanded this work and we also had a lot of help from Michael Watson who contributed his expertise on visits to us. Brian, and Andy and Harry when they joined the group, expanded our investigations into a number of mineral kingdom formative processes, e.g. fluid flow, crystallisation and solidification, which we sought to interpret in terms of stress fields in the space-energy acting on sustances. What we did was exploratory in nature and much further work is required to establish properly what was going on in our experiments. Thus, in this Part of our book we give a brief outline of these investigations to show the sort of phenomena that were involved.

Chapter 25

The Creation of Etheric Stress Forms

An *h*K-M Overview of Our Experiments

Before our presentation of our electrophotography experiments on etheric stress forms in this Chapter and our experiments on stress-produced forms in substances in Chapter 26, we need to reiterate the problem with which they are concerned. When we look at the world around us we see the mineral, plant, animal and human kingdoms in many forms and performing a variety of functions. Minerals and living organisms are made of various combinations of substances and scientists have made a detailed evaluation of their substance constitution but there is very little understanding of what gives rise to their forms and functions. The current view of science is that these somehow arise as a result of the forces of interaction of the substances of which they consist, i.e. the large-scale force of gravity and local interatomic forces that operate through space. As we have reported in Chapter 9, other cultures have taken the view that substances do not do what they do out of themselves but that there are energy systems associated with minerals, plants and animals that bring about their forms and functioning, e.g. Prana, Ch'I, pneuma, etc. (in our own culture Reichenbach claimed the existence of an Odic force and Reich an orgone), while mystics and clairvoyants claim to perceive auras of etheric, etheric+astral, and etheric+astral+mental energy fields associated respectively with plant, animal and human activities.

The *h*K-M view is that everything derives from a basic, initially dormant, 'space energy'. This became active and turbulent and the turbulence broke down into a hierarchy of activities within activities to give rise to the features of the Universe, as has been described in Parts I and II. In this way the forms that we observe in the mineral kingdom and in living organisms arise as a result of the interactions of the activities that developed in the space energy with substances (that also arose from developments in the space energy) as these have evolved on Earth.

The Earth planet started as a concentration of gases and cosmic dust that disrupted, and thereby separated off, a part of the Sun entity's activity, which then became the Earth Entity. The B-cell motion of the Earth entity concentrated the gas and dust to its centre to form the Earth planet. Some substances came together in stable enduring relationships to form the solid part of the planet, while some of the oxygen and hydrogen combined in fluid relationships to form water on the Earth's surface. In solids and liquids the atoms of which they consist are locked together by the localised stress fields that they create in the Earth Entity activity. As a result of forces arising from the interaction of the Sun and Earth, groups of substances in the watery environment underwent cyclic activities that gave the space energy involved a sense of self, so that it developed into prokaryotic, eukaryotic and multicellular self-actualising entities. In seeking sense of self these entities created stresses in the Earth Entity's activity that acted on the substances to cause them to take up the forms that they possess. By creating appropriate stresses in the Earth Entity's activity it is possible to simulate and register stress fields of this nature, which is what we do in our experiments described in this chapter. In the next chapter we deal with how such stress fields act on substances to produce mineral kingdom forms that are the forerunner of the basic forms of living organisms, particularly the forms of plants.

Forms Produced by Electrophotography

The essential feature of our electrophotography experiments was that we created a stress situation by applying a high voltage to metal electrodes close to, or in contact with, a glass photographic plate that registered the stress phenomena in this region of the space-energy caused by the high voltage. The high voltage was created by putting an excess of electrons into the electrode, to create a negative voltage or, conversely a withdrawal of electrons from the electrode to create a positive voltage. We applied potentials of 2,000 to 20,000 volts, at first using a Wimshurst machine and then a Van de Graaf generator. Although they produced some interesting results, these machines gave multiple complex, uncontrolled pulses of high voltage. Michael Watson then designed and built for us a power source with which we could apply a single controlled pulse of high voltage. With this we could better define the conditions that gave rise to the various phenomena that we observed.

[The details of this power source were given in the Loom of Creation but since this book has long been out of print we repeat the information in an Appendix. For the same reason we have included in the present book a selection of results from The Loom of Creation, along with results that we obtained subsequently].

When we rapidly applied a very high voltage the stress field that this produced disintegrated atoms, and gave rise to sparking, in the atmosphere around the electrode. But if we reduced the voltage and/or applied it more slowly nothing visible happened but there was a registration of an effect of the stress field on the 'boundary layer' of gas/space energy adjacent to the solid photoplate that was held in place by its stress field.

To begin with we worked with Ilford O250 plates; later we used Ilford Q2 scientific plates as we found that these registered the widest range of phenomena. With Ilford Q2 Scientific plates the silver halide grains are on the surface of a layer of gelatine, instead of buried within it. This makes them very sensitive but they require extremely careful handling so as not to disturb the surface layer. We also used colour film in some of our experiments. Sometimes, instead of a photographic plate, we used a glass plate coated with a fine, non-conducting powder then, when we applied the high voltage, the movement that it caused in the space-energy acted on, and created patterns in, the powder. We occasionally used a plastic plate, in which the high voltage created a stress pattern that was subsequently shown by coating it with powder of the sort used in photocopy machines.

We used many different experimental arrangements. The simplest was the application of a pulse of about 15KV to two short copper rods stood on a photo plate, which was set on a copper plate, fig. 25.1.

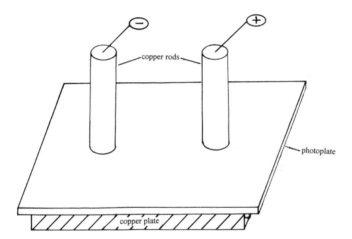

Fig. 25.1.   The experimental arrangement in which a high voltage was applied to two copper rods sitting on a photographic plate set on a copper backing plate.

Around the negative electrode a striated disc shape registered, a sort of rudimentary 'daisy-like' pattern, while a radial branching, 'streamer' pattern registered around the positive electrode, fig. 25.2.

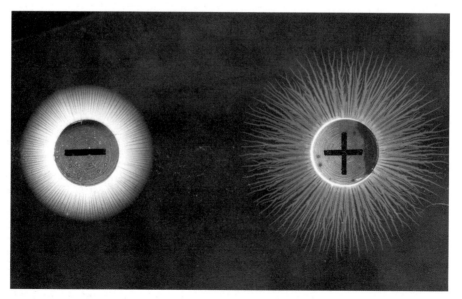

Fig. 25.2.   The daisy-like pattern registered around the negative electrode and the branching streamer pattern registered around the positive electrode, on a photographic plate with the experimental arrangement shown in fig. 25.1.

When the photoplate was replaced by a glass plate covered with a fine powder, this again showed radial patterns around the electrodes, fig. 25.3 but they were different to the patterns registered on the photoplate. Examination of the distribution of the powder under a microscope showed that there was a movement outwards of the powder away from the negative electrode and a movement inwards towards the positive electrode.

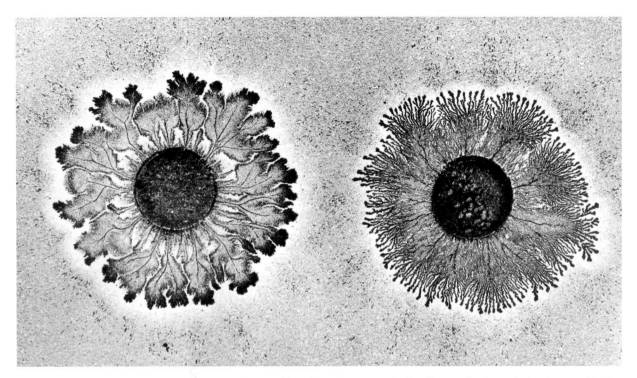

Fig. 25.3.   The result of the same experiment carried out with a glass plate covered with a fine powder, instead of a photographic plate.

We interpret the striated disc pattern around the negative electrode in fig. 25.2 as being created by a movement outwards of the space energy in the boundary layer of gas adjacent to the photoplate which was held in place by the rigid forces of the solid plate, so that a stress was set up in it and it divided into moving and stationary striations.   Where it moved this activated the gas and caused the molecules of it to radiate and this registered on the photoplate. Conversely the reduced electron pressure in the positive electrode created a suctional effect, giving rise to an inwards flow of etheric energy from the environment, akin to the suctional action of a plant root seeking moisture from the environment, with again the stress of interaction between the moving and stationary parts of the boundary layer causing splitting of the pattern, in the way shown by the registration of the radiations from the molecules in the moving parts.

The coarser response of the powder compared with that of the gas in the boundary layer adjacent to the photoplate changed the delicate daisy-like pattern around the negative electrode to something more like a spray of cabbage leaves. The suctional root-like action around the positive electrode encountered greater resistance with the powder, breaking it down into a multiplicity of 'fine roots' compared with the photoplate, fig. 25.3.

[Of the various powders that we tried, that were readily available to us, we found 'parting powder', a talc-based mixture used in the foundry industry that flows readily, gave us the best results, although other powders such as fine alumina were good too].

In the above experiments two etheric/space energy movements took place, one when the high voltage was switched on and another when it was switched off. To show clearly the effect of applying the negative or positive voltages the formation of the stress pattern on switching off was eliminated by using a large value of the resistance in the discharge circuit which slowed the rate of space energy/etheric movement to a level at which no effect was registered on the photoplate and it did not move the powder. The resistance in the charge circuit was zero to give the rapid application of stress that produced the stress patterns.

Patterns of equal intensity on switching on and off were produced by using a pointed electrode positioned a few mms above the photoplate, fig. 25.4, with zero resistance in both the charge and discharge circuits.

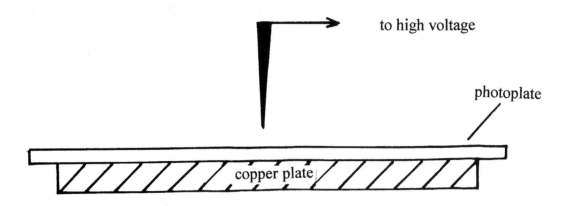

Fig.25.4. The experimental arrangement with a pointed electrode positioned above the photoplate.

The photoplate was then moved beneath the electrode between switching on and switching off the voltage, so as to separate the two stress patterns. Fig. 25.5 shows the striated disc pattern produced on switching on a negative voltage and the positive, converging streamer pattern on switching off. The effect of switching on and off with a positive electrode produced the same patterns but in reverse order.

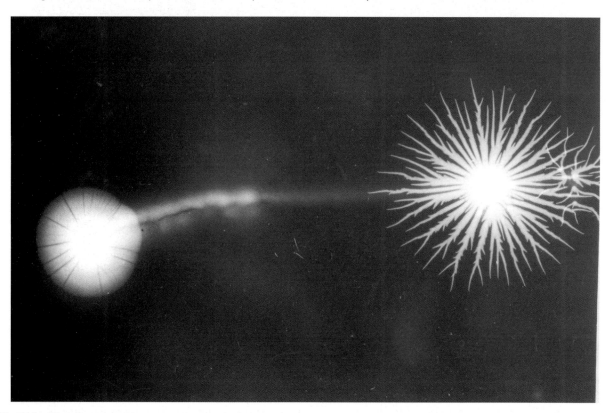

Fig.25.5. The effect of applying a negative voltage to the pointed electrode, showing the expansive, striated-disc pattern produced on switching on (on the left) and the contractile, streamer pattern on switching off (on the right), after moving the electrode.

Further information on the nature of the patterns was obtained by putting the two electrodes in close proximity on the photoplate and applying the same voltage to them. Two negative electrodes showed opposing circular/spherical emanations from them, fig. 25.6a, while two positive electrodes showed opposing radial streamer patterns, fig. 25.6b. The opposing circular/spherical patterns of fig. 25.6a we interpret as due to the collision of the outward etheric flows from each electrode while the opposing radial streamer patterns of fig. 25.6b we interpret as due to the inwards, suctional etheric flows acting on the environment, in a way akin to that in which the roots of two plants close together create fields of influence in which they seek competitively to suck in the desired substances from their environment.

a   b

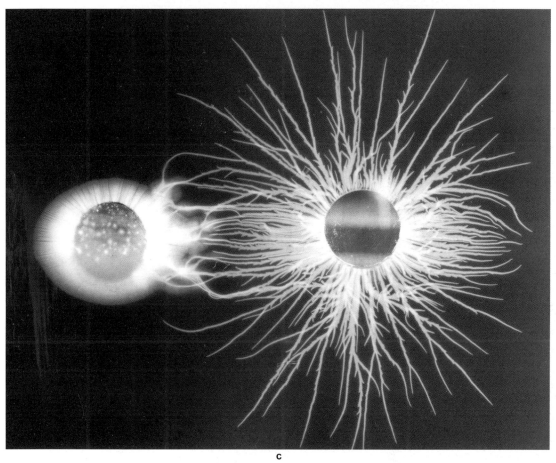

c

Fig. 25.6.   The repulsion between: (**a**) two negative expanding etheric sphere patterns, (**b**) two positive contractile streamer patterns;
(**c**) the interaction between the negative expansive etheric sphere pattern (on the left) and the positive contractile streamer one when
the electrodes were brought close together, showing the positive, inwards-moving streamer form (on the right) feeding off the negative,
outwards-moving disc-like form.

In fig. 25.2, in which one electrode was positive and the other negative, they were placed sufficiently far apart and with the applied voltage at a level such that they did not interact. Fig. 25.6c shows what happened when the electrodes were brought close together so that they did interact, in which the suctional effect of the positive electrode can be seen to 'feed off' the outwards etheric flow from the negative electrode.

The photographs in fig. 25.6 show the effects of creating an out-of-balance electrical stress in the space energy in the boundary layer of gas adjacent to a photoplate but other ways of creating stress fields produce similar results. Thus a drop of salt solution dropped into a layer of water on a glass plate creates a stress field in it. Fig. 25.7a shows how two drops of the same concentration of salt solution, containing ink to show up their behaviour, produce opposing stress fields, while fig. 25.7b shows the interaction between two drops of different concentrations, (from LEDUC). Similar stress fields are shown by the patterns of iron filings between similar and opposing poles of magnets. According to *h*K-M the reason for the similarity of electrical, magnetic and diffusion forms is because everything exists, and creates a disturbance/

stress, in the activity of the s-pressurised space energy, so it is the response of the space energy to the disturbance (whatever its cause), that determines the stress pattern. LEDUC has also shown how diffusion experiments of the type that produced fig. 25.7 will simulate the activities of cells, (see also D'arcy THOMPSON). This is because these processes arose in the first place from the s-pressure causing these types of activities to take place between substances, that gave the part of the space energy involved a sense of self so that it took it over and made it self-actualising, to give rise to procreating cells.

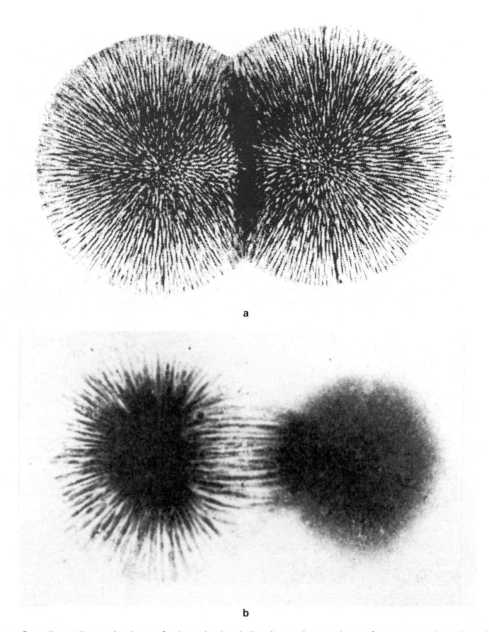

a

b

Fig.25.7. The configurations taken up by drops of coloured salt solution dropped onto a layer of water on a glass plate, (a) two drops of the same concentration of salt solution placed adjacent to each other, (b) two drops of different concentrations (from LEDUC).

The patterns around the negative electrodes in fig. 25.6a comprise an inner and an outer part. The inner part is like that in fig. 25.2 (which does not show the outer part) but not so clearly defined. (How the parts show up depends on the photographic processing). The outer part, that is more diffuse, we interpret as due to a general effect of the outwards spherical flow of etheric energy from the electrode into the atmosphere around it while the inner, more clearly defined, part we interpret as due to the outwards expanding etheric energy interacting with the thin layer of more rigidly held gas/space energy in the boundary layer. The patterns around the positive electrode also comprise two parts, an inner part due to the suctional etheric flow operating on the boundary layer, that was dominant in producing registrations (as in figs. 25.2, 25.3, 25.6b and 25.6c) and an outer, much more delicate effect on the surrounding environment, that only occasionally registered on the photoplate (we give an example later in fig. 25.11).

Changing the Response of the Boundary Layer

In the following experiments the response of the boundary layer to the etheric flows was varied by changing the gas and/or the gas pressure in our experiments. This was done by using the pointed electrode equipment in a chamber that could be evacuated and filled with different gases at the required pressure.

The patterns became more widespread as the pressure was reduced, as shown by the example of the positive electrode patterns in air, fig. 25.8. This can be attributed to less gas in the boundary layer that therefore presents less resistance to the etheric flow.

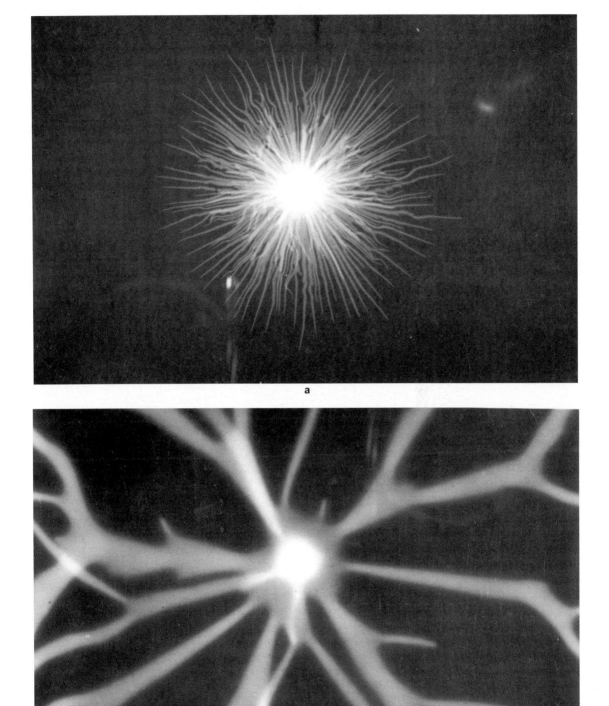

Fig. 25.8. An example of the way in which the etheric energy flow pattern became more widespread as the resistance of the boundary layer was reduced by decreasing the gas pressure. In this case with a positive voltage in air: (**a**) at 300 mm pressure; (**b**) at 50 mm pressure.

A comparison of different gases at the same, reduced pressure of 300mm. (which showed variations clearly) showed that the negative voltage disc form varied in size and in the degree to which it was broken up and striated. With hydrogen and helium there were no striations, as in fig. 25.9a; nitrogen, oxygen and carbon dioxide gave somewhat similar striated patterns of the type shown in fig. 25.9b, while argon gave a larger pattern, with more diffuse striations, fig. 25.9c. The reason for these differences we attribute to the variation in the mobility of the gas atoms/molecules. Thus hydrogen molecules and helium atoms, which are small and move rapidly and so do not cause so much resistance of the boundary layer to the outwards moving etheric flow, responded without causing break up and striations.

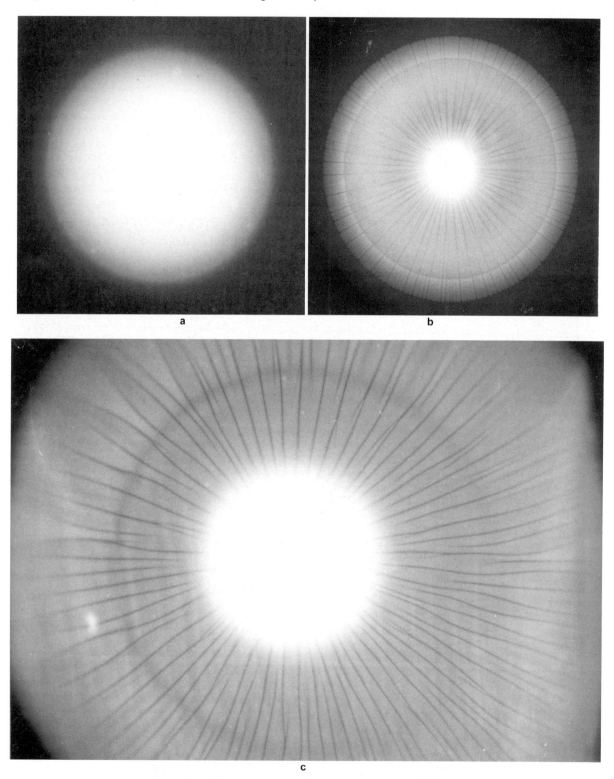

Fig. 25.9. The variation in the expanding patterns in the boundary layer, produced by a negative voltage, arising from different gases: (a) Hydrogen showing a uniform, undifferentiated pattern; (b) Carbon dioxide showing a striated disc; (c) Argon, showing a larger pattern with diffuse striations; (All at 300 mm pressure).

With electrode positive the contractile patterns varied from being diffuse, with hydrogen, helium and carbon dioxide, to being more precise with argon and nitrogen, fig. 25.10. With hydrogen we got the clearest registration that we observed in our experiments, of the outer zone around the positive electrode, fig. 25.11.

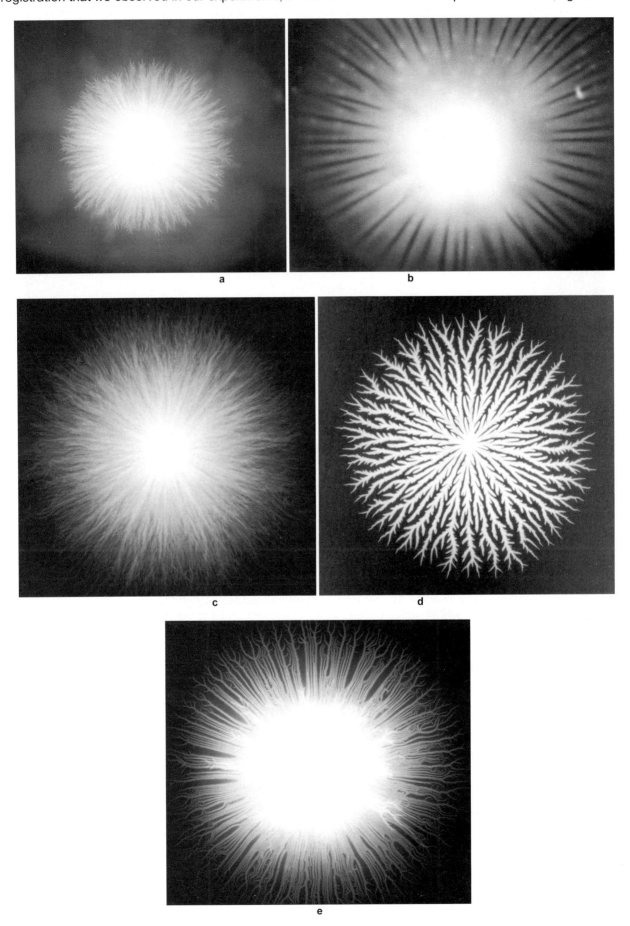

Fig. 25.10. The variation in the contractile patterns, produced by a positive voltage, arising from the response of different gases; (a) Hydrogen, (b) Helium, (c) Carbon Dioxide, (d) Argon, (e) Nitrogen.(All at 300 mm pressure).

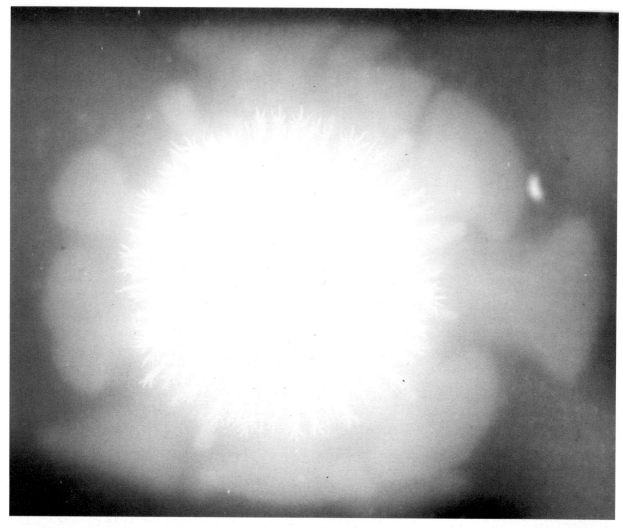

Fig. 25.11. An example of the 'dim outer surround', in this case registered with a positive voltage with hydrogen. (This is the same result as that shown for hydrogen in fig.25.10(a) but it has been printed to show the surround more clearly, while losing the detail in the central section).

In our interpretation of the forms that we observed we have used the analogy of plant forms and we do this even more so later. We envisage the early rudimentary proto-plant multicellular organism as experiencing a cycle of upwards and downwards etheric flows resulting from the interaction of Sun and Earth. These bring nutrients and warmth and light to the proto-plant that enhances its sense of self, so that the plant entity takes over these activities and makes them self-actualising. It then seeks further, increased sense of self by reaching out and enhancing these flows of nutrient and it is the stress of doing this that gives rise to the development of the plant's form, akin to the stress patterns that we registered in our experiments.

To explore further these two types of etheric flows, inwards moving and outwards moving, we carried out many experiments altering our experimental parameters where, essentially we were changing these basic factors, i.e. direction - inwards or outwards, and the rate of application and intensity of the stress field and the response of the material on which it acted.

Multi-differentiated Forms

In the experiments so far described it can be seen that the greater the resistance to the outwards etheric flow, generated by a negative electrical voltage, the more differentiated is the pattern that arises. This effect of increasing the resistance to the etheric flow was clearly demonstrated in an experiment in which, using the pointed electrode set up, its resistance to movement was increased by putting a confining sheet of glass above and close to, one part of the photoplate, fig. 25.12.

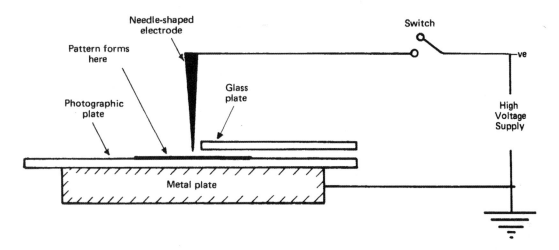

Fig. 25.12.   The experimental arrangement used to increase the resistance to the etheric energy flow on one side of the electrode, to which a negative voltage was applied.

As a result the flow pattern was more broken down and it differentiated into a group of expanding forms on this side, compared with the more 'free' side, fig. 25.13.

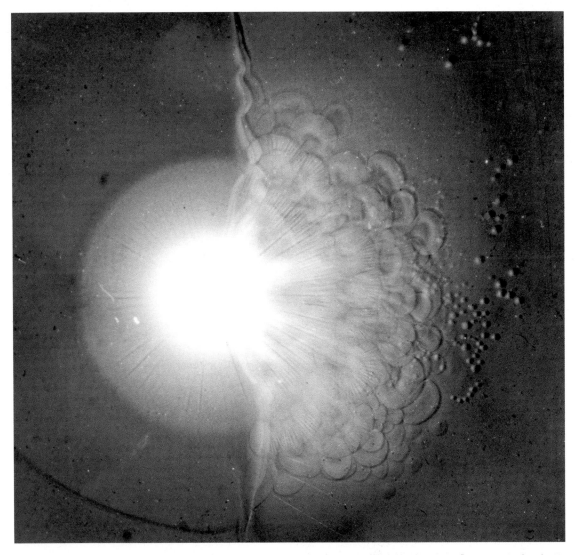

Fig. 25.13.   The more differentiated stress pattern on the side in which movement of the etheric energy flow was restricted, compared with the other, more free, side, obtained with a negative voltage.

This effect was explored more fully in experiments in which the electrode (in this case a stud) was set in a glass or plastic plate, with the photoplate closely above it. A copper backing plate, connected in the circuit, was next to the photoplate to spread the stress field, fig. 25.14.

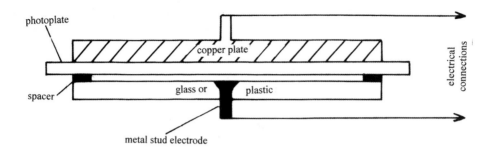

Fig. 25.14. The experimental set-up for applying a pulse to a more-restrained situation obtained by setting the electrode in a glass or plastic plate close to the photographic plate, with a copper plate above to spread the stress field.

By changing the experimental conditions, viz., the voltage level, its rate of application, the resistance to the etheric energy flow (the gap between the plates) and the material that it acted on (gas or liquid), a variety of forms was produced. Again these were similar to plant forms and some have already been presented in Chapter 15 (figs. 15.9 and 15.10). We give a few more here, with some details of how they were obtained, to illustrate the factors involved in their formation.

Fig. 25.15a shows a pom-pom flower-like form that was obtained by putting a disc of filter paper wet with salt solution on the electrode stud, where the restriction in all directions around the electrode has caused a circular differentiation. By wetting the filter paper with paraffin oil the differentiated, 'layered' (Sweet William plant-like) form of fig. 25.15b resulted. Setting the stud electrode in a bakelite sheet (instead of glass as with the previous two results) gave the simple petalled form of fig. 25.15c; carrying out the same experiment in nitrogen gave the 'bracket fungus' form of fig. 25.15d.

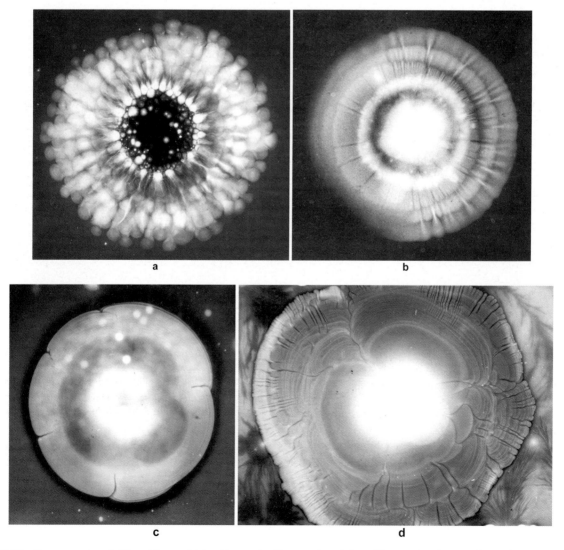

Fig. 25.15. Four examples of different forms obtained by varying the experimental conditions, using the experimental arrangement of fig. 25.14 and applying a negative, expansive voltage. (a), (b) and (c) have rudimentary flower forms while (d) has a rudimentary bracket fungus form.

Increasing the rate of application of the pulse caused the basic striated disc-like form to differentiate further into a group of feather-like forms, fig. 25.16a. Putting filter paper wetted with salt solution on the electrode stud and applying a rapid voltage pulse, gave shell-like patterns around the central disc, of which fig. 25.16b is an enlarged section. By making the restriction greater, by decreasing the gap between the plates, the central region lost definition and coherence but the outer zone became better defined, although irregular. This resulted in the 'fluid' seaweed frond-like forms of fig. 25.16c. All of these forms were obtained with a negative, outwards-flow-producing voltage applied to the electrode. With a suctional flow caused by positive voltage the root-like form of fig. 25.16d was obtained. (In this case the experimental set-up was modified so that, instead of a stud in the hole in the plate there was a cylinder of filter paper wet with salt solution wrapped around a short length of Perspex/lucite rod to which the voltage was applied).

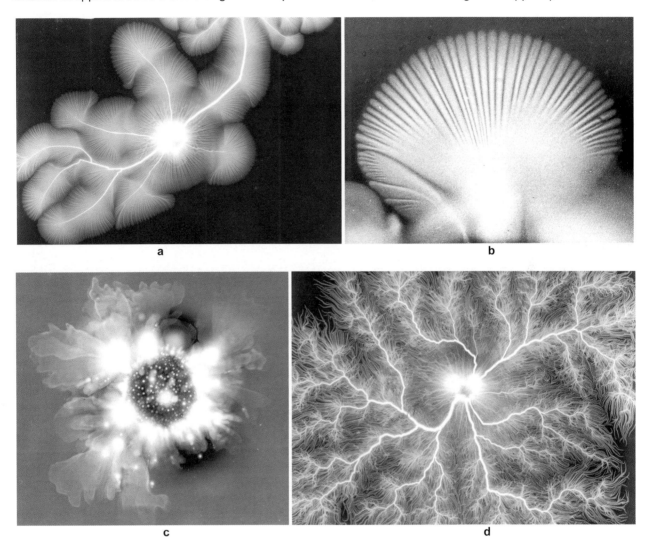

a

b

c

d

Fig. 25.16. Four further examples of patterns obtained by varying the experimental conditions using the experimental set-up of fig. 25.14, (**a**), a group of rudimentary feather-like forms, (**b**), a shell-like form, (**c**), seaweed-like forms, all obtained with a negative, expansive voltage, (**d**) a root-like form obtained with a positive contractile voltage.

A visually impressive result occurred with a negative voltage applied to the stud that was also heated, with a piece of wet filter paper on it, fig. 25.17. Here the increased mobility of the atoms/molecules of hot vapour around the stud have responded to the etheric flow with sufficient mobility that the boundary layer has not broken down and become striated, to give rise to a uniformly circular form: then, at the periphery of the circle, the stress has produced a series of spreading disc-like forms. As the voltage has decayed on switching off, the reversal to a contractile force has caused a branching, streaming-in form at each of the discs. The overall effect is like a cross- section of the Earth with expansive, tree-like, forms growing outwards which have contractile, root-like, forms growing inwards.

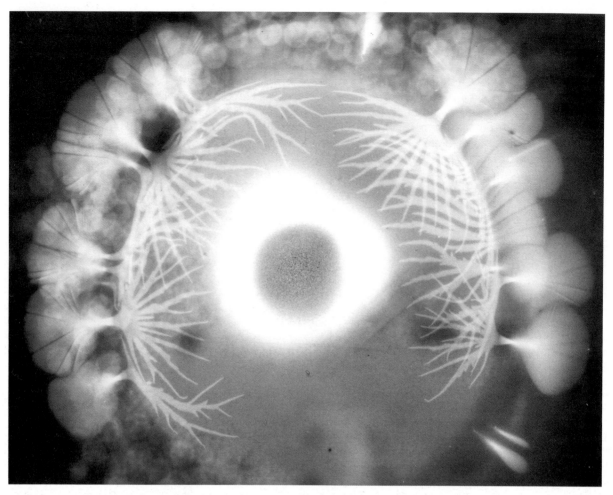

Fig.25.17. A rudimentary 'planet Earth' form obtained by heating the electrode, with wet filter paper on it, before switching on and off a negative voltage.

When we look at a plant we see its substance growth form, and scientists and horticulturists have established which substances it needs to develop this. The scientific view is that the genetic make up of the seed somehow determines which substances the plant absorbs from its environment and how it brings these together to create its form and function. According to hK-M, the essential feature of a plant is that it is a self-actualising, etheric/will, entity that derives from the Earth Entity energy and goes through a life cycle in accordance with the pattern of response to the etheric flows arising from the interaction of the Sun and the Earth. It reaches out for nutrients and brings these together in specific combinations that supply it with substance and energy to build its structure, form and functioning. Its form has developed from the stress pattern of its reaching out for nutrients, while its genetic structure has developed from the way in which the substances combine as it does this. According to hK-M, the substance (genetic) part is only half of the story and it requires an understanding of the etheric energy flow aspects to complete it. The scientific viewpoint deals only with the substances of the plant but if that is all that there is to the plant then we could eat, and thrive on, the chemicals of the substances, e.g. in tablet form, without bothering to grow and eat plants. According to hK-M when we eat plants we release etheric energies that are bound up with the substances and this supports the functioning of our own etheric bodies.

A 'Field' of Forms

By using two opposing photoplates, with copper backing plates in a 'sandwich' arrangement, fig. 25.18 (the configuration with which we found that we registered auras around leaves), we applied an overall space-energy stress field, instead of the centred stress and etheric energy flow from a central electrode used for the results so far described. Pursuing the analogy with the plant kingdom, whereas the previous experiments registered stress forms and etheric flow from a centre, analogous to a growth centre in a plant, this arrangement generated an overall etheric flow over the surface of the photoplate, in the way that the Sun's and Earth's etheric flows occur in relation to the Earth's surface. With this experimental configuration a 'field of forms' registered on the photoplate, that varied according to the distance between the plates and the characteristics of the pulse applied.

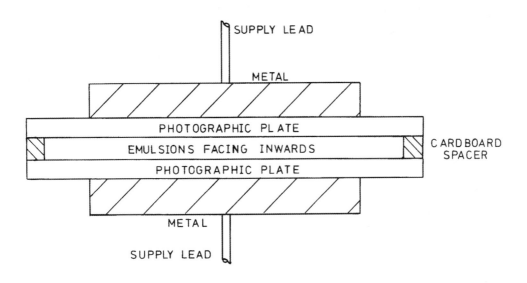

Fig. 25.18. The experimental 'sandwich' arrangement with two opposing photographic plates with an air gap in between and two copper backing plates, both connected in the circuit.

The simplest result was a recording of a multiplicity of small versions of the spherical etheric forms on the positive side of the sandwich and the streamer forms on the negative side, fig. 25.19.

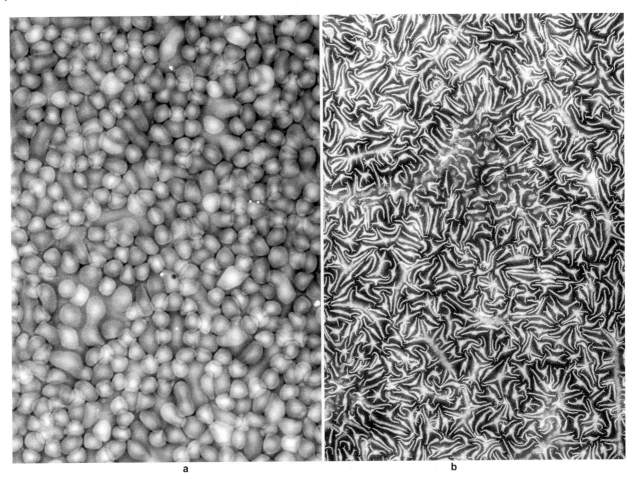

a   b

Fig. 25.19. The basic pair of results obtained with the sandwich arrangement with a negative pulse, (a) the field of etheric spheres that registered on the positive side of the sandwich, (b) the field of streamer shapes that registered on the negative side.

Our interpretation of this result is that the outwards etheric flow has taken place from many points on the negative side of the sandwich and registered on the positive side while the suctional inwards moving flow from the positive side has acted on the etheric spheres to derive streams of etheric flow from them (in a similar way to that shown in fig. 25.6) which has registered on the negative side. This pattern of etheric flow was shown clearly on a narrow strip of photographic plate inserted across the gap between the two sides of the sandwich, fig. 25.20.

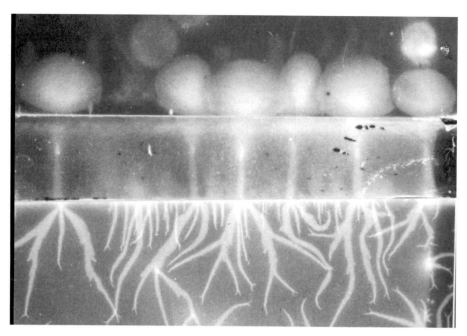

Fig. 25.20. The result obtained by inserting a slither of photoplate across the sandwich so as to register the flow of activity from the negative to the positive side. (The plates are very delicate and the black marks are damage caused by cutting off the slither and inserting it, in the dark).

The results of figs. 25.19 and 25.20 were obtained with a large discharge resistance to slow the etheric movement on switching off, so that only the effect of a rapid application of voltage was registered. With the discharge resistance reduced then the more rapid reduction of the stress was equivalent to applying a stress in the opposite direction. The etheric spheres produced on switching on then acted as preferential sites for etheric energy flow on switching off, so that positively-induced streamer energy flow forms took place in them, fig. 25.21.

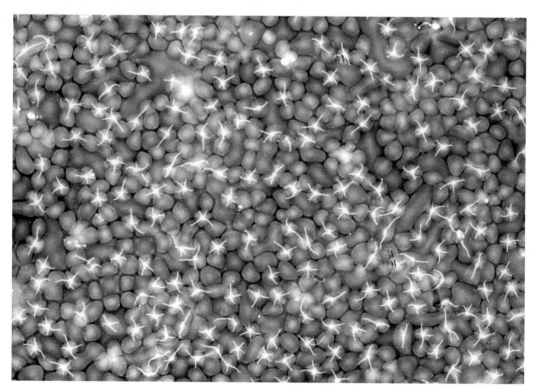

Fig. 25.21 The effect of switching the pulse off more rapidly so that the stress generated created streamer shapes in the etheric spheres that had formed on applying the pulse.

[At the time when we were carrying out these experiments and seeking an explanation for them, we were studying Steiner's cosmology in which the first stage of creation, which he designated the 'Saturn stage', consisted of the formation of 'warmth spheres':

338

Picture to yourself a mulberry or blackberry, composed as it is of ever so many tiny berries. To the supersensible observer Saturn looks like this in the evolutionary epoch here described .... Then, in a further development .... A life of light begins, flickering here and there within the Saturn world and dying down again. At some places a quivering of light will appear, at others something more like rapid lightning flashes. The Saturn warmth bodies begin to glisten, even to radiate light.

from Occult Science

This made us think that, perhaps, in our experiments we were simulating on a minute scale the processes that Steiner was observing in his mystical state of consciousness].

By eliminating the discharge resistance altogether the amount of positive stress-generated streamer shapes in the negative etheric spheres increased. When this happened, then, where the etheric spheres were dominant and exerted a confining effect on the raying out shapes, this gave rise to 'cotton ball' forms and where the raying out shapes were dominant, to spreading-out' tentacled' forms, fig. 25.22.

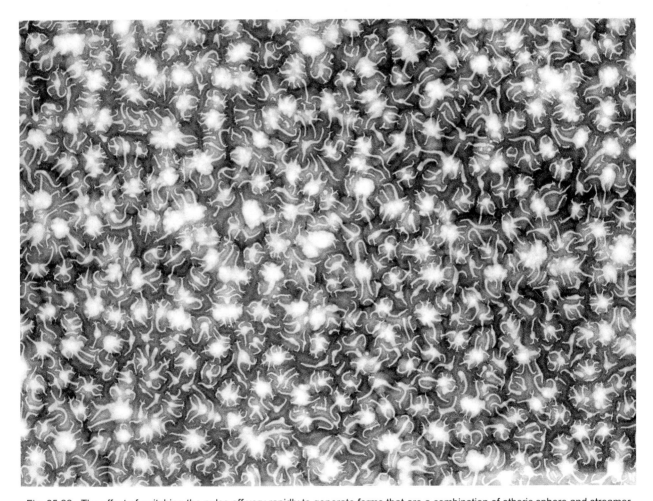

Fig. 25.22. The effect of switching the pulse off very rapidly to generate forms that are a combination of etheric sphere and streamer shapes, giving rise to rudimentary 'cotton ball' and 'tentacle' forms.

With an intermediate rate of voltage increase and decrease the result shown in fig. 25.23 was obtained, where a variety of 'rudimentary creature' forms has arisen in the etheric spheres.

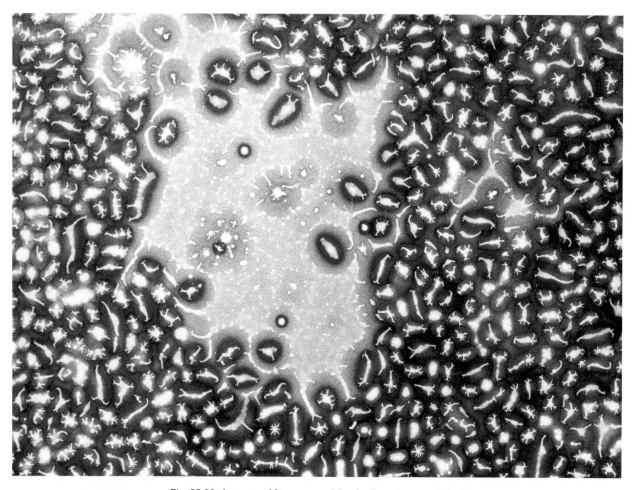

Fig. 25.23 An array of forms resembling 'rudimentary creatures'

By decreasing the stress intensity (reducing the applied voltage, or increasing the distance between the plates), the patterns became more diffuse, with fewer sites of initial breakdown and greater spreading out from these. The positive shapes then showed a resemblance to branching plant and multi-legged animal forms, fig. 25.24, while the etheric spheres became more spread out and diffuse, differentiating into spheres at their peripheries.

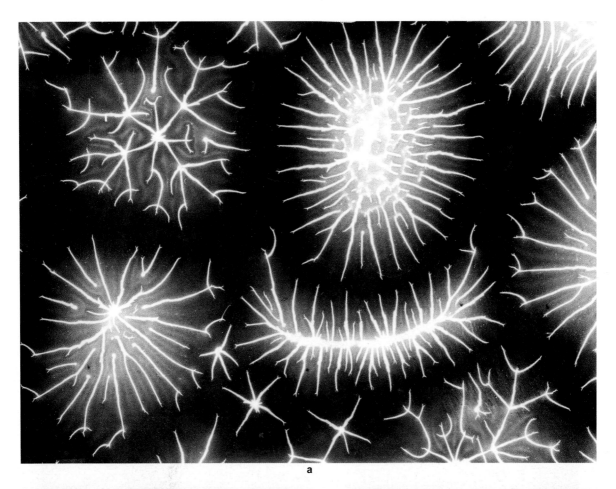

a

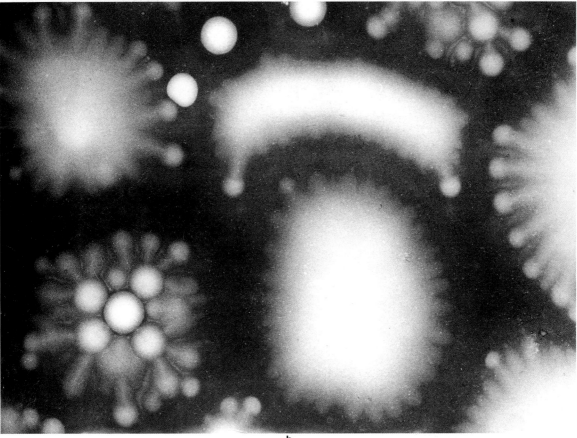

b

Fig.25.24 By increasing the air gap in the sandwich the patterns were less confined, giving rise to more extensive, insect-like and branching formations (**a**), and more extensive cloud-like etheric sphere forms that differentiate at their peripheries, (**b**).

With a yet larger air gap, the patterns became more varied and, on one occasion, the visually attractive form of fig. 25.25 was obtained.

Fig. 25.25.   A visually impressive result obtained on one occasion with a larger than usual air gap in the sandwich.

We are not, of course, the only people to have carried out experiments on Lichtenberg figures; for some references to other work see LICHTENBERG. We would like to draw attention in particular to the work of Lord ARMSTRONG who, over 100 years ago published impressive Lichtenberg figures recorded photographically and in powder (using a mixture of fine carbon and magnesia) and who noted their resemblance to living forms. We reproduce three of Armstrong's powder pictures here, fig.25.26.

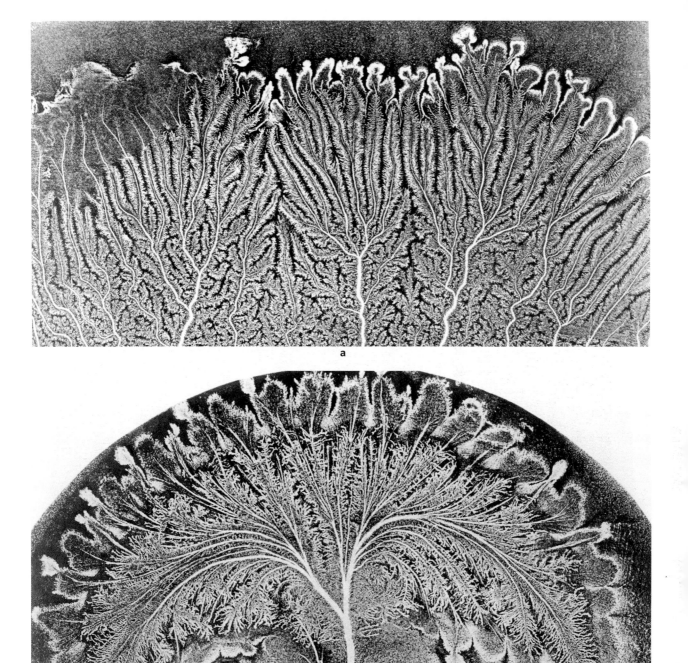

Fig.25.26a & b. Reproduction of two of Armstrong's results, (**a**) and (**b**) showing foliage and tree-like formations

Fig 25.26a Armstrong described as;

> '*arborescent forms showing trees and undergrowth, in which stems, branches and leaves find their approximate representation.*

Fig 26b is similar but shows a main trunk. Fig. 26c Armstrong describes as:

'a circle of independent figures, each complete in itself .... with a nucleus ...... like pictures of physiological cells .... in every stage of fission, from small beginnings to complete separation and in every case the divided form displays the same internal structure as the original from which it springs .... electrically organised motion carried apparently to the very verge of life.

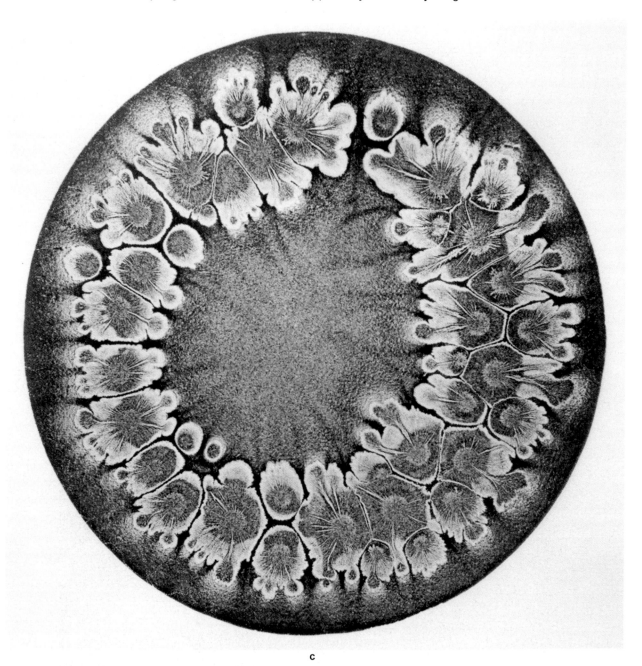

c

Fig.25.26c. Reproduction of another of Armstrong's results, that he related to cellular forms.

Forms Associated With Liquids

We also looked at the effect of having a layer of liquid on one side of the sandwich, containing this in a shallow dish, fig. 25.27a. Generally the liquids that we examined (alcohol, acetone, various acids and alkalis and solutions of a number of salts) gave similar results to those obtained with the sandwich technique with an air gap between the photoplates, i.e. etheric spheres and streamer shapes but at different rates of application of voltage to those used with the air gap sandwich. This was presumably due to the way that the vapour of the liquid altered the response to the etheric flow. However, water (and dilute aqueous solutions) exhibited an additional phenomenon, of subdividing bright spots on the photoplate, fig. 25.27b. Since these only occurred with water and aqueous solutions we assume that they were due to the presence of water vapour and that the internal etheric balance of this was disturbed by the externally-imposed etheric flow, possibly splitting it into hydrogen and oxygen, the 'etheric bodies' of which registered as the bright spots. In Harry's ECE on the nature of substances hydrogen and oxygen were portrayed as at opposing poles of creation (Luciferic and Ahrimanic in the terminology used to describe this), so that there would be a tension between them. In Chapter 27 we present results that we interpret as showing that water vapour molecules readily disintegrate into their atomic and sub-atomic constituents.

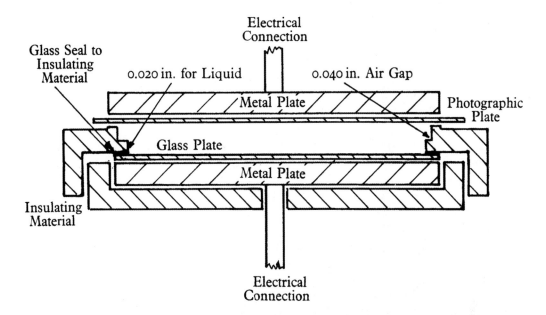

Fig.25.27a. The experimental arrangement used to examine the effect of having a liquid on one side of the sandwich-type set up.

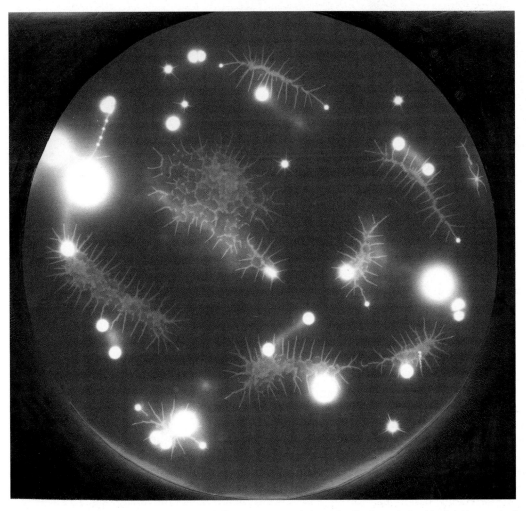

Fig.25.27b. The type of result obtained with water and dilute aqueous solutions, that is characterised by bright, seemingly moving, subdividing spots.

345

Phenomena Associated With Leaves

The 'auric' and other phenomena associated with leaves, that were shown in Chapter 15, were obtained by the 'sandwich technique' with a leaf in the air gap between the photographic plates, by the multi-pulse technique using a Wimshurst machine or a Van de Graaf generator.

A further example of the type of result obtained with the multi-pulse technique, in this case with a spray of mountain ash leaves, is shown in fig. 25.28.

Fig.25.28. An example of the type of result obtained by the multi-pulse technique, with a spray of mountain ash leaves in the gap in the sandwich.

There are many problems in interpreting these results. One is to know to what extent the electrophotography technique has registered something that was already there and to what extent it has brought about what it has registered. We would guess that the narrow band around the leaves, shown particularly clearly in fig. 15.3(a), is the etheric aura that exists around living organisms and is perceived by clairvoyant vision but that the extensive 'auras' that we registered around leaves, as in figs. 15.3(b), 15.4, 15.5 and 25.28, could be caused by the multi-pulse technique, with some pulses causing the emanation and others registering it. Examination of a spray of mountain ash leaves with the single-pulse technique, using the conditions that gave rise to etheric spheres with streamers, with nothing in the air gap, fig.25.21, show white spots, characteristic of those registered with water, at the tips of the leaves, fig. 25.29(a).

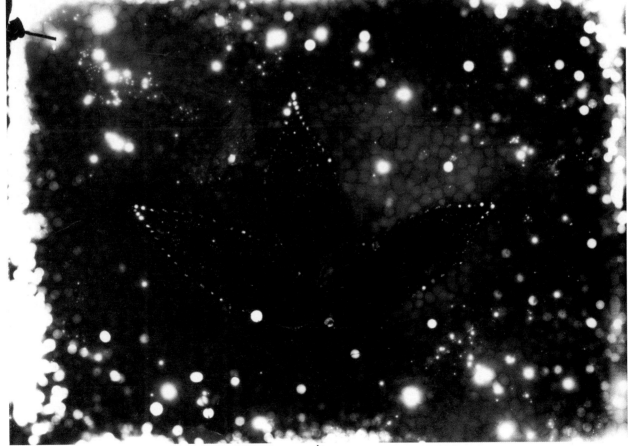

Fig.25.29. (a) The effect of a single rapid pulse with a spray of mountain ash leaves; (b) The result obtained when the high-voltage was maintained for much longer, (3 minutes).

With an extended pulse of 3 minutes the moisture in the leaves was driven off and they became dry and brittle and white spots that we have associated with water accumulated at the periphery of the sandwich, fig. 25.29(b).   Some sub-dividing bright 'water spots' can be seen among the background spots around the leaves in fig. 25.28 and also in some of the leaf pictures in Chapter 15. Fig. 15.5(a) seems to show an emanation from a privet leaf that is differentiating into bright spots at its periphery.

According to hK-M a plant comprises a pattern of etheric stress that has become self-actualising and has interacted with substances to build the form of the plant.   When a leaf is detached from the self-actualising activity of the plant entity it starts to die and its substance aspect reverts to being part of the mineral kingdom, while its etheric/life formative activity disperses into the etheric environment.   We think that applying the high voltage stress to it caused an outwards dispersion of its 'etheric body of activity' that accelerated the dying process.

Where we registered interactions between leaves, figs. 15.7 and 15.8(a), this could be of etheric energy flow but that water could be associated with this was shown by fig. 15.8(b) where there was a similar interaction between wet filter paper and a dying leaf.   As the etheric energy-water combination emanates from a leaf it could break down into 'droplets' like the prana that mystics and clairvoyants perceive being absorbed into a plant as it grows. It is all very difficult to unravel and sort out.

We carried out a number of 24-hour surveys of leaves, to see if we registered any evidence for etheric activity associated with the time of day or night.   Sometimes we seemed to register activity in the 'space ' around a leaf but we were not able to establish a regular pattern of behaviour. Two examples, obtained with the multi-pulse technique, are shown in fig. 25.30(a & b).

Fig 25.30(a). An example of seeming activity around a privet leaf in July at 01:00 registered with the multi-pulse technique

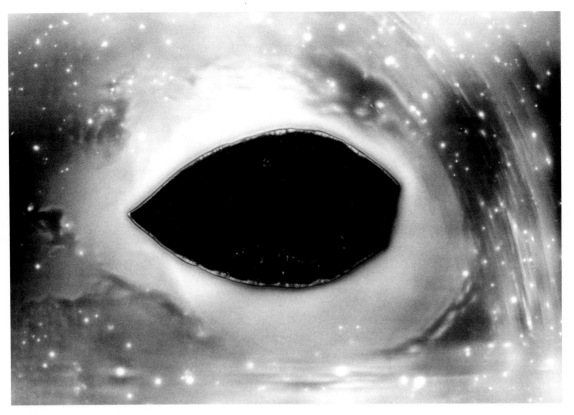

Fig.25.30(b). A further example of seeming activity in the environment around a privet leaf in July, registered with the multi-pulse technique at 13.00.

Experiments with Magnets

On the basis that magnets create a stress field in the space-energy around them, which might interact with the etheric flow created by the high-voltage, we carried out a number of experiments in which we put thin magnets in the sandwich and subjected them to the multi-pulse technique. Fig. 25.31 shows the result obtained with a horse-shoe magnet which registered an inner and an outer surround to it.

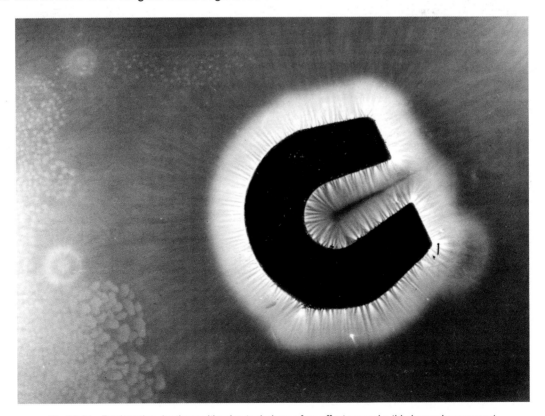

Fig.25.31. Registration, by the multi-pulse technique of an effect around a thin horseshoe magnet.

With a magnetic compass needle we registered bright zones at the tips, fig. 25.32.

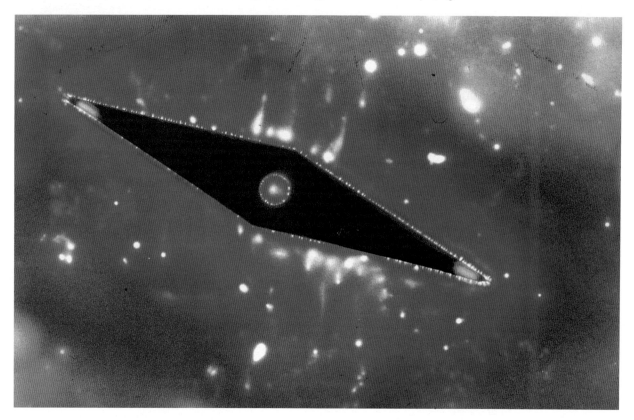

Fig.25.32. The registration of bright zones at the tips of a magnetic compass needle.

With two compass needles positioned with like poles opposing, the bright zones at one end were heightened while those at the other end were so dim as to be barely perceptible, fig. 25.33.

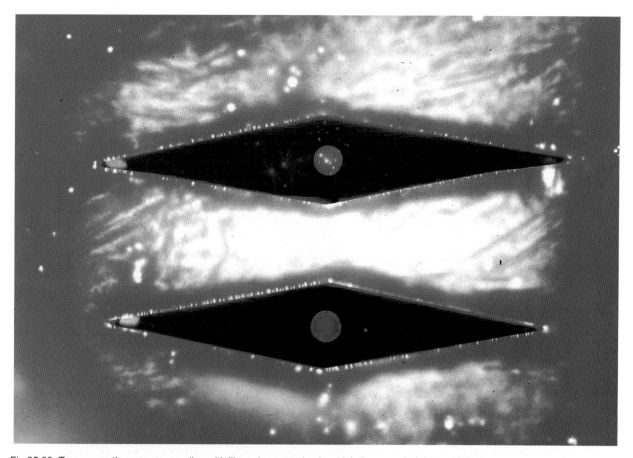

Fig.25.33 Two magnetic compass needles with like poles opposing in which there are heightened bright zones at one end while those at the other end are almost extinguished.

Fig, 25.34 shows an interaction between three magnetic compass needles and a demagnetised needle.

Fig.25.34 Three magnetic compass needles and a demagnetised needle (the largest one, on the right) showing evidence of considerable interaction.

In fig. 25.35 a compass needle has been placed near to a leaf and there seems to be some sort of interaction between them, while the bright zone at the tip of the compass needle away from the leaf has been heightened.

Fig.25.35 Seeming interaction between a leaf and a magnetic compass needle.

Some Other Phenomena That Registered

We mentioned in Chapter 19 the problem of a 'squaring activity', which at that time we associated with Steiner's 'life ether' and the formation of grid structures. We occasionally registered something suggestive of such an activity, thus in fig. 25.36a, obtained with a single pulse, there seems to be some sort of 'squaring activity' around a leaf while fig. 25.36b shows a similar phenomenon around a disc of wet filter paper.

a

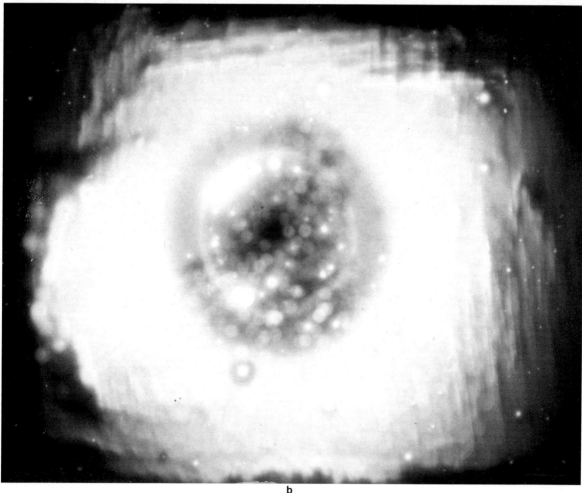

b

Fig.25.36. Suggestions of a 'squaring activity' obtained with a prolonged single pulse, (a) around a leaf, (b) around a disc of wet filter paper

We also registered this squaring activity in one of our experiments examining the behaviour of different gases using the needle electrode technique. It occurred with nitrogen but it was a phenomenon that, to some extent, crept into the results occasionally so that it was probably not specific to nitrogen. These registrations of a 'squaring activity in space' were comparatively rare events in the many hundreds of experiments carried out.

In Chapter 19 we described how we first used the ECEs to seek insight into what was going on in our experiments by asking Ted if he could perceive what happened when we applied a high voltage to a pointed electrode positioned above a photoplate. This produced a striated disc pattern and we asked:

G: Is there any detail in the structure of the disc?
T: Yes, I saw a honeycomb structure where you've got material forming networks with a pattern of holes running through it. It's as if the gas forms the networks but there are holes within it. It's a very fine thing though and you've really got to crawl right down into it to see it.

On occasions we seemed to register such a honeycomb pattern, as in fig. 25.37.

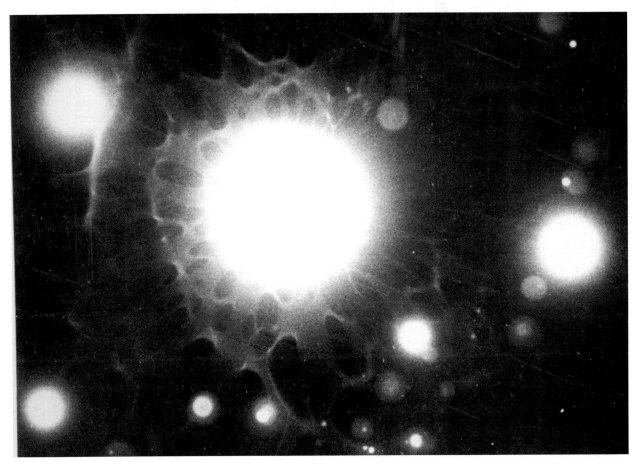

Fig.25.37 A honeycomb structure, which seems to be in accord with the ECE claim made with Ted as the receiver, that is suggestive of a breaking up of something (the etheric energy associated with the boundary layer of gas?) under stress. Magnification x10.

In our explanation for the striated disc, daisy-like, pattern around a pointed electrode, (fig.25.5) we proposed that this arose from the stress of interaction between the outwards flowing space energy from the electrode and the more static space energy associated with the boundary layer of gas adjacent to the photoplate. Fig. 25.37 was obtained when a planar stress (as opposed to a radial one) was applied to the space energy/gas boundary layer that could, perhaps, account for holes appearing in it. This gives the impression of something being stretched and breaking up under stress.

While we have put forward tentative interpretations of these experimental results there is much that we do not understand about them and about the nature and behaviour of space energy/etheric activity in general. Hopefully our results and interpretations may stimulate someone else to formulate a better understanding.

Chapter 26

Mineral Kingdom Forms Produced by Stress

According to *h*K-M the Universe consists of a hierarchy of patterns of activities within activities, with each activity disrupting and creating stress in the levels above and below and interacting with other activities at its own level. Any change in the configuration or intensity of one activity reverberates through, and impinges on, the other activities in an overall pattern of mutual development. In the last chapter we were concerned with generating and registering patterns of stress that occurred in the background Earth Entity energy activity when we introduced a change in our experimental set up by momentarily applying the stress created by a high voltage. When we did this to a glass photographic plate the applied stress interacted with a boundary layer of gas adjacent to the plate, which was restrained by the stress field of the rigid plate, to give rise to a transient stress form that acted on the sensitive particles in the photographic emulsion that showed up when it was developed. When we placed a leaf or a magnet adjacent to the photographic plate the applied stress interacted with the stress field created by life activity in the leaf, and the stress field of the magnet, which showed up in the photographic emulsion. Equally the movement involved in the formation of the stress pattern was shown up by substituting for the photographic plate a glass plate covered with a fine powder that took up the configuration of the stress pattern. When we used a Perspex (Lucite) plate it modified the structures of the molecules of the Perspex so that these responded to, and showed up, the stress patterns in carbonaceous dust subsequently applied to the Perspex plate. Since these stress patterns were created by transient stresses in the Earth Entity energy activity they had only an ephemeral existence. In this chapter we look at how some more substantial forms are created in the mineral kingdom by different stress conditions that occur when different substances interact. Where we see the living organisms of plants and animals, the Earth Entity's energy involved in these stress patterns has become self-actualising, so that forms produced in the mineral kingdom are the pre-self-actualising forms of living organisms, particularly of plants that have not developed the functions of feeling/emotion and thinking driven activity possessed by more evolved animal and human organisms.

To investigate how forms are produced by stress in solids and liquids we carried out various types of experiments. These were: a liquid subjected to mechanical stress, flow of one liquid over another, evaporation of a liquid containing solid in solution that crystallises out, the solidification of a liquid and the application of an electrical stress to a liquid containing dissolved solid. We present a selection of these experiments here; there is nothing special or original about them; it is a matter of trying to explain their formative activities in terms of the principles of *h*K-M.

Forms Produced in a Liquid by Mechanical Stress

We subjected a liquid - oil - to a mechanical stress by pulling apart two glass plates that had a thin layer of oil between them, fig. 26.1(a). As the plates were pulled apart the oil retracted to the narrower region of the gap between the plates in a way that depended on the rate at which the plates were pulled apart.

Oil on its own behaves as a liquid and flows under external forces e.g. when poured out of a container it flows downwards due to the Earth's stress field (force of gravity) but where the oil is in contact with a plate it comes under the influence of the stress field of the rigid glass and in a thin layer between two glass plates the rigidity of the glass stress field extends through it, so that it is in an intermediate state between rigid solid and fluid liquid. When the plates were pulled apart slowly the oil behaved as a liquid and moved as a collective, so that the moving front retracted uniformly back, fig. 26.1(b). But when the glass plates were pulled apart fast, there was insufficient time for the oil to adjust to the stress, so that it behaved like a 'semi-solid' and was 'torn apart' and the retracting front broke down, fig. 26.1(c) and the faster the application of stress, the more break down that occurred, fig. 26.1(d). Because only a simple mechanical stress is involved, this experiment shows unambiguously how stress gives rise to different forms in a simple case and it leads to the inference that, in more complicated situations the forms that arise are due to the underlying stress field.

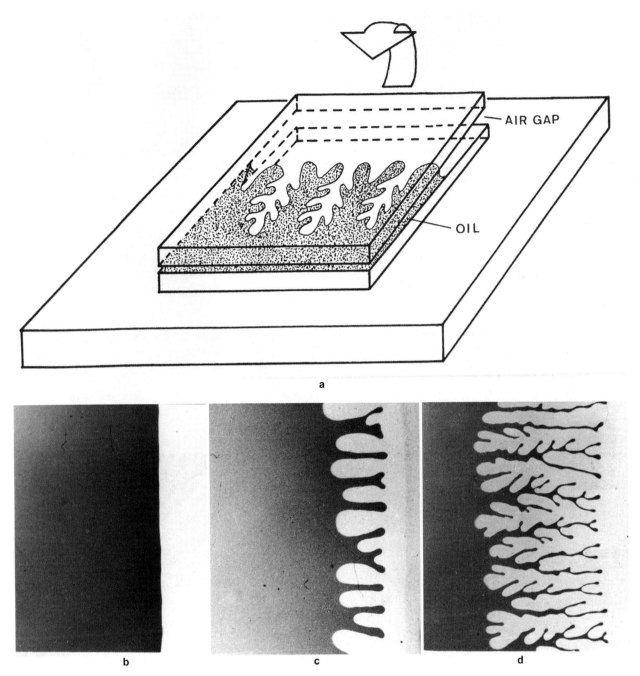

Fig.26.1. (a) The method of applying stress to a film of oil held between two glass plates: (b), (c) and (d) the way in which the moving front of the oil film breaks down under increasing stress.

The Universality of Stress Forms

Before we move onto a detailed consideration of the systems that we investigated, we present results that show that the stress forms observed with the mechanically stressed moving liquid front can be observed in other systems. Thus fig. 26.2(a) shows virtually identical patterns formed at increasing rates of solidification (stress-induced coming together of atoms into the solid state) of a liquid, (in this case the solidification of camphene, which is typical of the way that many substances solidify): fig. 26.2(b) shows patterns of breakdown of the front of a liquid drop spreading out into filter paper at increasing rates: fig 26.2(c) shows patterns made in gas subjected to the stress of an electrical discharge at increasing intensity of the discharge. Although the latter two examples are of circular spreading, the advancing fronts break down in the same way as the planar fronts in figs. 26.1 and 26.2(a).

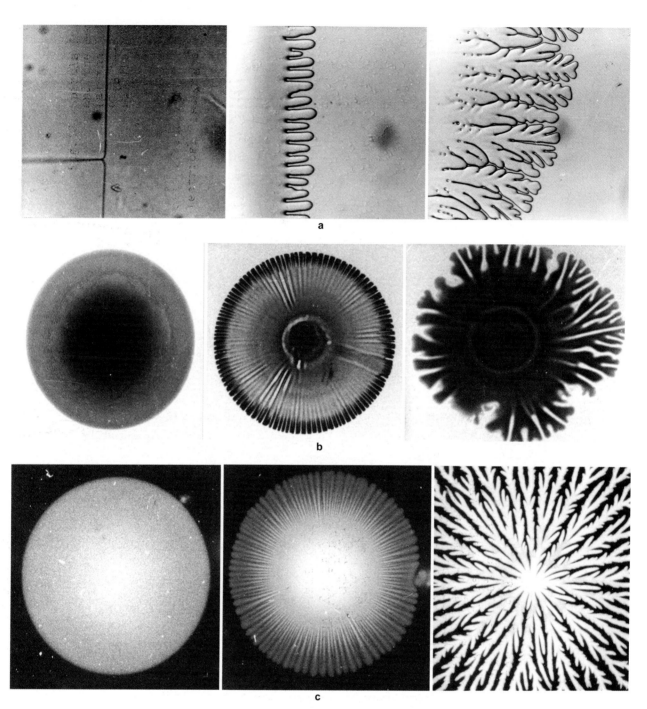

Fig.26.2 (a) Breakdown of the solidification front of camphene at increasing rates of solidification (increasing stress imposed on the liquid-solid front); (b) the breakdown of the front of a spreading drop at increasing rates of advance. (c) electrical discharge patterns obtained under increasing stress.

According to hK-M, the reason why all these patterns show marked similarities is because they are all due to similar patterns of stress in the Earth Entity space energy, acting on the substances involved.

Stress Forms in a Spreading Droplet

We investigated the breakdown of a moving liquid front when a drop of liquid spreads across the surface of a thin layer of another liquid that is on a glass plate, fig. 26.3(a).

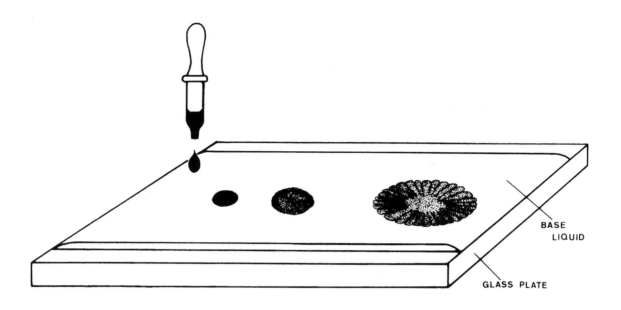

Fig. 26.3(a). The principle of the spreading drop experiments.

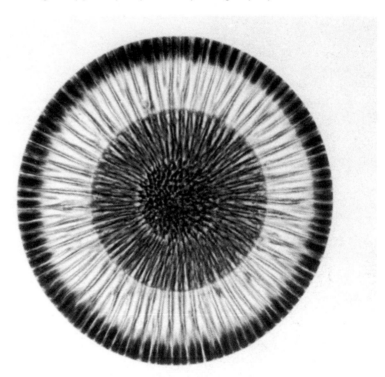

Fig. 26.3(b) The form taken by a drop of water, containing colloidal graphite as a 'marker', spreading on a thin (10^{-2}cms) layer of glycerine.

The transition of the space energy from its state within the droplet to its different state in the air outside creates a stress at their interface, which scientists know as surface tension. This is also the case at the surface of the liquid layer on the glass plate. The behaviour of the drop when it contacts the liquid layer depends on whether its surface stress interacts repulsively or attractively with that of the liquid layer. If the interaction is repulsive then the droplet remains a droplet, as with a drop of water on the surface of oil or vice versa. If the interaction is attractive, (as is the case in the experiments to be described) then the droplet spreads over the surface of the liquid layer. As it does so it creates a stress in the liquid layer by trying to take it with it, but this is held in place by the stress field of the plate, so that there is a stress on the spreading front of the droplet liquid that causes it to break down, (as with the advancing oil front between the two glass plates that are pulled apart), and parts of the front advance while other parts are retarded. The result obtained for a drop of water (containing colloidal graphite as a 'marker' to make its activity visible) spreading on a thin (10^{-2} cm thick) layer of glycerine shows these alternating striations of the advancing and retarded stress/flow, fig. 26.3(b). Where it flows readily the water dilutes the glycerine, which reduces its resistance and this creates a channel along which further water flows preferentially, so that 'fingers of flow' develop. This pattern has a rudimentary flower appearance. (The non-uniform distribution of the graphite is due to interactions between it and the two liquids - similar patterns of the distribution of substances can often be seen in flowers). This stress/flow pattern is similar to that of the breakdown of the gaseous boundary layer of carbon dioxide adjacent to the photoplate, brought about by a negative high-voltage pulse shown in fig. 25.9(b).

When the resistance to the flow of the spreading drop was increased, by replacing the glycerine layer by more viscous water glass (sodium silicate) solution, more of the front was retarded and there were fewer advancing 'fingers', each of which showed extensive side branching fig. 26.4(a). Further increasing the resistance of the layer on which the drop spread, by changing it to gelatine dissolved in water or to a pasty mix of fine alumina powder in water, reduced the number of fingers of flow and the preferential flow along these became more pronounced, figs. 26.4(b) and (c).

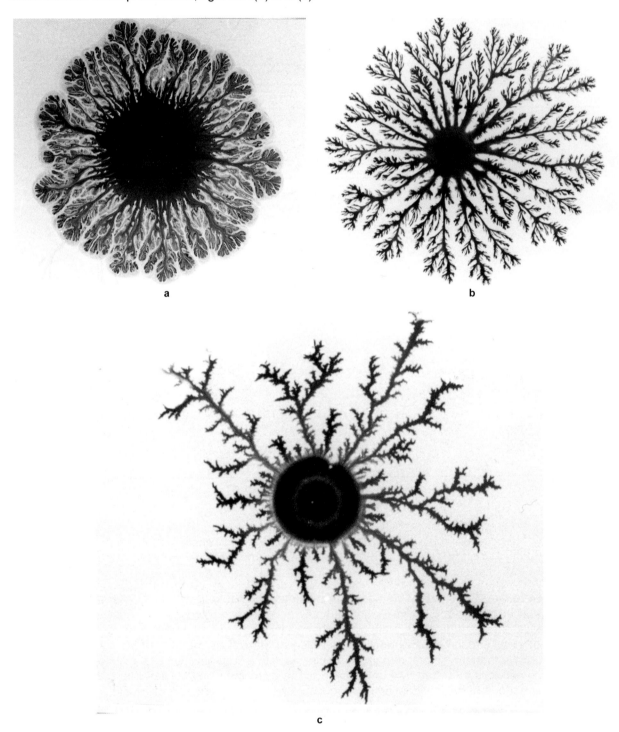

Fig.26.4 The increase in breakdown of the spreading drop caused by increasing the resistance to its flow by changing the layer of liquid on which it spreads from glycerine to (**a**) a more viscous sodium silicate solution, (**b**) gelatine dissolved in water and (**c**) a paste made of alumina powder in water.

Conversely, adding wetting agent to the water drop increased the ease of spreading, with increasing amounts of wetting agent showing a progression from fine, multiple but limited breakdown of the advancing front to more extensive spreading with a smaller number of much larger fingers of flow, fig. 26.5.

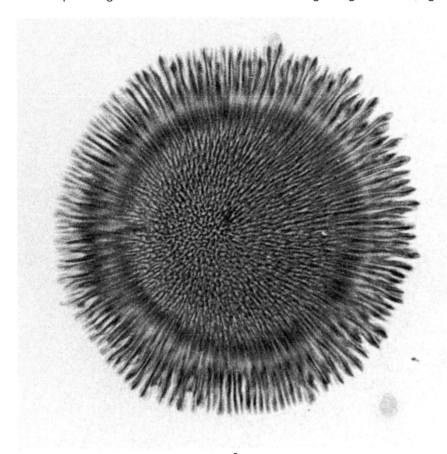

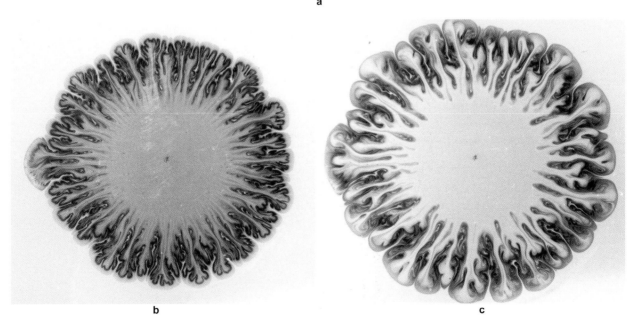

Fig.26.5. (a) to (c). The effect of adding increasing amounts of wetting agent to the droplet water. (In carrying out these experiments it is very important to apply a uniform droplet to a uniform thickness of glycerine layer to get symmetrical spreading. This is quite difficult to do and was not quite achieved in (**b**), which is the cause of the asymmetry in the spreading.

In the experiment with water spreading on a layer of glycerine, the glycerine layer on the glass plate was very thin (10^{-2} cm thick) so that it was held in place by the stress field of the underlying glass plate; as a result there was limited downwards penetration of the water into the glycerine and it therefore spread primarily outwards over the surface. When the glycerine layer was increased in thickness (by a factor of five), the water from the drop penetrated more into it and this resulted in more well-defined channels of flow and more well-defined breakdown of the advancing front, fig. 26.6.

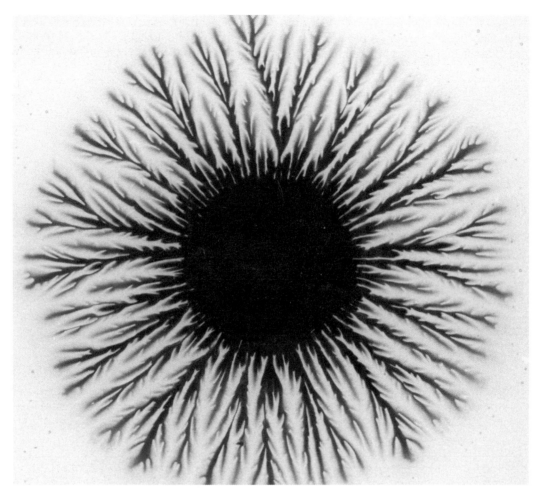

Fig.26.6. The more deeply penetrating and increased differentiation of the flow pattern of the spreading drop resulting from increasing the thickness of the glycerine layer from 1.10^{-2}cms to 5.10^{-2}cms.

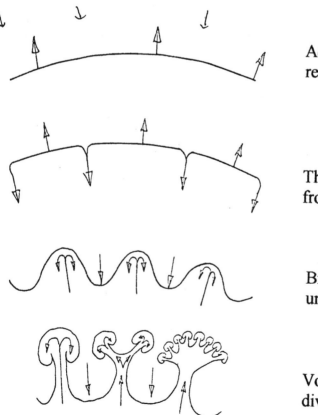

Advancing front encounters resistance

The resistance causes the front to break down

Breakdown gives rise to undulations and vortices

Vortex heads break down and divide by the same principle

Fig.26.7. Diagrammatic illustration of the principle of breakdown of the spreading front, leading to vortex formation and bifurcation.

As with the electrophotography stress forms, these flow patterns resemble rudimentary plant forms but because they develop more slowly than the electrophotography forms, it is possible to observe better how they arise. This is particularly so with the well-defined pattern of breakdown that occurred with water containing wetting agent addition, spreading on glycerine shown in fig 26.5 (b) and (c). What happens is that as the advancing front of the water breaks down into a number of channels the resistance acting along the sides of these slows the flow there, while the flow along the centre continues to advance. This then spreads out sideways to create a vortex head. The resistance acting on the sides of the vortex heads then causes these to bifurcate, fig. 26.7. This process is repeated again and again to cause a multiplicity of bifurcations, giving rise to a 'tree-like' formation. Vortices and their breakdown could also be perceived in some of the other, less extensive, channels of flow. But the formation of a vortex is not essential, the point is that any 'finger' caused by the breakdown of an advancing front is subjected to stresses along its sides, which cause it to split and bifurcate.

The plant, in expressing its will to be active strives to grow upwards to obtain light and warmth, and downwards to obtain the moisture and nutrients that it needs to maintain and enhance its sense of self. This (will/etheric) striving encounters the Earth Entity activity around the Earth, which is more static. Thus the etheric striving of the plant encounters the Earth Entity activity in a way comparable to that of the spreading drop encountering the resistance of the liquid layer on which it is spreading, giving rise to comparable stress forms. In this way the will/etheric striving of the plant creates a stress pattern in the environment that acts on substances to cause them to take up the form of the plant. Thus the forms of figs. 26.4(a) and (b) are akin to those of rudimentary flowers, while that of 26.4(c) is like a bramble.

The spreading drop is, however, not self-actualising and actively striving out of itself. It has been placed in an out-of-balance situation by the experimenter and it simply responds to the forces that then act on it but, in so doing, it manifests the stress-induced formation that arises. Once it has spread in the way that it does, the stress, and thereby the driving force for its movement, is dissipated. The degree of stress arising from the out-of-balance situation is comparable to the degree of inner striving of the plant and the form that this gives rise to is determined by the forces generated by its interaction with its environment.

The plant maintains its activity until it exhausts its will/etheric striving for its sense of self. It then gets a sense of fulfilment that comes to expression in the flower. Mystics state that in the flower the plant touches the astral, i.e. the realm of feelings; this means that the plant does not just exert its will to do something, that gives it a sense of self, but that it gets a rudimentary sense of fulfilment from what it does. When it has exhausted its will to be active the s-pressurised Earth Entity activity becomes dominant and clamps down on it and the plant substances revert to a 'dead' state. But the memory of its experience of sense of self remains in the EM-energy and as it closes down it retains a connection with this in the genetic configuration of the substances in the seed. Then, when the environmental conditions activate the seed, this reawakens this memory and its will to grow which it does according to the etheric striving (stress) pattern by which it did this before.

Forms in Capillary Dynamolysis

These experiments were concerned with investigating the role of substances in the creation of different types of forms, using the interaction between a flow of water or aqueous solutions, and substances. The experimental technique was to run a solution of the substance to be investigated, through a filter paper on a glass dish, from a central 'wick', fig. 26.8.

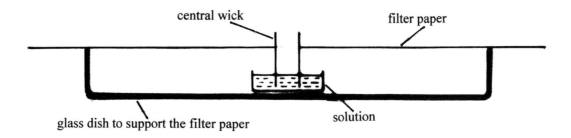

Fig. 26.8. The experimental arrangement for the capillary dynamolysis experiments.

The filter paper was then dried leaving the substance in it in a dispersed solid form and another liquid was run through it and the effect on the flow of this due to the presence of the substance observed. The following examples illustrate the types of behaviour that occurred.

Fig. 26.9. The disc of manganese sulphate deposit produced by a 12.5wt% solution, as the first stage of the experiment.

Fig. 26.9 shows the circular distribution of substance, in this case manganese sulphate, produced by the first run through. The solution and the area it spread through were colourless and to show the area of flow it has been exposed to ammonia vapour (as were the results of all experiments with manganese sulphate) which has caused it to darken.

In the simplest experiment, distilled water was used as the second liquid. As this spread out through the impregnated filter paper it dissolved the manganese sulphate. This manganese sulphate solution then continued to flow out followed by further distilled water flowing through filter paper now denuded of manganese sulphate. The manganese sulphate solution ahead of the distilled water then created a resistance to its flow. As a result the advancing front of the distilled water broke down, developing a vortex pattern, fig. 26.10, (in a similar way to that of the advancing front of the spreading drop in fig. 26.5), thereby sweeping the manganese sulphate solution aside and behind it.

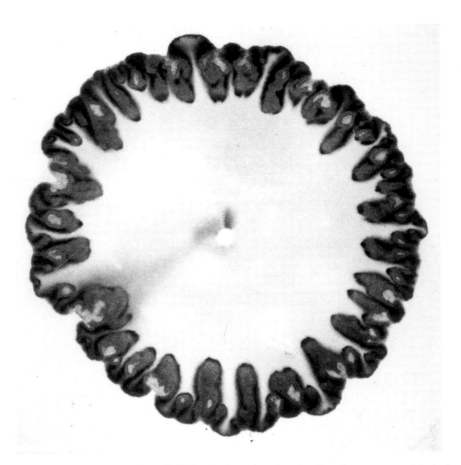

Fig.26.10. The vortex-type pattern that arose when distilled water flowed out into the disc of manganese sulphate deposit produced by a 12.5wt% solution, shown in fig. 26.9. The spreading front of distilled water has broken down into 'fingers' that have divided and swept back the manganese sulphate solution at their peripheries.

However, breakdown of the advancing front did not always occur, depending on the chemical that was used to impregnate the filter paper before flowing distilled water through it. With filter paper impregnated with potassium dichromate the distilled water flowed out uniformly, pushing the potassium dichromate ahead of it, to give a smooth advancing front, fig. 26.11.

Fig.26.11. The more uniform front of distilled water spreading into filter paper previously treated with a solution of 10wt% potassium dichromate and then dried.

An intermediate type of behaviour was observed with potassium ferricyanide, in which the advancing front broke down into a series of undulations, without vortex formation, fig. 26.12.

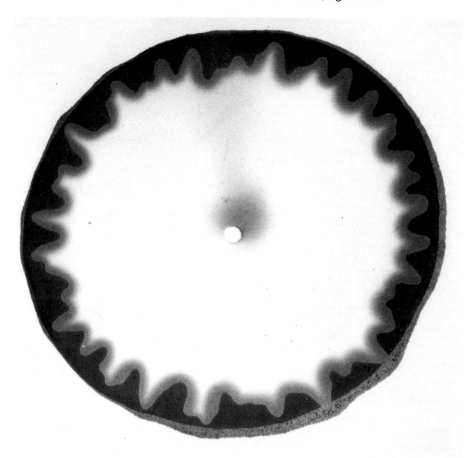

Fig.26.12. The 'fingered' front of distilled water spreading into filter paper treated with 15wt% potassium ferricyanide solution.

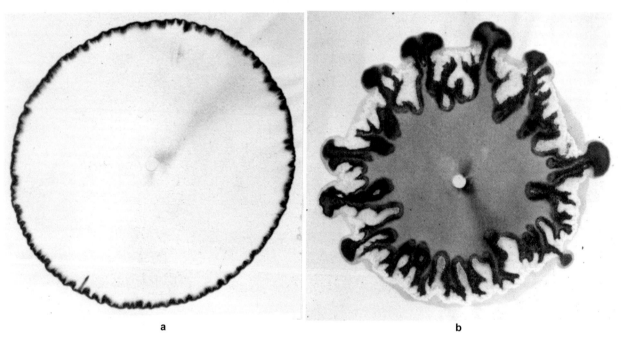

a   b

Fig.26.13. (a) The slight breakdown of the front of distilled water spreading into filter paper treated with 0.75wt% manganese sulphate solution. (b) The strongly differentiated front of distilled water spreading into filter paper treated with 30wt% manganese sulphate solution.

The degree of breakdown depended on the concentration of the substance in the solution that was first run through the filter paper. Thus fig. 26.13(a) shows the small breakdown of the advancing front with only 0.75wt% manganese sulphate and fig. 26.13(b) the much greater breakdown that occurred with 30wt%, which also shows clearly the 'mushroom-shape' of the vortex heads. All of the patterns could be changed by changing the concentration of the substance used in the first run through.

The factor that seemed to determine the breakdown of the spreading front of the distilled water was the affinity between the pre-deposited chemical and the filter paper. With the manganese sulphate type of breakdown, as the filter paper subsequently dried out the manganese sulphate was deposited as a matrix within the fibres of the filter paper, fig. 26.14(a).

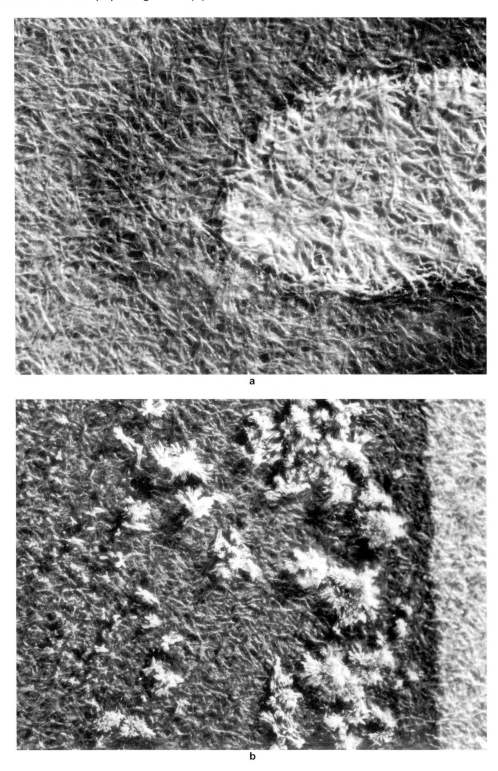

a

b

Fig.26.14. After the distilled water at the spreading front has flowed through and dissolved the manganese sulphate deposit, when the filter paper subsequently dries the manganese sulphate deposits out as a matrix within the fibres of the filter paper, (a), while potassium dichromate deposits on the surface of the filter paper, (b).

With potassium dichromate, where there was a smooth spreading front, as the filter paper dried out it was deposited on the surface of the filter paper, fig. 26.14(b). Thus for the distilled water to spread out it had to dissolve the manganese sulphate that blocked its flow, whereas with the potassium dichromate it could flow past it.

In other experiments, instead of running distilled water through the filter paper as the second liquid, an aqueous solution of another chemical was used, which reacted with the first chemical to produce deposits of substance in the filter paper, two examples of which are shown in fig. 26.15.

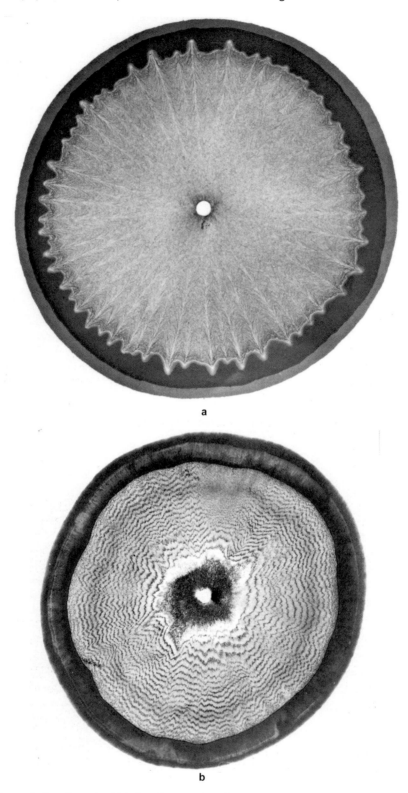

a

b

Fig.26.15. Capillary dynamolysis patterns in which there is a reaction of the substance in the second liquid with that in the first liquid, showing periodic precipitation that marks out the stress pattern. (a) First solution 15 wt% potassium ferricyanide second solution 15 wt% cobalt nitrate. (b) First solution 15 wt% potassium chromate, second solution 15 wt% manganese sulphate.

The deposits occurred in regular, often banded, patterns. This sort of periodicity is quite common with chemical reactions. Our suggested explanation for it is that as the second solution advances it dissolves the deposits laid down by the first solution until the build up of the two chemicals creates stresses in the space-energy/liquid combination beyond what it can accommodate, then the substances are rejected and become trapped in these regions. This relieves the stress in the second flow that dissolves more of the deposits of the first chemical and the build up of stress followed by the deposition process is then repeated, giving rise to deposits that outline the stress pattern. In some cases the deposits broke down the flow of the second liquid so that it divided into channels, which subsequently spread sideways to come together again, fig. 26.16.

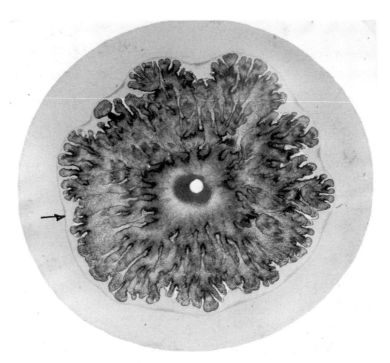

Fig.26.16. An example of a pattern where the deposit produced by the interaction between the chemicals in the two flows of solution caused the second flow to break down into subsidiary flows which then spread sideways to come together again. First solution 10 wt% potassium ferricyanide, second solution 10 wt% copper sulphate.

Processes of this nature could be a significant factor in producing flower forms, e.g. as in fig. 26.17.

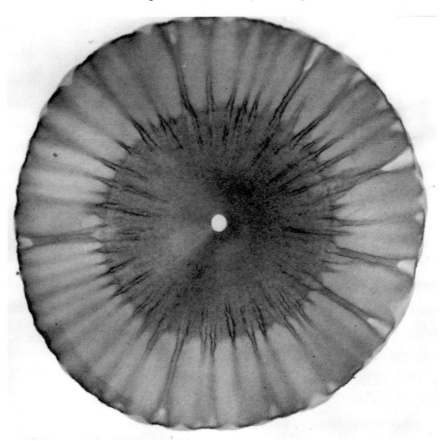

Fig.26.17. A 'flower form' pattern produced by the interaction of two dilute solutions. First solution 1 wt% ferric chloride, second solution 1 wt% potassium ferricyanide.

In further experiments, instead of running the liquids through filter paper we ran them through a thin layer (12 x 10^{-3} cm) of various pastes deposited and then dried on a glass plate. A hole was made in the glass plate to accommodate a filter paper wick. Figs. 26.18(a-c) show some results obtained with potassium dichromate solution (10 wt%) run through various pastes, allowed to dry and followed by distilled water. With a paste made of silica gel powder, the spreading front of the distilled water was largely uniform, but with some small undulations, fig. 26.18(a). With a paste of aluminium oxide powder it took on the 'fingered' pattern of breakdown, fig. 26.18(b). With cellulose powder paste part of the potassium dichromate was dissolved and swept into the advancing front of the distilled water and outlined a pattern of vortex heads but some of it was left behind where it had been swept into the 'neutral' zones between the advancing vortex heads, thus giving a pattern of radiating striations, fig. 26.18(c).

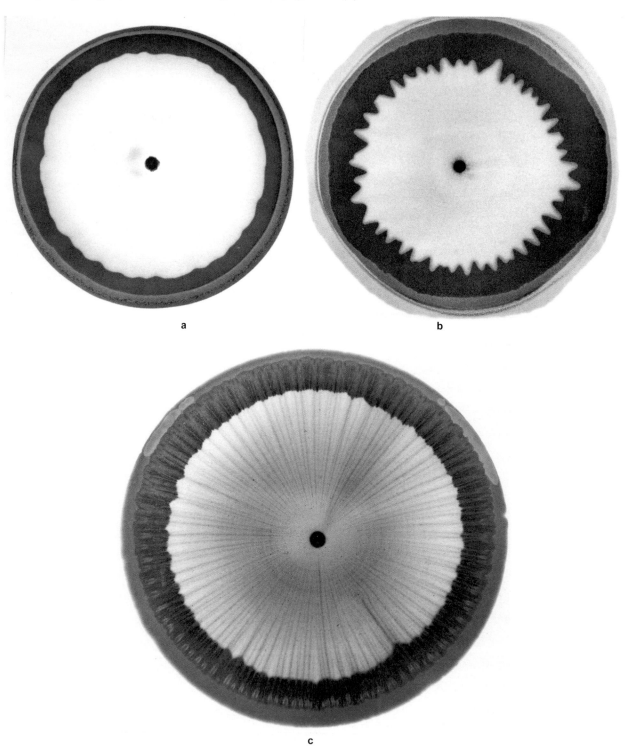

a   b

c

Fig.26.18. Capillary dynamolysis patterns produced by running distilled water through a layer of dried paste on a glass plate that had been impregnated with 10 wt% potassium dichromate solution. (**a**) With a paste of silica gel. (**b**) With a paste of aluminium oxide. (**c**) With a paste of cellulose powder.

The effect of changing the resistance of the paste layer was examined by changing its thickness. Figs.26.19(a-c) show the effect of reducing the thickness of a silica gel paste laid down on the glass plate and a first solution of 15 wt% cobalt nitrate run through it followed (after drying) by 15 wt% potassium ferricyanide solution. The thicker layer, $(5 \times 10^{-2} cm)$, which presented the least resistance to flow (less effect of the rigidity of the underlying glass plate), gave a more or less uniform spreading front but with an inner zone delineating a region of chemical reaction and deposition that showed small undulations, fig. 26.19(a). A reduction in thickness to 15×10^{-3} cm resulted in a strongly fragmented front that appeared to arise from undulations in the inner reaction zone, with deposition outlining the breakdown leading from the inner to the outer front, fig. 26.19(b); there was also a further less well defined inner zone. With the thinnest layer (6×10^{-3} cm) the inner zone has caused a breakdown of the spreading front into a petalled formation with a sort of 'fringe' of deposition bands at the periphery, fig. 26.19(c).

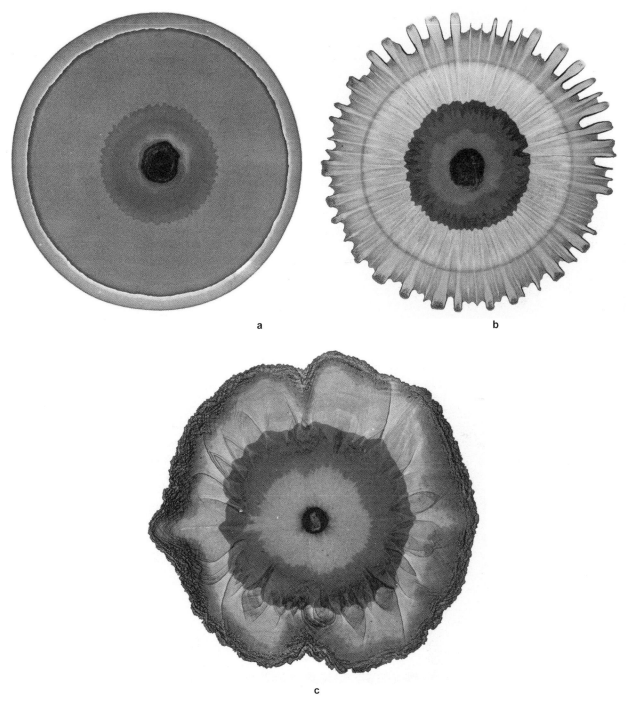

a   b

c

Fig.26.19. The effect of decreasing the thickness of a layer of silica gel paste on the glass plate and thereby increasing the resistance to flow. In this case the first solution was 15 wt% cobalt nitrate and the second solution 15 wt% potassium ferricyanide. (**a**) Paste layer 50×10^{-3} cm thick, (**b**) 15×10^{-3} cm, (**c**) 6×10^{-3} cm.

The point about the spreading drop and capillary dynamolysis experiments is that they demonstrate how the sort of forms that we see in plants can arise from stress fields in the Earth Entity activity and furthermore how, as with plants, a great many variations on the basic spreading-out form arise with changes in the substances involved and the environmental conditions. In our experiments the stress fields have been brought about by setting up a centre that creates an imbalance and a stress from which events develop, the drop or the wick. In plants there is a self-actualising centre which, in order to maintain and enhance its sense of self, creates striving etheric forces that spread outwards into its environment and it is the way that this spreading-outwards force interacts with the Earth Entity activity and the substances of the environment that gives rise to the forms that it produces and at the same time determines the distribution of substances. The forms of plants and animals can be affected by a deficiency or excess of substances in the soil or substances of their nutrition, even at the level of trace elements. It may be that experiments of the type that we have described could lead to principles of form production that would throw light on these matters. In these experiments there is a wealth of information on how plant-like forms are created in the mineral kingdom but to correlate the forces and factors involved with those active in plant growth requires an expertise and depth of understanding that we do not possess.

A self-actualising centre seeking to maintain/enhance its sense of self creates forces that act on, and determine the disposition of, substances that give rise to the genetic structures of organisms. However, the genetic distribution of substances is only half the story of the form and function of an organism; it needs the pattern of will activity expressed as etheric forces that moves substances to complete the picture.

On a larger, cosmic scale the stress fields of the Sun, Moon and other planets produce changes in the Earth Entity activity that manifest in the capillary dynamolysis patterns that we referred to in Chapter 18.

The Crystallisation of Copper Chloride

Steiner suggested crystallisation experiments as a way of revealing etheric force activity. Following this suggestion, using the crystallisation of copper chloride, ENQUIST carried out experiments in which she sought to reveal the inner qualities of plants, and found effects of light and shade and soil type and processes involved in germination, storage after harvesting, growth to ripeness and beyond. PFEIFFER applied the technique to the diagnosis of the human condition by the admixture of minute quantities of a subject's blood with the crystallising solution and, working with hospital physicians, claimed to make accurate diagnoses from the crystal patterns. This applied, not only to the subject's physical condition, because on three occasions Pfeiffer had schizophrenic subjects and in each case the crystal pattern was divided into two independent parts. Pfeiffer also studied the action of homoeopathic remedies on these patterns and claimed that a homoeopathic remedy could harmonise a disharmonised blood pattern. SELAWRY studied in detail the crystallisation process and its application to the study of human disorders and characterised many of the features involved. In the light of this work, as we reported in Part III, we took up the crystallisation of copper chloride as a method for investigating etheric forces and shape-forming processes.

In our overview of experimental work in Chapter 19, where we described the events that led us to hK-M, we gave some account of these researches. They centred on trying to understand the forces that gave rise to the crystallisation forms of copper chloride and the effects of various additions. The ECEs put forward the view that the needle form of copper chloride crystals represents a balance between the copper seeking to form a compact cube and the chlorine striving spherically outwards to form a gas, giving rise to the compromise of a radiating pattern of needles, (fig. 19.3). In the experimental result that was presented in Chapter 19, (of a drop of 1% copper chloride solution crystallising on a glass plate, fig. 19.2), the crystallisation pattern was of a comparatively random array of nuclei from many of which various configurations of needles radiated. Of the different additions that we made we showed a result when we added iron chloride, which strengthened and organised the radiating groups of needles, (fig. 19.4) and the effect of adding a tincture of mercurialis plant, which resulted in a high degree of overall organisation, (fig. 19.5). Here we give a more detailed account of these researches.

As we have stated, the ECEs claimed that copper chloride forms needles as a balance between the contracting, cube-forming activity of the copper and the spherical, outwards gas-forming activity of chlorine. On this view it might be expected that all metal chlorides would form needles but this is not so; for example, under our experimental conditions sodium and magnesium chlorides formed cubes, whereas chlorides of nickel, chromium, lithium, calcium and iron tended to form amorphous deposits without crystalline features. From the ECE viewpoint this could be interpreted as due to differences in the balance between the compacting, cube-forming activity and the dispersive gas-forming activity, fig. 26.20, with sodium and magnesium showing a dominance of the metal cube-forming nature, fig. 26.20(b), and chromium, lithium calcium and iron showing a dominance of the chlorine dispersing nature, fig 26.20(c). However, these results can only be regarded as specific to our experimental conditions because of the underlying influence of the stress field of the glass plate on which they were carried out.

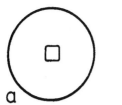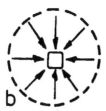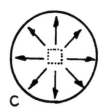

Fig. 26.20. A schematic representation of the range of interactions available to a cube and a sphere; **a** The starting point; a cube within a sphere; **b** The sphere is grasped by the condensing forces of the cube and pulled entirely within the cube; this gives rise to cubic crystals; **c** The cube is expanded outwards by the sphere, to fill it; this gives rise to non-crystalline, amorphous deposits; **d** A balanced interaction between the contracting and expanding forces, to create a radiating array of needles.

The patterns formed by drops of copper chloride solution of different concentrations, crystallising on a glass plate are shown in fig. 26.21. A 95% solution spread over the plate and, because of the high level of saturation, with very little evaporation it crystallised, to give rise to a mass of needle outgrowths in bushy formations, with very little left in the middle, fig. 26.21(a). A 10% solution retracted on the glass plate until it reached saturation and started to crystallise and then formed a solid mass of needles, fig. 26.21(b). A 1% solution started to crystallise at the edge of the droplet, where it first dried out, as rosettes of needles which pinned the droplet there, and then a mixture of rosettes, long straight needles and small crystals developed over the whole area, fig.26.21(c). This variation in the configurations of the copper chloride is comparable to the variations that a plant can take up in relation to its environment, e.g. alpine or lowland, dry or swampy, which in some cases vary from dense ground hugging to large and/or dispersed bushes.

Fig.26.21. The crystallisation patterns produced by drops of various dilutions of copper chloride solution on a glass plate; (a) 95% solution showing strong outwards growth of bush-like arrays of needles; (b) 10% solution showing the contraction of the drop before crystallisation starts and the subsequent tightly packed needles; (c) 1% solution. Rosettes of needles have formed at the edge and pinned the drop there, while a mixture of rosettes, long straight needles and small crystals have formed within the drop.

The stress fields responsible for the crystallisation patterns arise as the water in the copper chloride solution evaporates to a point at which there is too much copper chloride for the liquid/EM-energy combination to accommodate. If the solution is kept very still in a smooth surfaced glass dish and it is extremely free of extraneous dust or other solid particles, so that initiation of crystallisation is difficult, the water can be slowly evaporated off until the degree of supersaturation with excess substance creates a high level of stress in the liquid/EM-energy combination, which builds up until it 'cracks'. Then, when 'fracture' occurs, it does so extremely rapidly: there is very little time for any internal adjustments to take place and crystallisation follows the fracture path, looking like fracture in a brittle material, like glass. If on the other hand there is disturbance that stops the build up of stress, so that the substance crystallises as soon as there is excess copper chloride in the solution, small crystals form, which relieve the stress in that area, so that crystallisation stops until further evaporation builds up further stress and crystallisation starts again in a new region of stress. If there is an intermediate situation, in which some degree of stress builds up before crystallisation, but less than that which gives rise to 'glass cracks', then small regions of 'rosette cracks' occur - the sort of cracking pattern that occurs in a stiff material with some flexibility, such as toffee.

In the dilute, 1% solution all three types of crystallisation can be seen, (fig. 26.21(c). As evaporation has taken place around the edge of the drop, localised stress has built up in the EM-energy to form rosette crystals that have pinned the droplet there. Then as the water has evaporated from the main body of the droplet a stress has built up that has stressed the liquid/Earth Entity space-energy combination until it has 'cracked', to give rise to the long straight 'glass crack-like' needles. This has left regions with a reduced level of copper chloride where small crystals have then formed with the localised toffee-like crack configuration. This delicate balance of crystallisation of the 1% copper chloride solution makes it susceptible to, and thereby to show up, the effects of any changes imposed on it and the effects of additives.

[This pattern of behaviour, i.e. of seeking to maintain the status quo while a stress for change builds up until this takes place, either gradually or dramatically, is common in evolutionary developments be these biological, emotional or in ways of thinking].

The stress relationship between the drop and the environment of the glass plate also plays a part in determining the crystallisation pattern that forms because of the part played by the stress field of the plate acting on the drop. Fig 26.21(a) showed that with the 95% solution, this relationship caused the droplet liquid to spread over the glass plate, to give bushy outgrowths of needles, whereas with the 10% solution the droplet contracted, to give the solid mass of needle crystals, fig. 26.21(b). With the 95% solution crystallising on perspex/lucite instead of glass, the droplet did not spread and there were no outgrowths. With a glass plate that had been dipped in a detergent solution (Teepol) and dried, to promote spreading, the outgrowths were more spread out with the 95% solution and the contraction of the drop with the 10% solution was eliminated, giving a free, spaced-out pattern of crystals similar to, but denser than, the 1% solution,

We increased the rate of stress build up by changing the medium in which the copper chloride was dissolved, from water to methanol which evaporates more rapidly and we further increased the rate of evaporation by heating the solution. With a high concentration of copper chloride (95%), there was a multiplicity of crystallisation stress centres and rounded crystals formed throughout the drop, fig. 26.22.

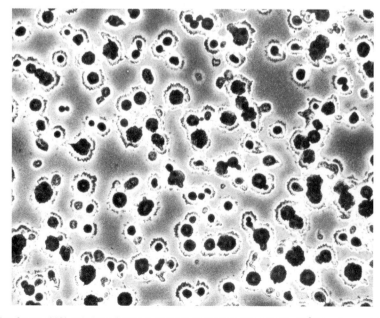

Fig.26.22. Crystallisation from a 95% solution of copper chloride in methanol heated to 50°C to give rapid crystallisation, showing rounded forms which at higher magnification are seen to consist of dense rosettes of needles, x13.

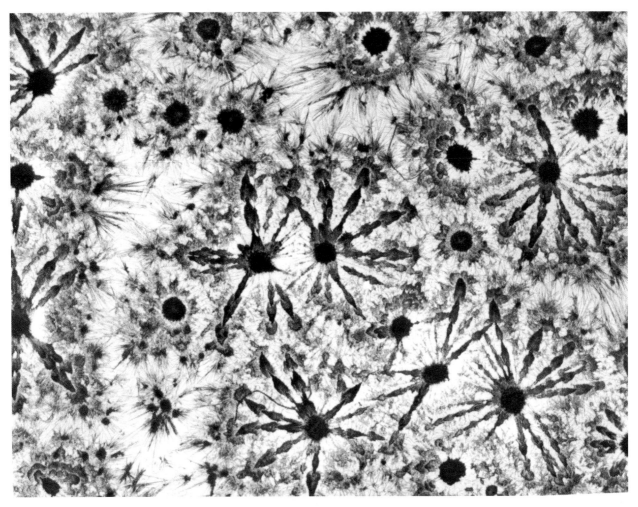

Fig.26.23. Crystallisation as fig. 26.22 but at room temperature, showing rosettes with arrow-like needles growing out from them, x 13.

Looking at these at high magnification they were seen to comprise dense, compact rosette patterns of needles. At the slower rate of crystallisation that took place at room temperature there was the opportunity for stresses to alleviate, so that there were fewer centres of growth, with more developed rosettes, in which needles had formed a sequence of arrow-head formations, fig. 26.23. These suggested a 'pulsing' of crystallisation as a result of a sequential build up and release of stress between the developing crystals and the EM-energy/liquid combination.

In our examination of the effects of additions to the copper chloride solution, we tried adding lactose, a sugary substance the common name for which is sugar of milk. We used two levels of concentration of lactose in the crystallising solution and we also examined the effect of changing the rate of evaporation by looking at the results obtained at two levels of humidity. At the higher concentration of lactose and higher rate of evaporation (conditions most conducive to crystallisation), the crystallisation of the copper chloride was totally suppressed and a sticky deposit formed.

With the same evaporating conditions the lower concentration of lactose suppressed a lot of the 'random' crystallisation, (that occurred without the lactose (fig. 26.21(c)) and resulted in fewer centres from each of which a mass of fine crystal needles grew radially, with a 'tabby cat' pattern, possibly due to a periodic build up of stress caused by the presence of the lactose, fig. 26.24(a). At this same concentration of lactose but with a decreased rate of evaporation and hence slower crystallisation that allowed readjustments to occur there were fewer centres with strong needles growing from them, that created more unified or homogeneous patterns, fig. 26.24(b).

a

b

Fig.26.24. The effect of lactose concentration and humidity (rate of crystallisation) on the crystallisation of 1% copper chloride solution. (a) With 0.02 molar concentration of lactose and humidity of 25% a number of nucleation centres has formed from which patterns of very fine radiating needles have developed. (b) At an increased humidity of 44%, (slower rate of crystallisation) for the same concentration of lactose as in a, there are fewer centres with stronger crystals radiating from them, x5.

In the examples of our experiments that we presented in our exposition of the path that our work has followed, (in Chapter 19), we showed a result where we added iron chloride to the copper chloride, which 'strengthened' the pattern of needles, (fig. 19.4). At that time we were pursuing the idea that strength is a basic contribution of iron in Nature, (e.g. iron is the main constituent of steel and lack of iron in the human

374

being leads to anaemia). We found that the addition of iron overcame the suppression of the copper chloride crystallisation by lactose and crystals formed where otherwise they did not occur, fig. 26.25(a), and strengthened crystallisation where it was weak, fig. 26.25(b). This was despite the fact that the level of iron chloride that we used (10%), on its own formed a non-crystalline, amorphous deposit.

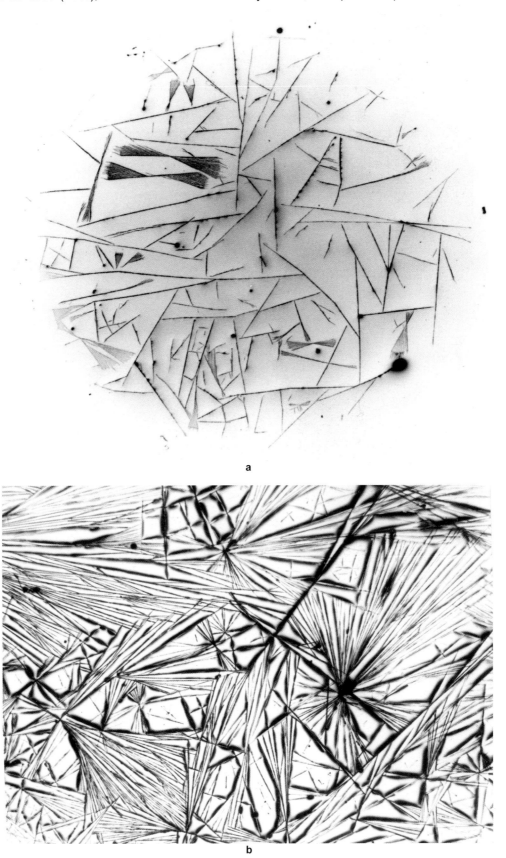

a

b

Fig.26.25 The effect of adding iron chloride ($FeCl_3$) to the lactose-containing solution; (**a**) 0.67% copper chloride in 0.02 molar lactose with 10% ferric chloride, x5. The lactose completely suppresses the crystallisation of the copper chloride at this low level, but the addition of the iron chloride has brought about the formation of thin but firm needles; (**b**) 1% copper chloride in 0.02 molar lactose with an addition of 10% iron chloride, x15. Here the iron chloride has produced an array of stronger needles.

The Addition of a Plant Extract

A plant is a self-actualising centre of activity (a plant I) that seeks to maintain/enhance its sense of self by channelling etheric flows from the Sun and Earth, that act on substances to create its substance form. When a piece of plant is disconnected from its I it comprises a cut off or 'frozen' part of the pattern of the stress/activity created by the plant's etheric striving and substance interaction. As it decays away or is consumed by an organism the etheric stresses disperse and the substances revert to their prior dead mineral state. If they are absorbed into a living organism they can affect the activity of this; if they are added to a non-living situation such as a crystallising solution they can modify what would otherwise be taking place in a way that is manifest by the effect that they have, which in turn could show something about the nature and behaviour of the plant.

Following on the work of Enquist, we added a number of plant extracts to a 1% copper chloride solution to see if the crystallisation patterns showed the formative forces that gave rise to the plants. We present a selection of these in figs 26.26 and 26.27.

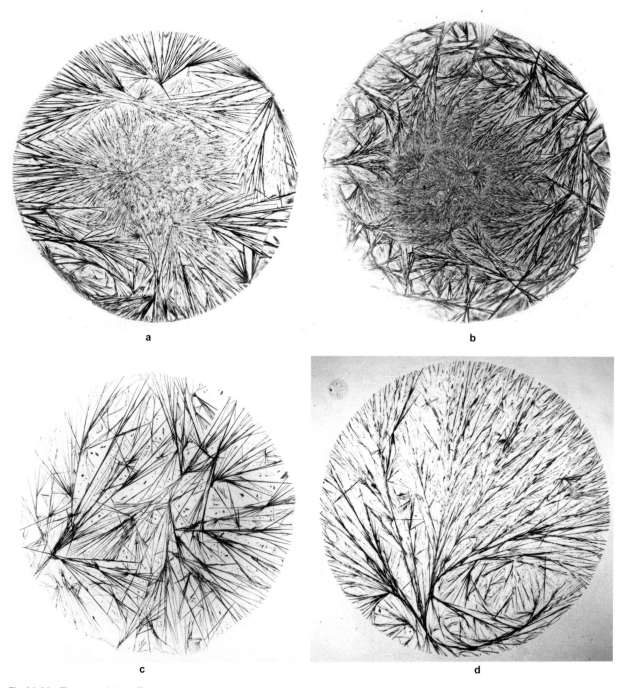

Fig.26.26. The organising effect on the crystallisation pattern of adding 10 drops of plant tincture to a 1% solution of copper chloride. (a) Archangelica x5, (b) Arnica x5, (c) Annanassae (pineapple) x5, (d) Chelidonium x4; (we showed the result for Mercurialis in fig. 16.5). These patterns should be compared with that where no addition was made, fig. 26.21(c).

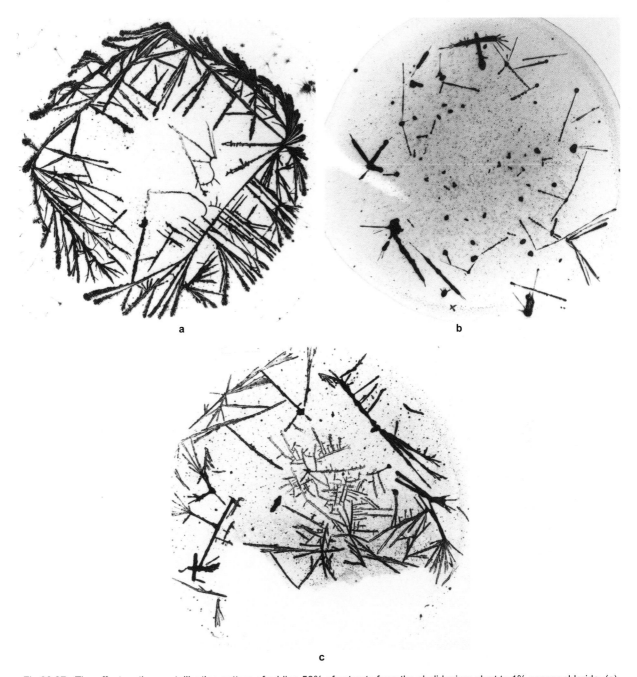

a

b

c

Fig.26.27. The effect on the crystallisation pattern of adding 50% of extracts from the chelidonium plant to 1% copper chloride, (**a**) extract from the root, (**b**) extract from the flower, (**c**) extract from the whole plant, which incorporates the root and flower forms of (a) and (b). All x 5.

They all have a marked effect on the crystallisation pattern and make it more unified. How much of this is due to etheric force activity associated with the plants and how much to the substances in them is not clear. We found that we could mimic some of the plant extract features by chemical additions to the crystallising solutions. Thus we obtained curved crystals by adding a small amount of glycerine to the copper chloride solution, fig. 26.28, plant extract-like patterns with certain levels of addition of iron chloride, fig. 26.29, and an overall organisation, by adding triethanolamine to the crystallising solution, fig. 26.30.

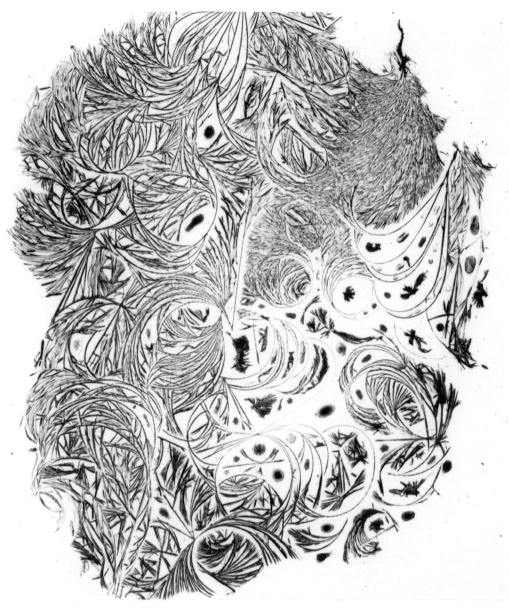

Fig.26.28. The curving of the needle crystals that occurred with the addition of 1.5% glycerine to 1% copper chloride solution.

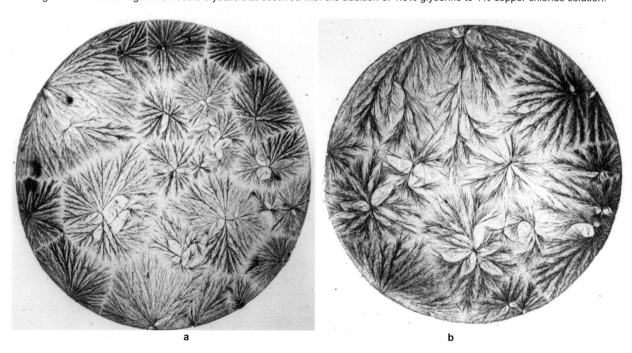

a   b

Fig.26.29. Examples of forms produced by the addition of various amounts of ferric chloride to the crystallising 1% copper chloride solution; (a) 0.0033 g/ml; (b). 0.005g/ml; (c) 0.010 g/ml.

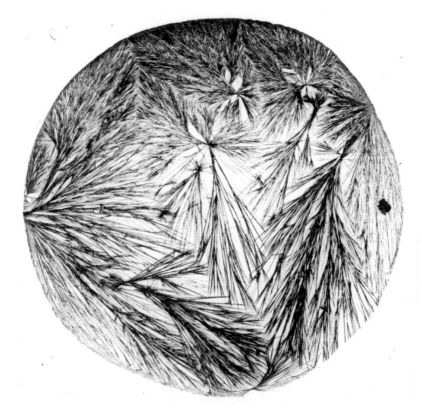

Fig.26.29(c)

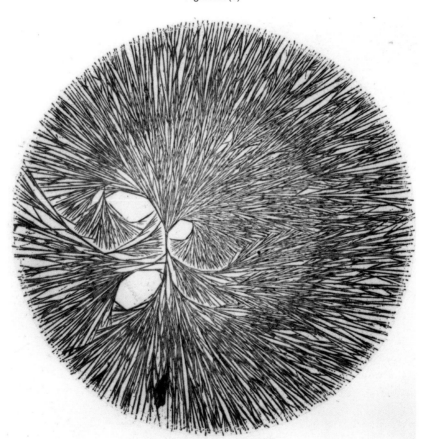

Fig.26.30. The overall organisation that occurred when triethanolamine was added to the crystallising copper chloride solution at a concentration of 1ml/60ml

In experiments with crystallisation from various alcohols we used a range of dilutions and crystallising conditions and got a variety of results. One result, 10% copper chloride in methanol, fig. 26.31, spanned many of the types of forms that we observed and it can be seen that these are akin to living forms that we see in Nature.

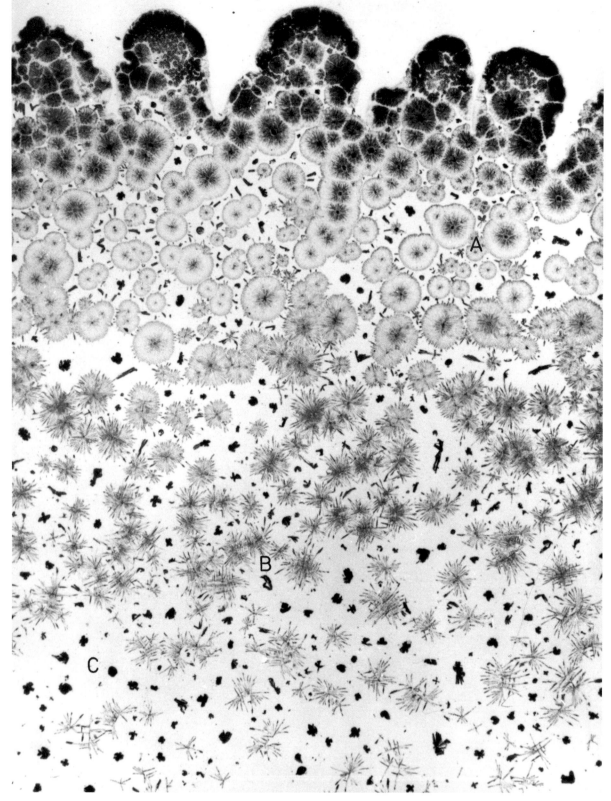

Fig.26.31. The crystallisation pattern obtained with a 10% solution of copper chloride in methanol.

These results show that the shape-forming forces of Nature can be examined by simple crystallisation experiments and that, according to the results of PFEIFFER, SELAWRY and ENQUIST this could have useful practical benefits. In our work we barely scratched at the surface of what could be a very rewarding field for investigation.

The Crystallisation of Ammonium Chloride

We looked at the crystallisation of ammonium chloride by making a saturated solution in water at a raised temperature of 35°C and then, through a microscope, watching it crystallise as it cooled down. This is a system that is often used to simulate the solidification of metals. Although a metal looks featureless it does in fact have a complex internal crystal structure but because of its opacity how this develops during solidification cannot be seen but only the end result observed by etching the surface and viewing it under a microscope. Since what is then seen is often similar to the crystal structures of ammonium chloride, it is assumed that the processes taking place during the solidification of a metal are similar to those that can be observed in the crystallisation of a transparent solution of ammonium chloride.

This system is simpler than the crystallisation experiments described previously, making it possible to discern more clearly the shape-forming processes that are at work. To do this we need first to reiterate some basic features of *h*K-M. According to *h*K-M, the dominant force in the Universe is the s-pressure that acts on all things to reduce their presence. This results in it causing atoms of substance to come together but as they do so the stress fields that they create in the Earth Entity space-energy interact and as they get closer this interaction builds up until it equals and opposes the s-pressure. The s-pressure operating uniformly from all directions acts to cause substances to take up spherical configurations, as it does with the collective of substances that make up the Earth planet and it acts similarly on isolated quantities of atoms, where these form a collective, as in a droplet of water which results in its spherical configuration. However, the stress fields of atoms (that are a manifestation of their individual characteristics) are not uniformly spherical and when they are forced into close proximity to form a solid, they fit together according to their natures. When atoms form solids this mostly results in them coming together in cubic crystal formations. Thus when ammonium chloride crystallises it forms a solid cubic structure. But this forces the Earth Entity space-energy in the liquid around the cube into this form, whereas its nature is to be spherical, as when liquids form drops. Our observations showed a conflict between these two tendencies and that the ammonium chloride crystal nuclei formed first as spheres, showing the dominance of the spheroidal-liquid-forming tendency, fig. 26.32(a). But then 'corners' developed on these spheres as the cubic-forming tendency of the solid ammonium chloride took over, fig. 26.32(b). The corners, penetrating into the liquid zone then acted like a 'chisel', to create a stress in it which caused the further crystallisation of the ammonium chloride to follow this direction. Thus spheres with outgrowths developed, figs. 26.32(c) and 26.33(a). The outgrowths at first were rod-like, showing a compromise between growing in the stress direction and forming a succession of spheres, to give rise to rods, fig. (26.32(c)). But the tendency for the ammonium chloride to form cubes caused the sequence of spheres that made up the 'rods' to develop 'corners' that created stresses in the Earth Entity energy, to give rise to the formation of secondary, rod-like 'side arms' that developed cubic protrusions fig. 26.32(d).

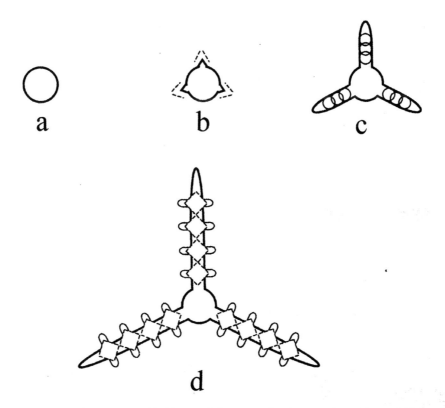

Fig 26.32. Stages of development of ammonium chloride growth forms, starting from a sphere (**a**), on which 'crystal corners' develop (**b**). The corners create a stress that causes further crystallisation to follow this direction while the nature of the liquid into which it is growing acts to create a sphere, so that the arms take on the form of rods (**c**). However, the cube-forming stresses of the ammonium chloride cause crystal corners to develop along the arms (**d**) and these create stresses to give rise to secondary arms, on which further 'crystal corners' develop to give rise to tertiary arms. (This explanation for the ammonium chloride forms that we observed, as a 'battle' between liquid spherical formations and solid cubic formations is akin to Steiner's chemical ether liquid forms and life ether cubic forms, described in Chapter 19).

Fig.26.33(a) The primary arm stage of ammonium chloride crystal formation. Six arms have formed from the spherical nucleus, three growing 'upwards' that can be clearly seen and three growing 'downwards' that are out of focus, x ~ 150.

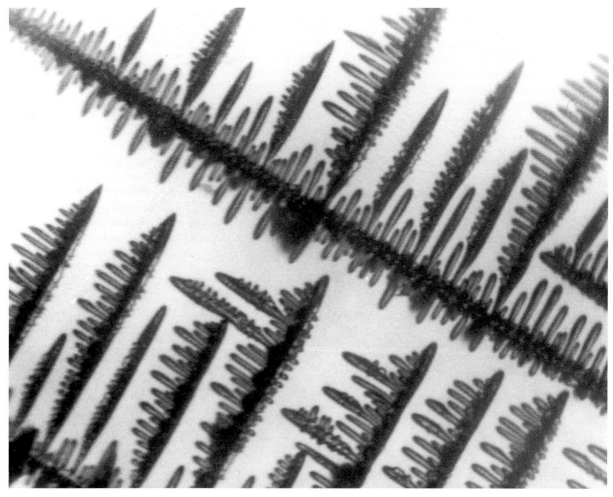

Fig.26.33(b) Part of a well-formed ammonium chloride primary-secondary-tertiary dendritic structure, x ~ 50.

The faster the rate of crystallisation, brought about by increasing the rate of cooling, the more secondary, and also tertiary, side arms developed, giving rise to a well-formed 'dendritic structure', fig. 26.33(b). (We showed an extreme example of extensive dendrite formation in fig. 19.9, as an illustration of cubic grid-forming structures). This showed that dendrite formation was due to solidification following the stress created by the cubic stress forming tendency of the solid taking over, and not allowing time for the liquid to create smooth rounded surfaces. Thus when crystallisation was stopped, by stopping the cooling, the spherical forming tendency of the dominant presence of the liquid took over and disintegrated the dendritic structure and rounded off the fragments, fig. 26.34.

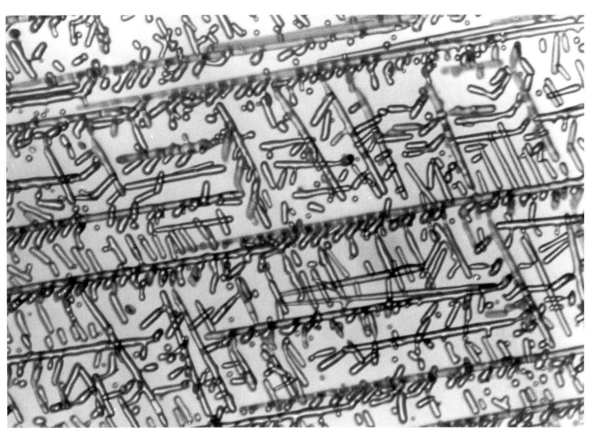

Fig.26.34(a) An ammonium chloride dendrite structure five minutes after crystallisation ceased, showing disintegration of the side arms which have then rounded off, x 150.

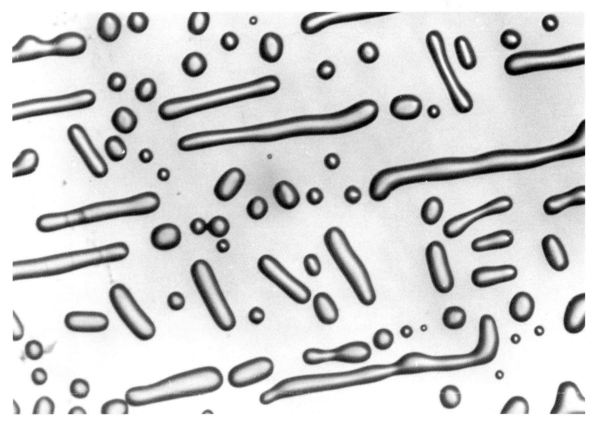

Fig.26.34(b) The same region as in fig. 26.34(a) after a further 30 minutes, x 150.

383

Having established the behaviour of ammonium chloride, we then investigated the influence of various metallic chlorides. Adding iron chloride suppressed the crystallisation of the ammonium chloride, so that undercooling way below that needed without the addition was required to create a nucleus and when nucleation did occur growth was very slow. The iron also eliminated the initial spherical-forming tendency of the nucleus, so that a cubic nucleus formed, from the corners of which cube shaped primary off-shoot arms developed, fig. 26.35(a), the cube-forming tendency of these resulted in them having a 'spade-like' shape, figs. 26.35(b and c).

Fig.26.35(a) The strongly cubic form at the commencement of crystallisation with the beginning of growth from the corners, when iron chloride was added to the ammonium chloride solution, x ~ 150.

Fig.26.35(b) The four side arms growing from the corners of the cube themselves take on cubic-like forms, x ~ 150.

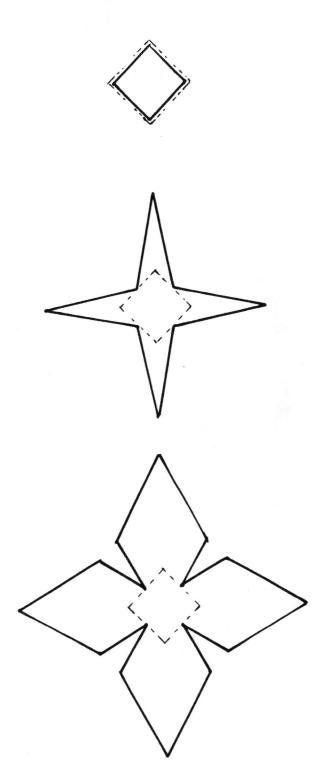

Fig.26.35(c) The cubic nucleus creates stresses at its corners which cause growth spikes in this direction. These then take on a cube-forming tendency.

Because of the suppressing effect of iron on crystallisation, we had to apply additional measures to get extensive crystallisation, by spraying the cell with alcohol that increased the rate of cooling. This gave secondary dendrite arms and also small tertiary arms that showed the cubic spade-like tendencies, particularly at their tips, fig. 26.36.

Fig.26.36 As secondary arms develop from the primary arms, these too show a cube-forming tendency at their growing tips, x ~ 150.

Calcium was also found to be a growth inhibitor: growth forms were small and restricted in their degree of dendrite development. As we have seen, copper chloride on its own crystallises readily, forming arrays of fine needles. However, the addition of copper chloride greatly reduced the crystallisation of the ammonium chloride: at first many spherical nuclei formed which remained spherical until they reached an appreciable size when they began to develop cubic facets, from which only occasional branches grew. Mercuric chloride additions rounded and softened the cubic tendency of the primary arms, making them more delicate and eliminated the secondary side arms, giving a more plant like structure, fig. 26.37.

Fig.26.37(a) The addition of mercuric chloride has resulted in an initial delicate four-petalled shape, x ~ 150.

Fig.26.37(b) The number of arms growing from the centre has increased but they remain delicate and without secondary arms growing from them, x ~ 150.

Antimony, added as the fluoride, because the chloride is insoluble in water, had only a small effect on the initial dendrite formations but after these had formed then, slowly over a period of several hours, wispy outgrowths formed from some of the tips, fig 26.38(a).

Fig.26.38(a). Wispy outgrowth from the tip of a dendrite arm, observed when antimony chloride was added to the ammonium chloride. This was a very delicate fragile structure but it remained intact as it developed slowly while at the same time the solution gelled and supported it, x ~ 150 .

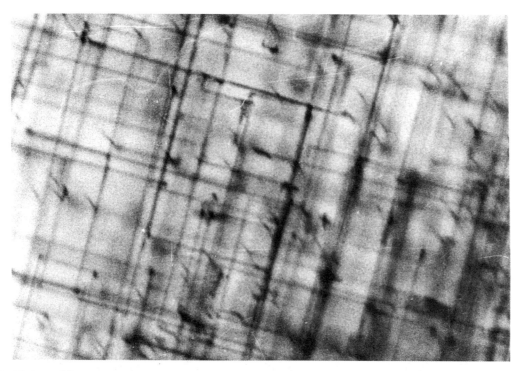

Fig.26.38(b). Part of the structure in 26.38a at higher magnification, showing that it comprised a very delicate cubic grid x~1200.

At high magnification these were seen to comprise very fine cubic grids, fig. 26.38(b). At the same time, the crystallising solution turned into a gelatinous mass that supported the growth of these delicate formations. As we reported in Chapter 18, the 'intelligences' behind the ECEs claimed to perceive a cubic grid structure around the tip of a growing bud, into which the bud unfolds. Perhaps there was something of this nature around the tip of the crystal growth structure that caused the cubic grid structure. It is certainly something that is difficult to account for in terms of the current scientific explanation for the growth fronts of crystals. The uniformity of this structure suggests that, over this small region there was a uniform stress field which acted on the substances crystallising in the gel, to cause something to precipitate and thereby mark it out. Sodium and caesium chlorides had little effect on the ammonium chloride structures. We looked at what happened when we modified the water by adding a wetting agent, Tupelo, to it. The Tupelo acted as a growth retarder and also increased the 'liquid action', rounding off the dendrites, fig. 26.39. Adding gelatine to the water produced a similar result.

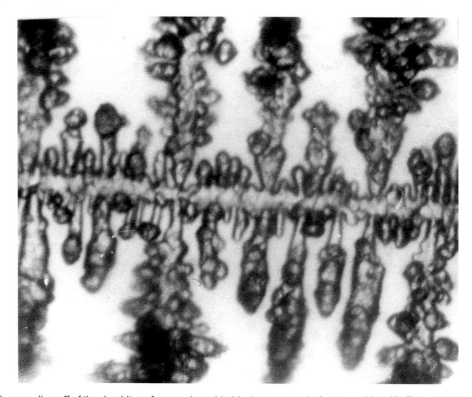

Fig.26.39 The rounding-off of the dendrites of ammonium chloride that occurred when we added 5% Teepol to the water, x ~ 75, (compare with fig. 26.33b).

Some Metal Solidification Forms

In our seeking to try and understand how different forms arise we also looked at some metal solidification forms, specifically those that arise in an alloy made of tin and aluminium. Aluminium has a higher melting point (660°C) than tin (232°C) and it is soluble in molten tin but insoluble in solid tin. This means that when a solution of aluminium in tin is melted and cooled, the higher melting point aluminium solidifies first in an environment rich in molten tin. When it has all solidified it is possible to dissolve away the tin, leaving the aluminium in the shapes that it took up as it solidified. These tended to be rows of faceted partial cube-like shapes, fig. 26.40, that followed the principle of a cube forming from a corner of a previous cube, as in fig. 26.35(c) but in this case in a continuous sequence.

Fig.26.40(a) Arrays of partial cuboid shapes of aluminium solidified out of a tin-20% aluminium alloy, x200.

Fig.26.40(b) The interconnecting aluminium cuboids that formed in a 4% aluminium-tin alloy, x 120.

The addition of a small amount of iron strengthened the cube-forming tendency and caused the aluminium structures to become more ordered, fig. 26.41.

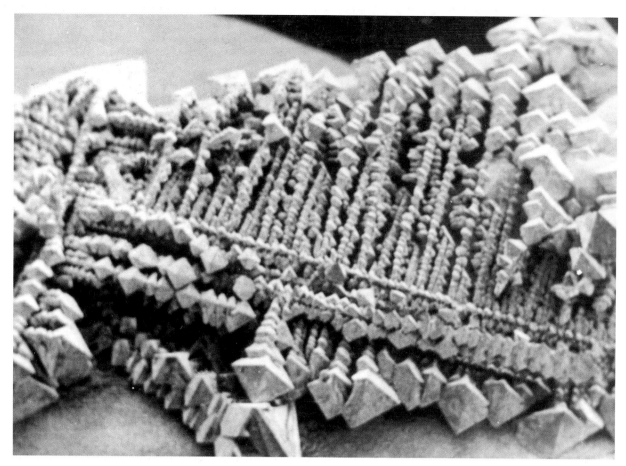

Fig.26.41. The more ordered type of aluminium cuboid dendrites that occurred with the addition of 1% iron to a 10% aluminium-tin alloy, x ~ 100.

A small addition of silver produced a similar result. Copper had a similar effect to iron but it also brought about the formation of occasional long needles of aluminium. The addition of silicon produced stunted rounded dendrite arms in the aluminium with some lumpiness due to incipient crystal corners, fig. 26.42.

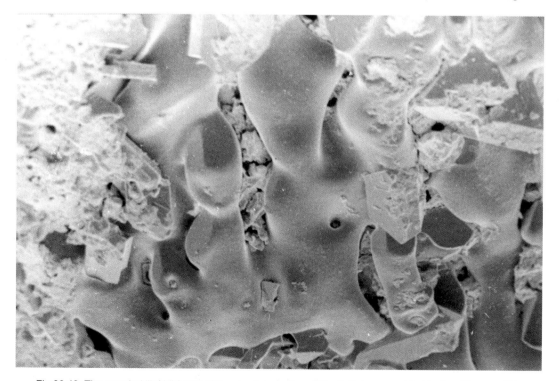

Fig.26.42 The rounded 'liquid' forms of the aluminium when 2% of silicon was added to the alloy, x ~ 400.

The addition of mercury, which is the only metal that is liquid in the normal conditions at the Earth's surface had a strong 'liquid' effect, in that it completely eliminated the cube-forming tendency and caused the aluminium to take on liquid forms, but of a 'negative' type, fig. 26.43, i.e. not outwards-rounded, but inwards rounded.

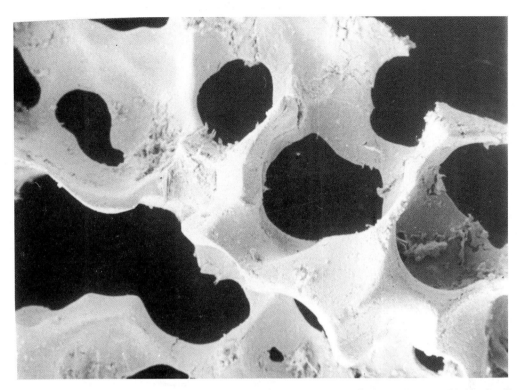

Fig.26.43 The 'negative' liquid-influenced structures formed by the aluminium when 2 % of mercury was added to the alloy, x ~ 400.

Zinc had a small effect, producing fragmented cubic forms, (as with aluminium without any extra addition, fig. 26.40), that were rounded-off at their corners. These results suggest an interplay between the cube-forming and the sphere-forming processes, while many of them are like miniature geological formations, showing that the same basic processes of 'creation' operate at all levels.

Forms Produced in a Liquid by Electrical Stress

According to hK-M, substances comprise a combination of ponderous s-entity derived energy (protons) and more active galaxy entity-derived energy (electrons). When these are separated from each other they give rise to what scientists know as negative and positive electrical stress fields that, on the electron-negative side, are greater, and on the proton-positive side less, than their stress field when they are together in their combined state. In this series of (electrochemical) experiments we subjected substances to these electrical stress fields and observed what happened. Once again we were using well-established scientific techniques, it was again a matter of creating forms that we sought to interpret in terms of hK-M.

We set up a 'cell' comprising a container of a solution of a metal salt, with two metal electrodes to which we applied the electrical stresses. The stresses caused the positive electrode to go into solution and metal from the solution to be deposited onto the negative electrode, where it produced growth forms. A problem with these forms was that they were very delicate and fragile and easily broken up by any movements, such as convection, in the solution in the cell. We overcame this in two ways; one was to put a substance in the solution to make it 'gel', so that it supported the structures that formed, the other way that we used was to make the liquid in the cell a very thin layer between two microscope slides, so that little convective movement could occur. This did, however mean that these structures tended to be two-dimensional and affected by the stress fields of the closely adjacent glass plates.

The form of lead growth in a sodium silicate gel was dendritic, fig. 26.44(a), with fairly regular radiating arms, which at low voltages (low stress) branched at $45°$ or $135°$ and at high voltages (high stress) branched at $90°$. On higher magnification it could be seen that during the early stages of growth the dendrite arms branched in a cubic grid structure, with some growing along the cube edges and some along the cube face diagonals, fig. 26.44(b), which could relate to the fact that lead atoms take up a cubic structure when they pack together in the solid metal. However, lead growth was quite different in an aga gel, fig. 26.45, more like a poplar tree, than the silica gel 'pine-tree' type.

Fig.26.44(a) The dendritic growth form of lead grown in a silica gel, potential applied 1.0 volt, magn x 1.5.

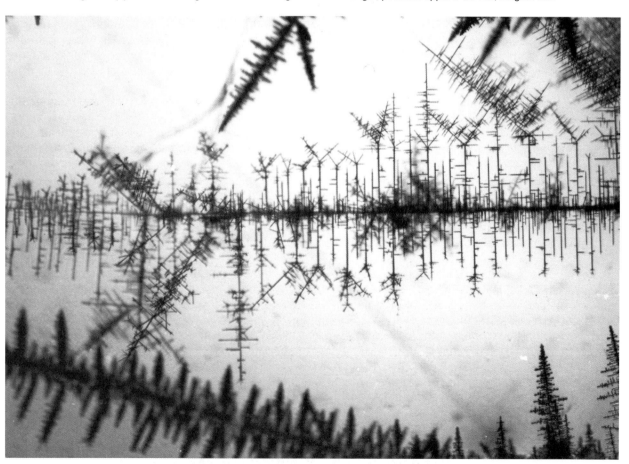

Fig.26.44(b) The early stages of development of lead dendrites, showing a cubic grid structure, x 22.

Fig.26.45   The different form of lead growth that occurred in agar gel, potential 1.0 volt, magn. x 13.5.

It was as though, as with plants that develop different forms when grown in different environments, this also happened with crystallisation. Cadmium in a silica gel gave a more varied, plant-like form, fig. 26.46(a), with branching occurring at 60° and 120° to the axis of growth, fig. 26.46(b), i.e. along the edges or face diagonals of a hexagon, which corresponds with the hexagonal atomic arrangement of a cadmium crystal.

Fig.26.46(a)   The growth form of cadmium in a silica gel, potential 0.9 volts, magn. x5

Fig.26.46(b)   Part of the growth form of fig. 26.46a at higher magnification (x 33) showing the branching of the dendrites at 60° and 120° to the axis of growth.

Silver and copper gave more amorphous structures with no clear branching direction, in growth forms similar to that of cypress trees, fig. 26.47.

Fig. 26.47   The cypress tree-like form obtained with silver, x 22

As we explained in the previous section, we attribute dendrite growth to the stress field of the developing cubic crystal defining the deposition of further atoms overpowering the rounding-off of the liquid environment. These two processes growing out and rounding off could play a major part in plant formation. The striving for light, nutrient etc giving rise to the outwards stress-induced form of foliage and roots and, when this is exhausted, the s-pressure of the environment giving rise to the rounding-off of bud, flower and seed

In our work with the thin cell we used two silver electrodes with a solution of silver nitrate, fig. 26.48 and we examined the different forms resulting from altering the current, the concentration of the silver nitrate solution and cell thickness.

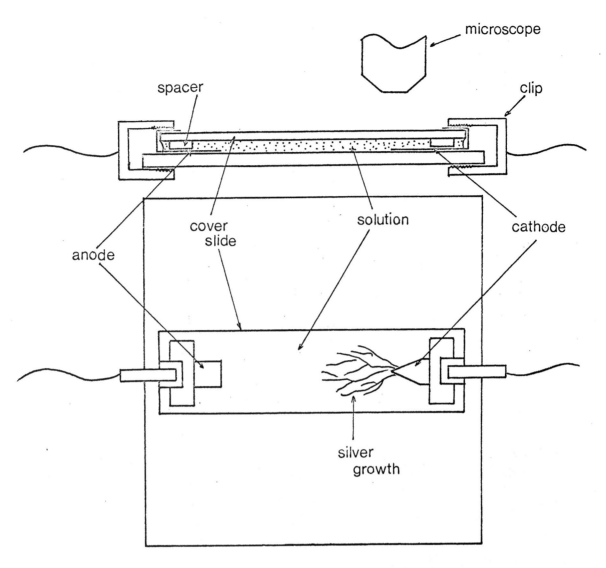

Fig.26.48. The thin cell arrangement that we used for observing growth forms.

At low electrical stress and hence low current density, the deposited silver forms developed slowly and were of a chunky, faceted, distorted cubic form, fig. 26.49, showing the dominance of the metal cube-forming activity.

Fig.26.49 The type of chunky, faceted growth of silver which formed at either low current density or high solution concentration.

As the electrical stress and current density were increased the forms grew faster and, as with the rapid cooling of the ammonium chloride, they spread out into dendritic shapes, fig. 26.50(a) and (b).

a   b

Fig.26.50 Two types of dendritic formations, (a) a structure that largely follows the line of stress between the two electrodes, observed with a solution concentration of 0.05M; (b) a structure obtained with the same solution as (a) but at a faster rate of growth, showing more branching out.

At a high electrolyte concentration the growth forms were the same as those at low current density i.e. heavy fragmented cuboids, as in fig. 26.49, showing the dominance of the cube-forming tendency where larger numbers of atoms were involved: as the concentration was decreased the forms became dendritic, as in fig. 26.50. When we made the gap between the glass plates very small we got plant-like forms, fig. 26.51, under conditions where with an increased gap size no growths formed.

Fig.26.51 A plant-like structure that we got when we made the gap between the glass plates very small.

Here we think the key factor was that with the glass plates very close together the stress fields of the plates extended through the thin layer of liquid and affected the growth forms. When we substituted Perspex/Lucite plates for the glass ones the growth form was more amorphous, fig. 26.52, presumably because of the different stress created by the perspex compared with the glass.

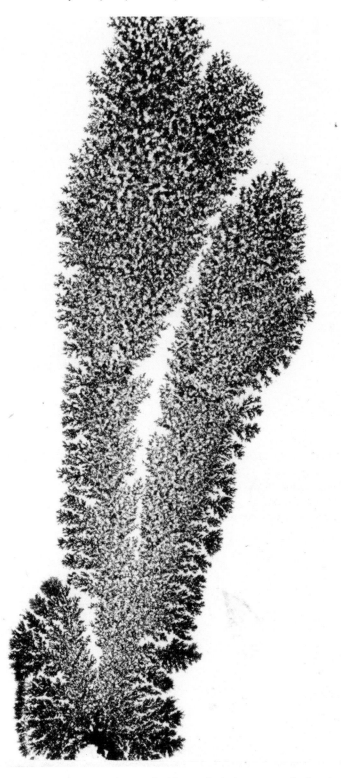

Fig.26.52 The more amorphous structure that resulted from substituting perspex for the glass plates.

We also obtained growth forms by simply putting a piece of copper in the silver nitrate solution, without any applied electrical stress. This is because the stress of the space-energy balance between the copper and the silver nitrate solution is reduced by copper diffusing into the silver nitrate solution, while silver diffuses out of it and is deposited onto the copper surface. The growth of the silver on the copper took four forms. First it formed a black spongy layer that covered the copper, this changed to a less dense growth of thin needles, in the third stage some of the needles grew outwards and thickened, fig. 26.53(a); when this growth slowed down, fine dendrite growth took place from the tips of some of the needles, fig. 26.53(b).

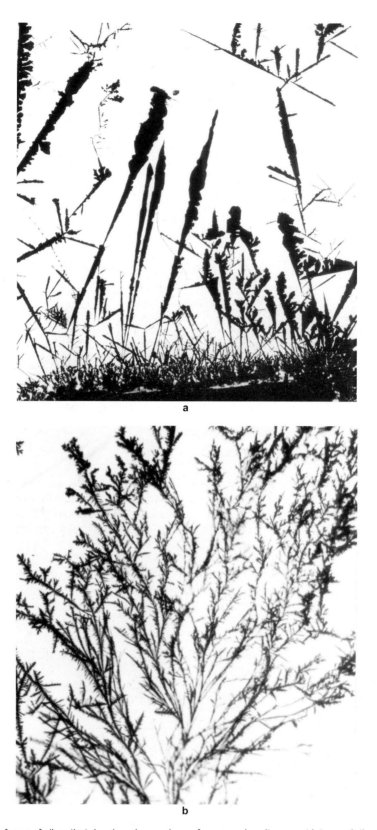

Fig.26.53(a) The growth forms of silver that developed on a piece of copper when it was put into a solution of silver nitrate; (b) the plant-like dendritic form that developed from the tips of the 'needles' in (a), after growth of these had slowed down. Overall the effect was akin to looking at a cross-section of growth from the Earth's surface, with layers of moss, grass and plants.

We have repeatedly drawn attention to the fact that many of our stress produced forms resemble the forms of plants and that our explanation for this is that the space energy involved in the creation of mineral kingdom forms gets a sense of self from this activity and makes it self-actualising. Thus the essential features of plant forms derive from, and can be simulated by, mineral kingdom activities. The form of the silver deposit in fig.26.53(a) is akin to looking at a cross section of growth from the Earth's surface, with layers of moss, grass and plants. In the early 1900s LEDUC showed that differential diffusion in colloidal solutions (osmosis) produced organic-like forms, fig.26.54.

Fig. 26.54. Organic forms produced by osmosis in colloidal solutions, (LEDUC).

A Final Comment on Our Researches Into Forms

In our researches described in this book we started off by carrying out experiments that gave us results that we could not understand. In trying to interpret these we got progressively involved in seeking a basic cosmology and we have described the path that we followed and the cosmology that emerged from it. What is required now is to interpret the results of our experiments in terms of the cosmology. To repeat part of one of Brian's ECEs that we recorded in Chapter 23:

B: The imagery is saying that we should be set on getting this total scheme of creation out clearly . Running it up and down and mirroring it. Experiments that repeat the processes of creation are what are needed.
G: We've got many experimental results and now we need to get to grips with them in terms of the basic processes of creation?
B: Right, this is it, yes. I think there is a lot in them that are glaringly obvious that we haven't seen. The strength will come from working from the bottom upwards as well as from the top down.

We have done what we could to try to fulfil this objective but we suspect that there is still 'a lot that is glaringly obvious that we haven't seen'. What is required is a clearer understanding of the cosmology and its workings in specific situations.

We have tried to examine forms produced in simple situations and to offer a rudimentary interpretation of them as being brought about by stress patterns in the Earth Entity space-energy. Everywhere that we look we see substances that have taken up various forms and activities as a result of the forces acting on them. By analysing the forms we should be able to come to an understanding of the forces/stresses that cause them. But because the forms of living organisms are difficult to manipulate it is difficult to work out how they have come about. The spreading drop, the capillary dynamolysis and the crystallisation experiments are examples of simple ways of producing a variety of forms that, in many cases, are like those observed in the living kingdoms of Nature, in which the factors involved can be altered to see their effects and thereby to evaluate the circumstances that give rise to them.

In a living system matter is continually crystallising out and dissolving away, either seasonally in the plant world or continuously in the animal world. In the mineral world a substance crystallises and so remains. During the time that it is crystallising and growing it could be regarded as exhibiting a 'slice' of living activity. In particular, nucleation centres in crystallisation and the centres in the spreading drop and capillary dynamolysis experiments may be looked upon as analogous to the forms that develop when seeds germinate and grow. When we look at the forms of animals we are looking at entities that have become aware of their ability to carry out these activities and have thereby taken these patterns of activity into themselves. Thus the forms of, for example, the nervous, blood and digestive systems are more evolved internalised versions of forms of plants and therefore have a similarity to some of the forms in our experiments.

If we could understand the space-energy stress fields that give rise to plants and how they interact with different substances, we should be able to understand the natures and roles of different plants and substances in Nature. For example, we interact with plants in the sense that we depend on them for sustenance and our well being. Ideally we should be able to discern from the form and substance of a plant its role in nutrition and healing but to do this would require a greater understanding of the forces and activities at work in Nature than we possess at present.

We have proposed that the underlying causes of the forms that we observed in our experiments are stress fields in the Earth Entity activity and, for example, we have suggested that in the ammonium chloride experiments we see two aspects of these at work, namely the solid crystallisation cube-forming stress field and the liquid spherical-forming stress field of the water. When a crystal nucleus forms it creates a centre from which a stress pattern develops which is dependent on how the cube-forming and sphere-forming stress fields are activated. By observing and putting together a sequence of the way in which forms develop in these terms, as in the formation of dendrites in figs. 26.32 and 26.35(c) we can perceive what is going on. Similarly we have suggested in fig. 26.7 principles underlying the shapes of the advancing front in the spreading drop experiments, which give rise to plant-like forms. If we see a form in our experiments and can work out the stress fields that give rise to it then, when we see the same form in the plant kingdom, we have to try and work out how stress fields of this type come about to create the plant form.

The scientific explanation for crystallisation or solidification patterns is that where the liquid becomes stressed by having too much substance dissolved in it or by being cooled below a temperature at which it should solidify, solid material starts to emerge where best it can, to form a nucleus. Growth of the solid then takes place by further atoms of substance attaching to the nucleus where they fit best, building up a growth front, without any overall organising force. The hK-M viewpoint is that the crystal patterns are the result of stress fields in the space-energy. For example, it is very difficult to envisage how the delicate cubic structure shown in fig. 26.38 could come about as a result of atoms fitting onto a growth front. It gives the appearance much more of deposition of substance onto a pre-existing grid pattern, as stated in Harry's (and other team member's) ECEs. It is as though, when conditions arise for substance to be deposited out, this activates the EM-energy's memory of a cubic forming mode, which the substance then takes up, in much the same way that when we encounter a situation our memory of past experiences is activated before we deal with the current situation, to structure us to deal with it in the same way as we did previously.

We have shown only a few examples of the types of forms that arose from our experiments. Experiments like these are very simple to carry out and offer an almost unlimited untapped field that awaits investigation, compilation of observations and their interpretation. However, we are not, of course, the only people who have looked at how forms come about; D'ARCY THOMSON, for example, many decades ago gave examples of the way in which the forms and behaviour of living structures, e.g. cells, cell division, the growth and forms of simple multicellular organisms can be simulated by physical experiments. In his work he pointed out that the forms that substances take up in organisms, e.g. the wings of birds, the flippers of penguins and whales, the skeletal and muscular structures of animals, are exquisitely designed to perform their functions. Among the specific examples that he considered was that of the head of the femur in the human body which is shaped according to the pattern of stress imposed on it, so that the material of the bone has been laid down along the lines of stress. Similarly plant tissues develop in a way that is determined by the stress imposed on them.

The exquisite design of organisms for their life styles has often been used as an argument for the existence of a Supreme Designer, or Creator God, who designed everything to be perfectly suited to its purpose. The current scientific view is that the complex design of organisms has arisen by evolution over millions of years, starting from the first form of life in minute prokaryotic single cells, as a result of small random changes and mutations in which those that benefit the organism's survival and evolution persist, in a 'survival of the fittest' explanation. The hK-M view is that everything started from a dormant energy state that became increasingly active and where this gave the active parts a sense of self, they took this over and became self-actualising and themselves increased in activity, thereby creating more activity and more self-actualising entities. Each new development has arisen, in the first place, inadvertently, out of the interplay of previous activities that then became shaped by the stresses of their striving to survive and maintain and enhance their sense of self. As the Earth Entity experienced these developments it built up a memory of them, the EM-energy, that served as a 'guide' for further developments, in the same way that out of the events of our lives we experience potentials for further developments in which we further express and experience our sense of self by applying our memory and mental abilities to develop these. On this basis there is no pre-existing God or plan of creation, creation develops further creation out of itself. But this does not occur as the result of a sequence of random events, with selection by survival of the fittest, but out of the positive striving of what has already developed, seeking to express and experience itself further. The space-energy with its memory and integrating nature, leading to the development of potentials that have inadvertently arisen, operates in the way in which our minds work and is the memory of the totality that, if so desired, could be called, 'the mind of God', that develops as evolution progresses in the same way that our minds develop as we evolve.

Chapter 27

Activity Tracks

A phenomenon that we recorded in our electrophotography experiments, which was not concerned with stress fields and their relationship to the creation of forms and requires separate consideration, was that of 'activity tracks'. These were registered when we put a disc of wet filter paper in the sandwich arrangement (fig. 25.18), and used a lower voltage of 5kv, compared with that which gave the other registrations (usually about 15kv) and a much longer exposure time of 10 or more seconds. Their occurrence did not seem to be influenced by the rate of pulse increase or decrease but they built up with increasing time of application of the pulse, so much so that with an exposure of 30 seconds the registration of tracks became very congested, fig. 27.1.

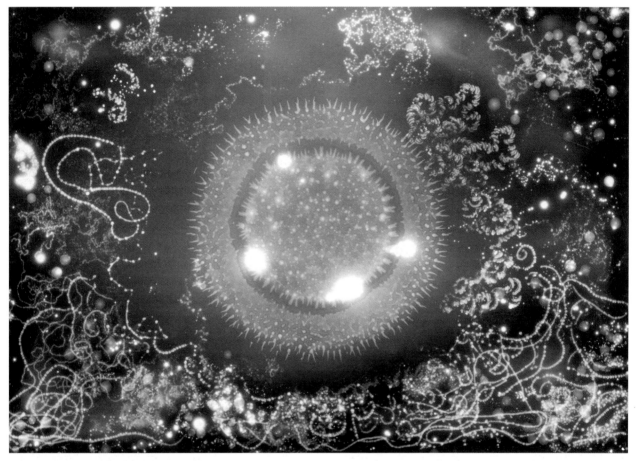

Fig 27.1. An example of the morass of 'activity tracks' that registered on the positive side of the sandwich when a 5kv pulse, that had no immediate effect, was maintained for a long period (30 seconds), with a disc of wet filter paper in the sandwich arrangement.

The tracks occurred regardless of what we wetted the filter paper with - water, various salt solutions, acids, alkalis, alcohols and, to a lesser extent, with oils. We also obtained them when we did not use wet filter paper but carried out the experiment in a chamber into which we passed air that had been bubbled through liquid or simply put a dish of liquid in the chamber. But they did not occur when we filled the chamber with dried air. This suggested that they were associated with water vapour and/or other molecules of vapour in the air between the plates.

There was an abundance of different types of tracks, as in fig. 27.1, some single and others duplex, some of which seemed to spread out, while others had a spiral formation. Fig. 27.2 shows examples of six types of single tracks, fig. 27.3 four types of duplex tracks and fig. 27.4 three examples of spiral tracks. (Because the tracks were quite small they have had to be enlarged considerably (about 6 to 10 times) which contributes to them being rather blurred).

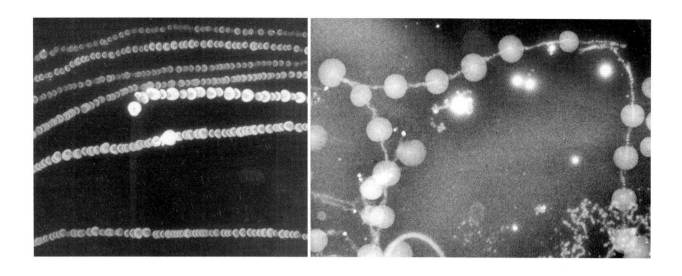

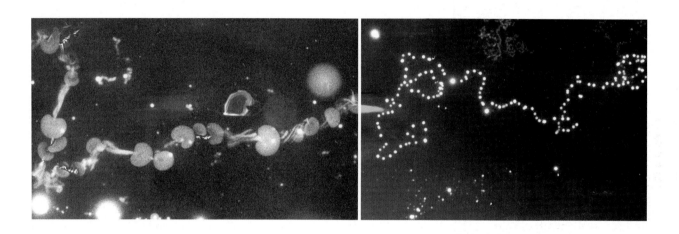

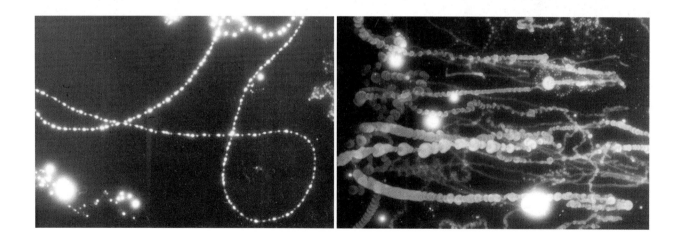

Fig. 27.2.   A selection of six different types of single activity tracks.

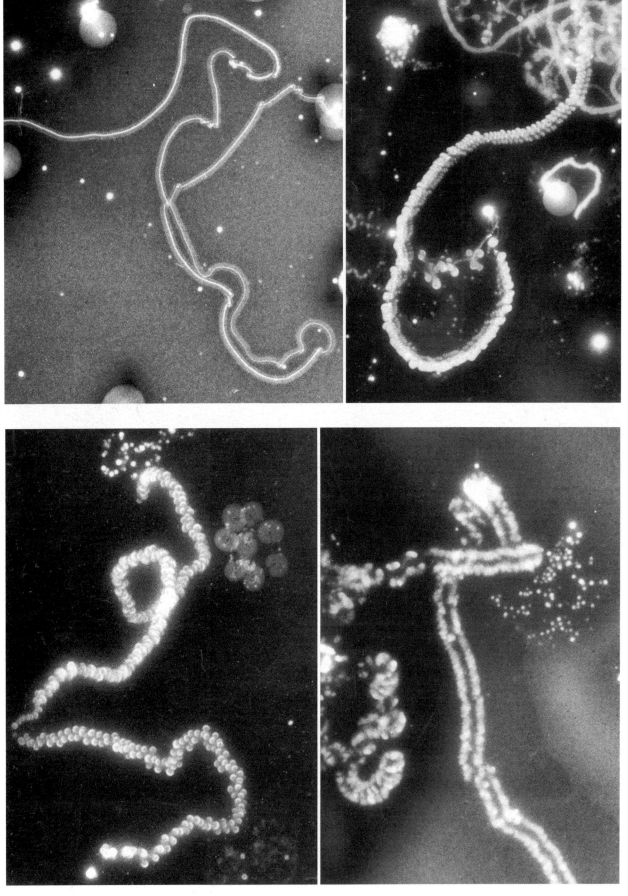

Fig 27.3. Examples of four types of duplex tracks

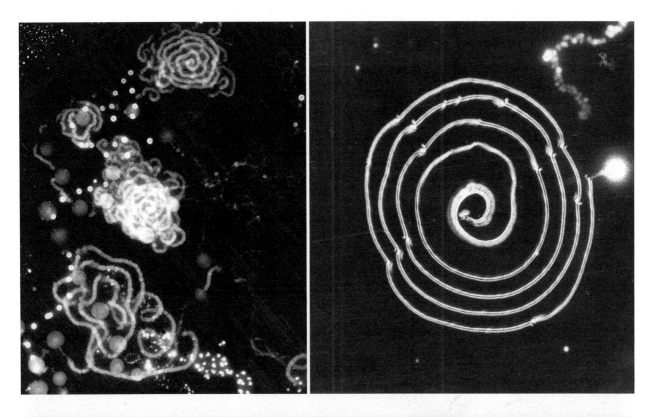

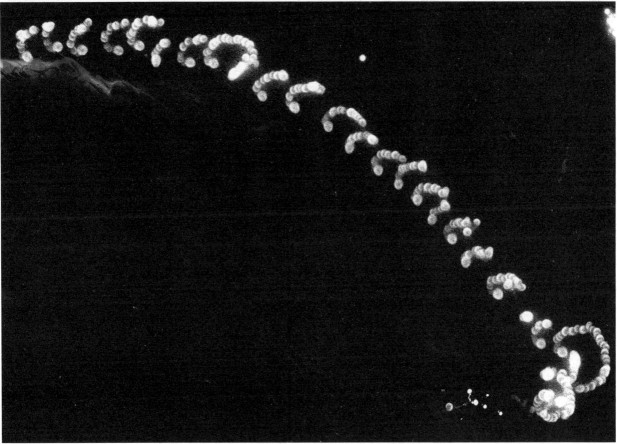

Fig. 27.4. Three types of spiral tracks. The bottom track gives the impression of a continuous spiral in 'space' that only registers as it passes through the boundary layer.

Most of the types of tracks did not seem to be specific to any particular liquid. However, on one occasion with a homoeopathic liquid, Aurum 12, we got the visually impressive chain shown in fig. 27.5.

Fig. 27.5　A somewhat different type of track that we obtained with a homoeopathic liquid, Aurum 12.

The tracks were registered on the photographic plate on the positive side of the sandwich and only in very blurred form, if at all, on the negative side. We found that we could also register the tracks with a plain glass plate lightly coated with fine powder. Another way in which we registered them was to use a 1.5 mm thick sheet of perspex/lucite, instead of a photoplate that, after the application of the pulse, we coated with the fine carbon powder used in photostatic printing. This gave results which, when photographed, were as clear and well-defined as the registrations on photographic plates and was a simpler and cheaper method. The problem was, what was the cause of the tracks?

In the early 20th century two Theosophically-oriented mystics, Besant and Leadbeater, claimed to be able to enter into a state of consciousness, by a technique taught to them by Indian yogis/mystics, in which they could will back the environment around an atom (in hK-M terms, the s-pressure) and the atom thereby opened up. They were then able to focus their consciousness so as to perceive the atom's internal structure. The essential feature of Besant and Leadbeater's observations is that physical atoms comprise assemblages of much smaller 'etheric atoms'. At the basis of all substance are two 'ultimate atoms', for which they used their Sanskrit name 'Anu'. They stated that if the origin of these ultimate atoms is traced further back, then one enters the spiritual or astral world. The ultimate atoms have currents of force entering and leaving them and the difference between the two ultimate atom types is that in one the force comes from the spiritual world into the etheric atom, whereas in the other the force flows from the etheric atom into the spiritual world, fig 27.6.

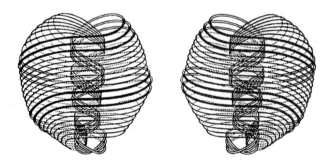

Fig. 27.6　The two types of ultimate atoms or Anu observed by Besant and Leadbeater. Both types comprise spirillae of activity that form a heart shape with a depression at the top. In the positive Anu the flow of spirillae is clockwise downwards from the top and back up again, while in the negative Anu it is anticlockwise.

In Besant and Leadbeater's account the two types of Anu are combined together in various numbers and configurations to form atoms at a second etheric level. The second level etheric atoms are combined together to give rise to further atoms at a third etheric level and the same thing happens again to give rise to a fourth etheric level which manifest as gaseous atoms. In this way, Besant and Leadbeater claimed, physical atoms comprise large numbers of Anu. Hydrogen contains the smallest number of 18 Anu, while heavier atoms contain many hundreds or thousands of Anu. The Anu are organised and grouped together in various ways to form the atoms of the higher etheric levels. The higher etheric atoms are in turn grouped together to form physical atoms.

The hydrogen atom is described as having an egg-like form that contains six small bodies each of which contains three positive or negative Anu, all undergoing rapid vibrations and gyrations. The six groups are divided into two, with each set of three linked to each other by lines of attraction, thus giving the whole the appearance of two interlaced triangles, fig. 27.7a. One triangle is more positive, i.e. comprising five positive and four negative Anu, while the other triangle is more negative, comprising five negative and four positive Anu. In the negative triangle the Anu within each set of three have a triangular relationship, while in the positive triangle one set has a triangular relationship while the two others have a linear one. When the investigator 'wills back' the containing wall, the two main triangles separate and form two spheres, fig. 27.7b. On willing back the surrounding spherical walls one set of three Anu separates off from each sphere, comprising two positive and one negative Anu in the positive triangle group and two negative and one positive in the negative triangle group, fig. 27.7c. On further disintegration all three sets of Anu separate from each other, fig 27.7d. In a final stage all the Anu become separate, fig. 27.7e.

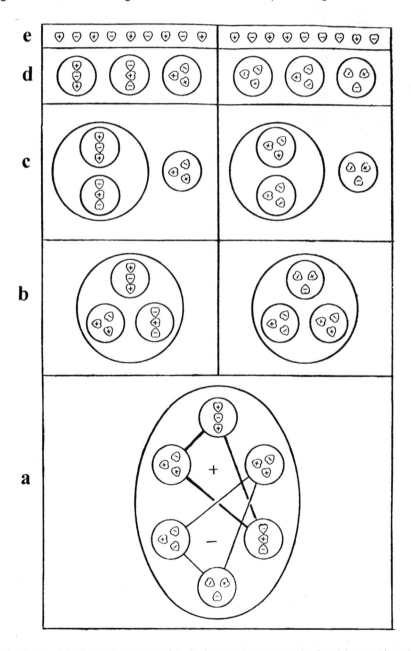

Fig. 27.7 The successive levels of the internal structure of the hydrogen atom as seen by the clairvoyant investigations of Besant and Leadbeater.

Besant and Leadbeater described the oxygen atom as an ovoid containing two spirally-coiled snake-like bodies, one negative and one positive, spinning in opposite directions around a common axis, fig.27.8.

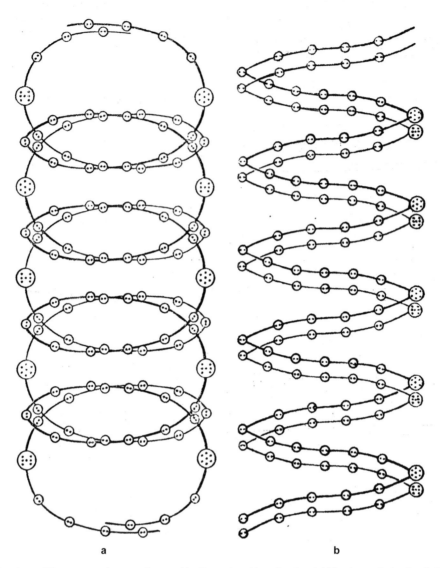

a   b

Fig 27.8 The structure of the oxygen atom as observed by Besant and Leadbeater, (a) The two spirals of activity that revolve in opposite directions around a common axis within the ovoid of the oxygen atom, (b) the double spiral in diagrammatic form to show its structure

Each 'snake' comprises five 'brilliant' spheres that contain seven Anu, that are linked by small spheres, each containing two Anu. The principle difference between the positive and negative snakes is that the brilliant sphere in the positive one has a positive Anu at its centre surrounded by three positive and three negative ones, while the negative snake has a negative Anu at its centre, again surrounded by three positive and three negative ones.

Over the period 1895 to 1933 Besant and Leadbeater described the structures of all the elements of the Periodic Table and a number of compounds. They found that the number of Anu in each atom corresponds with the atomic weight; that is, taking hydrogen which contains 18 Anu as the unit of atomic weight, then dividing the number of Anu which they observed in the atom of any other material by 18 gave its atomic weight as determined by science. In 1951 Jinarajadasa gathered together the results of these investigations, and some associated material and published it as a book with the title 'Occult Chemistry' by BESANT and LEADBEATER, © The Theosophical Publishing House, Adyar, Chennai -600 020, India.

With the exception of hydrogen, oxygen and nitrogen, Besant and Leadbeater observed the sub-atomic units to be organised into seven basic structures, namely spike, dumb-bell, tetrahedron, cube, octahedron, bar or star, which they related to the atoms' properties in their classification in the Periodic Table. Within these encompassing structures the basic constituents of atoms are organised in shell, or onion-like assemblages.

An atomic physicist, STEPHEN PHILLIPS has made a detailed comparison of Besant and Leadbeater's descriptions with current scientific concepts. Phillips relates Besant and Leadbeater's clairvoyant observations to the structure of atomic nuclei and finds that there is a considerable degree of correlation between the two viewpoints. Particularly remarkable is the fact that Besant and Leadbeater, in the early 1900's, from their clairvoyant investigations, described sub-atomic structures that scientists have only recently become aware of. They also described the structures of atoms of substances that, at the time, scientists had not discovered and the structures of isotopes, the existence of which was not then known to scientists.

Besant and Leadbeater stated that the sub-atomic constituents that make up an atom are enclosed in a sort of bubble on the walls of which they exert a pressure so that it is under tension. Space is filled with an invisible substance which they called 'koilon', (in hK-M terms the space-energy) and that there was a force associated with the bubble that radiated from, and returned to, its centre. According to hK-M this would be the electron energy which, driven by the nucleus at its centre, has a Bénard-cell type configuration that pushes back the space-energy, as we described in Chapter 9.

Besant and Leadbeater described the ultimate atom as:

> a sphere, slightly flattened, and there is a depression at the point where force flows in, causing a heart-like form ...

And that when an electric current is brought to bear on the atoms:

> they arrange themselves in parallel lines and in each line the heart-shaped depression receives the flow, which passes out through the apex into the depression of the next and so on ...(fig. 27.9)

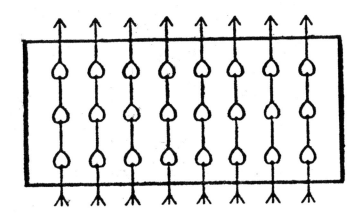

Fig. 27.9 Besant and Leadbeater's diagram of the way in which an electric current causes the Anu to become arranged in parallel lines, with a flow passing through the depression in one heart-shaped Anu and out through its apex into the depression in the next Anu. Note the similarity of this to some of the activity tracks in fig. 27.2.

Some of the 'chains of activity' that we registered conformed to this description (e.g. in fig. 27.2). Other descriptions by Besant and Leadbeater, of chains of 'bright beads' and duplex chains which intertwine and chains which, prior to unwinding are coiled spiral-wise, were like the activity tracks that we observed in our experiments and this led us to think that perhaps the electrical stress somehow caused atoms to unwind and it was this that registered on our plates.

We sought further insight into this viewpoint in our ECEs. Thus in seeking to understand the distinguishing features of different types of atoms, one of Brian's ECEs claimed that what gave different atoms their characteristics was not only the number of ultimate atoms of which they consist, but also how the flow through them varied:

B: *I've got an image of an ultimate physical atom that is made of little spiral fibres that go through a motion from periphery to centre to periphery, gathering experience and getting to the centre. At the centre you have the experience for yourself. Having got that you return to the outside.*
G: *Can we look at gold as an example?*
B: *The image is of a range of ultimate physical atoms. They've all got the same make up. In the gold atom these currents flow through it as a balanced flow. Other materials are imbalanced. This does not mean that they are wrong or out of harmony with basics. Their imbalances give them their characters.*
G: *It's really the circulations that differ?*
B: *Yes.*
G: *What does the circulation of say, lead look like compared to gold?*

B: Slow, turgid.

G: And hydrogen?

B: Fast. With gold there is a fine feeling of smooth rhythmic ease, no problems, nothing disruptive, just a constant steady fine cycling. Lead is like a flow with a valve in it and it's as if the valve is that entity called lead. Hydrogen is sheer joy. It's like absolute lightning. That is one end of a spectrum.

G: What does carbon look like?

B: Steady. Carbon is a steady plodder, chugging along like a machine. The circuit going into the centre and the circuit coming out don't show any change, there is no feeling associated with them.

G: What does iron look like?

B: The feeling is that its fibres are under pressure all the time. What is going through them is vibrant, like rippling muscles. The iron is spiralling vigorously into the centre and is reluctant to leave that centre.

G: In lead we also see a strong downwards flow but it is more sluggish than iron?

B: Yes, iron has a drive and a will to go down. It seeks this centre. Lead doesn't care. It is pulled down by its own weight and pushed up by the weight of lead wanting to come down.

G: Iron's job is to get down more than get up. It's a principle which in man carries him down to earth -- Is the flow which is more downward Ahrimanic and the one which is more upward Luciferic?

B: Ahriman and Lucifer are themselves based on these principles.

G: The principles come first and Ahriman and Lucifer come after?

B: Yes.

In our ECEs we sought further insight into what was happening in our experiments, with Ted as the receiver. At that time the ECEs were dominated by the Steiner-type cosmology, with everything described in terms of light and warmth ether beings and individualising beings. As we have explained we think that the so-called light and warmth ether beings are not beings but what science recognises as light and warmth quanta of energy, while the individualising activity is the boundary of interaction between a self-actualising entity and that of the s-pressurised space-energy around it.

G: Can you visualise the sandwich set up and look at the formation of the chains?

T: Right, O.K.

G: We will start with the question, 'Are these water molecules unwinding?

T: There was a 'Yes' to that.

G: Can you get a picture of the water molecules inside the sandwich?

T: Yes, I'm in the gap in the sandwich and I'm surrounded by hundreds and hundreds of water spheres.

G: Now ask if we can look at the disintegration process forming the chains and describe it as you go along.

T: The switch is pressed and light floats out from the top plate in the form of beings that are moving quickly through this cloud of water spheres. Some glance off the spheres, some pass between them and occasionally a light being strikes one of these spheres squarely and penetrates it and this begins to release the grip of the individualising beings and the end of the coil of heart-shaped atoms springs out through the gap. This then drags out the rest of the chain, expanding as it escapes from the confines of the sphere. This chain goes on unwinding until what was all packed down into one sphere is tracing a path which runs halfway round our plate.

G: How does it register on the photographic plate?

T: The light ether beings from the discharge seem to get a response from the spheres and cause them to illuminate. Then as the chain unwinds it's carried across by the light ether beings towards the opposite side and moves quite gently onto the surface of the plate (fig. 27.10) where the light goes out of it into the photographic emulsion. After that the image shows the individual heart shapes contracting to a very small centre and disappearing.

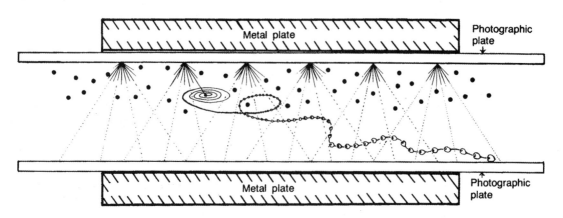

Fig. 27.10 The way in which Ted's ECE portrayed atoms unwinding and registering on the photo plate in the sandwich arrangement.

G: We get many different forms of chains, double chains, bright dots without a link between them, almost continuous tubes with only splodges instead of heart shapes?

T: I find myself looking at a string of bright dots. These have originated from inside one of the atoms in exactly the same way as the chain did. I can't see the connecting link between these dots, but it behaves exactly like a chain, it appears that there is a link that is not visible.

G: In some cases the water spheres unwind and in other cases they shatter?

T: I ask for a sphere to be opened in such a way that the chain comes out in pieces and the image shows a shell that is attacked in more than one place. One light ether being hit the sphere squarely on and the chain began to unwind, then others were striking at the sides, causing the shell to break away and the thing seemed to explode, with the chain shattering into pieces.

G: Do the individual units of the chain still look heart-shaped?

T: The image is showing all sorts of variations. It can be heart-shaped, heart-shaped elongated sideways, or an irregular circle. The heart was casting a shadow as it turned in space above me and the shape changes as the heart turns, so that from one angle it's throwing a complete heart shape, then as the heart shape moves the shape of the shadow changes.

G: Quite a lot of these forms are not proper chains made up of individual units but swirly masses?

T: I get 'lack of understanding'. And I'm shown the chain unwinding as a succession of heart shapes but the image registered on the plate as different from these heart shapes. I think it's our understanding that is lacking.

G: Can this individual unit be unravelled further?

T: I tried to unravel it and it just disappears, it doesn't break down to anything smaller.

G: Now repeat the experiment with the plate dusted with powder, what happens?

T: The chain impresses itself into the powder and carries on moving, making further impressions in the powder.

G: Can you get some imagery as to why this is?

T: No, I get again, 'lack of understanding'.

G: What happens when we do the experiment with a perspex plate and subsequently dust it with carbon powder?

T: I couldn't see anything at all on the surface, it looked quite clean. Then I dusted it with carbon powder and the outline of the chain showed up. The powder didn't go to where the chain had been in contact, it went to the periphery of the impressions.

G: When you see an atom of hydrogen you see a sphere with coiled up chains surrounded by individualising beings, ask, 'Is that an actual atom or is it a symbol?'

T: Symbol. Words came in that the actual atom isn't unlike this symbolic one but the symbolic atom is all we can cope with. At the moment the true atomic picture is beyond us. What we have is symbolism for it and symbolism for the way in which it reveals itself.

G: If we put two hydrogen atoms and one oxygen atom together to get water, again you see it as a sphere - much like the atom. From this we get the impression that the hydrogen and the oxygen lose their identities when they become water?

T: Yes, I saw the oxygen and the hydrogen come together, the three spheres merged and left one sphere which looked the same as the individual ones.

G: Science sees it totally differently. It sees atoms as retaining their individualities and being held together by attractions between them.

T: The image forms that way also.

G: Which is nearest to reality?

T: The words come in, 'serving one another'. The image is showing that they are still there as individuals and yet they've taken up the common role of water. Then when the light ether being comes along this thing unwinds as water.

Besant and Leadbeater state that when a compound is observed clairvoyantly a mingling of the component parts of the atoms is seen; sometimes the atoms retain their individuality and sometimes they are much broken up. With water the oxygen double snake retains its individuality and the two hydrogen atoms arrange themselves around it, while the group as a whole forms a sphere. (Is it possible that there are circumstances under which the constituents of atoms could intermingle and then separate as different atoms, as claimed by KEVRAN).

G: How is it that just one light ether being is able to bring about this unwinding?

T: The image shows this to be a very gentle process. The light ether being enters the water sphere and the outer shell begins to break down and then the thing begins to unwind. It appears to be finely balanced as if all that was needed was this almost soft push from the light ether being.

G: Can you get an image of a copper atom alongside the water molecule - does this unwind in the same way?

T: No, the light ether being seems to have much more difficulty here. The difference seems to be that the copper is much more securely grasped by the individualising beings and the light ether being finds it difficult to dislodge them.

G: How about a hydrogen atom?

T: This seems to be quite stable too and the light ether being has difficulty here also.

G: What about an oxygen atom?

T: The image looks similar to the copper one. The atom is very firmly grasped.

G: What feeling do you get for hydrogen?

T: One of floating off, drifting away.

G: And for oxygen?

T: Pulled down.

G: What happens when we put the two together?

T: There is the combination of the feelings of drawing to a centre and of wanting to move outwards. The light ether being moved into this and disturbed the balance, it added to the moving-out feeling and the sphere began to open up.

G: Change it to an ethyl alcohol molecule - does the light ether being enter this easily?

T: Yes, the system appears to be finely balanced and it can get in relatively easily and disturb this balance.

G: So, if we take anything that's firmly grasped, like any solid atom, this experiment won't work, but a liquid which is hovering on the borderline of changing to gas - water and alcohol evaporate readily - is amenable to unwinding?

T: Yes.

G: With the water molecule, what happens as we reduce the speed of the light ether being, does it still go in and cause unwinding?

T: It seems to be more difficult for it to penetrate.

G: What happens as we increase the speed of the light ether.

T: It has no trouble penetrating but tends to shatter the chains.

G: Now can we look at the Aurum picture and can you ask about where the chain comes from, is it the gold?

T: There was a 'No'.

G: Lactose?

T: There's a 'yes' and the word 'liquid' too.

G: So, was it due to the light ether being unwinding the potentised lactose in the solution and carrying it onto the photographic plate?

T: Yes.

G: In principle should it be possible to unwind atoms of any substance by potentising them?

T: A hesitant 'yes'.

Besant and Leadbeater do not give a clairvoyantly-observed structure for lactose but they describe several other benzene-ring based molecules and these show a fan-like structure, fig. 27.11, not unlike the string of fan-like forms that registered in the aurum photograph (fig. 27.5).

Fig. 27.11 The hexagonal fan-shaped structure that Besant and Leadbeater observed in a number of benzene-ring based molecules, in this case for phenol which has the specific structure on the upper right of the diagram attached to the hexagonal fan arrangement.

In one of Ted's ECEs on homoeopathic diluting we had been told that this caused the atom to unwind (Chapter 20), so we asked about this:

G: If we homoeopathically dilute, say, copper, is what's going on in the water the same as the pictures we've got of the unwinding atomic structures?
T: On yes, it shows it like that, yes. And the image shows the water very active with the beings in it.

We had also, of course, wondered about the relationship of these experiments to the conventional way in which science splits the atom:

G: Now change the image altogether and impact a high-energy particle on a piece of copper foil in a vacuum chamber, as conventional science does in splitting the atom and see what happens.
T: Well it appears to be very, very violent. The particle strikes the atom, the shell disintegrated, it breaks into pieces. The individualising beings are dispersed and the chain just explodes outwards, it doesn't even begin to unwind, it just shatters completely and the little heart-shaped bits are spread out all over the place.
G: Can you view it as a chain that is fractured in many places?
T: Yes, that image forms.
G: Is science doing a bad thing when it does this?
T: Yes, it appears to be interfering with the natural order of things but what comes in, is that man works in the material world and has freedom to work with the means available to him. So if he has developed along these lines these are the methods he will use. It's accepted.

G: In our unwinding atoms experiments we are doing the same thing as in splitting the atom, so is there the potential for getting energy out of substance in this way?
T: The image is saying that atomic energy is released as the result of the disintegration of atoms that in turn disintegrate other atoms around - I'm shown the uncontrolled state, in an atomic bomb cloud. In our sandwich a few of the light beings from the top plate penetrate spheres and cause them to unwind. These chains don't break up other atoms, only beings from the top plate are entering the sphere.
G: Is it possible to turn this into a system to generate light and heat in a way that would be gentle and yet be useful?
T: Nothing comes in.
G: Well, at the moment it's not on our programme to look into the generation of energy by alternative methods, would it be a good thing to do so?
T: Everything went misty and grey and the image of our experiment dissolved --- out of the mist came images of the crystallisation patterns - three big images, the copper chloride, the gold and the graphite, these images are very sharp and clear.
G: So we should concentrate on the crystallisation work and not think about liberating energy?
T: Our guides came in and pointed to the crystallisation patterns, they say that we have to make this decision. We would have to decide to work with energy -- they point strongly to the crystallisation patterns.
G: Our job is to advance the metaphysics and to do this we have to look at form in crystallisation and at homoeopathic remedies and things like that. But nevertheless there is a better way of liberating energy than Man is using at the moment - there is a job to be done there?
T: They nod at that but having nodded they turn and look at the patterns.
G: What about the perpetual lamp mentioned in Isis Unveiled, does that fall into this energy category?
T: An image formed of an ancient oil lamp, shaped like a genie lamp, the flame coming out of the spout. This was burning and there was an image of a clock alongside it that was racing round and round but the lamp kept burning without being filled -- and the guides still kept pointing to the crystal patterns.
G: Right, the message is clear enough.

The reference to the book *Isis Unveiled* relates to an interesting experience that we had. Many times during our researches things would happen, such as unsolicited encounters with people who gave us financial support which enabled us to keep going, or coming unexpectedly across information, books or articles, that helped us in what we were doing. In the photographic work we started by using sheet film of the sort that we used in our technology researches, then one day when Ted went to the stores to get more film, by mistake the storeman gave him a box of Ilford Q2 scientific plates that had not been stocked for some time but that someone had returned to stores. When, that evening, we went to continue with our experiments we realised the storeman's 'mistake' but we had only the Q2 plates so we used them instead of the usual film. They turned out to give much better results (the photographic sensitive particles in Q2 plates are on the surface and therefore directly in contact with what is taking place there, whereas in normal film they are embedded in a protective layer). It often seemed as though there was some invisible force trying to guide us. The most outstanding example of this was when we received through the post the two volumes of the Theosophical work, *Isis Unveiled* by BLAVATSKY, in which we came across the account of the ancient endlessly burning lamp, (the basis of Theosophy is that there existed an ancient wisdom which had a knowledge of things that has been lost). We had not ordered these books and when we phoned the bookseller who had sent them to us he could not remember doing so. So in an ECE, we asked the 'spiritual guides' about this:

G: Can we have a chat with the guides?
T: Your guide came in and mine appeared from behind him.
G: How on earth did they manage to land those two volumes of Isis Unveiled on my desk, which I hadn't ordered and the bookseller didn't even know he had sent me?
T: They shake hands on that.
G: And the bit that we dug out is the bit that the books were intended for?
T: Definitely.

There are many problems in understanding the significance of the activity tracks and whether or not they are unwinding atoms and, if so, their relationship to current scientific concepts of the nature of atoms and how this fits into *h*K-M and the relevance of what the ECEs have to say on this matter. In our searching for greater insight into the cause of the tracks we found that it was possible to create similar ones by putting small particles in the air gap in the sandwich.

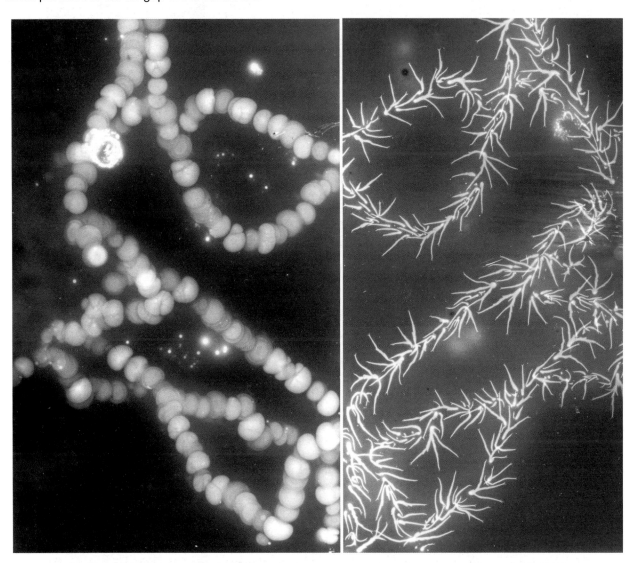

Fig. 27.12. Complementary registrations obtained on the negative and positive sides obtained by putting a particle of silica gel that was smaller than the air gap, in the sandwich. The particle has probably oscillated between the two sides, initiating break down of the boundary layer and light shapes on the negative side, with corresponding warmth spheres on the positive side.

Fig. 27.12 shows tracks made by putting a particle of silica gel (that was smaller than the air gap) in the sandwich. This produced 'light shapes' on the negative side and complementary 'warmth spheres' on the positive side, (of a type akin to those that occurred with the 'field type' break down that took place at higher voltage over the whole area of the photoplate, in fig. 25.19). We think this was due to the silica gel particle oscillating back and fore across the air gap, agitating a region of atoms in the boundary layer to give light shapes on the negative side, with corresponding warmth spheres on the positive side. When we put a glass sphere, (smaller than the silica gel particle) in the air gap we got the straight, regular tracks shown in fig. 27.13, while fig. 27.14 shows irregular tracks formed by irregular-shaped particles of ground glass. We assume that, as with the silica gel particle, the glass particles oscillated between the two plates but that because they were smaller they created only small regions of agitation of the atoms in the boundary layer which gave out light as 'spots'. Where the particle was symmetrical, as with the glass sphere, its movement followed a straight trajectory but if it was asymmetric, as with the ground glass particles, this force caused it to rotate as it oscillated back and fore, creating the tracks in the space-energy seen in fig. 27.14.

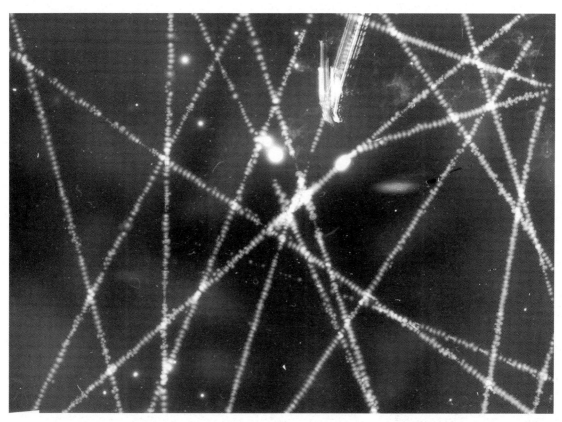

Fig. 27.13 Straight, regular activity tracks produced by putting a single spherical glass bead, that was smaller than the silica gel particle, in the air gap in the sandwich.

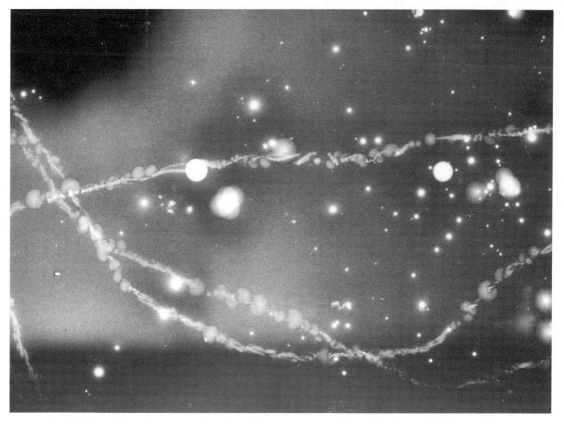

Fig 27.14 Irregular tracks produced by putting irregularly shaped pieces of ground glass in the sandwich

This asymmetrical movement occurred to a greater extent when we used short, highly asymmetric nylon fibres, (which had a length less than the air gap), fig. 27.15

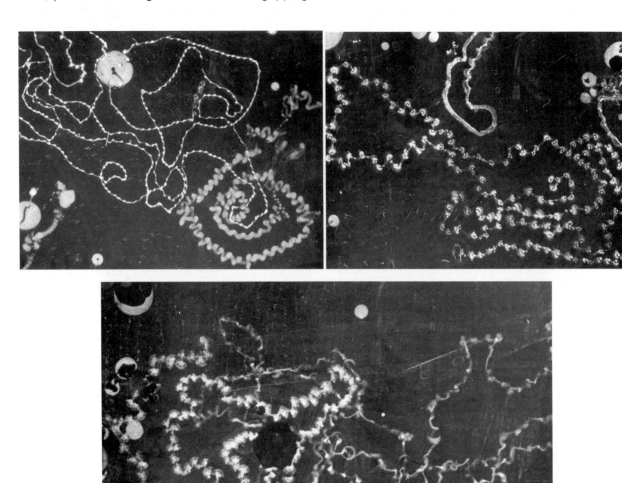

Fig.27.15 A selection of tracks obtained by putting short, fine nylon fibres in the sandwich. But in this case the photo plate on the positive side has been replaced by a thin sheet of perspex/lucite which has been subsequently dusted with fine carbon power (as used in Xerox printing) to show the tracks.

In some cases these tracks resembled some of the duplex tracks of fig. 27.3. We did not get tracks unless we deliberately put particles, or water vapour, in the air gap in the sandwich. This created the problem of the relationship of the particle-created tracks to the moisture-related 'atomic chains' and we asked about this in our ECEs:

G: Put a particle of dust in the gap between the plates and apply a voltage and see what happens.
T: When the light ether streams over, the particle glows and oscillates between the two surfaces, moving about as it does so.
G: So you get a series of glows created at the surface that are similar to the atomic chains?
T: Yes.
G: But the registrations that we get are much larger than the particle?
T: The image shows it like that. The particle is very small but it's surrounded by the activity of warmth and light that it has picked up and it's this that reacts with the plate to form an image - it appears to have acquired this on the other side of the sandwich.
G: With the atomic chains we register warmth and light forms that are nearly identical to those we get with particles, so, are these the aura of some little particle?
T: All I see is the sphere itself that is glowing. It contains its own light and warmth. But this increased enormously in size over when it was bound down inside the atom. I don't find a particle like the dust particle.
G: Do we have to have particles of dust there as well as the water vapour?

T: *Nothing comes for that.*

The tracks caused by the moving particles show that the size of the registration on the photo plate is much larger than the particle, presumably related to the size of the region of disturbance that it creates in the boundary layer that gives off light. In the same way, unwinding atom tracks could represent the areas of disturbance, where light is emitted, and not directly the size of the particles. But this still leaves the problem that if these are tracks of unwinding atoms, how does it come about that atoms have this inner structure?

The *h*K-M view that we have expounded is that atoms come into existence from the interaction and breakdown of the ponderous s-entity energy and the more-active galaxy energy, in which the fragmented ponderous s-entity becomes the nucleus, and the more-active galaxy energy becomes the electron energy, of a hydrogen atom. Then, in stars, hydrogen atoms are forced together to form larger atoms. When these come together, if they are compatible they form a molecule, as described in these ECEs for the formation of a water molecule from hydrogen and oxygen atoms. According to the ECEs, when a light ether entity enters the molecule it disturbs its internal balance, so that it breaks open and its internal components unwind, to give rise to the activity tracks registered in our experiments.

As we have stated, according to *h*K-M, atoms come about by the interaction of ponderous s-entity derived energy and the more active galaxy derived energy, both of which derive from the same space energy. We therefore carried out some fluid flow experiments on the interaction of a greater with a lesser activity. These consisted of observing the behaviour of a stream of oil (the more active part) poured into the same oil in a near static (less active) state. We put fine copper flake powder in the container of less-active oil and stirred it slightly before each experiment, so that it became reflecting and the behaviour of the impinging stream could be observed and photographed. If the oil was sufficiently viscous, as the active stream entered the oil in the container its impact caused it to spiral. If the viscosity of the oil was reduced, or it was moved faster across the surface, or it was dropped from a greater height, (thereby increasing its activity), instead of flowing smoothly into the oil below the flow pattern showed a sequence of 'bulges'. If the viscosity was further reduced or its impact increased, (further increasing its activity), the stream lost its coherence and broke up into droplets, often with smaller droplets in between, fig. 27.16.

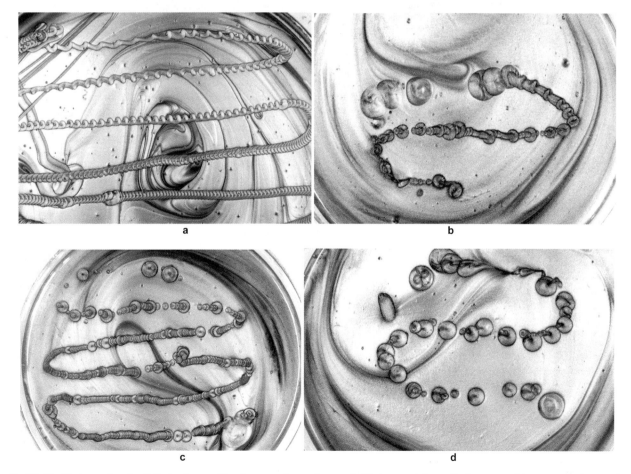

a   b

c   d

Fig.27.16. Photographs of activity tracks resulting from pouring a stream of oil into a container with the same oil in a near static state in it. (a) Spiral tracks produced with high viscosity oil (560). (b), (c), (d) the different tracks produced by progressively reducing the viscosity (115, 83, and 52). Note the similarity of these tracks to some of those registered in fig 27.2 and to Leadbeater and Besant's diagram in fig. 27.9. The background swirls arise from the slight stirring necessary to activate the copper powder in the oil in the container so that the tracks showed up.

These experiments show that when a flow of higher energy encounters the resistance of lower energy it breaks up into formations resembling those that we registered as 'activity tracks'.

It may be that the turbulence of interaction between the s-entities and galaxy entities forms chains of the type seen in our experiments, while the chain, as a whole would follow the rotating pattern of the turbulence. This would be compressed to a spiral by the s-pressure and form the nucleus of the atom that would unwind in our experiment. It would conform to the description of atomic structure given by Leadbeater and Besant and it could account for the fact that scientists find that the nucleus of the atom can be split up into many subatomic components.

Another possibility is that chains formed from disintegrating neutrons. In Chapter 8 we proposed that hydrogen atoms were formed by the flow of the higher activity g-entity energy passing over, and wrapping up the lower activity s-entity energy in a wave-like manner, to give rise to a low energy nucleus with a high energy electron surround, fig. 8.1(a). If the interaction was more intense we suggested that a 'swiss roll' structure of alternate layers of high and low energy resulted, fig. 8.1(b), to form a neutron. In this, the more active energy layer could then act on the low energy one, to produce a smaller version of the hydrogen atom structure, while the alternate layers of high and low energy could be a delicate balance that broke up under the impacting light energy entity. (Fig. 8.2 of the suggested structure of the neutron as a coiled up chain of 'miniature hydrogen atoms' was an image received by Ted in one of his ECEs dealing with atomic structures).

It seemed that the 'unwinding of atoms' occurred more readily with water vapour because, according to the ECEs, the water molecule is a delicate balance between an expansive nature of hydrogen and a concentrating nature of oxygen. In Chapter 25 we presented results that showed that when water vapour molecules were subjected to a stress in the sandwich (due to a higher voltage than used in the unwinding experiments) dividing bright spots were observed, (fig. 25.27(b)). Also bright spots were registered associated with water vapour being driven out of leaves by subjecting these to a prolonged high voltage pulse, (fig. 25.29(b)). Perhaps there is a connection between this behaviour and the chains of bright spots in the 'unwinding atom' experiments that required the presence of water vapour. This instability and division of water makes one wonder about its role in cell division. Since the major constituent of a cell is water, could cell division perhaps be related to the delicate balance of water, claimed by the ECEs, and that it divides under stress, as happens in prebiotic globules? However, other factors may be involved, as clairvoyants report observing 'prana', or 'vitality' globules associated with living organisms and Besant and Leadbeater state that when examined by clairvoyant vision the internal structure of these globules is similar to, but not identical with, that of the oxygen atom. Perhaps some of the bright spots emanating from leaves, shown in Chapter 25 are not of a chemical nature but are 'vitality globules'. We have suggested, in Chapter 20, that water could play a crucial role in the link by which etheric-willing, soul-feeling and spirit-thinking connect with, and bring about activities in, the physical substance body. Also there is the role that water plays in encapsulating and carrying the healing activities of homoeopathic remedies. There is much here to be sorted out by the next generation.

Résumé

We commenced this book by making the claim that humanity is now poised to make a further step in its understanding of existence, by adding to the knowledge that it has accumulated on the way in which the Universe works a comprehension of why it works in the way that it does and its underlying purpose. To make a contribution to this end we have set out a hypothetical Kosmic Metaphysics (hK-M) that seeks to demonstrate that such a goal is feasible, although we make no claim for the validity of all, or any part of this metaphysics.

Kosmic Evolution

According to hK-M our Universe is one of a sequence of Universes that comprise what we call the Kosmos, while the Kosmos itself is part of an 'Absolute' all-embracing totality. To describe how our Universe arises we trace back its origins beyond the beginning of life on Earth and beyond the existence of any kosmic phenomena, to a prior state of dormant energy that derives from the Absolute. As a result of stress due to unrealised potentials, generated in its prior 'Absolute' state, the energy stirs into activity, which then increases to become a state of turmoil. In this turmoil the energy becomes aware of its ability to be active and this gives it a sense of self, here there and everywhere, that results in the turmoil differentiating into multitudinous self-actualising centres of activity.

The activity flowing out from each centre encounters that of adjacent centres which return it to it, so that the activity takes on the pattern of a Bénard cell and the energy becomes organised into a collective of these cosmic Bénard cells, that we have called superstructure entities (s-entities) because these then comprise the superstructure of the Kosmos.

In seeking increased sense of self the s-entities increase in activity and, in so doing, they exert stresses on each other at their peripheries of interaction that causes these regions to breakdown into a state of turmoil, out of which further self-actualising centres arise that develop into a Universe.

By increasing in activity to a state of stress, the s-entities exhaust their impulse to experience a sense of self and they revert to a quiescent state. But they then lose their sense of self and the impulse to re-experience it arises in them so they become active again. They then repeat the cycle of increasing in activity to cause further break down at their peripheries, that generates another state of turmoil and another Universe and a state of stress that causes them to revert again to a quiescent state. This cycle is repeated, as a sort of breathing out and breathing in activity, that creates a succession of Universes.

In each cycle the s-entities seek increasing sense of self by increasing their level of activity. This means that each state of turmoil and the Universe that arises from it, is more active, develops further, is more differentiated and the parts are more 'substantial' before the s-entities becomes stressed and withdraw to a quiescent state. In this way each Universe creates, and exists at, its own level of activity, (i.e. in its own set of 'dimensions' or level of vibrations).

The continual seeking for ever-greater sense of self is the underlying reason for the evolutionary nature of the Kosmos and of everything of which it consists. The turmoil that this creates, giving rise to an increasing number of Universes and their activities and entities, is the cause of the ever-expanding variety of features that develop in the Kosmos in each subsequent Universe.

These developments all take place in the basic energy state, so that everything in the Kosmos comprises patterns of activity in which everything interacts with everything else and the evolution of the whole is the sum of the evolution of the parts and the evolution of each part is controlled by the evolution of the whole.

Universes are not independent of each other because they all exist within, and are subjected to, the pressure of the collective activity of the s-entities that make up the Kosmos. In particular, this causes each new Universe to interact with the previous generations of Universes, with the earlier generations acting to integrate the new generation into their established pattern of activity, while the new generations stimulate the older ones into a new, more active mode.

As a result of interacting with later Universes, the entities created in earlier Universes evolve. When they are first 'born' they are, like babies, entities of 'will', i.e. concerned with expressing the sense of self that they experience from being active. When they interact with the new entities from later Universes they experience sensations that evoke feelings of like or dislike in them, according to whether they experience these as a stress or a stimulus. Then, instead of blindly carrying on with their established activities, they adjust these to the activities of later Universes.

As more different entities and their associated interactions are created in further Universes these give rise to a wider range of sensations and a corresponding development of a range of more sensitive feelings in the entities of the earlier Universes. Thereby later developments bring about the evolution of the earlier ones.

As more Universes come into existence, the gap between early and later Universes and their entities increases and it becomes more difficult for the early generations of entities to relate directly to the increasingly remote activities of the later ones by their sensations and feelings. They have to evaluate them indirectly, through the changes that they produce in the activities of the Universes with which they are in direct contact. This evaluating activity causes them to develop thinking and thereby they begin to get some conscious understanding of what is going on.

Developments do not, however, take place at the same rate so that three streams arise. One stream 'lags behind', so that its understanding, thinking and activities relate to an earlier, more 'ethereal' and unified state than the way that things are developing at the 'working face': another stream gets an enhanced (Ego) sense of self from pushing ahead with new developments, so that its activities are directed towards greater differentiation and making things more substantial, without concern for any disharmony that its activities may have on the established situation: the third stream gets an enhanced sense of self from ensuring that its ideas and actions contribute to a harmonious evolution of the totality.

The Evolution of our Universe and Planet Earth

When the s-entities interact and break down at their peripheries in our Universe-creating Kosmic cycle this results in a state of turmoil out of which further self-actualising entities, galaxies, (g-entities) arise.

In seeking greater sense of self the newer, more active g-entities interact with the surrounding older, less active s-entities and their zone of interaction breaks down into a state of turmoil that comprises a mixture of high activity, more evolved g-entity energy and low activity, less evolved s-entity energy. Under the pressure of the activity of the surrounding s-entity, these two levels of activity 'grind each other down' into small bits that combine together to form a cloud of hydrogen atoms, in which the bits of the less evolved activity form nuclei surrounded by zones of the more evolved activity.

The hydrogen cloud disrupts the pattern of activity of the s-entity in this region and this part of it becomes separated off and is then compressed by the larger, unaffected part of the s-activity until the increase in intensity of its activity creates a stress in it that gives it a sense of self and it becomes a self-actualising star entity, with a B-cell pattern of activity.

The s-pressurised B-cell motion of the star entity compresses together the hydrogen atoms within it, to form larger atoms of different substances that then pervade this region of the cosmos as 'cosmic dust'.

The interaction between s-entities and g-entities, causing mutual breakdown and creating hydrogen, and the hydrogen creating stars that then form larger atoms from the hydrogen is continually taking place and is the basis of the cosmic phenomena that we perceive when we look out to the heavens.

As more hydrogen and stars form from the continuing interaction and break down of g-entities and adjacent s-entities, these encompass cosmic dust of substances formed by previous stars. This causes a stress in the B-cell pattern of activity of the later forming stars that results in some of it being ejected from the new star into the surrounding s-entity where it causes this region of the s-entity's activity to become separated off. This then becomes compressed so that it develops a B-cell motion, to create a Planetary Entity that carries the substances to its centre, to form a planet that orbits the star. This is the way in which an Earth planetary entity and our Earth planet come into existence.

The s-pressurised B-cell activity of the Earth Entity carries substances towards its centre and as these come closer together the stresses that their presence creates in the Earth Entity energy interact. Where interaction stresses are dominant and lock substances together and prevent them from flowing with the B-cell motion, solid substances separate out, to form the body of the Earth. Where interaction stresses are small, substances continue to circulate with the B-cell motion to form the gaseous atmosphere. Where interaction stresses are intermediate, substances cohere together and have movement imparted to them by the Earth Entity's B-cell motion, as the watery parts of the Earth's surface.

The Arising and Evolution of Life on Earth

In its initial hot state of turmoil the water on the surface of the planet takes in some of the gaseous atmosphere and some solid earth substances. Then, as it cools and contracts, these substances create stresses in it, causing minute droplets of one composition to separate out from the overall watery state of a different composition.

The interaction between substances inside the droplets with those outside them results in the formation of membranes around them. The s-pressure causes some substances to flow from their environment into the droplets and other substances to flow out of them, by diffusion/osmosis. Some of the substances going into the droplets interact in a way that reduces the stress in the droplets, thereby liberating energy in them. This gives the energy in the droplets a sense of self and they take over this activity of taking in substances that reduce the stress and interact to free energy and correspondingly rejecting substances that increase the stress, to give rise to minute living, prokaryotic cells in the watery environment that derive a sense of self from maintaining the pattern of activity that gives them their existence.

Groups of prokaryotic cells develop a pattern of interaction, whereby some prokaryotic cells live off substances rejected by other prokaryotic cells. This pattern of activity gives the space energy in this region a sense of self and it becomes self-actualising and it maintains and develops this activity. Thereby larger, eukaryotic cells arise that comprise a group of interacting prokaryotic cells under the control of a eukaryotic entity.

Groups of eukaryotic cells develop a pattern of interaction that gives the space energy involved in this a sense of self and it becomes self-actualising and maintains its sense of self by maintaining and developing this pattern of activity. Thereby larger, multicellular, organisms arise that comprise a group of interacting eukaryotic cells under the control of a multicellular entity.

In seeking increased sense of self multicellular entities develop the ability to maintain their patterns of activity with increasing numbers of eukaryotic cells. Thereby an increasing number and variety of larger multicellular organisms arise, first in the watery environment and then also on land.

In striving to maintain their existence and their sense of self in an increasing range of environments, multicellular entities experience a variety of stresses that cause them to develop an increasing variety of patterns of activities and skills, e.g. to swim, to fly, to penetrate into the earth, to climb trees and to move through and exist in, different terrains.

As parts of the Earth Entity become separated off in pursuing the life cycles of the organisms that develop in this way and then return to the collective state, they carry their experiences back with them. Thereby the Earth Entity contains the total memory of all the developments that have taken place on Earth. When it is 'incarnated' in a living organism, the stress/stimulus of the circumstances that it encounters activates the relevant memories and cause it to repeat its past behaviour and this results in the instinctive species behaviour of organisms, that is passed on from generation to generation.

Where members of a species are simultaneously subjected to the same stresses in the same environment this activates the same aspect of the Earth Entity memory in all of them so that they respond collectively to it, as in the behaviour of shoals of fishes and flocks of birds.

However, the Earth Entity is not simply a repository of past experience. The s-pressure causes it to integrate its experiences, in the same way that our memory organises our experiences into coherent patterns of relationships.

In some cases, e.g. honey bees and termites, the Earth Entity's memory-integrating behaviour is reflected in, and enacted out by, the behaviour of different members or groups in a species, to give rise to integrated patterns of organisation.

Out of this continual sorting and organising of experiences potential new relationships emerge that are subsequently activated by the circumstances that the Earth Entity finds itself in, in the various organisms in which it is 'incarnated'. In putting these into effect some work out and some don't, depending on how they fit into the overall pattern of evolution on Earth. Evolution of life on Earth thereby occurs by a combination of potentials for further developments arising out of the Earth Entity's memory integrating activity and the stresses encountered by organisms that activate relevant responses, in their striving to maintain their existence and enhance their sense of self. This is the same as the way in which human developments take place – by uniting possibilities that arise from the sorting and integration of past experiences with the stresses/needs/desires to maintain and develop our sense of self, in the conditions in which we find ourselves that, in turn, arise from the collective evolution of everything else around us.

Out of these developments there arises a particularly versatile creature, a hominid, that is able to swim, climb trees and traverse different terrains by walking upright and that has the dexterity to manipulate materials in its environment to make simple tools to support the activities of its existence.

The Arising of Humanity

In the same way that organisms on Earth explore new environments for new possibilities for enhanced sense of self, so do the hierarchy of spiritual, entities of the Kosmos, created in previous Universes, explore the environments of the new Universes that come into existence.

As a result some of these spiritual entities explore the developments that have taken place on planet Earth and they seek understanding and a sense of self by fostering them. As they explore the hominid situation they find that this offers new opportunities for a more substantial, enhanced sense of self and they get caught up in it and thereby they 'incarnate' into hominid bodies, to give rise to homo sapiens.

At first homo sapiens retain some awareness of their origins and existence in the hierarchy of entities generated by previous Universes (the world of the gods) and the role of these in the Kosmos. But, as they become more involved in developing an existence and sense of self in the complexities of hominid existence on Earth and in exploring its potentials, they lose their awareness of, and contact with, the Kosmic Hierarchy.

This gives them a sense of freedom and individuality to develop their sense of self. At the same time, as a result of becoming cut off from the Hierarchy they are forced to rely on their own resources and to think for themselves. At first their thinking is concerned with developing a more secure, satisfying, rewarding and fulfilling life on Earth. But then they begin to think about the situation in which they find themselves and to try to understand what it involves, how it has come about and what lies behind it all. In this way homo sapiens develop a 'cut off', 'outsider' view of the Kosmos by forming a conceptual understanding of its nature and workings, that gives the Kosmos a new level of self-consciousness.

Characteristics of Our Life on Earth

We are spiritual willing, feeling, thinking entities, incarcerated in bodies developed by biological evolution on Earth through which we express these qualities in the circumstances in which we find ourselves. Thereby, in our 'cut off' state we develop our will, feeling and thinking further than in our spiritual existence within the collective activity of the Omniverse Hierarchy.

The spiritual world comprises different levels of beings generated by previous Universes, all of which seek a sense of self by their activity at their particular level of development. At the 'top' are beings from the first Universe in our Kosmic sequence that are the oldest, most well-established beings of the Kosmic Hierarchy, who work together to stimulate harmonious evolution and who we know as 'God'.

By working through a series of developments of their will, feeling and thinking, these Beings have developed an understanding and loving concern for the well-being of later generations of entities in the struggles that they are going through, in their striving to survive and develop a sense of self, in the situations in which they find themselves. The higher levels exist in the patterns of activities of their own realms and they do not directly interact or interfere with the activities of lower levels but from their greater experience, more developed control of the cosmic energy and their larger viewpoint they can offer help and guidance for those beings of the lower levels who seek it.

Because of our need to concentrate on the activities that enable us to maintain our existence on Earth, we have largely lost contact with the spiritual world of our origins. However, a few people retain, or develop, the ability to contact the spiritual world even, in some cases to the extent of having contact with the Godhead level, and these people have been responsible for keeping an awareness of spiritual worlds alive and for founding the world's religions that, in their various ways, seek to give meaning and purpose to our lives.

Humanity, and correspondingly the Omniverse spiritual hierarchy comprises three streams of beings: those that are more concerned with seeking a sense of self from their Ego spiritual thinking activity: those that are more concerned with seeking a sense of self from realising the potentials of their material existence: a middle stream that seeks enhanced Ego sense of self by integrating spiritual and material advances to make a harmonious contribution to the evolution of the whole. We can tap into, and derive inspiration and strength from each of these streams. The first gives rise to spiritual ideals and, if pursued one-sidedly, to religious fanatics: the second gives rise to exploring and developing the potentials of the material world, in extreme cases to out and out materialists who do this with no awareness of, or concern for, the effects that their activities have on upsetting the balance of evolution. Tapping into the inspiration and strength of the third stream leads to balanced, harmonious spiritual-material evolution.

We find that life on Earth is, on the one hand, a lonely, stressful and demanding business and, on the other hand, that it is stimulating and challenging and offers opportunities for developing a greater sense of self.

We can develop our sense of self in many different ways, for example:

- We get a sense of self from playing a role in the activities of our society, e.g. activities that provide food, homes, education, medical and/or other support for people, industry, commerce, law and order, the arts, entertainment, transport, etc.

- The experience of living in and manipulating a physical body is, in itself, challenging and we get a sense of self by developing it and/or enhancing its appearance or in exploring its potentials in physical activities.

- We find ourselves in a world of minerals, plants and animals and we get a sense of self by working with, and developing, different aspects of these, or just in exploring the world at large.

- We are caught up in a biologically-developed system of interaction between male and female sexes and we get a sense of self from these interactions and from procreation and creating a family and fostering the development of off-spring.

- We experience a sense of self from a variety of social interactions with our fellow human beings.

Where we find it difficult to cope with the void created by losing contact with the collective activity and support provided by the spiritual hierarchy we invent activities to fill it, such as games the playing of which gives us a sense of self, or vicariously by watching others play, to fill our lives and keep the emptiness at bay.

Because of our feeling of insecurity that arises from being separated from the spiritual world of our origins, we seek stability from the activities, feelings, thoughts and beliefs that we acquire in striving for a sense of self but where these clash with those of other people in their striving for a sense of self this can lead to disharmony, conflict and, in the extreme case, to wars. If we wish to make a contribution to peace and harmony in the world we have to develop tolerance, compassion, understanding and peace in ourselves and become centres for the expression of these qualities.

When we die, we, i.e. our spirit, separates from its physical body. However, we then no longer fit into the spiritual world of the Omniverse Hierarchy because, as a result of our Earth experiences, we have developed different qualities, some of which are disharmonious to those of the spiritual world of our origins. So we exist in an intermediate state, along with other discarnate spirits. In our post-mortem existence we review what we did in our Earth life and the effect of our actions on other entities, and opportunities that we neglected. This causes impulses to arise in us to reincarnate into the Earth situation to sort out these issues. We do this a number of times until we have developed an inner spiritual harmony that enables us to return to the spiritual world, taking with us the experiences of our Earth lives. We are then prodigal sons/daughters returning to the Father.

A Tentative Look at the Future

Ancient myths show that from early times homo sapiens was concerned with the creation and workings of the world, which their myths attributed to the activities of a spiritual world of gods. These myths gave rise to beliefs and practices on which early cultures based their way of life. Working under the auspices of the gods homo sapiens learned to do many things which made them aware of their innate ability to operate out of their own resources and to think for themselves. Then, in the 5th century B.C. philosophers in ancient Greece thought that it is possible for humanity to comprehend the workings of the gods out of its own power of thinking and thereby, in Western Civilisation there developed the search for a conceptual understanding of the nature and workings of the world. With the arising of Christianity, the belief in creation by a world of gods was replaced by creation by a single God, (working through emissaries Seraphim, Cherubim, Archangels, Angels, etc). The understanding developed by the ancient Greeks was absorbed into the subsequent

Hellenistic and Roman cultures and revived, in Western Europe in the Renaissance. Then, in a new level of conceptual development, in the 16th century, it was found that the workings of the solar system could be described by the mathematical laws that govern mechanisms. However, understanding of the nature and workings of God and of the nature and role of humanity remained difficult. This led to the search for an understanding of existence being broken down into three aspects, the nature and workings of God/gods that became the province of religion and theology, the nature and activities of humankind that became the province of the humanities and the workings of the material world that became the province of science.

- We suggest that in the comparatively near future there will develop a Metaphysics, perhaps something like hK-M, that will provide a broader and more basic evolutionary-wholistic understanding of existence that will reintegrate the three aspects of religion/theology, the humanities and the workings of the material world, that were separated from each other at the beginning of the scientific era. We think that this will create major changes in our outlook and understanding of many aspects of existence.

Since the three culture split scientists have been determining in ever-greater detail the nature and laws of behaviour of the substances of the mineral kingdom. By examining the behaviour of substances in living organisms scientists have found that these take on more complex and evolved functions than in the mineral kingdom. Scientists have then attempted to explain the arising and evolution of life on Earth, feelings, thinking, consciousness and the whole of creation in terms of the behaviour of substances, as though substances have brought about all these evolutionary developments out of themselves. However, there is no evidence for substances possessing properties whereby they have the ability to bring these developments about. According to hK-M substances do nothing of themselves. They create stresses in the basic energy that results in these parts becoming active. This gives them a sense of self, which they take over and thereby they become self-actualising entities. These then seek enhanced sense of self by exploring the potentials of their interaction with substances for further developments. It is the same as the way that, when we seek a sense of self by achieving something in the material world, what we achieve results from the combination of our striving activity and the natures of the materials that we are working with.

In the arising of life on Earth, by using their energy to exert their will to be active in the world of substances, organisms create a body of will activity that permeates the physical substances of the body. Thereby it becomes an entity that seeks to fulfil its will nature (i.e. a plant). As it evolves and interacts with other entities it experiences sensations and feelings and it seeks fulfilment of these. Thereby it raises part of its energy to become a body of feeling activity that permeates its will activity and physical substance bodies i.e. it develops an animal nature. In seeking fulfilment of its feelings the organism evaluates and selects the best way to do this and thereby it develops thinking ability and raises part of its energy to become a mental-thinking body of activity that permeates its feeling activity, will activity and physical substance bodies: that is, it becomes a human being. Our body thus comprises substances acted on by a hierarchy of self-actualising patterns of activity, that give rise to prokaryotic cells, eukaryotic cells, and a multicellular hominid body into which we have incarnated from a spiritual world.

- We suggest that new areas of investigation will develop that are concerned with patterns of energy flow and the way that these give rise to the formations and functions of substances in living organisms, particularly in the workings of the human body. A growing number of people are developing the ability to perceive these energy fields. Also attempts are being made to register them photographically and/or instrumentally. We think that energy field research will become a growing area of activity that will enhance our understanding of the workings of our bodies and correspondingly our understanding of what is required for good health and the treatment of malfunctioning.

- The growing number of people experiencing higher states of consciousness suggests that increasing knowledge of, and integration with, the activities of the spiritual world is occurring. This could give us an enhanced contact with the Omniverse Hierarchy and, in particular, with the higher Godhead level and at a more prosaic level, with the part of us that remains in the spiritual world from which we derive, i.e. our Higher Selves. This could lead to a better understanding of the nature and purpose of our personal lives and greater understanding of the nature and workings of existence in general.

Technical Appendix

Electrophotography

We started this aspect of our investigations using an electrostatic generator, first a Wimshurst machine and then a Van de Graaf generator applied to the 'sandwich' set up of fig. 25.18. The spark gap decided the voltage applied to the sandwich, fig. TA.1(a), and we usually operated within the range 5 - 15 mm with about 20 sparks to give the registration on the photoplate.

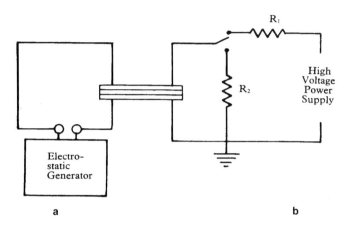

a   b

Fig TA.1 The arrangement used to apply pulses of high voltage to the 'sandwich' or similar type of experimental set up, (a) from an electrostatic generator, (b) by a single controlled pulse using the high voltage supply unit of fig. TA2 .

Figs. 15.3, 15.4, 15.5(a) and (b), 15.6, 15.7, 15.8, 15.9, 15.10, 25.28, 25.30, 25.32, 25.33, 25.34, 25.35, 25.36, 25.37(a) and (b), were obtained by this method.

Later we used a more controlled technique, applying a single pulse from a high voltage power source, fig. TA.1(b). This power source was designed and built for us by Michael Watson. The circuit for the power source is shown in fig. TA.2.

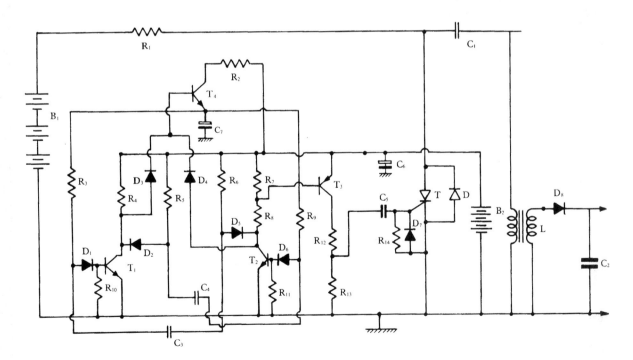

Fig. TA.2 The circuit for the high-voltage power supply unit designed and built for us by Michael Watson. Component values:R1 1.8kΩ 10w: R2 39Ω: R3, R9 3.9kΩ: R4, R5, R6 1kΩ: R7, R8 560kΩ: R10, R11 47kΩ: R12, R13 68Ω: R14 220Ω: D1 to 7 IN914: D8 LC180: T BT106: T1,T2 2N3705: T3 2N2905: T4 2N2219: C1 0.47 µF 350v: C2 typically 0.005µF 20 Kv working: C3, C4 1µF: C5 0.1µF: C6, C7 100µF 12v: B1 3x90v tapped batteries or variac-controlled rectifier unit: B2 9v battery: L oil-filled ignition coil

High voltage batteries B1 pass current through a charging resistor R1. This current charges the storage capacitor C1. The voltage across C1 rises until it is equal to the applied battery voltage. An electronic switch, the thyristor T, is used to connect C1 across the primary winding of a motor car ignition coil L. To operate the thyristor T an impulse is applied to its gate terminal, this results in T becoming a short circuit. This condition only occurs for current flowing in one direction. If an attempt is made to reverse the current flow then T passes into the non-conducting condition. This mechanism is used to return T to the open condition and allow C1 to recharge. Assume that C1 is fully charged and that a trigger impulse has been applied to T. C1 is now connected directly across the coil L. Current starts to flow in L and the rising current produces a voltage across L equal to that applied from C1. As current flows out of C1 the voltage across it falls. When the capacitor has discharged the voltage across it is zero. The magnetic field produced by the coil L now stores the energy which initially was stored in the capacitor. The collapse of the magnetic field causes the current flowing through L to continue. The continuing current charges C1 but the polarity is now in reverse to that of its original charge. The capacitor C1 discharges sending a current in the reverse direction through L. This current switches the thyristor into its non-conducting condition. A diode D is provided which allows the current to bypass the thyristor and partially recharge the capacitor C1. The capacitor is now polarised as it was initially. Some energy has been passed out of the coil through its secondary winding. The secondary winding has a larger number of turns than the primary winding. The output of the secondary winding is therefore larger. For a 300 volt charge on C1, the output voltage may be between 15- 28kv. The actual voltage depends on the coil used and various losses inherent in the circuit.

A rectifier is used to convert the oscillatory output of the coil into direct current for charging a storage capacitor C2.

The trigger impulse is provided by a transistor square wave generator. Each transistor alternately switches between the on and off condition. The frequency of oscillation is given by:

$$F = \frac{1}{1.4C3.R2}$$

where C3 is in farads, R2 is in ohms and F is in hertz.

The voltage produced at the output on C2 can be changed by altering the applied battery voltage or by changing the value of R1.

It must be emphasised that working with high voltages can be very dangerous. the author and publisher of this book cannot accept any responsibility for injury suffered as a result of constructing apparatus described in this book.

Table 1 gives the experimental conditions for the figures that were obtained by this method.

TABLE 1

Fig No.	Air gap 10^{-3} cms	Applied Voltage Kv	Charge Resist. ohms	Discharge Resist. ohms	Exposure secs
15.9(a)	70	3	1.5m	500m	10
15.9(b)	280	15	500m	1g	0.5
15.9(c)	300	18	0	500m	10
15.9(d)	130	18	0	500m	10
15.10(a)	280	20	1m	0	1/100
15.10(b)	370	20	1m	0	1/100
15.10(c)	200	17.5	28k	5g	1/100
25.2	-	20	0	5g	1/100
25.3	-	20	0	5g	1/100
25.5	-	18	0	0	-
25.6	-	10	0	0	1/100
25.8(a)	-	5	0	0	1/100
25.8(b)	-	5	0	0	1/100
25.9(a)	-	5.5	0	0	1/100
25.9(b)	-	15	0	0	1/100

25.9(c)	-	2	0	0	1/100
25.10(a)	-	10	0	0	1/100
25.10(b)	-	1.5	0	0	1/100
25.10(c)	-	2	0	0	1/100
25.10(d)	-	15	0	0	1/100
25.10(e)	-	10	0	0	1/100
25.13	-	20	0	5g	1/100
25.15(a)	70	18	1.5m	50g	0.5
25.15(b)	70	18	1.5m	5g	0.5
25.15(c)	300	18	1.5m	500m	0.5
25.15(d)	-	18	1.5m	5m	0.5
25.16(a)	140	18	0	500m	10
25.16(b)	70	18	1.5m	500m	10
25.16(c)	35	18	1.5m	500m	0.5
25.16(d)	-	18	0	500m	-
25.17	140	18	1.5m	500m	10
25.21	70	12.5	1m	5g	1/100
25.23	70	15	1m	500m	1/100
25.24	70	12.5	1m	0	1/100
25.25	300	15	28m	5g	1/100
25.27(b)	400	19	500	5g	1/100
25.29(a)	70	15	1m	1m	1/100
25.29(b)	70	10	1m	0	180
27.1	70	5	1.5m	0	30
27.2(a)	70	5	1.5m	10k	10
27.2(b)	70	5	1.5m	10k	10
27.2(c)	70	5	150	10k	10
27.2(d)	70	5	100k	10k	10
27.2(e)	70	5	1.5m	10k	10
27.3(a)	70	5	1k	10k	10
27.3(b)	70	5	1.5m	0	10
27.3(c)	70	5	10k	10k	10
27.3(d)	70	5	1k	10k	10
27.4(a)	70	5	1.5m	10k	10
27.4(b)	70	5	1.5m	3m	10
27.4(c)	70	5	100k	10k	10
27.5	70	5	1k	10k	10
27.12	150	5	0	0	5
27.13	70	5	1m	10k	10
27.14	280	9	1.5m	10k	10
27.15	70	5	0	0	5

The Spreading Drop Technique

The experimental arrangement for this technique is shown in fig. 26.3(a). The essential features were a dropper on a hinged arm positioned to allow a drop of liquid (about 0.05 cc) to fall a distance of 7mm onto the liquid layer below. The hinged arm was then moved to one side so that photographs of the spreading of the drop could be taken with the camera above. It was found vital to have a uniform layer of liquid on the plate below and for this to be level, hence the levelling screws which were adjusted in conjunction with a highly-accurate engineering spirit level. A ribbon of liquid was put onto the surface of the plate and this was then spread across it by a spreader made from an aluminium bar with a precisely machined step of the required height, so as to make a uniform layer. It was also found essential that the glass plates were uniform, flat and clean (so that they were wetted by the liquid layer and it did not retract). We used photographic half plates that were stripped of emulsion and then soaked in a mixture of 50% Analar Nitric acid and 50% Analar Sulphuric acid for a week after which they were washed in tap water, then distilled water, and dried.

Capillary Dynamolysis

These experiments were carried out in a glass chamber to reduce temperature fluctuations and prevent draughts. The dryness of the filter paper after running the first solution through it was found to be critical. We placed the filter paper in an air oven at $100^{\circ}C$ for 15 minutes.

A well-established and widely used technique similar to capillary dynamolysis is that of chromatography. Here a solution of a mixture of substances is run through the filter paper followed by a solvent and the different substances are separated out as bands in the solvent flow according to their affinity for the solvent and their affinity for adsorption on the fibres of the filter paper. The experimental arrangement in this case is designed to produce well-delineated bands of the different substances that can then be analysed and not to produce complex patterns of the capillary dynamolysis type.

The technique of capillary dynamolysis was suggested by Rudolf Steiner and worked out by KOLISKO to examine planetary effects and to examine the 'quality' of plant extracts, the growth potential of soils and the effects of composts on plant growth, judging the results by the 'amount of form' that was produced. A particularly extensive investigation of this type was carried out by FYFE who, over a twelve year period found a correlation between the patterns produced by mistletoe sap and the phase of the Moon].

However, long before this the German chemist RUNGE, examining the migration rates of various ions as they were drawn through filter paper by capillary action, was impressed by the forms produced by different substances. Fig. TA.3 shows a reproduction of the title page of his book, 'The Formative Urge of Matter', published in 1858. His work was later repeated and expanded by VON EUGEN.

Fig. TA.3 The title page of Runge's book, published in 1855, showing the range of patterns produced from different chemical solutions.

REFERENCES

As stated in the Introduction, the purpose of this book is to stimulate the seeking for an evolutionary-wholistic understanding. It is not designed to prove anything so that an exhaustive, supporting bibliography is not necessary. References are therefore confined to those specifically mentioned in the text that provide a basis for anyone wanting to get to know about these matters. In many cases the references quoted themselves contain bibliographies which could provide leads for the next generation to investigate these fields.

ADLER, Robert; Origin of Planetary Systems, New Scientist, 16 September 2000

ANANTHASWAMY, Anil: Scene set for the next mass extinction, New Scientist, 27 March, 2004, p.10.

ARMSTRONG, Lord W.G, Electrical Movement in Air and Water with Theoretical Inferences, Smith, Elder and Co. London 1897 and:
Supplement to Lord Armstrong's Work on Electric Movement in Air and Water with Theoretical Inferences by Henry Stroud, Smith, Elder and Co, London, 1899

ARP, Halton, Seeing Red: Redshifts, Cosmology and Academic Science, pub.Apeiron, Montreal, Canada, 1998.

BARADUC, H; The Human Soul, its Movements, its Lights (English translation) Libraire International de la Pensee Nouvelle, Paris, 1913.

BATTERSBY, Stephen; New Scientist, 17 April 2004.

BEARD, Paul; Living On: A Study of Altering Consciousness After Death; George Allen and Unwin, London, 1982.

BECKER, Robert and SELDEN, Gary; The Body Electric: Electromagnetism and the Foundation of Life, Quill, William Morrow, New York, 1985.

BERCIU, Dumitru, Romania before Burebista, Thames and Hudson, London, 1967.

BERLITZ, Charles; Mysteries of Forgotten Worlds, Souvenir Press, London, Doubleday & Co, New York, 1972.

BESANT, Annie and LEADBEATER, Charles. W, Occult Chemistry; Investigations by Clairvoyant Magnification Into the Structure of the Atoms of the Periodic Table and of Some Compounds, Theosophical Publishing House, Adyar, Madras India 1951.

BLAVATSKY, H.P, Isis Unveiled, originally published in New York in 1877, available now as a Theosophical University Press Edition, Pasadena, Calif. 1976. Volume 1 is a polemic against scientist's dismissal of the phenomena of spiritualism and occultism and an attempt to validate these, mainly by quoting large amounts of anecdotal evidence for them. Blavatsky claims that they are manifestations of phenomena and an understanding that is older and deeper than that of modern science. The statements about the unquenchable lamp are made on p. 224 et seq. Vol 2 is a polemic against modern religions and claims that these derive from, and are distorted versions of, an ancient mystery religion that emanated from the East. Both volumes are full of references that could be useful for anyone pursuing these ideas.

BRENNAN, Barbara Anne, Hands of Light: A Guide to Healing Through the Human Energy Field, Bantam New Age Books, New York, London, 1988. This book contains a list of references to works dealing with the human aura and researches into these energy fields.

BROWNE, Sylvia: Past Lives, Future Healing, Dutton/Penguin U.S., Piatkus London, UK, 2001

BRYSON, Bill; A Short History of Nearly Everything: Doubleday (A Black Swan Book), London, 2003.

BURR, Harold Saxton, Blueprint for Immortality: The Electric Patterns of Life, originally published by Neville Spearman, London, 1972, now published by C.W. Daniel, Saffron Walden, U.K.

CALLAHAN, Roger (with Richard Trubo) Tapping the Healer Within: Using Thought Field Therapy to instantly conquer your fears, anxieties and emotional distress; Piatkus, London, 2001.

CANNON, Dolores:
(1) Jesus and the Essenes: Fresh Insights into Christ's Ministry and the Dead Sea Scrolls; Gateway Books,Bath, U.K. 1992.
(2) They Walked With Jesus: Past Life Experiences with Christ; Gateway Books, Bath, U.K. 1994.
(3) The Custodians: Beyond Abduction; Ozark Mountain Publishers, Huntsville, USA, 1999.

CAPRA, Fritjof; The Web of Life; A New Synthesis of Mind and Matter; Harper-Collins, London, 1996.

CAREY, Kenneth X; The Starseed Transmissions, pub. Uni-Sun Books, Box 70, Mountain View, MO, 65548, U.S.A.

CARROLL, Sean B: Endless Forms Most Beautiful; The New Science of Evo Devo and the Making of the Animal Kingdom. W.W. Norton and Co U.S.A. 2005, Weidenfeld and Nicolson, London, UK 2006

CATTON, Chris and GRAY, James, Sex in Nature, pub. Croom Helm Ltd, Beckenham, Kent, UK, 1985.

CHOWN, Marcus (1), Taming the Multiverse, New Scientist, 14th July 2001, p 27. (2) Cycles of Creation, New Scientist, 16 March 2002, p.26, (3) Chaotic Heavens, New Scientist, 28 February, 2004, p.32.

CHRISTIE-MURRAY, David; Reincarnation: Ancient Beliefs and Modern Evidence, David and Charles, London, 1981.

CONSTABLE, Trevor James; The Cosmic Pulse of Life: The Revolutionary Biological Power behind UFOs, Merlin Press, Santa Ana, Calif. U.S.A. 1976.

COURTENEY, Hazel: (1) Divine Intervention, CiCo Books, London, 1999, revised ed. 2005, (2) The Evidence for the Sixth Sense, Cico Books, London, 2005.

CRAIG, Cary: The best way to access Gary Craig's EFT is via his website, www.emofree.com.

CRAWFORD, W.J: The Psychic Structures at the Goligher Circle; John M. Watkins, London, 1921.

CREMO, Michael A. and THOMPSON, Richard L: Hidden History of the Human Race, Bhaktivedanta Book Publishing Inc./Torchlight Publishing Inc. 1996

CROOKALL, Robert; The Study and Practice of Astral Projection, Aquarian Press, London, 1961.

DAVID-NEEL, Alexandra; Magic and Mystery in Tibet, University Books, New York, 1965 Edition.
(As well as giving an account of thought forms referred to in the text of the present book, David-Neel's book illustrates how a totally different culture, that is concerned with an inner path of development, can produce a completely different attitude to that of Western civilisation. What David-Neel describes is a way of life with a very low material level of existence but with a much greater understanding of the workings of the mind and, as a result, the production of phenomena which, by Western standards are unbelievable.

DAVIDSON, John, The Secret of the Creative Vacuum, C.W. Daniel Co, Saffron Walden, England, 1989.

DAVIES, Paul
(1) Superforce; The Search for a Grand Unified Theory of Nature, Counterpoint/Unwin Paperbacks, London 1984
(2) The Cosmic Blueprint, Heinemann, London 1987

DE BRATH, Stanley; The Physical Phenomena of Spiritualism, pub. College of Psychic Studies, London, 1947.

DICKERSON, Richard, E. and GEIS, Irving: Chemistry, Matter and the Universe, An Integrated Approach to General Chemistry, pub. W.A. Benjamin Inc. California, U.S.A. 1976.

DIONYSIUS the AREOPAGITE, The Mystical Theology and the Celestial Hierarchies, published by The Shrine of Wisdom, Godalming, Surrey, UK, 1965.

DOUGLAS, Kate;Article in New Scientist, 25th November 2000, p. 29.

DVIR, Adrian, X3 Healing Entities and Aliens, publisher Adrian Dvir, produced by BookMasters Inc. U.S.A 2003.

EISENBUD, Jule; The World of Ted Serios, Jonathan Cape, 1968.

ELIADE, Mircea; The Myth of the Eternal Return or Cosmos and History, Bollingen, Princeton University Press, USA, 1965.

EMOTO, Masuru; Messages from Water, Vols 1 and 2 pub Hado Kyoikusha Co Ltd, Tokyo, European Office Leiden Netherlands, Beyond Words Publishing Hillsboro, U.S.A. 2004. An account of Emoto and his work is given in 'The True Power of Water' by Masaru Emoto pub. Beyond Words Publishing, address above.

ENGQUIST, Magda; Gestaltkräfte der Lebenigen, Vittorio Klosterrmann, Frankfurt-am-Main, 1970.

EVELYN-WHITE, Hugh G; Hesiod; The Homeric Hymns and Homerica, William Heinemann, London; Macmillan, New York, 1914.

FAULKER, R.O.; The Ancient Egyptian Book of the Dead, British Museum Press, London, 1985.

FEYNMAN, Richard; the quote, that nobody understands quantum theory comes from New Scientist, 2nd September 1989, p.72

FOX, Sidney W. and DOSE, Klaus; Molecular Evolution and the Origin of Life, pub. Marcel Dekker Inc, New York and Basel, 1977.

FRANKFORT, H. WILSON, J.A. and JACOBSEN, T; Before Philosophy, Penguin Books, London 1949.

FUKURAI, T; Clairvoyance and Thoughtography, Pub. Rider, London, 1931.

FYFE, A; Moon and Plant, Society for Cancer Research, Arlesheim, Switzerland, 1967.

GARDNER, Edward L; Fairies: The Cottingley Photographs and Their Sequel, Theosophical Publishing House, London, Fourth Edition, 1966.

GARRETT, Eileen; My Life as a Search for the Meaning of Mediumship, Rider and Co, London, 1939.

GAUQUELIN, Michael, The Cosmic Clocks, Peter Owen, London 1969.

GERBER, Richard: Vibrational Medicine, Bear and Co, Santa Fe, New Mexico, 1996.

GILBERT, Adrian and COTTERELL, Maurice; The Mayan Prophesies, Element Books, Shaftesbury, Dorset, UK, 1995.

GLASKIN, G.M; Windows of the Mind: The Christos Experiment, Wildwood House, London, 1974 and Worlds Within: Probing the Christos Experience, Wildwood House, London, 1976.

GOOD, Timothy; Above Top Secret, Sidgwick and Jackson Ltd, London, 1987, updated in Beyond Top Secret, same publishers, 1996.
Alien Liaison; The Ultimate Secret, Century, London, 1991.
Alien Update, Random House, London, 1993.

GRANT, Joan:
(1) Winged Pharoah, Arthur Barker, London 1937
(2a) Eyes of Horus, Methuen, London, 1942
(2b) Lord of the Horizon, Methuen, London,1943
(3) So Moses Was Born, Methuen, London, 1952
(4) The Scarlet Feather, Methuen, London, 1945
(5) Return to Elysium, Methuen, London, 1947
(6) Life as Carola, Methuen, 1939
There have been a number of reprints and further republications of these books.
Grants description of how she experienced and developed recall of past lives is given in:
GRANT, Joan, Time Out of Mind, Arthur Barker, London, 1956, and in the next reference

GRANT, Joan and KELSEY, Denys: Many Lifetimes, Victor Gollancz, London, 1970.

GRIBBIN, John, In the Beginning, The Birth of the Living Universe, Penguin Books, London, 1994.

GUIRDHAM, Arthur; The Cathars and Reincarnation, Neville Spearman, London, 1970.
We Are One Another, Neville Spearman, London, 1974.
The Lake and the Castle, Neville Spearman, London, 1976.
A Foot in Both Worlds: A Doctor's Autobiography of Psychic Experience, Neville Spearman, London, 1973.

HANCOCK, Graham; Fingerprints of the Gods: A Quest for the Beginning and the End, William Heinemann, London, 1995.
(This book is a good source of references for the subjects that it covers).

HARDO, Trutz; Children Who Have Lived Before, C.W. Daniel C. Ltd. Saffron Walden, U.K. 2001.

HARTMANN, Silvia: Adventures in EFT, 6th Edition, Dragon Rising, Eastbourne, UK, 2003.

HASTED, John; The Metal Benders, Routledge and Kegan Paul, London, 1981.

HASTINGS, Arthur; With the Tongues of Men and Angels: A Study of Channelling, Holt, Rinehart and Winston Inc, Orlando, USA, 1991.

HAY, Louise; You Can Heal Your Life; 2005 Ed. Hay House Inc. Australia, Canada, Hong Kong, South Africa, United Kingdom, United States

HENBEST, Nigel; The Mysterious Universe, Ebury Publishers, London, 1981.

HEYWOOD, Rosalind; The Infinite Hive, Ch.9; Pan Books, London, 1964.

HODSON, Geoffrey; The Science of Seership, Rider and Co, London, 1929.

HOMOEOPATHY
There are so many books on homoeopathy that here we can only refer to a limited number. The following are by medical doctors who use homoeopathy.
LOCKIE, Andrew, The Family Guide to Homoeopathy, Penguin, London, 1989
BOYD, Hamish, Introduction to Homoeopathic Medicine, Beaconsfield Publishers, Beaconsfield, England, Second Edition, 1989. (This book is orientated towards medical doctors who are taking up homoeopathy).
SMITH, Trevor, Homoeopathic Medicine; A Doctor's Guide to Remedies for Common Ailments, Thorsons, Wellingborough, England, 1982.
SMITH, Trevor, The Homoeopathic Treatment of Emotional Illness, A Self-Help Guide to Remedies Which Can Restore Calm and Happiness, Thorsons, Wellingborough, England, 1983
In the UK homoeopathic remedies are prepared according to the methods laid down in The German Homoeopathic Pharmacopoeia, published by The British Association of Homoeopathic Manufacturers, 1999. The books by Lockie and Boyd contain extensive bibliographies for further homoeopathic books and useful information on organisations.

HOPE, Murry
(1) The Changeling, Light Publishing at the College of Psychic Studies, London, 1999
(2) The Ancient Wisdom of Atlantis, Thorsons/Harper Collins, London, 1998

HOUGH, Peter and RANDLES, Jenny; The Complete Book of UFOs, An Investigation into Alien Contacts and Encounters, Piatkus, London, 1994.

HUTTON, J. Bernard; Healing Hands, W.H. Allen, London, 1966.

HUXLEY, Aldous; The Doors of Perception, Penguin books, London, 1959.

IKIN, A. Graham; Studies in Spiritual Healing, World Fellowship Press, London, 1968.

JACOBS, David M; Alien Encounters, Virgin Books, UK, 1994. Published in the U.S.A. as Secret Life, Simon and Schuster, New York, 1992.

JANTSCH, Erich; The Self-Organising Universe; Pergammon Press, Oxford, 1980.

JUNG, C.G: Modern Man in Search of a Soul, Routledge and Kegan Paul, London, 1962.

KARAGULLA, Shafica; Breakthrough to Creativity, De Vorss and Co, Los Angeles, 1967.

KILNER, W.J.: The Human Atmosphere (The Aura); first published under the title, The Human Atmosphere in 1911, revised edition 1920(Kegan Paul, London), reprinted with an explanatory foreword by Leslie Shepard in 1965, University Books, New York.

KIRK. G.S, RAVEN J.E. and SCHOFIELD M. The Presocratic Philosophers, 2nd Edition Cambridge University Press, London 1983

KOLISKO, L: The Workings of Stars in Earthly Substances, 1927, Rudolf Steiner Bookshop, London.

KOLISKO, L: Agriculture of Tomorrow, Kolisko Archive, Stroud, Glos. 1939.

KOLLERSTROM, N; The Correspondence of Metals and Planets, J. Astrological Association, vol.18, No. 3, 1976.

KOLLERSTROM N. AND DRUMMOND M: Chemical Effects of a Mars- Saturn Conjunction, J. Astrological Association, vol. 19, No.3, 1977.

KRYSTAL, Phyllis: Cutting the Ties that Bind, Turnstone Press, 1982. Sai Baba - The Ultimate Experience, Sawbridge Enterprises Ltd, London, 1985.

LAING, Peggy and Ron; Embodiment of Love, Gateway, Bath, U.K. 1993.

LAKHOVSKY, Georges: The Secret of Life, The True Health Publishing Company, London, 1951, Reprinted Health Research, California U.S.A. 1970

LANG, Kenneth, R; Sun, Earth and Sky, Springer-Verlag, Berlin, Heidelberg, New York, 1997.

LAWTON, Ian: Genesis Unveiled; The Lost Wisdom of our Forgotten Ancestors. Virgin Books, London, 2003.

LEADBEATER, C.W; Man Visible and Invisible, Theosophical Publishing House, London, 1902.
The Chakras; Theosophical Publishing House, first edition 1927 with many subsequent reprints.

LEAKEY, Richard E: The Making of Mankind, Michael Joseph Ltd. London 1981

LEDUC, Stéphane; The Mechanism of Life, Rebman Ltd, London 1911, Théorie Physico-Chimique. de la Vie et Générations Spontanée, A.Poinat, Editeur, Publications Medicales et Scientifiques, Paris 1910.

LeSHAN, Lawrence; Cancer as a Turning Point, Revised Edition, Penguin Books, U.S.A. 1994, Gateway Books, U.K. 1996

LEWIN, Roger; Human Evolution: An Illustrated Introduction, Blackwell Scientific Publications, Oxford, 1984.

LICHTENBERG figures: There is an extensive literature dealing with the scientific investigation of Lichtenberg figures. A concise account of the interpretation offered by current science for some basic patterns is given in;
    Fundamentals of Gaseous Ionisation and Plasma Electronics by Essam Nasser, John Wiley and Sons, New York, 1971.
    A more detailed account is given in:
Electrical Coronas: Their Basic Physical Mechanisms, by Leonard B. Loeb, University of California Press, Berkeley and Los Angeles, 1965.
    An investigation of the patterns registered by circular electrodes on a photographic plate is reported by C. Edward Magnusson in:
Journal of the American Institute of Electrical Engineers, 1930, vol. 49, p. 756.
Some most beautiful Lichtenberg figures were recorded, both photographically and in layers of powder on a glass plate, by:
Lord W.G Armstrong, 'Electrical Movement in Air and Water with Theoretical Inferences' Smith, Elder and Co, London, 1897, and
Supplement to Lord Armstrong's Work on 'Electrical Movement in Air and Water with Theoretical Inferences' by Henry Stroud, Smith Elder and Co, London 1899.

LIPTON, Bruce; The Biology of Belief: Unleashing the Power of Consciousness, Matter and Miracles, Mountain of Love /Elite Books, Santa Rosa, CA 95404, U.S.A., Cygnus Books, PO Box 15, Llandeilo, SA19 6YX, UK, 2005.

LOYE, David: Darwin's Lost Theory of Love, pub.toExcel, iUniverse com, Inc U.S.A.

LUCKENBILL, D.D: Ancient Records of Assyria and Babylonia Vol. 2. University of Chicago 1927, Reprinted Greenwood Press 1968, New York, U.S.A.

McLEOD, Myles and BRADDY, Simon, New Scientist, 8 June 2002 p. 39.

McTAGGART, Lynne; The Field: The Quest for the Secret Force of the Universe, Harper Collins, London, 2001.

MALIN, David and MURDIN, Paul: The Colours of the Stars, Cambridge University Press, Cambridge, 1984.

MARCINIAK, Barbara; Bringers of the Dawn - Teachings from the Pleidians, Bear and Co, Santa Fe, New Mexico, 1992
Earth; Pleidian Keys to the Living Library, Bear and Co, 1995.

MARGULIS, Lynn: The Symbiotic Planet: a New Look at Evolution, Weidenfeld and Nicolson, London, 1998

MARGULIS, Lynn and SAGAN, Dorion (1): Microcosmos: Four Billion Years of Evolution from Our Microbial Ancestors, Allen and Unwin, London, 1987.

MARGULIS, Lynn and SAGAN, Dorion (2): What is Sex, Simon and Schuster, New York, 1997.

MARGULIS, Lynn and SAGAN, Dorion (3): What is Life, Weidenfeld and Nicolson, London, 1995.

MARGULIS, Lynn and SCHWARTZ, Karlene: Five Kingdoms: An Illustrated Guide to the Phyla of Life on Earth (3rd Edition), W.H. Freeman and Co, New York, 1997.

MARKIDES, Kyriacos C; The Magus of Strovolus, 1985: Homage to the Sun, 1987: Fire in the Heart, 1990. All published by Penguin/Arkana.

MASLOW, Abraham; (1) The Farther Reaches of Human Nature, Pelican Books, Penguin 1973, Harmondsworth Mddx.U.K.
(2) Motivation and Personality, 3rd Edition, Adison Wesley Longman, 1987, U.S.A.

MELLAART, James; Earliest Civilisations of the Near East. Thames and Hudson, London, 1965.

MILNER, Dennis and SMART, Edward; The Loom of Creation: A Study of the Purpose and the Forces that Weave the Pattern of Existence, Neville Spearman, London, 1976.

MILNER, Dennis (Ed.); Explorations of Consciousness, Neville Spearman, London, 1978.

MONROE, Robert A., (1) Journeys out of the Body, Doubleday, New York, 1971: (2) Far Journeys, Doubleday, New York, 1985.

MOODY, Raymond A; Life After Life - The Investigation of a Phenomenon - Survival of Bodily Death, Bantam Books, New York, 1975.

MORTON, Chris and THOMAS, Ceri Louise; The Mystery of the Crystal Skulls, Thorsons (HarperCollins) London, 1997.

MUIR, Hazel; New Scientist article 17 May 2003, 'Earth, Wind and Fire' Vol. 178 No 2395, p.26.

MURPHET, Howard; Sai Baba, Man of Miracles, Frederick Muller, London, U.K. 1971. Murphet has also written three other books, Sai Baba, Avatar: Invitation to Glory and The Undiscovered Country.

MYSS, Caroline; Anatomy of the Spirit: The Seven Stages of Power and Healing, Bantom Books, 1997.

OLDFIELD, Harry and COGHILL, Roger: The Dark Side of the Brain, Element Books, UK 1988.

OWEN, Iris M. and SPARROW, Margaret; Conjuring up Philip: An Adventure in Psychokinesis, Harper and Row, New York, 1976.

OXENHAM, John, (1). 'The Ways' from Bees in Amber, A Little Book of Thoughtful Verse, Methuen, London, 1913; (2) Out of the Body,Longmans Green and Co, London, 1941

PAGE, Christine R; Frontiers of Health, C.W. Daniel, Saffron Walden, U.K. 1992.

PATTERSON, Tom; Spirit Photography, pub. Regency Press, London, 1965.

PAYNE, Phoebe; Man's Latent Powers, first published by Faber and Faber, London, 1938. Reprinted Pelegrin Trust/Pilgrim Books, Norwich, U.K. 1992.

PEARCE-HIGGINS, Canon J.D and Rev. G. STANLEY WHITBY; Life, Death and Psychical Research, Churches Fellowship for Psychical and Spiritual Studies, Rider, London, 1973.

PEARL, Eric; The Reconnection; Heal Others, Heal Yourself, pub Hay House Books Carlsbad, California, U.S.A. London, U.K

PEARSALL, Paul, The Heart's Code, Broadway Books, New York, U.SA; Thorsons London, U.K, 1998.

PERRY, Julian, Mindweld: A Cosmic Embrace, Amethyst Books, New York/London, 1991.

PFEIFFER, Ehrenfried, Sensitive Crystallisation Processes, Graphic Crafts Ind, Lancaster, Pa. USA, 1968.

PHILLIPS, Graham; The Moses Legacy: The Evidence of History, Sidgwick and Jackson, London, 2002.

PHILLIPS, Stephen M: ESP of Quarks and Superstrings, New Age International Publishers New Delhi, 1999. This book can be difficult to obtain through booksellers but is available from Theosophical Society Bookshops.

PIERRAKOS, John: Core Energetics, LifeRhythm Publication, Mendocino CA 95460, U.S.A, 1990.

PLAYFAIR, Guy Lyon and HILL, Scott, The Cycles of Heaven: Cosmic Forces and What they are Doing to You, Souvenir Press, London, 1978.

POLLARD, John; Seers, Shrines and Sirens, George Allen and Unwin, London, 1965.

POWELL, Arthur; The Etheric Double and Allied Phenomena, Theosophical Publishing House, London, U.K. Adijar, Madras, India: Wheaton Ill. U.S.A. 1925.

RICHELIEU, Peter; A Soul's Journey; Turnstone Press, London, 1972.

REES, Martin, Our Cosmic Habitat; Princeton University Press, USA 2001, Weidenfeld and Nicolson, London, UK, 2002

REICHENBACH, Karl von; Researches on Magnetism, Electricity, Heat, Light, Crystallisation and their relation to the Vital Force, translated by Gregory, pub. Taylor, Wratten and Maberly, London, 1850.
A condensed version of this work was published as 'The Mysterious Odic Force' translated by Leslie O. Korth, pub. Aquarian Press, Wellingborough, Northamptonshire, U.K. 1977.
See also, 'The Odic Force. Letters on Od and Magnetism' by Karl von Reichenbach, Hutchinson, London, 1926, republished University Books, New York, 1968.

RITCHIE, George; Return From Tomorrow; Chosen Books Pub. Co, U.S.A. Kingsway Publications, Eastbourne U.K. 1978.

ROSE, Ronald; Living Magic; The Realities Underlying the Psychical Practices and Beliefs of Australian Aborigines, Rand McNally, New York, 1956.

RUNGE, F.F; Der Bildungstrieb der Stoffe, Oranienburg, 1855.

RUSSELL, Edward W, Report on Radionics, Neville Spearman, London, 1973.

SAI BABA: Books about Sai Baba are not generally in libraries and bookshops in the West. In the U.K. those referred to in this book, and many others, can be obtained from: Sai Bhavan, Kundra House, 33

Commercial Road, London, E1 1LD and in the U.S.A. from the Sathya Sai Book Centre of America, 305W First St. Tustin, Ca. 92680.

SANDWEISS, Samuel H: Sai Baba, The Holy Man and the Psychiatrist, Birth Day Publishing Co, San Diego, U.S.A. 1975

SCHIFF, Michel; The Memory of Water, Thorsons, London 1995.

SCHLEMMER, Phyllis V, and JENKINS, Palden; The Only Planet of Choice, Gateway Books, Bath, U.K. 1993.

SCHWARTZ, Gary; The Afterlife Experiments: Breakthrough Scientific Evidence of Life After Death, Simon and Schuster, New York, 2003

SCOTT-MUMBY, Keith; Virtual Medicine: A New Dimension in Energy Healing, Thorsons, London, 1999.

SELAWRY, A and O; Der Kupferchloridekristallisation, Gustav Fischer Verlieg, Stuttgart, 1957.

SHEALY, Norman and MYSS, Caroline; The Creation of Health: Merging Traditional Medicine with Intuitive Diagnosis, Stillpoint Publishing, Walpole NH, USA, 1988.

SHELDRAKE, Rupert; (1) The Presence of the Past: Morphic Resonance and the Habits of Nature, Collins, London, 1988. (2) Dogs that know when their owners are coming home and other unexplained powers of animals, Arrow Books, (Random House), London, 2000.

SHERWOOD, Jane (1) The Country Beyond, Neville Spearman, London, 1969.
(2) The Fourfold Vision, Neville Spearman, London, 1965

SHERWOOD-TAYLOR, F: The Fourfold Vision, Chapman and Hall, London, 1945.

SIMONTON, O. Carl, MATTHEWS-SIMONTON, Stephanie, CREIGHTON, James L; Getting Well Again, Bantom Books, New York, London 1978

SMITH, Cyril and BEST, Simon; Electromagnetic Man: Health and Hazard in the Electrical Environment, J.M Dent and Sons Ltd, London, 1989.

SMOLUCHOWSKI, Roman; The Solar System: The Sun, Planets and Life, Scientific American Books, Freeman and Co, New York, 1983.

SOLOMON, Grant and Jane; Harry Oldfield's Invisible Universe: The Story of One Man's Search for the Healing Methods That Will Help Us Survive the 21st Century, Thorsons, London, 1998.

SOSKIN, Julie; The Wind of Change, Barton House, Bath, U.K. 1990

SPARKS, H.F.D; The Apocryphal Old Testament, Clarendon Press, Oxford, 1984.

STARR, Cecie and TAGGART, Ralph; Biology: The Unity and Diversity of Life, Wadsworth Pub. Co. California, U.S.A.

STEINER, Rudolf; (1) Theosophy; Rudolf Steiner Press. This book gives a description of Steiner's observations on the nature of the human soul and the soul world, the human spirit and the spirit world and the human aura.
(2) Occult Science; Rudolf Steiner Press, gives an account of Steiner's cosmology.
(3) Atlantis, Selections from the work of Rudolf Steiner, Sophia Books, Rudolf Steiner Press, Forest Row, U.K. 2001
(4) Agriculture: this book records the lectures that Steiner gave in his Agriculture Course; Spiritual Foundations for the Renewal of Agriculture, in 1924, including the recipes for 'spiritual manures, together with an account of the discussions that followed these lectures with further notes and a bibliography relating to the work of the Biodynamic Association (set up on the basis of the lectures), the use of the spiritual manures, and other relevant work by the Anthroposophical Research Group at Dornach, published in 1993 by the Biodynamic Farming and Gardening Association Inc. PO Box 550, Kimberton, PA 19442, USA
For Steiner's account of his life, see An Autobiography, Rudolf Steiner Press,

STEMMAN, Roy (1); Reincarnation: True Stories of Past Lives; Pub. Judy Piatkus, London, 1997.

STEMMAN, Roy (2): Healers and Healing, Pub. Judy Piatkus, London, 1999

STRAY, Geoff; Beyond 2012; Catastrophe or Ecstasy: A Complete Guide to End-of-Time Predictions, Vital Signs Publishing, Lewes, Sussex, U.K. 2005

STRIEBER, Whitley; Communion, Arrow Books, London, 1997. Transformation: The Breakthrough, Century Books, UK, 1988.

TANSLEY, David; Radionics and the Subtle Anatomy of Man, Health Science Press, Rustington, Sussex, U.K. 1972.

TAYLOR, Gordon Rattray: The Great Evolution Mystery, Abacus Sphere Books, London, 1984.

TEMPLE, K.G: The Sirius Mystery: Was Earth Visited by Intelligent Beings from a Planet in the system of the Star Sirius, Sidgwick and Jackson, London, 1976.

THOMAS, Barry: The Evolution of Plants and Flowers, Pub. Peter Lowe/Eurobooks 1981

THOMPSON, D'Arcy Wentworth; On Growth and Form, in two volumes, Cambridge University Press, London, First Edition 1917, Second Edition 1942 (Many Reprints).

TOULMIN, S and GOODFIELD, J; The Architecture of Matter, Penguin Books, London 1965.

VALLEE, Jacques; Vallee has made an in-depth study of UFO phenomena for many years:
'Passport to Magonia: On UFOs, Folklore and Parallel Worlds', contains a summary of the essential features of 923 UFO-type encounters that occurred between 1868 and 1968, together with a survey of historical records and folklore from Biblical to modern times, showing their common features; pub. Regnery Co, Chicago, 1969, reprinted Contemporary Books, Chicago, 1993.
'Dimensions; A Casebook of Alien Contact' pursues this theme in greater depth. Contemporary Books Inc. U.S.A. Souvenir Press U.K. 1988.
Confrontations: A Scientist's Search for Alien Contact, Souvenir Press UK, Random House USA, 1990. In this book Vallee analyses the evidence: to estimate the power involved in UFO phenomena: the nature of physical substances associated with UFOs: biological effects causing deterioration or enhanced growth of plants: the clinical data on physiological effects on human beings: the value that can by placed on hypnotic recall of events during missing time.

VAN DYKE, Milton; An Album of Fluid Motion, Parabolic Press, Stanford, California, 1982.

VAN DER POST, Laurens; The Lost World of the Kalahari, Companion Book Club (Odhams Press), London, 1958.

VLASTOS, Gregory; Plato's Universe, Clarendon Press, Oxford, 1975.

VON DANIKEN, Erich; The Chariots of the Gods puts forward his thesis for Man's extra-terrestrial origins; more on the evidence on which he bases this, is presented in; 'According to the Evidence', Souvenir Press, U.K. 1977

VON EUGEN DEISS; Uber Runge-Bilder und Liesegange-Ringe auf Filtrierpapier, Kolloid Zeitschrift, vol. 89, p. 146, 1939.

WACHSMUTH, Gunther, The Etheric Formative Forces in Cosmos, Earth and Man, Anthroposophical Publishing Co, London, 1932

WALSCH, Neale Donald (1), (2) and (3); Conversations With God, Books One, Two and Three, 1997, 1999, (4) The New Revelations, 2002, (5) Tomorrow's God, 2004, (6) Home With God, 2006, all published by Hodder and Stoughton,. London, U.K.

WATSON, Lyall, Supernature, Hodder and Stoughton, London, 1973.

WEEKS, Nora, The Medical Discoveries of Edward Bach Physician, C. W. Daniel Co, Saffron Walden, England, 1940 and many reprints.

WEISS, Brian: Many Lives, Many Masters, Simon Schuster Inc, U.S.A. 1988; Judy Piatkus, London, U.K. 1994.

WHITE, John; Pole Shift, A.R.E. Press, Virginia, U.S.A.

WHITE, John and KRIPPNER, Stanley (Editors), Future Science, Anchor Books, Doubleday and Co Inc, New York, 1977.

WICKLAND, Carl; Thirty Years Among the Dead, orginally published in the U.S.A. in 1924 and later in abbreviated form by Amherst Press, Wisconsin, U.S.A. This is the 'classic' book about possession by discarnate entities and the freeing from these by a rescue circle.

WILSON, Colin; (1) Rudolf Steiner: The Man and His Vision, Aquarian Press, Wellingborough, U.K. (2) From Atlantis to the Sphinx: Recovering the Lost Wisdom of the Ancient World, Virgin Books, London, New York, Toronto, 1996

WOODARD, Christopher; A Doctor Heals by Faith, 1953; A Doctor's Faith Holds Fast, 1955; both published by Max Parrish, London. In these books the author quotes cases of 'possession' by discarnate entities.

YOGANANDA, Paramhansa; Autobiography of a Yogi, Rider and Co, London, 1950 and many reprints.

YOUNG M.L. Agartha: A Journey to the Stars, Stillpoint Publishing, Walpole, New Hampshire, U.S.A. 1984, Gateway Books, U.K.

INDEX

Beard, Paul 125
beavers 90, 159
Becker, Robert 148
bees 90, 96, 148
behaviour, 'instinctive' patterns of 32
behavioural skills 97
Bénard cells (B-cells) 14, 19-23, 56
  form, motion and activity 61, 64, 66-68, 323
  magnetic field 74, 244
Benveniste, Jaques 157-159, 284, 285
Berlitz, Charles 196
Besant, Annie 406-409, 411, 412
Best, Simon 148, 160
Bible 99, 114, 115, 117, 183
  Old Testament 318
Big Bang theory 17-18, 53, 66, 76, 262
  'background radiation' 63
  developing reaction against dominance of 59
  Kosmic metaphysics (hK-M) and 58-63
  creation of hydrogen and helium as galaxies
    break down 59-60
  distribution of galaxies 59
  redshift 58-59
bilocation 169
Binns, Dr James 288
bioelectricity 148
biological evolution, specific aspects of 89-90
  Earth-Memory (EM) energy 90-91
  genetic viewpoint 91-93
  hK-M and the Darwinian theory of evolution
    93-98
  symbiogenesis 89-90
bioplasma 145
bio-resonance therapy 157
bipedal movement 27, 33, 86
birds 85, 91, 93-95, 156, 244
birds, ability to use materials of their environment
  28, 31
birds' wings, form of 94, 400
'black holes' 66, 318
Blavatsky, H.P. 175, 413
blood pressure, high 234
bone growth, stimulating 148
bone implements, use made by homo sapiens 41
Book of the Dead 101
bow and arrow, development of 40
Brahma 298
  day and night of 56
brain damage 233
Brazil, UFOs in 175
Brennan, Barbara Anne 151-152, 208, 245
'Bringers of the Dawn: Teachings from the
  Pleiadians & Earth' 181-182
Brown, Frank A. 244-245
Browne, Sylvia 129
Bryson, Bill 186
Buddha 187
Burr, Harold Saxton 147, 148
bushmen, Kalahari 137, 168-169
butterflies 94-96
Byzantine Empire and Byzantium 116

C

Callahan, Roger 161
Camphene, solidification of 356
cancer 235
  detection of 146
  radiation and 157
  self healing 160-161
Cannon, Dolores 131, 172
'capillary dynamolysis' 244, 248
  forms in experiments 361-370
Carey, Kenneth X. 177-178
carrots 244
catastrophe, evidence of 84, 93-94, 196-197
catastrophe, impending, likelihood of 198-199
caterpillars 94
Cathars 128-129
cave paintings 38
Cayce, Edgar 147, 166
cell budding 79, 81, 83
cell division 79, 81, 83
cells, behaviour of 91, 92
cells, EM-energy of 92-93
cells, regeneration of 148
Celts 114-115
chakra energy systems 144, 150, 151, 155, 156,
  229, 236
channelled communications see communications,
  channelled
Chapman, George 165, 236
characters of people, correlating 251
chemical reactions, cosmic stress fields and 244
chemistry, early 111, 118
chemotropic cells 80
Chephren 101
Ch'i (space energy) 75, 145, 156
'chi gong' 173
children recalling previous lives 126, 127, 129
children's illnesses 235
chimpanzees 28, 95
China 43
  UFOs in 173
chitin 84, 88
Christ, Jesus 131, 134, 138, 179, 184
Christ, kingdom of 239-240
Christ force 289
Christ influences 231, 237
Christ path, ECEs portraying 305-312
Christ path and The Absolute 314
Christ phenomenon 114
Christ stream of activity 138, 171, 231
Christianity 115-119
Christie-Murray, David 129
chromosomes 91
civilisations of the Near East and Western Europe,
  development of 100-104, 119
clairaudience 125
clairvoyance 125
'clairvoyance, medical' 156
clairvoyant ability 167
clairvoyant observations of the body's energy
  fields 149-152
clairvoyants 145, 168, 170, 203-204, 323, 348
classification of organisms 78, 88-89
clay pots, early making of 41, 114

light (reverberations) 72-73, 80
  created by formation of larger atoms 23, 24
  given off by particle entity 58
lignin 87
limb joints 94
Lipton, Bruce 163
liquid, forms produced by electrical stress in
  391-399
liquid, forms produced by mechanical stress in
  354-356
lives, past, historic value of recall of 130-131
lodestone (magnetite) 68
Loom of Creation 324
Lovelock's Gaia concept 96
Lucifer, Kingdom of 238-239, 305, 312
Luciferic influences 231, 237, 249, 250, 251, 272,
  273
Luciferic stream of activity 138, 171, 231
Lucretius 111
lyre birds, male 95

M

magnetism 73-74
magnetite (lodestone) 68
magnets 244
  experiments with 349-354
  'hazes' round 150
mammary glands 85
man as a thinker 47, 109
'Man's Latent Powers' 145
mana (space energy) 75, 145
Marciniak, Barbara 181-182
Margulis, Lynn 88-89, 90
Marius, Emperor 113
Markides, Kyriacos C. 139-140, 165, 167
Mars 69, 244
marsupials 85, 95
Maslow, Abraham 121, 228
'Masters' 167, 175
materialist viewpoint 46
'Materialist' stream 35, 36, 48
Maya (illusion) 139, 140, 143
Mayan civilisation 181, 197, 198-199
McNeil, Dr Andrew ECE imagery 212, 223-224,
  227, 237-240, 279, 316, 321
  The Absolute 314-315
  Christ path 305, 307-312
  creation, seven stages of 299-302
  on formative behaviour of substances 258-259
  on homeopathy 279-281, 283
  junior school 'Godhead in evolution' cosmology
    298-299
  on pattern formation in crystallisation 259-261
mechanical stress, forms produced in liquid by
  354-356
medical facilities using homeopathy in UK 159
medical practice, integration of energy field
  concepts into 156-158
meditation 139, 169, 170
meditation practices 46
Meek, George 211
membrane-enclosed droplets 25, 49, 78-79

Mendel, Gregor 91
mental illnesses 167
'Mentor' 178, 179
Meredith, Dr Brian ECE imagery 212, 219-223,
  227, 316, 319, 321, 399
  The Absolute 313
  Christ path 306-307
  etheric force interpretation 262
  junior school 'Godhead in evolution' cosmology
    294-298
  sources of imagery in 286
  on 'ultimate' atoms 409-410
meridian energy flow lines 152, 156, 157
meridian energy healing 161-162
Mesoamerica 43
Mesolithic era 114
Mesopotamian civilisations, development of
  100-105
'messengers from the gods' 170-171
Messiah 114
metabolic activity, variations in 244-245
metal solidification forms 389-391
metals and homeopathy 279
metamorphosis in organisms 94
meteorites 23
microfossils 25
Milky Way 62, 175
mimicry as evolutionary feature 96
mind and the human aura, problem of 203-205
'Mindweld' 176-177
mineral kingdom forms produced by stress
  354-401
Minoan peoples 106
miracles 114, 138, 170
Mitchell-Hedges crystal skull 197-198
Mohammed 116
monkeys, arising of 27, 33, 86
Monroe, Robert A. 132, 133
Moon, influences of 244, 245, 248
morphology 212
Morton, Chris 198
Moses 318
Moslems 116
mountain ash leaves 346-347
movement, bipedal 27, 33, 86
movement, stresses for 84
multicellular organisms, arising of 26-27, 32, 33,
  49, 82-83
mushrooms 88
Mycenaen peoples 106
mycorrhizae 88
Myss, Caroline 156, 166
mystics 145, 147, 168, 175, 253, 267, 288, 348
  see also 'Daskalos'; Sai Baba; Steiner,
apporting objects 169
  and auras 323
  contemporary 138-141
  cosmology of 135 et seq
  and flowers 361
  healing by 165-167
  as 'Masters' 167, 211
  Tibetan 170
  viewpoint of *h*K-M on 142-143
  worlds of soul and spirit according to 133-135
mythology, Jewish 36

Erratum – penultimate picture, the death mask.

Hypo comes into the world
seeking sustenance to maintain
his bodily existence

Hypo becomes aware that there
is a multitude of happenings
in the world around him

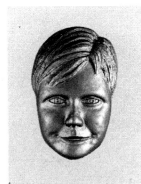

Hypo experiences the joy of
exploring his world and his ability to do so

This gives hypo an enhanced
experience of self, as a callow
youth

He then experiences the daunting
challenge of growing up into an adult
person

Hypo sees opportunities for enhanced
sense of self if only he can measure up to
them

Hypo gets down to the steady grind of
coping with the pressures of life

Hypo gets satisfaction in succeeding
according to society's view of success

But this does not give him the fulfilment
that he expected and he ponders this

By seeking understanding of his life's
experiences Hypo develops wisdom

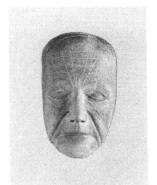

Having achieved what he is capable of ,
Hypo departs from the material world

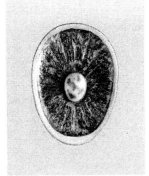

Hypo's achievements serve as a seed for
those of future generations

Fig.11.13b. The evolution through his life cycle of a hypothetical male.